Web Dynpro ABAP®

SAP PRESS

SAP PRESS is a joint initiative of SAP and Rheinwerk Publishing. The know-how offered by SAP specialists combined with the expertise of Rheinwerk Publishing offers the reader expert books in the field. SAP PRESS features first-hand information and expert advice, and provides useful skills for professional decision-making.

SAP PRESS offers a variety of books on technical and business-related topics for the SAP user. For further information, please visit our website: *www.sap-press.com*.

James Wood, Joseph Rupert
Object-Oriented Programming with ABAP Objects (2nd edition)
2016, 470 pages, hardcover and e-book
www.sap-press.com/3597

Kiran Bandari
Complete ABAP
2017, 1,047 pages, hardcover and e-book
www.sap-press.com/3921

Goebels, Nepraunig, Seidel
SAPUI5: The Comprehensive Guide
2016, 672 pages, hardcover and e-book
www.sap-press.com/3980

Paul Hardy
ABAP to the Future (2nd edition)
2016, 801 pages, hardcover and e-book
www.sap-press.com/4161

James Wood, Shaan Parvaze

Web Dynpro ABAP®

The Comprehensive Guide

Rheinwerk®
Publishing

Bonn • Boston

Editor Kelly Weaver
Copyeditor Miranda Martin
Cover Design Graham Geary
Photo Credit iStockphoto.com/Jdrim
Layout Design Vera Brauner
Production Graham Geary
Typesetting SatzPro, Krefeld (Germany)
Printed and bound in the United States of America, on paper from sustainable sources

ISBN 978-1-59229-416-9

© 2017 by Rheinwerk Publishing Inc., Boston (MA)
1st edition 2013, 1st reprint 2017

Library of Congress Cataloging-in-Publication Data
Wood, James, 1978-
Web Dynpro ABAP : the comprehensive guide / James Wood and Shaan Parvaze.
-- 1st edition.
pages cm
ISBN 978-1-59229-416-9 -- ISBN 1-59229-416-2 1. Web Dynpro. 2. User
interfaces (Computer systems) 3. Web sites--Design. 4. ABAP/4 (Computer
program language) I. Parvaze, Shaan. II. Title.
QA76.9.U83W66 2013
006.7'6--dc23
2012034255

Contents at a Glance

Dear Reader,

We editors are often faced with an interesting dilemma. On the one hand, we dream of impeccable authors who can write perfect manuscripts. On the other hand, when we get them…we find ourselves with nothing to do. And, indeed, as I "edited" this book, I spent most of my time marveling over how superfluous I was. Now you know, dear reader: James Wood and Shaan Parvaze don't need me.

Fortunately, my crippling existential crisis is your undeniable gain! You are now the proud owner of a brilliantly written, clear, and comprehensive book on Web Dynpro ABAP. And whether you're new to the game or a veteran programmer, I trust that you will find great value within these pages.

Of course, we at SAP PRESS are always interested in your opinion. Did I set the bar too high for *Web Dynpro ABAP — The Comprehensive Guide*? What do you think about the book? As your comments and suggestions are the most useful tools to help us make our books the best they can be, we encourage you to visit our website at *www.sap-press.com* and share your feedback.

Thank you for purchasing a book from SAP PRESS!

Kelly Weaver
Editor, SAP PRESS

Rheinwerk Publishing
Boston, MA

editorial@rheinwerk-publishing.com
www.sap-press.com

Contents

14   Working with the Floorplan Manager 607

15 WDA Integration 633

Development Workbooks

Introduction

Since its release in late 2005, Web Dynpro ABAP (WDA) has quietly emerged as the *de facto* technology for building interactive applications in ABAP. However, curiously, we've found that many ABAP developers still don't quite know what to make of WDA. Some of the developers we've talked to recognize its power but remain more comfortable developing dialog applications using classic Dynpro technology. Others dismiss WDA as yet another in a long line of web-based technology frameworks that are here today and gone tomorrow. And some simply don't have the time or resources to invest in learning a new skill set.

Regardless of the circumstances that drew you to this book, we'd offer that there's never been a better time to begin learning how to work with WDA technology. Indeed, given SAP's strong investment in WDA technology, it's becoming harder and harder to ignore WDA. So, whether you're an ABAP developer new to the world of web development or a novice developer looking to take your ABAP skills to the next level, you've come to the right place.

Target Group and Prerequisites

This book is intended for ABAP application developers who have some basic experience writing ABAP programs using the ABAP Development Workbench. Basic ABAP language concepts are not covered in this book, so if you have not worked with ABAP before, we recommend you start off by reading *ABAP Objects: ABAP Programming in SAP NetWeaver* (Keller and Krüger, SAP PRESS, 2007). In addition, since WDA makes liberal use of object-oriented programming techniques, you might want to check out *Object-Oriented Programming with ABAP Objects* (Wood, SAP PRESS, 2009).

Though some of the topics covered in this book extend beyond the context of ABAP (e.g., integration with the SAP Enterprise Portal, etc.), no pre-existing background knowledge on these subjects is required. In particular, we assume that readers may not be familiar with web development concepts. Therefore, we'll provide a gentle introduction to these topics as we approach them throughout the book.

WDA was first made available with the SAP NetWeaver 7.0 release. Therefore, if you're planning to follow along with the examples in the book, you'll need to have access to an AS ABAP system based on this release or higher. If you don't have access to such a system, you can download a trial version of the software from the SAP Developer Network online at *http://www.sdn.sap.com*. From the main page, select DOWNLOADS • SOFTWARE DOWNLOADS • SAP NETWEAVER MAIN RELEASES to find the version of the AS ABAP that matches your preferred operating system. Each download package comes with a set of instructions to help you get started. The SAP Developer Network forums can also provide useful tips if you run into problems.

At the time this book is being written, the latest SAP NetWeaver release is version 7.31. Where appropriate, we'll call out features unique to this release and earlier releases. However, for the most part, you'll find that the majority of the concepts described apply equally to prior versions of SAP NetWeaver.

To help you follow along with the examples demonstrated in the book, we've provided all the example code in a source code bundle you can install on your local AS ABAP system. You can download the code bundle from the book's companion site, which is online at *http://www.bowdark.com/books/wdabook*. You can also find it on the book's page at *www.sap-press.com*.

Structure of the Book

As we brainstormed how this book should be put together, one of the biggest challenges we faced was how to introduce core concepts without inundating readers with too many extraneous details. On one hand, we firmly believe many concepts are best described using examples. On the other hand, sometimes the complexity of WDA applications makes it difficult to provide an example without digressing into a lot of application setup details, etc. This phenomenon is particularly evident early on in the learning process since so many topics are interrelated.

Ultimately, we decided to present the material by introducing the concepts in the first part of the book, and giving you practical exercises in the second part of the book. The basic idea here is to keep most of the examples within the manuscript text short and to the point in relation to the concepts being introduced. That way, we can remain focused on the topic at hand. Then, once you grasp the basics, you can use the development workbook exercises to apply what you've learned and consider more broad application design topics. Sandwiched in between, you'll find a number of case studies, which apply several of the topics described toward the creation of WDA applications, at the end of the chapters. In the end, we hope this format will make the book easier to read, follow, and come back to for reference later on.

Within the chapters of the manuscript, you'll find detailed instruction on the development of WDA applications. Here, we'll start off with the basics and progress into more advanced topics in the later chapters. The first eleven chapters build upon one another as we continually peel back additional layers of the WDA programming model. Then, beginning in Chapter 12, the chapters become more topical, focusing in on particular aspects of WDA development. The chapters themselves are organized as follows:

▶ **Chapter 1: Getting Started**
We'll get things started in this chapter by looking at WDA from a big-picture perspective. Along the way, we'll spend some time exploring the genesis of the Web Dynpro application development framework and its relationship to other web development technologies. Finally, the chapter concludes by describing how WDA integrates with the rest of the SAP NetWeaver technology stack.

▶ **Chapter 2: The Anatomy of WDA Applications**
This chapter narrows the focus a bit from Chapter 1, concentrating on the physical makeup of WDA applications and their underlying WDA components. The concepts introduced here will set the stage for the remainder of the book.

▶ **Chapter 3: Developing Your First WDA Application**
Having looked at WDA applications from a conceptual point of view in the first two chapters, this chapter switches gears and allows us to roll up our sleeves and develop a fully functional WDA application from start to finish.

▶ **Chapter 4: Controller Development**
In this chapter, we'll look at the ins and outs of controller development in WDA. We begin by looking at the various elements that make up a controller

(e.g., attributes, methods, events, and so on) and then move into specifics of the various controller types contained within WDA components. The chapter closes by looking at how controllers interact with one another and the surrounding Web Dynpro runtime environment.

▶ **Chapter 5: Working with Contexts**
This chapter picks up where Chapter 4 leaves off by looking at a special feature of WDA controllers: *controller contexts*. Controller contexts are used to store the data displayed within a WDA application. In this chapter, we'll show you how to model data using the Context Editor tool and interact with the context API used to store and retrieve data from the context.

▶ **Chapter 6: Windows and Views**
In this chapter, we begin taking a closer look at the view layer by investigating window and view elements. Here, we'll show you how these elements are stacked on top of one another to produce all sorts of UI designs. Other topics of interest in this chapter include container layouts, navigation concepts, and pop-up windows.

▶ **Chapter 7: Basic UI Elements**
This chapter launches an introduction into the various UI element types provided within the Web Dynpro framework. We'll begin by looking at some of the more basic and well-known form element types such as the `InputField` and `Button` elements. From there, we'll branch out and look at more advanced element types such as menus, toolbars, and dropdown lists.

▶ **Chapter 8: Advanced UI Elements**
This chapter continues on from Chapter 7 by looking at some of the more advanced UI element types provided by the Web Dynpro framework. During the course of our analysis, we'll look at some real-world examples using the following UI element types:

- ▶ `Image`
- ▶ `ThresholdSlider`
- ▶ `FileUpload/FileDownload`
- ▶ `InteractiveForm`
- ▶ `Table`
- ▶ `Tree`
- ▶ `RoadMap`

We'll also spend some time looking at the drag-and-drop feature introduced with the SAP NetWeaver 7.01 release.

▶ **Chapter 9: Component-Based Development Concepts**
In this chapter, we'll look at how to apply componentization techniques to WDA development. Here, we'll see how WDA components can be mixed and matched to assemble WDA applications rather than starting from scratch. The chapter concludes by demonstrating several common use cases that call for a component-based design approach.

▶ **Chapter 10: User Interaction**
This chapter introduces some of the various facilities SAP provides to enhance the user interaction experience. Here, we'll look at options for developing input helps, accessing help texts, displaying pop-up dialog boxes, and more.

▶ **Chapter 11: Dynamic Programming**
Though user interfaces in Web Dynpro are primarily designed using a declarative programming model, there are occasions when it's useful to take more direct control of the rendering process. In this chapter, we'll demonstrate some of the various dynamic programming techniques, which provide us with this flexibility.

▶ **Chapter 12: Configuration and Adaptation**
This chapter takes a look at both the concept of configuration by *adaptation* in Web Dynpro as well as some of the features you may want to employ in the development of your applications to make them more adaptable and well rounded. Chapter content includes how to *configure*, *customize*, and *personalize* applications in Web Dynpro, as well as brief looks at accessibility, styling, and internationalization in the WDA context.

▶ **Chapter 13: Modification and Enhancements**
In this chapter, we will discuss how Web Dynpro interacts with ABAP's *Enhancement Framework*, thus allowing you to make code modifications to existing applications. We'll go over which WDA development objects are allowed to be enhanced and provide examples of how to do so.

▶ **Chapter 14: Working with the Floorplan Manager**
The *Floorplan Manager* is a Web Dynpro technology that helps you build composite applications from disparate components, as you might in the case of building an overview or a wizard for a complex business process. This chapter takes an in-depth look at the floorplan technology and gives a brief primer on the *ABAP Page Builder*, which similarly helps build composite applications.

► **Chapter 15: WDA Integration**

This chapter covers a broad range of integration topics for Web Dynpro. On one hand, it takes a look at how to integrate rich internet application technologies such as Adobe Flash and Microsoft Silverlight into your WDA applications. On the other hand, it provides an overview of common integration scenarios with other SAP technologies, such as SAP NetWeaver Portal.

► **Chapter 16: Security Concepts**

In this chapter, we examine some of the security aspects of introducing Web Dynpro into your system landscape from both development and configuration perspectives. As a developer, you need to be aware of some of the unique security challenges that web application development brings to the table and the general guidance that SAP provides on mitigating these risks through secure coding. As an administrator or configurator, you too need to be aware of how to approach and mitigate certain security scenarios that present themselves when exposing web applications on your ABAP system.

► **Chapter 17: Performance Tuning**

Nobody likes a slow-performing application. This chapter provides some tips and techniques for improving the performance of your applications, including some general development considerations and specific configuration options at your disposal.

Once you're through Chapter 17, you'll be ready to get your hands dirty. The Development Workbooks section contains eight exercises that allow you to apply what you've learned throughout the book. Each workbook exercise is supplemented with design tips to help guide you through the development process. Furthermore, fully functional solutions are provided online with this book's source code bundle.

Finally, to round off the book, we provide you with an appendix on debugging WDA applications.

Conventions

This book contains many code examples demonstrating syntax, functionality, and so on. To distinguish these sections, we're using a font similar to the one used in many integrated development environments to improve code readability (see

Listing 1). As new syntax concepts are introduced, we'll highlight these statements using a bold listing font (see Listing 1).

```
method WDDOINIT.
  DATA lo_nd_sales_orders TYPE REF TO if_wd_context_node.

  lo_nd_sales_orders =
    wd_context->get_child_element(
      name = wd_this->wdctx_sales_orders ).
endmethod.
```

Listing 1 Code Syntax Formatting Example

Acknowledgments

When you embark on a journey like this, you never know what sort of obstacles you might face along the way. Luckily, we've been fortunate to have been supported by so many friends, colleagues, and SAP community members along the way. In particular, we both extend a hearty thanks to our editor, Kelly Harris, for providing us with everything we've needed to complete this project. We couldn't have done it without you.

Since its release in the mid-2000s, Web Dynpro ABAP has quickly emerged as the standard technology for developing web-based user interfaces in the ABAP environment. In this chapter, we'll introduce you to Web Dynpro ABAP and highlight some of the key benefits it has to offer.

1   Getting Started

It has been estimated that roughly 65% of the people on this planet are visual learners. When you think about the implications of this in terms of a software user base, you begin to appreciate just how influential user interfaces can be. After all, the user interface (UI) represents that all-important first impression you make with a user. If users like what they see, they may be willing to take the time to explore the various features your application has to offer. On the other hand, if the application's UI is clunky or difficult to use, users will probably dismiss the application without a second thought. Indeed, history is littered with many wonderful applications that fell by the wayside due to poor UI designs.

These days, UI design is further complicated by the fact that users want the flexibility of accessing their applications via the web. So, in addition to dealing with typical UI development issues, developers must also come up with ways to seamlessly integrate their applications into a web infrastructure that wasn't really designed with interactive applications in mind. This is where frameworks like Web Dynpro ABAP (WDA) come in.

WDA is a framework designed by SAP that allows developers to create web applications using a model-based approach. This model-based approach provides a layer of abstraction that frees developers from having to worry about tedious web application development details such as HTTP protocol handling, stateful processing, HTML/JavaScript support, and so on. Ultimately, this newfound freedom empowers developers to focus their attention on what matters most: getting the business application logic right.

In this chapter, we'll introduce you to WDA and its surrounding framework. During the course of this introduction, we'll look back at some foundational technologies that have influenced the design of the WDA framework. We'll also explore the Web Dynpro metamodel, which drives the development of WDA applications. Finally, we'll wrap up by showing you how WDA fits into the overall SAP NetWeaver technology stack.

1.1 Foundations for Web Dynpro

Before we embark on our journey into the world of WDA programming, it's useful to first take a quick look at some of the foundational technologies that either support or have influenced the design of WDA over the years. Having a basic understanding of these technologies will help you to recognize and appreciate what Web Dynpro brings to the table.

1.1.1 HTTP and the World Wide Web

Whether you're designing a public web site or deploying a web application on a local intranet, the goal of web programming is the same: to serve up and manage resources. Here, the term *resource* can be used to describe static objects such as HTML files as well as more abstract concepts like the results of a database query. In any case, regardless of the content type, clients can access these remote resources by submitting requests to the target web server using the *hypertext transfer protocol* (HTTP).

HTTP is a request-response protocol that provides clients with various methods for accessing web resources hosted on remote web servers. Here, the general requirement is that the resources must be addressable using uniform resource locators (URLs). To demonstrate how this content exchange works, let's take a look at what happens behind the scenes when we try to access the resource located at *http://www.sap-press.com/products/ABAP-Cookbook.html* using our local web browser. Figure 1.1 illustrates this process:

❶ The process begins when you enter the URL into the address bar of your web browser and click the Go button.

❷ Next, the web browser uses the URL path information to construct an HTTP GET request that's sent to the destination web server. Besides the path of the resource being requested, the HTTP request also provides the server with information about your web client, the types of resources your client will accept, and so on.

❸ Upon receiving the GET request, the web server will locate the resource (or dynamically generate it) and attach it to the HTTP response message. For instance, in the illustration shown in Figure 1.1, you can see how the HTML markup contained within the requested *ABAP-Cookbook.html* file is embedded within the response message.

❹ Finally, the HTTP response message is received by the browser and the embedded HTML markup is used to render the screen shown at the bottom of Figure 1.1.

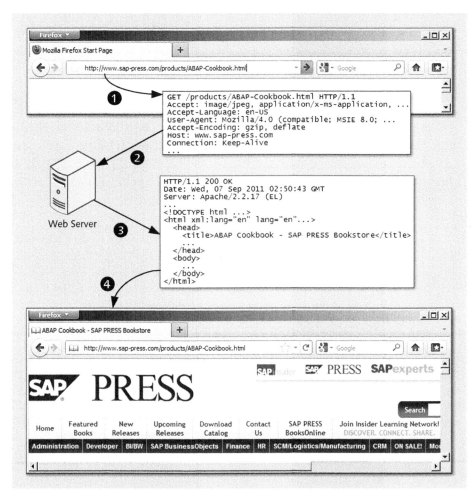

Figure 1.1 Process Flow for an HTTP GET Request

Though it's somewhat difficult to visualize in the sample messages illustrated in Figure 1.1, HTTP messages do have a certain structure to them. In general, an HTTP message can be broken down into three parts:

▶ The first line of the message contains either a *request line* in the case of request messages or a *status line* in the case of response messages. The request line declares the HTTP method being used to issue the request—see the box entitled "HTTP Request Methods" for more details. Status lines describe the status of the processing for the request initiated at the beginning of the request-response loop.

▶ Next, you have a series of one or more name-value pairs called *header fields,* which contain meta-information about the message. For instance, in the example shown in Figure 1.1, the request header *Accept-Encoding: gzip, deflate* tells the web server that the client will accept compressed content.

▶ Finally, after the header fields, you have the body of the message. In the example in Figure 1.1, the body of the message contains the contents of an HTML file. However, HTTP is not limited to simply text-based HTML content; just about any content imaginable can conceivably be exchanged (e.g., PDF files, Microsoft Office documents, etc.). The same also applies for those HTTP request methods that are used to upload data to the server.

HTTP Request Methods

In addition to the GET method illustrated in Figure 1.1, the HTTP protocol provides other methods that can be used to update and maintain resources. For example, the POST method is used to create a resource. The HEAD method can be used to access meta-data about a resource without having to read the entire resource. And the PUT and DELETE methods can be used to overwrite and/or delete a resource. You can find a comprehensive list of supported methods in the official W3C recommendation for the HTTP protocol online at *http://www.w3.org/Protocols/rfc2616/rfc2616-sec9.html#sec9*.

Collectively, the methods defined by the HTTP protocol make it possible for a wide variety of clients to interact with resources over the web. These clients include traditional web browsers installed on workstation clients as well as new age browsers included with tablet PCs, smartphones, and so on.

HTTP: A Stateless Protocol

Before we wrap up our discussion on HTTP processing, it's important that we highlight a key behavior of the HTTP protocol. Looking back at the HTTP request-response cycle demonstrated in Figure 1.1, you can see that the backend web server received a request and issued a response. Once that handoff was complete, the web server's job was finished. At this point, the server is free to clean up any used resources and effectively forget everything about the request(s) it just processed. This is because of the stateless nature of the HTTP protocol. In essence, you can think of web servers as being like amnesia patients: they never remember anything about previous requests issued by clients. We'll explore the implications of this a bit further in the upcoming sections.

1.1.2 Evolution of Web Programming Models

Now that you're familiar with the basic concepts of resource access using HTTP, let's take a look at how web programming models have evolved over the years and consider some of the lessons learned along the way.

Static HTML

The original World Wide Web, as envisioned by its creator, Tim Berners-Lee, was largely based on static content encoded using the *hypertext markup language* (HTML). As the name suggests, HTML is a markup language that allows you to mark up (or decorate) hypertext. Initially, HTML pages consisted mostly of plain text, a few images, and perhaps a table or two. However, it didn't take long for the HTML standard to expand to support more sophisticated UI elements such as text input fields, dropdown lists, and so on.

> **What is Hypertext Anyway?**
>
> The term *hypertext* refers to text content that contains references to other text. These references are realized in the form of hyperlinks. When chained together, hypertext documents make it possible for users to surf the web in search of interesting (and presumably related) content.
>
> These days, the term *hypermedia* might be more appropriate than *hypertext*, since much of the web content you see online also consists of various media objects such as images, movies, and so on. Still, no matter what you call it, hypertext still reigns supreme as the *de facto* format for exchanging information over the web.

Though the advent of HTML and the World Wide Web ushered in a level of information exchange unprecedented in all of history, users quickly became frustrated with the static nature of websites. They longed for more interaction and personalization—something static HTML simply couldn't provide in and of itself. This called for programming, and lots of it.

CGI: The Common Gateway Interface

In order to serve up more dynamic content, developers had to go back to the drawing board and revisit the architecture of web servers. In the beginning, the tasks performed by a web server were roughly equivalent to that of a file server. For example, the process of fulfilling an HTTP GET request basically consisted of fetching the physical file that corresponded with the path information encoded in the request URL. Thus, in the example illustrated in Section 1.1.1, the web server would use the path information in the URL (i.e., the */products/ABAP-Cookbook. html* part) to locate the file called *ABAP-Cookbook.html* and then embed its contents into the HTTP response message.

To achieve a more dynamic approach, developers needed a way to get their hands on HTTP requests in a programmatic context. After they considered several alternatives, the Common Gateway Interface (CGI) emerged in the early 1990s as a standard for enhancing web server software toward this end.

As the name suggests, the CGI provides an interface between the web server and a (typically) external application. To see how this works, consider the CGI process flow illustrated in Figure 1.2. In this scenario, the web server hands off an HTTP GET request to a Perl interpreter, which then executes a Perl script. This simple script uses the print command to output a series of environment variables. The output of this script is then dynamically appended to the HTTP response message via the CGI and sent back to the client.

With the CGI infrastructure in place, developers were able to produce all kinds of dynamic content for the first time. For example, a CGI program could be used to execute a database query and then tabulate the results in a dynamically generated HTML document. In this scenario, the dynamic HTML is produced via a series of print statements, as illustrated in Figure 1.2. Of course, CGI scripts weren't limited to just HTML: they could also be used to download dynamically generated images and other resources.

In addition to the generation of dynamic content, CGI scripts made it possible to develop interactive applications in which users could upload data from forms into a remote database using the HTTP POST method. This feature, when combined with the powerful content generation capabilities described earlier, gave rise to a whole new breed of web applications that could maintain some level of conversational state with the user.

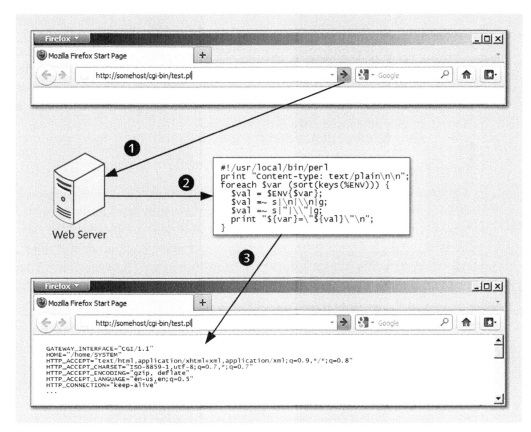

Figure 1.2 Processing an HTTP Request Using a CGI Script

Java Servlets and Web Application Servers

Right around the time CGI scripts reached the peak of their popularity, Sun Microsystems introduced its Java Servlet specification. Unlike CGI, which spawns a heavyweight OS-level process each time an HTTP request is received, Java Servlets execute inside a dedicated web container, which is always up and running. At runtime, HTTP requests to Servlets are dispatched to lightweight processor threads maintained in a thread pool within the Servlet container. Because Servlets run inside a container, they can maintain a closer relationship with the web server, which makes them more aware of their surroundings than their CGI counterparts. As such, the Java Servlet specification represented a huge leap forward in the development of web application servers—a concept we'll explore further in Section 1.3.

Despite their popularity early on, web developers quickly discovered that applications based on CGI programs or Java Servlets were rather difficult to maintain. This is because it was difficult to separate the UI concerns from backend data processing concerns. Indeed, the process of hacking HTML inside a series of print statements is a very nasty business, especially considering that typically only a fraction of the content truly needs to be dynamic.

Server Pages Technology

Recognizing the need for a more economical development model, Microsoft decided to turn the concept of web scripting on its ear by introducing its Active Server Pages (ASPs) in the late 1990s. Unlike CGI scripts and Java Servlets, ASPs are HTML-centric pages that embed custom programming logic inside special tags called *scriptlets*. This approach makes it easier to separate UI development concerns from the application logic.

Given the widespread success of ASP technology, Sun Microsystems quickly followed suit with its own JavaServer Pages (JSPs). Then, not too long after that, SAP also got on board with Business Server Pages (BSPs). For the most part, you'll find that all server pages technologies look and feel about the same. Listing 1.1 provides an example of a BSP page. As you can see, it consists mostly of HTML markup. Indeed, in this simple example, the only custom code is included within the scriptlet expression contained between the <% and %> tags.

```
<%@ page language="abap" %>
<html>
<head>
  <title>Sample BSP Application</title>
</head>
<body>
  <h1>Hello <%= sy-uname %>!</h1>
</body>
</html>
```

Listing 1.1 A Sample BSP Page

MVC and Web Frameworks

Though modern technologies such as server pages certainly made it easier to produce dynamic web content, developers still found themselves having a difficult time trying to build large-scale applications. Here, developers found that:

► It generally took much longer to build web screens than it did to build traditional rich client screens using tools such as Microsoft Visual Studio or the SAP Screen Painter.

► Web applications were difficult to maintain since even the simplest changes to the UI could trigger a domino effect of changes downstream.

► Due to the stateless nature of the HTTP protocol, it was difficult to keep track of the state of user sessions within the application.

► Transferring data between HTML forms and backend data sources was tedious and error prone.

► Users were often dissatisfied with the capabilities and performance of web applications when compared to the rich client applications they were accustomed to running on their local workstations.

In order to level the playing field, developers began to create various kinds of web frameworks, which provided baseline solutions to problems such as the ones described above. Common features that emerged from these frameworks included:

► The development of *tag libraries* (e.g., HTMLB in the BSP world), which expanded the default UI toolkit provided with HTML. With the advent of tag libraries, developers were finally able to integrate complex UI controls such as trees, interactive tables, and so on into web screens without having to write all the requisite HTML/JavaScript from scratch.

► Automated data binding between HTML form fields and backend data structures.

► The capacity for *session management*. Here, we're talking about an application's ability to keep track of a user's activity as they interact with the application. See the box entitled "HTTP Session Management" for more details about this feature.

HTTP Session Management

As you learned in Section 1.1.1, HTTP is a *stateless* protocol. This means that web servers don't have to remember anything about prior requests they've serviced. From a performance perspective, this makes good sense because it reduces the amount of system resources a web server requires to process incoming requests. On the other hand, it certainly complicates matters for developers trying to develop interactive web applications.

To get around this limitation of the HTTP protocol, a popular workaround for many developers is to come up with a mechanism for implementing session management at the application level. Though realized in different ways, the basic approach here is as follows:

▶ When a user first accesses the application, the application will allocate a session key that it passes back to the client in the HTTP response message. This session key is an arbitrary token shared between the client and the application and can be implemented in many different ways (e.g., as an HTTP cookie, URL query string parameter, etc.).

▶ Next, the application will use the derived session key as an index for allocating a chunk of memory somewhere on the application server (e.g., in memory, the database, etc.). This memory is used to keep track of user input, navigational state, and so on.

▶ Finally, once the session is established, users can continue interacting with the application as usual. The only difference is that now the HTTP requests contain the provided session key in the HTTP request headers. This key allows the application to correlate requests with an existing application session and updates the application state accordingly.

A familiar example of session management is the so-called *shopping cart,* which you've probably interacted with at one time or another at online retailer sites. Here, the session keeps track of the items you've added to your cart as you shop within the online store. Then, when you go to check out, the backend application can fetch this data and apply it toward the creation of a sales order (for example).

Overall, the use of HTTP session management has become so commonplace that most users simply assume web applications will be smart enough to keep track of where they are, the data they've entered, and so on. Of course, while HTTP session management seems easy enough to implement on paper, the devil is in the details. Fortunately, in the upcoming chapters, you'll see how the Web Dynpro framework takes care of these details for you automatically.

One of the common themes that seemed to resonate throughout the entire development community as web frameworks emerged was the application of the Model View Controller (MVC) design pattern. Here, the primary goal in applying the MVC pattern was to provide clearer lines of separation between the frontend UI and the backend application/data model. To understand how these lines of separation are drawn up, consider the MVC architecture diagram shown in Figure 1.3. Here, you can see how incoming requests are filtered through a controller. Internally, a controller processes an inbound request as follows:

1. First, the controller ascertains the nature of the request by validating user input provided from the view layer.

2. Next, based on its findings, the controller may determine that an update is required in the model layer. Here, the provided user input might be used to create or update a record, for example.

3. Then, once any required changes are applied to the backend data model, the next step is to select the appropriate view to be displayed next for the user. This determination is based on provided user input, navigational requests, etc. Naturally, the selected view will be filled with data from the updated data model.

4. Finally, the target view will be displayed for the user, and the cycle starts all over again as the user inputs more data, triggers events, and so on.

As you can see in Figure 1.3, the introduction of the controller layer makes it possible to decouple the UI from the underlying application model. Therefore, if a change needs to be made to a screen in the view layer, the change can be made with little to no impact on the underlying application data model and vice versa. Indeed, the coupling between these two layers is so loose, it's possible to swap out the UI or application layers with minimal impact to the application as a whole. Furthermore, such clear separation makes it possible for developers to specialize in particular areas of development (e.g., HTML and graphic design vs. backend application development).

With MVC-based web frameworks in place, developers finally had all the tools necessary to build full-scale web applications. Of course, this is not to say that web development became orders of magnitude easier—it was still very difficult to design and maintain large applications. Furthermore, it was very challenging in those days to find an experienced developer who had all the necessary skills to work in these environments.

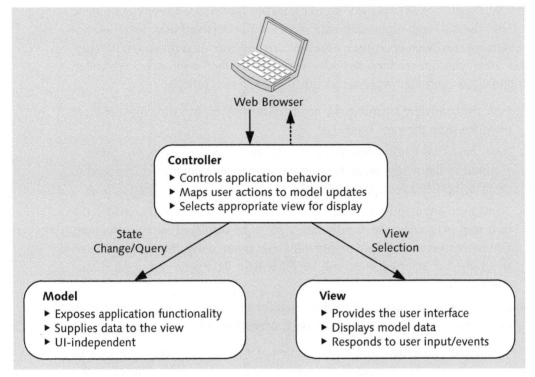

Figure 1.3 Overview of the MVC Design Pattern

Client-Side Programming and AJAX

Each of the approaches to web development considered thus far falls under the category of *server-side development*. This is to say that the custom programming logic executes on the server *before* the content is shipped down to the client. In these models, if you want to elicit any kind of response from the application, you must submit a request back to the HTTP server so that it can call a program, for example. This back-and-forth between the client and server is referred to as a *server roundtrip*.

From a user perspective, server roundtrips are obnoxious because they interrupt access to the application for seconds (or even minutes) at a time. Such interruptions are particularly annoying in cases when only a portion of the screen needs to be refreshed. For these reasons, and others, client-side scripting languages such as JavaScript were developed.

Client-side scripting languages make it possible to integrate custom programming logic within an HTML document to perform simple tasks such as form validation, dynamic screen rendering, and so on. With client-side scripting, all this is made possible without a server roundtrip, since the code runs locally inside a container embedded within the web browser (typically as a plug-in).

One of the most recent features added to the client-side scripting bag of tricks is the capacity for executing asynchronous calls to the backend web server in the background. This technique is commonly referred to as asynchronous JavaScript (or AJAX). Among other things, AJAX makes it possible to implement so-called "flicker-free" screens that greatly improve the user experience.

1.2   A Model-Based Approach to UI Development

As we examined the evolution of web programming models in Section 1.1.2, you may have noticed a trend: each evolutionary step introduced a deeper level of abstraction than the previous one. Naturally, as the quality of the abstraction improved, so did developer productivity. And yet, despite all these advances, developers still found themselves having to maintain a lot of code to perform even the simplest tasks.

In order to take the next step in terms of productivity, developers needed a programming model that would allow them to adopt a more *declarative approach* to UI development. Here, we're talking about more than just the introduction of some snazzy graphical development tools; we're talking about a comprehensive programming model that guides the UI development process from start to finish. As you might have guessed, Web Dynpro provides just such a declarative programming model. In this section, we'll introduce you to the Web Dynpro programming model and show you some of the key benefits it has to offer.

Declarative Programming vs. Imperative Programming

In computer science literature, you'll frequently find declarative programming defined as being the antithesis of *imperative programming*. Of course, this definition is only useful if you understand what imperative programming is. So, without further ado, let's attempt to put these two programming paradigms in perspective.

Like many words in the English language, the term *imperative* has different meanings depending on its usage. One usage type refers to verbs that express commands or requests.

In a programming context, imperative commands take on the form of statements and algorithms that codify program logic. Thus, from a developer's perspective, the use of the imperative approach involves the detailed development of source code that specifies each of the steps required to achieve a particular goal. In essence, imperative programming is all about the *how*. If you've ever developed ABAP programs using procedural programming techniques, you know what the imperative approach is all about.

As opposed to the code-intensive imperative approach, the declarative approach is focused primarily on specifying *what* the program should do instead of worrying about *how* it should be done. As a result, the declarative methodology promotes a division of labor between higher-level application components and lower-level technical components. In the end, the declarative approach makes it possible for developers to effectively weave together applications using graphical development tools, as opposed to having to write/integrate all the underlying code from scratch.

When you look at these two paradigms in this light, you can see that they really complement one another. For instance, base-level components are typically implemented using an imperative programming approach. Then, once these base components are in place, application developers can come along and use declarative programming techniques to integrate and configure these components in an application. We'll see this concept on display again and again as we progress throughout the course of this book.

1.2.1 Understanding the Web Dynpro Framework

Unlike other web programming models, which allow you to implement UI designs using anything from an IDE to a simple text editor, WDA requires you to lay out and configure UI components exclusively through a graphical editor tool called the Web Dynpro Explorer. In keeping with the declarative approach, this tool provides you with a convenient WYSIWYG (what you see is what you get) editor that allows you to develop UI layouts quickly and easily. Behind the scenes, the various UI settings are expressed in terms of a platform-independent data model called the Web Dynpro metamodel, as opposed to—for example—HTML markup. Though this metadata-based approach may seem overly restrictive at first, we'll see in Section 1.2.2 that there's a method to SAP's madness here.

The Web Dynpro metamodel itself is part of a larger framework generically referred to as the Web Dynpro framework. This framework brings structure to the development process, providing developers with predefined hooks in which they can supplement statically defined UIs with custom event handler methods, dynamically generated UI components, and so on. Collectively, the framework makes it possible for developers to quickly weave applications together using a healthy blend of declarative and imperative programming techniques.

Figure 1.4 illustrates the programming model made possible via the Web Dynpro framework. On the one hand, you can see how a UI is declaratively defined in terms of the Web Dynpro metamodel using a drag-and-drop view editor. On the other hand, you can see how custom ABAP code is integrated at predefined points within the framework. When the application is activated, the Web Dynpro metadata is fed through a code generator, which translates portions of the generic model data into ABAP code. This generated code is then combined with any custom ABAP code that may exist and fed into the ABAP compiler. Once the compilation process is finished, the Web Dynpro application is complete and ready to run.

As you can see in Figure 1.4, Web Dynpro applications run inside a specialized runtime environment called the Web Dynpro runtime environment. The Web Dynpro runtime environment exists in two parts:

▶ On the server side, the runtime environment provides a container for Web Dynpro applications much like the Java Servlet container described in Section 1.1.2. As such, it takes care of a lot of low-level technical issues, such as HTTP protocol handling, session management, and more. Furthermore, it's also in charge of rendering UI screens at runtime. We'll have more to say about this in Section 1.2.2.

▶ On the client side, the runtime environment takes advantage of various features available in the user agent to improve the overall user experience. For example, when rendering screens for HTML-based browser clients, the client-side runtime environment may use innovations in JavaScript and CSS technologies to reduce the time it takes to render and/or refresh screens. Naturally, the scope of such enhancements will vary among different client types.

We'll have an opportunity to investigate the technical side of the Web Dynpro runtime environment further in Section 1.3.

Like a lot of web-based development frameworks, the Web Dynpro framework has its basis in the aforementioned MVC design pattern. Among other things, this enforces a very clear separation between the UI design and the backend application model. We'll see how these lines of separation are drawn up when we begin to explore the anatomy of WDA applications in Chapter 2.

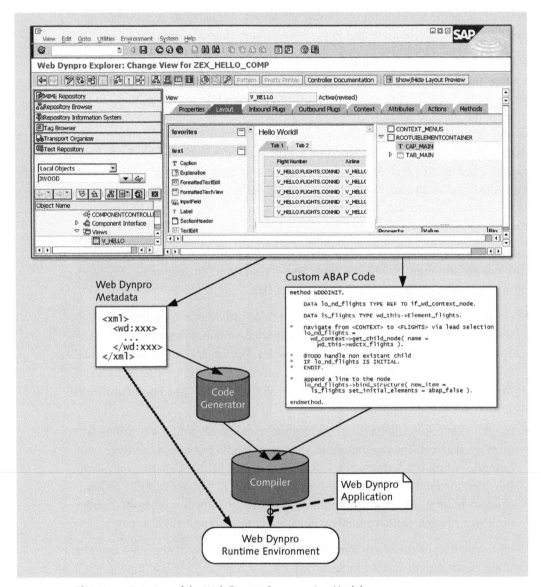

Figure 1.4 Overview of the Web Dynpro Programming Model

1.2.2   The Benefits of a Model-Driven Architecture

Now that you're familiar with the Web Dynpro framework, you might be wondering why there's a need for so much abstraction. After all, if the end game is just to produce a series of web screens anyway, why not just encode the UI layout using HTML? As it turns out, there are quite a few benefits to using a model-based approach. In this section, we'll explore several of these benefits.

Multichannel Access and Adaptability

One of the primary benefits of utilizing an intermediate metamodel to represent the UI layout is that it makes applications much more portable. To understand what that means, let's consider a real-world example. Imagine you've built a web application using a conglomeration of HTML 4, CSS, and JavaScript. Now, let's fast-forward to the future and think about what happens when the standards for UI development change. For example, clients now want the application to utilize the latest widgets provided with HTML5. Or, they want the application to be more user-friendly on next-generation mobile devices.

With Web Dynpro, you don't have to worry about keeping up with the latest and greatest web technologies. In terms of development inventory, you don't have a single line of HTML or JavaScript written anywhere. Instead, you just have a collection of metadata that describes the UI in generic terms: a label with this set of properties goes here; a button goes there, and so on. Therefore, the only thing you need to render the UI in HTML5 or some Rich Internet Application (RIA) technology like Adobe Flex is an extension to the Web Dynpro runtime environment. What's more, the end-user experience doesn't change all that much as the technology evolves. To them, a button's a button; only one button is rendered in HTML5, and another one is rendered using an Adobe Flex control.

At the time this book is being written, SAP has already extended the Web Dynpro runtime environment to include an Adobe Flex–based rendering engine, and plans for an HTML5-based rendering engine are currently underway. Furthermore, the clear separation between the UI design and runtime components has also allowed for various other innovations along the way, such as the Unified Rendering Light Speed (URLS) rendering engine added in SAP NetWeaver 7.0, EHP 1. This engine offers huge performance boosts for HTML-based clients in that it utilizes AJAX and other cutting-edge HTML rendering technologies to reduce the number of roundtrips to the server.

Reducing the Learning Curve

In the beginning, it takes a little while to familiarize yourself with the Web Dynpro development model. However, unlike other fleeting web technologies, the time investment involved in learning Web Dynpro is essentially a one-time proposition. In other words, you don't have to constantly invest time in learning next-generation technologies such as HTML, JavaScript, ActionScript, and so on to develop state-of-the-art web applications. Instead, the burden of enhancing the Web Dynpro runtime environment falls to SAP. From a developer's perspective, once you've invested the time to understand the Web Dynpro framework, you'll be able to leverage these skills again and again over time.

While we're on the subject, we should also point out that Web Dynpro is not unique to ABAP; SAP also provides Web Dynpro Java (WDJ). In fact, WDJ actually predates WDA by about a year, since it was first made available with the SAP NetWeaver 2004 release. Naturally, there are some major differences between the two platforms. Besides the obvious disparity in the underlying code structure, WDJ components are developed in an Eclipse-based, client-side development environment called the SAP NetWeaver Developer Studio (NWDS). Once you get past these fundamental differences, though, you'll find that the process of developing UIs in either platform to be remarkably similar. If you're interested in learning more about WDJ, we highly recommend the second edition of *Inside Web Dynpro for Java* (Whealy, SAP PRESS, 2007).

Repeatable Results and Reusability

One of the things you'll notice about Web Dynpro is that the development process is very structured. Everything has its place, and there is a clear separation of concerns at each step within the development process. Among other things, such order makes it possible to achieve *repeatable results* in the UI development process. This is to say that the UI development process should be fairly predictable and that you should see productivity improvements over time.

Another benefit of the structure of the Web Dynpro development model is that it naturally introduces component boundaries. Once you understand how these boundaries work, you can begin to organize your development into reusable components. Furthermore, you'll find that SAP has provided quite a few useful components that you can utilize right out of the box. We'll explore the Web Dynpro component concept beginning in Chapter 2.

1.3 Technical Integration Concepts

Up until now, we've talked about WDA in fairly generic terms. Now, as we get ready to segue into more practical discussion points, it's appropriate to take a look at some technical integration concepts for WDA. Having an understanding of these concepts will help you understand how WDA applications work from a technical perspective.

1.3.1 Legacy Web and UI Technologies

As we mentioned earlier, WDA is not SAP's first foray into the world of web development. Before WDA was released in 2005, SAP provided several different options for implementing web-based applications. In this section, we'll look at some of the challenges and growing pains SAP faced at the time the web exploded onto the scene in the mid-1990s.

Classic Dynpros and the SAP GUI

In order to appreciate how web technology frameworks evolved in the ABAP world, you first need to understand a little bit about the UI technology that preceded them. In the more than twenty years prior to the advent of web technology in the ABAP world, SAP UIs had evolved from mainframe console-based screens to a proprietary client-server-based UI technology in the late 1980s called *Dynpro*.

> **Note**
>
> The term *dynpro* is an abbreviation for "dynamic program." Though the term is also used in the context of Web Dynpro, the two UI technologies have very little in common.

Classic Dynpro technology, like many UI technologies developed during that time period, is based on a rich client application architecture:

▶ On the server side, a classic Dynpro application consists of an ABAP program and one or more Dynpro screens. Dynpro screens are created using a specialized editor tool integrated into the ABAP Workbench called the Screen Painter. Within the Screen Painter, developers can define the layout of the Dynpro screen using a fixed set of UI controls. In addition, developers can also specify the screen's *flow logic*. The screen's flow logic determines how the application will behave whenever specific events are triggered.

► On the client side, users access classic Dynpro screens using a proprietary application client called the SAP GUI. Among other things, the SAP GUI client is responsible for rendering screens, responding to user input, and in some cases, performing local tasks like sorting or filtering. Behind the scenes, the SAP GUI client communicates with the backend application server using SAP's proprietary DIAG protocol.

Legacy Dynpro Technology vs. Web Dynpro

In order to differentiate between legacy Dynpro technology and Web Dynpro, you'll frequently see legacy Dynpro technology referred to as "classic Dynpro," a convention we'll follow in this book.

Figure 1.5 shows an example of a classic Dynpro screen in the SAP GUI for Windows. If you've spent much time around SAP, you probably interact with classic Dynpro screens like this all the time. Indeed, at the time of this writing, more SAP users interact with classic Dynpro screens than any other UI technology employed by SAP. To some degree, this is a testament to the effectiveness of the technology. However, it also speaks to the inflexibility of the framework as compared to MVC-based UI frameworks—a concept we'll explore further in the next section.

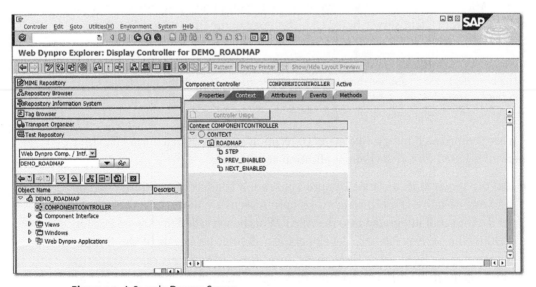

Figure 1.5 A Sample Dynpro Screen

SAP GUI for HTML and the Internet Transaction Server

In terms of establishing a web presence, SAP got its start in 1995 with the release of the *Internet Transaction Server* (ITS). At the time, the ITS was positioned as a makeshift solution for bridging fundamental gaps in the ABAP technology stack. Here, SAP faced several sizeable obstacles to providing web-based access:

▶ First and foremost, the underlying SAP Basis application server at the time didn't provide native support for web technologies (for example, HTTP).

▶ Secondly, there was nothing about the proprietary Dynpro architecture that made for an easy transition to web technologies like HTML.

▶ Finally, after more than a decade of investment in Dynpro technology, SAP discovered that many Dynpro-based applications didn't draw clear lines between the Dynpro flow logic and application logic. Consequently, the prospects of web-enabling such applications went much deeper than swapping an HTML screen for a Dynpro screen. To do this right, SAP would effectively have to rebuild many applications from scratch.

In the short term, SAP decided that the quickest path to web enablement was to interject the ITS component as a sort of middleware that would sit between a web server (e.g., Apache or Microsoft IIS) and a backend SAP application server. Much like the CGI approach described in Section 1.1.2, the ITS served as a gateway that allowed web servers to forward requests on to an SAP application server. Internally, the ITS had the responsibility of translating an HTTP request into a DIAG request and vice versa. Furthermore, it was also tasked with converting Dynpro screens into comparable HTML markup. Figure 1.6 illustrates the basic architecture of the ITS.

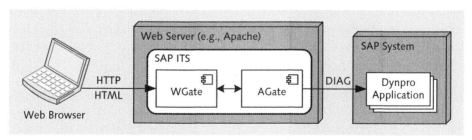

Figure 1.6 High-Level Architecture of Standalone ITS

Over time, as the ITS evolved, various programming models were developed to give developers more control over the page-rendering process. SAP also introduced the SAP GUI for HTML, which allowed users to access most of the standard transactions they were accustomed to working with via their local web browsers. Still, despite these incremental innovations, it's fair to say that the ITS was received with mixed results from the SAP community:

▶ In terms of user experience, ITS-based solutions were definitely lacking when compared to some of the shiny new web applications being introduced by competing vendors at the time.

▶ For some users, use of the SAP GUI for HTML felt like a step backward since the ITS-generated screens were not nearly as robust or responsive as the same Dynpro screens accessed via the SAP GUI for Windows or SAP GUI for Java.

▶ On the development side of the house, many developers found the programming models overly complex and cumbersome to work with.

Despite these limitations, the ITS is still used today in situations when companies want to web-enable Dynpro-based transactions. However, as of the SAP NetWeaver 2004 release, customers no longer have to install the ITS as a bolt-on to an external web server such as Apache or Microsoft IIS. Instead, the ITS has been integrated within the SAP NetWeaver technology stack. We'll look at the communication components that make this possible in the upcoming sections.

1.3.2 Internet Communication Manager

While the ITS provided a somewhat workable alternative for providing web access to SAP transactions, it was never intended to be anything more than a temporary solution. The longer-term solution involved retrofitting the SAP Basis application server to provide native support for web technologies. This effort culminated with the release of the SAP Web Application Server ABAP (hereafter referred to as the AS ABAP) in 2001.

Though positioned as a replacement for the legacy SAP Basis application server, it's probably more accurate to think of the AS ABAP as a web-based extension to the legacy SAP Basis application server. This extension was realized in the form of the Internet Communication Manager (ICM) component. Figure 1.7 illustrates the high-level architecture of the AS ABAP. As you can see, the core elements of the predecessor SAP Basis application server remain intact: the dispatcher, work processes, and so on. The ICM sits outside all this as a standalone executable program. At runtime, communication requests between the ICM and core application server are routed through the dispatcher component in much the same way that SAP GUI requests are processed.

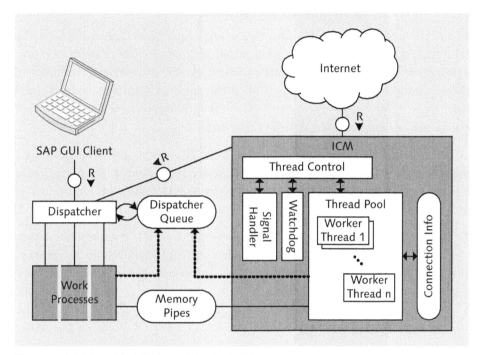

Figure 1.7 High-Level Architecture of the AS ABAP

From a communications perspective, the ICM supports bidirectional communication between an AS ABAP instance and the outside world using Internet protocols such as HTTP, HTTPS, and SMTP. Thus, in addition to handling incoming HTTP requests, the ICM can also be used to:

▶ Initiate HTTP client requests from an ABAP program (for example, calling a web service)

▶ Send and receive mail messages using SMTP

▶ Encrypt incoming and outgoing HTTP requests using SSL

For the purposes of this book, our investigation of the ICM will be limited to the processing of HTTP requests within the context of WDA. However, if you're interested in learning how to utilize some of the other features of the ICM (e.g., submitting HTTP client requests or sending and receiving e-mail), we recommend that you check out *ABAP Cookbook* (Wood, SAP PRESS, 2010).

1.3.3 Internet Communication Framework

As a developer, you'll typically find yourself to be pretty well insulated from the complexities of the ICM and the communication it brokers. This insulation is provided in the form of a communication framework that sits between the ICM and the application programming layer called the Internet Communication Framework (ICF). From a developer's perspective, the ICF offers a convenient API that can be used to send and receive HTTP requests.

To better understand the role the ICF plays in HTTP request processing, let's trace the path of an HTTP request through the ICM and ICF and up to the point where it's processed in ABAP. The UML sequence diagram in Figure 1.8 illustrates this process flow:

1. The process begins when the ICM takes receipt of an HTTP request and hands it off to an available worker thread within the ICM thread pool. The worker thread will then process the request by forwarding it on to the ABAP dispatcher node (see Figure 1.7).

2. Next, the dispatcher node will select an available dialog process to process the HTTP request.

3. The dialog process begins processing the request by forwarding it on to the *ICF Controller* node, which is the gateway into the ICF.

4. The ICF Controller then sends the request on to an *ICF Manager* instance for internal processing.

5. The ICF Manager is responsible for introspecting the request and selecting an HTTP request handler module to process it.

6. Within the *request handler module* (which is an ABAP Objects class that implements the standard IF_HTTP_EXTENSION interface), we can include custom ABAP code to process the HTTP request within the predefined HANDLE_ REQUEST() method.

7. Finally, the results of the request (i.e., the HTTP response) are forwarded back through the framework and on to the client.

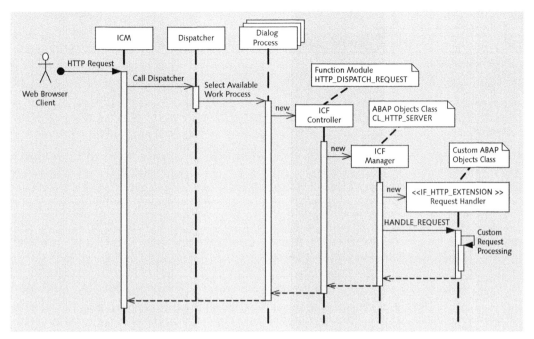

Figure 1.8 Process Flow of an HTTP Request through the ICM and ICF

As you can see in Figure 1.8, all the low-level HTTP protocol processing is handled upstream by standard ICM/ICF components. So, by the time an HTTP request is handed off to a custom request handler class, everything we need to process the request is packaged up within easy-to-use ICF object references.

Understanding ICF Service Nodes

Looking at the process flow depicted in Figure 1.8, you might be wondering how the ICF Manager knew how to route an incoming HTTP request to a particular HTTP request handler module. For this task, the ICF Manager looks up this routing information at runtime using ICF server node definitions maintained in Transaction SICF.

Figure 1.9 shows the initial screen of Transaction SICF. As you can see, this initial screen provides a selection screen that can be used to narrow a search to specific ICF service nodes. For now, let's take a look at the entire list so you can see how things are organized. To access the entire list of service nodes, click the EXECUTE button.

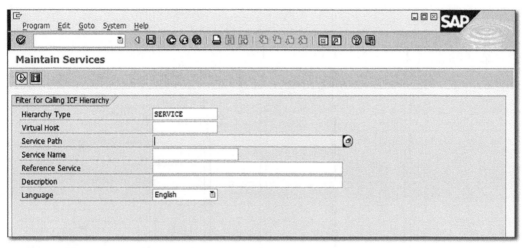

Figure 1.9 Initial Screen of Transaction SICF

Figure 1.10 shows the maintenance screen for ICF service nodes in Transaction SICF. Here, you can see that the service hierarchy is broken up into *virtual hosts* and *service nodes*:

▶ **Virtual hosts**
A virtual host is a specialized node that gets bound to a particular HTTP port defined within the ICM. Most of the time, you'll work with the default_host virtual host that gets set up out of the box during the AS ABAP installation process. This virtual host is normally bound to the default HTTP port for the AS ABAP.

Note

The default HTTP port for the AS ABAP is an 8000-series port, where the last two digits represent the system number of the AS ABAP system.

▶ **Service nodes**
Underneath a given virtual host, you have a series of hierarchically defined service nodes (which can be nested arbitrarily deep). From an addressing perspective, each service node represents a path segment in a URL. Thus, for example, to access the bsp service node highlighted in Figure 1.10, we would construct a URL like this: *http(s)://host:port/sap/bc/bsp*.

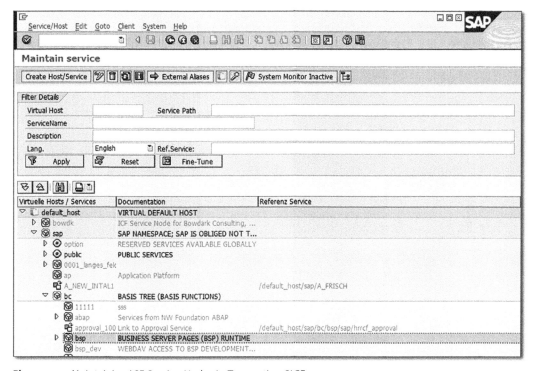

Figure 1.10 Maintaining ICF Service Nodes in Transaction SICF

Once a server node's place is established within the service hierarchy, you can begin specifying various attributes of the node's behavior. To see some of these attributes on display, consider the service node definition for the Web Dynpro runtime environment shown in Figure 1.11. As you can see, there are quite a few settings you can configure for a given service node: basic service details, logon data, error handling procedures, and so on. Perhaps most importantly, you have the HANDLER LIST tab, in which you can configure one or more request handlers for the node (i.e., ABAP Objects classes that implement the IF_HTTP_EXTENSION interface). At runtime, the ICF Manager component will select the handler(s) specified in this list to process a given request.

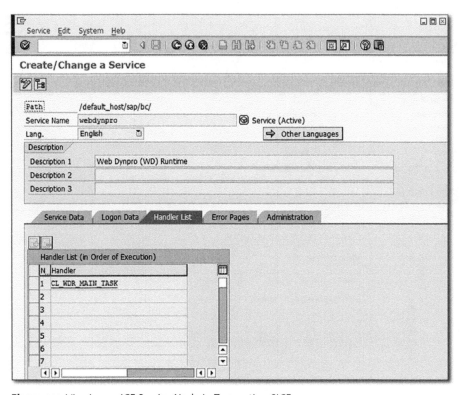

Figure 1.11 Viewing an ICF Service Node in Transaction SICF

As you browse through the set of service nodes provided by SAP, you'll find various nodes that provide some familiar web-based functionality in the AS ABAP world, including:

▶ /sap/bc/bsp
This service node provides the runtime environment for BSP applications. If you expand this node, you'll find many subnodes, each of which represents a separate BSP application. As you create new BSP applications within the ABAP Workbench, you'll see that new nodes are automatically created within this hierarchy.

▶ /sap/bc/gui
This service node implements the integrated ITS described in Section 1.3.1.

▶ /sap/bc/webdynpro
This service node implements the Web Dynpro runtime environment. We'll learn more about how this node works in Section 1.3.4.

1.3.4   The Web Dynpro Runtime Environment

Now that you have a feel for how HTTP requests are processed through the ICF, let's take a look at how the Web Dynpro runtime environment fits into all this. As you can see in the ICF service node definition in Figure 1.11, the ICF handler class for the Web Dynpro runtime environment is called CL_WDR_MAIN_TASK. Figure 1.12 shows how this class is defined in the ABAP Class Builder tool. Here, among other things, you can see how the class implements the IF_HTTP_EXTENSION interface.

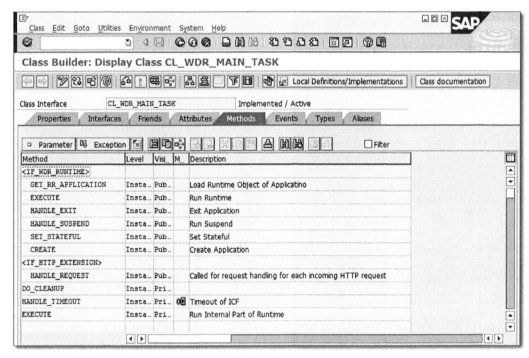

Figure 1.12 ICF Handler Class for Web Dynpro Runtime Environment

At runtime, all requests for WDA applications are ultimately routed through the HANDLE_REQUEST() method of class CL_WDR_MAIN_TASK. Figure 1.13 shows the signature of this method, which consists of a single importing parameter called SERVER (which is of reference type IF_HTTP_SERVER). The SERVER parameter provides the handler method with everything it needs to process an incoming request:

▶ The public attribute REQUEST (of reference type IF_HTTP_REQUEST) can be used to access basic request info, header fields, the contents of the request body, and so on.

▶ The public attribute RESPONSE (of reference type IF_HTTP_RESPONSE) provides various methods that can be used to build the HTTP response.

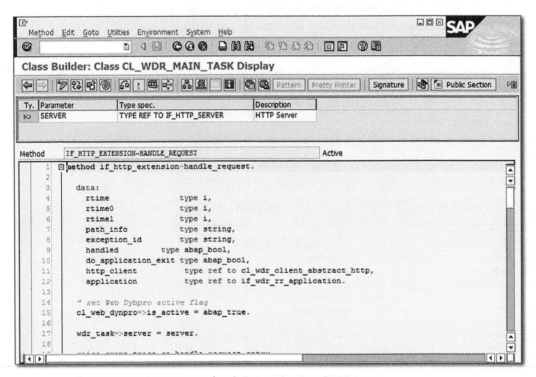

Figure 1.13 Implementation of Web Dynpro Runtime Environment

If you look at the code in the HANDLE_REQUEST() method of class CL_WDR_MAIN_TASK, you can get a feel for how the Web Dynpro runtime environment is initialized during request processing. Once the framework is bootstrapped, the runtime environment assumes the responsibility for request processing from that point forward. Therefore, as you dig through the code, you can see how different components within the runtime environment collaborate to process events, render screens, and so on. It's at this layer that SAP can provide innovations such as the aforementioned URLS rendering engine, for example.

1.3.5 System Requirements

As we mentioned earlier, WDA was first made available with the SAP NetWeaver 7.0 release (sometimes called SAP NetWeaver 2004s) in 2005. Therefore, in order to develop WDA applications, you must have access to an SAP NetWeaver system based on the 7.0 release or later. If you don't have access to such a system, SAP does provide a 90-day trial download of current SAP NetWeaver systems on the SAP Developer Network at *http://www.sdn.sap.com/irj/scn/downloads*.

Since the initial release of WDA in 2005, SAP has been making incremental improvements to the WDA framework by adding new UI elements, improving performance of the runtime environment, and so on. However, despite these incremental enhancements, you'll find that the core framework hasn't really changed over the years. Therefore, most of the concepts you'll learn in this book apply equally to any SAP NetWeaver 7.0 system or later.

At the time this book is being written, the current version of SAP NetWeaver is version 7.3. Therefore, where appropriate, we'll point out new features added with this release. However, if you're developing WDA applications on an older version of SAP NetWeaver, don't worry; you'll find everything you need to get started in the upcoming chapters.

1.4 Summary

In this chapter, you were introduced to WDA and its surrounding framework. During the course of this introduction, you learned about some foundational technologies that contributed to the development of Web Dynpro. You also learned about the model-driven approach to UI development at the heart of Web Dynpro. Finally, we wrapped everything up by looking at how WDA integrates within the overall SAP NetWeaver technology stack.

Collectively, the knowledge you attained in this chapter should provide you with a solid foundation to build on in the upcoming chapters. As we progress through the book, you'll see many of the concepts described in this chapter applied during the course of development.

In the next chapter, we'll transition away from the conceptual side of things and begin dissecting the elements that make up a WDA application.

Conceptually speaking, WDA applications have a lot of moving parts. As a result, it can be difficult to get started with WDA development without knowing your way around the Web Dynpro component architecture. Therefore, in this chapter, we'll explore this architecture as we survey the anatomy of WDA applications.

2   The Anatomy of WDA Applications

In the previous chapter, we learned that Web Dynpro employs a model-based approach to UI development. From a development perspective, this implies that there's a certain order to how WDA applications are structured. Therefore, as an ABAP developer working within the framework, it's important that you understand how all the various pieces fit together.

In this chapter, we'll take a look at the anatomy of WDA applications. During the course of this investigation, we'll examine WDA applications at varying degrees of magnification so you can understand the roles and relationships among the different core elements. This analysis begins with the exploration of component-based software development concepts and then works its way outward as we consider Web Dynpro components and Web Dynpro applications as a whole. Once you've mastered these concepts, you'll be ready to begin creating WDA applications of your own.

2.1   Component-Based Software Development Concepts

Unlike other ABAP development objects you might have worked with in the past (e.g., report programs, module pools, etc.), the basic unit of development in WDA isn't a program or application. Instead, WDA development is focused on the manufacture of *components*. If you've never worked with components before, a brief introduction to component-based software concepts is in order. Therefore, in this section, we'll review these concepts and take a look at some reasons why a component-based development approach makes sense when developing user interfaces with Web Dynpro.

2.1.1 Componentization Overview

Common sense will tell you that one of the best ways to approach a complex task like UI development is to break the software down into a series of smaller modules that are easier to understand and maintain individually (a technique sometimes referred to as *decomposition*). However, while the decomposition technique may make sense intuitively, it's not always easy to figure out how to apply it at an implementation level. This is especially the case in large software projects when significant functionality is being delivered. Here, modularization involves much more than breaking a program up into a series of subroutines, functions, etc.

In recent years, a popular approach to software decomposition has been to break the software down into a series of reusable *software components*. This approach borrows from the manufacturing field in the sense that you can think of software components as being analogous to parts and materials used within the manufacturing process. For example, consider the way automotive manufacturers build a car. This process begins with the fabrication and acquisition of a series of discrete parts, which compartmentalize various aspects of the car design into smaller units that are easier to understand and maintain individually: fuel injectors, pistons, crankshafts, and so on. Then, once all the requisite parts are in place, the final manufacturing process consists mostly of combining these parts together to create a finished product (see Figure 2.1).

Figure 2.1 Integrating Components to Create an Assembly

In general, there are several important observations one can make regarding the use of componentization techniques in the manufacturing process:

▸ Breaking the design up into a series of discrete parts makes it easier for more production steps to execute in parallel (or, in many cases, before the production process even begins). This, in turn, reduces the amount of time it takes to complete the production cycle. Here, imagine the alternative of having to build each car from scratch using nothing but a series of bolts, wires, hoses, and so on.

▸ The component-based approach allows various parties to specialize in the fabrication of different parts. Such focused attention allows parties to innovate and figure out ways to produce higher-quality parts in a shorter amount of time. In the end, this makes it possible to produce parts in a much more cost-effective manner.

▸ As familiar part types emerge, their design specifications frequently become standardized. Such standardization makes it possible for competing vendors to develop compatible parts. This opens up the field such that manufacturers can choose whether or not they want to build parts in house or procure them from external suppliers.

2.1.2 Characteristics of Software Components

While it's easy to visualize how componentization works in a traditional manufacturing context, many developers have a difficult time figuring out how to apply these concepts toward the creation of software components. Here, it's important to realize that despite their abstract nature, software components should basically embody the same characteristics as physical parts. Indeed, with the automotive part metaphor in mind, let's think about some of the main characteristics that software components should exhibit:

▸ First of all, software components should have a simple and well-defined interface. Such interfaces make it easier to integrate components into larger component assemblies. It also makes it possible to swap out different components as needed.

▸ Next, software components should be *cohesive*. In other words, the functions performed by a component should be related in a meaningful way. This not only keeps things simple but also makes it easier to troubleshoot larger subassemblies because there is a clear separation of duties among the components.

▶ Finally, the implementation details for software components should be hidden from the outside world and shielded from tampering. This is to say that components should be well *encapsulated*. Proper encapsulation techniques reduce the number of dependencies between components and the assemblies that use them. This in turn makes it easier to maintain and enhance the components over time.

When you combine these characteristics, you end up with a self-contained module that can perform a handful of related tasks in an autonomous manner.

2.1.3   Understanding the Positioning of Web Dynpro Components

Now that we've observed some of the benefits of componentization, you might be wondering what all this has to do with the development of user interfaces with Web Dynpro. After all, since the rapid development tools provided with the Web Dynpro framework make it relatively easy to create new WDA applications, all this up-front component-based design work may seem like overkill.

The important thing to remember here is that one of the main goals of componentization is to improve the overall quality of the abstraction we're working with. In other words, we want to create building blocks that are flexible and easy to use. For example, imagine we're tasked with creating a series of interactive report applications. Here, rather than reinventing the wheel each time we want to build an interactive report, it makes sense to create a separate and standalone reporting component that can be reused in multiple scenarios. Or, better yet, we might be able to leverage an SAP standard component such as the familiar *SAP List Viewer* (ALV) component for this purpose. Figure 2.2 illustrates how this separation of duties works. Naturally, by delegating the report output to the ALV component, we avoid duplicate efforts and ensure that if a change needs to be made to the report output at some point, it only has to be made once.

Besides the obvious benefits of reuse, componentization also makes the software easier to understand and maintain in the long run. Here, instead of having a single module overburdened with too much responsibility, we have a series of standalone modules that specialize in particular tasks. Due to their cohesion, each of the standalone modules is much easier to maintain individually: we don't have to sift through a lot of cross-cutting concerns to figure out what's going on underneath the hood.

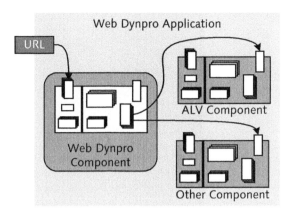

Figure 2.2 Leveraging Components to Create New Applications

We'll have an opportunity to see how componentization works on a practical level in Chapter 9. In the meantime, we'll narrow our focus a bit and look at the organization and design of individual components.

2.2 Web Dynpro Components

Before we can begin developing WDA applications, we must first create one or more WDA components. Conceptually, you can think of WDA components as building blocks that can be mixed and matched to build WDA applications. However, as we'll soon see, these building blocks are much more than just a loose collection of technical artifacts. When designed correctly, WDA components can be used to encapsulate entire steps within a business process. In this section, we'll introduce you to WDA components and the various types of elements that can be defined within them.

2.2.1 Architectural Overview

Developers new to WDA often make the mistake of assuming that WDA components basically play the same role as a function group or folder. In other words, they assume WDA components only exist to group a series of related UI development objects together. However, this overly simplistic view fails to take into account the structure and boundaries that WDA components enforce. The component architecture diagram contained in Figure 2.3 illustrates these boundaries.

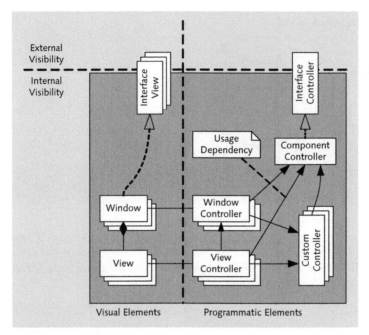

Figure 2.3 Architecture of a WDA Component

As you look over the component model depicted in Figure 2.3, you can see that there are clear boundaries that define the visibility and access of internal elements. Here, it is important to note that:

▶ The only entities that are visible to the outside world are *interface views* and the *interface controller*. Collectively, these two entities make up a WDA component's *component interface*. We'll look at component interfaces in more detail beginning in Chapter 9.

▶ In keeping with the MVC design paradigm, a WDA component distinguishes between elements that exist at the *view layer* and elements that exist at the *controller layer*. You can see this breakdown by looking at the vertical dotted line in the component model in Figure 2.3: the view layer elements are shown on the left-hand side of the line, while the controller elements are depicted on the right-hand side.

▶ WDA components can define different types of controllers: component controllers, custom controllers, window controllers, and view controllers. We'll explore the function of these controllers in more detail beginning in Section 2.2.4.

Figure 2.4 shows how WDA components are organized within the Web Dynpro Explorer perspective of the ABAP Workbench. In Chapter 3, we'll have an opportunity to see how these elements are created as we develop a WDA application from scratch. In the meantime, we'll explore these elements from a conceptual point of view, thinking about the role each element plays within the Web Dynpro component architecture.

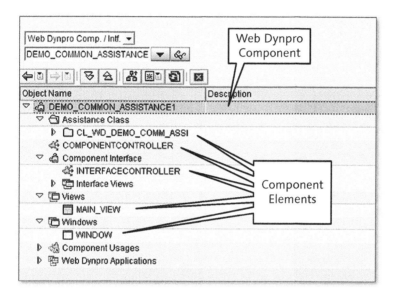

Figure 2.4 Viewing a Web Dynpro Component in the Web Dynpro Explorer

2.2.2   Views

Like many UI toolkits, Web Dynpro employs a layered approach to UI development. This implies that UI components are stacked on top of one another in hierarchical fashion. At the base of this hierarchy lies the *window* component, which we'll describe in more detail in the next section. Underneath the window component, you have a series of embedded *view* components.

According to SAP, a view "describes the layout and behavior of a rectangular area of the user interface." In other words, you can think of views as a canvas upon which you can lay out various *UI elements* (e.g., labels, input fields, buttons, and so on). Figure 2.5 illustrates the relationships among windows, views, and UI elements.

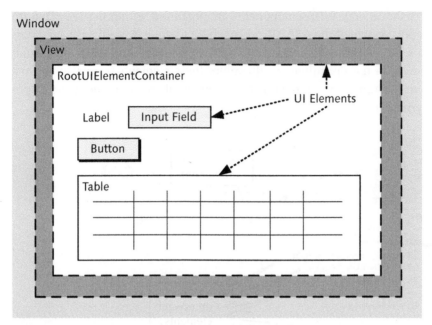

Figure 2.5 Web Dynpro UI Component Hierarchy

In keeping with the layered approach to UI design, each view maintains a UI element hierarchy. At the top of this hierarchy, you have the default `RootUIElement-Container` element, which serves as the base-level container for embedding UI elements within the view. Within this container, you can embed various UI elements, which can be divided conceptually into two broad categories:

▶ **Interactive elements**
Interactive elements allow users to view and edit data and trigger various kinds of events. Examples of interactive elements include input fields, dropdown lists, buttons, and so on.

▶ **Layout elements**
Layout elements organize interactive elements (and sometimes other layout elements) within the layout. Examples of layout elements include groups, panels, tab strips, and other container-like elements.

Figure 2.6 shows how the UI element hierarchy is organized on the LAYOUT tab of the VIEW EDITOR screen (which can be found in the Web Dynpro Explorer perspective of the ABAP Workbench). Here, you can see how various UI elements are nested underneath the `RootUIElementContainer` UI element on the right-hand side of the screen. As new UI elements are added to the hierarchy, the layout preview on the left-hand side of the VIEW EDITOR screen will adjust so that you can observe a close approximation of what the UI will look like at runtime (see Figure 2.6).

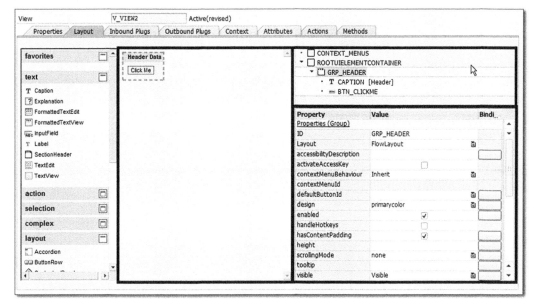

Figure 2.6 Organization of the View Editor in the Web Dynpro Explorer

Each UI element that gets added to the UI hierarchy maintains a set of *properties*, which allow you to configure different aspects of the UI design, such as the UI element's background color, font, and so on. We can configure these properties by statically assigning values in the properties editor contained in the lower right-hand corner of the VIEW EDITOR screen shown in Figure 2.6. Alternatively, we also have the option of dynamically assigning values at runtime by binding the UI element property with a special kind of variable defined within the view's *context*. We'll learn more about contexts and data binding in Section 2.2.5.

2.2.3 Windows

As you may recall from Chapter 1, the UI layout specified within WDA components is expressed according to the Web Dynpro metamodel, as opposed to some specific UI rendering language like HTML. At runtime, this implies that the Web

Dynpro runtime environment must translate Web Dynpro metadata into specific UI constructs (e.g., HTML form controls, Adobe Flex controls, and so on). This transformation process begins with the mapping of the outermost UI element: *windows*.

For the most part, you can think of windows in Web Dynpro as a type of frame or panel that sets the boundaries for the user interface. Typically, the dimensions of these frames correspond with those of the application client screen (i.e., a browser window). However, it's also possible to use windows to create popup dialog boxes (see Figure 2.7). In either case, windows serve as a top-level container for embedding one or more view components.

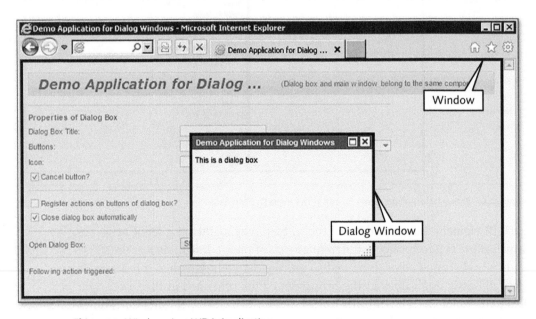

Figure 2.7 Windows in a WDA Application

The relationship between windows and views is defined within the WINDOW EDITOR screen shown in Figure 2.8. As you can see, it is possible to embed multiple views within a window. However, only one of those views can be visible at a given time within the UI. Normally, when you access a window for the first time, the first view you'll see is the one selected as the *default view* in the Window Editor (see Figure 2.8). From there, which view gets displayed next is largely based on how you choose to navigate within the application.

> **Note**
>
> In Chapter 6, we'll learn that there is an exception to this rule: a given view may define one or more `ViewContainerUIElement` UI elements within the UI hierarchy, which makes it possible to embed other views within the context of the embedding view.

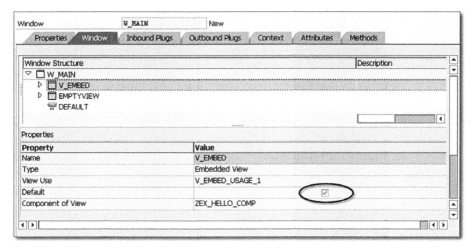

Figure 2.8 Embedding Views in the Window Editor Screen

Navigational Concepts

In order to navigate between the views embedded in a window, we must statically define *navigational links* between the views in the Window Editor at design time. These links are established by connecting a pair of *navigation plugs* defined in the source and target views, respectively. Figure 2.9 illustrates this relationship between a source view *A* and a target view *B*. Here, you can see that there are two different types of navigation plugs you can define for a given view: *outbound plugs* and *inbound plugs*. Outbound plugs define a navigational exit point from a view, while inbound plugs define a navigational entry point to a view.

Outbound plugs and inbound plugs are defined within the corresponding tab pages of the View Editor. As you can see in Figure 2.10, a plug definition consists of the plug's name and some optional parameters. After we create a plug definition in the View Editor, a corresponding event handler method will be created behind the scenes in the view's controller.

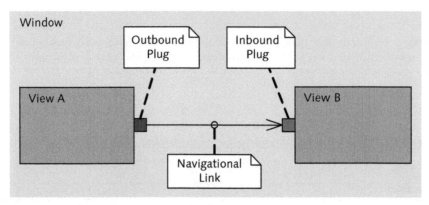

Figure 2.9 Understanding Navigational Links

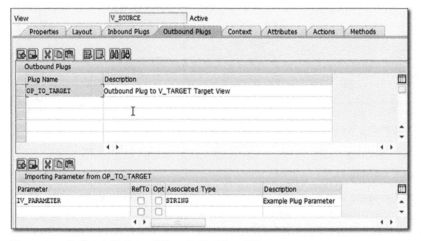

Figure 2.10 Defining Outbound Plugs in the View Editor

> **Note**
>
> As you may have noticed in Figure 2.8, it's also possible to define outbound and inbound plugs for windows. However, since the navigation scenarios for these plug types are more complex, we'll defer this topic until we cover windows in further detail in Chapter 6.

At runtime, navigation is triggered within a source view by calling the auto-generated method associated with an outbound plug. This method call *fires* the outbound plug, which in turn activates the Web Dynpro framework to initiate the navigation sequence. From here, the Web Dynpro framework takes over, using navigational link metadata defined within the overarching window element to determine which view it should display next. Once this selection process is complete, we have the opportunity to perform some last-minute initialization within the auto-generated event handler method created for the inbound plug in the target view. Here, the optionally defined parameters in the outbound and inbound plugs provide a mechanism for passing contextual information about the event that triggered the navigation to the target view.

If all this still seems a bit fuzzy, don't worry; we'll spend quite a bit of time looking at various navigation scenarios in Chapter 6. Furthermore, we'll also have an opportunity to see how this works interactively as we develop our first WDA application in Chapter 3.

2.2.4 Controllers

Looking back at the WDA component architecture diagram shown in Figure 2.3, you can see a dotted line that separates the visual elements that make up the user interface (windows and views) from the programmatic elements that respond to user input (controllers). From an MVC perspective, this line represents the natural separation between the view layer and the controller layer. One of the primary reasons for establishing boundaries like this is to separate "those parts of a program responsible for generating data, from those parts of the program that consume the generated data."[1]

Many MVC purists have taken the concept of separating producers and consumers to such extremes that it's become an unwritten rule that no custom logic should exist within the view layer. However, such a hard-line stance fails to take into account the fact that the view layer may need to perform certain housekeeping tasks, such as:

▶ Populating dropdown lists and input helps with data that makes it easier for users to input data

▶ Responding to events triggered by interactive elements within the user interface

▶ Validating data entered in the various input fields

---

[1] This concept is described at length in a whitepaper written by Chris Whealy called *The Structural Concepts of Web Dynpro Components*. You can find this reference guide at the SDN online at *http://www.sdn.sap.com/irj/scn/go/portal/prtroot/docs/library/uuid/a048387a-0901-0010-13ac-87f9eb649381?QuickLink=index&overridelayout=true*.

▶ Processing navigation requests

▶ Initializing and adjusting the user interface as needed

Recognizing these circumstances, SAP chose to extend the MVC controller concept such that you have two different classes of controllers: those that have a visual interface and those that don't. This slight departure from conventional MVC wisdom is not a license to violate the producer/consumer separation principle highlighted above. Rather, it further establishes those boundaries in a more natural and intuitive way. In the upcoming sections, we'll see how both controller types work in tandem to make WDA applications come alive.

Controllers without a Visual Interface

Within the Web Dynpro component model, there are three different controller types that are not associated with a visual interface:

▶ **The Component controller**
Each Web Dynpro component has a central controller called the *component controller*. The component controller is initialized whenever a component is first created and is visible to all other controllers within the component. Given its status as a sort of master controller, the component controller is usually at the center of data exchange between component elements. Furthermore, it also serves as the central point of control for the behavior of the Web Dynpro component.

▶ **Custom controllers**
In addition to the component controller, it's also possible to define one or more *custom controllers*. These optional controller types play a similar role to that of the component controller in terms of their global stature and behavior. We'll take a closer look at when and where custom controllers should be used in Chapter 4.

▶ **Interface controller**
We'll explore this controller type further when we look at component-based development concepts in Chapter 9. For now, suffice it to say that the interface controller represents a point of contact between two components that enter into a usage relationship with one another. Here, the using component utilizes the interface controller of the used component in order to interact programmatically with the used component.

In general, the primary responsibility of each of the controller types listed above is to provide a two-way conduit for data to flow back and forth between the view layer and the model layer. As a developer working with these controller types, you'll find that you can implement this logic in much the same way that you would implement a normal ABAP Objects class. Indeed, as you can see in Figure 2.11, the Controller Editor has a similar look and feel to the Class Builder tool. Here, we can define attributes, methods, and events to—for example—store and process data.

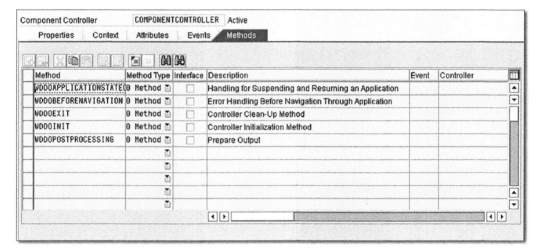

Figure 2.11 Working with Custom Controllers

Looking closely at the Methods tab of the Controller Editor shown in Figure 2.11, you can see that the framework automatically provides several methods. These methods are referred to as *hook methods,* since they provide us with hooks for hanging custom code to perform various housekeeping tasks, custom validations, and so on. For example, if we want to implement some custom initialization logic whenever a component is first created, we can insert code into the WDDOINIT() method. We'll explore each of the standard hook methods in depth in Chapter 4.

Controllers with a Visual Interface

As you may have guessed, the two types of controllers that have a visual interface are *view controllers* and *window controllers*. Within the framework, these two controller types are relegated to performing some of the various housekeeping duties required within the view layer.

Though defined as controllers, it's probably more appropriate to think of view and window controllers as being extensions of the view layer within the MVC model. In essence, they provide the presentation logic. As such, they shouldn't be used to interact directly with the model and bypass the traditional MVC boundaries. Rather, window and view controllers are used to separate the coding that manipulates the UI layout from the UI elements themselves, a concept which will become much clearer in Section 2.2.5.

To a large degree, window and view controllers are structured very similarly to the faceless controller types described in the previous section. For example, as you can see in Figure 2.8 and Figure 2.12, the CONTROLLER EDITOR screen for windows and views allows you to define attributes and methods to cache data, implement custom program logic, and so on.

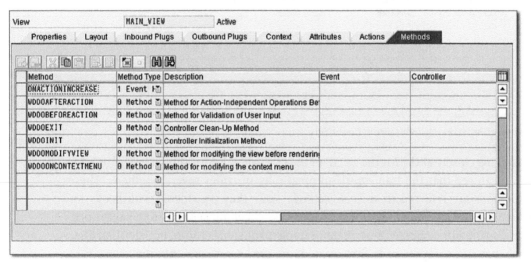

Figure 2.12 Working with View Controllers

Though frequently depicted as being separate for illustrative reasons, we should point out that there's no actual separation between a window or view and its corresponding controllers—they are in fact one logical entity. Thus, as you can see in the VIEW EDITOR screen shown in Figure 2.12, there are tabs provided to edit the UI layout, create outbound/inbound plugs, etc.

2.2.5 Context and Binding Concepts

As we reviewed the different controller types that can be defined within a WDA component in Section 2.2.4, we considered some of the various elements of controller design: attributes, methods, navigation plugs, and so on. However, one important facet of controller design we've glossed over up to this point is *controller contexts*. This omission has been purposeful since it's difficult to grasp the notion of controller contexts without first understanding the relationship between Web Dynpro controller types. Now that we have a better feel for these concepts, let's take a look at how controller contexts can be used to facilitate the exchange of data between the different layers of a WDA component.

Understanding the Context: A Nuts-and-Bolts Overview

From a conceptual point of view, the context is a specialized data storage area within a controller. Here, you can model just about any data structure imaginable by arranging entities known as *context nodes* and *context attributes* in hierarchical fashion. For example, in Figure 2.13, you can see how a list of sales orders was modeled in terms of context nodes and context attributes.

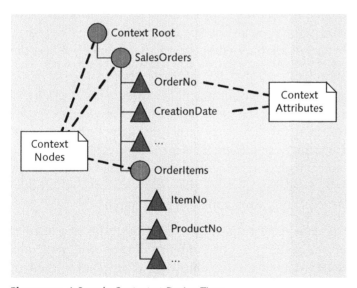

Figure 2.13 A Sample Context at Design Time

Looking at the sample context hierarchy in Figure 2.13, you can see that the data is organized as follows:

▶ At the base of the hierarchy, we have a specialized node referred to as the *context root*. This node is always the first node in any context.

▶ Nested underneath the context root, you have a `SalesOrders` context node, which is used to model a sales order entity. Here, notice the plurality of the context node name `SalesOrders`. This isn't an accident, since it's possible to define context nodes with different *cardinalities*. In this example, the cardinality for the `SalesOrders` node is set to `0..n` so that zero or more sales orders can be stored in the context. Had we wanted to model a single sales order, we could have set the cardinality to `0..1` or `1..1`.

▶ Beneath the `SalesOrders` context node, we have a series of context attributes, such as `OrderNo` and `CreationDate`, which describe the various attributes of a sales order. Within the hierarchy, context attributes are the leaf elements. As such, they should only be used to represent atomic values such as strings, dates, or numbers.

▶ In addition to the context attributes, you can see that the `SalesOrders` node also contains a child context node called `OrderItems`. As you might expect, this node represents the line items associated with a particular sales order. Here, the context attributes `ItemNo`, `ProductNo`, and so on describe various attributes of a sales-order line item. In addition to these attributes, we also could have defined further subnodes to represent schedule lines, for example. In general, context nodes can be nested arbitrarily deep in order to accurately reflect the target data model.

At design time, the context for a given controller is modeled using the CONTEXT EDITOR screen shown in Figure 2.14. During the modeling process, context nodes and context attributes are assigned various properties that describe how the context will be structured at runtime. For example, as mentioned earlier, the `cardinality` property of a context node determines how many instances of a node can be generated at runtime. Similarly, the `type` property for a context attribute determines the attribute's data type from a runtime perspective.

Figure 2.15 demonstrates how the example `SalesOrders` context is structured at runtime. As you can see, the context takes on a different dimension at runtime as *context elements* are added to the mix. Conceptually speaking, you can think of context elements as being *instances* of a context node at runtime. In other words, if you wanted to store ten sales orders within the context, the `SalesOrders` node would have ten context elements nested beneath it: one for each of the sales orders being represented (see Figure 2.15).

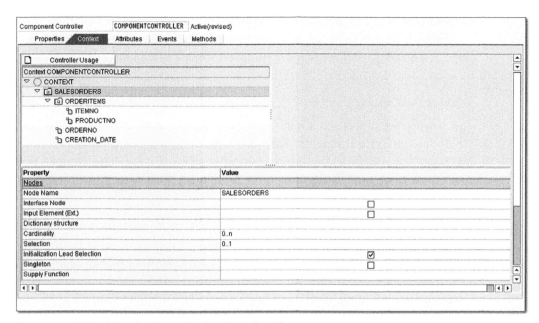

Figure 2.14 Maintaining the Context in the Controller Editor

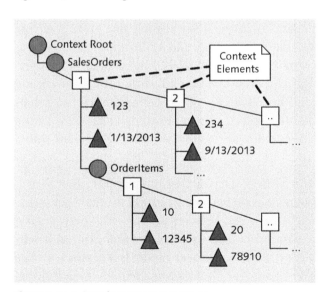

Figure 2.15 A Sample Context at Runtime

Each context element is an independent entity constructed in the image of its corresponding context node. As such, the context elements maintain their own copies of the attributes defined within the context node as well as any nested sub-nodes. In Chapter 5, we'll see how the context API allows you to traverse through these relationships and manipulate context elements at runtime.

What is the Context Used For?

Given what we've learned about controllers already, you might be wondering what the context is used for. After all, since it's possible to define various attributes (i.e., variables) within a controller, why is a separate storage area needed? Rest assured, there is a method to SAP's madness here, and it centers on the notion of *data binding*.

Generically speaking, the term *data binding* refers to a technique in which two data sources are linked together in an automated fashion. In terms of UI development with Web Dynpro, data binding implies a linkage (or *binding*) between UI elements displayed in a view and nodes/attributes within the view controller's context. Thus, whenever a data binding relationship is in effect, any change that is made to a value in a UI element of the view is automatically synchronized with the corresponding element in the view context, and vice versa.

From a technical perspective, data binding is made possible due to the structure afforded by the context. With a defined structure and API to work with, SAP was able to implement full-scale data binding at the Web Dynpro framework layer. Thus, instead of having to write a lot of custom source code to copy data back and forth between UI elements and the context, you can define these relationships declaratively using the View Editor. Indeed, as you can see in Figure 2.16, only a few clicks of the mouse are required to declaratively bind a UI element with a context node/attribute.

In addition to the simplification it offers, data binding also makes it easier to realize the producer/consumer boundaries that lie at the heart of the MVC paradigm. To put this in perspective, imagine how data between the view and controller layers would be synchronized without data binding. Here, we're looking at having to write a bunch of custom code within controller methods to extract a value from one layer and copy it over to another. Besides being tedious, time consuming, and error prone, this approach also clutters up the controller with a lot of view-level minutiae. With data binding, these extraneous details can be left up to the framework, allowing us to focus our attention on getting the business logic right.

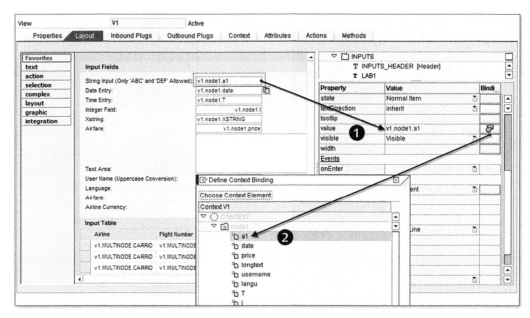

Figure 2.16 Binding a UI Element to a Context Attribute

Context Mapping

In the previous section, we observed how UI elements in a view could be bound to elements of the corresponding view controller context. This feature greatly simplifies the process of synchronizing data between the view and view controller layers. However, looking at the bigger picture, you might be wondering where the view controller gets its data from in the first place. After all, as we mentioned earlier, view controllers are positioned within the framework as extensions of the view layer. As such, they shouldn't be producers of data, per se. Instead, this duty resides with faceless controller types, such as the component controller or custom controllers.

In order to facilitate the transfer of data between faceless controllers and view/window controllers, the Web Dynpro framework allows us to define *context mappings*. Conceptually, you can think of context mappings as another form of data binding, only this time between the contexts of a pair of controllers. Here, two contexts are linked together by *mapping* a context node from one controller's context to another. Figure 2.17 illustrates this relationship, demonstrating how a context node called SALESORDERS is mapped from a component controller's context to a view controller's context.

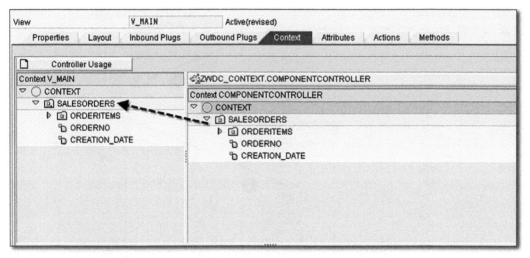

Figure 2.17 Mapping a Context Node between Controllers

Before we begin looking into how context mapping works from a conceptual point of view, it is helpful to first understand how context mapping relationships are established. In general, there are two basic steps required in order to define a context mapping:

1. First of all, before we can define a context mapping between a pair of controllers, we must define a *usage relationship* between the controllers. From the source controller's perspective, this is akin to declaring the target controller a *data source*. Figure 2.18 demonstrates how this works, illustrating the default relationship defined between a view controller and the component controller.

> **Note**
>
> There are rules within the Web Dynpro framework that define the types of usage relationships you can define. For example, a component controller cannot define a usage relationship to a view controller because this violates the producer/consumer principle. We'll explore these rules in greater detail in Chapter 4.

2. As soon as a usage relationship is established, the context of the used controller will be available for selection on the right-hand side of the using controller's

CONTEXT tab, as shown in Figure 2.17. At this point, we can define a context mapping by simply dragging and dropping a node from the used controller's context onto the top-level context node of the using controller's context. This action will automatically create a mapped version of the selected context node in the using controller's context (see Figure 2.17).

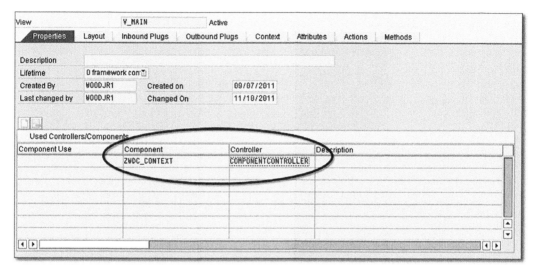

Figure 2.18 Declaring Usage Relationships between Controllers

If you look carefully at the mapped SALESORDERS node in the view controller context shown in Figure 2.17, you'll notice that its icon has a little arrow underneath it to signify that it is a *mapped node*. This subtle distinction is important, as it indicates that the mapped node gets its data from somewhere else. In effect, you can think of these mapped nodes as being *aliases* for the nodes they map to. Of course, this doesn't change the way you use them; you can still bind mapped nodes to UI elements. The only difference is that they get their data from an upstream controller (e.g., the component controller).

Putting it All Together

Now that you understand how data binding and context mapping work conceptually, let's take a step back and see how these concepts work in tandem to facilitate data flow between the different layers of a WDA component. Figure 2.19 illustrates this data flow from a runtime perspective.

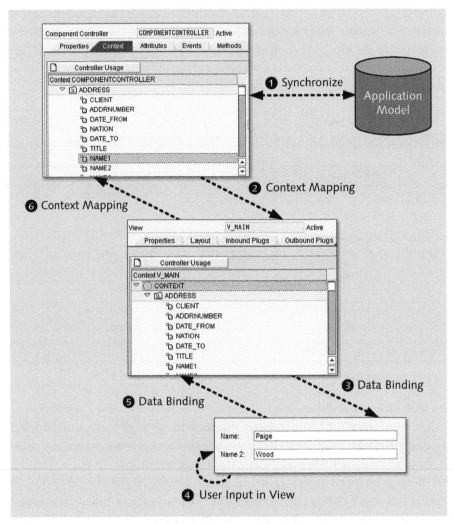

Figure 2.19 Data Flow between Different Layers of a WDA Component

Following along with the diagram in Figure 2.19, let's trace the flow of data between the different layers of a WDA component:

❶ In many applications, the process begins with the loading of data from an application model into the context of a global controller such as the component controller. Here, the application model could be defined in terms of BAPIs, a custom database schema, or web services, and accessed via one or more hook methods of the controller.

❷ Next, data flows from a component or custom controller down to a view controller via context mappings. Here, it's important to note that the data isn't copied from one context to the other. Instead, the view controller simply *references* (or points to) the context nodes mapped from the upstream controller. Thus, there's little to no overhead involved in this data transfer step.

❸ At the view layer, mapped data nodes are bound to UI elements as usual. Therefore, any data loaded in step 1 will be automatically populated in the UI elements displayed within the view layout.

❹ Once the view is rendered, users can enter and adjust data in the UI elements and initiate a server roundtrip by triggering some kind of event (e.g., clicking a button).

❺ At the onset of the server roundtrip, the data binding relationship between UI elements and the view context kicks in and data between the two layers is automatically synchronized.

❻ This, in turn, causes the corresponding component or custom controller nodes to be updated as a result of the context mapping relationship(s) defined within the view controller.

❼ Finally, the component or custom controller, having been updated via data entered at the view layer, can synchronize its context with the application model, and the cycle starts all over again.

Clearly, there are a lot of moving parts involved in the data exchange between WDA component layers. However, one of the great things about the Web Dynpro framework is that you hardly even realize all this is going on behind the scenes. This frees you up to worry about synchronizing data between the controller/model layers; the framework handles everything else. We'll see how this works on a practical level beginning in Chapter 5.

2.3 Web Dynpro Applications

In the previous section, we briefly described the symbiotic relationship between WDA components and WDA applications. There, we learned that it is impossible to create a WDA application without first building one or more WDA components. At this point, you now know why this is: the WDA components contain all the application logic.

From a technical perspective, WDA applications do little more than associate a URL link with a window in a WDA component (see Figure 2.20). In this regard, you can think of WDA applications as analogous to transaction codes assigned to ABAP reports or classic Dynpro programs.

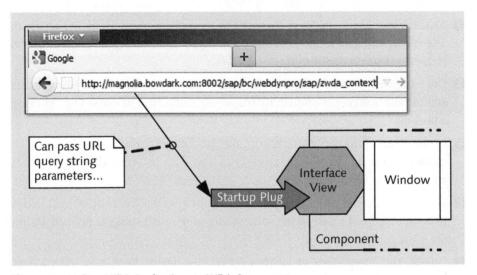

Figure 2.20 Linking WDA Applications to WDA Components

Though tightly associated with WDA components, WDA applications are defined as separate and standalone objects within the ABAP Repository. Figure 2.21 shows a sample application called ZWDA_CONTEXT in the WDA application editor. As you can see on the PROPERTIES tab, the main properties that need to be configured are:

▶ The target component

▶ The target window (or *interface view*) within the selected component

▶ The target inbound plug of the selected interface view

Once these properties are set and the WDA application is saved, a corresponding ICF service node will be created underneath the default */sap/bc/webdynpro/sap* service node to represent the application within the ICF. Thus, the general form of a WDA application URL is *http(s)://host:port/sap/bc/webdynpro/bc/<WDA Application Name>*.

Application ZWDA_CONTEXT New

| Properties | Parameters |

Description Test WDA Application
Component ZWDC_CONTEXT
Interface View W_MAIN
Plug Name DEFAULT
Help Links
Handling of Messages
● Show Message Component on Demand
○ Always Display Message Component

Figure 2.21 Defining a WDA Application (Part 1)

Besides the basic properties defined on the PROPERTIES tab of the WDA application editor, it is also possible to define one or more parameters for a WDA application on the PARAMETERS tab shown in Figure 2.22. Here, you can see that there are several standard parameter types to choose from. These parameters influence various aspects of the application's behavior. Furthermore, in addition to the standard parameter types, we can also define our own custom parameter types as needed.

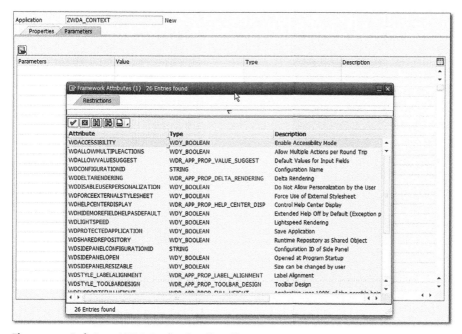

Figure 2.22 Defining a WDA Application (Part 2)

At runtime, parameters are passed from the application layer to correspondingly named parameters defined in the inbound plug of the selected interface view. From here, we can use the parameters to initialize the application and take further steps. We'll take a closer look at how this parameter flow works in Chapter 6.

2.4   Summary

In this chapter, we took you on a whirlwind tour that covered the mechanics of WDA applications from an architectural perspective. Along the way, we learned about component-based software design concepts, WDA components, and more.

Overall, there's a lot of theory to digest when trying to wrap your head around Web Dynpro—so much so that figuring out where to begin is a dilemma of the chicken-and-egg variety. On one hand, you need to know a little bit about the Web Dynpro component model in order to get started with development. On the other hand, it's hard to digest all this theory without some practical, hands-on application.

So, at this point, we'll use the foundation we've established thus far as a basis for branching out into more practical discussions. As we proceed through the upcoming chapters, many of the concepts reviewed in this chapter will become much clearer. To get things started, we'll roll up our sleeves and start getting our hands dirty in the next chapter by creating a custom WDA application from start to finish.

The English poet John Keats once remarked that "Nothing ever becomes real 'til it is experienced." Though he probably didn't have WDA development in mind when he penned this adage, it still rings true. Therefore, in this chapter, we'll take his advice to heart and apply the knowledge gained in the previous two chapters toward the creation of a WDA application.

3   Developing Your First WDA Application

In Chapter 1, we described how the Web Dynpro programming model leans toward the use of declarative programming techniques wherever possible. While this inclination certainly lends itself to an economical and efficient programming model, it also presents certain challenges from a learning perspective. Recognizing these challenges, we came to realize very early on that Web Dynpro is not something you can learn by only reading this book; you also have to interact with it and experience it for yourself.

So, now that we've had an opportunity to acquaint ourselves with the Web Dynpro framework, we think that the logical next step in the learning process is to roll up our sleeves and see how WDA applications are built from a hands-on perspective. This little excursion should help reinforce the concepts we learned in Chapter 2. Furthermore, it should also provide us with a visual frame of reference to draw upon as we approach more advanced topics later in the book.

3.1   Requirements Overview

Throughout the course of this chapter, we'll be developing a custom WDA application that will allow users to lookup contact information for user master records in an SAP NetWeaver system. This information will be obtained via an SAP standard BAPI module called `BAPI_USER_GET_DETAIL`. At this early stage in the book, we'll stick to the basics and concentrate on getting a working application up and running. As we move forward in later chapters, we'll have plenty of opportunities to worry about best design approaches, aesthetics, and so on.

To support the lookup of contact information, the application will have two views: a selection view and a details view. The selection view, shown in Figure 3.1, provides a selection screen that allows users to input a user name and initiate the lookup. After the lookup is complete, the user contact information will be displayed on the details view shown in Figure 3.2. From here, users can either close the application or click on the SEARCH AGAIN button to look up contact information for another user.

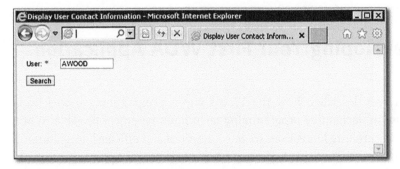

Figure 3.1 Sample Application Selection View

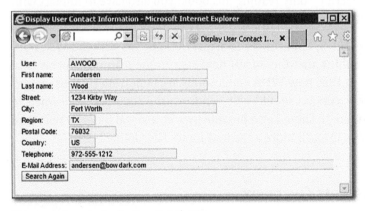

Figure 3.2 Sample Application Details View

Despite its relative simplicity, this sample application will provide us with the opportunity to design a couple of views, create some navigation links, and pass data around using controller contexts. Furthermore, we'll have an opportunity to work with the Web Dynpro Explorer toolset and see how the various WDA elements fit together in a real and tangible way. So, without further ado, let's get started.

3.2 Getting Started with the Web Dynpro Explorer

WDA components and applications are developed in a special perspective of the ABAP Workbench called the *Web Dynpro Explorer*. To open up the ABAP Workbench, execute Transaction SE80. This will bring you to the editor screen shown in Figure 3.3.

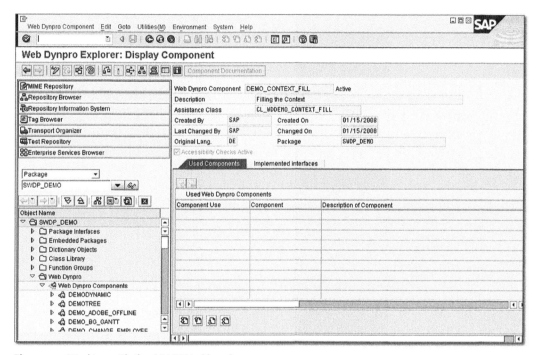

Figure 3.3 Working with the ABAP Workbench

If you haven't had an opportunity to work with the ABAP Workbench before, a brief introduction is in order. As you can see in Figure 3.3, the ABAP Workbench editor screen is organized as follows:

▶ The top left-hand portion of the screen provides us with several different browser tools. We can use these browser tools to search for various types of development objects within the system. For the purposes of Web Dynpro development, we'll be working mostly with the default repository browser selected in Figure 3.3.

▶ On the bottom left-hand portion of the screen, we have an explorer-like selection view called the *navigation area*. Within the navigation area, we can browse through and/or create various development objects within the *ABAP Repository*. We'll discuss the ABAP Repository in further detail in just a moment.

▶ On the right-hand portion of the screen, there is a generic editor area called the *tool area*. The tool area changes in accordance with the objects selected in the navigation area. For example, if we double-click on a view within a Web Dynpro component in the navigation area, the View Editor will be loaded into the tool area so that you can edit the view in its native editor. Similarly, controllers will be opened up in the Controller Editor, and so on.

Overall, the ABAP Workbench has a similar look and feel to most modern integrated development environments (IDEs). However, from a logistics perspective, things are definitely managed a little differently behind the scenes. Therefore, in the upcoming sections, we'll take a look at how development objects are stored and organized within the ABAP Repository. Having an understanding of how this works is particularly important for WDA developers because WDA development lends itself toward the creation of many development objects. Here, things can get out of hand in a hurry if we don't have a plan for organizing the various objects you'll be creating beforehand.

3.2.1   Working with the ABAP Repository

Unlike other popular client-based IDEs, such as Microsoft Visual Studio.NET or Eclipse, which edit source code artifacts in a file system on your local machine, the development objects you create within the ABAP Workbench are maintained within a logical database on the server called the *ABAP Repository*. In a way, you can think of the ABAP Repository as a sort of virtual file system mounted on top of the AS ABAP system database. Here, development objects are persisted within ABAP Dictionary tables in much the same way that master data objects are stored. Indeed, if you open up table TADIR in the Data Browser tool (Transaction SE16), you can find a listing of all the development objects in the database of the SAP NetWeaver system you are logged onto.

While it is not essential that you know how the ABAP Repository works from a technical perspective, it is important that you recognize that development objects maintained within the ABAP Repository are in effect *global objects*. Here, you are basically given up to a maximum of forty characters (usually fewer) to uniquely define a development object's name within the repository. This limitation includes any namespace prefix that might be used. For example, a namespace prefix like /BOWDK/ reduces the number of characters that can be used in a name by seven.

Without a doubt, one of the biggest challenges with creating objects within the ABAP Repository is coming up with intuitive and meaningful names to identify the objects within a global context. Often, despite the most rigorous of naming standards, we may end up with a long and mangled object name that may not be very easy to remember. Fortunately, the object name is not all we have to go on when searching for development objects within the ABAP Repository. In addition to the object's name, each development object within the ABAP Repository is also tagged with the following metadata:

▶ The object's type (e.g., WDA component, ABAP Objects class, etc.)

▶ A language-specific short text description for the object

▶ The name of the user who created the object

▶ The date the object was created and last changed

The aforementioned browsers in the ABAP Workbench use this metadata to allow us to search for development objects in many different ways. However, even with these additional search criteria, we still really have to know what we're looking for. This can be particularly challenging in a WDA development context where development normally occurs in layers. With that in mind, we'll take a look at some more effective ways of organizing development objects within the ABAP Repository in Section 3.2.2.

3.2.2 Package Organization Concepts

Each development object created within the ABAP Repository must be assigned to a special repository object called a *package*. To some extent, you can think of packages as a type of folder in that they collect related development objects together. In this sense, packages also play a similar role to projects in other IDEs you might have worked with in the past.

Packages can be nested together to form a *package hierarchy*. Within this package hierarchy, we can organize development objects using three different types of packages:

▶ **Structure packages**
As the name suggests, structure packages are used to provide structure to software projects. Structure packages sit at the top of the package hierarchy and are made up of one or more *main packages*.

▶ **Main packages**
Underneath structure packages, we have main packages. Much like structure packages, main packages are grouping objects that organize one or more development packages together—ideally by function.

▶ **Development packages**
At the bottom of the hierarchy, we have *development packages*, which contain the actual development objects being created (for example, WDA components). Ideally, the development objects contained within a development package should be closely related.

In general, the package concept is very flexible, giving us the option to choose how complex we want our package hierarchy to be. Indeed, technically speaking, it is possible to simply create one big standalone development package to store all of your custom development objects in one place. On the other end of the spectrum, you can have a nested package hierarchy like the one depicted in Figure 3.4. This is the hierarchy that we'll be using to organize the examples developed within this book. As you can see, at the top of the package hierarchy, we have provided a structure package called ZWDA_BOOK, which will encapsulate all of the development objects created in conjunction with this book. Underneath the ZWDA_BOOK structure package, we have a main package called ZWDA_BOOK_EXAMPLES that will house all of the book's example code. Finally, underneath the ZWDA_BOOK_EXAMPLES main package, we have a series of development packages, such as ZWDA_BOOK_EXAMPLES_CHP03, that contain the various development objects created with the examples.

Looking at the package hierarchy in Figure 3.4, you might be wondering why we didn't just create a series of standalone development packages, such as ZWDA_BOOK_EXAMPLES_CHP03. As it turns out, there are a couple of major benefits to organizing packages this way:

▶ First of all, having a fine-grained package hierarchy like this makes it easier to search for objects within the development catalog. For instance, looking at Figure 3.4, you can see how we've organized the object list in the navigation area by package. Thus, starting at the top-level ZWDA_BOOK structure package, we can navigate through the package hierarchy to search for objects in much the same way you might scan through a book's table of contents or index.

▶ Second, the package concept allows us to lock down packages and restrict the use of certain development objects contained within. These encapsulation features can come in handy on many levels as we endeavor to protect certain development objects that are sensitive to change. These concepts are described at length in the SAP NetWeaver online help documentation in the "Package Builder" section.

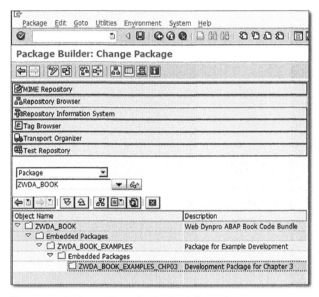

Figure 3.4 Package Hierarchy for Book Examples

Though it is possible to develop WDA applications using just about any approach to package organization, we strongly recommend that you structure your packages in such a way that they complement the layered approach utilized for WDA development. For example, in larger applications, it probably makes sense to have one development package to store objects within the persistence layer, another development package for the application/model layer, and one or more development packages for the various WDA visual components. Not only does this approach make it easier to keep track of related development artifacts, but it also helps you establish clear boundaries between layers from a logistical perspective. But enough about software logistics; let's get on with the good stuff and begin creating our sample application.

Packages and the SAP Application Hierarchy

As packages are created within the ABAP Workbench, they must be assigned to an application component within the *SAP Application Hierarchy* (see Figure 3.5). If you're not familiar with the SAP Application Hierarchy, you can think of it as a functional overview of the application components installed on an SAP NetWeaver system. You can view this hierarchy using Transaction SE81.

While there are no hard and fast rules regarding which application component you assign a package to, we recommend that you try to align your packages as closely to the standard SAP Application Hierarchy as possible. For instance, in Figure 3.5, you can see that SAP assigned a package called SWDP_DEMO containing WDA demo applications to the BC-WD-ABA (Basis Components—Web Dynpro—Web Dynpro ABAP) application component. If you think about it, this assignment to the WDA component makes intuitive sense. After all, when looking for WDA demo components, it stands to reason that the first place you'd look would be within the WDA application component. Similarly, if a developer needed to find an enhancement to purchase order processing in an SAP ERP system, it would make sense for them to start looking in the MM-PUR-PO (Materials Management—Purchasing—Purchase Orders) application component.

Once all the proper assignments are in place, it's easy for other developers to come along and look for development artifacts without knowing much about project naming standards. Instead, all they have to do is open up Transaction SE81 and browse to the desired application component within the hierarchy. From there, they can see all the packages nested underneath this component and begin narrowing down their search for specific development objects from there.

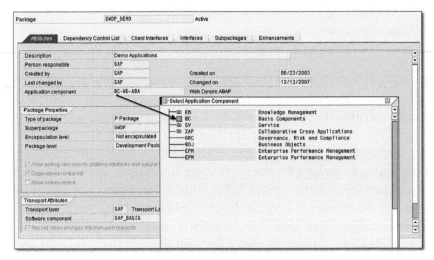

Figure 3.5 Assignment of a Package to an Application Component

3.3   Creating a WDA Component

Now that you know your way around the Web Dynpro Explorer, we're ready to begin developing our sample application. As we learned in Chapter 2, this process begins with the creation of a WDA component. Therefore, in this section, we'll walk through this creation process step-by-step.

3.3.1   Defining the Component

For the most part, you'll find that the process of creating a WDA component is no different from the process used to create other objects within the ABAP Workbench. For our example component, we'll proceed as follows:

1. Before we can create the WDA component, we must first select the package in which we want to store the generated component and related artifacts. For the purposes of this demonstration, we'll utilize the ZWDA_BOOK_EXAMPLES_CHP03 package described in Section 3.2.2. Of course, as you're following along with the book, you can choose a different package name or even define the WDA component as a local object (i.e,. package $tmp). In any case, we can create the component by right-clicking on the package in the navigation area of the ABAP Workbench and selecting the menu option CREATE • WEB DYNPRO • WEB DYNPRO COMPONENT (INTERFACE) as shown in Figure 3.6.

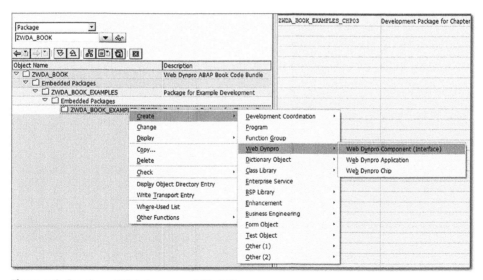

Figure 3.6 Creating a WDA Component (Part 1)

2. This will open up the WEB DYNPRO: COMPONENT/CREATE INTERFACE dialog box shown in Figure 3.7. As you can see, this dialog box provides us with an edit mask that allows us to select the WDA component name as well as some other basic attributes, including:

   ▷ A short text description of the component

   ▷ The component type (e.g., regular component vs. component interface)

   ▷ An optional default window/view

Figure 3.7 Creating a WDA Component (Part 2)

3. For the purposes of our example, we'll create a normal WDA component called ZWDC_USER_DISPLAY, with a window called W_MAIN and an initial view called V_SELECT. Once the WDA component properties are set, we can click on the button with the green checkmark on it to proceed.

4. Before the component can be created within the ABAP Repository, it must be assigned to a package in the CREATE OBJECT DIRECTORY ENTRY dialog box shown in Figure 3.8. Here, if desired, you can click on the LOCAL OBJECT button to create the WDA component as a local object. Otherwise, select the target package name and click on the SAVE button.

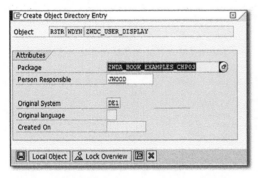

Figure 3.8 Creating a WDA Component (Part 3)

5. If you choose not to create the WDA component as a local object, you will next be prompted to add your component to a transport request in the dialog box shown in Figure 3.9.

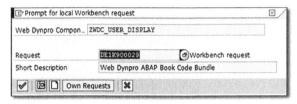

Figure 3.9 Creating a WDA Component (Part 4)

6. Finally, once all the requisite ABAP Repository housekeeping is in order, the WDA component will be opened up in the Web Dynpro Explorer as shown in Figure 3.10. At this point, we can activate our changes and begin working on the individual component elements.

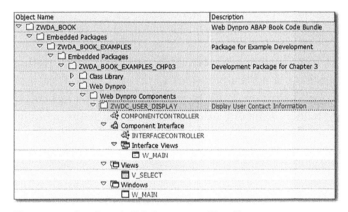

Figure 3.10 Creating a WDA Component (Part 5)

3.3.2   Modeling the Application Data

With our WDA component now in place, the next step is to begin modeling the data that will be displayed during the user lookup. Since this data will be shared between the selection and details view, we'll model the data centrally within the component controller's context. Here, we'll define a simple context node called USER_CONTACT which will contain attributes to represent user contact information (e.g., user name, phone number, etc.). To create this context node, we'll proceed as follows:

1. First of all, we need to open the component controller up in the Controller Editor. This can be achieved by double-clicking on the COMPONENTCONTROLLER node underneath the newly created WDA component in the navigation area on the left-hand side of the Web Dynpro Explorer (see Figure 3.10).

2. To edit the component controller's context, we need to select the CONTEXT tab. From there, we can create a new context node by right-clicking on the top-level CONTEXT node and selecting the CREATE • NODE menu option (see Figure 3.11)

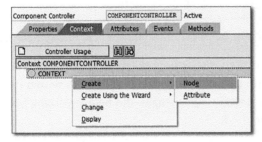

Figure 3.11 Defining the Component Controller Context (Part 1)

3. This will open up the CREATE NODES dialog box shown in Figure 3.12. As you can see, this dialog box provides you with many different options for creating context nodes. We'll have an opportunity to look at the semantics of each of these attributes in Chapter 5. For now, we'll keep things simple and just create the USER_CONTACT node with a cardinality of 1..1. Click on the button with the green checkmark on it to continue.

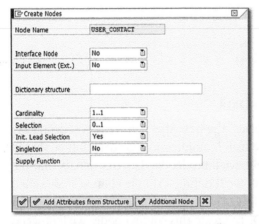

Figure 3.12 Defining the Component Controller Context (Part 2)

4. After the context node is created, we can proceed with the definition of the various context attributes. You can do this by right-clicking on the newly created USER_CONTACT node and selecting the menu option CREATE • ATTRIBUTE as shown in Figure 3.13.

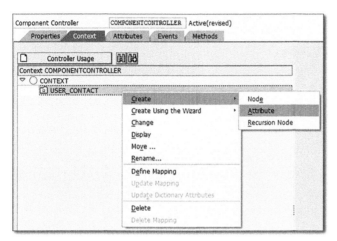

Figure 3.13 Defining the Component Controller Context (Part 3)

5. In the CREATE ATTRIBUTE dialog box shown in Figure 3.14, we can specify the attribute properties. For example, in Figure 3.14, you can see that we've defined an attribute called USERNAME and assigned it the XUBNAME type. Here, we could have assigned built-in types such as STRING, but, as we'll learn in later chapters, there are many benefits to using predefined data elements from the ABAP Dictionary.

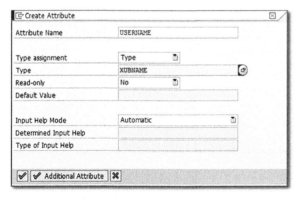

Figure 3.14 Defining the Component Controller Context (Part 4)

6. The remainder of the attributes are created in the same way that the USERNAME attribute was created (see Figure 3.15). In order to keep things simple, we have typed the remaining attributes to correspond with the fields returned in the exporting ADDRESS parameter from BAPI_USER_GET_DETAIL (which is of type BAPIADDR3).

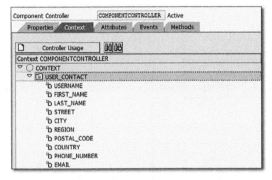

Figure 3.15 Defining the Component Controller Context (Part 5)

7. After all your changes are complete, you should save and activate the component controller.

3.3.3 Implementing the Lookup Method

From a data flow perspective, all roads within a WDA component lead to the component controller. Therefore, given its role as a central data broker, it makes sense that we would implement the user contact lookup logic within the component controller. Here, we'll encode this logic within a custom instance method called GET_USER_CONTACT_INFO() (see Figure 3.16).

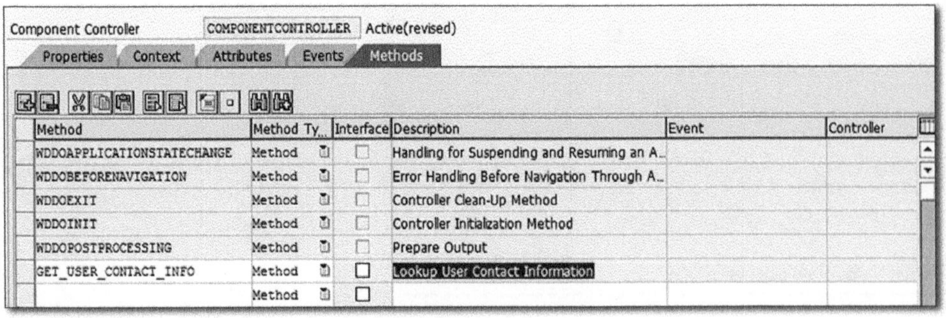

Method	Method Ty	Interface	Description	Event	Controller	
WDDOAPPLICATIONSTATECHANGE	Method	☐	Handling for Suspending and Resuming an A...			
WDDOBEFORENAVIGATION	Method	☐	Error Handling Before Navigation Through A...			
WDDOEXIT	Method	☐	Controller Clean-Up Method			
WDDOINIT	Method	☐	Controller Initialization Method			
WDDOPOSTPROCESSING	Method	☐	Prepare Output			
GET_USER_CONTACT_INFO	Method	☐	Lookup User Contact Information			
	Method	☐				

Component Controller · COMPONENTCONTROLLER · Active(revised)
Properties · Context · Attributes · Events · Methods

Figure 3.16 Defining the Contact Lookup Method

As we create the new method on the METHODS tab shown in Figure 3.16, we have the option of defining method parameters just as we would in the traditional Class Builder tool. However, in this case, we don't need to define any parameters because data exchange will flow through the component controller context automatically (through data binding and context mapping). So, we can bypass this step and begin implementing the logic by double-clicking on the newly created method. However, before we begin writing custom ABAP code, we need to think a little bit about our development approach.

From a logical perspective, our GET_USER_CONTACT_INFO() method will be called after a user enters a user name and clicks on the SEARCH button shown in Figure 3.1. When this occurs, two things will happen in short succession:

1. First, the proposed user name value will be propagated from the InputField UI element on the frontend view all the way back to the bound USERNAME attribute in the component controller context.

2. Then, the button-click event will trigger an action that will ultimately result in the invocation of the GET_USER_CONTACT_INFO() method.

Without digressing into a lengthy discussion on the WDA phase model (which is covered in Chapter 4), the main takeaway here is that, by the time control arrives at GET_USER_CONTACT_INFO(), the selected user name will be sitting there waiting for us in the component controller context. From there, we can use the data to perform the lookup and copy the results back into the context.

Listing 3.1 shows what the finished method looks like. For now, we won't spend a lot of time looking into the various context-related API calls; we'll have plenty of time to look at these calls in Chapter 5. In the meantime, we can follow along with the comments to see what's going on here from a conceptual point of view:

1. First, we're extracting the value of the USERNAME attribute from the top-level USER_CONTACT node's first and only context node element. (Remember, we defined the cardinality of the USER_CONTACT node as 1..1.)

2. Then, once we have the user name value in hand, we use it in a call to BAPI_USER_GET_DETAIL to extract the user contact information.

3. Finally, the extracted address results are copied into a structure that gets bound to the context via the SET_STATIC_ATTRIBUTES() method.

```
method GET_USER_CONTACT_INFO.
  "Method-Local Data Declarations:
```

```abap
DATA lo_nd_user_contact TYPE REF TO if_wd_context_node.
DATA lo_el_user_contact TYPE REF TO if_wd_context_element.
DATA lv_username TYPE REF TO
      wd_this->Element_user_contact-username.

DATA ls_address TYPE bapiaddr3.
DATA lt_return TYPE STANDARD TABLE OF bapiret2.
DATA ls_user_contact TYPE wd_this->Element_user_contact.

"Read the selected user name into context:
lo_nd_user_contact =
  wd_context->get_child_node(
    name = wd_this->wdctx_user_contact ).
lo_el_user_contact = lo_nd_user_contact->get_element( ).
lv_username ?=
  lo_el_user_contact->get_attribute_ref( 'USERNAME' ).

"Lookup the user's contact information:
CALL FUNCTION 'BAPI_USER_GET_DETAIL'
  EXPORTING
    username = lv_username->*
  IMPORTING
    address  = ls_address
  TABLES
    return   = lt_return.

"Copy the results to a structure and bind it to the context:
ls_user_contact-username = lv_username->*.
ls_user_contact-first_name = ls_address-firstname.
ls_user_contact-last_name = ls_address-lastname.
ls_user_contact-street = ls_address-street.
ls_user_contact-city = ls_address-city.
ls_user_contact-region = ls_address-region.
ls_user_contact-postal_code = ls_address-postl_cod1.
ls_user_contact-country = ls_address-country.
ls_user_contact-phone_number = ls_address-tel1_numbr.
ls_user_contact-email = ls_address-e_mail.

lo_el_user_contact->set_static_attributes(
  ls_user_contact ).
endmethod.
```

Listing 3.1 Implementing the GET_USER_CONTACT_INFO( ) Method

From a practical standpoint, we recognize that you might be looking at the code excerpt contained in Listing 3.1 and wondering what in the world you've gotten yourself into. This is particularly the case for developers not accustomed to working with object-oriented programming techniques. For now, we recommend that you simply copy the code from Listing 3.1 into your method in order to get started. In the meantime, rest assured that by the time we're done with Chapter 5, the mechanics of all this will make a lot more sense.

3.3.4 Laying Out the Selection View

At this point, we have completed the development in the backend model/controller layers and are now ready to turn our attention to the view layer. We'll start with the initial selection view, which is displayed whenever the application is started (see Figure 3.1). This view was created for us automatically when we first created the WDA component in Section 3.3.1. Looking back at Figure 3.7, you can see that we decided to name this view V_SELECT.

Before we begin defining the UI layout for the V_SELECT view, we first need to configure the view context that we'll bind the UI elements to. Here, since we already modeled this data in the component controller, we simply need to map the pre-existing USER_CONTACT node from the component controller over to the view context. We can do this by dragging and dropping the context node from the component controller context over to the view controller context on the CONTEXT tab of the View Editor as shown in Figure 3.17.

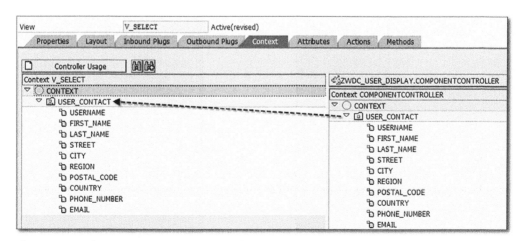

Figure 3.17 Implementing Context Mapping in the V_SELECT View

After the context is defined, we can switch to the LAYOUT tab and begin laying out the user interface. As you can see in Figure 3.18, we have an empty canvas to work with by default.

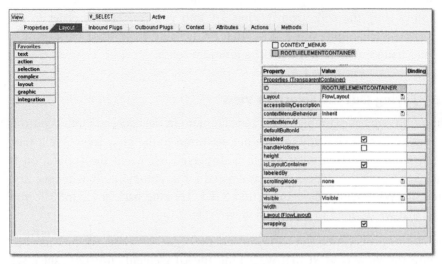

Figure 3.18 Defining the V_SELECT View UI Layout (Part 1)

Before we begin adding UI elements to the view, we need to select a layout, which will define how the elements are arranged on the screen. If you click on the dropdown list for the LAYOUT property in the PROPERTIES panel on the lower right-hand portion of the View Editor, you can see that you have several different options to choose from. We'll consider each of these layout options in detail in Chapter 6. For now, since we're building a selection form, we'll choose the Grid-Layout option as shown in Figure 3.19.

Once the layout is set, we can begin adding UI elements to the canvas. We can do this by either dragging and dropping UI elements from the toolbox on the left-hand side of the View Editor or adding elements in hierarchical fashion to the ROOTUIELEMENTCONTAINER node shown in Figure 3.18. For this first example, we'll stick to the latter approach by proceeding as follows:

1. Our selection form will contain three UI elements: an input field to select a user name, a corresponding label to annotate the input field, and a button that will allow the user to trigger the search. We'll start by creating the label. We do this by right-clicking on the ROOTUIELEMENTCONTAINER node and selecting the INSERT ELEMENT menu option (see Figure 3.20).

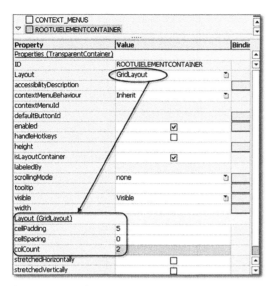

Figure 3.19 Defining the V_SELECT View UI Layout (Part 2)

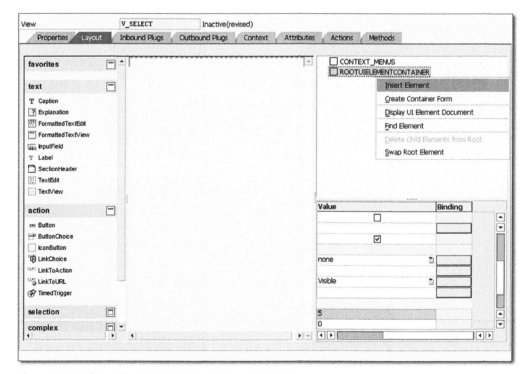

Figure 3.20 Defining the V_SELECT View UI Layout (Part 3)

2. This will cause the CREATE ELEMENT dialog box shown in Figure 3.21 to open. Here, we'll specify the UI element name (LBL_USERNAME) and select the Label element type in the TYP dropdown list. Click the button with the green checkmark on it to continue.

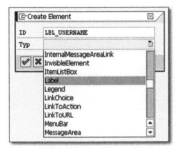

Figure 3.21 Defining the V_SELECT View UI Layout (Part 4)

3. Next, we'll next create the InputField element (INP_USERNAME) as shown in Figure 3.22. Click the button with the green checkmark on it to continue.

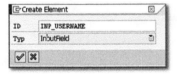

Figure 3.22 Defining the V_SELECT View UI Layout (Part 5)

4. At runtime, we want to be able to capture the text input provided from the end user in the INP_USERNAME input field. Therefore, we need to bind this UI element with a context attribute—namely, the USER_CONTACT.USERNAME context attribute. This can be achieved by clicking on the button on the right-hand side of the VALUE attribute (in the BINDING column). Then, in the DEFINE CONTEXT BINDING dialog box shown in Figure 3.23, we can select the USERNAME attribute and click on the button with the green checkmark on it to confirm our selection.

5. At this point, it's probably a good idea to go ahead and save our changes and run a quick syntax check to make sure everything has been configured correctly thus far. To run the syntax check, select the VIEW • CHECK • SYNTAX menu option. If you don't see any errors, you're definitely on the right track. Otherwise, you may want to re-trace your steps and see if you missed a step somewhere along the way.

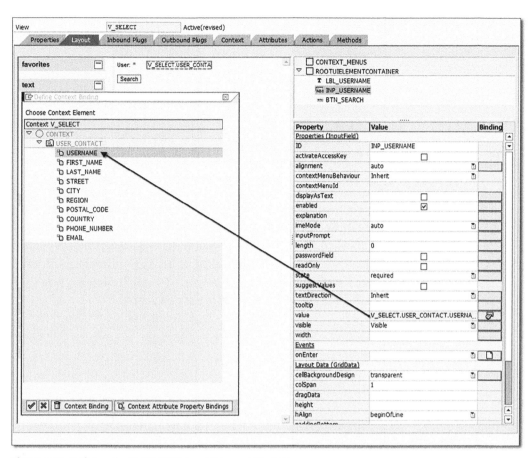

Figure 3.23 Defining the V_SELECT View UI Layout (Part 6)

6. Looking over the results of the syntax check performed in the previous step, you should see a warning indicating that the `labelFor` property of the `LBL_USERNAME` element does not contain a value. We can remedy this problem by selecting the `INP_USERNAME` element in the dropdown list shown in Figure 3.24. Once this attribute is set, the `Label` and `InputField` UI elements will be formally associated with one another. Among other things, this relationship allows the framework to derive the label text automatically—a concept we'll explore in further detail in Chapter 7. Of course, if you wish to specify your own label text, you can do so by filling in the `text` property for the `LBL_USERNAME` UI element.

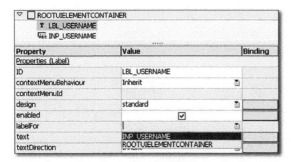

Figure 3.24 Defining the V_SELECT View UI Layout (Part 7)

7. Once the form elements are set, the last thing we need to do is create the SEARCH button that users will click on to initiate the search. Here, we will add a Button element called BTN_SEARCH as shown in Figure 3.25. After the button is created, you can specify its label by filling in its text property. For now, that's as far as we'll take it. However, in Section 3.3.7, we'll circle back and see how to activate this button by associating it with an action.

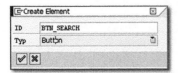

Figure 3.25 Defining the V_SELECT View UI Layout (Part 8)

3.3.5   Laying Out the Details View

In order to display the user contact information, we'll need to create another view. Within the Web Dynpro Explorer, we can do this by right-clicking on the VIEWS node for the selected component and selecting the CREATE menu option (see Figure 3.26). Then, in the CREATE VIEW dialog box shown in Figure 3.27, we can choose a name for the view (V_DETAILS) and enter an optional short text description. Click on the button with the green checkmark on it to confirm your selection.

For the most part, you'll find that the process for designing the V_DETAILS view is pretty similar to the one we used to lay out the V_SELECT view. Here, we will once again bind attributes from the USER_CONTACT context node to a series of Input-Field elements. Though we could repeat the UI element creation process illustrated in Section 3.3.4, it turns out there is a faster way.

Figure 3.26 Creating the V_DETAILS View (Part 1)

Figure 3.27 Creating the V_DETAILS View (Part 2)

Within the View Editor, there is a form creation wizard we can use to automatically create a form based on the attributes defined within a given context node. To initiate the form creation wizard, simply right-click on the ROOTUIELEMENTCONTAINER node and select the CREATE CONTAINER FORM menu option as shown in Figure 3.28. This will open the CREATE FORM ELEMENTS dialog box shown in Figure 3.29. Here, we must select the context node that will act as a source for the generated form fields: the USER_CONTACT context node. Once the context node is selected, you can see that the form wizard will automatically create form fields for each of the individual attributes defined within the context node (see Figure 3.29).

Figure 3.28 Creating a Container Form in the View Editor (Part 1)

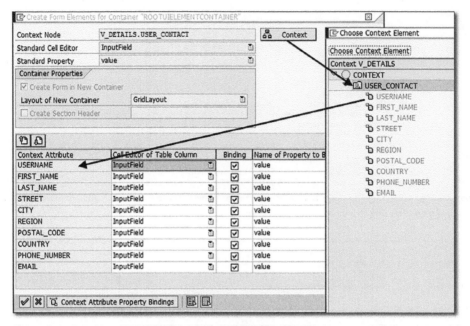

Figure 3.29 Creating a Container Form in the View Editor (Part 2)

For our simple example, we'll accept all the defaults proposed by the form creation wizard by clicking on the button with the green checkmark on it. However, if you wish to adjust the layout of the form, you can do so by editing form elements in the table contained in the bottom portion of the CREATE FORM ELEMENTS dialog window shown in Figure 3.29. Within this table, we can:

▶ Change the cell editor of the form element by selecting from the list of available UI elements in the CELL EDITOR OF TABLE COLUMN column. As you can see in Figure 3.29, the default UI element selected is the familiar InputField element.

▶ Remove elements from the form by de-selecting the checkbox in the BINDING column.

▶ Select the property of the UI element you wish to bind a given context attribute to.

Once the form generation wizard is complete, you'll notice that a series of Label and InputField elements have been added to the view layout. Since we're only displaying user contact information, not editing it, we should gray out these fields so users don't get the wrong impression. This can be achieved by selecting the readOnly property for each of the generated InputField elements, as shown in Figure 3.30.

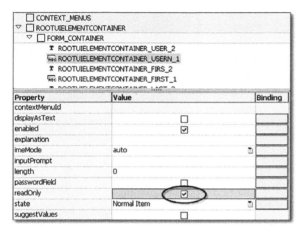

Figure 3.30 Setting the readOnly Property for the InputField Elements

The last thing we need to do on the V_DETAILS view is add a Button element called BTN_BACK to the bottom of the view layout. This button will be used to start the user lookup process over again if the user so desires.

3.3.6 Window Organization and Navigation Links

Now that we have completed the view layer design, we're ready to begin connecting everything together. To a large degree, much of this configuration happens within the window element. However, before we start down this path, there are a couple of loose ends we need to tie up in the view layer.

As we learned in Chapter 2, navigation between a pair of views is achieved by defining navigational links. These navigational links connect a pair of navigation plugs: an outbound plug in the source view and an inbound plug in the target view. Therefore, in order to be able to navigate back and forth between the V_SELECT and V_DETAILS views, we need to create some navigation plugs.

In our example, we'll define simple navigation plugs that don't contain any parameters. For instance, Figure 3.31 shows how we've defined an outbound plug called TO_DETAILS that will be used to trigger navigation from the V_SELECT view to the V_DETAILS view. On the flip side, Figure 3.32 shows how we have defined an inbound plug called FROM_SELECT in the V_DETAILS view. To navigate from the V_DETAILS view back to the V_SELECT view, we'll create two more navigation plugs called TO_SELECT and FROM_DETAILS, respectively.

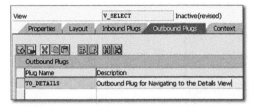

Figure 3.31 Defining an Outbound Plug in the V_SELECT View

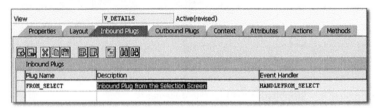

Figure 3.32 Defining an Inbound Plug in the V_DETAILS View

With the navigation plugs now in place, we can turn our attention to window design. For this task, we'll open up the W_MAIN window in the Window Editor by double-clicking on it in the navigation area. As you can see on the WINDOW tab shown in Figure 3.33, the V_SELECT view has already been embedded in the window. This step happened automatically behind the scenes when we first created the WDA component. Now we need to embed the V_DETAILS view in the window. We can do this by right-clicking on the top-level W_MAIN node in the WINDOW STRUCTURE tree table and selecting the EMBED VIEW menu option (see Figure 3.33). Then, in the EMBED VIEW dialog box shown in Figure 3.34, we can select the V_DETAILS view by opening the input help on the VIEW TO BE EMBEDDED input field. Click on the button with the green checkmark on it to confirm your selection.

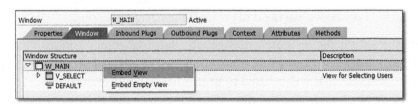

Figure 3.33 Embedding the V_DETAILS View (Part 1)

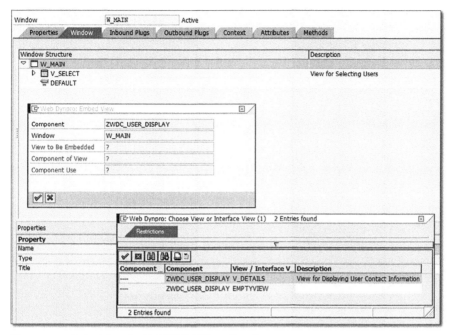

Figure 3.34 Embedding the V_DETAILS View (Part 2)

Once the V_DETAILS view has been embedded into the window, we can begin defining navigation links between the two views. To demonstrate how this works, let's see how the navigation link from the V_SELECT view to the V_DETAILS view is defined. The steps required here are as follows:

1. To begin, we need to locate the TO_DETAILS outbound plug of the source V_SELECT view within the Window Structure table shown in Figure 3.35. Then, we can initiate the creation of the navigation link by right-clicking on it and selecting the Create Navigation Link menu option.

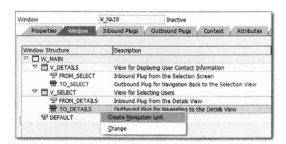

Figure 3.35 Creating a Navigation Link (Part 1)

2. This will open the CHOOSE DESTINATION FOR NAVIGATION dialog box shown in Figure 3.36. Here, we can select the destination view and target inbound plug in the correspondingly named input fields.

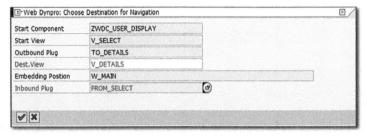

Figure 3.36 Creating a Navigation Link (Part 2)

3. Finally, once the destination view/inbound plug is selected, we can confirm your changes by clicking on the button with the green checkmark on it. Figure 3.37 shows the completed navigation link.

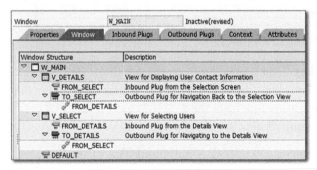

Figure 3.37 Creating a Navigation Link (Part 3)

To define the navigation link going the other direction, we can simply right-click on the TO_SELECT outbound plug of the V_DETAILS view and repeat the steps outlined above.

3.3.7 Defining Actions and Event Handler Methods

In order to make our application come alive, we need to associate the Button elements on the V_SELECT and V_DETAILS views with special event handler modules called *actions*. These actions will be triggered whenever a user clicks on the Button elements at runtime.

We'll begin by defining an action called SEARCH that will be invoked whenever a user clicks on the BTN_SEARCH button in the V_SELECT view. We'll do this by opening up the V_SELECT view in the View Editor, selecting the LAYOUT tab, and then clicking on the NEW button adjacent to the onAction property of the BTN_SEARCH button. This will open the CREATE ACTION dialog box shown in Figure 3.38. Here, you must select a name for the action (in this case, SEARCH) as well as an optional short text description. Furthermore, in the lower left-hand corner of the CREATE ACTION dialog box, you can see that we also have the option of selecting an outbound plug that will be fired whenever the action is invoked. This suits our particular use case because we want to navigate to the DETAILS view to display our search results. To confirm our selection, we can simply click on the button with the green checkmark on it.

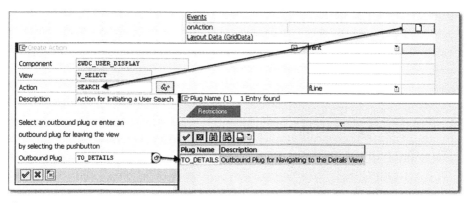

Figure 3.38 Creating an Action (Part 1)

Figure 3.39 shows the newly created action on the ACTIONS tab of the View Editor. If we had wanted to, we could have created the action separately and then linked it with the BTN_SEARCH button after the fact. In any case, once the action is created, we can double-click on it to open up the auto-generated action handler method. Figure 3.40 shows what this auto-generated method looks like.

View		V_SELECT		Inactive				
Properties	Layout	Inbound Plugs	Outbound Plugs	Context	Attributes	Actions	Methods	

Action	Action Type	Description	Event Handler
SEARCH	Standard	Action for Initiating a User Search	ONACTIONSEARCH
	Standard		

Figure 3.39 Creating an Action (Part 2)

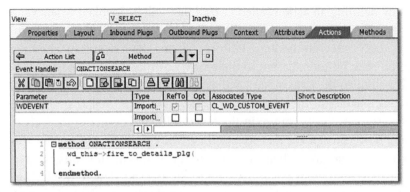

Figure 3.40 Creating an Action (Part 3)

Looking closely at the generated code displayed in Figure 3.40, you can see that the code generation wizard automatically implemented the call to the FIRE_TO_ DETAILS_PLG() plug method, which fires the TO_DETAILS outbound plug on the V_SELECT view. Thus, whenever a user clicks on the BTN_SEARCH button on the V_SELECT view, the SEARCH action will fire the TO_DETAILS outbound plug, and navigation to the V_DETAILS view will commence. However, somewhere along the way, we need to perform the lookup of the user contact information.

Though there are several different places to interject the user lookup logic, we chose to put this logic in the auto-generated handler method associated with the FROM_SELECT inbound plug defined in the V_DETAILS view. As you can see in Listing 3.2, we're simply delegating the user lookup to the GET_USER_CONTACT_INFO() method described in Section 3.3.3. We'll explore the nature of this method call syntax in further detail in Chapter 4.

```
method HANDLEFROM_SELECT.
  "Invoke the component controller method to load the user
  "contact info:
  wd_comp_controller->get_user_contact_info( ).
endmethod.
```

Listing 3.2 Implementing the User Contact Lookup

Going the other way, things are much simpler. For the BTN_BACK button element on the V_DETAILS view, we'll simply create an action called BACK, which will fire the TO_SELECT outbound plug on the V_DETAILS view. No further customization is required.

3.3.8 Input Validation and Messaging

At this point, our WDA component is almost finished. However, before we wrap everything up, we should probably tighten things up a little bit on the V_SELECT view. Right now, there's nothing stopping a user from initiating a search without first entering a proper user name. To prevent this from happening, we should make the INP_USERNAME input field a required field. This process begins with the configuration of the state attribute for the InputField, as shown in Figure 3.41. Once this attribute is set, the corresponding label in the UI display will contain a red asterisk that indicates that the field is a required field.

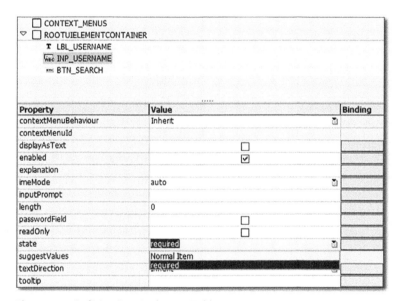

Figure 3.41 Defining Required Input Fields

Though the state attribute of an InputField element allows us to identify required fields in the UI, it does not actually enforce user input. For this task, we must implement some custom validation code in ABAP using the WDDOBEFOREACTION() hook method defined within the V_SELECT view. As the method name suggests, this method gets called *before* any actions are fired. Therefore, it is the perfect place for performing input validations.

Listing 3.3 shows how we have implemented the WDDOBEFOREACTION() method. We'll defer the description of the individual API calls until Chapter 4 when we talk about controller APIs in depth. However, even without knowing a lot of the nitty-gritty details, you can see that the CHECK_MANDATORY_ATTR_ON_VIEW() class method of class CL_WD_DYNAMIC_TOOL is doing most of the heavy lifting. Behind the scenes, this method is sophisticated enough to introspect UI element meta-data to determine whether or not the user has entered data in all the required fields. Furthermore, if an error is detected, the previous navigation request will be aborted, and error messages will be displayed to inform the user of the problem (see Figure 3.42).

```
method WDDOBEFOREACTION.
  "Method-Local Data Declarations:
  DATA: lo_api_controller TYPE REF TO if_wd_view_controller,
        lo_action          TYPE REF TO if_wd_action.

  lo_api_controller = wd_this->wd_get_api( ).
  lo_action = lo_api_controller->get_current_action( ).

  IF lo_action IS BOUND.
    CASE lo_action->name.
      WHEN 'SEARCH'.
        cl_wd_dynamic_tool=>check_mandatory_attr_on_view(
          EXPORTING
            view_controller = lo_api_controller ).
    ENDCASE.
  ENDIF.
endmethod.
```

Listing 3.3 Implementing Required Field Checks

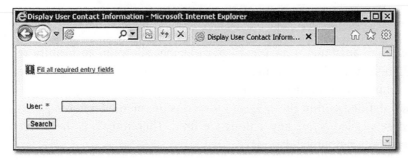

Figure 3.42 Checking for Required Fields in the V_SELECT View

3.4 Creating and Testing the WDA Application

At long last, our WDA component is complete, and we're ready to create our WDA application. Fortunately, this can be accomplished in a few easy steps. To begin, we'll right-click on the Web Dynpro node in our selected package and select the CREATE • WEB DYNPRO APPLICATION menu option as shown in Figure 3.43. This will open the CREATE WEB DYNPRO APPLICATION dialog box shown in Figure 3.44. Here, we'll create a new WDA application called ZWDA_USER_DISPLAY. To confirm your selection, click on the button with the green checkmark on it.

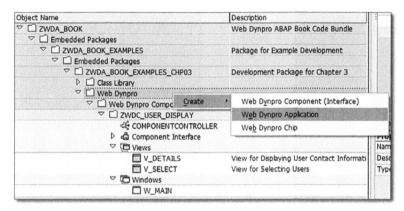

Figure 3.43 Creating the WDA Application (Part 1)

Create Web Dynpro application		⊠
Application	ZWDA_USER_DISPLAY	
Description	Display User Contact Information	

Figure 3.44 Creating the WDA Application (Part 2)

By default, the newly created WDA application won't be associated with any particular WDA component. We can define this association on the PROPERTIES tab of the Application Editor screen shown in Figure 3.45. As you can see, we have associated our new application with the ZWDC_USER_DISPLAY component developed in Section 3.3. Once you're satisfied with your selection, click on the SAVE button to save the application.

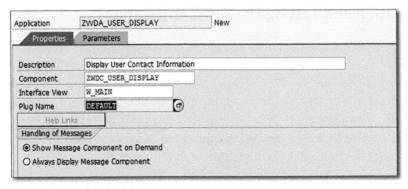

Figure 3.45 Creating the WDA Application (Part 3)

As the WDA application is being saved, the application will be added as a new ICF service node underneath the */sap/bc/webdynpro* node behind the scenes. Thus, as soon as you save the application, you can test it by clicking on the TEST/EXECUTE button in the toolbar of the Web Dynpro Explorer screen shown in Figure 3.46. Assuming all goes well, the application should load into a browser window as shown in Figure 3.47.

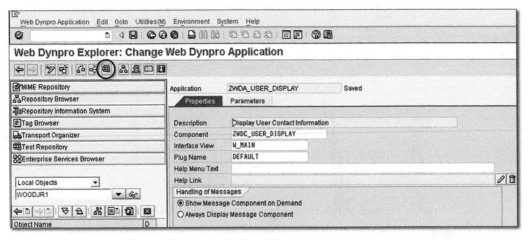

Figure 3.46 Testing the WDA Application (Part 1)

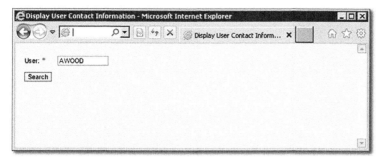

Figure 3.47 Testing the WDA Application (Part 2)

As you play around with the application, you can use the ABAP Debugger tool to trace through the code and see what's happening behind the scenes. Here, all you need to do is set an external breakpoint somewhere within the source code. You can do this by placing the cursor on a particular line in the code and clicking on the SET/DELETE EXTERNAL BREAKPOINT button as shown in Figure 3.48.

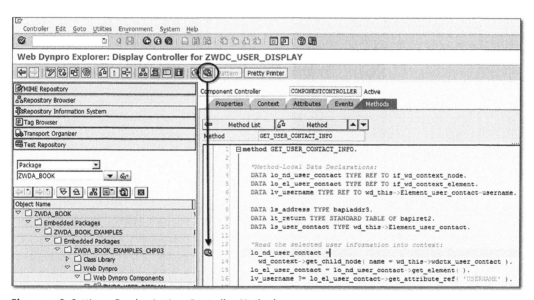

Figure 3.48 Setting a Breakpoint in a Controller Method

After the breakpoint is set, you can restart the application and the Debugger tool will open whenever the breakpoint is reached (see Figure 3.49). From here, you can step through the code in much the same way you would trace through a method in an ABAP Objects class.

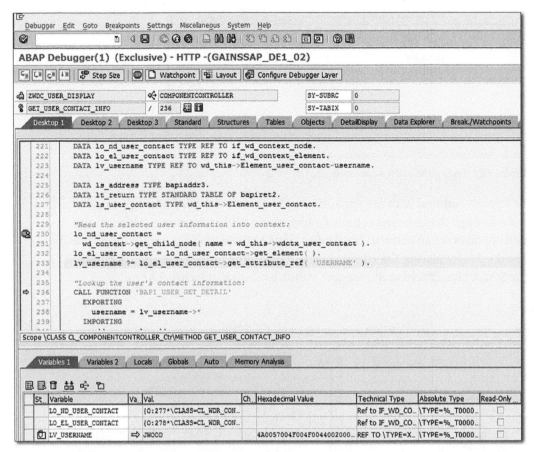

Figure 3.49 Debugging a Method in the ABAP Debugger Tool

In addition to the standard debugging tools you may have worked with in the past, the Debugger tool also provides us with a custom Web Dynpro debugger tool that allows us to trace through WDA-specific elements such as the WDA context, UI element properties in the view, etc. We can enable this tool by clicking on the REPLACE TOOL button on the right-hand side of the Debugger tool screen and selecting the Web Dynpro tool (see Figure 3.50).

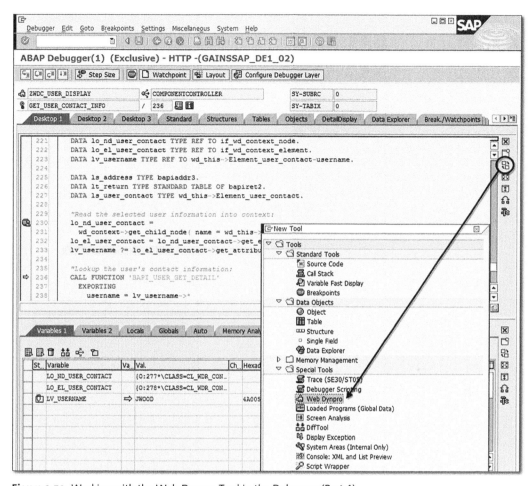

Figure 3.50 Working with the Web Dynpro Tool in the Debugger (Part 1)

Figure 3.51 demonstrates what the Web Dynpro tool looks like. We'll have an opportunity to explore these features in greater detail throughout the course of this book.

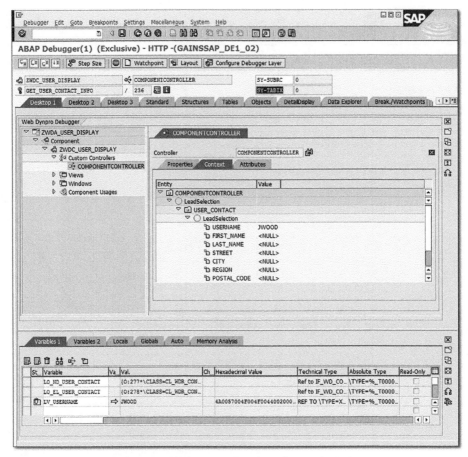

Figure 3.51 Working with the Web Dynpro Tool in the Debugger (Part 2)

3.5 Summary

In this chapter, we were able to experience the development of a complete WDA application from start to finish. Hopefully this journey helped to solidify some of the WDA concepts and principles described thus far. At the same time, while this excursion helped reinforce what we've already learned, it also shed some light on certain aspects of Web Dynpro development that we've glossed over before now. At this point, we'll attempt to bridge these gaps by probing into specific areas of Web Dynpro programming up close. We'll begin this process in the next chapter by looking at controllers and related runtime APIs.

Controllers make up the active parts of a WDA component. In other words, they are in charge of orchestrating what goes on behind the scenes as users interact with WDA applications. In this chapter, we'll explain how controllers work in tandem with the Web Dynpro framework to define the behavior of WDA applications.

4   Controller Development

In Chapter 3, we had an opportunity to get our hands dirty building a custom WDA application from scratch. There, we were able to accomplish quite a bit without writing much ABAP code. However, as we progressed through the development of our sample application, it quickly became obvious that there was an upper bound on what we'd be able to accomplish without knowing our way around controllers and the Web Dynpro runtime APIs. Therefore, in this chapter, we'll attempt to bridge this knowledge gap by looking at controllers from a nuts-and-bolts perspective.

We'll begin our analysis by looking at the various elements that are common to all controller types (e.g., attributes, methods, and so on). Then, we'll explore specific controller types and see how each controller type is tailor-made to fulfill its specific role within the Web Dynpro framework. From there, we'll look at the bigger picture and see how the different controller types are utilized at runtime. Finally, we'll wrap up by considering some tools and APIs that can be used to simplify the controller development process.

4.1   Controller Element Overview

In many ways, you can think of a WDA controller as a specialized version of an ABAP Objects class. Indeed, looking at the Controller Editor screen shown in Figure 4.1, you can see many similarities to the Class Builder tool used to maintain ABAP Objects classes. Here, for example, we can define attributes, methods, and events within a controller in much the same way that these elements are defined in ABAP Objects classes. Of course, there are a few controller-specific wrinkles to these elements that we need to be mindful of. Therefore, in this section, we'll go over the various elements you can define within a controller and see how to utilize these elements within the Web Dynpro framework.

Component Controller	COMPONENTCONTROLLER	Active				
Properties	Context	Attributes	Events	Methods		

Method	Method Type	Interface	Description	Event	Controller	
WDDOAPPLICATIONSTATE	O Method	☐	Handling for Suspending and Resuming an Application			
WDDOBEFORENAVIGATION	O Method	☐	Error Handling Before Navigation Through Application			
WDDOEXIT	O Method	☐	Controller Clean-Up Method			
WDDOINIT	O Method	☐	Controller Initialization Method			
WDDOPOSTPROCESSING	O Method	☐	Prepare Output			

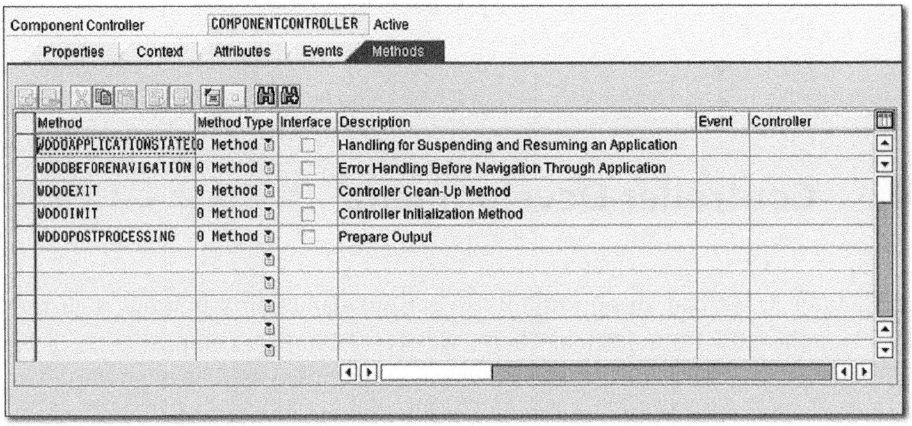

Figure 4.1 Similarities between the Controller Editor and Class Builder

4.1.1 Methods

Behind the scenes, all the functionality of a WDA component is encoded within the methods of its various controllers. In this section, we'll look at the different types of methods you can create within a controller and see how these methods work in concert with the surrounding Web Dynpro framework to respond to user events and coordinate the flow of data between the view and model layers.

Hook Methods

When you create a controller, you'll notice that the system takes the liberty of automatically creating a handful of methods for you: the so-called *hook methods*. From a technical perspective, a hook method is a type of callback method that gets invoked by the Web Dynpro framework at predefined points within the application flow. As such, hook methods are analogous to user exits in that they provide us with a *hook* for integrating custom logic designed to respond to various events within the controller lifecycle. Put a different way, hook methods represent the intersection between the Web Dynpro framework and our custom application code.

Naturally, the types of hook methods contained within a controller vary between controller types. For example, a window controller provides hook methods such as WDDOONOPEN() and WDDOONCLOSE() to handle the window open and close events, respectively. Similarly, as you can see in Figure 4.2, view controllers provide hook methods called WDDOBEFOREACTION() and WDDOAFTERACTION()that allow you to react to user actions triggered within a view. We'll learn about the specific hook methods provided with the different controller types in the upcoming sections. Furthermore, we'll also learn about the call sequence for these hook methods in Section 4.4.

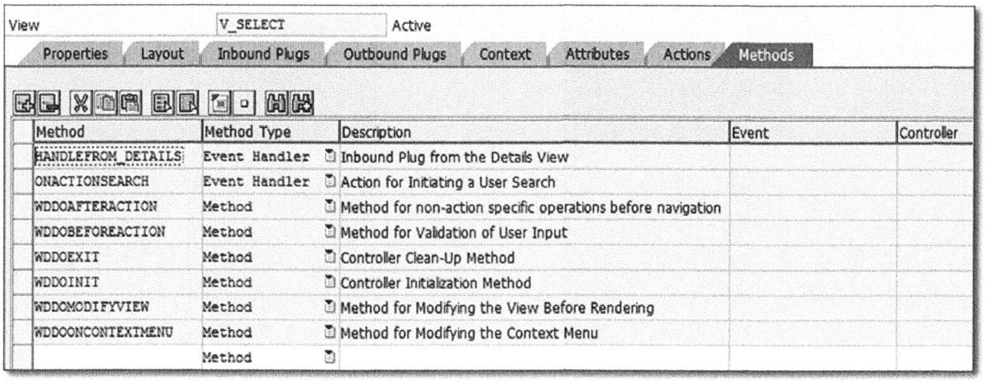

View		V_SELECT		Active					
Properties	Layout	Inbound Plugs	Outbound Plugs	Context	Attributes	Actions	Methods		

Method	Method Type	Description	Event	Controller
HANDLEFROM_DETAILS	Event Handler	Inbound Plug from the Details View		
ONACTIONSEARCH	Event Handler	Action for Initiating a User Search		
WDDOAFTERACTION	Method	Method for non-action specific operations before navigation		
WDDOBEFOREACTION	Method	Method for Validation of User Input		
WDDOEXIT	Method	Controller Clean-Up Method		
WDDOINIT	Method	Controller Initialization Method		
WDDOMODIFYVIEW	Method	Method for Modifying the View Before Rendering		
WDDOONCONTEXTMENU	Method	Method for Modifying the Context Menu		
	Method			

Figure 4.2 Predefined Hook Methods for a View Controller

Collectively, the hook methods defined within a controller make up the controller's interface. We use the term *interface* loosely here since there is not a specific ABAP Objects interface that controllers implement. Nevertheless, from a developer's perspective, the experience is much the same. Indeed, as you can see in Figure 4.2, the hook methods are locked down for editing within the Controller Editor; we cannot change the signature of these methods or modify the way in which they are called. As developers, all we can do is open up the method (by double-clicking on it) and define its implementation by inserting custom code within the METHOD...ENDMETHOD block, as shown in Figure 4.3.

Within a hook method, we are given license to implement pretty much whatever ABAP code is needed to process a given event. However, best programming practices call for modularization and separation of duties. In particular, we recommend that the implementation of a hook method be minimalistic; deferring most of the heavy lifting to helper classes or methods, or better yet, the model layer.

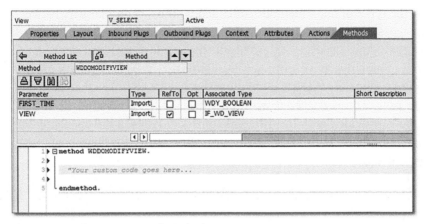

Figure 4.3 Implementing a Hook Method

This is analogous to decoupling events such as AT SELECTION-SCREEN or START-OF-SELECTION in ABAP report programs from the actual application logic. This separation of concerns will simplify the design and make it easier to adapt the application logic over time.

Instance Methods

Besides the standard hook methods described in the previous section, we can also create our own custom *instance methods* within a controller. This can be achieved by simply keying in the desired method name in the METHOD column of the methods table contained within the METHODS tab shown in Figure 4.4. Here, we must select the default METHOD option in the METHOD TYPE dropdown list.

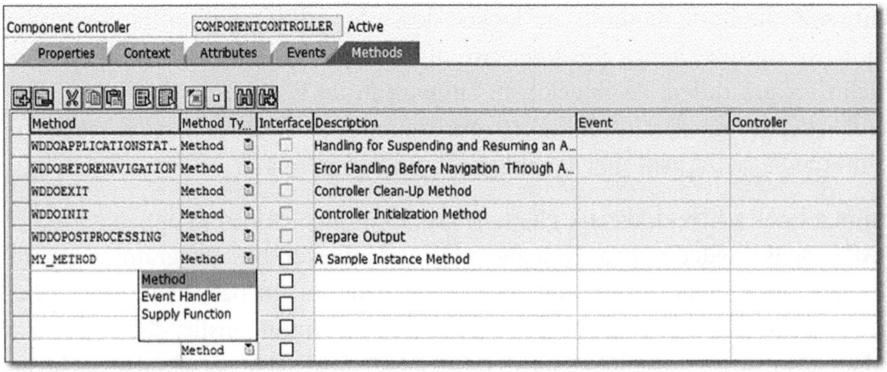

Figure 4.4 Creating an Instance Method (Part 1)

Once the instance method is created, we can implement it by double-clicking on it. This will open up the editor screen shown in Figure 4.5. Here, we can insert the requisite ABAP code into the METHOD...ENDMETHOD block as usual. Furthermore, we can also define method parameters, just as we would for a normal ABAP Objects method using the parameter table shown in Figure 4.5.

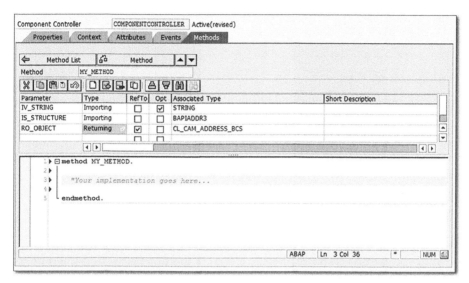

Figure 4.5 Creating an Instance Method (Part 2)

As we mentioned earlier, instance methods are frequently used to support the standard hook methods. This best practice simplifies the design and helps to maintain healthy boundaries between the controller and model layers. Here, one of the primary goals is to avoid unnecessary entanglements between WDA controllers and model objects. In general, the model layer should not know or care that it is being accessed from a WDA component. In order to bridge this gap, instance methods often take on the role of adapter; facilitating the exchange of data between the controller context and model layers. We'll see this on display quite a bit when we look at context programming concepts in Chapter 5.

Syntax Restrictions

As you develop your controller methods, it's important to be aware of certain syntax restrictions in effect. In particular, we should point out that there are certain ABAP statements that aren't allowed within a WDA controller method.

> For example, Dynpro screen processing statements such as LEAVE SCREEN don't really make sense in a WDA context. Similarly, WDA controller methods are subject to the same language restrictions imposed on methods in regular ABAP Objects classes. If you're not familiar with these restrictions, don't worry; the compiler will tell you where you've gone wrong. These restrictions are also described at length in the SAP online help documentation, in the section entitled "Special Features of Web Dynpro ABAP Programming." Another excellent reference on this topic is *The Official ABAP Reference* (Keller, SAP PRESS, 2011).

Event Handler Methods

If you look closely at the method editor screen in Figure 4.4, you'll notice that there are a couple of other types of methods we can define within a WDA controller. One of these method types is the so-called *event handler* method type. These methods register themselves as listeners for events that may be triggered by other controllers. We'll learn more about how these methods are used in Section 4.1.4.

Supply Function Methods

As the name suggests, supply function methods supply context nodes with data on demand. This feature can be particularly useful in situations where we have a complex context hierarchy that may contain a lot of data. Here, it makes sense to utilize the lazy loading technique afforded with supply functions to load data into the context only when it is needed. We'll see how supply functions work in Chapter 5.

4.1.2   Attributes

Throughout the lifetime of a controller, we may need to keep track of certain data objects behind the scenes. Examples of such data objects include references to model objects, cached data, and state information such as search indexes. Whatever the use case might be, we can store these data objects as *attributes* within a given controller.

As you would expect, attributes are maintained in a table on the ATTRIBUTES tab of the Controller Editor, as shown in Figure 4.6. Here, we can define attributes by filling in the properties contained within the following columns:

▶ ATTRIBUTE

In the ATTRIBUTE column, we must specify the attribute's name. As attributes are controller specific, we needn't use special naming conventions to qualify them; just a meaningful name will do. Within the controller methods, the attribute will be accessed using syntax like this: wd_this->attribute_name.

▶ PUBLIC

We can use the PUBLIC checkbox to assign the public access specifier to attributes defined in component/custom controllers. Whenever this property is set, other controllers within the same WDA component can access the attribute directly (i.e., wd_comp_controller->attribute_name).

▶ REFTO

The REFTO checkbox is used to define attributes that refer to instances of ABAP Objects classes or generic data objects.

▶ ASSOCIATED TYPE

In the ASSOCIATED TYPE column, we must assign a data type to the attribute using elementary types, ABAP Dictionary types, class types, and so on.

▶ DESCRIPTION

In the DESCRIPTION column, we can provide an optional description of what the attribute is used for.

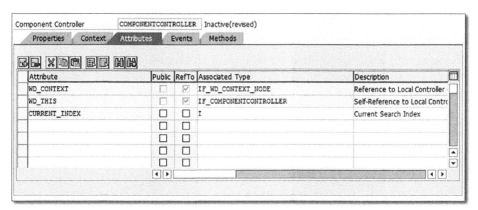

Figure 4.6 Defining Attributes in a Controller

Given what you already know about controller contexts, you might be wondering when data should be stored in attributes instead of the controller context, and vice versa. The general rule of thumb here is that the context should be used to model data that will be displayed in the UI: either directly via data binding in the view or indirectly via context mapping. For everything else, the use of the context and its associated overhead is overkill. Therefore, if you need to keep track of state information and other details behind the scenes, attributes are the way to go.

4.1.3 Contexts

As we learned in Chapter 2, each controller type maintains a context that is used to store data displayed within the UI. For now, we'll defer our discussion on context design and development issues to Chapter 5.

4.1.4 Events

As we've seen, controllers can communicate and share resources with one another in a variety of different ways. For instance, we've observed that context mapping allows a pair of controllers to share common data objects used within the UI. Also, in Chapter 3, we demonstrated how one controller could invoke a method provided by another controller. In the latter case, the communication was *synchronous* in nature. In other words, the source controller invoked a method at a predefined point within its process flow and then waited for the method to respond before proceeding.

Sometimes, it may be desirable for controllers to be able to communicate with one another behind the scenes *asynchronously*. For example, a global controller might want to notify dependent controllers of an event such as the arrival of data, etc. To set up such a scenario, we can define an event in the global controller and then register each of the dependent controllers as *listeners* for the event. Then, when the event is triggered at runtime, the dependent controllers can respond to the event by executing the logic encoded within their event handler methods. We'll learn how all this works in the upcoming sections.

Understanding the Event Process Flow

Before we begin exploring the mechanics of event processing from an implementation perspective, it is first helpful to trace through an event processing scenario to see how the various elements involved interact with one another at runtime. Once we have a better grasp of these concepts, we'll be in a better place to determine when and how to configure such scenarios.

To illustrate the event process flow, let's take a look at the process flow diagram in Figure 4.7. Here, we've depicted a fairly typical scenario in which a view controller is listening for an event defined by the component controller called DATA_LOADED. At runtime, the DATA_LOADED event is processed as follows:

1. The event is triggered within the component controller via a call to an auto-generated event trigger method whose name is of the form FIRE_<Event>_EVT(). So, in our example, this call would be to the FIRE_DATA_LOADED_EVT() method.

2. After the event trigger method is invoked, the Web Dynpro framework will intercept the call and broadcast the event to any subscribing controllers. Here, it's important to note that even though our sample diagram only contains one listening controller, it's possible that multiple controllers could be listening for a particular event simultaneously.

3. Once the list of subscribers is determined, the Web Dynpro framework will invoke the event handler methods linked to the event on the target controllers. So, for instance, in the scenario illustrated in Figure 4.7, the ON_DATA_LOADED() method will be invoked on the listening view controller.

4. Finally, within the ON_DATA_LOADED() method, the view controller can execute the logic needed to respond to the event. Here, it is possible that event parameters may be used to provide additional information, such as information about the nature of the event.

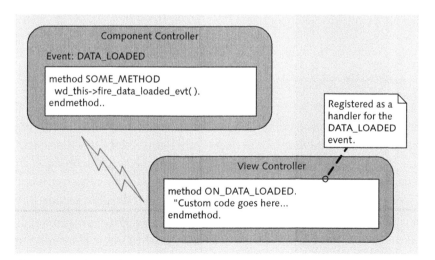

Figure 4.7 Understanding Event Process Flow

Event Wiring and Configuration

Now that we've seen how event processing works from a runtime perspective, let's take a look at how such scenarios are implemented at design time. Here, we'll use the event example illustrated in Figure 4.7 as the basis for our demonstration. In this case, the steps required to define the event flow are as follows:

1. First, we must define the event itself within the source controller. We can do this by opening the controller and navigating to the EVENTS tab shown in Figure 4.8. Here, we must provide a meaningful name for the event (e.g., DATA_ LOADED) and an optional description. If we like, we can also define one or more parameters in the PARAMETERS table directly beneath the EVENTS table (see Figure 4.8).

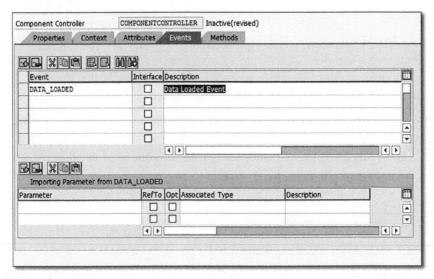

Figure 4.8 Defining an Event

2. Next, before we can register other controllers as listeners for the event, we must first define *usage declarations* between those controllers and the source controller. Fortunately, since the system takes the liberty of defining such usage relationships for view controllers, no additional steps are required in our sample scenario. We'll cover usage declarations in further detail in Section 4.3.

3. After the proper usage declarations are in place, we can register a controller as a listener for an event by creating an event handler method that will respond to

the event at runtime. We can do this by opening up the listening controller, selecting the METHODS tab, and defining a method with method type EVENT HANDLER (see Figure 4.9). We can then use the input help provided with the EVENT column to help us select the event that we want to listen for (e.g., the DATA_LOADED event).

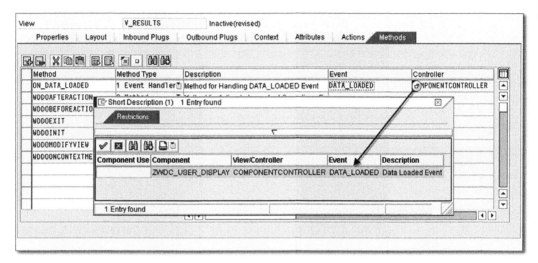

Figure 4.9 Defining an Event Handler Method (Part 1)

4. The last step is to provide an implementation for the event handler method just like we would for any other method. We can do this by double-clicking on the method and plugging in custom ABAP code in the METHOD...ENDMETHOD block (see Figure 4.10). By default, we're provided with a parameter called WDEVENT, which is of type CL_WD_CUSTOM_EVENT. In some scenarios, the WDEVENT parameter can be used to access event parameters dynamically. We'll see how to access some of these parameters in upcoming chapters. You can also find detailed documentation for class CL_WD_CUSTOM_EVENT in the Class Builder tool.

If you'd like to see how event processing works firsthand, you can find some live examples in package SWDP_TEST, which is installed by default in your AS ABAP system. There, you can trace through the event-handling logic built into the WDR_TEST_EVENTS_RT_00 and WDR_TEST_EVENTS_RT_01 components by setting breakpoints in the event handler methods.

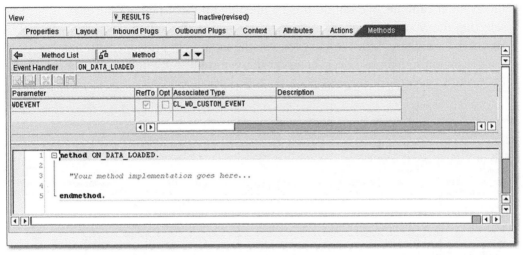

Figure 4.10 Defining an Event Handler Method (Part 2)

Event Parameters

Most of the time, the raising of the event itself is sufficient for relaying the occurrence of a particular event or milestone to interested controllers. However, there are times when some additional information might be needed to put the nature of the event into the proper context. In these scenarios, we can define event parameters to pass along additional data.

To a large degree, it's appropriate to think of event parameters as being like importing parameters to the auto-generated event trigger method that gets generated behind the scenes for an event. Indeed, as you can see in Figure 4.11, the event editor screen provides a table that allows us to define parameters for an event in the same way we'd define importing parameters for a method. At runtime, these parameters are passed into the auto-generated event trigger method as usual.

On the receiving side of things, in order to receive the parameter values, we must align the signature of the event handler methods with the event definition. We can do this within the listening controller by selecting the event handler method on the METHODS tab and then clicking on the ADJUST PARAMETERS button shown in Figure 4.12. Note that the same process also applies in situations when additional parameters are added to an event after the fact.

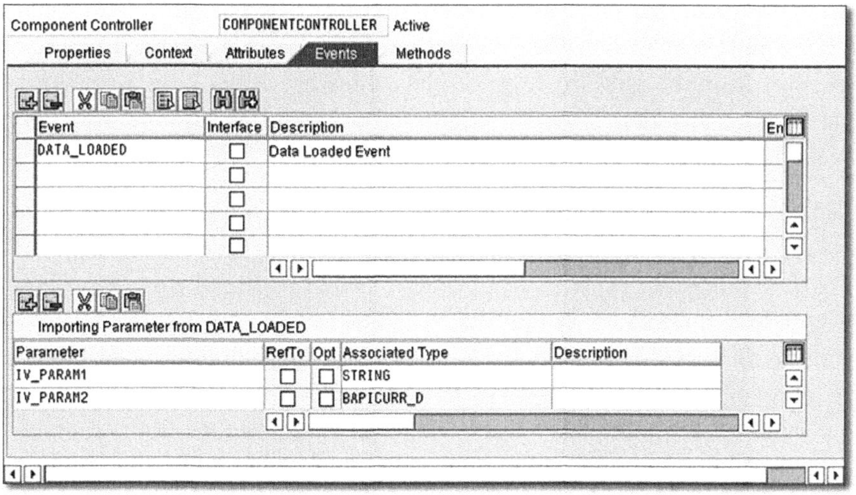

Figure 4.11 Adding Parameters to an Event

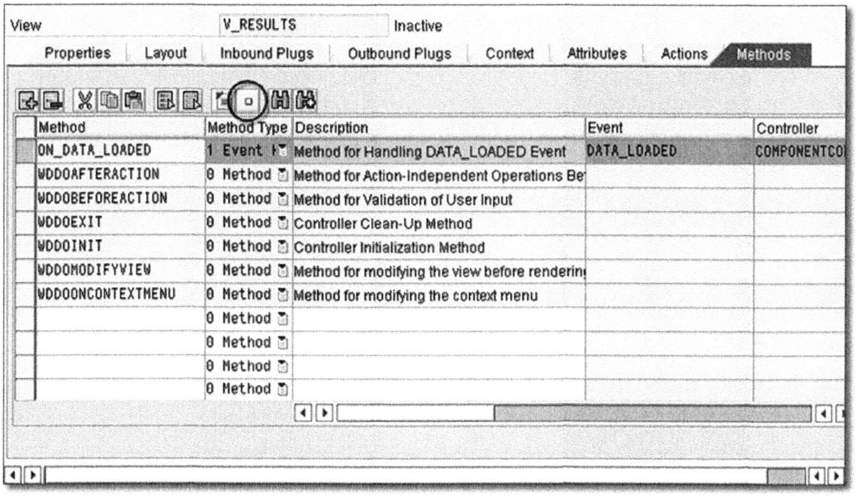

Figure 4.12 Adjusting the Parameters in an Event Handler Method

When to Use Events

Now that we've seen how events work, you might be wondering when events should be used within your own developments. Though there are no hard and fast rules concerning their usage, we recommend you only use events in situations when asynchronous messaging is truly required. For example, using an event to replace a simple synchronous method call between a pair of controllers in a WDA component is overkill. The goal here is to keep the code simple and transparent, and event handling logic can be somewhat difficult to trace. Not to mention the fact that there is some additional overhead at runtime associated with event handling.

One scenario when events really show their value is when we get into cross-component communication scenarios. Here, let's imagine we're defining a generic component that can be leveraged by multiple components. In this case, if our generic component needs to communicate with its using component(s), it can do so by raising an event. That way, the generic component doesn't need to keep track of the set of listening components. Instead, it simply fires the event and lets the Web Dynpro framework sort things out from there. We'll see how this works in Chapter 9.

> **Event Usage Restrictions**
>
> Most of the time, events are used to notify other controllers of the arrival of data and other similar occurrences. Therefore, in keeping with the principle of separation of producers and consumers described in Chapter 2, you can only define events within component or custom controllers. When you think about it, this makes sense because view and window controllers shouldn't be publishing data. If this rule seems confusing, don't worry; the system won't allow you to create an event by mistake. In other words, if you're editing a controller and you see an EVENTS tab in the Controller Editor, then you know you're in the right place.

4.1.5 Actions

If you've ever worked with HTML forms before, you know that form elements (UI elements, in Web Dynpro parlance) are associated with events. These events make it possible to respond to specific actions triggered by the user within the Web UI. For example, if a user clicks on a button in an HTML form, the button's `onclick` event will be fired, and you as a programmer can determine if you want to respond to this action by linking the `onclick` event with a custom event handler method.

Though the HTML forms metaphor begins to break down when we start talking about event handling concepts in Web Dynpro UIs, it's nevertheless useful in illustrating the relationships among UI elements, the events they trigger, and the event handler methods that respond to these events. Within the Web Dynpro framework, the glue that binds all of these pieces together is the *action*.

According to the SAP help documentation, an action is defined as "a view controller-specific mechanism for responding to events raised on the client device as a result of user interaction." To understand how this event handling mechanism works, consider the diagram in Figure 4.13.

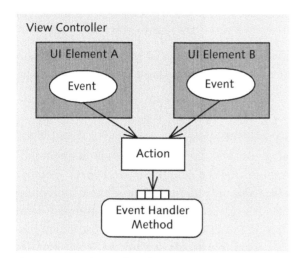

Figure 4.13 Understanding the Relationship between UI Elements and Actions

At the top of the stack, we have the UI elements that users are interacting with at the view layer. Many of these UI elements define event properties. For example, a `Button` UI element has an event property called `onAction` that gets triggered whenever the button is clicked in the UI. Similarly, the `DropDownByKey` UI element has an event property called `onSelect` that gets triggered whenever an entry is selected in a dropdown list. We'll see plenty of other UI element events as we proceed throughout this book. You can also find detailed information concerning events supported by each of the UI elements included in the Web Dynpro framework in the SAP online help documentation.

Whenever we want to handle an event triggered by a given UI element, we can associate its event property with an action. Although it's possible to create the action on the fly within the View Editor tool, it's important to note that actions are in fact independent elements defined within a view controller. This independence allows us to reuse actions to process the events triggered by multiple UI elements. For instance, in Figure 4.13, you can see that UI elements A and B are both leveraging the same action.

Each action is associated with an event handler method, which allows us to process the event(s) triggered upstream in the UI. Within the event handler method, we might perform some validations, invoke a method on the component controller, fire an outbound plug, and so on.

Creating Actions

From an implementation perspective, actions consist of little more than an action name and an event handler method. As such, you'll find that they're relatively easy to create. Here, we have two basic options:

▶ We can create an action on the fly within the View Editor tool by clicking on the CREATE button adjacent to the event property, as shown in Figure 4.14. Then, in the CREATE ACTION dialog box, we can define a new action by providing a name and optional description for the action. For certain UI element types (e.g., `Buttons`), we'll also be given the opportunity to select an outbound plug to fire whenever the event is triggered. As you may recall from our demonstration in Chapter 3, this selection causes the system to go ahead and implement the outbound plug call for us automatically within the event handler method.

> **Note**
>
> If you like, you can also select the COPY UI EVENT PARAMETERS checkbox to enable event parameterization for the action. For more information about this feature, consult the SAP online help documentation in the section entitled "Working Dynamically with Parameter Mappings."

▶ Alternatively, we can create an action directly on the ACTIONS tab, as shown in Figure 4.15. Here, we once again fill in the action name and an optional description for the action. We also have the option of specifying the action's *type*. As you can see in Figure 4.15, we can choose between the STANDARD and VALIDATION-INDEPENDENT action types. We'll learn more about the difference between these two action types in Section 4.4.

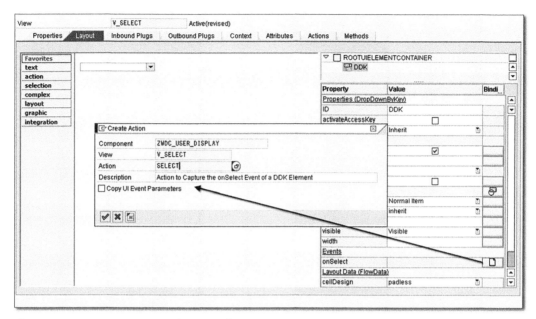

Figure 4.14 Creating an Action in the View Editor (Part 1)

Figure 4.15 Creating an Action in the View Editor (Part 2)

Regardless of the approach taken to create an action, we'll ultimately maintain them in the ACTIONS tab, as shown in Figure 4.15. From here, we can navigate to the auto-generated event handler method by double-clicking on the method name in the EVENT HANDLER column shown in Figure 4.15. As you can see in Figure 4.16, the interface of the auto-generated event handler method mirrors that of the server-side event handler methods described in Section 4.1.4. We'll see plenty of examples of action event handler methods as we proceed throughout the rest of this book.

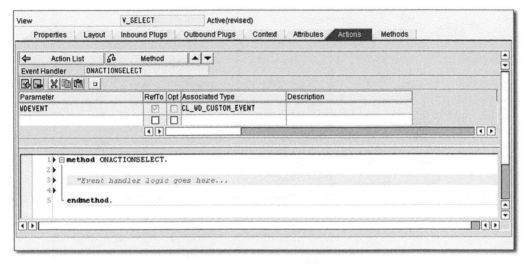

Figure 4.16 Implementing an Event Handler Method for an Action

4.2 Working with Specific Controller Types

Now that you have a feel for the types of elements included with Web Dynpro controllers, let's take a look at the roles and responsibilities fulfilled by each of the controller types within the framework. Having an understanding of these concepts will help you to better understand the organization and flow of WDA applications.

4.2.1 The Component Controller

Within a given WDA component, there's only one controller type whose presence is 100% guaranteed: the component controller. As we've seen, the component controller is generated automatically whenever a WDA component is created, and it cannot be deleted. Because of this symbiotic relationship, the component controller is characterized in the online help documentation as being "hierarchically superior" to all the other controllers within a WDA component.

From a runtime perspective, the component controller is instantiated when a component is first loaded by the framework and remains in context for the duration of the component's lifecycle. Consequently, due to its elevated stature and long lifespan, the component controller represents a natural place for implementing core application logic, storing data shared among controllers within the WDA component, and brokering communications with the model layer. In other words, the component controller is the central point of control for the behavior of the WDA component.

Understanding the Component Controller Interface

Behind the scenes, a component controller is realized in terms of a generated class that closely resembles a traditional ABAP Objects class. We can view the definition of this application class by clicking on the DISPLAY CONTROLLER INTERFACE button in the toolbar of the Controller Editor (see Figure 4.17). This will open the controller interface source view shown in Figure 4.17. Here, we can see the generated interface code maintained behind the scenes as we edit controller methods, context nodes, and so on.

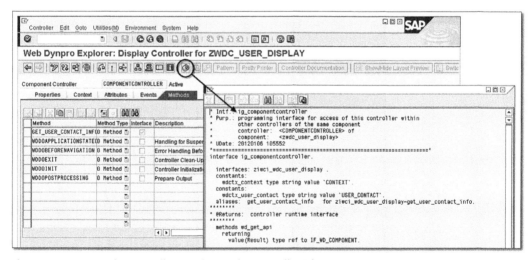

Figure 4.17 Viewing the Controller Interface in the Controller Editor

As you look over the controller interface source view, you'll notice the presence of several generated ABAP Objects interfaces. These interfaces define the programming interface used to access the component controller, both within the controller itself and outside the controller. In order to understand the scope of these different interfaces, consider the UML class diagram depicted in Figure 4.18.

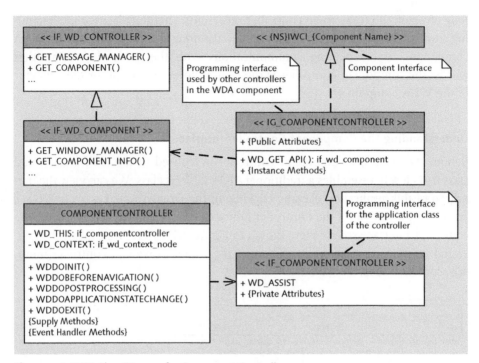

Figure 4.18 UML Class Diagram for Component Controllers

Here, we can trace through the generalization relationships to see that there are three different interfaces used to access the component controller:

▶ The {NS}IWCI_{Component Name} interface makes up the component's interface to the outside world. Here, the {NS} prefix refers to the namespace prefix of the component (e.g., Z or /BOWDK/). We'll defer detailed analysis of this interface to Chapter 9 when we talk about component-based development concepts. For now, suffice it to say that this interface exposes methods, events, and context nodes that need to be accessed by external components.

▶ The IG_COMPONENTCONTROLLER interface represents the programming interface that other controllers within the WDA component use to interact with the component controller. As you can see in Figure 4.18, this interface provides us with access to the component controller's instance methods and public attributes. Furthermore, the IF_WD_COMPONENT reference returned from the WD_GET_API() method call can be used to obtain access to component-wide services such as the message manager.

Coincidentally, we've seen the IG_COMPONENTCONTROLLER interface on display already when we demonstrated a call to a component controller method from a view controller in Chapter 3. There, we used the WD_COMP_CONTROLLER attribute of the view controller as the object reference for initiating an instance method call. If you look carefully at the specification of the WD_COMP_CONTROL-LER attribute in a window or view controller, you can see that it's of the reference type IG_COMPONENTCONTROLLER.

▶ Finally, at the bottom of the inheritance tree, we have the IF_COMPONENTCON-TROLLER interface, which makes up the programming interface utilized within the component controller itself. As you can see in Figure 4.18, this interface defines the WD_THIS attribute used (either explicitly or implicitly) within methods of the component controller.

Hook Method Overview

As we mentioned earlier, one of the primary objectives of this section was to identify the roles and responsibilities assumed by the various controller types within a WDA component. Here, we can gain a sense of a controller type's role by looking at the hook methods it provides. Table 4.1 describes each of the hook methods provided with the component controller in detail. As you can see, these methods are generally used to perform initialization and cleanup activities as well as component-wide validation or processing. We'll see where these hook methods fit into the overall Web Dynpro phase model in Section 4.4.

Method Name	Description
wddoinit	This method is called immediately after the component controller is instantiated. As such, it represents a logical place for inserting code used to initialize a WDA component (for example, prefilling the context).
wddobeforenavigation	This method allows us to perform any last-minute, component-wide validations before the navigation cycle begins.

Table 4.1 Hook Methods of the Component Controller

Method Name	Description
wddopostprocessing	This method is the last called before the Web Dynpro framework begins the rendering process. It's often used for cleanup of resources utilized within a single server-side roundtrip.
wddoapplicationstatechange	This method provides us with an opportunity to handle situations where the surrounding WDA application is suspended or resumed. We'll explore this concept in further detail in Chapter 6.
wddoexit	This method is called when the component controller, and by extension, its overarching WDA component, is being removed from context. Therefore, if the component controller is holding on to some kind of system resource or lock, this method can be used to release that resource gracefully.

Table 4.1 Hook Methods of the Component Controller (Cont.)

What Is the Component Controller Used For?

Now that you have a feel for how the component controller is organized from a technical perspective, let's broaden our focus a bit and think about what the component controller should be used for. As we mentioned earlier, the component controller represents the central point of control for the behavior of the WDA component. Given this, the component controller should be tasked with the following:

▶ Providing a shared data store (via its context) that can be leveraged by subordinate controllers (e.g., view controllers)

▶ Maintaining component-wide resources such as application-level locks, connection metadata, and so on

▶ Exposing business methods and services to subordinate controllers

▶ Brokering communications between the controller and model layers

In some respects, you can think of the component controller as a hub, facilitating communications among subordinate controllers, the Web Dynpro framework, and the model layer. As such, it should not be responsible for doing much of the heavy lifting application-wise; it's more of a pass-through. It's important to keep this in mind from a design perspective, since methods within a component controller tend to run more slowly than methods in traditional ABAP Objects classes. So, the leaner you keep the component controller, the better your application will perform.

> **SQL Restrictions**
>
> While it's easy to be tempted to cut corners and plug in application logic within component controller methods, we should point out that SAP forbids the use of `SELECT` statements within the WDA programming context. Although the syntax check in the Web Dynpro Explorer does not yet enforce such restrictions, we highly recommend that you not tempt fate by heading down this path. For more information about restrictions in the WDA programming context, check out the SAP online help documentation in the section entitled "Special Features of Web Dynpro ABAP Programming."

4.2.2 Custom Controllers

In addition to the component controller, the Web Dynpro framework provides another faceless global controller type called the *custom controller*. Architecturally, custom controllers have a similar look and feel to component controllers. However, unlike component controllers, custom controllers are created on an as-needed basis by developers. Indeed, within a given WDA component, you can have many custom controllers.

> **Note**
>
> You'll find the term *custom controller* used generically to describe both custom controllers and the component controller in a lot of Web Dynpro literature.

In this section, we'll take a look at custom controllers and see what they are used for within the Web Dynpro development paradigm.

Creating a Custom Controller

Before we look into the specifics of custom controllers, let's first see how they're created within a WDA component. Here, the process is pretty straightforward:

1. To begin, we can right-click on the WDA component in the left-hand navigation area and select the CREATE • CUSTOM CONTROLLER menu option (see Figure 4.19).

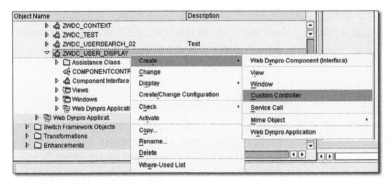

Figure 4.19 Creating a Custom Controller (Part 1)

2. Then, in the ensuing CREATE CONTROLLER dialog box, we must provide a name
   and an optional description for the custom controller (see Figure 4.20).

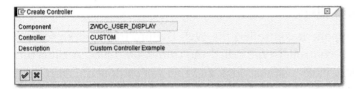

Figure 4.20 Creating a Custom Controller (Part 2)

3. Finally, we can confirm our changes by clicking on the button with the green
   checkmark on it.

Once a custom controller is created, we can maintain it in the Controller Editor
just as we would a component controller (see Figure 4.21). Here, we can edit the
custom controller's context, define attributes, methods, events, and so on.

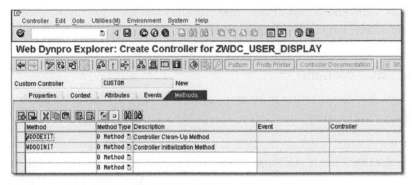

Figure 4.21 Maintaining a Custom Controller

Hook Method Overview

As we've seen, global controllers are primarily used to provide data and services to other controllers (e.g., view controllers). As such, they don't really interact with the Web Dynpro framework all that much. This is evidenced by the condensed list of hook methods provided with custom controllers (see Table 4.2).

Method Name	Description
wddoinit	This method is called immediately after the custom controller is instantiated. As such, it provides us with a hook for initializing the custom controller as necessary (e.g., prefilling the context, and so on).
wddoexit	This method is called whenever the custom controller, and by extension, its overarching WDA component, is being removed from context. Therefore, if the custom controller is holding on to some kind of system resource or lock, this method can be used to release that resource gracefully.

Table 4.2 Hook Methods for Custom Controllers

What Are Custom Controllers Used For?

Given their stature as an optional element within the Web Dynpro programming paradigm, you might be wondering what custom controllers are used for. Conceptually, you can think of custom controllers as extensions of the component controller. As such, they are typically used as a means for organizing code and reducing some of the burden on the component controller. For example, we might use a custom controller to encapsulate all the logic used to support input helps at the view layer. That way, the component controller isn't encumbered with extraneous details that are ancillary to the core application logic.

Ultimately, the use of custom controllers is mostly a matter of preference. However, before you get carried away with defining custom controllers galore, it's important to be mindful of an important design point. As you may recall from Chapter 2, WDA components are designed to encapsulate a particular business process. As such, they should be scoped in such a way that they perform a handful of related tasks well (i.e., they should have strong cohesion). Therefore, if you're finding yourself needing to create many custom controllers just to keep things organized, your WDA component is probably much too big. Overall, we recommend that you develop at most between one and three custom controllers per component.

4.2.3 View Controllers

According to the SAP help documentation, a view controller is "the controller within a Web Dynpro component that handles both the presentation of business data, and processing of responses to user input." Though the terms *view* and *view controller* are often used separately, they are in fact one logical entity. Consequently, there are no special steps required to create a view controller; they're generated automatically whenever a view is created.

As you can see in the View Editor screen depicted in Figure 4.22, view controllers have many elements in common with other controllers (e.g., attributes, methods, and so on). Of course, in addition to these common elements, view controllers also maintain a handful of view-specific elements, including:

▸ The view layout, which describes the look and feel of the user interface

▸ Navigation plugs (i.e., outbound and inbound plugs), which make it possible to navigate back and forth between views

▸ Actions, which are used to respond to events triggered in the user interface

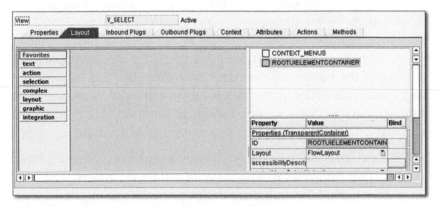

Figure 4.22 Editing a View Controller in the View Editor

Because this is a chapter on controller development, we'll defer view-specific topics, such as UI layout and navigation, to later chapters. For now, we'll focus our attention for the remainder of this section on controller-specific development concepts.

Hook Method Overview

Given their close proximity to the user interface, view controllers come equipped with a number of hook methods, which allow us to react to events triggered within the user interface. Table 4.3 summarizes these methods, showing you the different hook methods that can be used to validate user input, dynamically adjust the UI, and so on.

Method Name	Description
wddoinit	This method is called immediately after the view controller is instantiated. As such, it provides us with a hook for initializing the view controller as necessary. Of course, because view controllers shouldn't really be responsible for managing shared resources, you'll find that you won't need to use this method very often.
wddobeforeaction	This method is used to validate user input within the view. As the method name suggests, this method is called *before* any actions are processed within the framework. We saw this method on display in Chapter 3, when we performed required field input validations in our sample application.
wddoafteraction	Much like WDDOBEFOREACTION( ), this method is typically used for input validations. However, since it's called after action processing, it provides a convenient location for performing validations that may be applicable regardless of the action that was fired.
wddomodifyview	This method can be used to dynamically modify the view layout before rendering occurs. Here, for example, we can add or remove UI elements from the layout, hide elements, and so on. We'll have an opportunity to experiment with this method in Chapter 11.
wddooncontext-menu	By default, whenever you right-click on a view, a context menu will appear. If you like, you can influence the design and layout of this menu within the WDDOONCONTEXTMENU( ) method. For more information about context menus, consult the SAP online help documentation in the section entitled "Dynamic and Static Context Menus."
wddoexit	This method is called whenever the view controller is being removed from context. Naturally, this method affords us the opportunity to perform various view-specific cleanup tasks.

Table 4.3 Hook Methods for View Controllers

What Are View Controllers Used For?

For you MVC purists: You might be a little bit skeptical about what view controllers are used for. After all, there's quite a bit of MVC documentation out there that suggests that absolutely no coding should reside within the view layer. However, as we pointed out in Chapter 2, this stance is unrealistic in its dismissal of commonly occuring use cases within the UI development process, such as event handling, navigation, UI manipulation, and so on.

As we touched upon in Chapter 2, SAP elected to take its own slant on MVC by distinguishing between traditional controller types (e.g., component/custom controllers) and controllers that have or support a user interface (e.g., view and window controller) within the Web Dynpro framework. While this design approach often raises eyebrows among MVC purists, it's important to note that such a distinction does not open a loop hole or violate the core principles of MVC. Instead, restrictions have been put in place in view controllers to create a controlled environment in which developers can only perform basic housekeeping tasks with the UI layer.

The basic takeaway from all this is that you should respect the boundaries of the Web Dynpro framework and use view controllers to do what they were intended to do: namely, perform basic input validations, process user events, and dynamically manipulate the UI as needed. For most other tasks, it makes sense to delegate responsibility to the upstream global controllers and/or the model layer. Suffice it to say that if you find yourself encoding application logic or performing complex calculations within a view controller method, you've definitely gotten off track somewhere along the way.

4.2.4 Window Controllers

The last type of controller we'll consider is the *window controller*. Hierarchically, window controllers lie somewhere between view controllers and global controllers in terms of their stature within the framework. Much like view controllers, window controllers are created automatically whenever a window is created. Figure 4.23 shows a window controller in the Window Editor tool. As you can see, window controllers share some resemblances to view controllers in terms of the elements they provide.

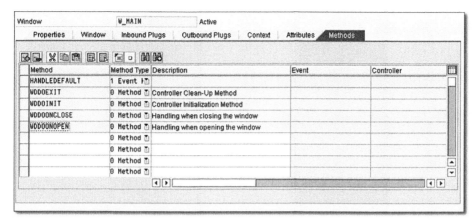

Figure 4.23 Maintaining Window Controllers in the Window Editor

We'll have an opportunity to look at window-specific issues in Chapter 6. In the meantime, we'll spend the remainder of this section looking at programming concepts for window controllers.

Hook Method Overview

For the most part, the hook methods for window controllers are limited to the familiar WDDOINIT() and WDDOEXIT() methods used for initialization and cleanup. However, as you can see in Table 4.4, hook methods are also provided for popup handling.

Method Name	Description
wddoinit	This method is called immediately after the window controller is instantiated. As such, it provides us with a hook for initializing the window controller as necessary (e.g., prefilling the context, and so on).
wddoonopen	This method is used to perform any initializations that might be required whenever a window is opened as a dialog window. At runtime, the provided WINDOW_DESCR parameter can be used to obtain a reference to the window. This reference, in turn, can be used to adjust the window properties, etc.

Table 4.4 Hook Methods for Window Controllers

Method Name	Description
wddoonclose	This method allows us to perform any cleanup required whenever a dialog window is closed.
wddoexit	This method is called whenever the window controller, and by extension, the window itself, are being unloaded from context. Here, we can perform cleanup tasks as needed.

Table 4.4 Hook Methods for Window Controllers (Cont.)

In additon to the standard hook methods, window controllers come equipped with another entry point from a programming perspective: the event handler methods associated with their defined inbound plugs. These event handler methods provide us with a hook for implementing complex navigation scenarios and/or application initialization.

To understand how the event handler methods for inbound plugs are used within a window controller, let's think about the process flow for a WDA application as it's accessed for the first time. As you can see in Figure 4.24, a WDA application is defined in terms of a WDA component, a particular window within that component, and, finally, an inbound plug within the selected window. At runtime, the Web Dynpro framework uses this information to load the target component or window into context. Then, once the window is created, its corresponding inbound plug is invoked. This, in turn, causes the configured event handler method (e.g., HANDLEDEFAULT()) to be executed (see Figure 4.25).

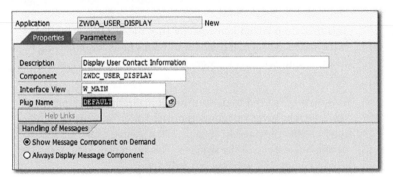

Figure 4.24 Selecting an Inbound Plug for a WDA Application

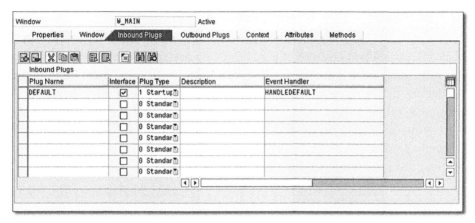

Figure 4.25 Relationship between an Inbound Plug and an Event Handler

Within this plug event handler method, we can invoke methods on a used global controller to initialize the application or use application parameters to selectively route incoming requests. We'll see how all this works in detail in Chapter 6.

What Are Window Controllers Used For?

Most of the time, you'll find that window controller programming is pretty well limited to custom navigation scenarios. Though it's technically possible to use window controllers to provide application functionality to view controllers, we highly recommend that you stick to using component/custom controllers for this purpose because this practice makes for a more intuitive application design.

4.3 Controller Usages

Conceptually speaking, each controller within a WDA component is an independent entity. In other words, controllers are designed to operate in isolation, fulfilling their duties when called upon. Of course, as we've seen, there are many occasions when we may want one controller to leverage functionality provided by another controller. While this is allowed (and encouraged), there are some rules that determine when and where such usages are possible. In this section, we'll analyze these rules as we consider the notion of controller usages.

4.3.1 Creating Controller Usages

Within the Web Dynpro framework, a controller is only allowed to utilize the resources of another controller if it has formally declared its intentions to do so. This pronouncement comes in the form of a *usage declaration*. Here, a controller can declare that it wants to leverage services of another controller by adding a declaration in the USED CONTROLLERS/COMPONENTS table shown in Figure 4.26. Most of the time, this declaration refers to another controller within the same WDA component. However, as we'll see in Chapter 9, it's also possible to declare references to the component interfaces of external components.

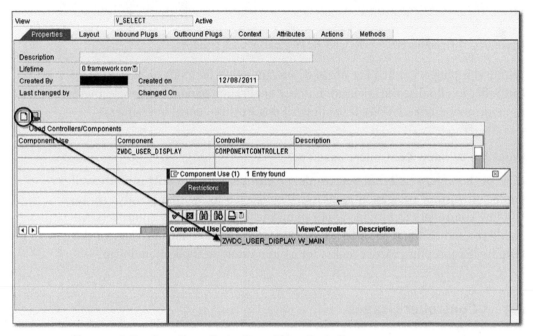

Figure 4.26 Creating a Usage Declaration within a Controller

As you can see in Figure 4.26, the process of defining a usage declaration consists of navigating to the PROPERTIES tab of the Controller Editor and clicking on the CREATE CONTROLLER USAGE button. This will open a COMPONENT USE dialog box in which we can select from the set of available controllers. Once we select the target controller, we can click on the button with the green checkmark on it to confirm our selection.

4.3.2 Leveraging Used Controllers

Whenever we create a controller usage within a given controller, the Controller Editor will take the liberty of creating a getter method behind the scenes that can be used to obtain a reference to the referenced controller. The generated method name is of the form GET_<Controller Name>_CR(). So, for example, if we want to obtain a reference to the component controller from a view controller, we could do so by calling method GET_COMPONENTCONTROLLER_CTR() as demonstrated in Listing 4.1.

```
METHOD some_view_method.
  DATA: lo_comp_ctrl TYPE REF TO ig_componentcontroller.
  lo_comp_ctrl = wd_this->get_componentcontroller_ctr( ).
  lo_comp_ctrl->some_instance_method( ).
ENDMETHOD.
```

Listing 4.1 Obtaining a Reference to a Used Controller

4.3.3 Restrictions for Creating Controller Usages

Now that you have a feel for how controller usages are established and utilized, you might be wondering why they are even necessary. The short answer here is that controller usages make it possible to keep a strict separation between those parts of the business application that display data (for example, data consumers), and those that process data (for example, data generators).

To understand how this works, let's consider the relationship between a view controller and the component controller. Here, the component controller assumes the responsibility of procuring data from the model and making it available for display in the view. To consume this data, the view will (by default) contain a usage relationship to the component controller. This usage relationship allows the view controller to interface with the component controller in a variety of ways, including:

▸ Mapping context nodes from the component controller's context
▸ Invoking instance methods provided by the component controller
▸ Listening for events that might be raised by the component controller

Collectively, these mechanisms allow the view controller to consume data provided via the component controller.

Now, if we look in the other direction, we can see why it wouldn't make sense for a component controller to be able to define a usage relationship to the view controller. After all, since the view controller shouldn't be producing any data in the first place, there's really nothing for the component controller to consume. Therefore, not surprisingly, it's not permitted to define a usage relationship from the component controller to a view controller.

When you think about controller usages in these terms, the rules for creating a controller usage should be fairly intuitive. However, even if they aren't, the Controller Editor tools will take the guesswork out of the equation by restricting you from being able to define invalid usages. So, if the Controller Editor allows you to create a controller usage, you can rest assured that you've gotten the relationship(s) right.

4.4   Understanding the Web Dynpro Phase Model

In the previous section, we learned about the various hook methods provided with the different controller types contained within a WDA component. Though it was useful to see how these hook methods work on an individual basis, it's important to realize that they don't operate in isolation. Instead, the hook methods of the various controller types within a WDA component work in tandem to help implement the process flow of a WDA application. Within the Web Dynpro parlance, this process flow is referred to as the *Web Dynpro phase model*.

From a technical perspective, the term *phase model* refers to the various phases that occur during the processing of an HTTP request within the Web Dynpro framework. This process flow is hardwired into the Web Dynpro framework and cannot be changed. However, with the hook methods, we can influence the behavior of the process flow by performing validations, managing navigation, and so on.

In this section, we'll take a look at the Web Dynpro phase model and show you how it can be used to influence the behavior of your WDA applications. Having an understanding of this process will help you get the most out of the hook methods that the framework provides within the various controller types.

4.4.1 Case Study: Tracing through the Web Dynpro Phase Model

To understand how the Web Dynpro phase model is designed, it's helpful to trace through the process from beginning to end using an example. Here, let's think about a simple WDA application with two views called A and B, respectively. Now, imagine that a user has clicked on a button in view A that triggers navigation to view B. The process flow within the Web Dynpro phase model for this navigation request is illustrated in the UML sequence diagram in Figure 4.27.

As you can see in Figure 4.27, the navigation request is processed as follows:

▶ **Phase ❶**
First, the WDA runtime environment (which, as you may recall from Chapter 1, consists of both client-side and server-side components) fields the HTTP request and takes care of translating the request to a client/protocol-independent format. During this transformation process, basic checks are carried out to verify input validity (e.g., making sure that the user didn't enter an invalid date value in a date field, and so on).

▶ **Phase ❷**
Then, after the incoming request has been validated, data from the UI input fields will be synchronized with the controller context(s) via data binding.

▶ **Phase ❸**
Once the request has been validated and the context(s) have been synchronized, the framework invokes the WDDOBEFOREACTION() hook method on view A. This method can be used to perform customized input validations before the action is executed.

▶ **Phase ❹**
After the request has been validated in phase ❸, the framework is ready to begin processing the event handler methods. Here, the framework will invoke the event handler method associated with the action that triggered the HTTP request in the first place (i.e., the button click in view A). In the diagram shown in Figure 4.27, the event handler method is triggering navigation to view B by firing an outbound plug. Of course, we could have programmed additional logic into this event handler method as needed.

▶ **Phase ❺**
As soon as the event handler method completes, the framework will invoke the WDDOAFTERACTION() hook method in view A. This method is kind of a catch-all method for performing any last-minute validations, etc.

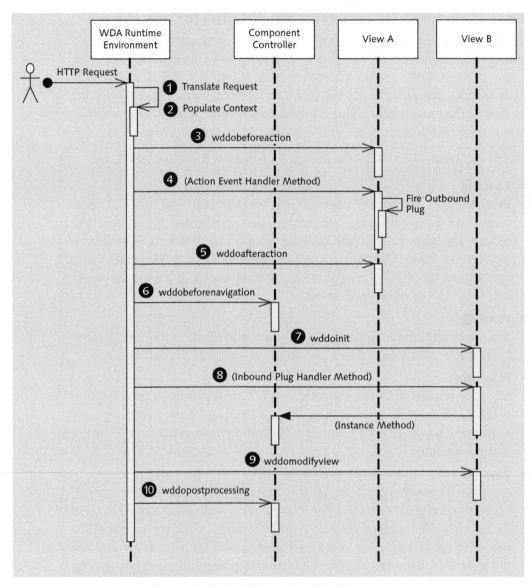

Figure 4.27 Tracing Through the Web Dynpro Phase Model

▶ **Phase ❻**

At this point, the framework is ready to begin the navigation process. However, before it proceeds, it will make a call to the WDDOBEFORENAVIGATION()

hook method of the component controller. This method offers the possibility of implementing complex validations on a more component-wide scale.

▶ **Phase ❼**
During the navigation cycle, the framework will determine that it needs to load view B into the view layout. If view B has not yet been accessed within the application session, the framework will call method WDDOINIT() on view B to allow for any view-specific initializations to occur.

▶ **Phase ❽**
After view B is initialized, the framework will complete the navigation process by invoking the event handler method associated with its target inbound plug. Within this method, additional initialization can be performed within the view. For example, in Figure 4.27, you can see how the event handler method is invoking an instance method on the component controller.

▶ **Phase ❾**
At this point, the framework is just about ready to begin rendering view B. However, before it does so, it will invoke the view's WDDOMODIFYVIEW() method. This method makes it possible to dynamically change the layout of the view as needed. We'll see how this works in detail in Chapter 11.

▶ **Phase ❿**
Finally, before completing the request/response cycle, the framework will make one last call to the WDDOPOSTPROCESSING() method of the component controller. This method is primarily used to perform any last-minute cleanup or, in some cases, respond to exception conditions stemming from supply functions gone awry. As mentioned earlier, we'll look at supply functions in more detail in Chapter 5.

The last phase in the Web Dynpro phase model that's not shown in the UML sequence diagram in Figure 4.27 is the *rendering phase*. During this phase, the Web Dynpro framework will render view B for display within the user's application client or browser. At this point, the user is free to enter data and start the processing cycle all over again by triggering an event in the UI.

4.4.2   Handling Actions and Events

For the most part, the process flow in Figure 4.27 can be used as a guide for determining how a particular event will be processed by the Web Dynpro framework.

However, one aspect of the process flow not shown in Figure 4.27 is what happens when an error occurs at some point during the event processing. For example, imagine a simple report application with two views: a selection view and a results view. Here, users enter data in the selection view and click a button that will execute the report and take them to the results view. Thus, in logical terms, the button click event causes the following steps to occur:

1. The data from the selection view will be validated for correctness.

2. The data from the selection view will be used as input to execute the report.

3. The user will be navigated from the selection view to the results view so that users can view the results.

However, what happens if an error is detected at step 1 or step 2? Should we proceed with the navigation request? Or is the nature of the error such that we should allow the event processing to proceed knowing there may be certain errors we need to contend with downstream?

In order to provide flexibility for dealing with these kinds of situations, the Web Dynpro framework allows us to define two different types of actions:

▸ **Standard actions**
Standard actions define event handler methods that are only invoked if there's not a pre-existing error condition detected earlier in the phase model processing. To put this into perspective, suppose we implemented the validation logic for our sample report in the WDDOBEFOREACTION() method of the selection view and the data lookup/navigation steps in the event handler method of a standard action. In this case, if a validation error is detected in the WDDOBEFOREAC-TION() method, the event handler linked to that standard action *will not* be executed. Instead, processing picks up a phase ❺ with the WDDOAFTERACTION() hook method. So, in effect, the error condition detected upstream causes the process to halt and allow the user to circle back and correct the error(s) in the selection view before proceeding.

▸ **Validation-independent actions**
Unlike standard actions, the event handler methods of validation-independent actions always execute, regardless of whether or not any errors were detected in previous phases. Thus, they can be used to implement catch-all logic that should be applied regardless of the circumstances.

As we learned in Section 4.1.5, selecting between these two action types requires that we select the proper value in the ACTION TYPE dropdown list on the View Editor screen (see Figure 4.15). By default, the system will choose the standard action type, and this is usually what you want. However, this is definitely one area within the Web Dynpro phase model where we can override the standard behavior of the process flow as needed.

4.5   Web Dynpro Programming Interface Overview

As we've explored controller development concepts, we've encountered several classes and interfaces that can be used to interact more closely with the Web Dynpro framework and some of the individual elements that make up the WDA component architecture. These classes and interfaces compose the core Web Dynpro runtime API.

While a detailed reference covering the ins and outs of the Web Dynpro runtime APIs is beyond the scope of this book, we would be remiss if we didn't draw your attention to certain key classes and interfaces you'll find useful during the course of your day-to-day development. Therefore, in this section, we'll introduce you to these APIs so you'll know to look for them when particular tasks arise. Of course, for an official, up-to-date reference on these APIs, we recommend you check out the class/interface documentation available in the Class Builder tool.

4.5.1   The Web Dynpro Runtime API

Within the Web Dynpro framework, you'll find that each of the core elements (i.e., components, controllers, and so on) is represented internally in the form of an interface. Collectively, these interfaces make up the Web Dynpro Runtime API.

From a developer's perspective, these interfaces allow us to interact with these elements programmatically. Table 4.5 highlights some of the more prominent interfaces contained within the API. Throughout the remainder of this book, we'll see these interfaces utilized quite a bit for various tasks.

Runtime Class/ Interface	Description
IF_WD_ACTION	This interface makes it possible to obtain information about an action in a view controller.
IF_WD_APPLICATION	This interface can be used to obtain information about the currently executing WDA application and its surrounding client environment. We can use this interface to adjust the title of the main application window, determine the user agent, and so on.
IF_WD_COMPONENT	This interface provides us with access to do just about anything we'd want to do with a WDA component from a runtime perspective. As you may recall from Section 4.2.1, we can obtain an object reference, which implements this interface, by calling the WD_GET_API() method on the component controller. We'll see several methods provided via this interface on display as we progress through the book. For everything else, we recommend you consult the documentation for this interface using the Class Builder tool (Transaction SE24).
IF_WD_CONTROLLER	This interface provides a controller with access to various elements contained within (e.g., actions and context nodes). It can also be used to access external resources, such as the message manager and the controller's surrounding component (via interface IF_WD_COMPONENT).
IF_WD_MESSAGE_ MANAGER	This interface provides various methods that allow us to write messages to a message area displayed within the UI. We'll have an opportunity to work with messages in Chapter 10.
IF_WD_VIEW	This interface provides us with most everything we need to interact with a view. We'll see this interface on display in Chapter 11 when we look at dynamic programming concepts.
IF_WD_WINDOW	This interface defines the types of operations you can perform programmatically on a window. Here, for example, you'll find methods such as OPEN() and CLOSE() to open and close a dialog window, respectively, and so on. We'll see this interface on display in Chapters 1 and 6.
IF_WD_WINDOW_MANAGER	As the name suggests, this interface is used to manage windows. We'll see how this works in Chapter 6.

Table 4.5 Selected Interfaces in the Web Dynpro ABAP Runtime API

4.5.2 Service Classes and Interfaces

In addition to the classes and interfaces that make up the Web Dynpro runtime APIs, the system provides us with some general service APIs that can be used to assist with various tasks that are routinely encountered with WDA development. Table 4.6 summarizes some of the more frequently used classes within this API.

Service Class/Interface	Description
CL_WD_CONTEXT_SERVICES	This class can be used to monitor context nodes for changes. For more information about this concept, check out the SAP online help documentation in the section entitled "Context Change Log."
CL_WD_DYNAMIC_TOOL	This class provides various helper methods that simplify dynamic programming tasks within Web Dynpro. We have already seen this class on display in Chapter 3, when we looked at the validation of required fields in a view. We'll have an opportunity to work with some of the other methods provided with this class in Chapter 10.
CL_WD_COMPONENT_ASSISTANCE	This abstract class defines the core functionality for assistance classes. We'll see what assistance classes are used for in Section 4.6.
CL_WD_RUNTIME_SERVICES	This class provides some utility methods that allow you to interact with the Web Dynpro runtime environment.
CL_WD_UTILITIES	This class provides some general utility methods for Web Dynpro programming.
CL_WD_TRACE_TOOL and IF_WD_TRACE_TOOL	The CL_WD_TRACE_TOOL class can be used to add data to a trace file produced by the *Web Dynpro Trace Tool*. To access this functionality, we must reference the class's static INSTANCE attribute, which is of type IF_WD_TRACE_TOOL. For more information about this feature, consult the SAP online help documentation in the section entitled "Web Dynpro Trace Tool."
CL_WEB_DYNPRO	We can use the static IS_ACTIVE attribute of this class to determine if the code we're running was initiated within the Web Dynpro runtime environment.

Table 4.6 Service Classes and Interfaces Supporting Web Dynpro

4.6   Assistance Classes

Performance-wise, controller methods run a little bit more slowly than methods of a regular ABAP Objects class. Therefore, if we have a requirement for some complex processing logic, it's best to implement that logic outside our WDA component. Naturally, most of this logic should reside in the model layer. However, there are times when we may need to implement some application-specific logic that sits somewhere between the controller and model layers. For these situations, we can enlist the help of *assistance classes*.

As the name suggests, assistance classes assist WDA components by providing them with services that are not linked directly with the layout or with the function of a controller. Such services include the procurement of localized texts, data transformations, and pretty much any trivial task a controller wishes to delegate to it.

In this section, we'll see how assistance classes are created and how they can be used to simplify the design of your WDA components.

4.6.1   Creating an Assistance Class

For the most part, you'll find the creation of an assistance class to be very straight-forward. Here, we simply open the component in the Web Dynpro Explorer and plug in a class name in the ASSISTANCE CLASS field, as shown in Figure 4.28. If the class doesn't already exist, the system will prompt us to create the class. If we click the YES button in the CREATE CLASS dialog box, the system will take care of creating the assistance class for us automatically. Otherwise, we can create the assistance class separately using the Class Builder tool. The only requirement here is that the class inherit (either directly or indirectly) from the abstract base class CL_WD_COMPONENT_ASSISTANCE.

4.6.2   Maintaining Assistance Classes

Aside from their linkage to a WDA component, assistance classes are basically like every other ABAP Objects class. As you can see in Figure 4.29, assistance classes are maintained in the Class Builder tool as usual. There, we can define additional methods, maintain attributes, and so on.

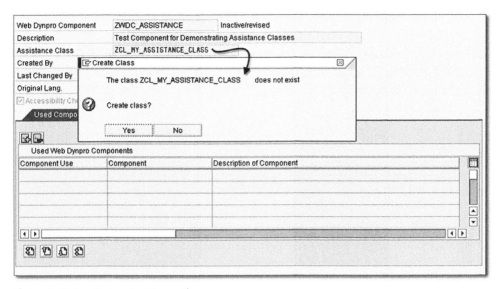

Figure 4.28 Creating an Assistance Class

Class Interface	ZCL_MY_ASSISTANCE_CLASS	Implemented / Inactive

Properties | Interfaces | Friends | Attributes | **Methods** | Events | Types | Aliases

□ Parameter | Exception | | | | | | | | | □ Filter

Method	Level	Visibility	M	Description
<IF_WD_COMPONENT_ASSISTANCE>				
GET_TEXT	Instance	Public		Returns a text of the model class
<CL_WD_COMPONENT_ASSISTANCE>				
SET_NOT_FOUND_TEXT_KEY	Instance	Protecte		Sets the key for the text if text not found

Figure 4.29 Method Overview for an Assistance Class

As we mentioned earlier, assistance classes should inherit from CL_WD_ COMPONENT_ASSISTANCE if we want them to have full access to some of the specialized services offered to assistance classes within the Web Dynpro framework.

You can see the inherited methods in Figure 4.29. If we let the Web Dynpro Explorer tool create the assistance class for us automatically, we can see that the system has taken the liberty of assigning this superclass on our behalf. Otherwise, we'll have to assign the superclass ourselves on the PROPERTIES tab of the Class Builder (see Figure 4.30).

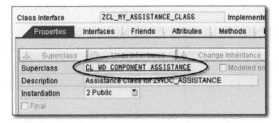

Figure 4.30 Defining the Superclass for Assistance Classes

One thing to keep in mind as you select the superclass for your assistance class is that it's also possible to inherit from a custom base class, which extends the default CL_WD_COMPONENT_ASSISTANCE class. Within this custom base class, we might provide certain utilities that may be used across WDA development projects.

4.6.3 What Should Assistance Classes Be Used For?

Now that you have a feel for the relationship between WDA components and their assistance classes, you might be wondering what assistance classes are used for. The short answer here is just about anything. However, there are a couple of caveats to be mindful of:

▶ First of all, assistance classes should not be used to modify the UI layout or perform other controller-specific tasks.

▶ Second, assistance classes should not be used to replace the model layer, although they can certainly be tasked with brokering and/or adapting calls to the model layer.

Another important function that assistance classes provide within the Web Dynpro framework is the management of dynamic texts. Here, we're talking about texts that are displayed within the UI at runtime. Examples of these texts include field labels, message texts, and so on. These texts can be obtained via a call to the assistance class's GET_TEXT() method (see Figure 4.29). We'll explore this concept in much more detail when we talk about internationalization in Chapter 12.

Before we wrap up our discussion on assistance classes, we should point out that their usage is not limited to any one controller within a WDA component. Indeed, after you assign an assistance class to your WDA component, you'll notice that the system has defined an attribute called WD_ASSIST in each of the WDA component's constituent controllers (see Figure 4.31). This attribute can be used to access the assistance class from within a given controller method. Naturally, the framework will take care of instantiating the assistance class object and assigning a reference to it in the WD_ASSIST attribute. So, by the time you get your hands on it, the assistance class is loaded and ready to service your requests.

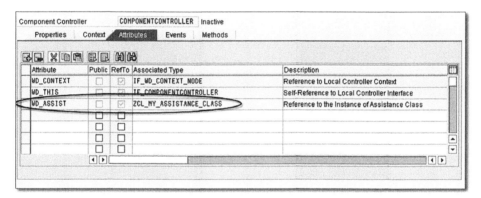

Figure 4.31 Accessing the Assistance Class in a Controller

4.7 Tool Support for Controller Development

Now that you've been exposed to controller development up close, you should have a pretty good feel for how things work. However, while it's not too difficult to wrap your head around the basic concepts of controller development, keeping track of controller-specific call syntax can prove challenging. Fortunately, SAP has integrated quite a few tools into the ABAP Workbench to help you jog your memory. In this section, we'll take a look at some of these tools and see how they can be used to speed up the development process.

4.7.1 Web Dynpro Code Wizard

The first, and perhaps most useful, tool in the toolset is the Web Dynpro code wizard. This tool can be used to automatically insert Web Dynpro–specific calls into your controller methods. In this sense, the code wizard plays a similar role to the familiar pattern insert feature commonly used to insert function or method calls in the ABAP Editor. We can access the code wizard within a controller method by clicking on the WEB DYNPRO CODE WIZARD button in the toolbar (see Figure 4.32).

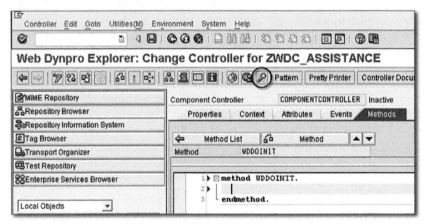

Figure 4.32 Initiating the Web Dynpro Code Wizard

When we open up the code wizard, we'll be presented with the WEB DYNPRO STATEMENT STRUCTURE dialog box shown in Figure 4.33. As you can see, the wizard provides us with quite a few options for implementing method calls, raising events, and so on. Of course, before you get irate with us for not showing you this tool sooner, keep in mind that the wizard is not 100% clairvoyant. In other words, it does a pretty good job of defining skeleton code but requires us to fill in the gaps in certain places. So, suffice it to say that you need to know a little bit about what you're doing in order to use this tool. Now that we've attained this knowledge, we'll be using this wizard quite a bit as we progress through the rest of this book. We'll also look at some of the context-specific operations supported by this tool in Chapter 5.

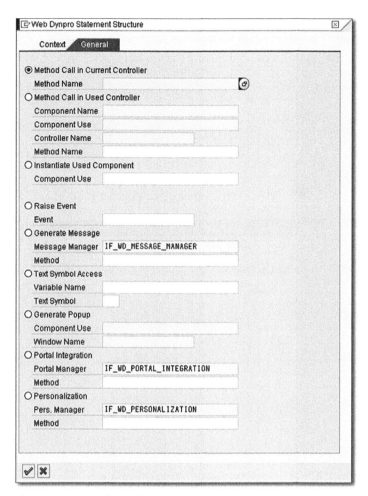

Figure 4.33 Using the Web Dynpro Code Wizard

4.7.2 Screen Design Time Conversion

Frequently, the design requirements for new WDA applications are defined in terms of pre-existing classic Dynpro screens. Here, for example, we might be asked to create views that look like screens from a particular transaction. Although it's possible to create such views by hand, it's much more efficient to use the Screen Design Time Conversion tool built into the View Editor.

Within a given view, the process involved in translating a particular classic Dynpro screen is as follows:

1. First of all, we need to identify the target program or screen we want to leverage. We can do this by opening the target transaction in the SAP GUI, placing the cursor in one of the input fields, and hitting the F1 key (see Figure 4.34).

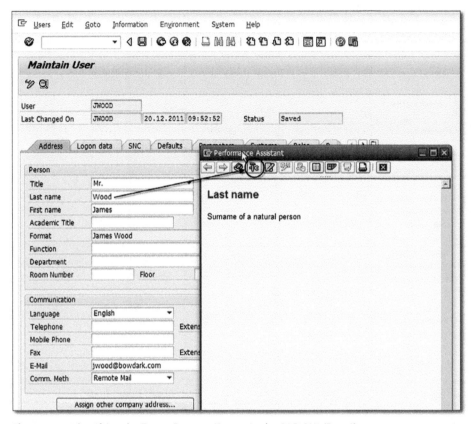

Figure 4.34 Identifying the Target Program/Screen in the SAP GUI (Part 1)

2. Then, if we click the TECHNICAL INFORMATION button (see Figure 4.34), the TECHNICAL INFORMATION dialog box shown in Figure 4.35 will be displayed. Here, the target program/screen number will be located at the top of the screen.

3. After we identify the target program/screen, we can open a view in the WDA component to perform the translation. Here, we'll click on the WEB DYNPRO CODE WIZARD button at the top of the screen to kick off the translation wizard (see Figure 4.36). On the TEMPLATE GALLERY screen, we'll select the SCREEN node and click on the CONTINUE button.

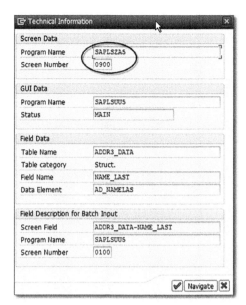

Figure 4.35 Identifying the Target Program/Screen in the SAP GUI (Part 2)

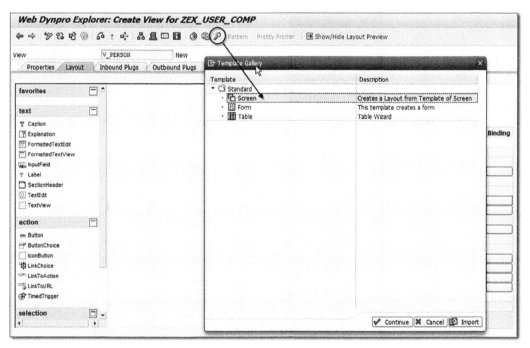

Figure 4.36 Initiating the Screen Design Time Conversion Wizard

4. Finally, on the CREATE LAYOUT FROM SCREEN dialog box shown in Figure 4.37, we can plug in the target program/screen and click the button with the green checkmark on it to kick off the translation process.

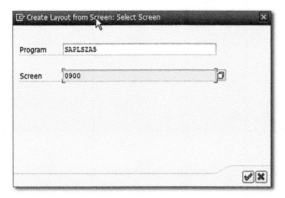

Figure 4.37 Translating a Classic Dynpro Screen

During the translation process, the wizard will do its best to translate between UI element types provided in the different technologies. Naturally, some UI elements will translate more cleanly than others, so your mileage may vary. In general, the simpler the classic Dynpro screen, the better it will translate. Fortunately, if the wizard makes a mistake or doesn't produce the layout you want, you can always tweak the UI layout in the View Editor after the fact.

You can find out more about the Screen Design Time Conversion tool in the SAP online help documentation, in the section entitled "Screen Design Time Conversion." There, you can find information about certain restrictions in the translation process, and so on.

4.7.3 Service Calls

For faceless controller types like the component or custom controller, you'll likely spend a fair amount of time implementing *service calls*. Here, the term *service call* refers to calls that are made to services provided by the model layer of the WDA application. From a technical standpoint, these services may be implemented in terms of BAPIs/function modules, classes, or web services.

To assist you in wiring up these service calls, the Web Dynpro Explorer provides you with the service call wizard. You can initiate this wizard for a given WDA component by right-clicking on the component and selecting the CREATE • SERVICE CALL menu path (see Figure 4.38). From there, the wizard will guide us through a series of steps to determine which controller will execute the service call, how the selected controller will derive the arguments for the call (i.e., via context node elements, method parameters, or a combination of both), and so on.

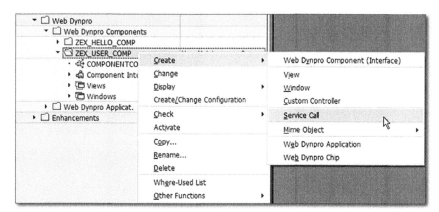

Figure 4.38 Initiating the Service Call Wizard

Once completed, the generated service call will be encapsulated within a controller method that can be triggered via an action or event, hook method, or instance method. For more information about this feature, check out the SAP online help documentation in the section entitled "Service Calls in a Web Dynpro Application."

4.7.4 Refactoring Assistant

In his now-classic software engineering text *Refactoring: Improving the Design of Existing Code*, Martin Fowler describes refactoring as a process whereby we "...restructure software by applying a series of refactorings without changing its observable behavior" (Addison-Wesley, 1999). In other words, refactoring is all about tidying up code whenever it becomes unmanageable for one reason or another. This effort proves its worth in the long run as it makes the software easier to understand and maintain.

Even if you've not heard of the term *refactoring* before, you probably do it all the time. For example, you might find that a method is too large and unwieldy, so you split it into two. Or, you want to rename an attribute or method to more accurately describe what it is and what it's used for.

Depending on the scope of your refactoring, you may find even the simplest of changes to have wide-reaching impacts. Indeed, something as innocuous as renaming a method could lead to serious syntax errors. However, with the right tool support, such risks are greatly mitigated. Fortunately, SAP provides just the tool we're looking for in the ABAP Workbench, and it's called the *Refactoring Assistant*.

Within the Web Dynpro programming environment, the Refactoring Assistant can be used to remove or rename elements within a WDA component (e.g., views and windows), remove or rename elements of a controller (e.g., context nodes, and events), and adjust navigation links. Plus, since the Refactoring Assistant is also built into the Class Builder and regular ABAP Editor tools, it can also be used to make relevant changes to the model layer. You can find detailed documentation about the Refactoring Assistant in the SAP Help Portal by performing a search on the phrase "refactoring for Web Dynpro ABAP."

4.8 Summary

In this chapter, we considered the ins and outs of WDA controller development. Along the way, we observed the different types of elements that can be defined within controllers, what those elements are used for, and how controllers work together to implement the Web Dynpro phase model. Collectively, the knowledge we've gathered should provide us with a solid foundation as we approach more specialized topics in the upcoming chapters.

Of course, by now you're probably itching to begin looking at all the shiny UI elements Web Dynpro has to offer in the view layer. However, we still have a little way to go in the controller layer before we're ready to begin looking at more advanced view-related concepts. In particular, we need to spend some time looking into context programming concepts. Here, it is important to bear in mind that, while controller development may not be the most glamorous of Web Dynpro topics, it's arguably one of the most important ones. Indeed, once you have a firm foundation in the model and controller layers, setting up the view layer should be a piece of cake.

If we trace the flow of data through WDA components, we can see that data is extracted from the model layer, filtered in the controller layer, and ultimately displayed in the view layer. At the intersection between these layers lie controller contexts, which broker the transfer of data in both directions. In this chapter, we'll learn how to work with these contexts in order to facilitate data exchange in WDA components.

5   Working with Contexts

In the early days of web programming, developers spent quite a bit of time coming up with ways to shuffle data back and forth between form fields in the UI and the backend data model. Fortunately, with the advent of modern web development frameworks like Web Dynpro, developers can now rely on built-in data binding facilities to automate this synchronization of data. Here, data binding greatly simplifies the application development process since the framework assumes the responsibility of making sure that data is where it's supposed to be when we need it.

Within the Web Dynpro framework, the glue that binds UI elements with the backend data model is the *context*. Therefore, in order to master the Web Dynpro programming model, we must learn how to work with controller contexts. In this chapter, we'll spend quite a bit of time looking at contexts from three different angles: conceptual overview, design time, and runtime. Collectively, these various perspectives will provide us with the insight we need to model and exchange various kinds of data using contexts.

5.1   Contexts: Revisited

Developers who are new to Web Dynpro often have a difficult time wrapping their heads around the notion of a context. This is perhaps due to the fact that the term *context* takes on different meanings depending on when and where it's being used. For instance, at design time, a context is a hierarchical data structure that is declaratively defined using graphical editor tools. However, at runtime, a context more closely resembles a complex structure or object collection that is manipulated programmatically using object-oriented APIs.

Recognizing that all this may still seem a bit abstract, we'll spend some time in this section revisiting some of the context-related concepts explored in Chapter 2. Along the way, we'll try to fill in some gaps now that you're more familiar with surrounding elements of the Web Dynpro framework. Alas, with a streamlined framework like Web Dynpro, it's difficult to comprehend one concept without having at least a cursory understanding of several others. Fortunately, by the close of this chapter, this circuitous journey through the core of the Web Dynpro framework will be almost complete.

5.1.1 What Is a Context?

The textbook definition of a context in Web Dynpro literature typically reads something like this: "A context is a hierarchical data storage area contained within a controller." While this definition accurately describes what a context *is*, it fails to illustrate what contexts are used for. So, to take things in a different direction, we'll define contexts as the interface between the UI and the backend data model. As such, contexts provide a convenient mechanism for passing data back and forth between the view and model layers.

5.1.2 Context Data Flow Concepts

Before we delve into the mechanics of context design and development, it's useful to take a moment to reflect once again on how contexts are used to facilitate data transfer between the different layers of a WDA component. Therefore, in this section, let's trace through this data flow by looking at an example. Here, we'll follow the flow of data from the point it's extracted from the model to the point it's displayed in the UI. Then, we'll see how changes to data in the UI are propagated back along the same path to the model layer.

As a basis for our analysis, let's consider the data flow diagram in Figure 5.1. As you can see, this flow is initiated in a global controller method via a series of API calls that copy data from the model layer into the controller context. This data is then propagated down to the view layer via a technique called *context mapping*.

Finally, the data from the mapped view context is displayed within the UI via *data binding* relationships established between UI elements in the view layout and selected context nodes and attributes. As users modify data within the UI, the Web Dynpro framework takes care of transmitting those changes back upstream to the global controller. Then, the global controller can take that data and use it to synchronize the model via API calls as necessary.

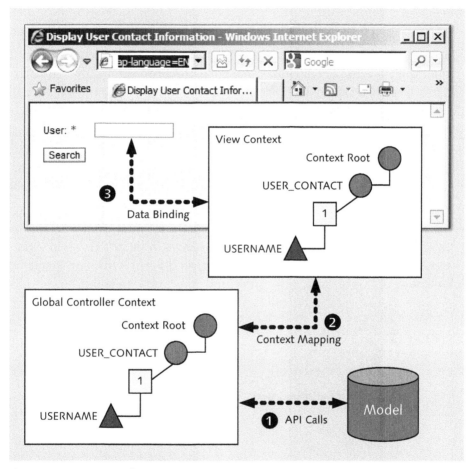

Figure 5.1 Context Data Flow Diagram

Throughout the remainder of this chapter, we'll see how each leg of this data transfer sequence is implemented.

5.1.3 The Building Blocks of a Context

As we stated earlier, contexts are hierarchical data structures made up of context nodes and context attributes. Looking at Figure 5.2, we can see that context hierarchies are organized as follows:

▸ At the base of the hierarchy, there's a specialized context node called the *context root*. This node is always the first in any context and cannot be changed or removed.

▸ Underneath the context root node, we can model various types of complex data objects (e.g., sales orders, materials, and so on) using a series of nested child context nodes. Each context node has a defined cardinality that determines how elements the node can maintain at runtime.

▸ Child context nodes are defined in terms of context attributes and additional child context nodes—more on the latter in a moment. As you can see in Figure 5.2, context attributes are analogous to leaves in a tree data structure. In other words, they're used to represent atomic values such as strings, dates, or numbers. So, when modeling a sales order, for example, context attributes would be used to represent the order number, order creation date, and so on.

▸ Since each context node can define one or more child nodes, a context hierarchy can be nested arbitrarily deep. So, for example, with the SalesOrders context node depicted in Figure 5.2, we might have a three-tier hierarchy consisting of SalesOrders, OrderItems, and ScheduleLines nodes.

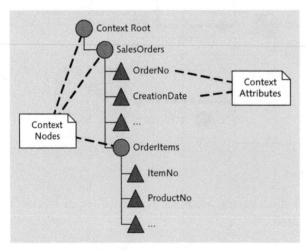

Figure 5.2 A Sample Context at Design Time

182

5.1.4 Contexts at Runtime

Contexts take on a different dimension at runtime, expanding as necessary to provide adequate storage for data displayed within the UI. In this regard, context nodes have certain characteristics in common with internal tables:

▶ Just as internal tables have a *line type* (which is defined in terms of a structure type), the entities of a context node (i.e., context attributes and child nodes) are aggregated into a unit called a *context element*. At runtime, a context element is analogous to a record in an internal table.

▶ Depending on its defined cardinality, a context node may contain zero or more context elements at runtime.

▶ As is the case with internal tables, it's possible to access individual elements within the collection by index. Furthermore, it's also possible to append, remove, and modify context nodes individually or en masse.

Though the internal table metaphor is useful for illustrating the relationship between context nodes and context elements, perhaps a more accurate analogy is to think of context nodes as being like *classes* from the object-oriented programming (OOP) paradigm. In OOP, classes are used to model some kind of real-world phenomenon at design time using a series of *attributes*. At runtime, class definitions are used as a template for creating an *object instance*. Naturally, these object instances are created in the image of their template class. Therefore, they inherit all the attributes from their defining class. Similarly, you can think of context elements as being *instances* of their defining context node.

To put all these relationships in perspective, let's take a look at what the sample context hierarchy from Figure 5.2 might look like at runtime. Figure 5.3 illustrates this relationship. Here, we can see how the SalesOrders context node contains multiple context elements: one per sales order. Each SalesOrders context element gets its own copy of the OrderNo and CreationDate context attributes, as well as its own copy of the OrderItems child node. The OrderItems node in turn contains its own context elements: one for each of the line items within the corresponding parent sales order. We could continue to traverse our way through the tree to look at item schedule lines and so forth, but you get the idea.

Looking at the context nodes depicted in Figure 5.3, you can see that context nodes effectively take on the role of *container* from a runtime perspective. In other words, they are placeholders from which we can traverse the context hierarchy and access individual context elements and attributes. This will become clearer as we learn how to work programmatically with these constructs in Section 5.4.

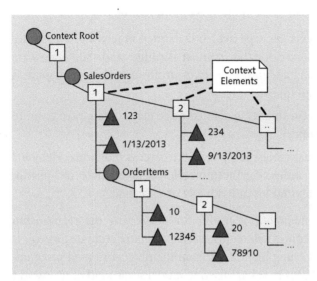

Figure 5.3 A Sample Context at Runtime

5.2 Context Nodes and Context Attributes: Up Close

Now that you have a feel for the positioning of context nodes and context attributes within the overall context hierarchy, let's narrow our focus a little bit and take a look at some of the properties of these elements. As we'll soon see, these properties go a long way toward defining the structure and behavior of a context at runtime.

5.2.1 Properties of Context Nodes

Whenever we define a context node, there are quite a few properties that we must configure. We'll see how this configuration is carried out in the Context Editor tool in Section 5.3.1. However, in the meantime, we need to spend some time reflecting on the semantic meaning of these properties. Table 5.1 describes each of these properties in detail.

Property	Description
Node Name	This property defines the context node's *name*. The name property is used extensively within the context API to access nodes and traverse the context hierarchy.
Interface Node	This Boolean property determines whether or not the context node is part of the *component interface*. As such, it can only be selected for context nodes created within the component controller.
Input Element (Ext.)	If the Interface Node property is selected for a context node, this Boolean property can be used to determine whether or not the node can be used in external mapping scenarios. We'll explore these scenarios when we look at component-based development concepts in Chapter 9.
Dictionary Structure	Frequently, we'll want to define context nodes in terms of pre-existing ABAP Dictionary structures. In these situations, we can use the Dictionary Structure property to make such an assignment for a context node.
Cardinality	This property is used to define the *cardinality* of a context node. In other words, this property determines how many instances of a context node (i.e., context elements) may exist at runtime. The possible values that we can choose from here are as follows: ▶ 0..1 ▶ 1..1 ▶ 0..n ▶ 1..n In effect, the cardinality property specifies a range for context elements within a node collection, with the minimum number of elements in the collection on the left-hand side of the ellipsis and the maximum number of elements on the right-hand side. So, for example, if we were to choose a cardinality of 0..n, there could be an unlimited number of context elements within the context node at runtime, but the collection could also be empty. Conversely, if we were to choose a cardinality of 1..n, there must be at least one context element within the collection at all times, but there could be many more.

Table 5.1 Properties of Context Nodes

Property	Description
Selection	Ultimately, the elements within a context node collection are intended to be displayed within UI elements at the view layer. Here, users may pick and choose particular elements within the collection for further processing.
	To control the number of elements that may be selected at any given time, we can utilize the Selection property. This property has the same domain of values the Cardinality property has. So, if we want to declare that at most one element can be selected at any given time, we might specify a value of 0..1. Similarly, if we want to allow for multiple selection, we might specify a value of 0..n.
	One thing to keep in mind as you configure the Selection property is that the value you select must coincide with the Cardinality property. In other words, if you've defined the cardinality of a context node as 0..1, it doesn't make sense to configure the Selection property with a value of 1..n. Of course, if you accidentally make a mistake, the syntax check will let you know.
Init. Lead Selection	Provided that a node collection is not empty at runtime, the system will designate a particular element within the collection as the *lead selection*. As we'll learn in Section 5.4, this designation simplifies the way context elements are accessed at runtime.
	Though it's possible to specify the lead selection directly via the context APIs, it's oftentimes much more convenient and effective to let the framework take care of it. You can do this by selecting the Init. Lead Selection property (which is selected by default whenever we create a new context node). We'll consider the lead selection concept in further detail in Section 5.2.3.
Singleton	This property is used to determine whether or not a context node is defined as a *singleton*. We'll describe this property in further detail in Section 5.2.4.
Supply Function	With this property, we can select a supply function method which will *supply* a context node with data on demand at runtime. We'll see how supply functions work in Section 5.5.

Table 5.1 Properties of Context Nodes (Cont.)

5.2.2 Properties of Context Attributes

Much like context nodes, context attributes also require the maintenance of a fair number of properties. These properties are described in Table 5.2.

Property Name	Description
Attribute Name	This property defines the context attribute's *name*. The name property is used within the context API to access and modify attribute values.
Type Assignment	This property determines whether or not the attribute refers to an elementary type such as an integer or string, or a reference type such as an object instance. Thus, the values we have to choose from include: ► TYPE ► TYPE REF TO In practice, you'll find that context attributes are rarely defined using reference types because these types don't lend themselves towards data binding in the UI. In time, this may change, though, so it's nice to have the option there just in case.
Type	This property defines the type of the context attribute. Here, we can choose between built-in types or ABAP Dictionary types as desired. However, as we progress through this book, we'll see several benefits that can be gained by using ABAP Dictionary types.
Read-Only	This property determines whether or not a context attribute is *write-protected*. When this Boolean property is set, attribute value cannot be modified.
Default Value	If desired, this property can be used to set a default value for the context attribute. This property can come in handy when we're developing input forms that need to contain default input values.
Input Help Mode	Depending on the nature of the data contained within a context attribute, it may make sense to provide an input help to assist the user in data entry within the UI.

Table 5.2 Properties of Context Attributes

Property Name	Description
Input Help Mode (Cont.)	As we'll learn in Chapter 10, the Web Dynpro framework provides several different options for delivering input helps. Therefore, the Input Help Mode property can be used to determine the method of input help selection. The list of options you have to choose from for this property are as follows: ▶ Automatic ▶ Deactivated ▶ Dictionary Search Help ▶ Object Value Selector ▶ Freely Programmed
(Input Help)	Once an input help mode is selected, we can plug in a specific input help using this property. Note that the name of this property will vary based on the selection made in the Input Help Mode property.

Table 5.2 Properties of Context Attributes (Cont.)

In addition to the static properties outlined in Table 5.2, we should also point out that context attributes maintain a handful of *dynamic properties* at runtime. As we'll see in Section 5.4.4, these dynamic properties can prove quite useful for adjusting the characteristics of certain types of UI elements on the fly.

5.2.3 Understanding the Lead Selection Concept

In Section 5.2.1, we briefly touched on the lead selection concept as it relates to the definition of context nodes. However, as this concept plays a significant role in determining how certain context operations are interpreted at runtime, it deserves a closer look.

Lead selections come into play whenever we have context nodes with a cardinality of 0..n or 1..n. Here, whenever the node collection contains more than one context element at runtime, it is important to be able to identify which context element is currently being processed. The Web Dynpro framework identifies such context elements using the lead selection designator.

For the most part, you can think of the lead selection designator as a convenience mechanism for simplifying node access expressions. For example, as we'll see in

Section 5.4, the context API uses the lead selection to implicitly refer to the currently selected context element within a given context node. We'll also see this property at work in Chapters 7 and 8 when we look at complex UI elements used for the purposes of selection.

Setting the Lead Selection

As we learned in Section 5.2.1, the Init. Lead Selection property of a context node determines whether or not a multi-element node collection contains a pre-selected lead selection element. If the Init. Lead Selection Property is selected, the first element within the node collection will be given the lead selection designator by default. Otherwise, the property is undefined.

In either case, the lead selection property for a context node can subsequently be adjusted in one of two ways:

▶ It can be set explicitly using methods provided via the context API.

▶ It may be adjusted via selection within a UI selection element that is bound to the corresponding context node.

5.2.4   Understanding the Singleton Property

As described in Section 5.2.1, it's possible to define a context node as a *singleton*. Of course, if you're not familiar with the concept of a singleton, a brief description is in order. The singleton design pattern is derived from the field of mathematics. There, the term *singleton* is used to describe a set with exactly one element. In their classic software engineering text, *Design Patterns: Elements of Reusable Object-Oriented Software*, Erich Gamma, et al. demonstrated how this concept could be applied to the creation of objects (Addison-Wesley, 1995). Here, the singleton pattern is employed to ensure that only a single object instance may exist for a class at runtime.

If we think of context nodes as a type of class, it follows that the *Singleton* property for context nodes is used to ensure that only a single instance of a context node may exist at runtime. To understand how this works, let's look at how the Singleton property affects the way a child node such as OrderItems is loaded into our sample SalesOrders context at runtime. As you can see in Figure 5.4, without the Singleton property set, multiple OrderItems nodes will be created at runtime: one for each sales order element in the SalesOrders node collection. However, if we were to mark the Singleton property on the `OrderItems` node, only *one* instance of the `OrderItems` node would exist at any given point in time. Here, the only `OrderItems` node created is the one that corresponds with the lead selection element (see Figure 5.5). Of course, if the lead selection in the `SalesOrders` node collection were to change, then the `OrderItems` node would need to be refreshed to reflect the item records associated with the selected sales order. As we'll learn in Section 5.5, this refresh process can be performed automatically by *supply functions*.

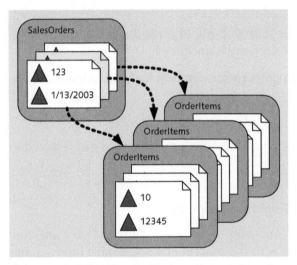

Figure 5.4 Understanding the Singleton Property (Part 1)

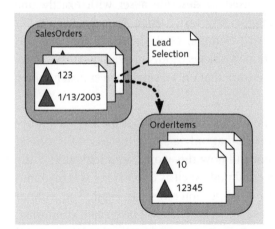

Figure 5.5 Understanding the Singleton Property (Part 2)

This distinction between singleton and non-singleton nodes is subtle, but often-times crucial to the overall design of a context. For instance, with our sales orders example, imagine the overhead associated with loading all the line items for every sales order a user might select for processing. For a couple of orders, it's not such a big deal. On the other hand, if the user were to load in hundreds or thousands of orders, we could have some serious memory utilization problems on our hands. By selecting the Singleton property for the `OrderItems` node, we can avoid such overhead since we'll only ever have a single `OrderItems` node in context at one time. Naturally, this can lead to huge performance benefits from a runtime perspective.

One final thing we should point out is that the performance benefits described in this section really only apply to context nodes that aren't direct descendents of the root node. If you think about it, this makes sense because there is only ever a single instance of the root node. So, even though direct descendant nodes of the root node are technically classified as singletons, there are no real performance benefits to be gained in this particular case.

5.3   Defining a Context

Having seen how contexts are organized and configured from a conceptual point of view, let's now turn our attention toward more practical matters and see how contexts are maintained using the graphical editor tools. As we'll see, this process is pretty straightforward once you understand how all the various pieces fit together.

5.3.1   Defining Context Nodes

Context nodes are defined and maintained using the Context Editor tool, which can be accessed via the CONTEXT tab of the Controller Editor. Here, we can define new context nodes by performing the following steps:

1. In order to create a new context node, we must locate an existing node within the context that will serve as the node's parent. Initially, the default root node will be all we have to choose from here. Of course, as additional nodes are added to the mix, those nodes will become parent candidates as well. In any case, once we select the target parent node, we can create a new child node by

right-clicking on the parent node and selecting the CREATE • NODE menu option as shown in Figure 5.6.

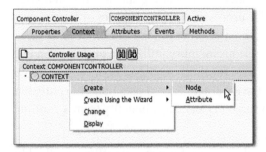

Figure 5.6 Creating a Context Node (Part 1)

2. This will open the CREATE NODES dialog box shown in Figure 5.7. Here, we can configure the individual properties of the context node as we like. (See Table 5.1 for a detailed description for each of the individual properties.)

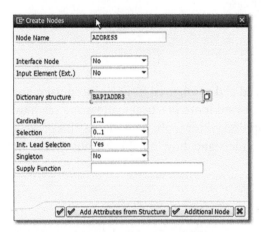

Figure 5.7 Creating a Context Node (Part 2)

3. At this point, we can save our changes by clicking on the button with the green checkmark on it. However, if the context node we're creating is modeled in terms of a pre-existing ABAP Dictionary structure (e.g., the BAPIADDR3 structure depicted in Figure 5.7), then we also have the option of going ahead and creating context attributes based on selected component fields of that structure. We can do this by clicking on the ADD ATTRIBUTES FROM STRUCTURE button (see Figure 5.7).

4. In the SELECT COMPONENTS OF STRUCTURE dialog box shown in Figure 5.8, we can pick and choose among the various structure components that will be used to model the context attributes for the selected context node. If we wish to select all the component fields, we can do so by clicking the SELECT ALL button in the toolbar.

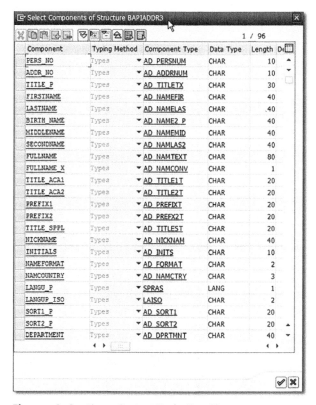

Figure 5.8 Creating a Context Node (Part 3)

5. Finally, once we're satisfied with our selections, we can finish the node creation process by clicking on the button with the green checkmark on it.

After the new context node is defined, we can maintain its properties after the fact in the properties editor shown in Figure 5.9. Here, as needed, we can click on the button adjacent to the DICTIONARY STRUCTURE property to reopen the SELECT COMPONENTS OF STRUCTURE dialog box shown in Figure 5.8. Within this dialog box, we can add or remove context attributes by selecting or de-selecting component fields within the structure. Alternatively, we can access this editor screen by

right-clicking on the context node and selecting the CREATE USING THE WIZARD •
ATTRIBUTES FROM COMPONENTS OF STRUCTURE menu option.

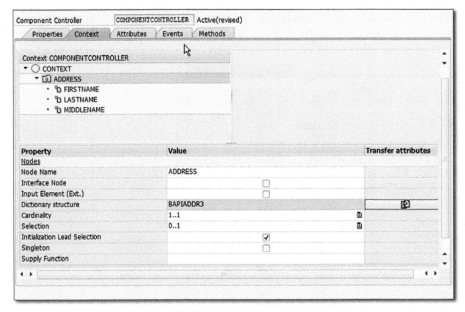

Figure 5.9 Maintaining Context Node Properties

Before we wrap up our discussion on context node maintenance, we should also
point out that the Context Editor offers an alternate tabular view that can be used
to edit context nodes and attributes en masse. To toggle between these different
views, simply click on the SWITCH CONTEXT EDITOR VIEW button in the toolbar.
Figure 5.10 illustrates the tabular view.

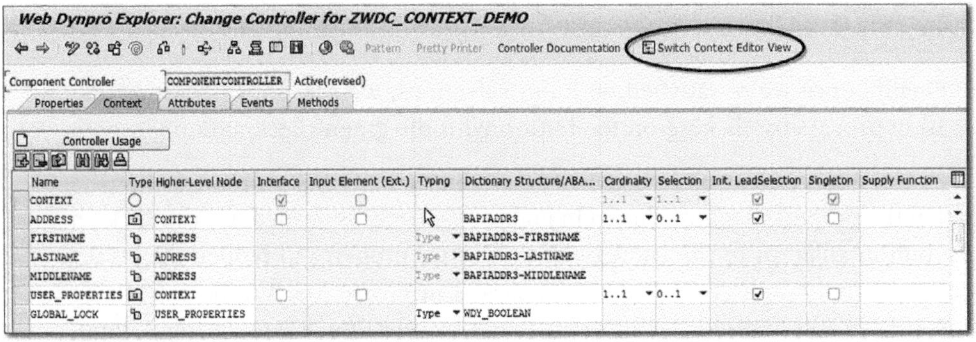

Figure 5.10 Switching the Context Editor View

5.3.2 Defining Context Attributes

In the previous section, we observed how the context node creation wizard could be used to automatically create context attributes in reference to component fields of an ABAP Dictionary structure. Though this feature is handy, there will be times when we need to create context attributes by hand. In these situations, we can perform the following steps:

1. First, we'll need to select the context node that will contain the context attribute.

2. Then, once we've selected the target node, we can right-click on the target node and select the CREATE • ATTRIBUTE menu option as shown in Figure 5.11.

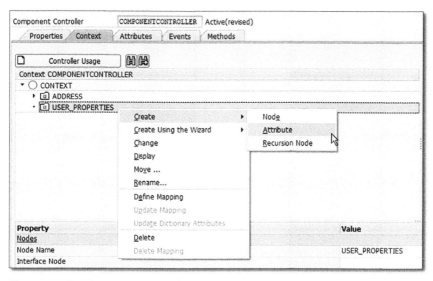

Figure 5.11 Creating a Context Attribute (Part 1)

3. In the CREATE ATTRIBUTE dialog box shown in Figure 5.12, we can configure the attribute properties as needed. Refer to Section 5.2.2, for more details about the properties of context attributes.

4. Finally, we can confirm our changes by clicking on the button with the green checkmark on it.

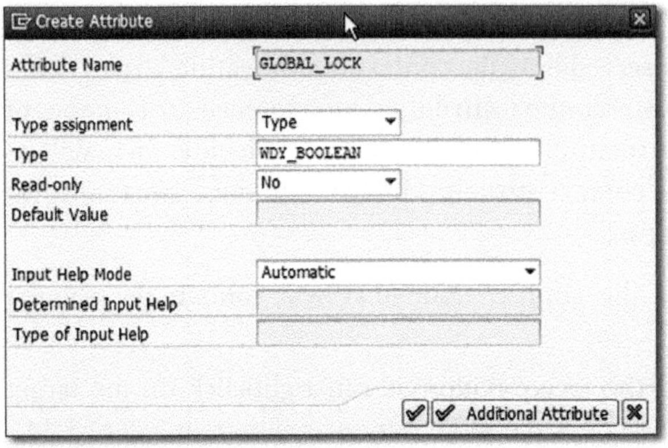

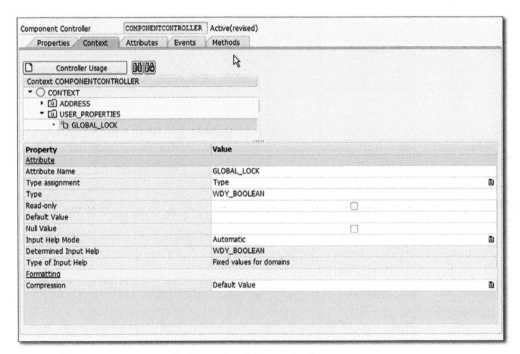

Figure 5.12 Creating a Context Attribute (Part 2)

Once the context attribute is created, we can maintain its properties in the editor screen shown in Figure 5.13. This also goes for auto-generated context attributes created in reference to component fields of ABAP Dictionary structures.

Figure 5.13 Maintaining the Properties of Context Attributes

One note worth mentioning here is that the Context Editor will not allow us to create context attributes underneath a context node whose `Dictionary Structure` property is maintained. One way to bypass this limitation is to simply clear out the property value after we're done with it. For example, if we need to define 90% of a node's context attributes in terms of a structure from the ABAP Dictionary, we can plug the structure into the `Dictionary Structure` property and use the wizard to define the bulk of the attributes we need. Then, we can remove the structure reference and manually create the remaining attributes from there.

5.3.3 Recursion Nodes

Most of the time, whenever we're defining a context, the depth of the node hierarchy will be known up front. For instance, when modeling a sales order, we know that the node hierarchy will be three levels deep:

▶ `SalesOrders`

　▶ `OrderItems`

　　– `ScheduleLines`

However, what happens if we don't know the depth of the node hierarchy up front? Here, a classic example is a node hierarchy used to model a file system. In this scenario, the node hierarchy could be arbitrarily deep depending on the number of subdirectories contained within a given file system.

To model such arbitrary node hierarchies, we must enlist the aid of *recursion nodes*. From a conceptual perspective, a recursion node is a special kind of context node whose structure is recursively defined in terms of some superordinate context node. In effect, recursion nodes are design time placeholders that can be used to model complex node hierarchies whose depth is unknown at design time. In this section, we'll learn how work with recursion nodes.

What Is Recursion?

Recursion is the process of repeating items in a self-similar way. A classic example used to demonstrate recursion is the factorial function from the field of mathematics. Since it's probably been a while since your last high school math class, the factorial function calculates the product of all the positive integers less than or equal to a number n. So, for instance, if n = 3, then `factorial(3)` = 3 x 2 x 1 = 6.

While it's possible to define the factorial function using looping structures, it's much more elegant to define the solution using a divide-and-conquer approach in which the function is defined in terms of itself. For example, in the ABAP Objects class listing below, you can see how the factorial() method repeatedly calls itself using the argument n − 1. The recursion sequence bottoms out whenever n becomes less than or equal to 1, at which point the program call stack unwinds and the factorial values calculated at the lower levels bubble their way back up the call stack.

```
CLASS lcl_recursion DEFINITION.
  PUBLIC SECTION.
    CLASS-METHODS:
      factorial IMPORTING n TYPE i
                RETURNING VALUE(re_factorial) TYPE i.
ENDCLASS.

CLASS lcl_recursion IMPLEMENTATION.
  METHOD factorial.
    IF n LE 1.
      re_factorial = 1.
    ELSE.
      re_factorial = n * factorial( n - 1 ).
    ENDIF.
  ENDMETHOD.
ENDCLASS.
```

To put the nature of this recursive solution into perspective, let's trace through a call to the factorial() method. Here, if we were to pass in an argument of 3, the final product would be calculated as follows:

```
factorial(3) =
  3 * factorial( 3 - 1 ) = 3 * 2 * 1 ✓
    2 * factorial( 2 - 1 ) = 2 * 1
      1
```

Once we reach the bottom of the recursion stack, we can begin plugging in the calculated values for each recursion step. So, for example, the expression factorial(2 − 1) evaluates to 1, factorial(3 − 1) evaluates to 2, and so on until we have 3 x 2 x 1 = 6.

Regardless of whether or not we're using recursion to define a function or a complex context node hierarchy, there are a couple of important observations we can take away from the implementation of the recursive factorial() solution:

▶ First, notice that the `factorial()` method made no assumptions about the depth of the recursion. So, whether we pass in an argument of 2 or 100,000, `factorial()` just goes about its business as usual.

▶ In order to avoid an infinite loop, we must define a *base case* that can be solved without recursion. In the case of the `factorial()` method, the base case occurs whenever n is less than or equal to 1.

Though recursive solutions are not always intuitive at first glance, they're very effective for solving certain types of complex problems. This will become apparent as we search for ways to model certain types of complex context node hierarchies.

Defining Recursion Nodes

In order to understand how recursion nodes work, it's useful to see how they're defined. That way, we can begin to visualize how recursive node hierarchies are realized at runtime. To guide us through this process, let's try to model the file system node hierarchy described earlier.

To begin, we'll first define a regular context node called DIRECTORY as shown in Figure 5.14. This context node has a cardinality of 0..n and defines a single context attribute called FILENAME. Thus, at runtime, we can use the DIRECTORY node to enumerate all the files contained within a single directory.

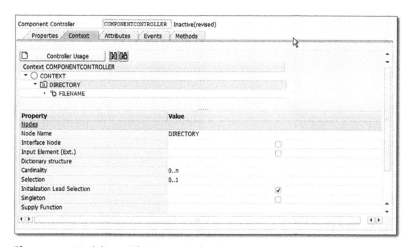

Figure 5.14 Modeling a File System in the Context

As you can see in Figure 5.15, our DIRECTORY node is rather limited in that it only allows us to model the files contained within a single directory. Here, the

DIRECTORY node collection contains a separate element per file, with the file name being represented by the FILENAME context attribute.

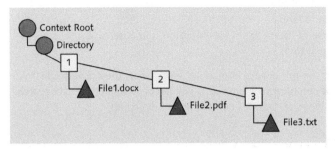

Figure 5.15 Visualizing the Directory Context Node at Runtime

In order to be able to model subdirectories, we need to add a recursion node called SUBDIRECTORY as a child of the DIRECTORY node. We can create this node by right-clicking on the DIRECTORY node and selecting the CREATE • RECURSION NODE menu option. This will open the CREATE RECURSION NODE dialog box shown in Figure 5.16. As you can see, recursion node definitions consist of a node name and a reference node that's used to describe the layout of the recursion node(s) at runtime. We can confirm our selection by clicking on the button with the green checkmark on it. After the recursion node is created, we can view its definition by clicking on the folder with the circular blue arrows on it (see Figure 5.17).

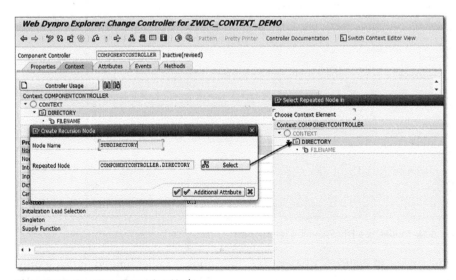

Figure 5.16 Creating a Recursion Node

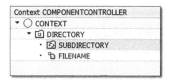

Figure 5.17 Recursion Nodes within the Context Editor

Recursion Nodes at Runtime

Getting back to our file system example, let's once again take a look at our DIRECTORY node at runtime now that we've added the SUBDIRECTORY recursion node. As you can see in Figure 5.18, the addition of the SUBDIRECTORY node now allows us to represent subdirectories within a given directory. Now, we have two different types of context elements within a DIRECTORY (or SUBDIRECTORY) node collection:

▶ If the context element represents a file, the FILENAME attribute contains the file name and the SUBDIRECTORY node collection is empty.

▶ If the context element represents a directory, the FILENAME attribute contains the directory name and the SUBDIRECTORY node collection will contain additional elements (and subelements) to represent the underlying directory structure.

We can then extend this structure out indefinitely to represent arbitrarily nested file structures as needed. Of course, not all of this happens by magic; we still have to programmatically create SUBDIRECTORY elements to represent the various subdirectories. We'll see how this is accomplished in Section 5.4.

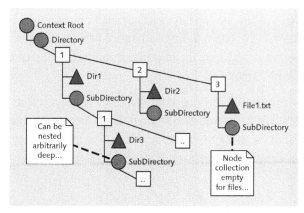

Figure 5.18 Viewing a Recursion Node Hierarchy at Runtime

Restrictions for Using Recursion Nodes

When working with recursion nodes, there are a couple of restrictions we need to be aware of:

▶ First of all, we cannot use the root node of a context as the repeated node for a recursion. When you think about it, this makes sense because it would lead to circular references.

▶ Secondly, we cannot map a recursive node from one context to another (via context mapping). In other words, in our file system example, we could not map the SUBDIRECTORY node by itself. However, this isn't to say that we couldn't map the superordinate DIRECTORY node. The point is that recursion nodes cannot exist in isolation.

5.4 Context Programming

Up until now, we have been primarily focused on the design-time characteristics of contexts. With this foundation in place, we're now ready to begin looking at contexts from a runtime perspective. Therefore, in this section, we'll explore the use of the provided context API and see how contexts are built and manipulated using good old-fashioned ABAP code.

5.4.1 Getting Started

Behind the scenes, the Web Dynpro framework is responsible for coming up with in-memory representations of the context node hierarchies we define within the graphical Context Editor tool. As you might expect, defining such an in-memory representation is no trivial matter, especially when you begin to think about all the different properties that can be configured for individual context nodes and context attributes within a node hierarchy.

In order to shield developers from the underlying complexity of context implementation details, SAP has provided a simplified API that allows us to traverse through and manipulate contexts in a straightforward and intuitive manner. Figure 5.19 contains a UML class diagram, which shows the primary interfaces we'll interact with when utilizing this API.

Further Reference

If you haven't worked with interfaces before, *Object-Oriented Programming with ABAP Objects* (Wood, SAP PRESS, 2009) provides a detailed description.

As you can see, these interfaces embody basic elements of a context: context nodes are represented via interface IF_WD_CONTEXT_NODE, context elements are represented via interface IF_WD_CONTEXT_ELEMENT, and so on.

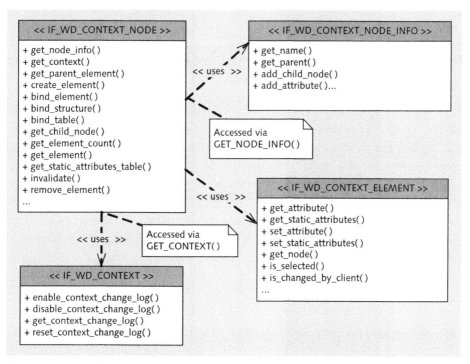

Figure 5.19 UML Class Diagram for Context API

In order to understand the positioning of the context API, let's take a closer look at how contexts are constructed behind the scenes. Whenever a controller is instantiated at runtime, the Web Dynpro framework assumes the responsibility of building an in-memory representation of a context. This representation is based on the design time metadata contained within a controller's context definition. The implementation of this representation, while proprietary, is realized in the form of objects, which implement the interfaces shown in Figure 5.19.

In order to tap into this auto-generated context hierarchy, we must obtain a reference to the context root node. Fortunately, as it turns out, this reference is provided to us automatically via the default WD_CONTEXT attribute, which is included with every controller within a WDA component. As you can see in Figure 5.20, this attribute is defined as an object reference, which points to an object that implements the IF_WD_CONTEXT_NODE interface.

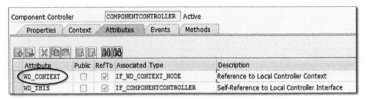

Figure 5.20 Accessing the Local Controller Context

Once we have access to the context root node, we can use the methods of the IF_WD_CONTEXT_NODE interface to begin traversing through the context hierarchy, adding and removing context elements, and so on. In the upcoming sections, we'll see how all this works by considering some practical programming use cases. To guide us through these exercises, we'll work with the SALES_ORDERS context hierarchy shown in Figure 5.21. Here, each of the nested context nodes (SALES_ORDERS, ORDER_ITEMS, and SCHEDULE_LINES) have a cardinality of 0..n. As we progress through these examples, we'll refer back to this sample context periodically to see how its properties influence the approaches we'll take to manipulate the context at runtime.

> **Note**
>
> You can also see how this context is defined by looking at component ZWDC_CONTEXT_DEMO within the chapter examples provided with the code bundle for this book.

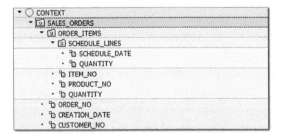

Figure 5.21 Sample Context Used for Examples

5.4.2 Maneuvering within a Context

At the end of the day, context programming is mostly about performing CRUD operations on the context node collections contained within a context hierarchy. Of course, in order to perform these operations, we must figure out a way to get our hands on the individual context nodes and context elements contained within a context hierarchy. Therefore, in this section, we'll spend some time looking at ways to traverse through the context nodes and context elements contained within a context.

Accessing Child Nodes Directly

As we learned in the previous section, each controller within a WDA component contains a default attribute called WD_CONTEXT, which points to the root node of the controller's context. We can use the methods of the WD_CONTEXT attribute to traverse the node hierarchy in several different ways.

One of the most common approaches for navigating from one context node to another is to use the GET_CHILD_NODE() method provided via the IF_WD_CONTEXT_NODE interface. Listing 5.1 demonstrates how this method works. Here, we're using the method to traverse two levels down in the sample context depicted in Figure 5.21:

▶ First, we use the method to traverse from the context root node to the SALES_ORDERS node.

▶ Then, we call the method on the provided sales orders object reference to traverse down to the child ORDER_ITEMS node.

```
METHOD wddoinit.
  DATA lo_sales_orders_node TYPE REF TO if_wd_context_node.
  DATA lo_item_node TYPE REF TO if_wd_context_node.
  lo_sales_orders_node =
    wd_context->get_child_node( 'SALES_ORDERS' ).

  lo_item_node =
    lo_sales_orders_node->get_child_node(
      name  = 'ORDER_ITEMS'
      index = 5 ).
ENDMETHOD.
```

Listing 5.1 Accessing a Child Node Using the GET_CHILD_NODE() Method

Looking at the signature of the GET_CHILD_NODE() method illustrated in Figure 5.22, you can see that the method can receive two importing parameters:

▶ **NAME**
As you would expect, the NAME parameter refers to the name of the node being accessed (e.g., SALES_ORDERS or ORDER_ITEMS).

▶ **INDEX**
The INDEX parameter is an optional parameter that can be used to specify *which* context element within the node element collection of the referenced context node we want to perform the lookup on. For example, in Listing 5.1, notice that we passed a value of 5 for the INDEX parameter in the call to look up the ORDER_ITEMS node. This call can be interpreted as a lookup for order items for the fifth sales order element in the referenced SALES_ORDERS node's element collection. If the INDEX parameter isn't specified, the method will use the lead selection element by default (see Figure 5.22).

Interface	IF_WD_CONTEXT_NODE		Implemented / Active			

Properties | Interfaces | Attributes | Methods | Events | Types | Aliases

Method parameters: GET_CHILD_NODE

Methods | Exceptions

Parameter	Type	Pass Value	Optional	Typing Method	Associated Type	Default value	Description
INDEX	Importing	☐	☑	Type	I	USE_LEAD_SELECTION	Index of Context Element
NAME	Importing	☐	☐	Type	STRING		Name of Lower-Level Node
CHILD_NODE	Returning	☑	☐	Type Ref To	IF_WD_CONTEXT_NODE		Lower-Level Node
		☐	☐	Type			
		☐	☐	Type			
		☐	☐	Type			

Figure 5.22 Signature of the GET_CHILD_NODE() Method

The GET_CHILD_NODE() method is useful in situations when we need to access a specific child node. However, sometimes we may need to look up *all* the child nodes for a given context node at once. In these situations, we can use the GET_CHILD_NODES() method of the IF_WD_CONTEXT_NODE interface. This method will return a table of context node references we can manipulate in a loop as per usual.

Finally, if we already happen to have our hands on a context element, we can access a child node for that element directly using the GET_CHILD_NODE() method defined in the IF_WD_CONTEXT_ELEMENT interface. The primary difference here is that this version of the GET_CHILD_NODE() method doesn't provide an INDEX parameter since the parent context element is implied from the context element object reference. We'll learn how to obtain references to context elements shortly.

> **Best Practices: Avoiding the Use of String Literals**
>
> For demonstration purposes, we used the string literal `SALES_ORDERS` to access the SALES_ORDERS child node in the code excerpt in Listing 5.1. However, from this point forward, we'll be utilizing constants from the controller interface for this purpose. You might ask, where do these constants come from? They're defined automatically by the system whenever we define context nodes within a controller context. So, if we define a context node called SALES_ORDERS, a constant called WDCTX_SALES_ORDERS will be created behind the scenes within the controller interface (which can be accessed via the WD_THIS attribute). We can then plug in this constant within the call to GET_CHILD_NODE() like this:
>
> ```
> lo_sales_orders_node =
>   wd_context->get_child_node( wd_this=>wdctx_sales_orders ).
> ```
>
> What's the difference? Well, by using constants, we allow the ABAP syntax check to verify that we're accessing a proper node name. Otherwise, there's nothing to stop us from accidentally entering a typo and having the lookup fail at runtime.

Accessing Descendant Nodes Using Paths

Though it's possible to use the GET_CHILD_NODE() method repeatedly to access the descendant nodes of a given context node, it can be much more efficient to bypass these steps and access descendant nodes directly using path lookup methods. To understand how these path methods work, consider the code excerpt in Listing 5.2. As you can see, we're using the PATH_GET_NODE() method to access the SCHEDULE_LINES node from our sample hierarchy. Here, you can evaluate the path expression `SALES_ORDERS.ORDER_ITEMS.SCHEDULE_LINES` in the same way you'd evaluate a path used to access a file in the file system of your local computer: C:\Folder1\Folder2\MyFile.txt.

```
DATA: lo_schedule_lines_node TYPE REF TO if_wd_context_node.

lo_schedule_lines_node =
  wd_context->path_get_node(
    `SALES_ORDERS.ORDER_ITEMS.SCHEDULE_LINES` ).
```

Listing 5.2 Accessing Descendant Nodes via Paths

When building path expressions, we must be careful to take node cardinalities into account. For example, the path expression contained in Listing 5.2 uses the lead selections for the SALES_ORDERS and ORDER_ITEMS nodes to obtain the targeted SCHEDULE_LINES node reference. If we want to access the schedule lines of the second line item of the third sales order, we would have to build a path expression like the one in Listing 5.3. In this case, the target index is specified after the context node using the syntax <context node>.<index>.

```
DATA: lo_schedule_lines_node TYPE REF TO if_wd_context_node.

lo_schedule_lines_node =
  wd_context->path_get_node(
    `SALES_ORDERS.3.ORDER_ITEMS.2.SCHEDULE_LINES` ).
```

Listing 5.3 Building Path Expressions with Specific Indices

Most of the time, we'll probably know the node path we want to query ahead of time. However, if we need to derive the node path dynamically in relation to a particular node, we can use the GET_PATH() method against that node to determine the current node path and then build our path expression from there. In addition, we can also use the PATH_GET_ELEMENT() and PATH_GET_ATTRIBUTE() methods to navigate to context elements and context attributes, respectively.

Accessing Context Elements

Once we get our hands on a context node reference, we can use the methods of the IF_WD_CONTEXT_NODE interface to access context elements contained within the context node's element collection. Table 5.3 describes each of these methods in turn.

Method Name	Description
| get_element | This method uses index-based semantics to access a particular context element within the referencing context node's element collection. If a specific index value is not provided via the optional INDEX parameter, the method will return the context element designated as the lead selection. Otherwise, the method will attempt to return the context element at the specified position. So, for example, if we want to access the fifth sales order element within the SALES_ORDERS node collection, we could do so like this:<br><br>```
DATA: lo_sales_orders
TYPE REF TO if_wd_context_node,
lo_sales_order
TYPE REF TO if_wd_context_element.
lo_sales_order =
lo_sales_orders->get_element( 5 ).
IF NOT lo_sales_order IS INITIAL.
"Do stuff...
ENDIF.
```<br><br>As you can see in the code excerpt above, it's always a good idea to perform a null check on the resultant context element because it may not always be mapped. For example, if we were to pass an index value of 11 to the GET_ELEMENT() method for a context node whose node collection contained only 10 context elements, the operation would be undefined. In this case, the GET_ELEMENT() method would return the null value instead of an instance of IF_WD_CONTEXT_ELEMENT. Naturally, this leads to null reference exceptions at runtime. |
| get_elements | If we want to obtain a list of all the context elements contained within a node collection, we can utilize the GET_ELEMENTS() method. This method returns a table of IF_WD_CONTEXT_ELEMENT references, which represent each of the elements in the collection.<br><br>If we like, we can use the provided FROM and TO parameters to whittle down the list to a subset of values like this:<br><br>```
DATA: lo_sales_orders
TYPE REF TO if_wd_context_node,
lt_order_elems
TYPE wdr_context_element_set.
``` |

Table 5.3 Methods for Accessing Context Elements within a Node Collection

Method Name	Description
| get_elements (Cont.) | ```
FIELD-SYMBOLS:
<lfs_order> LIKE LINE
OF lt_order_elems.
lt_order_elems =
lo_sales_orders->get_elements(
from = 2
to = 4 ).
LOOP AT lt_order_elems
ASSIGNING <lfs_order>.
"Process the order element...
ENDLOOP.
``` |
| get_element_count | As the method name suggests, this method provides us with a count of the number of context elements contained within a node collection. This method can come in handy when accessing context elements within a loop. Here, the resultant value can be used as an upper bound on the loop to make sure that calls to GET_ELEMENT() are made with valid index values. |

Table 5.3 Methods for Accessing Context Elements within a Node Collection (Cont.)

In addition to the methods provided for accessing context elements contained within a node's collection, the IF_WD_CONTEXT_NODE interface provides a method that allows us to access the parent element of the selected node: GET_PARENT_ELEMENT(). This method can be handy for dynamic programming situations when we need to walk up the node hierarchy one step at a time.

Working with the Lead Selection Property

In Section 5.2.3, we observed the ways in which the Web Dynpro framework uses the lead selection property to identify which context element is currently being processed within a node collection. In practice, the lead selection provides us with a very convenient way to address context elements within a node hierarchy without having to worry about keeping up with indices. Of course, in order for all this to work, we must be careful to make sure the lead selection is kept up to date. For these tasks, we can use the methods outlined in Table 5.4.
```

Method Name	Description
get_lead_selection	This method returns the context element at the lead selection. Behavior-wise, it's semantically equivalent to calling the GET_ELEMENT() method without passing in a specific index value.
get_lead_selection_index	This method returns the index of the lead selection element as an integer. As such, it can be useful for determining where the lead selection is with respect to the rest of the elements within the node collection.
move_first	This method marks the first context element in the node collection as the lead selection.
move_last	This method marks the last context element in the node collection as the lead selection.
move_next	This method moves the lead selection indicator to the next element in the node collection. So, if the lead selection index is currently at 2, a call to MOVE_NEXT() will move the lead selection index to the element at position 3. If the last element within the collection is currently designated as the lead selection, the method will return without making any changes to the lead selection.
move_previous	This method is the analog of MOVE_NEXT() in that it moves the lead selection pointer to the previous element in the context node collection. If the first element in the list is marked as the lead selection, the method will return without making any changes to the lead selection.
move_to	This method allows us to move the lead selection pointer to the element at the specified index, assuming it exists.
set_lead_selection	Unlike the other methods we've seen that have used index-based semantics, this method allows us to pass in the actual context element we wish to designate as the lead selection.

Table 5.4 Methods for Querying and Setting the Lead Selection

Method Name	Description

`set_lead_selection` (Cont.)	The code excerpt below demonstrates how this works for a context element reference `LO_SALES_ORDER`, which could be obtained in a number of different ways.
	
	`DATA:`
	`lo_sales_orders`
	`TYPE REF TO if_wd_context_node,`
	`lo_sales_order`
	`TYPE REF TO if_wd_context_element.`
	
	`lo_sales_orders->set_lead_selection(`
	`lo_sales_order ).`

`set_lead_selection_index`	This method uses the provided index parameter to identify the element within the node collection to mark with the lead selection indicator. One thing to note with this method is that it will raise an exception if the provided index is out of bounds.

Table 5.4 Methods for Querying and Setting the Lead Selection (Cont.)

5.4.3 Filling a Context

Now that we've seen how to maneuver within a context, let's spend some time exploring ways to fill a context. In this section, we'll consider some of the methods we have at our disposal for carrying out these tasks.

Creating New Context Elements

For the most part, the context representation generated by the Web Dynpro framework is empty by default. So, in order to begin loading data into a context, we must create new context elements to fill in the context nodes contained within the node hierarchy. However, since the only representation of a context element we have to work with is the `IF_WD_CONTEXT_ELEMENT` interface, we cannot instantiate new context elements using the `CREATE OBJECT` statement. Instead, we must rely on a series of factory methods provided within the `IF_WD_CONTEXT_NODE` interface. In this section, we'll take a look one of these methods in particular: the `CREATE_ELEMENT()` method.

As the name suggests, the CREATE_ELEMENT() method creates a brand new context element. Listing 5.4 demonstrates how this works.

```
DATA: lo_sales_orders TYPE REF TO if_wd_context_node,
      lo_sales_order  TYPE REF TO if_wd_context_element.

lo_sales_orders =
  ld_context->get_child_node( wd_this=>wdctx_sales_orders ).
lo_sales_order = lo_sales_orders->create_element( ).
```

Listing 5.4 Creating a Context Element Using CREATE_ELEMENT()

By default, the context attributes for the generated context element returned from the call to CREATE_ELEMENT() will be set to the initial values of their corresponding data types. We can pre-initialize these values using the STATIC_ATTRIBUTE_VALUES parameter as demonstrated in Listing 5.5. Here, notice that we're using the wd_this->Element_sales_orders structure type to prefill the context attributes. This structure type was generated for us automatically within the controller interface when we created the SALES_ORDERS node in the Context Editor and provides a convenient way for us to specify context attribute values en masse. Of course, we're also free to define our own structure type if we prefer. In either case, the Web Dynpro framework will map the component fields of the structure in much the same way component fields are copied from one structure to another using the MOVE-CORRESPONDING statement in ABAP.

```
DATA: lo_sales_orders TYPE REF TO if_wd_context_node,
      lo_sales_order  TYPE REF TO if_wd_context_element,
      ls_sales_order  TYPE wd_this->Element_sales_orders.

"Initialize the attributes of the new sales order:
ls_sales_order-order_no = '1234567890'.
ls_sales_order-creation_date = sy-datum.
ls_sales_order-customer_no = '3456789012'.

lo_sales_orders =
  ld_context->get_child_node( wd_this=>wdctx_sales_orders ).
lo_sales_order =
  lo_sales_orders->create_element( ls_sales_order ).
```

Listing 5.5 Creating a Pre-Initialized Context Element

Adding Context Elements to a Node Collection

In the previous section, we learned how the CREATE_ELEMENT() method could be used to create new context elements. By default, these newly created context elements exist in isolation. In other words, they aren't yet part of the element collection of the context node whose reference was used to create them.

In order to add the context element to the node's element collection, we must *bind* the element to the context node. This bind operation is similar to the APPEND statement used to add new lines to an internal table.

The IF_WD_CONTEXT_NODE interface provides four different methods for binding context elements to a node collection. The first method we'll look at is the BIND_ELEMENT() method. This method's three importing parameters influence its behavior at runtime:

► NEW_ITEM
  This parameter contains the context element that will be added to the node collection.

► SET_INITIAL_ELEMENTS
  This optional Boolean parameter determines whether or not we want to refresh the node collection before appending the selected context element.

► INDEX
  This optional integer parameter can be used to specify the precise index into which we want to insert the selected context element. If this parameter is not specified, the context element will be added to the end of the node collection.

Assuming we want to accept the default behavior for the BIND_ELEMENT() method, we can extend our element creation example from Listing 5.5 to append the generated sales orders element to the SALES_ORDERS node collection as demonstrated in Listing 5.6.

```
DATA: lo_sales_orders TYPE REF TO if_wd_context_node,
      lo_sales_order  TYPE REF TO if_wd_context_element,
      ls_sales_order  TYPE wd_this->element_sales_orders.

"Initialize the attributes of the new sales order:
...

lo_sales_orders =
  ld_context->get_child_node( wd_this=>wdctx_sales_orders ).
```

```
lo_sales_order =
  lo_sales_orders->create_element( ls_sales_order ).
lo_sales_orders->bind_element( lo_sales_order ).
```

Listing 5.6 Adding a Context Element to a Node Collection

To add a series of context elements to a node collection in one fell swoop, we can use the BIND_ELEMENTS() method. This method behaves in much the same way that the BIND_ELEMENT() method does. The primary difference is in that BIND_ELEMENTS() allows us to pass a table of context elements in its NEW_ITEMS parameter.

As we've seen, the CREATE_ELEMENT() and BIND_ELEMENT() methods are fairly straightforward to work with. However, if we find ourselves having to build a complex node hierarchy, this repeated call sequence can get tedious in a hurry. Fortunately, the IF_WD_CONTEXT_NODE interface provides a couple of shortcut methods to simplify this process.

The first shortcut method we'll look at is the BIND_STRUCTURE() method. This method consolidates the calls to CREATE_ELEMENT() and BIND_ELEMENT() into single method call as demonstrated in Listing 5.7. This call has the same effect as the previous two calls, providing us with the same parameters that BIND_ELEMENT() uses to determine how the element is added to the node collection.

```
DATA: lo_sales_orders TYPE REF TO if_wd_context_node,
      ls_sales_order  TYPE wd_this->element_sales_orders.

"Initialize the attributes of the new sales order:
ls_sales_order-order_no = '1234567890'.
ls_sales_order-creation_date = sy-datum.
ls_sales_order-customer_no = '3456789012'.

lo_sales_orders =
  ld_context->get_child_node( wd_this=>wdctx_sales_orders ).
lo_sales_orders->bind_structure( ls_sales_order ).
```

Listing 5.7 Creating and Appending Elements Using BIND_STRUCTURE()

In addition to the BIND_STRUCTURE() method, the IF_WD_CONTEXT_NODE interface provides the BIND_TABLE()method for appending context elements en masse. In effect, a call to this method is equivalent to building a series of context elements using CREATE_ELEMENT(), storing them in an internal table, and then adding them to the node collection via the BIND_ELEMENTS() method.

Listing 5.8 shows how the BIND_TABLE() method works. As you can see, the majority of this code is business as usual in ABAP: we're simply building an internal table. The type of this internal table was defined for us automatically within the controller interface when we created the SALES_ORDERS node. So, rather than reinventing the wheel, we simply define the local table variable LT_SALES_ORDERS using the Elements_Sales_Orders table type. Finally, once the table is built, we can simply pass it to the BIND_TABLE() method in order to create the context elements. If you look at the signature of the BIND_TABLE() method, you'll see that it provides us with the same parameter choices as BIND_ELEMENTS(), allowing us to influence how the elements are appended at runtime.

```abap
DATA: lo_sales_orders TYPE REF TO if_wd_context_node,
      lt_sales_orders TYPE wd_this->Elements_sales_orders.
FIELD-SYMBOLS:
  <lfs_sales_order> LIKE LINE OF lt_sales_orders.

"Create a couple of sales orders elements:
APPEND INITIAL LINE TO lt_sales_orders
            ASSIGNING <lfs_sales_order>.
<lfs_sales_order>-order_no = '1234567890'.
<lfs_sales_order>-creation_date = sy-datum.
<lfs_sales_order>-customer_no = '3456789012'.

APPEND INITIAL LINE TO lt_sales_orders
            ASSIGNING <lfs_sales_order>.
<lfs_sales_order>-order_no = '234567890'.
<lfs_sales_order>-creation_date = sy-datum.
<lfs_sales_order>-customer_no = '3456789012'.

lo_sales_orders =
  ld_context->get_child_node( wd_this=>wdctx_sales_orders ).
lo_sales_orders->bind_table( lt_sales_orders ).
```

Listing 5.8 Adding Elements to a Node Collection Using BIND_TABLE()

5.4.4 Working with Context Attributes

Since we learned how to create context elements in the previous sections, let's now turn our attention to the maintenance of the context attributes contained within these context elements. For the most part, you'll find these operations to be quite straightforward. After all, there's only so much you can do to a set of name-value pairs. However, as we'll soon see, context attributes also maintain a handful of dynamic properties that can be used to influence the behavior of certain types of UI elements.

To query or set the values of context attributes, we must use the methods described in Table 5.5. As you might expect, these methods are provided via the IF_WD_CONTEXT_ELEMENT interface. Thus, you can think of the attribute access operations from the perspective of the referencing context element.

> **Note**
>
> For convenience, you'll also find versions of the same methods provided with interface IF_WD_CONTEXT_NODE. However, these methods are really just wrapper methods in that they delegate the request to a selected context element behind the scenes (either via lead selection or explicit index selection).

Method Name	Description
get_attribute	This method can be used to obtain the value of a context attribute. The code excerpt below demonstrates what this call looks like. Here, assume the object reference LO_SALES_ORDER points to some context element. As you can see, the method call simply takes in a context attribute name and returns the attribute's value. DATA: lv_order_date TYPE datum. lo_sales_order->get_attribute(EXPORTING name = `CREATION_DATE` IMPORTING value = lv_order_date).

Table 5.5 Methods for Working with Context Attributes

Method Name	Description
get_attribute_ref	This method is similar to GET_ATTRIBUTE() in that it allows us to access the value of a given context attribute. However, in this case, the attribute value is returned using *reference semantics*. This subtle variation allows us to avoid a potentially expensive memory copy operation in certain situations.

The code excerpt below demonstrates how the GET_ATTRIBUTE_REF() method works. If you're unfamiliar with data references, we recommend you check out the ABAP help documentation in the section entitled "Data References."

```
DATA: lr_order_date TYPE REF TO datum.
DATA lv_order_date TYPE datum.

lr_order_date ?=
lo_sales_order->get_attribute_ref(
`CREATION_DATE` ).

"We can access the value by dereferencing
"the reference variable like this:
lv_order_date = lr_order_date->*.
``` |
| set_attribute | This method is the analog of the GET_ATTRIBUTE() method, allowing us to map a value onto a context attribute by name. The code excerpt below demonstrates how this works.

```
DATA: lv_order_date TYPE datum.
lv_order_date = sy-datum + 7.

lo_sales_order->set_attribute(
EXPORTING
name = `CREATION_DATE`
value = lv_order_date ).
``` |
| get_static_attributes | This method is used to obtain the values of all the statically defined context attributes contained within a context element in one fell swoop. |

Table 5.5 Methods for Working with Context Attributes (Cont.)

Method Name	Description
`get_static_attributes` (Cont.)	The values are copied over to a structured data type, whose component fields mirror the context attributes contained within the referencing context element as demonstrated in the code excerpt below: ``` DATA: lo_order TYPE REF TO if_wd_context_element, ls_order TYPE wd_this->element_sales_orders. lo_order->get_static_attributes(IMPORTING static_attributes = ls_order). ```
`get_static_attributes_ref`	Much like the `GET_ATTRIBUTE_REF()` method considered earlier, this method uses reference semantics to pass back a reference to the statically defined attributes of a context element. As was the case with `GET_ATTRIBUTE_REF()`, this method comes in handy whenever we need to avoid expensive memory copy operations for large context elements.
`set_static_attributes`	This method is the analog of `GET_STATIC_ATTRIBUTES()` in that it allows you to initialize the values of the statically defined attributes of a context element in one fell swoop using a structured data object. The code excerpt below demonstrates how this method is used. ``` DATA: lo_order TYPE REF TO if_wd_context_element, ls_order TYPE wd_this->element_sales_orders. "Adjust the static attributes of an "order: ls_order-order_no = '1234567890'. ls_order-creation_date = sy-datum. ls_order-customer_no = '3456789012'. lo_order->set_static_attributes(ls_order). ```

Table 5.5 Methods for Working with Context Attributes (Cont.)

Runtime Properties of Context Attributes

At the end of the day, context attributes are intended to be used as a means for transfering data back and forth between UI elements in the view layer and the backend data model. Here, the properties of UI elements are bound to context attributes in such a way that data is synchronzied automatically.

Normally, when we talk about data binding with UI elements, we're talking about binding the value of a context attribute to a property of a UI element used for displaying data. For example, to display the value of a context attribute using an `InputField` UI element, we'd bind the `value` property of the `InputField` element with the context attribute. However, it's also possible to use data binding to define the values of other UI element properties, such as the `enabled` property, `readOnly` property, and so on.

Recognizing the benefits of using data binding to determine the values of certain common UI element properties, SAP elected to extend context attributes to include additional runtime properties that could be used for this purpose. The benefit here is that we don't have to incur the overhead of defining additional context attributes to specify these UI element properties. So, for instance, we could use a single context attribute to define not only the `value` property of an

`InputField` element, but also its `enabled` property, `readOnly` property, and so on. This leads to much better performance at runtime.

Table 5.6 describes the set of runtime properties available for a given context attribute. Each of these properties is Boolean in nature and can be maintained using methods provided via the `IF_WD_CONTEXT_ELEMENT` interface as described in Table 5.7.

Property Name	Description
`enabled`	This property can be used to determine whether or not a UI element is enabled within the view.
`readOnly`	This property can be used to adjust the `readOnly` property of UI elements.
`state`	This property can be used to determine whether or not a UI element is considered to be a required field in the view layout.
`visible`	This property can be used to determine whether or not a UI element is visible within the view layout.

Table 5.6 Runtime Properties of Context Attributes

Method Name	Description
`set_attribute_property`	This method is used to set a single runtime property of a context attribute. The individual runtime properties are enumerated via the `E_PROPERTY` constant defined within the `IF_WD_CONTEXT_ELEMENT` interface. The code excerpt below demonstrates how this method call works.

```
DATA:
lo_order TYPE REF TO
IF_WD_CONTEXT_ELEMENT.

lo_order->set_attribute_property(
EXPORTING
attribute_name = `ORDER_NO`
property       =
lo_order->e_property-read_only
value          = abap_true ).
```

Table 5.7 Maintaining the Runtime Properties of a Context Attribute

Method Name	Description
`set_attribute_props_for_elem`	This method allows us to set the runtime properties for a set of context attributes en masse. The attribute properties are specified within the `PROPERTIES` table parameter provided in the method signature.
`get_attribute_properties`	This method allows us to query the status of each of the runtime properties of a context attribute. Here, we simply pass in the attribute's name in the `ATTRIBUTE_NAME` parameter and the method will return a structure containing the current property values.
`get_attribute_props_for_elem`	This method performs a wholesale lookup of attribute runtime properties for the referencing context element.

Table 5.7 Maintaining the Runtime Properties of a Context Attribute (Cont.)

Once the runtime properties for a context attribute are in place, we can use them to define context bindings for UI elements in a view using the familiar DEFINE CONTEXT BINDING dialog box, shown in Figure 5.23. However, in this case, we'll want to choose the target runtime property in the PROPERTY list underneath the BIND TO THE PROPERTY OF THE SELECTED ATTRIBUTE radio button as shown in Figure 5.23.

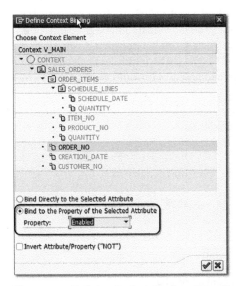

Figure 5.23 Defining Context Bindings Using Runtime Properties

If you look closely at Figure 5.23, you can see that there's also an INVERT ATTRIBUTE/PROPERTY ("NOT") checkbox that can be used to invert the value of a runtime property as needed. So, for example, if the readOnly property for a context attribute has a value of abap_false, the value abap_true will be used for the purposes of data binding.

5.4.5 Performing Housekeeping Duties within a Context

During the course of a WDA application session, we may need to move context elements around or even remove them from a context node collection altogether. In this section, we'll see how these tasks are carried out using methods of the IF_ WD_CONTEXT_NODE interface.

Removing Context Elements from a Node Collection

To remove a context element from a node collection, we can use the REMOVE_ELE- MENT() method. Listing 5.9 shows how this method can be used to remove the lead selection element from a node collection. We can determine whether or not the operation was successful using the resultant Boolean value from the method call.

```
DATA: lo_sales_orders_node TYPE REF TO if_wd_context_node,
      lo_sales_order_elem  TYPE REF TO if_wd_context_element,
      lv_removed           TYPE abap_bool.

"Remove the lead selection element from the collection:
lo_sales_orders_node = wd_context->get_child_node(
  name = wd_this->wdctx_sales_orders ).
lo_sales_order_elem = lo_sales_orders_node->get_element( ).

"The variable LV_REMOVED will tell us whether or not the
"operation was successful.
lv_removed =
  lo_sales_orders_node->remove_element(
    lo_sales_orders_elem ).
```

Listing 5.9 Removing Elements from a Node Collection

Once a context element is removed from the node collection, the context elements to the right of the removed element will be shifted to the left by one position. So, for example, if we have a node collection containing ten elements, and we remove the element at index five, the elements at indexes six through ten will shift left such that the element formerly at index six is now at index five, and so on.

Moving Context Elements within a Node Collection

Occasionally, we may want to adjust the order of context elements within a node collection. For instance, if we're using a node collection to represent the contents of a `Table` UI element, we may need to provide methods for sorting the elements in the node collection to correspond with sorting criteria specified within the view layer. For this task, we can enlist the aid of the `MOVE_ELEMENT()` method.

As the name suggests, the `MOVE_ELEMENT()` method allows us to move a context element from one index to another. Listing 5.10 demonstrates how this works. Here, we're using the `FROM` and `TO` parameters to determine the source and target indexes for the move operation.

```
DATA: lo_sales_orders_node TYPE REF TO if_wd_context_node.

"Move the element at position 4 to position 8:
lo_sales_orders_node = wd_context->get_child_node(
  name = wd_this->wdctx_sales_orders ).
lo_sales_orders_node->move_element( from = 4 to = 8 ).
```

Listing 5.10 Moving Elements Around Using MOVE_ELEMENT()

When working with the `MOVE_ELEMENT()` method, be aware that the underlying method implementation will silently adjust erroneous index values before performing the move operation. For example, if we were to pass a `FROM` value of –1 or a `TO` value greater than the size of the node collection, the method would move the context element at position 1 to the end of the list. Sometimes, this may be what you want, but it's nevertheless dangerous to leave this to chance. Therefore, when sorting node collections, we recommend you double-check your index-derivation logic and use the `GET_ELEMENT_COUNT()` method to make sure your indexes are in bounds.

5.4.6   Working with the Context Change Log

During the course of the lifecycle of a context, there will be many changes made to context nodes. At the outset, nodes collections will be filled in a controlled manner using API methods as demonstrated throughout the course of this section. From that point forward, however, changes may be initiated from a couple of different places:

▶ From users entering data in UI elements bound to context elements or context attributes contained within the node's element collection

▶ From event handler methods in controllers that are designed to add, change, or remove context elements on demand

Most of the time, any changes made to a context will need to be synchronized with the model layer. Though it's possible to perform these updates using a "kill-and-fill" approach in which updates are performed indiscriminately *en masse*, it can be much more efficient to update only the values that actually changed. Of course, the problem with the latter approach is trying to figure out exactly what was changed. In particular, we need to know what was changed by users at the view layer. Fortunately, the Web Dynpro framework provides us with a *context change log* that can be used to track changes made by users on the frontend. In this section, we'll see how to put this change log to use.

Flipping the Switch on the Context Change Log

Strictly speaking, the context change log is not associated with any particular context node. Instead, it's used to track changes made by users for *all* of the context nodes contained within the overarching controller context. Therefore, instead of being aligned with an instance of IF_WD_CONTEXT_NODE, the context change log is accessed via methods provided within the IF_WD_CONTEXT interface.

To turn on the context change log, we can use the ENABLE_CONTEXT_CHANGE_LOG() method demonstrated in Listing 5.11. Similarly, we can later turn off the context change log by calling the DISABLE_CONTEXT_CHANGE_LOG() method, which is also demonstrated in Listing 5.11.

```
"Obtain a reference to the overarching controller context:
DATA: lo_context TYPE REF TO if_wd_context.
lo_context = wd_context->get_context( ).
```

```
"Turn on the context change log:
lo_context->enable_context_change_log( ).

...

"Turn off the context change log:
lo_context->disable_context_change_log( ).
```

Listing 5.11 Turning on the Context Change Log

Accessing the Change Log

Once the context change log is turned on, it will begin silently tracking changes behind the scenes. At any point along the way, we can view the contents of the change log by invoking the GET_CONTEXT_CHANGE_LOG( ) method of the IF_WD_CON-TEXT interface. This method will return a table with a line type based on the WDR_CONTEXT_CHANGE structure illustrated in Figure 5.24. As you can see, this table provides us with access to the type of change, the corresponding context node/element/attribute, and the old/new values.

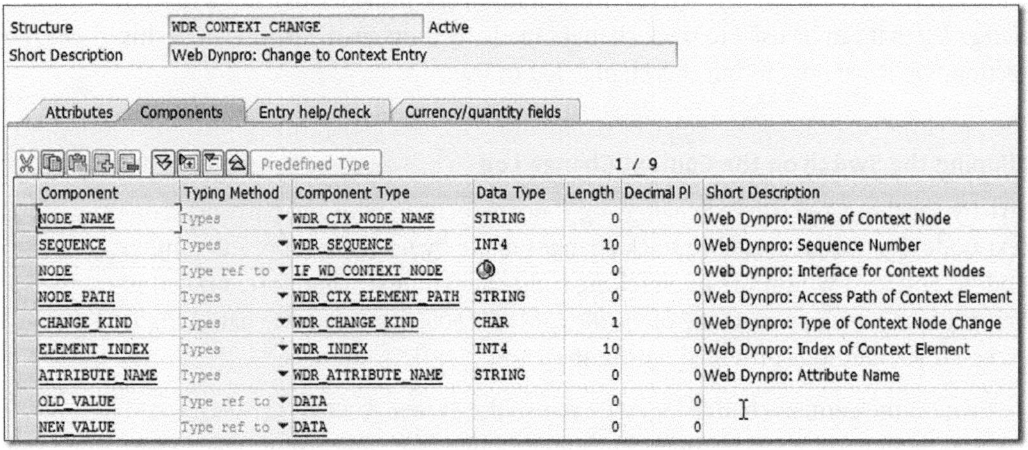

Structure	WDR_CONTEXT_CHANGE		Active			
Short Description	Web Dynpro: Change to Context Entry					

Attributes	Components	Entry help/check	Currency/quantity fields

Predefined Type   1 / 9

Component	Typing Method	Component Type	Data Type	Length	Decimal Pl	Short Description
NODE_NAME	Types	WDR_CTX_NODE_NAME	STRING	0	0	Web Dynpro: Name of Context Node
SEQUENCE	Types	WDR_SEQUENCE	INT4	10	0	Web Dynpro: Sequence Number
NODE	Type ref to	IF_WD_CONTEXT_NODE		0	0	Web Dynpro: Interface for Context Nodes
NODE_PATH	Types	WDR_CTX_ELEMENT_PATH	STRING	0	0	Web Dynpro: Access Path of Context Element
CHANGE_KIND	Types	WDR_CHANGE_KIND	CHAR	1	0	Web Dynpro: Type of Context Node Change
ELEMENT_INDEX	Types	WDR_INDEX	INT4	10	0	Web Dynpro: Index of Context Element
ATTRIBUTE_NAME	Types	WDR_ATTRIBUTE_NAME	STRING	0	0	Web Dynpro: Attribute Name
OLD_VALUE	Type ref to	DATA		0	0	
NEW_VALUE	Type ref to	DATA		0	0	

Figure 5.24 Evaluating Changes in the Context Change Log

If you're interested in seeing how all this works in an actual application, check out the DEMO_CONTEXT_CHANGES component in the SWDP_DEMO package. You can also find further details concerning the use of the context change log in the documentation for interface IF_WD_CONTEXT.

5.4.7 Tool Support for Context Programming

Hopefully by now you should feel comfortable enough with the context API to be able to perform basic CRUD operations within a context. However, if you forget how to perform a particular operation along the way, you can lean on the Web Dynpro code wizard to help jog your memory. As we learned in Chapter 4, we can access the code wizard within a controller method by clicking on the WEB DYNPRO CODE WIZARD button in the toolbar (see Figure 5.25).

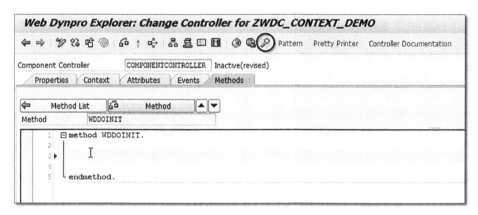

Figure 5.25 Accessing the Web Dynpro Code Wizard (Part 1)

After you initiate the wizard, you'll be presented with the familiar WEB DYNPRO STATEMENT STRUCTURE dialog box shown in Figure 5.26. Here, on the CONTEXT tab, you can use the input help for the NODE/ATTRIBUTE input field to select the target context node or attribute you want to access. Then, you can select from the available radio buttons to define the type of operation you want to perform. You can also select the AS TABLE OPERATION checkbox to perform bulk operations.

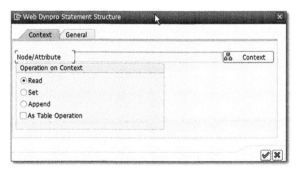

Figure 5.26 Accessing the Web Dynpro Code Wizard (Part 2)

As is the case with most code wizards, the generated code will most likely require some tweaking in order for everything to work correctly. Still, more often than not, this is much better than having to write the code from scratch.

5.5 Supply Functions

So far, our context programming examples have assumed that data is loaded into a context via regular controller methods (i.e., hook methods or instance methods). However, as we learned in Chapter 4, controllers also offer a specialized method type for this purpose: supply functions.

As the name suggests, supply functions are used to supply a context node with data on demand. As such, their implementations are relatively straightforward. In the upcoming sections, we'll look at how supply functions are used to streamline the context node initialization process.

5.5.1 Creating a Supply Function

Despite the use of the term *function*, supply functions are in fact controller methods. Therefore, they're created in much the same way that regular controller methods are created. Here, we have two options for creating a supply function:

1. We can manually create a supply function by navigating to the METHODS tab of the Controller Editor and filling in the method details in the provided input table, as shown in Figure 5.27. Then, once the supply function is created, we can associate it with a context node in the Context Editor, as shown in Figure 5.28.

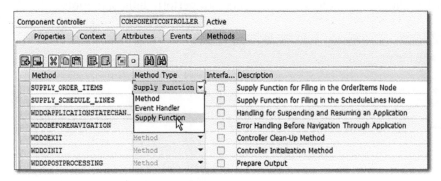

Figure 5.27 Creating a Supply Function (Part 1)

2. Alternatively, we can let the system automatically create the method for us by filling in the desired supply function name for the selected context node in the Context Editor screen, as shown in Figure 5.28. In this case, the supply function will be created silently behind the scenes if it doesn't exist already.

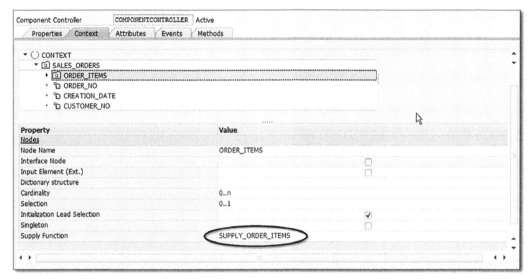

Figure 5.28 Creating a Supply Function (Part 2)

5.5.2 Implementing Supply Functions

Regardless of the approach taken to create a supply function, we'll end up with an empty method that defines two importing reference parameters:

▶ NODE

This parameter refers to the node whose element collection is being filled by the supply function. Naturally, this parameter is defined using the interface type IF_WD_CONTEXT_NODE.

▶ PARENT_ELEMENT

This parameter provides a reference to the parent element of the context node. It's defined using the interface type IF_WD_CONTEXT_ELEMENT.

With these two parameters in hand, we can implement a supply function by filling in the element collection for the selected context node using methods of the IF_WD_CONTEXT_NODE interface. Listing 5.12 demonstrates how this works for a supply function called SUPPLY_ORDER_ITEMS, which is used to fill in the ORDER_ ITEMS context node. As you can see, this implementation is mostly business as usual from a context programming perspective.

```
method SUPPLY_ORDER_ITEMS.
  "Method-Local Data Declarations:
  DATA: lt_order_items TYPE wd_this->Elements_order_items.
  FIELD-SYMBOLS:
    <lfs_order_item> LIKE LINE OF lt_order_items.

  "Add the sales order items to the node collection;
  "Note: This data would be normally obtained from
  "the model. We can use context attributes from the
  "PARENT_ELEMENT parameter as a key for performing
  "the lookup:
  APPEND INITIAL LINE TO lt_order_items
             ASSIGNING <lfs_order_item>.

  <lfs_order_item>-item_no    = `12345`.
  <lfs_order_item>-product_no = `1234567890`.
  <lfs_order_item>-quantity   = 10.

  node->bind_table(
    new_items = lt_order_items
    set_initial_elements = abap_true ).
endmethod.
```

Listing 5.12 A Supply Function Example

5.5.3 Understanding How Supply Functions Are Invoked

In general, supply functions are invoked automatically by the Web Dynpro framework to fill a context node whenever one of the following conditions is satisfied:

▸ The context node is initial or not yet filled.

▸ The context node has been *invalidated* at a previous step.

While the first condition makes intuitive sense, the second condition requires some additional description.

During the lifecycle of a context node, there may be times when the contents context node becomes *dirty*. This could be as a result of a change in the model layer, upstream node changes, etc. Regardless of the root cause, we need to make sure the node gets refreshed so that data remains in sync. Here, we could manually clean up the node using context API methods, or we could defer the initialization to supply functions. In the latter case, we must *invalidate* the context node in order for the Web Dynpro framework to determine that it needs to be refreshed.

Context nodes can be invalidated in two ways:

▸ The Web Dynpro framework will automatically invalidate a singleton node whenever the lead selection in the parent node changes.

▸ You can also manually invalidate context nodes using the INVALIDATE() method provided with the IF_WD_CONTEXT_NODE interface.

Once a context node is invalidated, the Web Dynpro framework will take care of invoking the node's corresponding supply function behind the scenes. We'll examine how this works for singleton nodes in the next section.

5.5.4 Supply Functions and Singleton Nodes

One of the most common use cases for supply functions is to automate the synchronization of singleton child nodes. To understand how this works, let's take a closer look at how the ORDER_ITEMS singleton node is filled using the SUPPLY_ORDER_ITEMS() supply function, as shown in Listing 5.12.

If you recall from Section 5.2.4, only a single instance of a singleton node will be created at runtime. This single node instance corresponds with the lead selection element of the parent node. So, in the case of our SALES_ORDERS context, we want to use the SUPPLY_ORDER_ITEMS() supply function to populate the ORDER_ITEMS node collection each time the lead selection changes in the parent SALES_ORDERS node.

Fortunately, the Web Dynpro framework will initiate the synchronization process automatically by invalidating the ORDER_ITEMS node each time the lead selection for the SALES_ORDERS node changes. Then, it will invoke the SUPPLY_ORDER_ITEMS() method, passing to it a reference to the ORDER_ITEMS singleton node and the lead selection element from the parent SALES_ORDERS node. The supply function can then use these references to fill in the ORDER_ITEMS node collection based on the selected SALES_ORDERS context element, as demonstrated in Listing 5.12.

5.6   Context Mapping and Data Binding: Up Close

Before we conclude our discussion on contexts, we should take a moment to revisit the concepts of context mapping and data binding in light of what we've learned in this chapter. That way, you'll have a clearer picture of what's going on behind the scenes.

5.6.1   How Context Mapping Works

As we observed in Section 5.1.2, the data within a WDA component flows downstream from the model layer to the view layer as follows:

1. First, data is extracted from the model layer via a service call performed in a global controller method.
2. Then, the extracted data is loaded into the global controller's context using the context API, as demonstrated in Section 5.4.
3. Once the data is loaded into the global controller context, it will be made visible to downstream views via context mapping relationships.
4. Finally, the data will become visible in UI elements through data binding relationships.

From a conceptual point of view, there's an invisible line that separates steps one and two from steps three and four. This line represents the virtual barrier that exists between the controller and view layers. Here, the controller layer *produces* data by loading model data into a global controller context, and the view layer then *consumes* this data using declaratively defined mapping relationships. The question is: how does this implicit data transfer occur?

As we've seen, context mapping relationships are declaratively defined within a controller by dragging and dropping a context node from a used controller into the controller's context. Once the relationship is defined, a copy of the mapped context node will be created within the referencing controller's context (see Figure 5.29). As evidenced by the little arrow icon underneath it, this copied node effectively points to the node it's mapping from. In other words, you can think of this copied node as an alias that can be used to address the mapped node at runtime.

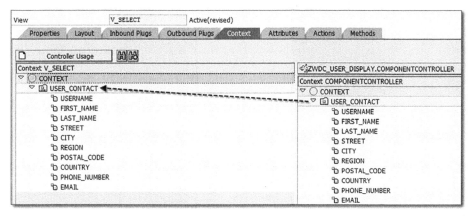

Figure 5.29 Defining a Context Mapping Relationship

If we think about the implied meaning of terms like *pointer* and *alias*, we can begin to grasp the nature of context mapping relationships from a runtime perspective. Though there are two copies of the mapped node at design time, there is in fact only *one* copy of the context node data at runtime: the one maintained within the used controller. Thus, any references to the copied node indirectly refer to the mapped node in the used controller. There are a couple of major benefits to this approach:

1. First of all, it improves performance by avoiding unnecessary memory copy steps between controllers.

2. Secondly, it further reinforces the principle of strict separation of producers and consumers from the MVC paradigm by ensuring that data is transferred between controller and view layers in a controlled and automated manner.

The great thing about all this from a developer's perspective is that the Web Dynpro framework takes care of managing these references for us behind the scenes. Therefore, not a single line of ABAP code is required to shuffle the data back and forth between controllers.

5.6.2 How Data Binding Works

Once data makes its way into a view controller context, it can be made available to selected UI elements within the view layout by declaratively defining *data binding relationships*. As you can see in Figure 5.30, these data bindings formally associate a UI element property with a context node or context attribute. This bi-directional relationship provides the Web Dynpro framework with the meta-data it needs to determine how to map values back and forth between a UI element property and the corresponding context node or context attribute it's bound to.

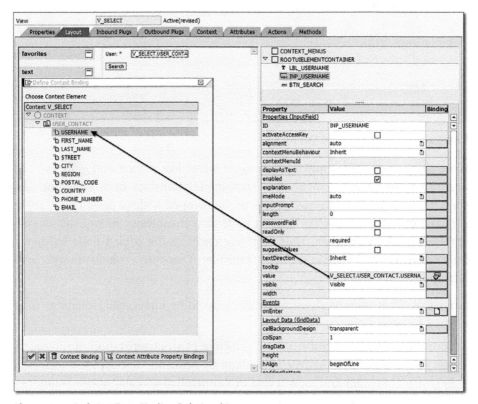

Figure 5.30 Defining Data Binding Relationships

At runtime, data transfer is carried out automatically by the Web Dynpro framework in two distinct places:

► At the beginning of the request/response cycle, data input by the user is transported from the various UI elements to their corresponding context nodes and context attributes.

► At the end of the request/response cycle, data is copied from context nodes and context attributes into the UI elements during the client rendering phase so that it can be displayed on the screen.

Though all this is shielded from developers, rest assured that this data transfer does not occur by magic. Behind the scenes, the Web Dynpro framework is utilizing the context API to transfer data to and from the context. On the other side of this exchange, the framework queries/sets the properties of UI elements using their corresponding runtime classes. Here, for example, to copy data to or from an `InputField` UI element, the framework would utilize the standard runtime class `CL_WD_INPUT_FIELD`. This class provides getter and setter methods such as `GET_VALUE()` and `SET_VALUE()`, which allow the framework to access the `value` property of an `InputField` element programmatically. We'll get a taste for some of this when we look at dynamic programming concepts in Chapter 11.

5.7   Summary

In this chapter, we explored the Web Dynpro context from several different angles. We began by analyzing the structure of contexts from both a conceptual and technical point of view. From there, we observed how these context hierarchies are declaratively defined using the Context Editor tool. Next, we surveyed the interfaces and methods that make up the context programming API, demonstrating how this API could be used to manipulate a context at runtime. Finally, we concluded our discussion by reviewing context mapping and data-binding concepts.

While context programming is certainly not one of the flashier topics related to WDA programming, it's right up there among the most important ones. So, suffice it to say that we'll see the concepts described in this chapter again and again as we progress through the rest of this book.

In the next chapter, we'll shift gears and begin looking at UI development concepts. Specifically, we'll take a closer look at windows and views and see how they're used to arrange the UI layout within the view layer.

Windows and views lay the foundation for user interfaces that are rendered via the Web Dynpro framework. Therefore, in this chapter, we'll get the ball rolling with user interface design by taking a look at these core elements and their interdependencies.

6   Windows and Views

With such a rich palette of UI elements to draw from, it can be very tempting to develop the user interface of WDA applications in an ad hoc manner by simply dragging and dropping UI elements onto the canvas and moving them around until we come up with a design that looks good on the screen. Of course, while this approach may work out okay for smaller applications, it can get us into trouble when we begin tackling more advanced application scenarios. Here, one of the subtle challenges of UI design is figuring out how to organize the content in such a way that users can easily find what they're looking for.

In her book *Designing Interfaces*, Jenifer Tidwell suggests that in order to guide users through a user interface, we must define a layout that "conveys meaning, sequence, and points of interaction." In effect, we must plan "the informational 'space' where people will dwell" (O'Reilly, 2006). Within the Web Dynpro framework, we can define these layouts and set the boundaries for the user interface using the properties of windows and views. Then, once the overall layout patterns are established, the rest of the application design process should flow much more smoothly.

In this chapter, we'll take a closer look at windows and views and see how they're used to design user interfaces. Once we've mastered these concepts, we'll be ready to begin considering advanced user interface design techniques in Chapters 7 and 8.

6.1   Windows

Ever since graphical user interfaces (GUIs) first exploded onto the scene in the mid-1980s, the "window" metaphor has become so commonplace that its description requires little introduction. Put simply, windows are used to provide a frame around a user interface, presenting a 2-D viewport to the user. In this regard, it's appropriate to think of windows as containers for other graphical objects (e.g., views, UI elements, and so on).

Within the Web Dynpro framework, windows are positioned as the top-level container within the logically defined user interface. Therefore, they play a key role in fixing the boundaries of the user interface. For example, when accessing a WDA application through a traditional web browser, there's a one-to-one correspondence between a window in a WDA component and the browser window on your local machine. Once these boundaries are established, the Web Dynpro framework has a clear baseline to work from when rendering the user interface.

In this section, we'll take a closer look at windows and the roles they play within the Web Dynpro framework. Along the way, we'll show you how windows are used to organize the view layout, create interactive dialogs, and more.

6.1.1   Windows as a View Container

As we've seen, the majority of the details of a UI design are captured within views. However, in order for a view to be displayed within the user interface, it must first be *embedded* within a window. Figure 6.1 illustrates this relationship for a WDA application displayed within a web browser. Here, we can see that the embedded view defines the visual area within the window, while the window itself acts as a container element that corresponds with the overarching user agent window.

Though it's possible to embed multiple views within a window, only one of those views can be visible within the UI at a time. There are several factors that determine which view should be displayed at a given point in time:

▶ By default, the initial view that will be displayed within a window is the one whose Default property is selected within the Window Editor (see Figure 6.2).

▶ Alternatively, a window can dynamically determine its initial view within the event handler method of a defined inbound plug. Here, parameters mapped from the overarching WDA application might be used to initialize the display.

▶ Once the initial view is loaded, users can navigate to other views by triggering events that fire navigation plugs.

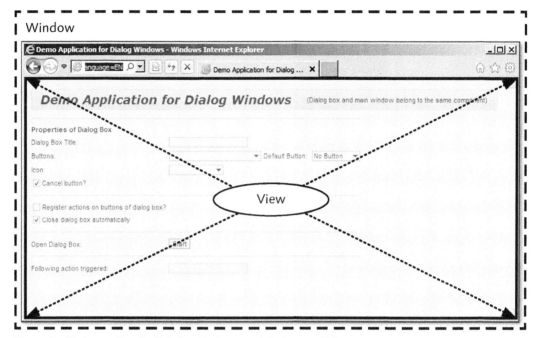

Figure 6.1 Understanding the Relationship between Windows and Views

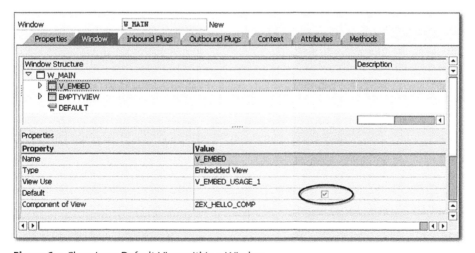

Figure 6.2 Choosing a Default View within a Window

Embedding Views in Windows

As we observed in Chapter 3, the process of embedding a view in a window is very straightforward. Here, we must perform the following steps:

1. First, we must open the window within the Window Editor and select the WINDOW tab.

2. Then, in the WINDOW STRUCTURE tree table, we must right-click on the window node and select the EMBED VIEW menu option (see Figure 6.3).

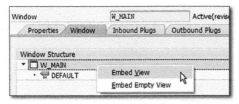

Figure 6.3 Embedding a View in a Window (Part 1)

3. This will open the WEB DYNPRO: EMBED VIEW dialog box shown in Figure 6.4. Here, we can use the input help in the VIEW TO BE EMBEDDED input field to select the target view we want to embed. This input help allows us to select only from the list of available views that haven't been embedded in the window already.

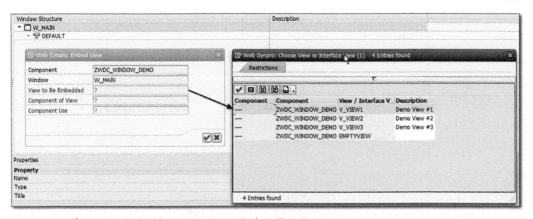

Figure 6.4 Embedding a View in a Window (Part 2)

4. Finally, once we confirm our selection, the embedded view will be displayed within the WINDOW STRUCTURE hierarchy shown in Figure 6.5.

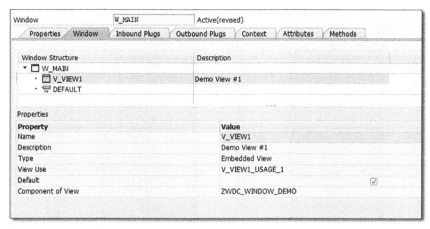

Figure 6.5 Embedding a View in a Window (Part 3)

Nested View Hierarchies

As we've seen, it's possible to display only a single view within a window at a given time. However, there may be times when we want to build a more complex view set within a window. For example, imagine we're building a WDA application to maintain a complex transactional document like a purchase order. Here, we'd want to divide the user interface in such a way that we isolate header and line item level data, etc. Though it's possible to organize this content within a single monolithic view, such an approach would limit our ability to reuse these elements in other scenarios since the overarching view is so complex.

Fortunately, we can get around this limitation by using a special UI element type called `ViewContainerUIElement`. This UI element can be used to embed one or more child views within a given view. To understand how this works, let's consider the window structure diagram depicted in Figure 6.6. Here, at the outermost layer, you can see we have a window that has embedded a view we'll assume to be the default view. This default view maintains a UI element hierarchy nested underneath the default `RootUIElementContainer` element as usual. It's underneath this element that things start to get interesting. Rather than directly appending a series of UI elements (e.g., labels, input fields, buttons, etc.) to the UI element hierarchy, the default view has embedded several `ViewContainerUIElement` elements. These `ViewContainerUIElement` elements, in turn, allow us to embed child views within the UI element hierarchy similarly to subscreens in classic Dynpro or iframes in HTML.

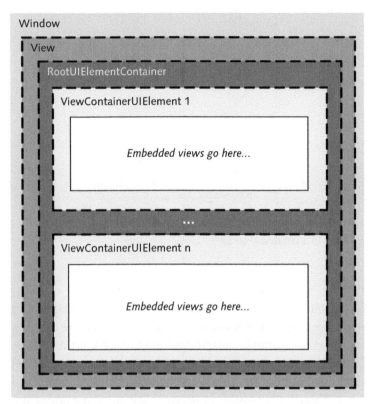

Figure 6.6 Understanding the Positioning of Nested Views

Since a view is defined as an element that describes the layout and behavior of a rectangular area of a user interface, we can insert views into places where we might otherwise plug in generic UI element containers such as panels, groups, or trays. In this regard, it's appropriate to think of the ViewContainerUIElement element as a placeholder for embedding reusable portions of a user interface defined in other views. Here, we could be talking about other views within the same WDA component, or interface views provided with a used component.

Now that you have a feel for the positioning of the ViewContainerUIElement within the UI element hierarchy, let's see how they're used to embed views using the View and Window Editor tools. To guide us through this exercise, we'll demonstrate the embedding of two child views within a parent view, yielding a window structure similar to the one illustrated in Figure 6.6.

1. To begin, we must open the parent view in the View Editor and navigate to the LAYOUT tab. Here, we'll insert a couple of `ViewContainerUIElement` elements into the UI element hierarchy by right-clicking on the top-level `RootUIElement-Container` node and selecting the INSERT ELEMENT menu option (see Figure 6.7).

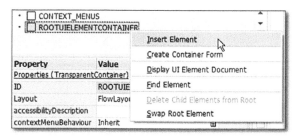

Figure 6.7 Working with ViewContainerUIElement Elements (Part 1)

2. Then, in the CREATE ELEMENT dialog box shown in Figure 6.8, we can create the new `ViewContainerUIElement` as usual. For the purposes of this exercise, we'll perform this step twice to create two view containers: `VCUI_TOPVIEW` and `VCUI_BOTTOMVIEW`.

Figure 6.8 Working with ViewContainerUIElement Elements (Part 2)

3. After we activate our changes in the parent view, we can open the view's parent window to view the changes in the window structure. As you can see in Figure 6.9, our parent view (`V_VIEW1`) now has two child view containers nested underneath it: the `VCUI_TOPVIEW` and `VCUI_BOTTOMVIEW` view containers created in the previous step. To embed a view within these view containers, we can right-click on them and select the EMBED VIEW menu option (see Figure 6.9).

4. This will open the familiar WEB DYNPRO: EMBED A VIEW dialog box (see Figure 6.10). Within this dialog box, we can choose from views defined within the same WDA component, or in used components.

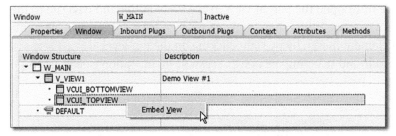

Figure 6.9 Embedding a View within a ViewContainerUIElement (Part 1)

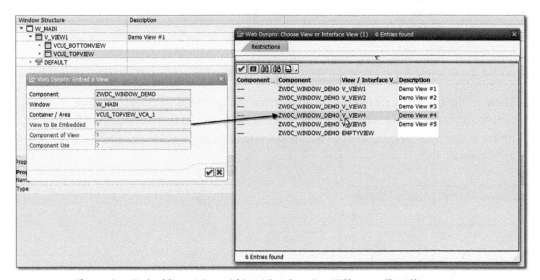

Figure 6.10 Embedding a View within a ViewContainerUIElement (Part 2)

5. After we confirm our selection(s), the nested views will show up in the WIN-DOW STRUCTURE hierarchy, as shown in Figure 6.11.

Figure 6.11 Embedding a View within a ViewContainerUIElement (Part 3)

If we want, we can continue to extend the window structure out by embedding additional child views underneath nested views. However, most of the time, it's a good idea to avoid building nested hierarchies that are too deep, if you can help it. Indeed, if you have to build such a nested hierarchy, it's very likely that your UI layout is probably too complicated.

Empty Views

Whenever we build complex view hierarchies like the ones demonstrated in the previous section, there may be times when you'll want certain portions of the user interface to be blank. For instance, a best practice in UI design is to *reveal* portions of the user interface in stages. That way, a user isn't overwhelmed with a busy user interface that's difficult to comprehend at first glance.

To achieve an incremental UI design, we can enlist the aid of *empty views*. As the name suggests, empty views are basically just empty placeholder views that can be embedded within a view hierarchy. To understand how empty views are used, consider the view hierarchy depicted in Figure 6.12. As you can see, we're using the `ViewContainerUIElement` element to define the layout of a simple report, which contains a selection view up top and a results view down below. However, the results view in the bottom portion of the screen is not displayed by default. Instead, the bottom portion of the screen is occupied by a default empty view. This approach helps to draw the users' attention to the selection view area, allowing them to focus on filling in the requisite selection criteria. Then, when the user executes the report (by clicking a button, let's say), the results view can be swapped in via navigation plugs as usual.

Technically speaking, empty views don't really exist in the same way that normal views do within a WDA component. Therefore, we cannot open them in the View Editor tool, define navigation plugs within them, and so on. However, aside from this base-level difference, you'll find that working with empty views is no different from working with normal views. For example, as you can see in Figure 6.13, empty views are embedded within the window structure in the same way that normal views are. Once an empty view is embedded within a window/view, you can also promote it to default view by right-clicking on it and selecting the SET AS DEFAULT menu option (see Figure 6.14).

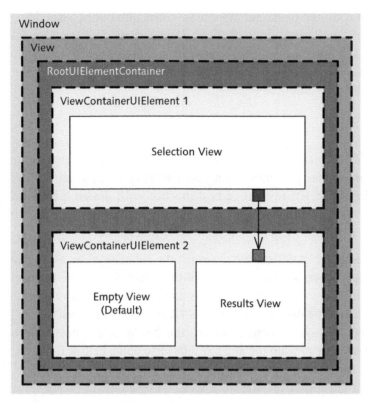

Figure 6.12 Working with Empty Views

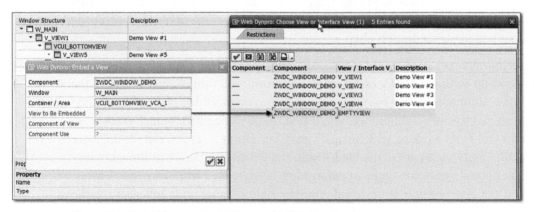

Figure 6.13 Embedding an Empty View to the Window Structure

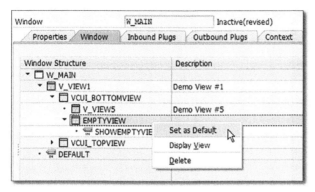

Figure 6.14 Setting an Empty View as the Default View

Besides making the user interface more intuitive, the use of empty views in certain situations can lead to improved performance on the client side. After all, it's much faster to render an empty view than it is to render a complex results view. So, if we know ahead of time that a particular view area isn't needed, it's in our best interest to hide it so we can avoid the overhead of having to render it on the frontend.

6.1.2 Interface Views

So far, we've seen how windows are used to combine a series of related views together. However, if we zoom out a bit and look at the larger picture, we can see that windows also play another important role within the Web Dynpro framework: exposing the visual interface of a WDA component to the outside world. This visual interface is referred to as an *interface view*. In this section, we'll look at how interface views are used to link windows with WDA applications and other WDA components.

What are Interface Views?

Conceptually speaking, interface views are logical constructs that are implicitly defined in reference to a window. Indeed, whenever we create a window, the system will automatically create an interface view with the same name behind the scenes underneath the COMPONENT INTERFACE • INTERFACE VIEWS node (see Figure 6.15).

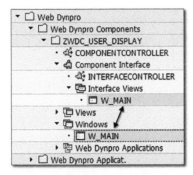

Figure 6.15 Relationship between a Window and an Interface View

Once an interface view is created, we can view its definition by double-clicking on it. This will open up the interface view in the read-only editor window shown in Figure 6.16. As you can see, an interface view definition consists of the view's name and a series of outbound and inbound plugs. We'll see how these plugs are defined and maintained in Section 6.3.2.

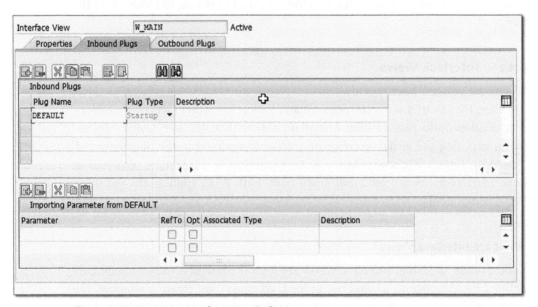

Figure 6.16 Viewing an Interface View Definition

From a logical perspective, it's appropriate to think of interface views as representing the virtual interface of a window. In other words, interface views provide an integration point into the navigation structure of a window. This navigation structure is realized in the form of navigation plugs, as is the case for views. As it turns out, these resemblances aren't coincidental. Rather, SAP purposefully defined windows this way in order to support advanced composition scenarios — a concept we'll explore further in just a moment.

Interface Views and WDA Applications

One place where we've seen interface views at work already is in the definition of WDA applications. Here, as demonstrated in Figure 6.17, the interface view provides an integration point between a WDA application and a window via a specialized inbound plug designated as the *startup plug*. Whenever a WDA application is accessed at runtime, the runtime environment will use these bindings to determine which window to load into the user interface.

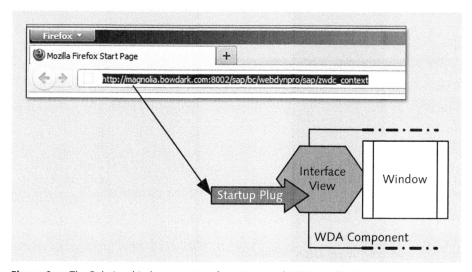

Figure 6.17 The Relationship between Interface Views and WDA Applications

In some respects, the relationship between a WDA application and an interface view is analogous to the one maintained between a transaction code and the initial screen to be displayed in classic Dynpro applications. These similarities are illustrated in Figure 6.18 and Figure 6.19, respectively. In the former case, you can see the definition for the familiar ABAP Dictionary Transaction SE11. Here, the transaction definition binds Transaction SE11 with program DD_START and screen 1000. In the latter case, you can see that WDA application ZWDA_USER_DISPLAY is linked to the W_MAIN interface view of component ZWDC_USER_DISPLAY. This linkage provides the Web Dynpro runtime environment with the information it needs to determine which inbound plug to fire on the interface view of the target WDA component.

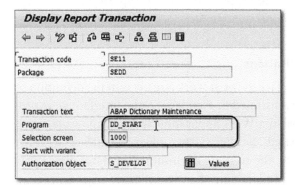

Figure 6.18 Linking a Transaction to a Classic Dynpro Screen

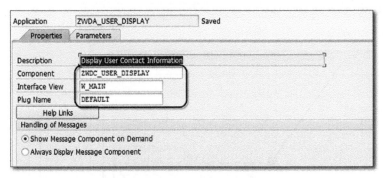

Figure 6.19 Linking a WDA Application with an Interface View

Cross-Component Integration Scenarios

So far, we've been focused primarily on the development of simple WDA applications based on a single WDA component. However, in the real world, many WDA applications are *composites*, weaving together functionality from a multitude of WDA components. These inter-component linkages are made possible through a WDA component's interface, which consists of:

▶ **Interface controller**
The interface controller provides a programmatic interface that can be used to integrate with a WDA component. Here, the interface controller exposes

selected elements (e.g., methods, events, etc.) from the component controller to the outside world.

▸ **Interface views**
Interface views make up the visual part of the component interface. As we've seen, interface views provide an integration point into the navigation structure of a window.

Though we'll have an opportunity to explore component-based development scenarios in more detail in Chapter 9, we do need to take a moment to consider the roles interface views play in all this.

Back in Section 6.1.1, we observed how user interfaces are designed by embedding various views within a window. However, when it comes to leveraging portions of another WDA component's user interface, it would seem we have a gap on our hands since views aren't included within the component interface. As it turns out, this perceived disparity is of little concern since windows are positioned as composites within the Web Dynpro framework.

Understanding the Composite Design Pattern

In their classic software engineering text, *Design Patterns: Elements of Reusable Object-Oriented Software* (Addison-Wesley, 1995), Erich Gamma, et al. introduce a series of structural design patterns that can be used to combine various objects to form larger structures or assemblies. One of the most prominent patterns in this collection is the *composite pattern*, which allows (software) clients to "treat individual objects and compositions of objects uniformly."

The key to the composite pattern is coming up with a uniform interface that clients can work off of. Once this interface is established, a client doesn't care if it's interfacing with an individual object or a set of objects; the behavior is the same in both cases.

Relating this back to Web Dynpro, we can see that the only thing a window really needs in order to embed a view is the view's name and a series of navigational plugs to enable navigation. Since interface views provide all this, the framework can use views and interface views interchangeably. In other words, from the window's perspective, since the *interface* is the same for both objects, it doesn't really care what kind of view it's embedding as long as the view provides the hooks it needs to integrate with the user interface.

When we look at interface views in this light, it's appropriate to think of them as being interchangeable with views from a conceptual point of view. However, there is a catch to all this. While it's perfectly acceptable to embed an interface view of *another* WDA component in a window structure (see Figure 6.20), it's not permitted to embed an interface view from within the *same* WDA component. So, for example, if we have a WDA component that defines two windows called W_WINDOW1 and W_WINDOW2, we can't embed the W_WINDOW2 interface view within the window structure of W_WINDOW1.

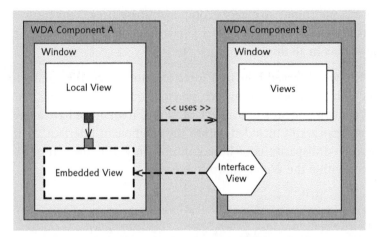

Figure 6.20 Embedding an Interface View into a Window Structure

We'll get back into cross-component development scenarios in Chapter 9. However, now that you're aware of these reuse possibilities, we encourage you to be mindful of these concepts as we take a closer look at UI layouts in Chapters 7 and 8. Once you realize that you can reuse portions of a user interface in multiple scenarios, it dramatically changes the way you approach the UI design process.

6.1.3 Dialog Boxes and Popup Windows

Most modern UI toolkits provide us with a means for presenting users with dialog boxes and popup windows, and Web Dynpro is no exception. Such dialog boxes and popup windows can be used to prompt users for specific pieces of information crucial for completing a dialog step. For example, some common usages include:

▶ Displaying alert messages.

▶ Prompting the user to confirm some sort of selection or event using a series of buttons (e.g., YES or NO, OK or CANCEL, and so on).

- Providing the user with more information about a particular element within the user interface in the manner of the ⌑F1⌑ help offered with classic Dynpro screens.

- Presenting users with an input help screen to assist them in making various selection choices.

- Partitioning off optional parts of dialog steps. For instance, when a user clicks a button to add a record to a table, the input mask for the record entry might be displayed in a popup window so the user doesn't have to navigate away to create the new record.

Figure 6.21 demonstrates an example of a popup window in an SAP demo application called DEMO_POPUPS_01. As you can see, this popup window contains a title bar with familiar window controls that can be used to close the popup window, shrink or expand it, and so on.

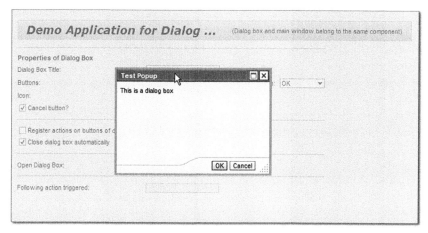

Figure 6.21 A Popup Window in a WDA Application

In the upcoming subsections, we'll take a closer look at popup windows and see how they can be utilized within various application scenarios.

Creating Popup Windows

From a development perspective, a popup window is nothing more than a regular window that's been opened programmatically via an API call. Listing 6.1 demonstrates the basic call sequence. As you can see, there are three basic steps required:

1. First, we obtain a reference to the Web Dynpro window manager.

2. Then, we use the window manager's CREATE_WINDOW( ) method to create a new window object.

3. Finally, we use the window's OPEN( ) method to open the window.

Along the way, we may choose to tweak various aspects of the window layout and orientation, but the basic steps required to create the window remain the same.

```
METHOD open_window.
  DATA: lo_comp_api   TYPE REF TO if_wd_component,
        lo_window_mgr TYPE REF TO if_wd_window_manager,
        lo_window     TYPE REF TO if_wd_window.

  "Obtain a reference to the Web Dynpro window manager:
  lo_comp_api = wd_comp_controller->wd_get_api( ).
  lo_window_mgr = lo_comp_api->get_window_manager( ).

  "Create the window reference:
  lo_window =
    lo_window_mgr->create_window(
      window_name = 'W_POPUP'
      title       = `Demo Popup`
      "Window properties go here...
      ... ).

  "Open up the window:
  lo_window->open( ).
ENDMETHOD.
```

Listing 6.1 Opening a Popup Window

Looking over the code excerpt in Listing 6.1, you can see that popup windows utilize a couple of interfaces that we haven't had much opportunity to work with before now. The UML class diagram in Figure 6.22 describes the makeup of these interfaces and their relationship to other core elements within the framework. As you can see, the API provides quite a few methods that can be used to customize the look and feel of a popup window at runtime. In particular, we can use the IF_WD_WINDOW interface to adjust the popup window's size, position, and so on.

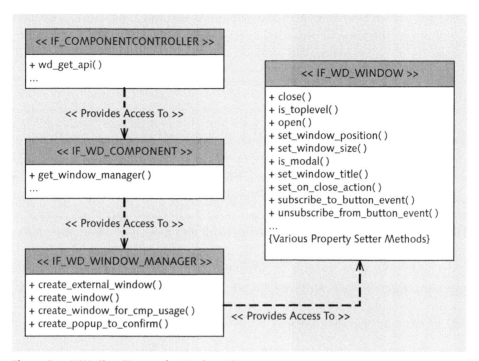

Figure 6.22 UML Class Diagram for Window API

As you browse through the UML class diagram in Figure 6.22, pay attention to several nuances within the window API:

▶ First of all, we should point out that most Web Dynpro popup windows are classified as *modal*. In effect, this means that, while the child window is open, a user cannot access the parent window. In order to get back to the parent window, the user must close the popup window.

▶ The only exception to the modal rule is for popup windows created using the CREATE_EXTERNAL_WINDOW( ) method of interface IF_WD_WINDOW_MANAGER. In this case, though, we're not opening a window defined within a WDA component. Instead, the CREATE_EXTERNAL_WINDOW( ) method uses its URL parameter to determine which URL to open up in a separate browser window. The application loaded into this external window runs in its own session, and is independent of the WDA application that spawned it.

▶ Finally, note that the IF_WD_WINDOW_MANAGER interface provides a method called CREATE_WINDOW_FOR_CMP_USAGE( ) that can be used to open a window from a used WDA component as a popup. As you might expect, this method utilizes the interface view defined in relation to the window, and not the window itself. We'll see how this works in Chapter 9.

The Lifecycle of Popup Windows

Unlike normal windows, whose lifecycles mirror that of their overarching WDA application, popup windows have a finite shelf life that begins when they're created and ends sometime shortly after they're no longer referenced somewhere within the defining WDA component. This reference can be either *implicit* or *explicit*. For example, with the code excerpt in Listing 6.1, the popup window reference LO_WINDOW goes out of scope once the VIEW_METHOD() method is complete. Thus, from that point forward, the framework will hang onto an implicit reference to the window as long as the window remains open on the frontend. Once it's closed, the reference is lost forever. On the other hand, had we defined our window reference as a controller attribute, we'd have an explicit reference to the window we could open and close as needed using the OPEN() and CLOSE() methods of the IF_WD_WINDOW interface.

In general, we recommend you define your popup window references as controller attributes, preferably within a global controller such as the component controller. That way, you have fine-grained control over the window reference throughout the course of its lifespan. Furthermore, defining the window reference in a global controller makes it easier to leverage the popup window at various locations within a WDA component.

Event Coordination Concepts

Once you get past all the initial setup required to open a popup window, you'll find that life inside a popup window is not all that different from what we've already seen with regular windows. In other words, you still have all the same elements to work with that you have in any other window: embedded views, navigational plugs, and so on. Furthermore, the embedded views still receive their data from upstream global controllers as usual.

For the most part, the biggest challenge popup windows present is with *event coordination*. Here, an action triggered in a child popup window might cause elements within the parent window to need to be refreshed. For example, imagine we've created a WDA application to maintain purchase orders. Within this application, suppose we're using a popup window to provide an input help that allows users to search for and select purchase orders. In this case, whenever the user makes a selection in the popup dialog box, we need to communicate that change back to the parent window so it can load the selected PO document into context.

In general, when it comes to event coordination between windows in a WDA component, we can employ several different techniques:

▶ Often, we can rely on features of the Web Dynpro context to automatically synchronize the two windows. For example, with our PO example above, we could simply invalidate the PO context node within the popup window and then rely on a supply function to take care of synchronizing the data displayed within the parent window.

▶ We can use methods or events defined in global controllers to trigger synchronization.

▶ For popup windows managed within a view, we can use the SUBSCRIBE_TO_BUTTON_EVENT() method to link a button from the popup window with an action defined in the managing view.

Having seen how to perform the first two techniques in Chapters 4 and 5, let's take a closer look at the third technique on the list. To demonstrate this technique, we'll extend our example from Listing 6.1 to include the registration of a pair of window buttons and actions defined with the triggering view. Listing 6.2 shows the resulting code. As you can see, we're registering these actions via the SUBSCRIBE_TO_BUTTON_EVENT(), which takes in the button we wish to monitor, the name of the action used to capture the event, and a reference to the view's controller, which is needed to dynamically bind these elements together.

```
METHOD open_window.
  DATA: lo_comp_api   TYPE REF TO if_wd_component,
        lo_view_api   TYPE REF TO if_wd_view_controller,
        lo_window_mgr TYPE REF TO if_wd_window_manager.

  "Obtain a reference to the Web Dynpro window manager:
  lo_comp_api = wd_comp_controller->wd_get_api( ).
  lo_window_mgr = lo_comp_api->get_window_manager( ).

  "Also obtain a reference to the view controller:
  lo_view_api = wd_this->wd_get_api( ).
```

```
"Create the window reference:
wd_this->popup_window =
  lo_window_mgr->create_window(
    window_name = 'W_POPUP'
    title       = `Demo Popup`
    button_kind = if_wd_window=>co_buttons_yesno ).

"Register actions with the Yes and No buttons:
wd_this->popup_window->subscribe_to_button_event(
    button      = if_wd_window=>co_button_yes
    action_name = 'YES_CLICKED'
    action_view = lo_view_api ).

wd_this->popup _window->subscribe_to_button_event(
    button      = if_wd_window=>co_button_no
    action_name = 'NO_CLICKED'
    action_view = lo_view_api ).

"Open up the window:
wd_this->popup_window->open( ).
ENDMETHOD.
```

Listing 6.2 Registering Actions with Buttons in a Popup window

Figure 6.23 illustrates the event process flow at runtime. As you can see, whenever the popup buttons are clicked, the event will be propagated back to the subscribing view's registered action. From there, we can use the view's action handler method to react to the event as necessary.

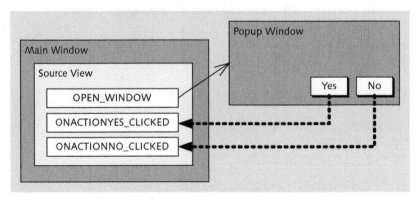

Figure 6.23 Understanding the Event Flow for Button Subscription

Usage Recommendations

As we've seen throughout the course of this section, it's relatively easy to open a popup window and pass data back and forth. However, it's important not to get too carried away with popup windows because they can degrade the performance of WDA applications. In general, we recommend you use popup windows sparingly, preferring to use regular window navigation where it makes sense.

Also, it's a good idea to avoid building nested popup stacks whenever possible. Here, we're talking about popup windows spawned from within popup windows. This can get confusing for the user in a hurry, and will probably come off as an annoyance.

Finally, in Chapter 10, we'll take a look at some of the built-in input help technologies that SAP provides within the Web Dynpro framework. Often, these built-in solutions can be used in the place of custom popup windows with little to no custom development required.

6.2 Views

According to the SAP help documentation, and as we explained earlier, a view "describes the layout and behavior of a rectangular area of a user interface." Therefore, it's appropriate to think of views as like a canvas upon which we can lay out and configure various parts of a user interface. From here, views can then be integrated into the overall user interface design by embedding them in windows as described in the previous section.

In this section, we'll have a closer look at views and see how UI elements are arranged within them internally. Having a firm grasp on these concepts will serve us well as we consider advanced UI design techniques in Chapters 7 and 8.

6.2.1 Views: Revisited

Whenever a WDA application is accessed by a user agent at runtime, the Web Dynpro runtime environment must translate the logical user interface defined using Web Dynpro metadata objects into a physical user interface. This transformation process begins with the mapping of the outermost UI element in the Web Dynpro UI element hierarchy—windows—and proceeds on from there with the rendering of embedded views. So, for instance, if we were to access a WDA application using a web browser, the transformation process would proceed as follows:

▸ First, the window/interface view associated with the application would be mapped to the browser window.

▸ Then, the embedded view elements would need to be translated into corresponding HTML elements.

In order to ensure a smooth transformation process, UI elements must be organized hierarchically within a view using various container elements, as illustrated in Figure 6.24. At the base of this hierarchy, we have the default `RootUIElement-Container` element, which serves as the top-level container for embedding UI elements within the view. Within this container, we can embed various UI elements, which can be divided conceptually into two broad categories:

▸ **Interactive elements**
Interactive elements allow users to view and edit data and trigger various kinds of events. Examples of interactive elements include input fields, dropdown lists, buttons, and so on.

▸ **Layout elements**
Layout elements organize interactive elements (and sometimes other layout elements) within the layout. Examples of layout elements include groups, panels, tab strips, and other container-like elements.

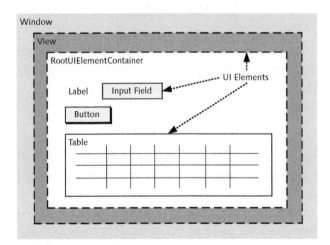

Figure 6.24 Web Dynpro UI Element Hierarchy

As we've seen, the UI element hierarchy is defined within the View Designer tool, which can be accessed via the LAYOUT tab of the View Editor, as shown in Figure 6.25. Here, we have the option of dragging and dropping UI elements onto the canvas or manually appending elements to the UI element tree structure in the upper right-hand corner of the View Designer. In either case, the UI elements will be added to the tree structure with default property values. We can then configure these properties to determine the look, feel, and behavior of the user interface. This task is carried out using the PROPERTIES table in the lower right-hand corner of the View Designer screen.

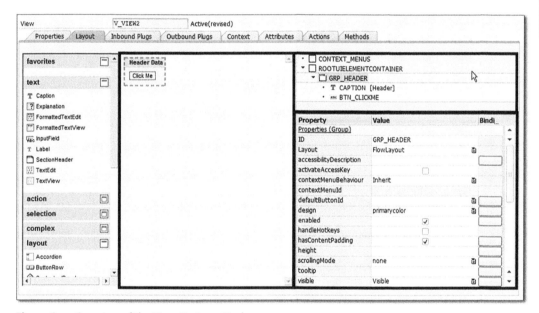

Figure 6.25 Overview of the View Designer Tool

Generally speaking, you'll find that UI elements maintain two or three sets of properties:

▶ **General properties**
Each UI element type has its own general set of properties that are used to define the element's ID within the layout, its look and feel, and so on. Naturally, the nature of these properties varies greatly between different UI element types.

▶ **Layout properties**

UI elements also maintain a series of layout properties, which determine the approximate positioning of the UI element within the user interface. We'll take a closer look at these properties in Section 6.2.3.

▶ **Event properties**

Finally, most UI elements define one or more *event properties,* which link events that may be triggered by the UI element on the frontend with actions defined in the view controller.

To a large degree, you can determine the values of these UI element properties either statically by keying in values into the properties table or dynamically in reference to elements defined in the corresponding view controller. In the latter case, we begin to see the touch points between UI elements in the view layout and the backend view controller. For example, we've already observed how context data binding techniques are used to define the values of UI element properties. Similarly, we've seen how event properties are linked with action definitions. Collectively, these bindings link the view layout with the backend Web Dynpro controller hierarchy in order to make the user interface come alive.

6.2.2   Working with Layout Elements

In the previous section, we learned how the UI elements within a view are integrated into a UI element hierarchy. This UI element hierarchy is organized such that:

▶ Nodes are represented by layout elements (or container elements), which aggregate/group one or more child UI elements.

▶ Leaves are represented by interactive elements, which don't contain any child elements.

At the root of the UI element hierarchy, we have the default `RootUIElement Container` element, which is the base-level container for all the UI elements within a view. As additional UI elements are added to the view layout, they must be added to either the `RootUIElementContainer` or a child layout element defined at a lower level within the hierarchy. Ultimately, this will yield a nested hierarchy like the one depicted in Figure 6.26.

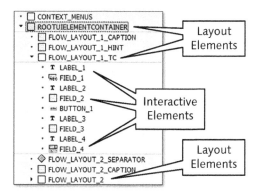

Figure 6.26 Understanding the Organization of the UI Element Hierarchy

As you can see in Figure 6.26, layout elements form the backbone of a UI element hierarchy, defining a logical organization of UI elements contained within the view layout. Within the Web Dynpro UI element catalog, you'll find that there are a number of layout elements to choose from when designing user interfaces. Therefore, in the upcoming subsections, we'll take a look at some of the more commonly used layout elements and see how they're used to group related UI elements together.

TransparentContainer

As the name suggests, the TransparentContainer element creates a transparent container within the view layout that can be used to group related UI elements. If you're familiar with HTML, you can think of the TransparentContainer element as roughly equivalent to the HTML <div> element, which is used to define a logical division or section within a page.

Given its overall simplicity and flexibility, you'll find that the Transparent Container element is used extensively in the definition of view layouts. As a matter of fact, we've actually seen the TransparentContainer element on display already, since it's used to define the default RootUIElementContainer element. So, in effect, the outer boundaries of *most* views are defined by a Transparent-Container element (see the sidebar below for clarification on this point). Of course, we can also use TransparentContainer elements to group related form elements together, partition off subsections within a view layout, and so on.

Swapping the Root Element in the UI Element Hierarchy

By default, the root element of a view's UI element hierarchy will be defined using the `TransparentContainer` element. Sometimes though, this may not be exactly what we want. For example, imagine that we're defining a simple view whose UI elements are organized within a `Group` element. In this case, the `TransparentContainer` element isn't really needed; it just adds an extra layer of complexity. Instead, it would be better (and more efficient) for us to simply define the root of the UI element hierarchy using the `Group` element. Fortunately, we can achieve this very thing within the View Editor tool.

In order to swap out the root element of a view's UI element hierarchy, simply right-click on the ROOTUIELEMENTCONTAINER element and select the SWAP ROOT ELEMENT menu option. This will open up a dialog box in which you can choose your preferred layout element. The only prerequisite to launching this function is that the UI element hierarchy for the view in question must be empty.

Figure 6.27 demonstrates how we're using a `TransparentContainer` to group a handful of form elements. Here, we should point out that the dashed line depicting the container boundaries is only present in the View Designer tool; at runtime, the container borders will be transparent as advertised.

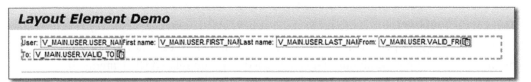

Figure 6.27 Grouping UI Elements Using a TransparentContainer

Once a `TransparentContainer` element has been appended to the UI element hierarchy, we can begin appending child elements to it just as we would for the `RootUIElementContainer`. For example, in Figure 6.28, you can see that we're using the INSERT ELEMENT context menu option to add a child element to a `TransparentContainer` called `TCO_TEST`. Alternatively, as `TransparentContainer` elements are frequently used to group form elements, we could choose the CREATE CONTAINER FORM menu option to create a form underneath the `TCO_TEST` element. We'll have a chance to work with `TransparentContainer` elements quite a bit as we progress through this book.

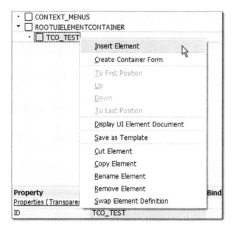

Figure 6.28 Adding Child Elements to a TransparentContainer Element

PageHeader

In recent years, the web landscape has experienced a not-so-subtle transition away from static HTML web pages to a more dynamic web focused on delivering full-fledged web applications. However, while this new breed of web applications may look and feel more like traditional desktop applications, the page metaphor remains a very popular design idiom among web developers and users. Recognizing this, SAP provides the PageHeader element that can be used to portray a page-like container within a view.

Figure 6.29 provides an example of the visual display of the PageHeader element. As you can see, it consists of a top-level title bar and a content area referred to as the PageHeaderArea. Within the PageHeaderArea, we can embed all kinds of content, including toolbars, other layout elements, and so on.

In order to understand how the page layout illustrated in Figure 6.29 is realized, let's take a look at the steps required to work with a PageHeader element:

1. First, we must add a PageHeader element to the UI element hierarchy as usual. Here, it normally makes sense to append the PageHeader element directly beneath the RootUIElementContainer element.

2. Next, we must insert a child PageHeaderArea element by right-clicking on the newly created PageHeader element and selecting the INSERT AREA context menu option (see Figure 6.30). Here, we can also use the INSERT TITLE CONTENT menu option to insert content into the title bar area (e.g., toolbars, and so on).

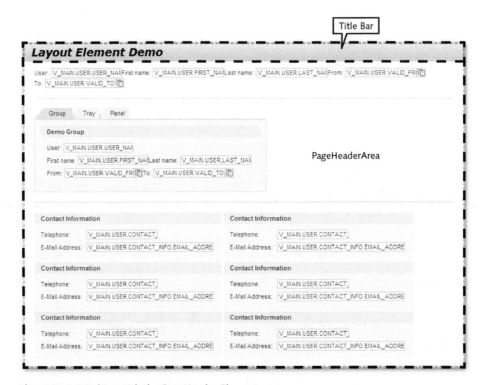

Figure 6.29 Working with the PageHeader Element

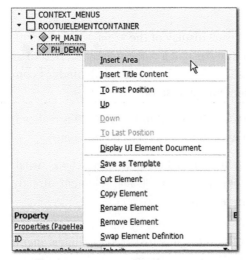

Figure 6.30 Defining the Content Area of a PageHeader Element

3. Finally, once the child `PageHeaderArea` element is defined, we can proceed with the layout of the `PageHeader` element's content area. However, since the `PageHeaderArea` element doesn't allow us to append multiple child elements to it, we must append a layout element such as the `TransparentContainer` element to define a container for the elements within the `PageHeader` element's context area. From here, we can lay out the remainder of the UI elements within the `TransparentContainer` element as usual.

If you're interested in seeing how all these pieces fit together in a concrete example, check out the `V_MAIN` view contained within the `ZWDC_LAYOUT_DEMO` component included with this chapter's sample code.

TabStrip and Accordion

These days, the tabbed document interface (TDI) metaphor is used extensively in GUI designs to group multiple content panes within a single window or view. For example, if you happen to be reading this book online, it's likely that the book page is being displayed within a tab in your web browser (see Figure 6.31). Here, the tabs are indexed with some kind of meaningful name (e.g., the title of the loaded web page) so users can easily navigate back and forth between pages.

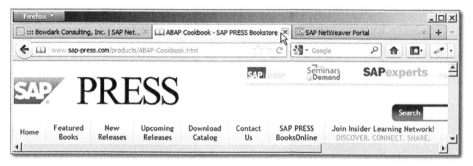

Figure 6.31 Example of the TDI Metaphor in a Web Browser

The Web Dynpro UI element catalog defines two different types of TDIs that can be used to group a set of related content areas: the `TabStrip` element and the `Accordion` element. As you can see in Figure 6.32, the `TabStrip` element has the familiar look and feel of most any TDI you might come into contact with on a daily basis. It consists of:

- A series of `Tab` subelements that define a `Caption` element, which represents the tab label
- A content area that can contain additional nested containers, forms, and so on

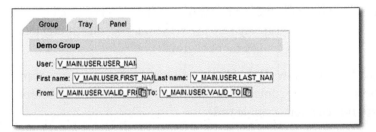

Figure 6.32 Working with the TabStrip Element

Unlike the `TabStrip` element, which arranges its items horizontally, the `Accordion` element arranges its items vertically, as shown in Figure 6.33. These items are defined using the `AccordionItem` subelement, which consists of, basically, a title and an internal content area. Users can choose among different accordion items by clicking on the triangle icons located in the top left-hand corner of the item. As is the case with the `TabStrip` element, only one item can be selected at a time. However, unlike the `TabStrip` element, the `Accordion` element does allow users to contract all the items at once. The SAP standard sample component `WDR_TEST_ACCORDION` demonstrates how all this works.

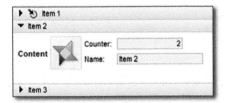

Figure 6.33 Working with the Accordion Element

Besides the described cosmetic differences, the `TabStrip` and `Accordion` elements are very much alike in terms of configuration and behavior. In particular, both elements define an `onSelect` event, which can be used to react to an item selection event. Here, we can ascertain the selected item in the event handler method and react accordingly.

Group, Tray, and Panel

The next set of layout elements we'll explore have something in common with the TransparentContainer element in that they're all used to group related UI elements under one umbrella. However, unlike the TransparentContainer element, whose boundaries are completely invisible, these elements implement a title bar and stylized backgrounds.

The Group element, as demonstrated in Figure 6.34, groups a series of UI elements underneath a common title. The look and feel of both the title bar and background area can be influenced by the design property.

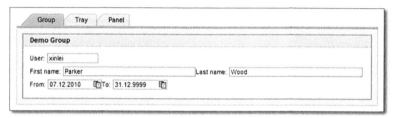

Figure 6.34 Working with the Group Element

In many respects, the Tray element, as demonstrated in Figure 6.35, can be viewed as an extension of the Group element that provides additional functions. These functions can be accessed via the toolbar-like buttons in the top right-hand corner of the title bar, as shown in Figure 6.35. Here, moving from right to left, we have:

▶ A toggle button, which can be used to expand and collapse the tray. Whenever the tray is collapsed, none of its constituent elements are visible within the view layout. This frees up more space within the view layout, which is automatically adjusted on the fly. If we like, we can use the onToggle event to respond to user interactions with this button.

▶ An optional context menu, which can be used to integrate related menu options associated with the grouped elements.

The last element in this group we'll consider is the Panel element, which is demonstrated in Figure 6.36. As you can see, this element has a similar look and feel to the Tray element in that its content area is collapsible. However, with the Panel element, the toggle button is represented by the little triangle button on the left-hand side of the title bar. As was the case with the Tray element, we can track user interactions with the toggle button by listening to the onToggle event.

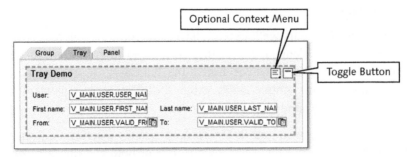

Figure 6.35 Working with the Tray Element

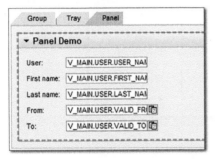

Figure 6.36 Working with the Panel Element

RowRepeater and MultiPane

The last two layout elements we'll consider are used to lay out UI elements in a type of grid: the RowRepeater element and the MultiPane element. These flexible layout element types can be used to build lightweight report layouts, dashboards, and so on.

As the name suggests, the RowRepeater element is used to display a series of related elements in rows. The row content area is defined by a child layout element appended to the RowRepeater element. Figure 6.37 illustrates this relationship for a sample RowRepeater element called RR_DEMO. Here, the row content area is defined via a TransparentContainer element called TCO_ROW. At runtime, a separate instance of the TCO_ROW element will be created for each context element contained within the context node bound to the RowRepeater element's data-Source property (see Figure 6.38). Naturally, it makes sense that the bound context node have a cardinality of 0..n or 1..n, though it's not a strict requirement. Figure 6.39 demonstrates how the RowRepeater element is rendered at runtime.

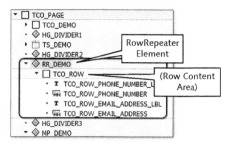

Figure 6.37 Working with the RowRepeater Element (Part 1)

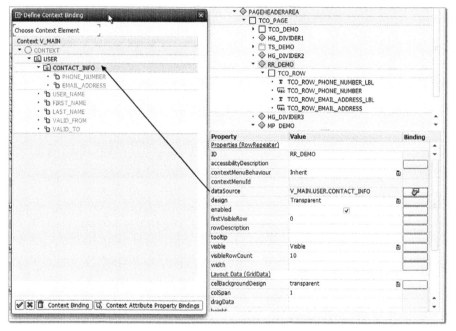

Figure 6.38 Working with the RowRepeater Element (Part 2)

Telephone:	V_MAIN.USER.CO	E-Mail Address:	V_MAIN.USER.CO
Telephone:	V_MAIN.USER.CO	E-Mail Address:	V_MAIN.USER.CO
Telephone:	V_MAIN.USER.CO	E-Mail Address:	V_MAIN.USER.CO
Telephone:	V_MAIN.USER.CO	E-Mail Address:	V_MAIN.USER.CO
Telephone:	V_MAIN.USER.CO	E-Mail Address:	V_MAIN.USER.CO
Telephone:	V_MAIN.USER.CO	E-Mail Address:	V_MAIN.USER.CO
Telephone:	V_MAIN.USER.CO	E-Mail Address:	V_MAIN.USER.CO
Telephone:	V_MAIN.USER.CO	E-Mail Address:	V_MAIN.USER.CO
Telephone:	V_MAIN.USER.CO	E-Mail Address:	V_MAIN.USER.CO
Telephone:	V_MAIN.USER.CO	E-Mail Address:	V_MAIN.USER.CO

Figure 6.39 Working with the RowRepeater Element (Part 3)

For the most part, the `MultiPane` element works like the `RowRepeater` element in that it repeatedly displays a content area using the elements contained within a bound context node. The primary difference is that the `MultiPane` element also splits the content up into rows *and* columns, as demonstrated in Figure 6.40. The number of columns to be displayed is based on the `MultiPane` element's `colCount` property. As was the case with the `RowRepeater` element, the content area is defined via a layout element. In the example shown in Figure 6.40, we're using a `Group` element for this purpose in order to define column headings.

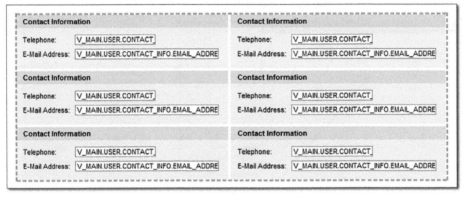

Figure 6.40 Working with the MultiPane Element

When working with `RowRepeater` and `MultiPane` elements, it's important to keep the layout simple by avoiding the use of nested container layouts and so on. Also, it's forbidden to embed UI elements from the complex category (e.g., `Tree` elements, `ViewContainerUIElement` elements, and so on) because such nested layouts become too taxing from a rendering perspective.

6.2.3 Working with Container Layouts

Up until this point, we've talked about appending UI elements to the view layout in fairly general terms, paying little attention to where the elements actually end up on the screen. However, while the geographic location of UI elements may not matter all that much in simple demo applications, it matters a great deal when it comes to the development of production-ready WDA applications. Therefore, in this section, we'll take a look at ways of organizing UI elements within layout elements.

If you've worked with other UI toolkits, such as Microsoft Windows Forms, you may be accustomed to affixing UI elements at fixed coordinates within the view layout. Here, for instance, we might specify that a button element should be located two hundred pixels from the top of the window and one hundred pixels to the left. Naturally, such precision gives us maximum control when specifying the layout of a user interface. However, such exactitude can only be achieved if boundaries of the user interface are predetermined up front—a luxury not afforded to the Web Dynpro framework.

In order to support a wide array of client devices with varying degrees of fidelity, the Web Dynpro framework must be flexible enough to render a consistent user interface, regardless of:

▶ The amount of space on the screen

▶ Limitations of the underlying UI toolkit

To achieve such flexibility, the Web Dynpro framework offers several different types of *container layouts* that can be used to organize UI elements within UI element containers in a view. In the following subsections, we'll take a look at each of the provided container layout types in turn.

FlowLayout

By default, layout elements such as `TransparentContainer`, `Group`, `Tray`, and so on are assigned the `FlowLayout` container layout. This simple layout sequentially arranges child elements one after another horizontally in a flow until it runs out of space in the container. Whenever this occurs, the layout shifts to a new "row" and continues on from there until all the child elements are rendered.

Given this approach, it's only natural that the final appearance of layout elements may vary greatly, depending on the size and type of the user agent screen. Figure 6.41 illustrates how this works for a `TransparentContainer` used to display an input form. Here, notice that the last two form fields are shifted over to a second row. If the user were to resize the screen to make it smaller, it's likely additional form fields would be shifted to the second row. Conversely, if the user were to make the screen area larger, it's possible the layout might adjust to fit all the form fields on a single row.

Figure 6.41 Working with the FlowLayout Container Layout

We can assign the FlowLayout container layout to a layout element by selecting it in the Layout property, as shown in Figure 6.42. Once assigned, we can configure the layout in the LAYOUT properties section shown at the bottom of the PROPERTIES table in Figure 6.42. As you can see, the only option we have is the wrapping property, which is used to control the automatic wrapping behavior for the FlowLayout. Whenever this property is turned off, any UI elements that don't fit into the first row are cut off, making them invisible within the display. Because of this, we recommend you only turn the wrapping behavior off if you know for certain that the child elements will fit into the defined container area.

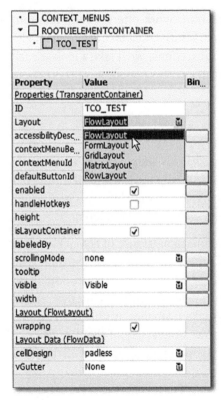

Figure 6.42 Assigning a Layout to a Layout Element

Though the `FlowLayout` container layout doesn't allow us much control over row breaks, it does provide us with some level of control over the rendering of the individual child UI elements. For each child UI element, we have two properties to work with:

▶ The `cellDesign` property allows us to control the padding around a given cell in the `FlowLayout`. For example, if we were to select the `lPad` value for this property, the cell would be padded to the left by four pixels. Similarly, if we were to select the `rPad` value, the cell would be padded on the right by four pixels.

▶ The `vGutter` property allows us to define additional horizontal space between cells, sometimes with a horizontal rule (line) as a divider.

RowLayout

The `RowLayout` container layout is very similar to the `FlowLayout` container layout in most respects. The primary difference between the two is that `RowLayout` allows us to control line breaks for individual elements, as shown in Figure 6.43.

Figure 6.43 Defining Rows Using RowLayout (Part 1)

As was the case with `FlowLayout`, we can specify the use of the `RowLayout` container layout by configuring the `Layout` property for the selected layout element (see Figure 6.42). Once this property is set, we can configure the individual rows as follows:

1. First, we must organize the child UI elements in the proper order from top to bottom within the UI element hierarchy.

2. Then, after the UI elements are organized, we can begin defining rows by selecting the desired row header element and configuring its `Layout Data` property. As you can see in Figure 6.44, we have two options to choose from here. To define a new row, we can select the `RowHeadData` value. Otherwise, we should keep the default `RowData` value.

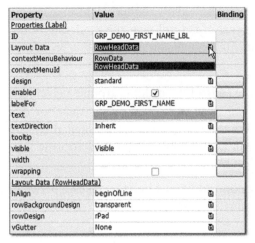

Figure 6.44 Defining Rows Using RowLayout (Part 2)

3. After a new row is defined, each of the subsequent UI elements will be added to that row definition until the RowLayout encounters another UI element with a Layout Data property value of RowHeadData. The look and feel of each row is defined in the row header element using the LAYOUT DATA properties shown at the bottom of the PROPERTIES table in Figure 6.44:

▶ The hAlign property defines the horizontal alignment of content within the row.

▶ The rowBackgroundDesign property allows us to specify the background color of the selected row.

▶ The rowDesign property allows us to define the padding between rows.

▶ The vGutter property allows us to define additional horizontal space between cells, sometimes with a horizontal rule (line) as a divider.

MatrixLayout

In the previous section, we saw how the RowLayout container layout could be used to control the way rows are defined within a container. However, one limitation of RowLayout is that it provides minimal control over the vertical spacing between UI elements. In general, each row simply defines one long column independent from all the other rows in the container. So, if one row happens to have wide elements and an adjacent one has narrow ones, the layout can become rather choppy.

In situations when horizontal alignment is crucial to the overall design, we can use the MatrixLayout container layout. From a usage perspective, MatrixLayout is very similar to RowLayout in that:

▶ We can define rows by selecting a row header element from an organized list of UI elements. We do this by configuring the familiar Layout Data property. However, in the case of MatrixLayout, the value set is different:

  ▸ We define new rows by selecting the MatrixHeadData value.

  ▸ We define regular cells by selecting the MatrixData value.

▶ Both layouts provide similar properties that can be used to decorate a row or individual cells.

However, unlike RowLayout, MatrixLayout organizes row elements into a grid so that the column widths are uniform throughout the container. The number of columns in the grid is determined dynamically via the row that happens to contain the most elements within it. Thus, there's nothing, configuration-wise, required to define uniform column layouts, as illustrated in Figure 6.45. However, if we want, we can use the stretchedHorizontally and stretchedVertically properties to stretch the grid to fill the entire container.

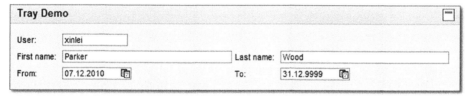

Figure 6.45 Working with the MatrixLayout Container Layout

From a customization perspective, each of the cells within a MatrixLayout can be configured using the layout properties described in Table 6.1. Overall, these properties provide tremendous flexibility for defining the layout.

Property Name	Description
cellBackgroundDesign	This property allows us to specify the background color of an individual cell.
cellDesign	This property defines the padding within a cell.

Table 6.1 Properties of MatrixLayout Cells

Property Name	Description
colSpan	This property can be used to define a cell that spans multiple columns within the virtual grid.
height	This property can be used to specify the height of a cell using CSS-based sizes such as pixels, percentages, and so on.
hAlign	This property can be used to define the horizontal alignment of the UI element within the cell.
vAlign	This property can be used to define the vertical alignment of the UI element within the cell.
vGutter	This property allows us to define additional horizontal space between cells, sometimes with a horizontal rule (line) as a divider.
width	This property can be used to specify the width of a cell using CSS-based sizes such as pixels, percentages, and so on.

Table 6.1 Properties of MatrixLayout Cells (Cont.)

GridLayout

Much like the MatrixLayout container layout, GridLayout can be used to build a grid of UI elements. However, instead of dynamically deriving the column count, GridLayout defines a fixed number of columns via its colCount property. For example, in the Panel element in Figure 6.46, you can see how we've defined a grid with a fixed column count of two. Table 6.2 outlines the properties that can be used to configure a GridLayout.

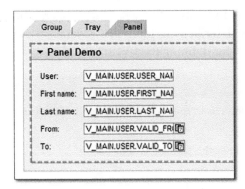

Figure 6.46 Defining a Fixed Grid Using GridLayout

Property Name	Description
cellPadding	This property allows us to define the amount of padding (in pixels) added to each of the cells in the grid. So, if we were to configure the cellPadding property with a value of three, each cell within the grid would have three pixels of padding on all sides.
cellSpacing	This property determines the amount of spacing between cells in pixels.
colCount	This property determines the fixed column count within the grid.
stretchedHorizontally stretchedVertically	These properties can be used to stretch the grid to match the boundaries of the surrounding container element.

Table 6.2 Properties for the GridLayout Container Layout

Each cell within a GridLayout defines a number of design properties similar to the ones used to define MatrixLayout cells. These properties are outlined in Table 6.3.

Property Name	Description
cellBackgroundDesign	This property allows us to specify the background color of an individual cell.
colSpan	This property can be used to define a cell that spans multiple columns within the virtual grid.
height	This property can be used to specify the height of a cell using CSS-based sizes such as pixels, percentages, and so on.
hAlign	This property can be used to define the horizontal alignment of the UI element within the cell.
paddingBottom paddingLeft paddingRight paddingTop	These properties can be used to define the amount of padding (in pixels) on all sides of the cell.

Table 6.3 Properties of Cells in a GridLayout

Property Name	Description
vAlign	This property can be used to define the vertical alignment of the UI element within the cell.
width	This property can be used to specify the width of a cell using CSS-based sizes such as pixels, percentages, and so on.

Table 6.3 Properties of Cells in a GridLayout (Cont.)

FormLayout

The last container layout we'll consider also happens to be the newest. The Form-Layout container layout was introduced with the SAP NetWeaver 7.02 release and makes it possible to define a layout using a newspaper-like page metaphor. Figure 6.47 demonstrates how this works. As you can see, the layout is divided horizontally into a series of pages, each of which maintains an invisible grid in the manner of GridLayout. Much like the RowLayout and MatrixLayout, FormLayout also allows us to identify page and row breaks via the Layout Data property of individual UI elements:

▸ To create a new page within the layout, we can select the FormTopData value.

▸ To create a new row within a page, we can select the FormHeadData value.

▸ All other cells are assigned the FormData value.

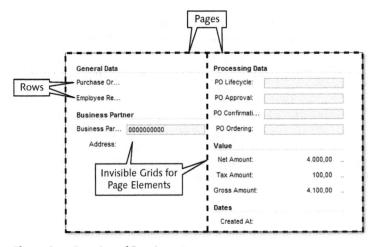

Figure 6.47 Overview of FormLayout

Each of the cells within a `FormLayout` can be configured using many of the same formatting properties we've seen with the other container layouts. Table 6.4 shows which properties are available for each of the different cell types.

	FormTopData	FormHeadData	FormData
`cellBackgroundDesign`	Yes	Yes	Yes
`colCount`	Yes	No	No
`colSpan`	Yes	Yes	Yes
`rowSpan`	Yes	Yes	No
`vAlign`	Yes	Yes	Yes

Table 6.4 Formatting Properties of FormLayout Cells

For more information about the `FormLayout` container layout, check out the WDA reference section of the SAP online help documentation in the subsection entitled "FormLayout." SAP also provides a sample component called `WDR_TEST_FORM_LAYOUT` that demonstrates its usage and configuration.

6.3   Navigation Concepts

In Section 6.1.2, we learned how interface views provide a link between a WDA application and a window within a WDA component. At runtime, this linkage provides the Web Dynpro framework with the information it needs to begin constructing the user interface. Here, the framework will load the selected window, which, in turn, determines the initial view that will be displayed for the user. From here, users are free to navigate among various views as desired.

In this section, we'll take a closer look at how navigation works within the Web Dynpro framework. Along the way, we'll consider some advanced navigation scenarios involving multiple components, external applications, and more.

6.3.1   Navigation between Views

Back in Chapter 2, we briefly introduced the notion of *navigation plugs* and *navigation links* and the roles they play in the navigation between views. However, since we've covered quite a bit of ground since then, these concepts deserve another look. Naturally, things should make a lot more sense this time around since we now understand the relationships between windows and views more clearly.

In order to comprehend how navigation works, let's consider the navigation diagram depicted in Figure 6.48. Here, we're depicting a navigation scenario between two views embedded within the same window: view A and view B. In order to navigate from view A to view B, an outbound plug from view A must be *linked* with an inbound plug from view B at design time. This link is referred to as a *navigation link*. At runtime, the navigation is triggered by *firing* the outbound plug on view A. From that point forward, the Web Dynpro framework will take over and complete the navigation request. In this section, we'll examine the mechanics of all this from a design time and runtime perspective.

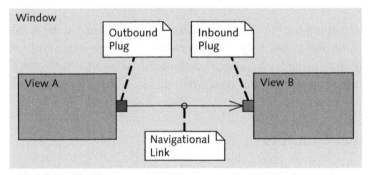

Figure 6.48 Navigation Plugs and Navigation Links: Revisited

Defining Navigation Plugs in Views

As we've seen, navigation between views is made possible via navigation links, which connect a pair of navigation plugs together. These navigation plugs can be divided into two distinct categories:

► **Outbound plugs**
These plugs define a navigational exit point from a view.

► **Inbound plugs**
These plugs define a navigational entry point to a view.

In either case, you'll find that navigation plugs are relatively easy to set up and configure.

Since navigation plugs are part of the view controller, we can edit them using the familiar View Editor tool. To define an outbound plug, we can navigate to the OUTBOUND PLUGS tab and add a plug definition to the OUTBOUND PLUGS table in the middle of the screen (see Figure 6.49). Here, we simply define a plug name and an optional description. Conventionally, outbound plug names are of the form OP_*, where the free-form suffix is used to provide a meaningful description for why the view is being exited.

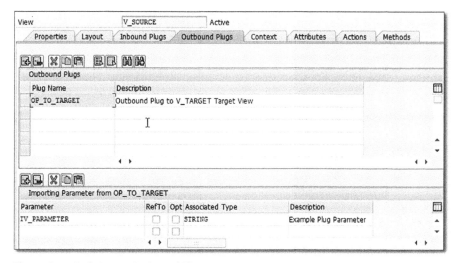

Figure 6.49 Defining an Outbound Plug

Looking closely at the outbound plug definition shown in Figure 6.49, you can see that outbound plugs can optionally define plug parameters that can be used to pass contextual information about a navigation event to the target view. These parameters are defined in much the same way that parameters would be defined for a method in an ABAP Objects class. For example, in Figure 6.49, you can see how we've defined a parameter called IV_PARAMETER for the OP_TO_TARGET outbound plug. We'll show you how parameters like this are used during a navigation sequence shortly.

As you might expect, inbound plugs are maintained on the INBOUND PLUGS tab of the View Editor as shown in Figure 6.50. As was the case with outbound plugs, inbound plug definitions consist of a plug name and an optional description. Conventionally, inbound plug names are of the form IP_*, where the free-form suffix is used to provide a meaningful description for why the view is being entered.

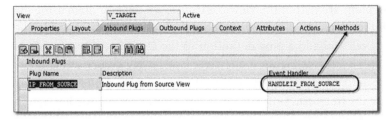

Figure 6.50 Defining an Inbound Plug

In the example shown in Figure 6.50, you can see how we've defined an inbound plug called IP_FROM_SOURCE. Here, notice that the system has automatically taken the liberty of associating the inbound plug with an event handler method of the form HANDLE<inbound plug name> (e.g., HANDLEIP_FROM_SOURCE). This event handler method will be invoked when the inbound plug is triggered at runtime. We'll take a closer look at how these event handler methods are used in a moment.

Creating Navigation Links between Views

Having seen how navigation plugs are defined in the previous section, let's now turn our attention to the creation of navigation links. Since navigation between views is defined at the window layer, this activity takes place within the Window Editor. Here, we can use the provided graphical tools to define links between a pair of views embedded within the selected window.

In order to demonstrate how navigation links are established, let's imagine that we have a window called W_MAIN that has embedded two views called V_SOURCE and V_TARGET. The V_SOURCE view defines an outbound plug called OP_TO_TARGET, and the V_TARGET view defines an inbound plug called IP_FROM_SOURCE. The steps required to link these two views together are as follows:

1. First, we must open the W_MAIN window in the Window Editor and navigate to the WINDOW tab.

2. Before we can create the navigation link, we must first locate the initiating OP_TO_TARGET outbound plug within the WINDOW STRUCTURE hierarchy as shown in Figure 6.51.

3. Then, we can create the navigation link by right-clicking on the outbound plug and selecting the CREATE NAVIGATION LINK menu option. This will open up the dialog box shown in Figure 6.52. Here, we must select the destination view (V_TARGET) and the corresponding inbound plug (IP_FROM_SOURCE).

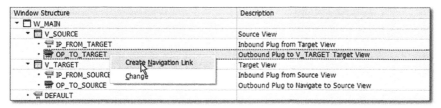

Figure 6.51 Creating a Navigation Link (Part 1)

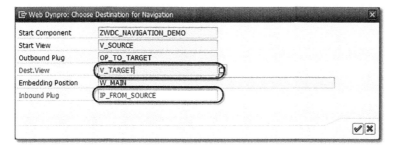

Figure 6.52 Creating a Navigation Link (Part 2)

4. Finally, once we've confirmed our selection, the newly created navigation link will show up in the WINDOW STRUCTURE hierarchy as demonstrated in Figure 6.53. If needed, we can verify the details of the link in the PROPERTIES table in the lower portion of the screen.

Window	W_MAIN	Active(revised)				
Properties	Window	Inbound Plugs	Outbound Plugs	Context	Attributes	Methods

Window Structure	Description
▼ ☐ W_MAIN	
▼ ☐ V_SOURCE	Source View
• IP_FROM_TARGET	Inbound Plug from Target View
▼ OP_TO_TARGET	Outbound Plug to V_TARGET Target View
• IP_FROM_SOURCE	
▶ ☐ V_TARGET	Target View
• DEFAULT	

Properties	
Property	**Value**
Name	IP_FROM_SOURCE
Type	Navigation Link
Target View	V_TARGET
TargPlug	IP_FROM_SOURCE
Component of Target View	ZWDC_NAVIGATION_DEMO
Embedding Position of Target	

Figure 6.53 Creating a Navigation Link (Part 3)

Beginning with the SAP NetWeaver 7.02 release, we now also have the option of defining navigation links using the WYSIWYG graphical editor tool shown in Figure 6.54. If you've worked with Web Dynpro Java and the SAP NetWeaver Developer Studio tool, you may be more at home with this graphical editor tool since it has a similar look and feel to the Java-based editor. To toggle back and forth between the different editor views, simply click on the SWITCH WINDOW EDITOR VIEW button in the toolbar.

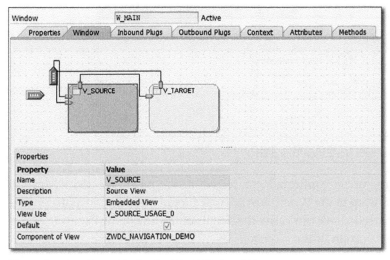

Figure 6.54 Working with the Graphical Window Editor

As we've seen, the process of defining navigation links is pretty straightforward. This process can be repeated to define all the different navigation options between the views embedded in a window. However, as you define additional navigation links, we should point out that:

▶ Only one navigation link can originate from an outbound plug. Of course, this link can lead to a series of target views.

▶ An inbound plug may be controlled by one or more outbound plugs.

The primary takeaway on these last two points is that you shouldn't think of outbound and inbound plugs as having a one-to-one correspondence with one another. Instead, think of navigation plugs as exit and entry points to a view, which may be leveraged in multiple navigation scenarios as needed.

Triggering Navigation at Runtime

Once the requisite navigation links are established within the window layer, we can trigger navigation within a source view by *firing* an outbound plug. As we have seen, outbound plugs are fired by invoking an auto-generated plug method whose name is of the form FIRE_<Outbound_Plug>_PLG(). So, if we have an outbound plug called OP_TO_TARGET, the corresponding view controller would define a method called FIRE_OP_TO_TARGET_PLG(). We could then fire the outbound plug within a controller method using a call syntax like this: wd_this->fire_op_to_target_plg().

Most of the time, navigation is triggered via an event handler method associated with an action defined in the source view. To demonstrate how this works, let's imagine that the V_SOURCE view we've considered throughout the course of this section has a view layout like the one demonstrated in Figure 6.55. When a user wants to navigate from the V_SOURCE view to the V_TARGET view, they'll click on the To TARGET VIEW button shown in Figure 6.55. Here, let's assume that the To TARGET VIEW button is tied to an action called NEXT. Listing 6.3 provides an example of what the event handler method behind this action might look like.

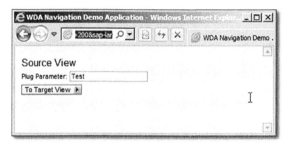

Figure 6.55 Triggering Navigation via a View Action

```
method ONACTIONNEXT.
  "Method-Local Data Declarations:
  DATA lo_el_context TYPE REF TO if_wd_context_element.
  DATA ls_context TYPE wd_this->Element_context.
  DATA lv_plug_parameter TYPE
    wd_this->Element_context-plug_parameter.

  "Read the plug parameter from context:
  lo_el_context = wd_context->get_element( ).
```

```
lo_el_context->get_attribute(
  EXPORTING
    name = `PLUG_PARAMETER`
  IMPORTING
    value = lv_plug_parameter ).

"Fire the outbound plug to trigger navigation:
wd_this->fire_op_to_target_plg(
  iv_parameter = lv_plug_parameter ).
endmethod.
```

Listing 6.3 Firing an Outbound Plug

As you can see in Listing 6.3, we're passing a parameter called IV_PARAMETER to the FIRE_OP_TO_TARGET_PLG() method. This parameter matches the one defined in the OP_TO_TARGET outbound plug shown in Figure 6.49. In this simple example, the value of the IV_PARAMETER came from a local context attribute called PLUG_PARAMETER, but we could have obtained the value from anywhere. The point is that we can pass in one or more parameter values to an outbound plug and have them routed automatically over to the target view by the framework.

Of course, in order to receive plug parameters in the target view, the signature of the event handler method for the target inbound plug must be adjusted to match the interface of the outbound plug. For instance, in Figure 6.56, you can see we've added the IV_PARAMETER parameter to the signature of the HANDLEIP_FROM_SOURCE() method defined to react to the firing of the IP_FROM_SOURCE inbound plug. This parameter value can be used just like any other method parameter. Frequently, the values are used to provide the target view with contextual details about the navigation sequence. These details can be used to allow the target view to dynamically initialize itself, and so on. Listing 6.4 demonstrates how we're loading the parameter into a local context attribute called PLUG_PARAMETER in the V_TARGET view. To trace how this navigation sequence works end-to-end, check out the ZWDC_NAVIGATION_DEMO component included with the book's source code bundle.

```
method HANDLEFROM_SOURCE.
  "Method-Local Data Declarations:
  DATA lo_el_context TYPE REF TO if_wd_context_element.
  DATA ls_context TYPE wd_this->Element_context.
  DATA lv_plug_parameter TYPE
```

```
wd_this->Element_context-plug_parameter.

"Copy the plug parameter into context:
lo_el_context = wd_context->get_element( ).

lo_el_context->set_attribute(
  name =  `PLUG_PARAMETER`
  value = iv_parameter ).
endmethod.
```

Listing 6.4 Event Handler Method for an Inbound Plug

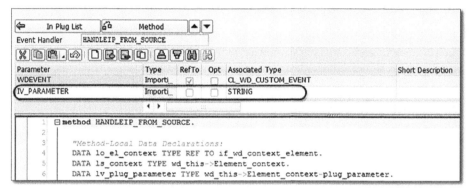

Figure 6.56 Accepting Parameters in an Inbound Plug Event Handler Method

6.3.2 Working with Window Plugs

The American poet James Whitcomb Riley once remarked, "When I see a bird that walks like a duck and swims like a duck and quacks like a duck, I call that bird a duck." Little did he know that some one hundred years later a Python developer named Alex Martelli would apply this observation toward the description of a brand-new dynamic typing scheme called *duck typing*. Without digressing into a lengthy discussion on the merits of static vs. dynamic typing schemes, the basic premise of duck typing is that if an object looks and behaves like another object, then it should be possible for the two objects to be used interchangeably (or *polymorphically*).

So what does all this have to do with window plugs? Well, if you recall from Section 6.1.2 that interface views define a series of navigation plugs, it stands to reason that interface views could be used interchangeably with views in navigation scenarios. After all, the only thing the Web Dynpro framework needs to define a navigation link is a pair of navigation plugs; the framework doesn't care where these plugs come from.

In this section, we'll take a look at window plugs and see how they're used to build advanced navigation scenarios. Here, we'll see that window plugs can be used for navigating within a window as well as in cross-component scenarios in which the window's interface view plays the role of a view within the navigation chain.

Defining Outbound Plugs in Windows

For the most part, you'll find that outbound plugs for windows are defined in much the same way they're defined in views (see Figure 6.57). However, with window plugs, there are a couple of additional attributes we must define:

- If the outbound plug is to be used in cross-component scenarios, you must add it to the interface view by clicking on the INTERFACE checkbox (see Figure 6.57).
- When the outbound plug is created, we must select a plug type from the correspondingly named dropdown list. Table 6.5 describes the options we have to choose from.

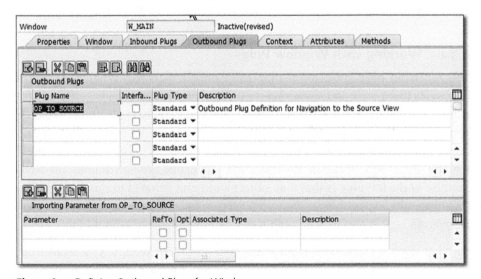

Figure 6.57 Defining Outbound Plugs for Windows

Plug Type	Description
Standard	This plug type should be chosen for outbound plugs used to navigate from the window to an inbound plug of an embedded view. This can come in handy whenever we wish to dynamically determine the default view displayed when a window is first loaded. Here, the outbound plug to select the target view would be fired within the event handler method of an inbound plug defined within the window. This scenario is demonstrated in Section 6.3.3.
Exit	This plug type is used to close the associated WDA application. We'll demonstrate how this plug type works in Section 6.3.4.
Suspend	This plug type is used to suspend a WDA application so the user can navigate to another application for a time and then eventually come back to the suspended application. We'll take a closer look at this feature of the Web Dynpro framework in Section 6.3.5.

Table 6.5 Outbound Plug Types for Windows

As you can see in Figure 6.57, window plugs can define plug parameters that are passed downstream during navigation scenarios. Since we demonstrated how plug parameters work in Section 6.3.1, we won't revisit these concepts here.

Defining Inbound Plugs in Windows

As was the case with outbound plugs, inbound plugs for windows are defined in the same way as they're defined in views. The only difference is that inbound plugs for windows provide two additional attributes that determine how the plug will be used at runtime (see Figure 6.58):

► The `Interface` attribute determines whether or not the inbound plug will be included within the window's corresponding interface view.

► The `Plug Type` attribute determines the role the inbound plug will play within the framework. Table 6.6 describes each of the available plug types we have to choose from.

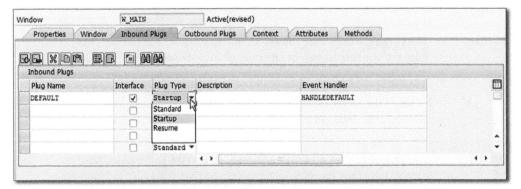

Figure 6.58 Defining Inbound Plugs for Windows

Plug Type	Description
Standard	This plug type is used in situations when a window is used in cross-component navigation scenarios. We'll see how this plug type is used in Chapter 9.
Startup	This plug type is used in conjunction with WDA application definitions to define the startup plug for the main window of a WDA application. A window may contain only one startup plug.
Resume	This plug type is the analog of the suspend plug type defined for outbound plugs. A window may contain only one resume plug. We'll take a closer look at how these plug types work with one another in Section 6.3.5.

Table 6.6 Inbound Plug Types for Windows

6.3.3 Case Study: Dynamically Selecting the Initial View for a Window

Now that we've observed the various types of navigation plugs that can be defined for a window, we're ready to see how these plug types are used to implement complex navigation scenarios. The first scenario we'll look at involves the use of WDA application parameters to influence the selection of the initial view displayed within a window. Here, for example, we might want to use application parameters to determine whether or not to bypass a selection screen, set the mode for a WDA application, and so on.

Figure 6.59 demonstrates how this navigation flow works. Here, we have a WDA application with defined application parameters whose values are determined at runtime via URL query string parameters. The Web Dynpro framework automatically maps these parameters to correspondingly named parameters in the event handler method associated with the startup inbound plug linked with the WDA application. Thus, at runtime, the parameter values can be used to build logical expressions within this event handler method to determine which view should be displayed first. From here, navigation to the selected view is initiated by firing an outbound plug defined within the window linked to an inbound plug of the view.

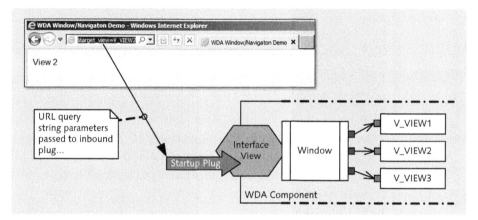

Figure 6.59 Navigation Flow for Dynamic View Selection

In order to understand the mechanics of the navigation flow depicted in Figure 6.59, let's take a closer look at each of the elements included within the navigation chain by looking at an example. In this example scenario, we're going to define a WDA component that has a window called W_MAIN, which embeds three views: V_VIEW1, V_VIEW2, and V_VIEW3. By default, the application will open to display the default V_VIEW1 view as usual. However, we're going to enhance the navigation flow such that users can pass in an application parameter to choose which view they want to display first. This dynamic flow is implemented by performing the following configuration steps:

1. As you can see in Figure 6.59, the dynamic nature of the navigation flow is determined via an application parameter defined at the WDA application level. These parameters can be defined on the PARAMETERS tab of the WDA Application Editor tool as shown in Figure 6.60. In our example, we've defined an

application parameter called TARGET_VIEW and assigned it the STRING data type. At runtime, we can pass this parameter to the WDA application by defining a URL query string parameter with the same name (e.g., *http://host:port/wda_ url?target_view=v_view2*).

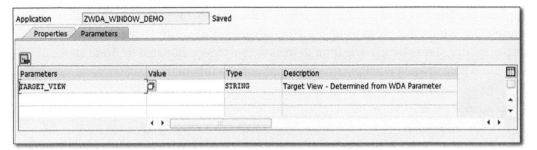

Figure 6.60 Defining WDA Application Parameters

2. As the Web Dynpro runtime environment loads the WDA application into context, it will fire the startup plug in the main window of the selected WDA component. In order to feed our application parameter to this plug, we must enhance the signature of the plug's event handler method. We can do this by double-clicking on the startup plug (see Figure 6.61) and adding a new importing parameter to the event handler method (see Figure 6.62). Here, notice that the name/type of the importing parameter in the event handler methodmust match that of the calling WDA application. Also, since users aren't required to pass in application parameters to a WDA application, you should mark this parameter as optional by clicking on the checkbox in the Opt column (see Figure 6.62).

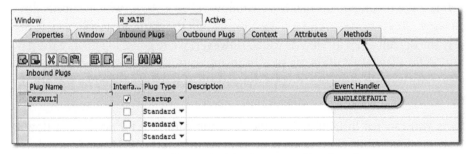

Figure 6.61 Editing the Event Handler Method for the Startup Plug (Part 1)

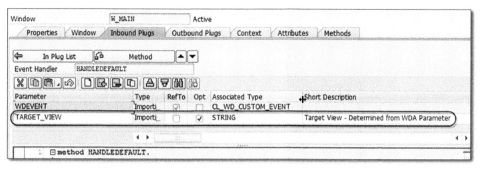

Figure 6.62 Editing the Event Handler Method for the Startup Plug (Part 2)

3. In a moment, we'll look at the program logic required to trigger dynamic navigation within the startup plug's event handler method. However, before we can do that, we must first define the outbound plugs within the main window that will be used to initate the navigation. Figure 6.63 demonstrates how we've created three outbound plugs for this purpose. Each of these plugs will be used to navigate to V_VIEW1, V_VIEW2, and V_VIEW3, respectively.

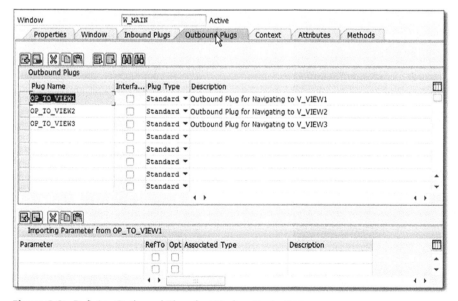

Figure 6.63 Defining Outbound Plugs for Window Navigation

4. Next, we'll need to define inbound plugs on each of the target views, as demonstrated in Figure 6.64.

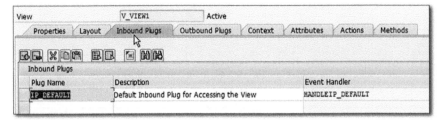

Figure 6.64 Defining Inbound Plugs on the Target Views

5. Finally, once the requisite navigation plugs are in place, we can define navigation links between the outbound plugs of the window and the inbound plugs of the views on the WINDOW tab of the Window Editor, as shown in Figure 6.65 and Figure 6.66.

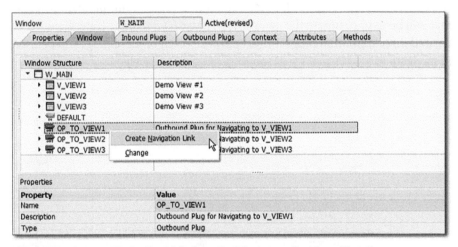

Figure 6.65 Creating Navigation Links from the Window to the Views (Part 1)

Figure 6.66 Creating Navigation Links from the Window to the Views (Part 2)

After we perform the configuration steps outlined above, all the requisite fixtures are in place to implement the dynamic view selection logic. This logic is contained within the event handler method associated with the startup plug for the main window. As you can see in Listing 6.5, we are using the TARGET_VIEW parameter in a CASE statement to determine which outbound plug to fire in order to trigger navigation to the selected view.

```
method HANDLEDEFAULT.
  CASE target_view.
    WHEN 'V_VIEW1'.
      wd_this->fire_op_to_view1_plg( ).
    WHEN 'V_VIEW2'.
      wd_this->fire_op_to_view2_plg( ).
    WHEN 'V_VIEW3'.
      wd_this->fire_op_to_view3_plg( ).
  ENDCASE.
endmethod.
```

Listing 6.5 Implementing Dynamic Routing within an Inbound Plug Method

6.3.4 Case Study: Closing WDA Applications

Sometimes, we may have a requirement for which we need to allow users to close or exit a WDA application in a graceful manner. In these scenarios, we can utilize a special type of outbound plug within a window called an *exit plug*. Whenever an exit plug is fired, the associated WDA application will be ended automatically.

Like most plug types, the behavior of exit plugs can be customized through the definition of plug parameters. With exit plugs, the Web Dynpro framework looks for three parameters in particular:

▶ URL

This STRING parameter is used to provide the Web Dynpro framework with a URL to navigate to after the associated WDA application is closed.

▶ `CLOSE_WINDOW`

This Boolean parameter (of type `WDY_BOOLEAN`) can be used to request that the Web Dynpro framework close the browser window after the associated WDA application is closed. Here, we should note that this may not be possible in all circumstances. You can verify whether or not this is the case using the `GET_IS_CLOSE_WINDOW_SUPPORTED()` of the `IF_WD_APPLICATION` interface.

▶ `LOGOFF`

This Boolean parameter (of type `WDY_BOOLEAN`) can be used to request that the user's session be removed whenever the associated WDA application is closed. You can test this behavior by watching the user sessions disappear in Transaction SM04.

Figure 6.67 demonstrates what an exit plug looks like for a window called `WDR_TEST_EXIT_CLOSE` in the SAP demo component `WDR_TEST_WINDOW_SUITE`.

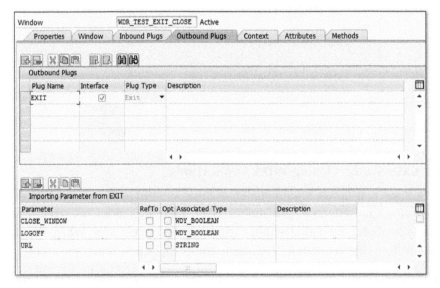

Figure 6.67 Defining an Exit Plug

We can test the behavior of exit plugs using the SAP demo application called `WDR_TEST_EXIT_WITH_CLOSE`. As you can see in Figure 6.68, this application allows us to pass in values for each of the defined exit plug parameters to see how they influence the closing of a window or application. We highly recommend you fire up this application and take exit plugs for a test drive as a reader exercise so you can see how the different parameters work.

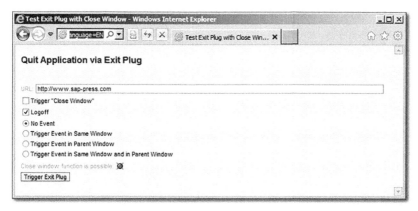

Figure 6.68 Testing the Behavior of Exit Plugs

6.3.5 Case Study: Suspend and Resume Calls

In Section 6.3.4, we observed how exit plugs can be used to close a WDA application and redirect the user's browser window to some alternate URL. This sort of functionality is useful when we want to allow users to navigate to different applications within the IT landscape (e.g., another WDA application, BSP applications, and so on). However, there may be times when we want to allow a user to navigate to another application for a bit and then come back to the running WDA application when they're done. In these situations, we can utilize *suspend* and *resume* plugs.

We touched on suspend and resume plugs briefly in Section 6.3.2 when we looked at the different plug types that could be defined for windows. To some extent, suspend plugs are similar to exit plugs in that both plug types are used to exit a WDA application. However, unlike exit plugs, suspend plugs don't cause the associated WDA application to be terminated. Instead, the running WDA application is merely suspended. It can then be reactivated later via a special kind of inbound plug type called a resume plug.

In this section, we'll take a look at how suspend and resume calls are implemented in real-world application scenarios.

Conceptual Overview

To demonstrate how suspend and resume calls work, we're going to trace the navigation flow between a WDA application and a BSP application included with the book's code bundle. These applications are called ZWDA_WINDOW_DEMO and ZBSP_RESUME, respectively. If you haven't worked with BSPs before, don't worry; we won't dig very deep into the details of BSP programming. Instead, our focus will be on demonstrating how WDA applications can play along with other web application technologies.

To put this application scenario into perspective, let's take a look at how the navigation sequence is implemented from a conceptual point of view. Figure 6.69 illustrates this navigation sequence:

1. As you can see, we initiate the navigation sequence within the WDA application by firing an outbound plug on view V_VIEW1 within the W_MAIN application window. This plug is fired within an action linked with a Button UI element in the V_VIEW1 view layout.

2. The outbound plug from step one is linked with a standard inbound plug defined within the W_MAIN window. Inside the event handler method for this inbound plug, we're suspending the WDA application by firing a suspend plug on the W_MAIN window.

3. Whenever the suspend plug is fired, the URL to the BSP application is provided as a plug parameter. This parameter enables the Web Dynpro framework to redirect the user to the ZBSP_RESUME application.

4. Finally, when the user is finished with the ZBSP_RESUME application, they can return to the ZWDA_WINDOW_DEMO application by clicking on a button. This button contains some JavaScript code to redirect their browser to the resume URL provided to the BSP application by the Web Dynpro framework when the BSP application was loaded in step 3.

As you can see in Figure 6.69, the Web Dynpro framework takes care of the majority of the heavy lifting when it comes to suspending and resuming the WDA application. The target application (i.e., the BSP in this case) is only responsible for hanging onto the resume URL and loading it when the user wants to navigate back to the WDA application. Given these minimal requirements on the part of the target application, we can implement suspend and resume calls using almost any type of web technology. So, while our target application was based on BSP technology in this example, we could have just as easily utilized JavaServer Pages (JSPs), ASP.NET, PHP, and so on.

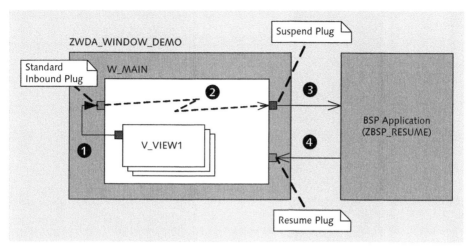

Figure 6.69 Implementing Suspend and Resume Calls

Though not depicted in Figure 6.69, there's a hook method that gets called before an application is suspended and right after it is resumed: the WDDOAPPLICATION-STATECHANGE() method of the component controller. This method allows us to release locks, clean up used resources, and so on, much like the WDDOINIT() and WDDOEXIT() methods.

Defining the Suspend and Resume Plugs

To a large degree, suspend and resume plugs are defined like any other navigation plug within a window. However, there are several things we need to be aware of when defining these plug types:

▸ First of all, since suspend/resume plugs are used for communication from the active component, they must be included within the window's interface view definition. Indeed, the Window Editor tool won't allow us to create these plug types without first specifying this attribute.

▸ Secondly, suspend plugs must be defined with a parameter called URL (of type STRING). Without this parameter, the framework has no idea which URL to navigate to when the WDA application is suspended.

▸ Finally, a window may contain only one resume plug.

Figure 6.70 and Figure 6.71 demonstrate how we've defined the suspend and resume plugs used to navigate to/from our sample BSP application.

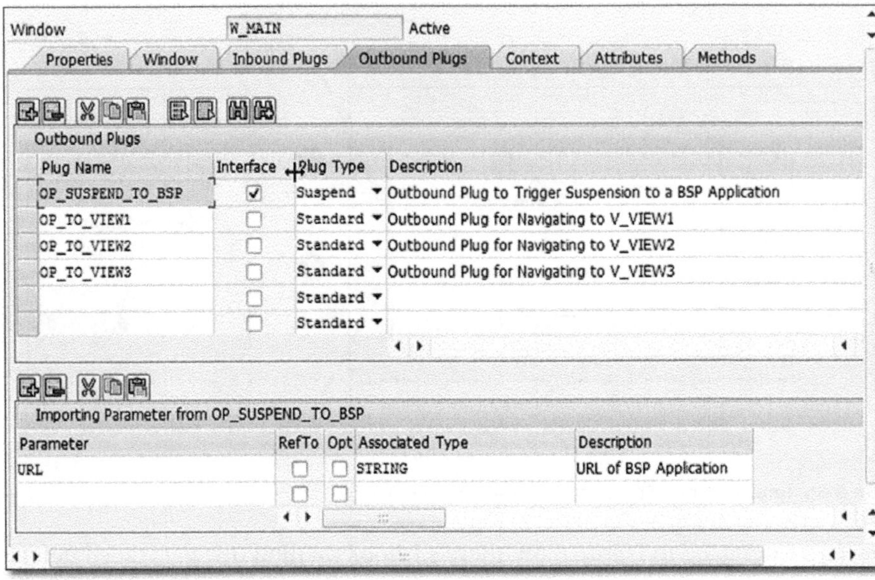

Figure 6.70 Defining a Suspend Plug

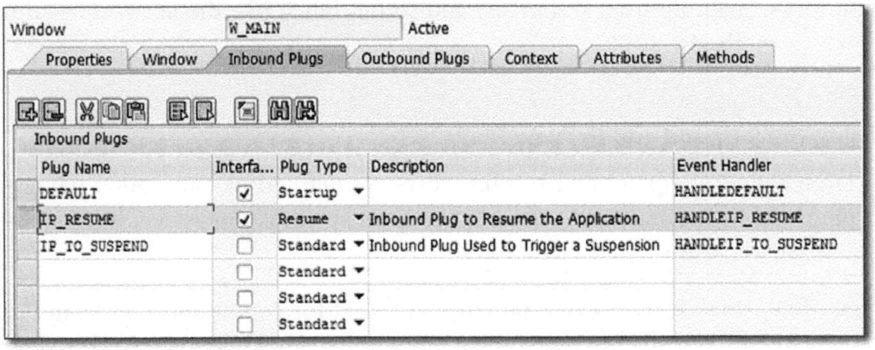

Figure 6.71 Defining a Resume Plug

One additional aspect we should point out regarding resume plugs is that their event handler methods can define importing parameters just like any other inbound plug type. These parameters can come in handy in situations when we want to implement inter-application communication. Here, for instance, the target application might pass data back to the calling WDA application via URL query string parameters that are ultimately passed in to the event handler method for the resume plug. From here, the data can be copied to the context, stored in the database, and so on.

Triggering Navigation Back to the WDA Application

When the Web Dynpro framework builds the call to the target (BSP) application, it will pass along a return/resume URL in the HTTP request message's form fields. The form field name is `sap-wd-resumeurl`. In order to call back to the WDA application at some later point in time, the target web application will need to keep track of this URL.

In our sample BSP application, we're storing the WDA resume URL in a page attribute, as demonstrated in Figure 6.72. If you're working with some other web technology, naturally the syntax will be different. However, the basic concept remains the same.

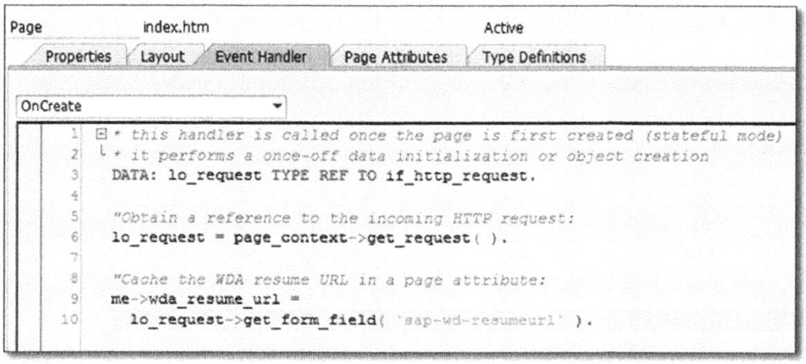

Figure 6.72 Storing the WDA Resume URL in a Page Attribute

Once the WDA resume URL is stored somewhere in memory, we can use it to trigger navigation back to the calling WDA application. For example, in Listing 6.6, we've implemented some JavaScript to change the user's browser location when they click on a button labeled RESUME WDA APPLICATION. We'll see how all this plays out on the screen in a moment.

```
<%@page language="abap"%>
<%@extension name="htmlb" prefix="htmlb"%>
<htmlb:content design="design2003">
  <htmlb:page title = "Main Page">
    <htmlb:form>
      <htmlb:textView
        text   = "Hello WDA from BSP!"
        design = "HEADER1" />
      <br /><br />
      <htmlb:button
```

```
      text            = "Resume WDA Application"
      design          = "PREVIOUS"
      onClientClick =
    "javascript:location.href = '<%= wda_resume_url %>'" />
  </htmlb:form>
 </htmlb:page>
</htmlb:content>
```

Listing 6.6 Navigating Back to the WDA Application

Resume Calls from WDA Applications

In Listing 6.6, we're firing the resume plug in the primary WDA application by changing the user's browser location. However, if the secondary application in a suspend/resume call scenario is a WDA application, this step can be omitted. In this case, the secondary WDA application need only fire an exit plug to trigger the navigation. Here, the secondary WDA application will be closed and the resume plug of the primary WDA application will be fired automatically by the Web Dynpro framework. Thus, we needn't worry about hanging onto the `sap-wd-resumeurl` form field within the secondary WDA application.

Putting It All Together

Now that we have an understanding of all the different elements involved in the navigation sequence, let's take a look at our finished application(s). Figure 6.73 shows what the ZWDA_WINDOW_DEMO application looks like in a user browser window. As you can see, users can suspend the WDA application by clicking on the button labeled SUSPEND WDA APP. Whenever a user clicks on this button, an action will be triggered within the V_VIEW1 view and an outbound plug within the view will be fired. This outbound plug is linked with a standard inbound plug called IP_TO_SUSPEND within the enclosing W_MAIN application window.

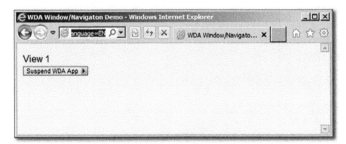

Figure 6.73 Suspending the WDA Application

Listing 6.7 contains the implementation of the event handler method behind the IP_TO_SUSPEND inbound plug. Here, we're using the CONSTRUCT_BSP_URL() method of class CL_BSP_RUNTIME to derive the URL for the BSP application. Then, we pass the derived URL to the FIRE_OP_SUSPEND_TO_BSP_PLG() method to fire the suspend plug.

```
method HANDLEIP_TO_SUSPEND.
  "Method-Local Data Declarations:
  DATA: lv_bsp_url TYPE string.

  "Derive the target BSP application URL:
  CALL METHOD cl_bsp_runtime=>construct_bsp_url
    EXPORTING
      in_application = `ZBSP_RESUME`
    IMPORTING
      out_abs_url    = lv_bsp_url.

  "Fire the suspension plug:
  wd_this->fire_op_suspend_to_bsp_plg(
    url = lv_bsp_url ).
endmethod.
```

Listing 6.7 Firing the Suspend Plug

> **Note**
>
> The class CL_WD_UTILITIES provides a similar method called CONSTRUCT_WD_URL() that can be used to derive the URL for a WDA application.

Once the suspend plug is fired, the Web Dynpro framework will take over and trigger navigation to the BSP application, as shown in Figure 6.74. From here, users can click on the RESUME WDA APPLICATION button to navigate back to the WDA application. This will cause the button-click event on the BSP page to execute the aforementioned JavaScript code and change the user's browser location to point at the WDA resume URL.

Figure 6.74 Resuming the WDA Application

6.4   Summary

In this chapter, we were able to formally establish the relationships between windows and views within WDA components. Here, we learned how windows embed one or more views, which are swapped in and out of the user interface at runtime based on user navigation requests. Each of these views maintains a complex UI element hierarchy, which is organized using layout elements and container layouts.

Now that we've put the pieces together with windows and views, we're ready to begin looking at some of the different interactive elements provided within the Web Dynpro UI element catalog. We'll pick this up in the next two chapters, starting with basic UI elements in Chapter 7 and moving to more complex UI element types in Chapter 8.

Most modern web development frameworks provide a set of GUI widgets (or controls) that can be used out of the box to display and/or manipulate data on the screen. Examples of these GUI widgets include labels, input fields, buttons, and so on. In this chapter, we'll begin an in-depth survey of the rich set of GUI widgets supported by the Web Dynpro framework.

7   Basic UI Elements

In the previous chapter, we considered a handful of nouns used to describe the visual layout of WDA applications: windows, views, and layout elements. As we observed, these elements are quite useful for describing the overall structure and flow of the application. However, if we want to make our WDA applications come alive, we need to mix in some UI elements that allow users to interact with the application and do things: display and edit data, fire events, trigger navigation, and so on. In other words, we're looking for the *verbs* of the user interface.

In this chapter, we'll begin exploring some of the basic UI elements that can be used to facilitate user interaction in WDA applications. Along the way, we'll also take a closer look at how UI elements are implemented from a technical point of view. Having a grasp of these concepts will help you understand how UI elements integrate with the rest of the Web Dynpro framework and also give you a leg up on understanding some of the dynamic programming concepts we'll discuss in Chapter 11.

7.1   Introduction to UI Elements

According to the SAP online help documentation, UI elements "support general user interaction and screen display within a web application." As such, they're used to display and edit data, trigger events, and so on. Throughout the course of this book, we've encountered several commonly used UI elements, such as the `Label`, `InputField`, and `Button` elements. We also demonstrated a series of layout-related UI elements in the previous chapter when we looked at the `TransparentContainer`, `Group`, and `Tray` elements, among others.

Overall, the UI elements considered thus far represent only a fraction of the UI elements we have to work with within the Web Dynpro framework. Indeed, as of the SAP NetWeaver 7.30 release, there are almost one hundred different UI element types to choose from. And that number is likely to increase over time as newer SAP NetWeaver versions are released.

In the upcoming sections, we'll begin looking at specific UI element types up close. However, in the meantime, we should spend a few moments looking over some basic concepts so we can better understand how UI elements fit into the overall Web Dynpro framework.

7.1.1 Basic Concepts

UI elements make up the basic visual building blocks of the Web Dynpro user interface. If you've worked with other UI toolkits, you can think of UI elements as analogous to GUI widgets, controls, and so on. Regardless of what we call them, though, the main takeaway here is that UI elements are reusable elements that can be mixed and matched to rapidly build input forms and create interactive reports and various other UI application types using declarative programming techniques.

As we've seen, UI elements are laid out and configured using the View Designer tool shown in Figure 7.1. Once a UI element has been added to the view layout, its appearance and behavior can be configured using a combination of:

▶ **Properties**
Each UI element type defines a number of properties that can be configured using the PROPERTIES table in the lower right-hand corner of the View Designer screen (see Figure 7.1). These properties are used to specify the UI element's dimensions, look and feel, data sources, and more.

▶ **Events**
Many UI elements define events that can be triggered by users interacting with the application on the frontend. For example, a `Button` UI element defines an `onAction` event triggered whenever the button is pressed by a user. These events are linked to actions defined within the view controller for the purposes of server-side event handling.

▶ **Aggregations**

Many UI element types are *aggregates* that embed one or more child UI elements. In Chapter 6, we observed this relationship with layout elements such as the `Group` element, which groups together a series of child UI elements. However, as we'll see soon, there are quite a few other aggregate UI element types defined within the Web Dynpro framework.

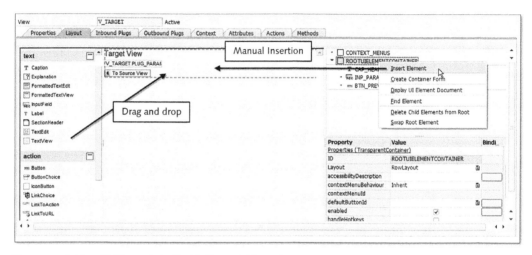

Figure 7.1 Adding UI Elements to the UI Element Hierarchy

As compared to other Web UI toolkits whose widgets are defined using some flavor of markup language (i.e., HTML and/or tag libraries), UI elements in Web Dynpro are quite easy to work with. Indeed, even the most complex of UI element types can usually be configured with just a few clicks of the mouse. However, such ease of use doesn't imply a tradeoff in terms of flexibility or sophistication. We're still dealing with high-fidelity UI elements here; the only difference is that much of the complexity in configuration is abstracted by the declarative nature of the Web Dynpro toolset.

As developers working within the framework, we can use the View Designer tool to weave together a user interface by simply dragging-and-dropping UI elements onto the canvas (as demonstrated in Figure 7.1). During this design process, we needn't concern ourselves with implementation-specific details, such as how a particular UI element will be rendered in a particular user agent type, and so on. Instead, we can simply add UI elements to the UI element hierarchy and let the

Web Dynpro runtime environment sort out all the low-level technical details at runtime.

7.1.2 Runtime Classes

As we've seen, the graphical tools provided by the Web Dynpro framework allow us to define a view layout without having to write a single line of source code. Behind the scenes, this is all made possible via the UI element's underlying *runtime class*, which is based on ABAP Objects. Internally, these runtime classes take care of mundane details, such as:

- Maintaining the UI element's properties and events
- Keeping track of child UI elements
- Interfacing with the surrounding Web Dynpro framework

Figure 7.2 illustrates the runtime class for the InputField UI element: class CL_WD_INPUT_FIELD. As you can see, this class defines a series of getter/setter methods that correspond with the configurable properties provided with the InputField element. Internally, the Web Dynpro framework interfaces with these methods to implement automatic data binding, and so on. The framework also has touch points with any events that might be defined within the runtime class (e.g., the ON_CHANGED event of the CL_WD_INPUT_FIELD class).

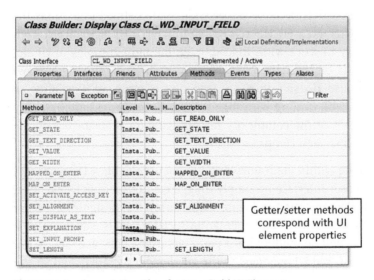

Figure 7.2 Implementation Class for InputField UI Element

If you look at the PROPERTIES tab of the CL_WD_INPUT_FIELD class, you can see that it's defined within the SWDP_UIEL_STANDARD package. If you navigate to this package within the Object Navigator tool, you'll find most of the other runtime classes for UI elements contained within the framework (see Figure 7.3).

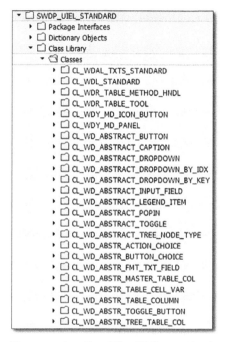

Figure 7.3 Locating Other UI Element Implementation Classes

Specific details about UI element runtime classes can be found online in the SAP Help Portal (*http://help.sap.com*) by searching for the expression *Web Dynpro ABAP, User Interface Elements*. There, you can find details about each of the provided UI element types, including:

▶ The UI element's runtime class

▶ UI element properties and their corresponding value domains

▶ Dynamically programmable properties and events

We'll revisit the topic of UI element runtime classes when we discuss dynamic programming concepts in Chapter 11.

7.1.3   UI Element Categories

Given the vast array of UI elements supported by the Web Dynpro framework, SAP decided to group together related UI elements into a series of logical *UI element categories*. Table 7.1 describes the list of UI element categories available as of the SAP NetWeaver 7.3 release.

UI Element Category	Description
Text	As the category name suggests, UI elements in this category are used to display and/or edit text-based content. Here, we have the `Label` and `InputField` elements we've seen already, as well as text boxes, captions, and so on. We'll look at UI elements from this category up close in Section 7.2.
Action	UI elements in this category are designed to allow users to trigger events. Examples of UI elements in this category include the `Button` and `LinkToAction` elements. We'll look at UI elements from this category in Section 7.3.
Selection	Within this category, we have a series of UI elements used to allow the users to make various kinds of selections: ▶ Checkboxes ▶ Radio buttons ▶ Dropdown lists and list boxes We'll look at UI elements from this category in Section 7.4.
Complex	This UI element category contains a host of complex UI elements used to display complex data structures, facilitate selections, and provide road maps for users traversing through the user interface. We'll look at selected elements from this category in Chapter 8.
Layout	This UI element category defines the set of layout elements (or containers) used to organize UI elements within the view layout. Here, we're talking about UI elements such as `Group`, `TabStrip`, `TransparentContainer`, and so on. Refer back to Section 6.2.2 for more details about UI elements in this category.
Graphic	This UI element category contains all the UI elements used to display graphics, dials, maps, and so on. We'll look at selected elements from this UI element category in Chapter 8.

Table 7.1 UI Element Categories

UI Element Category	Description
Integration	UI elements from this category are used to integrate WDA applications with external applications and technologies. Here, you'll find UI elements to upload and download files, embed PDF forms or Microsoft Office documents, and so on. We'll look at selected elements from this UI element category in Chapter 8.

Table 7.1 UI Element Categories (Cont.)

Throughout the remainder of this chapter and the next, we'll explore the use of many of these UI element types up close. Realistically, it wasn't feasible for us to cover every possible UI element type in depth. Therefore, our focus will be more on understanding how the different UI elements work, how they interface with other view elements such as actions and context nodes and attributes, and where to go to find examples and documentation for particular application use cases. Also, since you should now be comfortable appending UI elements to the UI element hierarchy, we'll skip over the screenshot-by-screenshot step list used to demonstrate UI elements earlier in the book so we can focus on the more obscure details of particular UI elements. So, without further ado, let's get started.

7.2 UI Elements from the Text Category

At the end of the day, most WDA applications contain at least some amount of textual content. Examples of textual content include page headings, labels, input fields, and so on. Since we interface with text elements like this all the time—both within and outside Web Dynpro—you'll find most of the text-based UI elements in the text category to be highly intuitive. We'll demonstrate the uses of most of these UI element types in the upcoming sections. You can find working examples of the other element types in the SAP sample component `WDR_TEST_EVENTS`.

7.2.1 UI Element Overview

As of the SAP NetWeaver 7.3 release, there are nine UI element types in the text category. Table 7.2 describes each of these UI element types in turn.

UI Element Type	Usage Description
Caption	The Caption UI element is used to display a heading or title in several complex UI elements, including the Group, Table, and Tray UI elements.
Explanation	This UI element is used to display translatable help texts that assist users in understanding and navigating within the user interface.
FormattedTextEdit	As the name suggests, this UI element is used to edit formatted text. The provided formatting options are based on the XHTML standard. Here, we can: ▶ Format text with boldfaced or italic font ▶ Organize text using three different heading levels ▶ Indent text ▶ Define ordered and unordered lists
FormattedTextView	This UI element is used to display formatted text based on the XHTML standard. However, unlike its FormattedText-Edit cousin element, it supports a somewhat wider selection of markup options, including links, images, and more.
InputField	The InputField UI element defines a basic input field for editing and displaying simple data types (e.g., strings, numbers, etc.). It corresponds with the familiar <input> tag in HTML and is used extensively in forms development.
Label	As the name suggests, the Label UI element is used to label other UI elements. For example, when defining an input form, Label elements are used to help the user understand the types of data that should be entered in InputField elements.
SectionHeader	This UI element is used to display a header for a section in a form.
TextEdit	The TextEdit UI element is used to edit plain text within a multi-line text field, much like the HTML <textarea> element. The text in this UI element uses a uniform font, font size, and font style. The text content area is displayed with borders and can scroll as necessary. The frame size is specified by the row and col properties.

Table 7.2 UI Elements from the Text Category

UI Element Type	Usage Description
TextView	This UI element is the read-only counterpart to the `TextEdit` UI element. As such, it's used to display plain, free-form text in a multi-line text field. However, unlike `TextEdit`, the `TextView` UI element isn't rendered with a surrounding border. The text can also be styled in different ways: font size, color, and so on.

Table 7.2 UI Elements from the Text Category (Cont.)

In the following sections, we'll take a closer look at some of the more predominant UI element types used within the text category.

7.2.2 Building Input Forms Using Label and InputField

Perhaps the most common of UI element types within the Web Dynpro toolkit are the `Label` and `InputField` elements. These elements are used to create basic input forms like the one shown in Figure 7.4. Here, data is captured in the `Input-Field` element, and the `Label` element is used to help the user understand what kind of data to enter into the `InputField`.

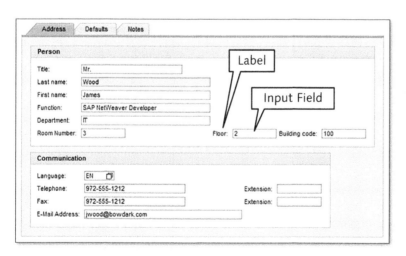

Figure 7.4 Working with the Label and InputField Elements

Working with the InputField Element

As we've seen, InputField elements are very straightforward to work with. Basically, once we append an InputField to the UI element hierarchy, all we really have to do is assign it an ID and link its value property with a context attribute, as shown in Figure 7.5. This will yield input fields like the ones shown in Figure 7.4 at runtime.

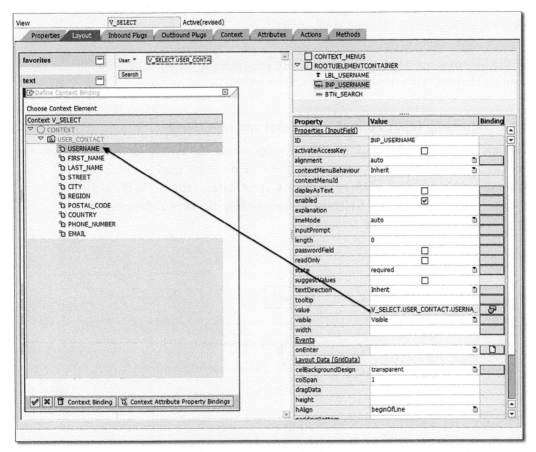

Figure 7.5 Binding an InputField with a Context Attribute

Though the contents of an InputField element are represented as a string on the screen, we can use the InputField element to edit *any* simple data type, including integers, floating point decimals, dates and times, and so on. This is made possible via the Web Dynpro framework, which performs automatic field conversions behind the scenes. Here, if an error occurs during field conversion (e.g., a user enters an invalid date in a date field), the framework will flag the InputField with a red border and issue an error message in the application message area.

In addition to the value property, InputField elements define quite a few other properties that can be used to influence the look, feel, and behavior of the input field at runtime. Table 7.3 describes a handful of the more prominent properties used to configure InputField elements.

Property Name	Description
displayAsText	This Boolean property determines whether or not a box will be drawn around the InputField. If selected, the contents of the text field will be displayed as plain text.
enabled	This Boolean property can be used to disable an InputField such that users cannot edit its contents, trigger events on it, and so on. Naturally, InputField elements are enabled by default.
explanation	This property can be used to display an explanation text that assists users in determining what kind of data to enter into the InputField. Since the topic of help texts in WDA is fairly involved, we'll defer further discussion on this property to Chapter 10.
inputPrompt	This property can be used to provide a help text that assists users in determining the format/type of data entered into an InputField. For example, in Figure 7.6, you can see how we've defined an input prompt for an InputField used to enter a telephone number. Here, the input prompt guides the user in entering a telephone number using the pattern XXX-XXX-XXXX. Whenever a user clicks on the InputField element, the input prompt will go away, and they can begin keying in data as usual.
passwordField	If an InputField is used to edit sensitive data such as passwords, we can mask the input/output using the passwordField property. If this Boolean property is selected, the data contained within the InputField will be masked using asterisks (*).
readOnly	This Boolean property determines whether or not the InputField is *editable*. If selected, the field will be grayed out within the user interface.

Table 7.3 Selected Properties of the InputField Element

Property Name	Description
state	This property can be used to determine whether or not the InputField is a required field. As we observed in Chapter 3, whenever the state property is assigned the required value, a couple of things happen: ▶ The corresponding Label element will be tagged with a red asterisk, indicating that the field is required. ▶ The InputField is treated as a required field. We can verify user input using the CHECK_MANDATORY_ATTR_ON_VIEW( )method of class CL_WD_DYNAMIC_TOOL. Refer back to Section 3.3.8 for an example.

Table 7.3 Selected Properties of the InputField Element (Cont.)

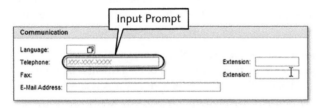

Figure 7.6 Working with the inputPrompt Property

Sometimes, it may be desirable to trigger a server roundtrip when users enter data in an InputField. In these situations, we can link the onEnter event with an action defined in the corresponding view controller. From here, we might perform a partial validation, refresh data, and so on.

Working with the Label Element

In order for users to know what to enter in InputField elements, we must label these elements with descriptive names. Naturally, we use the Label UI element for this purpose.

In and of themselves, Label UI elements are fairly simplistic in nature. Their sole function is to provide a label for other UI elements whose purpose/function may not be obvious on their own. Here, we should point out that, although you will often see Label and InputField elements used side by side, Label elements are also used to provide labels for dropdown lists, radio buttons, and so on. See the online help documentation for a complete listing of UI elements that can be associated with a Label.

Property Name	Description
text	This string property defines the Label element's text. The value for this property can be configured in several different ways: ▶ Within the properties table, we can statically define a label text. ▶ If we want the label text to be easily translatable, we can assign an OTR text from the Online Text Repository tool using the provided input help. We'll learn more about OTR texts in Chapter 12 when we discuss internationalization concepts. ▶ We can bind the property with a context attribute that contains the label text. If no value is specified, the Label text may also be derived dynamically at runtime via the Web Dynpro framework. We'll see how this works in a moment.
labelFor	This property is used to bind the Label element with another UI element (e.g., an InputField, ItemListBox, and so on).
tooltip	If the label text itself isn't sufficient for describing an input field, we can use the tooltip property to provide some additional descriptive text for the user. This text will show up as a tooltip when users hover their mouse pointers over the Label (see Figure 7.7).

Table 7.4 Selected Properties of the Label Element

Figure 7.7 Displaying a Tooltip for a Label Element

As we mentioned earlier, if the text property for a Label element isn't configured, the Web Dynpro framework *may* be able to derive its value dynamically at runtime. This derivation process is driven off of the UI element pointed to by the labelFor property and is implemented as follows:

1. First, the framework checks to see if the used UI element's *primary property* is bound against a context attribute whose type is based on a data element from the ABAP Dictionary (see Figure 7.8 and Figure 7.9).

Note

For more information about primary properties, check out the Web Dynpro ABAP online help documentation in the section entitled "Primary Property."

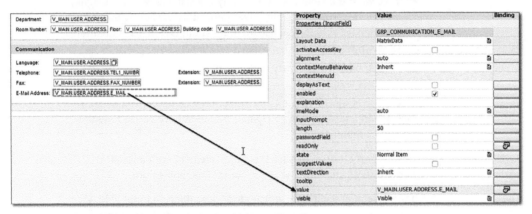

Figure 7.8 Dynamically Deriving Label Text (Part 1)

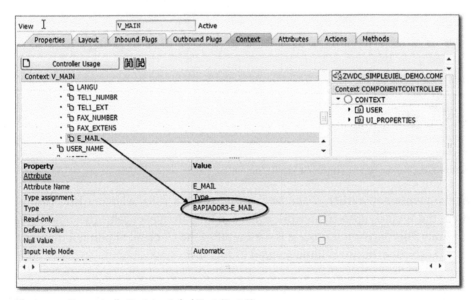

Figure 7.9 Dynamically Deriving Label Text (Part 2)

2. If it is, the framework will introspect the data element to extract the medium-length field label text as shown in Figure 7.10. This is the value that will be proposed for the Label text at runtime.

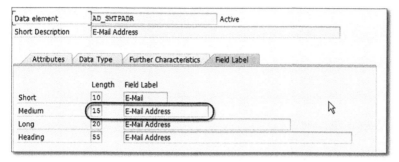

Figure 7.10 Dynamically Deriving Label Text (Part 3)

Working with the Container Form Wizard

Back in Section 3.3.5, we demonstrated how the container form wizard could be used to automate the creation of input forms. Now that we're more familiar with how such forms are defined, let's take a closer look at what this wizard is doing behind the scenes. As you may recall, the steps for creating an input form using the container form wizard are as follows:

1. First, we must select a layout element that will contain the form fields. This could be the default RootUIElementContainer, a nested Group element, and so on. In any case, we can right-click on the layout element and select the CREATE CONTAINER FORM menu option as shown in Figure 7.11.

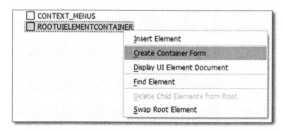

Figure 7.11 Working with the Container Form Wizard (Part 1)

2. This will open the dialog box shown in Figure 7.12. Here, we can select a context element and determine which context attributes should be used to define

the form fields. As you can see in Figure 7.12, the wizard automatically derives the default cell editors for each of the form fields.

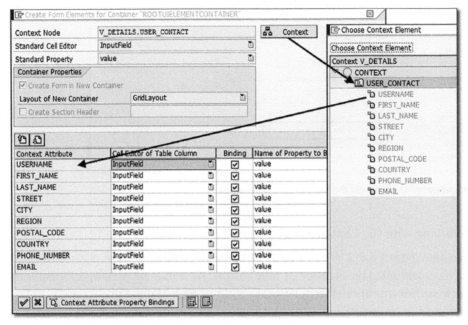

Figure 7.12 Working with the Container Form Wizard (Part 2)

3. After we're finished with our configuration, we can click on the button with the green checkmark on it to confirm our selection. At this point, the wizard will begin creating a `Label` and `InputField` elements within the selected container behind the scenes: a pair for each context attribute selected in the dialog screen shown in Figure 7.12.

4. Finally, the input form will be created and we can begin tweaking the resultant `Label` and `InputField` elements within the properties table as usual.

Naturally, the primary benefit to using the wizard is that it reduces the amount of manual configuration necessary to create all the required `Label` and `InputField` elements. This is particularly the case for context elements whose attributes are defined using data elements in the ABAP Dictionary. Here, we can avoid having to specify the `text` property for each of the generated `Label` elements by letting the Web Dynpro framework dynamically derive these texts on our behalf at runtime.

7.2.3 Displaying Plain Text Using TextView

Frequently, we may run into situations when we need to display a relatively large amount of free-form text on the screen. For example, we might want to display notes, user comments, and so on. For this task, we can utilize the TextView element.

Figure 7.13 illustrates how the TextView element is rendered on the screen using the SAP example application WDR_TEST_UI_ELEMENTS. As you can see, the text is displayed in a frame with an invisible border. Within this frame, we can use the design and semanticColor properties to determine the font size and color of the text being displayed. We can also influence wrapping behavior using the wrapping property. Alternatively, if we want to set hard line breaks within the text, we can do so using the newline character (represented by the NEWLINE_CHARACTER constant defined in class CL_ABAP_CHAR_UTILITIES).

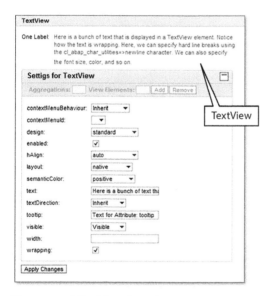

Figure 7.13 A TextView Example

7.2.4 Editing Plain Text with TextEdit

The InputField element demonstrated in the previous section is useful in situations when we need to enter small amounts of text. However, if we need to support larger amounts of text, we can enlist the aid of the TextEdit element. Figure 7.14 demonstrates what the TextEdit element looks like on the screen. As you can see, it has a similar look and feel to the HTML `<textarea>` element in that it provides a simple, plain-text editing area.

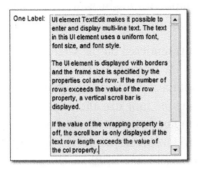

Figure 7.14 A TextEdit Example

From a design-time perspective, `TextEdit` elements are configured much like `InputField` elements. Here, we have the same familiar properties for specifying the text alignment, value, and so on. However, in addition to all that, the `TextEdit` element also defines a handful of properties for defining the look and feel of the surrounding text frame. Table 7.5 describes these properties in detail.

Property	Description
cols	The `cols` property defines the width (in characters) of the `TextEdit` field. Since the text contained within a `TextEdit` field is not displayed using a monospace font type, this width is something of an approximation. Furthermore, the width can be superceded by the `width` property.
rows	The `rows` property defines the height of the text frame in terms of lines, or rows, of text. If the number of lines of text contained within the `TextEdit` field exceeds the value specified in this property, a vertical scrollbar will be provided, as demonstrated in Figure 7.14.
wrapping	This property determines how text is wrapped within the text frame—if at all. Here, we're provided with three different configuration options: ▶ `off` If wrapping is turned off, text will be displayed continually on one line without line breaks. If the number of characters exceeds the width of the text frame (as specified by the `cols` and/or `width` properties), a horizontal scrolling bar will be displayed to allow users to scroll over and view the text.

Table 7.5 Selected Properties of the TextEdit Element

Property	Description
wrapping (Cont.)	▶ **hard** When this property value is selected, hard line breaks will be inserted using carriage returns whenever a row of text exceeds the width specified by the `cols` property. ▶ **soft** When this property value is selected, soft line breaks will be inserted whenever a row of text exceeds the width specified by the `cols` property.

Table 7.5 Selected Properties of the TextEdit Element (Cont.)

7.2.5 Displaying Formatted Text using FormattedTextView

In Section 7.2.3, we demonstrated the `TextView` element, which can be used to display free-form text on the screen. As we observed, the formatting options provided with the `TextView` element are pretty much limited to font size and color. Therefore, if we need to display more stylized text, we must utilize the `FormattedTextView` element, which is demonstrated in the `DEMO_UIEL_FORMATTED_TEXT_EDIT` sample application shown in Figure 7.15.

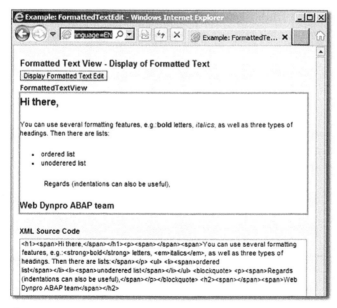

Figure 7.15 A FormattedTextView Example

325

As you can see in Figure 7.15, the `FormattedTextView` element supports a number of common formatting features, including:

- Boldface and italic font
- Headings
- Paragraphs
- Indentations
- Lists
- Links
- Images

Behind the scenes, the formatted text is encoded using a subset of XHTML, as shown in the XML SOURCE CODE text area in Figure 7.15. Here, you can see familiar tags, such as `<h1>`, `<strong>`, and so on. You can find a list of supported tags in the online help documentation in the reference section for the `FormattedTextView` element.

Working with the CL_WD_FORMATTED_TEXT Service Class

For the most part, `FormattedTextView` elements are configured by binding the `text` property with a string attribute containing XHTML markup. This markup might be contained within a database table or derived dynamically. In either case, we may need some help formatting the text that will be displayed on the screen. Fortunately, SAP provides a service class called `CL_WD_FORMATTED_TEXT` that can be used for this purpose. Table 7.6 describes some of the methods offered with this class.

Method Name	Method Type	Description
CREATE	Static	Factory method used to create an instance of the class using XML markup.
CREATE_FROM_ SAPSCRIPT	Static	Factory method used to transform SAPScript text into XML markup that can be displayed in a `FormattedTextView` element.

Table 7.6 Methods of Class CL_WD_FORMATTED_TEXT

Method Name	Method Type	Description
CREATE_FROM_HTML	Static	Factory method that can be used to generate compliant XHTML markup from an excerpt of HTML markup. Here, non-supported tags are removed from the markup as needed.
MAKE_TEXT	Static	Factory method that can be used to chain together a series of formatted text objects (also defined as instances of CL_WD_FORMATTED_TEXT) to build larger paragraphs, and so on. See the online help documentation in the reference section for the CL_WD_FORMATTED_FIELD for a demonstration of this method.
MAKE_IMG_TAG	Static	Factory method used to construct an \<img\> tag.
MAKE_A_TAG	Static	Factory method used to construct an anchor tag (i.e., the familiar \<a\> tag). This tag will be rendered as a hyperlink in the FormattedTextView. Whenever users click on this link, the onAction event of the FormattedTextView element will be fired.
MAKE_SAP_FIELD	Static	Factory method used to construct an \<sap:field\> tag. SAP fields are used as placeholders within the XHTML markup. The values of these placeholders are replaced at runtime with the values contained in bound context attributes. To understand how this works, consider the XHTML excerpt below. Here, you can see how we've defined two SAP fields with the names CONNID and CARRID, respectively. These names refer to context attributes defined with the context node bound against the FormattedTextView element's dataSource property. Places \<em\>available\</em\> for flight \<code\>\<sap:field name="CONNID"/\>\</code\> of line \<sap:field name="CARRID"/\>.

Table 7.6 Methods of Class CL_WD_FORMATTED_TEXT (Cont.)

Method Name	Method Type	Description
MAKE_SAP_FIELD (Cont.)		At runtime, both tags will be replaced with the values contained within the linked context attributes like this: Places available for flight <code>0017</code> of line AA. As you might expect, SAP fields are quite useful in situations when we need to construct formatted text on the fly. Here, we can weave static text with the dynamic text contained within SAP fields using the aforementioned MAKE_TEXT() method. This is demonstrated in the online help documentation.
RENDER	Instance	This instance method can be used to adjust and customize the rendering of the XHTML markup as needed.
SET_XML_TEXT	Instance	This method can be used to overwrite the existing markup for a CL_WD_FORMATTED_TEXT instance.
VALIDATE	Instance	This method is used to ensure that the generated XHTML markup is valid according to the requirements of the FormattedTextView element. It's always a good idea to use this method to validate texts before displaying them on screen.
REPLACE_ PLACEHOLDER	Instance	Whenever texts are created using the MAKE_TEXT() method, it's possible to define placeholders within the text using syntax like this: &placeholder&. The REPLACE_PLACEHOLDER() method is used to replace these placeholders with another formatted text object. This is another way class CL_WD_ FORMATTED_TEXT allows us to chain together text objects.

Table 7.6 Methods of Class CL_WD_FORMATTED_TEXT (Cont.)

7.2.6 Editing Formatted Text with FormattedTextEdit

In the previous section, we learned how the FormattedTextView element can be used to display formatted text. To edit formatted text, we can use the FormattedTextEdit element, which is demonstrated in Figure 7.16. As you can see, this element provides a simplified text editor with a handful of familiar formatting options in the integrated top-level toolbar.

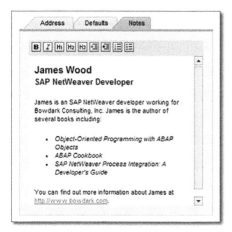

Figure 7.16 A FormattedTextEdit Example

Much like the `FormattedTextView` element, the text content contained within a `FormattedTextEdit` element is encoded using a subset of XHTML. However, in the case of the `FormattedTextEdit` element, the set of supported tags is condensed down even further. So, if you don't see a tag represented via one of the toolbar buttons, it's not supported via the `FormattedTextEdit` element.

7.3 UI Elements from the Action Category

Each of the elements within the action category provides users with the opportunity to trigger actions at runtime. As you may recall from Chapter 4, these actions provide "a view controller-specific mechanism for responding to events raised on the client device as a result of user interaction."[1] In this section, we'll survey the elements within this category and take a look at a couple of related element types that don't have an official category: the `Menu` and `ToolBar` elements. You can find working examples for each of the element types within the action category in the SAP sample component `WDR_TEST_EVENTS`.

---

1 This quote was taken from an SAP whitepaper entitled *The Structural Concepts of Web Dynpro Components*. This reference guide can be found online at *http://scn.sap.com/docs/DOC-2574*.

7.3.1 UI Element Overview

As of the SAP NetWeaver 7.3 release, there are seven UI element types within the action category. Table 7.7 describes each of these UI element types in turn.

UI Element Type	Visualization	Usage Description
Button	Text for Attribute: text	This UI element is used to represent a push button on the screen. Users can click on these buttons to trigger actions on the backend.
ButtonChoice	Text for Attribute: text Text for Attribute: text Text for Attribute: text Text for Attribute: text Text for Attribute: text	This UI element combines the look and feel of the Button UI element with a dropdown menu.
IconButton		This UI element defines a push button with an icon/image on it instead of text like the Button UI element. It can also be configured to display a dropdown menu like the ButtonChoice UI element.
LinkChoice	Text for Attribute: text Text for Attribute: text Text for Attribute: text Text for Attribute: text Text for Attribute: text	This UI element is similar to the ButtonChoice UI element in that it displays a dropdown menu. However, instead of rendering the menu items as buttons, the menu items are displayed as hyperlinks.
LinkToAction	Text for Attribute: text	This UI element renders a hypertext link to an action.
LinkToURL	Text for Attribute: text	This UI element also renders a hypertext link like the LinkToAction element. However, in this case, the link points to a physical URL (e.g., *http://www.bowdark.com*), and not an action. The URL is opened in a separate window.

Table 7.7 UI Elements from the Action Category

UI Element Type	Visualization	Usage Description
TimedTrigger	N/A	This UI element is used to asynchronously trigger actions on the backend on a periodic interval (à la AJAX). As such, it's not displayed within the user interface. Instead, it runs silently in the background using a timer whose interval can be configured using the delay property. If you're interested in seeing how this works firsthand, check out the SAP demo component WDR_TEST_UI_ELEMENTS for a live demonstration.

Table 7.7 UI Elements from the Action Category (Cont.)

7.3.2 Basic Concepts

For the most part, UI elements from the action category can be classified as either a *button* or a *link*. Within these subcategories, certain button/link types may also be further enhanced with submenus. Collectively, these items allow users to trigger actions by pressing buttons, clicking on links, or selecting menu items.

UI elements from the action category are linked with actions defined on the corresponding view controller via the onAction event, as demonstrated in Figure 7.17. We can then attach custom logic to these actions via the auto-generated event handler method associated with the action. For example, in Listing 7.1, you can see how we're invoking an instance method called SAVE_USER() on the component controller whenever a user clicks on the SAVE button, as shown in Figure 7.17. In general, we can use these event handler methods to:

- ▶ Trigger navigation
- ▶ Initiate server roundtrips to refresh the view
- ▶ Call methods on global controllers to process data and/or sync up with the model layer
- ▶ Perform housekeeping within the view layer

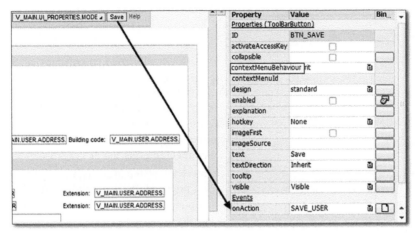

Figure 7.17 Linking a Button with an Action

```
method ONACTIONSAVE_USER.
  "Save the user record:
  wd_comp_controller->save_user( ).
endmethod.
```

Listing 7.1 Responding to an Action Triggered via a Button Element

7.3.3 Working with Menus

As discussed in Section 7.3.1, several UI elements from the action category may contain a nested dropdown menu. The items within these menus are represented using the abstract `MenuItem` element, which may be used to define several different types of menus within WDA applications, including:

► Traditional menus nested within a menu bar, as illustrated in Figure 7.18

► Context menus (i.e., menus that are opened by right-clicking on an element)

► Sub-menus for certain types of UI elements

As you can see in Figure 7.18, menus in Web Dynpro have a similar look and feel to menus found in traditional desktop applications, so much so that their use requires little introduction for users. As a result, you'll find that there are a number of UI element types that utilize nested submenus to enhance the element's selection capabilities in an intuitive and straightforward manner. The hierarchy diagram contained in Figure 7.19 illustrates how these relationships are established.

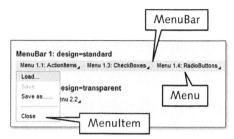

Figure 7.18 Working with Menus

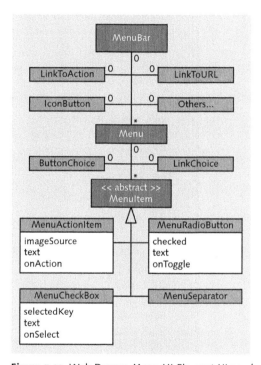

Figure 7.19 Web Dynpro Menu UI Element Hierarchy

Looking at the UI element hierarchy diagram in Figure 7.19, you can see that most of the elements toward the top of the hierarchy are aggregates. In other words, the top-level `MenuBar` and `Menu` elements do little more than group one or more child `Menu` or `MenuItem` elements, respectively. As such, the process of embedding child elements within these element types is quite similar to the one used to embed child elements to a layout container such as the `TransparentContainer` element.

From a functional perspective, the heavy lifting for menus is carried out by menu item elements based on the abstract `MenuItem` element type. Table 7.8 describes the various menu item types we have at our disposal when creating menus using Web Dynpro. The `DEMO_UIEL_MENU` sample component demonstrates each of these menu item types within a live WDA application.

Element Type	Visualization	Description
`MenuActionItem`		This element type is used to define a traditional menu item. Menu items of this type contain a label text and/or an optional image/icon. Whenever users click on this menu item type, the `onAction` event will be fired to process the user selection.
`MenuCheckBox`		This element type renders a menu item that acts like a switch. As users make selections, the menu item will be toggled on/off, the `onToggle` event will be fired, and the selected menu item will be annotated with a little checkmark on the left-hand side of the menu item text.
`MenuRadioButton`		This element type allows users to choose between several menu options in much the same way they would select a radio button in a radio button group. As selections are made, the `onSelect` event will be fired and the selected element will be rendered with a little dot icon on the left-hand side of the menu item text.
`MenuSeparator`		For large menus, the `MenuSeparator` element can be useful for defining a horizontal gutter between menu items.

Table 7.8 Menu Item Type Overview

7.3.4 Grouping Action Elements with the ToolBar Element

In some application scenarios, we may run into situations when we need to group a series of related action elements together. While this can be achieved using familiar layout elements such as the `TransparentContainer` or `ButtonRow` elements, another option would be to use the standard `ToolBar` element to create a toolbar.

Figure 7.20 demonstrates what the `ToolBar` element looks like on screen. Here, we've embedded the `ToolBar` element in the header area of a `PageHeader` element (see the sample component `ZWDC_SIMPLEUIEL_DEMO` in this book's sample code bundle for more details). Overall, `ToolBar` elements can be embedded as child elements of a number of UI element types, including tables, layout elements, and so on.

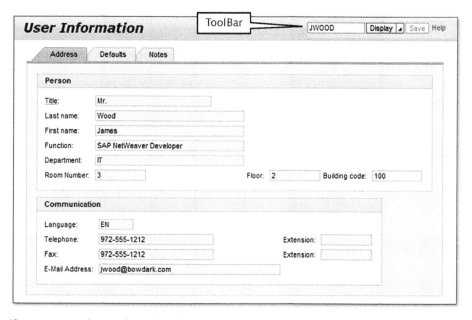

Figure 7.20 Working with ToolBar Elements

As you can see in Figure 7.20, `ToolBar` elements can contain a number of different UI element types: input fields, buttons, links, and so on. However, these UI elements aren't represented using familiar UI element types such as `InputField` or `Button`. Instead, there are `ToolBar`-specific UI subelements that, although they look like their regular counterpart elements, are optimized for use within a `ToolBar` element. Table 7.9 enumerates these elements. Since these elements have the same look, feel, and behavior as their regular counterpart elements, we won't get into further details on these UI element types here.

Element Type	Visualization
`ToolBarButton`	Save
`ToolBarButtonChoice`	Change ◢
`ToolBarDropDownByIndex`	Text for Attribute: texts ▼
`ToolBarDropDownByKey`	
`ToolBarInputField`	5.00
`ToolBarLinkToAction`	Text for Attribute: text
`ToolBarLinkToURL`	Text for Attribute: text
`ToolBarLinkChoice`	Text for Attribute: text Text for Attribute: text Text for Attribute: text Text for Attribute: text Text for Attribute: text
`ToolBarSeparator`	Display ◢ Save Help
`ToolBarToggleButton`	Text for Attribute: text

Table 7.9 Sub-Elements of the ToolBar Element

7.4 UI Elements from the Selection Category

In Section 7.2, we looked at several UI element types used to allow users to input various types of data: `InputField`, `TextEdit`, and so on. While these element types can be used to capture almost any kind of information, they can be cumbersome for users to work with in situations when users need to make a selection from a finite set of values rather than entering free-form text. In these scenarios, we can enlist the aid of UI elements from the selection category.

In this section, we'll survey the set of available UI elements within the selection category. Along the way, we'll take an up-close look at a couple of UI element types whose use may not be all that intuitive at first glance. You can find working examples of the other element types in the SAP sample component WDR_TEST_EVENTS and the sample component included with this book's code bundle for this chapter.

7.4.1 UI Element Overview

As of the SAP NetWeaver 7.3 release, there are eleven UI element types within the selection category. Table 7.10 describes each of these UI element types in turn.

UI Element Type	Visualization	Usage Description
CheckBox	☑ A Checkbox	This UI element type can be useful for displaying flags and other Boolean-type values. The checkbox state is maintained within the checked property. As users toggle the checkbox on and off, the onToggle event will be fired behind the scenes.
CheckBoxGroup	☐ Text for Attribute: texts ☐ Text for Attribute: texts ☐ Text for Attribute: texts ☐ Text for Attribute: texts ☐ Text for Attribute: texts	This element is used to display a group of CheckBox elements: one for each context element contained within the context node bound against the texts property. As users make selections within the checkbox group, the corresponding context element will be marked as selected within the parent context node.

Table 7.10 UI Elements from the Selection Category

UI Element Type	Visualization	Usage Description
DropDownByIndex and DropDownByKey	Text for Attribute: texts ▼	These UI element types are used to produce a dropdown list box in which users can select an input value from a predefined list of values. As opposed to a free-form text field, dropdown lists display a finite set of input values so that users don't have to remember all the possible input options. Naturally, dropdown lists are useful in situations when a field's value set is constrained by a predefined domain of values (e.g., state or country codes). In Section 7.4.2, we'll take a closer look at dropdown lists and consider the options we have for defining value domains.
ItemListBox	Text for Attribute Text for Attribute Text for Attribute Text for Attribute Text for Attribute	This UI element type is similar to the DropDownBy* element types in that it displays a selection list based on a predefined domain of values. However, from a functional perspective, there are a couple of key differences: ▶ The list box is permanently expanded to display a configurable number of entries, scrolling as necessary. ▶ Users can select multiple items within an ItemListBox simultaneously. The contents of the list are defined via the dataSource property, which gets bound to a context node with a cardinality of 0..n or 1..n.

Table 7.10 UI Elements from the Selection Category (Cont.)

UI Element Type	Visualization	Usage Description
RadioButton	⊙	RadioButton elements are used to choose only one of a predefined set of options. Normally, RadioButton elements are arranged in groups such that whenever a given RadioButton element is selected within the group, all other RadioButton elements will be deselected. We'll look at ways of defining RadioButton groups in Section 7.4.3.
RadioButtonGroup (ByIndex) (ByKey)	⊙ Text for Attribute: texts ◯ Text for Attribute: texts ◯ Text for Attribute: texts ◯ Text for Attribute: texts ◯ Text for Attribute: texts	
ToggleButton	Text for Attribute: text	This element type is functionally similar to the CheckBox element in that it provides users with a basic on/off switch. However, in this case, the switch is denoted by a push button instead of a checkbox. If the Toggle-Button is selected, the push button will be displayed in a *pressed down* state; otherwise, it will be represented as a normal push button.
ToggleLink	▼ Text for Attribute: text	This element type is functionally equivalent to the ToggleButton element. However, in this case, a link, instead of a push button, is displayed.
TriStateCheckBox	☑ ☒ ☐	This element type renders a specialized checkbox field that allows users to toggle between three different statuses (as defined in the standard data element WDUI_TRI_STATE): ▸ True (01) ▸ Undecided (00) ▸ False (02)

Table 7.10 UI Elements from the Selection Category (Cont.)

7.4.2 Working with Dropdown Lists

As we observed in Section 7.4.1, there are a couple of overlapping element types within the selection category that can be used to generate dropdown lists: DropDownByIndex and DropDownByKey. Though both of these element types look identical on screen, they're implemented quite differently behind the scenes. From a technical perspective, the differences lie in the way the the lists of values are derived. Here, we have the option of choosing between two different data binding techniques: *index binding* and *key binding*. In this section, we'll explore each of these techniques.

Index Binding and the DropDownByIndex Element

As the name suggests, the DropDownByIndex element utilizes the index binding technique. With index binding, the set of possible input values is defined by via a context node whose cardinality is 1..n or 0..n.

In order to understand how all this works, let's look at an example. In the diagram shown in Figure 7.21, you can see how we're using index binding to configure a DropDownByIndex element. This configuration basically consists of binding the DropDownByIndex element's texts property with a context attribute that will contain the text description for the dropdown list items. In the example shown in Figure 7.21, we're using the DESCRIPTION attribute for this purpose. At runtime, a separate list item will be displayed within the list box for each context element contained within the DESCRIPTION attribute's parent context node: DATE_FORMATS.

As users make selections on the frontend, the selected context element will be marked using the lead selection indicator. Therefore, we can use this index value to capture user selections and react accordingly in event handler methods. Indeed, the DropDownByIndex defines an event called onSelect that can be used for this purpose.

Key Binding and the DropDownByKey Element

One of the downsides to index binding is that it requires us to represent the set of input values displayed within the dropdown list using a separate context node that contains multiple elements: one for each possible selection entry. If we happen to have one of these context nodes lying around already, this is probably no big deal. On the other hand, if we don't already have a multi-element context node defined, it's a lot of work to create one just to supply a dropdown list with selection data.

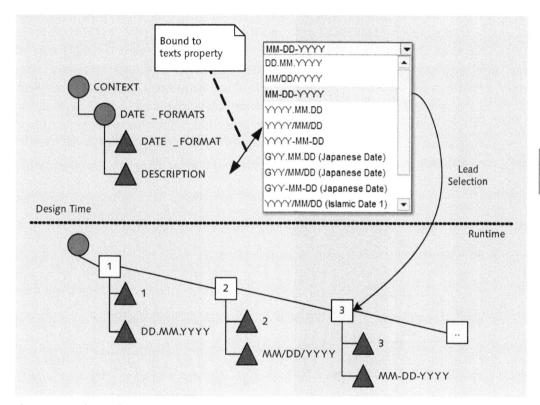

Figure 7.21 Index Binding Overview

To put this in perspective, let's imagine a scenario in which we have a context node called USER_DEFAULTS that has a cardinality of 0..1. Within the USER_DEFAULTS node, we've defined a context attribute called LANGU that's used to capture a user's default language in the form of a language key: e.g., EN for English, DE for German, and so on. Rather than forcing users to manually enter language keys, we want to bind the LANGU context attribute with a dropdown list. However, instead of having to define a separate context node to contain the set of possible input values, we'd like to figure out a way to store the data in one place. That way, we don't have to worry about having to manually synchronize values between the dropdown list and the LANGU attribute. As you may have guessed by now, we can achieve this by utilizing the key binding technique.

In order to understand how key binding works, let's look at how we'd implement the default language dropdown list described earlier in this section. In the diagram shown in Figure 7.22, you can see how we've bound the selectedKey property of a DropDownByKey element with a context attribute called LANGU. As you can see, the parent context node for the LANGU attribute, USER_DEFAULTS, has a cardinality of 0..1. However, this isn't a problem since the DropDownByKey element doesn't rely on the parent context node of its bound context attribute to determine its input value set. Instead, the DropDownByKey element derives its input value set from a set of name–value pairs attached to the metadata of the context attribute bound against the selectedKey property (e.g., the LANGU context attribute).

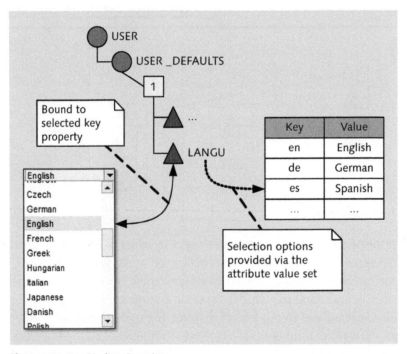

Figure 7.22 Key Binding Overview

From an implementation perspective, we have a couple of options for building our attribute value set:

▶ If the data type of the context attribute bound to the `selectedKey` property is defined using a data element from the ABAP Dictionary, the Web Dynpro framework can automatically derive the attribute value set using the data element's corresponding domain object (see Figure 7.23). This is the default behavior.

▶ Otherwise, we can always create the attribute value set by hand using the `IF_WD_CONTEXT_NODE_INFO` interface. We'll look at how this is accomplished in just a moment.

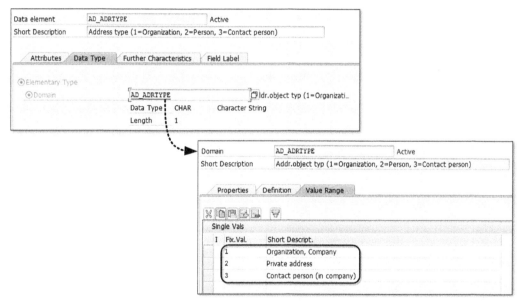

Figure 7.23 Deriving Attribute Value Sets via the ABAP Dictionary

Listing 7.2 demonstrates how we're using the `IF_WD_CONTEXT_NODE_INFO` interface to manually define the list of possible language keys in our example scenario.

```
method INIT_LANGUAGE_KEYS.
  DATA lo_nd_defaults TYPE REF TO if_wd_context_node.
  DATA lo_node_info   TYPE REF TO if_wd_context_node_info.
  DATA ls_value_set   TYPE wdy_key_value.
  DATA lt_value_set   TYPE wdy_key_value_table.
```

```
DATA lt_lang_keys   TYPE
        zcl_wda_simpleuiel_assist=>ty_language_key_tab.
FIELD-SYMBOLS:
  <lfs_lang_key>  LIKE LINE OF lt_lang_keys,
  <lfs_value_set> LIKE LINE OF lt_value_set.

"Lookup the set of language keys:
CALL METHOD wd_assist->get_language_keys
  IMPORTING
    et_lang_keys = lt_lang_keys.

"Copy the language keys to a set of name-value pairs:
LOOP AT lt_lang_keys ASSIGNING <lfs_lang_key>.
  CLEAR ls_value_set.
  ls_value_set-key = <lfs_lang_key>-spras.
  ls_value_set-value = <lfs_lang_key>-sptxt.
  APPEND ls_value_set TO lt_value_set.
ENDLOOP.

"Load the attribute value set into context:
lo_nd_defaults =
  wd_context->path_get_node( path = `USER.DEFAULTS` ).
lo_node_info = lo_nd_defaults->get_node_info( ).
lo_node_info->set_attribute_value_set(
  name = 'LANGU'
  value_set = lt_value_set ).
endmethod.
```

Listing 7.2 Defining an Attribute Value Set

As you can see in Listing 7.2, the process of defining an attribute value set is relatively straightforward:

1. First, we must obtain the raw selection values from the backend data model or ABAP Dictionary. For instance, in the code excerpt from Listing 7.2, we looked up the set of language keys from table T002 via an assistance class method called GET_LANGUAGE_KEYS().

2. Once the raw selection values are loaded, we must copy them to a name–value table of type WDY_KEY_VALUE_TABLE.

3. Then, in order to access the context attribute metadata, we must call the GET_NODE_INFO() method on the context attribute's parent context node. This method will return an object instance that implements the IF_WD_CONTEXT_NODE_INFO interface.

4. Finally, we can load the attribute value set into context by calling the SET_ATTRIBUTE_VALUE_SET() method of the IF_WD_CONTEXT_NODE_INFO interface.

Once the attribute value set is derived, the DropDownByKey element will pick up the changes automatically. Therefore, from a UI configuration perspective, once the selectedKey property is bound with the target context attribute, our work is done, and the Web Dynpro framework will handle everything else from there.

7.4.3 Working with Radio Buttons

As we mentioned earlier, RadioButton elements provide a sort of on/off switch that can be used to allow users to make selections. Though it's possible to define RadioButton elements in isolation, they're normally organized into groups using the RadioButtonGroupByIndex and RadioButtonGroupByKey elements. Much like their dropdown list counterparts, these UI elements use index binding and key binding techniques to build radio button groups. Indeed, from a configuration perspective, you'll find that the process for defining radio button groups corresponds with the one described for dropdown lists in the previous section:

▶ With the RadioButtonGroupByIndex element, we must bind the texts property with a context attribute whose parent context node has a cardinality of 0..n or 1..n. The value of the bound context attribute will be used to define the label text for the radio buttons defined within the group. As users make selections on the frontend, the lead selection for the linked context node will be adjusted automatically by the Web Dynpro framework the next time a server roundtrip is triggered. However, if we want to trigger this server roundtrip automatically, we can do so by wiring up the onSelect event.

▶ With the RadioButtonGroupByKey element, we must bind the selectedKey property with a context attribute that has an attribute value set attached to its metadata (see Figure 7.24). As users make selections on the frontend, the value of the bound context attribute will be updated automatically during the next server roundtrip. Alternatively, as was the case with the RadioButtonGroupByIndex element, we can force this synchronization to occur immediately by wiring up the onSelect event.

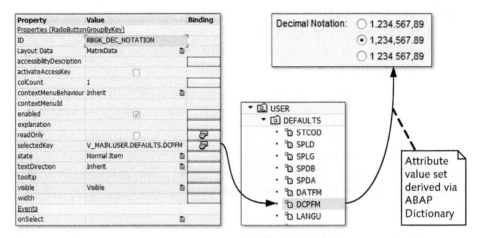

Figure 7.24 Working with the RadioButtonGroupByKey Element

7.5 Summary

In this chapter, we further acquainted ourselves with UI elements and the roles they play in defining user interfaces within the view layer. As we observed, the Web Dynpro framework provides so many types of UI elements that the UI element types are broken down into several distinct categories. Within this chapter, we surveyed some of the basic UI elements from the text, action, and selection categories. With this experience under our belts, we're now ready to dig into some of the more complex UI element types offered by the framework. Therefore, in the next chapter, we'll pick up where this chapter leaves off and continue looking at some of the other UI element types provided by the Web Dynpro framework.

In this chapter, we'll pick up where Chapter 7 left off by considering some of the more advanced UI element types provided with the Web Dynpro framework. Along the way, we'll also look at some new features supported in the latest versions of SAP NetWeaver, including drag and drop, popins, and more.

8   Advanced UI Elements

In the previous chapter, we examined some of the basic UI element types provided by the Web Dynpro framework. For the most part, these UI element types correspond with many of the common UI elements used to build traditional form-based web applications: input fields, buttons, and so on. Therefore, as we observed, their configuration was both straightforward and predictable.

In addition to the basic element types introduced in Chapter 7, the Web Dynpro framework also provides a number of more sophisticated UI element types that can be used to construct heavyweight GUI widgets such as trees or tables, integrate with various external media types, and more. In this chapter, we'll examine these more advanced UI element types.

8.1   UI Elements from the Graphic Category

Throughout the course of this book, we've seen that Web Dynpro, like its distant cousin, classic Dynpro, is well suited to building interactive, dialog-based applications. Of course, while this style of application may be the most common, Web Dynpro can also be used to build many other application types, including web-based reports. Here, in addition to displaying raw report data, we often need to display various types of graphics such as charts, graphs, and so on. For this task and others, we can enlist the services of UI elements from the graphic category.

8.1.1 UI Element Overview

As of the SAP NetWeaver 7.3 release, there are eight UI element types within the graphic category. Table 8.1 describes each of these UI elements in turn.

UI Element Type	Usage Description
BusinessGraphics	This UI element works in conjunction with the *Internet Graphics Service* (IGS) to display various types of charts and graphs, including pie charts, bar graphs, and so on. The data for the charts is supplied via the categorySource and seriesSource properties, respectively. There are also properties provided that allow us to specify the chart type, the URL for the target IGS, and a background image for the chart display. You can find more information about the capabilities of this UI element and the IGS in general online at the SAP Help Portal (*http://help.sap.com*) by performing a search on "BusinessGraphics" and "Internet Graphics Service," respectively.
Gantt	As the name suggests, this UI element is used to produce Gantt charts. However, unlike the BusinessGraphics element, which relies on the IGS to render its charts, the Gantt element is based on Java™ Applet technology, which requires that users have a Java Runtime Environment (JRE) installed as a plug-in on their user agent/browser. The data for the Gantt chart is provided via the dataSource property, which must be bound to a context attribute of type XSTRING. This context attribute must contain a serialized XML document that conforms to the XML Schema expected by the JGantt control on the frontend. You can find an example of this XML format in the SAP sample component WDR_TEST_EVENTS. Here, simply expand the MIMEs folder in the Web Dynpro Explorer tool and open up the gantt.xml file to see how the XML is structured.
GeoMap	This UI element is used to display a portion of a geographical map in the manner of Google Maps™. However, in order for this control to work, we must install a plug-in that must be purchased separately via a third party provider to the IGS (see SAP Note #994568 for more details).

Table 8.1 UI Elements from the Graphic Category

UI Element Type	Usage Description
Image	This UI element is used to display various types of graphical images on the screen. It supports several different types of image formats, including the familiar GIF, JPEG, and PNG formats. From a configuration perspective, the Image element is similar to the HTML <img> tag, providing properties to specify the dimensions of the image, whether or not a border should be displayed, and so on. We'll take a closer look at how images are displayed with the Image element in Section 8.1.2.
Network	This UI element type can be used to edit and display various types of network graphics: trees, E-R model diagrams, UML activity diagrams, and so on. In other words, it's a control that can be used to visualize graphs that are made up of nodes and edges.
	Much like the Gantt element, the Network element utilizes a Java applet called JNet to render the network graphics on the frontend. It also utilizes the same XML Schema to display the network graphics. See the tree.xml file in the WDR_TEST_EVENTS component for a sample of this XML format.
ProgressIndicator	The ProgressIndicator element is used to display a progress bar that indicates, percentage-wise, how much progress has been made for a particular activity. The completion percentage of a task is represented by the percentValue property, which must be bound to a context attribute of type I.
	One common way of synchronizing the status of a Progress-Indicator element is to utilize the TimedTrigger element described in Chapter 7. Here, we can use the onAction event of the TimedTrigger element to periodically query the status of a task in the background and update the percentage complete value on the ProgressIndicator element.
	Another option is to utilize the new *Web Dynpro Notification Service*, which was introduced in the SAP NetWeaver 7.02 release. For more information about this service, check out the class documentation for class CL_WD_NOTIFICATION_SERVICE in the Class Builder tool.

Table 8.1 UI Elements from the Graphic Category (Cont.)

UI Element Type	Usage Description
ThresholdSlider	This UI element displays a slider bar that allows users to graphically specify a value by dragging the bar back and forth within a predefined value range. The ThresholdSlider element is often used for the input of integer values bound by some minimum and maximum value. Here, instead of forcing users to enter a raw integer value using a free-form InputField element, we can use the ThresholdSlider element to constrain the value domain as necessary (e.g., between zero and one hundred). Furthermore, we can also define intermediate thresholds, which help users interpret the semantic meaning of a range of values within the value domain. We'll see how all this works up close in Section 8.1.3.
ValueComparison	In some respects, you can think of this UI element as like a display-only version of the ThresholdSlider element. Here, a value is displayed in a horizontal bar that can be partitioned off into different value buckets. This visualization helps users see where a particular value falls within a given value domain. You can find a live example of this UI element in the sample WDR_TEST_UI_ELEMENTS component provided by SAP.

Table 8.1 UI Elements from the Graphic Category (Cont.)

8.1.2 Displaying Images with the Image Element

The Image element makes it very easy to add images to the view layout. For the most part, all we have to do is bind the Image element's source property with a URL that points to the image we want to display. Here, there are several different URL formats to choose from. Table 8.2 provides an overview of the supported formats. If you're interested in learning more about specific syntax rules, check out the Web Dynpro ABAP online help documentation in the section entitled "Handling Images and Web Icons."

URL Syntax Format	Description
~Icon/Attachment ~IconLarge/AudioFile	These URLs are used to point to SAP-defined web icons provided out of the box. The input help for the source property allows us to browse interactively through this list of web icons.

Table 8.2 Supported URL Formats for the Image Element

URL Syntax Format	Description
`$EXT_SERVER_HTTP$/img/a.jpg` (where `EXT_SERVER_HTTP` is an RFC destination of type G)	This URL syntax is used to construct an absolute URL that points to image files stored on an HTTP-based server. Here, the `$DESTINATION$` variable refers to an RFC destination of type G (HTTP connection) maintained in Transaction SM59. It should be noted that this scheme could also be used to point to images that are dynamically created on the fly via some kind of server-side component (e.g., an ICF service, Java Servlet, and so on).
`/sap/public/images/hello.gif`	This URL scheme is used to point to images stored within the SAP MIME Repository. We'll learn more about how to access image files from the MIME Repository in just a moment.
`hello.gif` `images/hello.gif`	This URL scheme can be used to point to files uploaded to the MIMEs folder of a WDA component. We'll see how this works in just a moment.
`{WDR_TEST_EVENTS}/s_lr_11417.jpg`	This URL scheme allows us to reference image files uploaded to the MIMEs folder of another WDA component. For instance, in the provided syntax example, we're referencing a JPEG file called *s_lr_11417.jpg* from the `WDR_TEST_EVENTS` component.

Table 8.2 Supported URL Formats for the Image Element (Cont.)

Displaying Images from the MIMEs Folder of a WDA Component

Every WDA component contains a special folder called MIMEs, which can be used to upload image files that can be displayed using the `Image` element. As these image files are in effect local to the WDA component that defines them, they can be accessed using a relative URL syntax, as demonstrated in Table 8.2. To upload an image file into the MIMEs folder of a WDA component, we must perform the following steps:

1. The first step is to right-click on the target WDA component and select the CREATE • MIME OBJECT • IMPORT menu option.

2. This will open a dialog box in which we can browse to an image file somewhere on our local machine. Once we locate the target file, we can select it by clicking on the OPEN button.

3. Next, in the CREATE NEW DOCUMENT dialog box, we can confirm the image selection, provide an optional short text description for the image (see Figure 8.1), and click on the SAVE button to confirm our changes.

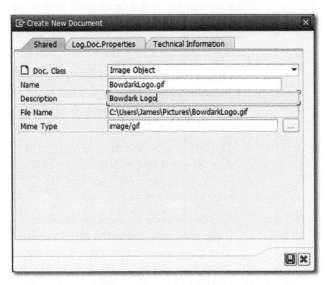

Figure 8.1 Uploading an Image to the MIMEs Folder of a WDA Component

4. Finally, we'll be prompted to create an object directory entry within the MIME Repository for the uploaded MIME object. Here, we can simply confirm the proposed package assignment and click on the SAVE button to upload the image.

Once the image file has been uploaded into the MIME Repository, we can display it in an `Image` element by assigning the uploaded file name to the `Image` element's `source` property, as shown in Figure 8.2. Here, we can use the provided input help to locate the target file as needed.

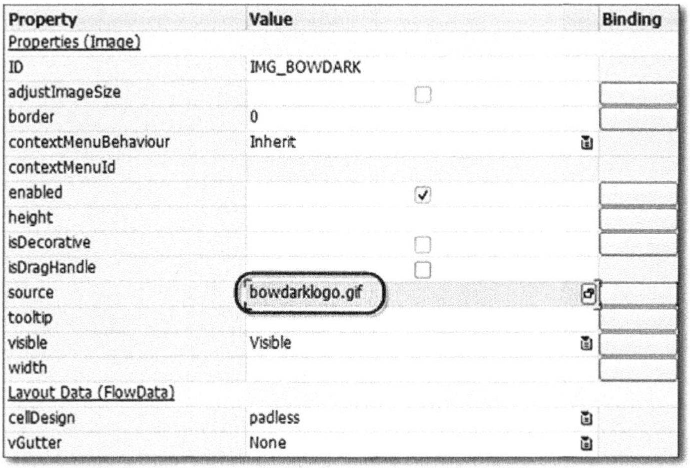

Property	Value	Binding
Properties (Image)		
ID	IMG_BOWDARK	
adjustImageSize	☐	
border	0	
contextMenuBehaviour	Inherit	
contextMenuId		
enabled	☑	
height		
isDecorative	☐	
isDragHandle	☐	
source	bowdarklogo.gif	
tooltip		
visible	Visible	
width		
Layout Data (FlowData)		
cellDesign	padless	
vGutter	None	

Figure 8.2 Displaying an Image from the MIMEs Folder

Displaying Images from the MIME Repository

In the previous section, we demonstrated how to upload image files into the MIMEs folder of a WDA component. However, technically speaking, what we really did was create a MIME object within a special folder carved out for WDA components within the *SAP MIME Repository*. If you haven't had an opportunity to work with the MIME Repository before, a brief description is in order. As the name suggests, the MIME Repository provides a repository for storing various types of MIME objects in an SAP system: image files, PDF files, XML configuration files, and so on. Behind the scenes, these MIME objects are stored within the ABAP Repository along with traditional development objects such as ABAP report programs and ABAP Objects class definitions. Thus, we can transport MIME objects via the Change and Transport System (CTS) as usual.

The MIME Repository can be accessed via the MIME Repository browser view of the ABAP Workbench, shown in Figure 8.3. As you can see, MIME objects are organized within the repository in hierarchical fashion, beginning with the default /sap root node and working downward. Here, for instance, we can find MIME objects uploaded into the MIMEs folder of a WDA component using the path /sap/bc/webdynpro/sap/<wda_component_name>.

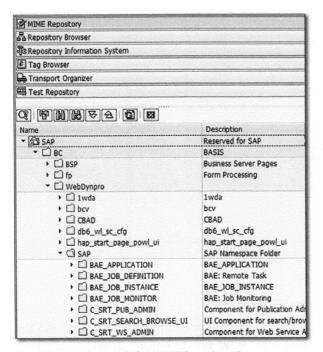

Figure 8.3 Working with the MIME Repository Browser

Generally speaking, we can access any image file contained within the MIME Repository by simply keying its path into the `source` property of an `Image` element (see Figure 8.4). At runtime, the Web Dynpro runtime environment will browse to the configured MIME Repository path, fetch the selected image file, and stream its contents into the `Image` element displayed within the view layout.

Property	Value	Binding
Properties (Image)		
ID	IMG_LOGO	
adjustImageSize	☐	
border	0	
contextMenuBehaviour	Inherit	
contextMenuId		
enabled	☑	
height		
isDecorative	☐	
isDragHandle	☐	
source	/sap/public/bc/nwdemo_model/images/company_logo.jpg	
tooltip		
visible	Visible	
width		

Figure 8.4 Referencing Image Files from the MIME Repository

8.1.3 Working with the ThresholdSlider Element

As we mentioned earlier, the `ThresholdSlider` element can be used to represent integral values in the form of a slider bar. Figure 8.5 illustrates what the `Threshold-Slider` element looks like on screen. Here, we're presenting a slider bar to represent a numeric grade scale in the range `0..100`. The values are aligned from left to right much like a number line with the minimum value on the far left and the maximum value on the far right. In between, we can display a series of tick marks that help users orient themselves along the slider bar (sort of like a ruler). Once all this is set up, users can interact with the `ThresholdSlider` element by sliding the slider bar back and forth to adjust the underlying value as needed.

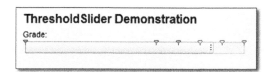

Figure 8.5 Working with the ThresholdSlider Element

Figure 8.6 demonstrates how we've configured the `ThresholdSlider` element depicted in Figure 8.5. Here, pay attention to four key properties:

▶ `maxTickMarks`
This property determines the total number of tick marks displayed on the bottom side of the control.

▶ `tickMarkSpacing`
This property determines the gap between a pair of tick marks. The spacing is measured in units whose length is determined by the `unitWidth` property.

▶ `unitWidth`
This property determines the width (in pixels) of an individual unit.

▶ `Value`
This property must be bound to a context attribute of type I. The value of the bound context attribute will be adjusted in step with changes made to the slider bar by users on the frontend. We can track these changes interactively using the defined `onAction` and `onChange` events, respectively.

Collectively, the four key properties described above determine the width and value range of the `ThresholdSlider` element as follows:

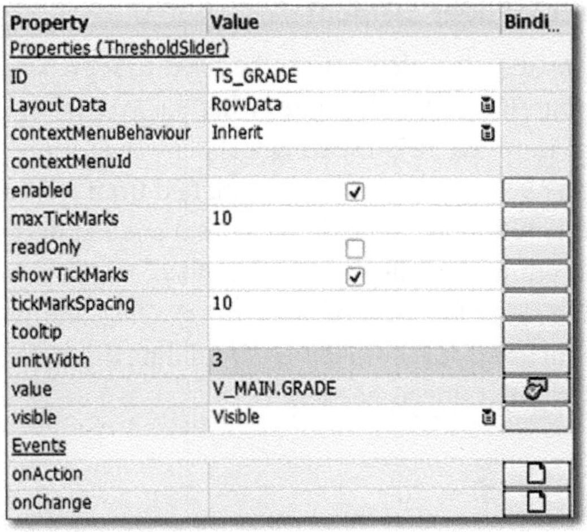

Property	Value	Bindi..
Properties (ThresholdSlider)		
ID	TS_GRADE	
Layout Data	RowData	
contextMenuBehaviour	Inherit	
contextMenuId		
enabled	☑	
maxTickMarks	10	
readOnly	☐	
showTickMarks	☑	
tickMarkSpacing	10	
tooltip		
unitWidth	3	
value	V_MAIN.GRADE	
visible	Visible	
Events		
onAction		
onChange		

Figure 8.6 Configuring the ThresholdSlider Element

▶ The width of the ThresholdSlider element on the screen is calculated as maxTickMarks x tickMarkSpacing x unitWidth. Thus, in our grade scale example shown in Figure 8.6, we have 10 x 10 x 3 = 300 pixels.

▶ The value range is calculated as [0..(maxTickMarks x tickMarkSpacing)]. In Figure 8.6, you can see how we configured both the maxTickMarks and tickMarkSpacing properties in our grade scale example with a value of 10 such that 10 x 10 = 100. Note that it's not permitted to assign a value to the value property outside this range at runtime.

As you can see in Figure 8.5, tick marks on the bottom side of the slider bar assist users in visualizing the data represented in a ThresholdSlider element on a quantitative scale. However, depending on the nature of the data we're representing, we may also want to define a qualitative scale, which is more intuitive for users from a semantic point of view. For instance, in our grade scale example, we want to visually demarcate the thresholds between letter grades (i.e., 90-100 for an A, 80-89 for a B, and so on). This can be achieved by embedding one or more Threshold child elements underneath the parent ThresholdSlider element. Figure 8.7 illustrates how we've defined letter grade thresholds in our grade scale example. Here, we've defined a separate Threshold element for each letter grade, A–F. Alternatively, we could have used the MultipleThreshold element to define these thresholds dynamically via the context.

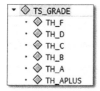

Figure 8.7 Defining Thresholds within a ThresholdSlider Element

As you can see in Figure 8.8, each `Threshold` element defines a `value` property that represents the lower bound of the threshold. The upper bound of a threshold is defined by the next `Threshold` element in the collection (which is assembled from top to bottom). So, to define the threshold for an "F," we assigned a value of 0 to the `TH_F Threshold` element and a value of 60 to the `TH_D Threshold` element. Thus, any value between 0 and 60 displayed on the `ThresholdSlider` element falls under the "F" threshold. We can use selected properties of the `Threshold` element to visualize individual thresholds as follows:

▶ The lower bound on a threshold can be demarcated by a small triangular icon on the top of the `ThresholdSlider` element (see Figure 8.5). We can turn on the display of this icon using the `showMarker` property.

▶ The `tooltip` property can be used to provide a tooltip label for the threshold marker icon whenever it's displayed.

▶ The color of the slider bar will change in accordance with the color value selected in the `color` property of each individual `Threshold` element. In our grade scale example, we're using the `color` property to assist users in understanding how the grade scale works. Here, we're leveraging the familiar traffic light color scheme to differentiate between bad marks and good marks (i.e., red for an "F," green for an "A," and so on). If you look at the online help documentation for the `Threshold` element, you can see that there are quite a few color schemes supported to represent different types of data displayed within a `ThresholdSlider` element.

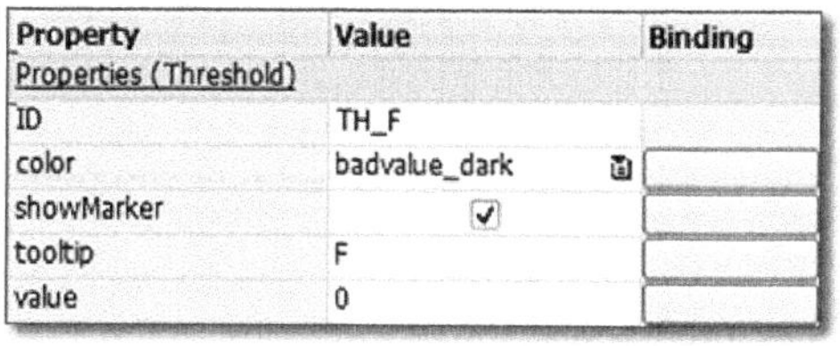

Property	Value	Binding
Properties (Threshold)		
ID	TH_F	
color	badvalue_dark	
showMarker	☑	
tooltip	F	
value	0	

Figure 8.8 Configuring a Threshold Element

8.2 UI Elements from the Integration Category

In the early days of web development, most web applications existed in isolation, with the majority of the application content being created from scratch. However, as the web matured, it quickly became apparent that such segregation failed to take advantage of all the rich content available online. Around this time, Web 2.0 was introduced, and with it, a new breed of web applications called *mashups*.

The term *mashup* is a name given to web applications that integrate content from a variety of sources. For the most part, there are no hard and fast rules to specify how external content should be integrated. The point is that, rather than building new content from scratch, we should try to leverage existing content as much as we can.

The Web Dynpro framework provides a number of UI element types that can be used to integrate external resources and create mashups. In this section, we'll survey these elements and consider how they can be used to integrate resources, both within the SAP landscape and beyond.

8.2.1 UI Element Overview

As of the SAP NetWeaver 7.3 release, there are eight UI element types within the integration category. Table 8.3 describes each of these UI elements in turn.

UI Element Type	Usage Description
AcfExecute	This UI element leverages functionality provided by the *Active Component Framework* (ACF) to integrate external applications into a WDA application. So, for example, we could use the AcfExecute element to start up a local desktop application such as Notepad or MS Paint. This is demonstrated in the WD_TEST_APPL_ACFEXECUTE sample component.
	From a technical perspective, the ACF leverages features of the Java Runtime Environment (JRE) to faciliate application integration. You can find details about supported JRE versions in SAP Note 1178747.

Table 8.3 UI Elements from the Integration Category

UI Element Type	Usage Description
AcfExecute (Cont.)	You can find more information about the capabilities and functions of the ACF online at the SAP Help Portal (*http://help.sap.com*) by performing a search using the term *Active Component Framework*.
AcfUpDownload	This UI element is designed to upload and download files from a *Knowledge Provider* (KPro) content server, though it can be configured to work with almost any HTTP handler. Because it leverages functionality of the ACF, it can support much larger files than the standard FileDownload and FileUpload elements used for general purpose file I/O.
BIApplicationFrame	This UI element provides a container for embedding web templates based on BEx Web Applications delivered via SAP NetWeaver Business Warehouse (BW). Various UI element properties are provided to allow us to customize the URL query string parameters passed to SAP NetWeaver BW at runtime.
FileDownload	As the name suggests, this UI element is used to download a file from the server to the client. The contents of the linked file are supplied via the data property (which is of type XSTRING). How the file contents are retrieved is an implementation-level detail left up to the developer. So, we can read from a file on the local application server host or mounted share, extract a serialized file from the database, or even build the file dynamically on the fly. We'll look at how this works from a technical perspective in Section 8.2.2.
FileUpload	This UI element is the analog of the FileDownload element, supporting the upload of files from the client to the server. As was the case with the FileDownload element, the contents of the file are serialized through the data property, which is of type XSTRING. We'll demonstrate how all this works in Section 8.2.2.
IFrame	This UI element is based on the HTML <iframe> tag used to define an inline frame within a page. Within this inline frame, we can embed other web pages, documents, or images: basically anything that can be reached via a URL.

Table 8.3 UI Elements from the Integration Category (Cont.)

UI Element Type	Usage Description
IFrame (Cont.)	However, there are some caveats to all this. Because the contents of the inline frame are isolated from the overarching WDA application context, it's almost impossible to synchronize the contents of the inner frame with the outer frame. For this reason, and others, SAP tends to discourage developers from using this UI element unless absolutely necessary. The WDR_TEST_UI_ELEMENTS sample component demonstrates the use of this control.
InteractiveForm	This UI element is used to embed PDF documents into the view layout. This includes regular PDF documents as well as interactive forms based on SAP Interactive Forms by Adobe®. We'll take a closer look at this element in Section 8.2.3.
OfficeControl	This UI element can be used to embed Microsoft Office™ documents within the view layout (i.e., Word or Excel documents, and so on). This is made possible via an ActiveX component that links in portions of the Microsoft Office libraries to host the applications. Because of this reliance on ActiveX technology, the OfficeControl element can only be used by browsers that support ActiveX controls (e.g., Internet Explorer).
	For the most part, all the heavy lifting for the OfficeControl is handled by the aforementioned ActiveX control on the client side. However, the OfficeControl does provide a handful of events that can be used to track changes to the document such as close and save. In the latter case, the onSave event allows us to upload the users' changes and serialize them out to whichever file location we retrieved the Office document from in the first place. You can find examples of this UI element in sample WDA applications provided within the SIOS package.

Table 8.3 UI Elements from the Integration Category (Cont.)

8.2.2 Uploading and Downloading Files

A common requirement of many WDA applications is the ability to upload and download content via files. For example, we might want to upload an XML configuration file or download the contents of a table to Microsoft Excel. For these tasks, we can use the FileUpload and FileDownload elements, respectively. In this section, we'll demonstrate how to work with both of these UI element types.

Uploading Files Using the FileUpload Element

For the most part, the `FileUpload` element looks and behaves very similarly to the HTML `<input type="file">` element used to upload files in HTML forms. As you can see in Figure 8.9, the `FileUpload` element is an aggregate that combines an `InputField` element with a `Button` element. The `InputField` element is used to capture the directory path of the file being uploaded, while the `Button` element is used to open a file selection dialog window.

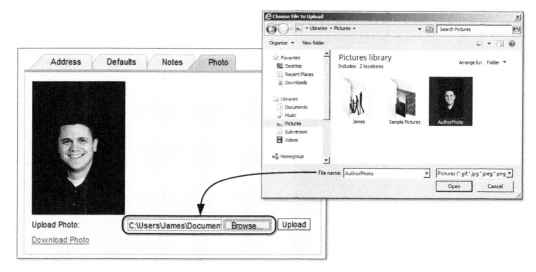

Figure 8.9 Working with the FileUpload Element

After the target file is located, an event must be triggered to initiate a server roundtrip. Here, since the `FileUpload` element doesn't define any events of its own, we must trigger the upload process via some other UI element. For instance, in Figure 8.9, you can see how we've defined an UPLOAD `Button` element to initiate the upload process. Of course, we could have just as easily used a `LinkToAction` element; the point is that we have to initiate a server roundtrip in order to cause the file to be uploaded.

> **Note**
>
> Since it's possible that *any* server roundtrip could trigger a file upload, SAP recommends that file upload operations based on the `FileUpload` element be driven through a dedicated screen or popup window. That way, users won't accidentally trigger file uploads before they're ready.

Once a server roundtrip is initiated, the contents of the file being uploaded will be streamed into the data property of the FileUpload element, which is of type XSTRING. We can also ascertain additional properties of the file by binding the fileName and mimeType properties with context attributes of type STRING. These properties can be used to determine the uploaded file name and MIME type, respectively. In general, we recommend that these file-related attributes be stored in a separate context node set aside for this purpose.

With this information in hand, it's up to us to determine what to do with the file once it's uploaded. Then, after we're done processing the file, it's a good idea to go ahead and invalidate the context node containing the file using the INVALI-DATE() method defined by the IF_WD_CONTEXT_NODE interface. That way, we can free up the memory resources used to facilitate the file upload.

Downloading Files Using the FileDownload Element

The FileDownload element is the inverse of the FileUpload element, making it possible to download the contents of a file as an XSTRING payload from the server down to the client. As you can see in Figure 8.10, the FileDownload element has a similar look and feel to the LinkToAction element. Users can click on the displayed hyperlink to initiate the file download process.

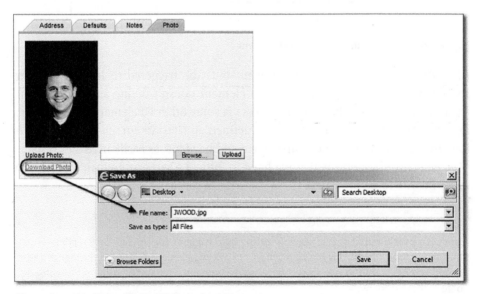

Figure 8.10 Working with the FileDownload Element

To configure the `FileDownload` element, we must define two key properties:

▶ The `text` property determines the hyperlink text displayed on the screen (e.g., the DOWNLOAD PHOTO link shown in Figure 8.10).

▶ The `data` property determines the source of the file being downloaded. It must be bound against a context attribute of type `XSTRING`.

When binding the `data` property, there are a couple of prerequisites we must be mindful of. First of all, the overarching context node of the bound context attribute must not contain additional attributes. In other words, it must be a context node containing a single context attribute of type `XSTRING`. Secondly, context node must be assigned a supply function. These prerequisites were put in place to allow the Web Dynpro framework to optimize the file download process. At runtime, whenever a user clicks on the download link, the download process will be carried out as follows:

1. First of all, even though the `FileDownload` element does not define any explicit events, a server roundtrip will be initiated.

2. On the server side, the supply function for the context node bound against the `FileDownload.data` property will be invoked to supply the file contents on demand. We can obtain the file's contents within this supply function however we like.

3. After the supply function is finished loading the file, the file will be downloaded to the client. Here, it's a good idea to utilize the `fileName` and `mimeType` properties to provide the user agent with some hints about the nature of the file being downloaded.

4. We can also use the `behaviour` and `target` properties to influence how the user agent opens up the file.

5. Finally, as soon as the file has been downloaded, the context node containing the file contents will be invalidated automatically by the Web Dynpro framework in order to conserve memory resources.

Downloading Files Using the File Export Feature

Though the `FileDownload` element is typically used to facilitate file downloads, we should point out another way to download files independently of the `FileDownload` element. This is made possible via the `ATTACH_FILE_TO_RESPONSE()` method of the `CL_WD_RUNTIME_SERVICES` utilities class. To see how this works, we recommend that you trace through the event handling logic contained within the BUTTON view provided with the WDR_TEST_EVENTS sample component.

8.2.3 Integrating PDF Forms with the InteractiveForm Element

In Section 8.2.1, we briefly described how the InteractiveForm element could be used to embed PDF documents within the view layout. Here, we could be talking about regular PDF documents or PDF forms generated via the SAP Interactive Forms by Adobe® framework. In either case, the PDF content is embedded within a scrolling container, as illustrated in Figure 8.11.

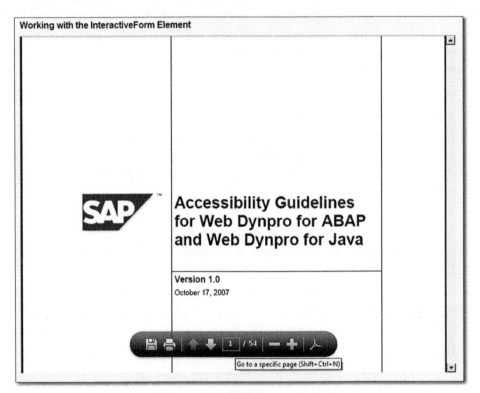

Figure 8.11 Working with the InteractiveForm Element

To demonstrate how the InteractiveForm element works, let's look at an example. In this book's source code bundle, there's a WDA component called ZWDC_PDF_DEMO, which reads the contents of a PDF document uploaded to the component's MIMEs folder and displays it on screen. Here, the contents of the

PDF document are passed to the `InteractiveForm` element via the `pdfSource` property, which is of type `XSTRING` (see Figure 8.12). Listing 8.1 demonstrates how the PDF content is uploaded into the `PDF_DOCUMENT.PAYLOAD` context attribute. From here, the `InteractiveForm` element takes over and displays the PDF document in its defined content area.

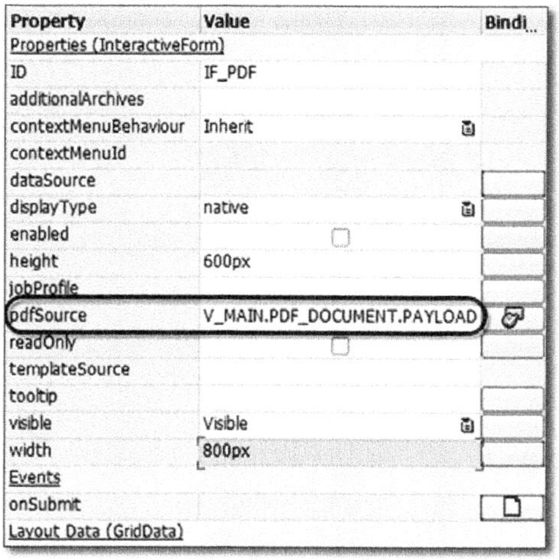

Property	Value	Bindi..
Properties (InteractiveForm)		
ID	IF_PDF	
additionalArchives		
contextMenuBehaviour	Inherit	
contextMenuId		
dataSource		
displayType	native	
enabled		
height	600px	
jobProfile		
pdfSource	V_MAIN.PDF_DOCUMENT.PAYLOAD	
readOnly		
templateSource		
tooltip		
visible	Visible	
width	800px	
Events		
onSubmit		
Layout Data (GridData)		

Figure 8.12 Configuring the InteractiveForm Element

```
method SUPPLY_PDF.
  "Method-Local Data Declarations:
  DATA ls_pdf_doc TYPE wd_this->Element_pdf_document.
  DATA lo_mr_api  TYPE REF TO if_mr_api.

  "Use the CL_MIME_REPOSITORY_API to download a sample file:
  lo_mr_api = cl_mime_repository_api=>get_api( ).
  lo_mr_api->get(
    EXPORTING
      i_url = 'sap/bc/webdynpro/sap/zwdc_pdf_demo/...'
    IMPORTING
      e_content = ls_pdf_doc-payload ).

  node->bind_structure(
    new_item            = ls_pdf_doc
    set_initial_elements = abap_true ).
endmethod.
```

Listing 8.1 Reading a PDF File from the MIME Repository

In our simple example, we simply read the contents of a PDF document uploaded to the MIME Repository. Of course, we could have just as easily derived that PDF content dynamically using SAPScript, Smart Forms, or better yet, SAP Interactive Forms by Adobe®. In the first two cases, it's just a matter of converting the PDF output into a hex-binary payload of type XSTRING. However, as you might expect, integrating SAP Interactive Forms technology is quite a bit more involved. Since a detailed description of the integration points between WDA and SAP Interactive Forms is beyond the scope of this book, we won't cover these concepts here. However, if you're interested in learning more about how this integration is realized, we highly recommend you pick up a copy of the second edition of *SAP Interactive Forms by Adobe* (Hauser et al., SAP PRESS, 2011). You can also find some live example scenarios in the WDR_TEST_ADOBE sample component.

> **Note**
>
> To test this component, you will need to have a connection to the *Adobe Document Services* (ADS) set up in the host AS ABAP system.

8.3   UI Elements from the Complex Category

The last set of UI elements we'll look at are those elements that belong to the complex category. According to the SAP online help documentation, this element group contains all those UI elements that are "...particularly complex in terms of their structure and content." As we'll soon see, much of this complexity stems from the fact that many of the UI elements in this category are *composites*, which combine several of the UI element types we've seen already to match GUI widgets users are accustomed to working with in rich client environments.

8.3.1   UI Element Overview

UI elements within the complex category are, well, complex. Given this overall level of complexity, it can be difficult to visualize and understand what these element types are all about without some additional background information. Therefore, in this section, we'll take a slightly different approach to presenting the UI elements within this category by addressing each UI element type within its own section. That way, we can take a closer look at the visualization of the UI elements and dig a little deeper into functional issues and so on.

BreadCrumb Element

The BreadCrumb element is modeled after the popular breadcrumb navigation metaphor used in many modern Web applications. If you're not familiar with this metaphor, a brief description is in order. The term *breadcrumb* is borrowed from the famous fairytale *Hansel and Gretel*, in which Hansel lays down a trail of breadcrumbs to help he and his sister find their way back home after a long journey into the woods. In the web application context, breadcrumb navigation is implemented via a series of breadcrumb steps that provide a hyperlink to a particular page or location a user has visited during the course of their application session. Normally, breadcrumb steps are arranged horizontally from left to right in the order in which navigation occurred. Users can then access these breadcrumb steps to navigate back to specific pages or locations they've visited already.

From an implementation perspective, the BreadCrumb element is an aggregate that groups together one or more BreadCrumbStep elements. Each BreadCrumb-Step element is rendered as a hyperlink with a label that refers to a particular page or location (see Figure 8.13). Whenever a user clicks on the link rendered by the BreadCrumbStep element, the onSelect event of the parent BreadCrumb element will be fired, providing a hook that allows us to react to the selection event and navigate accordingly.

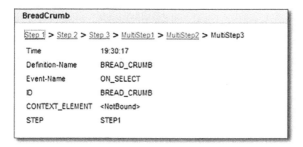

Figure 8.13 Working with the BreadCrumb Element

The BreadCrumb element can be configured statically or dynamically as needed. With static configuration, a finite set of breadcrumbs is defined by embedding a series of BreadCrumbStep elements underneath the parent BreadCrumb element, as shown in Figure 8.14. With dynamic configuration, the MultipleBreadCrumbStep element type is used. Here, the dataSource property of the MultipleBreadCrumb-Step element is linked to a context node whose cardinality is 0..n or 1..n.

Figure 8.14 Defining a BreadCrumb Element

RoadMap Element

The RoadMap element is conceptually similar to the BreadCrumb element in that it displays a navigation trail. However, in contrast to the BreadCrumb element, the navigation trail displayed within a RoadMap element is used to mark the steps followed within a wizard or guided procedure. Figure 8.15 demonstrates how the RoadMap element is visualized on screen. We'll take a closer look at the steps required to set up a wizard using the RoadMap element in Section 8.3.4.

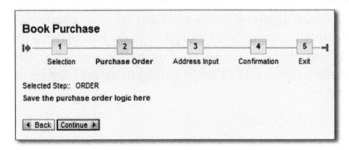

Figure 8.15 Working with the RoadMap Element

PhaseIndicator Element

Much like the RoadMap element, the PhaseIndicator element is used to display the steps taken within a wizard. Figure 8.16 shows what the PhaseIndicator element looks like on screen. As you can see, it has a very similar look and feel to the RoadMap element. The only real difference lies in the way the steps are outlined on the screen; while the RoadMap element renders the steps as hyperlinks, the PhaseIndicator element renders the steps as push buttons.

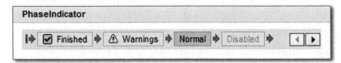

Figure 8.16 Working with the PhaseIndicator Element

From a technical perspective, both the RoadMap and PhaseIndicator element types are implemented in almost exactly the same way. Therefore, once you know how to work with one of the elements, you know how to work with the other. Given these similarities, it can be confusing at times to figure out which element to use for a particular use case. While we would submit that such choices are rather subjective, the SAP online help documentation does point out one distinguishing characteristic of the PhaseIndicator element: it's intended to be used to display larger steps that are more time consuming for the user. With this in mind, it follows that the general rule of thumb would be to use the RoadMap element for basic wizards and the PhaseIndicator element for complex wizards with long-running steps.

DateNavigator Element

The DateNavigator element is used to display a customizable calendar control on screen (see Figure 8.17). Users can interact with this calendar control to make various date selections, including:

▶ A specific date

▶ A particular week/month/year

▶ A range of dates, which can span weeks or even months

Figure 8.17 Working with the DateNavigator Element

The provided event types (e.g., onDaySelect) can be used to track these selections and react accordingly behind the scenes. To see a live demonstration of how all this works, check out the WDR_TEST_EVENTS sample component and the DATE-NAVIGATOR view.

Legend Element

The Legend UI element is a flexible UI element that can be used to explain the symbology/pictorial language used in one or more UI elements contained within the view layout. Figure 8.18 provides an example of what the Legend element looks like on screen. As you can see, even if you didn't happen to study cartography in college, the semantic meaning behind the Legend element should be quite clear. That's because Legend elements are designed to have a very similar look and feel to legends you might see on a map.

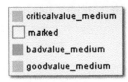

Figure 8.18 Working with the Legend Element

From a technical point of view, Legend elements are aggregates, embedding one or more LegendItem or MultipleLegendItem child elements. Each LegendItem element represents a different symbol displayed within the Legend display (see Figure 8.18). This symbol can be visualized in the form of an icon or a color scheme. See the properties for the LegendItem element in the online help documentation for more details about the options available here.

Though Legend elements can be used as standalone UI elements, they're typically integrated directly into the UI elements they're describing. For example, if we're using a specialized color scheme for rows or columns in a Table element, we might embed a Legend element at the bottom of the Table element so that users would have a clear understanding of the semantic meaning behind each of the different colors. Legend elements are also frequently used to help annotate calendars displayed via the DateNavigator element (see the bottom of Figure 8.17 for a demonstration).

Shuttle Element

As the name suggests, the Shuttle element is used to shuttle data back and forth between a pair of UI elements. As such, it's a natural extension of the familiar "browse-and-collect" pattern in which users *browse* for data in a source UI element and *collect* that data in a target UI element.

As you can see in Figure 8.19, the `Shuttle` element provides four directional buttons that can be used to move either a single item or all items within the source or target UI elements. These buttons are linked with two events: `onAdd` and `onRemove`, respectively. Within the event handler methods for these events, we must manually implement the logic to move the data back and forth; the `Shuttle` element doesn't do this for us automatically. As you'd expect, this basically amounts to the movement of context elements between the context nodes that are bound to the source/target UI elements. In Section 8.4, we'll look at another way of implementing the browse-and-collect pattern when we explore the drag-and-drop capabilities of the Web Dynpro framework.

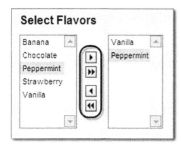

Figure 8.19 Working with the Shuttle Element

Table Element

Despite its overall complexity and broad set of capabilities, the `Table` element is perhaps one of the most intuitive UI elements for users within the entire Web Dynpro UI element catalog. In essence, it's used to organize a series of records into a two-dimensional grid made up of rows and columns. The contents of the `Table` control are supplied via a multi-element context node bound against the `dataSource` property. As you can see in Figure 8.20, a separate row is created for each context element contained within the bound context node. Once this relationship is established, we can pick and choose the context attributes we want to display via a series of `TableColumn` child elements.

Figure 8.21 demonstrates what a `Table` element looks like on screen. As you can see, the `Table` element comes packed with a number of useful features out of the box. In Section 8.3.2, we'll take an up-close look at how many of these features are configured and/or implemented.

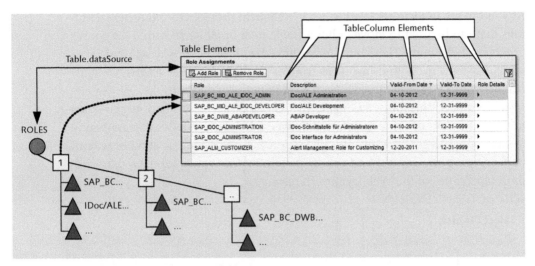

Figure 8.20 Anatomy of a Table Element

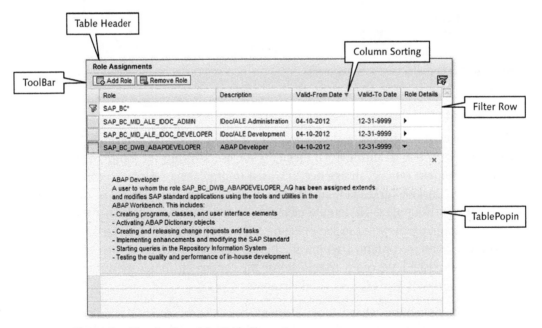

Figure 8.21 Visualization of the Table Element

Client Table (CTable) Element

This CTable element was made available with the SAP NetWeaver 7.31 release. It expands upon the basic Table element, providing additional customization options that influence the table's display/behavior. Also, on the client side, users benefit from several nice features built into the CTable element, including (but not limited to):

- ▶ The ability to resize the CTable element on the client side without a server roundtrip and custom coding
- ▶ Vertical and horizontal scrolling with asynchronous reload behind the scenes
- ▶ Support for pagination in lieu of scrolling

If you have access to an SAP NetWeaver 7.31 system, you can find a live demonstration of this element in the WDR_TEST_C_TABLE sample component.

Tree Element

The Tree element is used to display hierarchical data. As you can see in Figure 8.22, it has a similar look and feel to hierarchical display elements like the ones you might find in Windows Explorer or the Mac Finder. Here, users can expand nodes, click on leaves, and generally traverse the hierarchy.

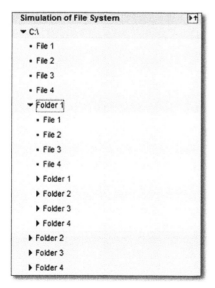

Figure 8.22 Working with the Tree Element

The Tree element is primarily used for selection and navigation. For example, in the screenshot shown in Figure 8.22, the Tree element is being used to navigate through a simulated file system. Whenever a user makes a selection within the tree, the onAction event will be fired, providing us with a reference to the selected context element. From here, we can process the user's selection in a number of different ways. We'll take a look at how to do this in Section 8.3.3.

8.3.2 Displaying Tabluar Data with the Table Element

A common requirement for many WDA applications is the ability to display tabular data such as that contained within an internal table. For this task, we can enlist the aid of the Table element, which is a flexible composite element that can be used to display tabular data in a two-dimensional grid made up of rows and columns.

In this section, we'll examine the Table element and see how it can be used to display (and edit) complex data objects. Along the way, we'll consider some of the more advanced functions of the Table element, including sorting, filtering, and popins. To guide us through this discussion, we'll look at how the Table example in Figure 8.21 was implemented to display the set of roles assigned to a user master record. The complete example is provided with the ZWDC_TABLE_DEMO component included in this book's source code bundle.

UI Element Configuration

Before we begin our in-depth analysis of the Table element and its aggregations, it's useful to first see how tables are constructed in the first place. In general, the steps required here are as follows:

1. First, we must insert a Table element into the UI element hierarchy just as we would any other UI element. As you can see in Figure 8.23, Table elements consist of simply a single header-level Caption element by default.

2. The data source for the Table element is assigned via the aptly named dataSource property. Here, we must assign a context node with a cardinality of 0..n or 1..n. In our user role assignments example, we are mapping to the USER.ROLES context node shown in Figure 8.24.

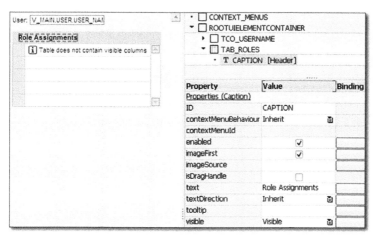

Figure 8.23 Configuring the Table Element

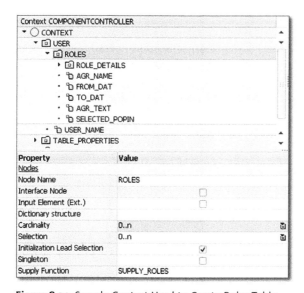

Figure 8.24 Sample Context Used to Create Roles Table

3. Once the data source for the `Table` is assigned, we can define a binding between the mapped context node's context attributes and a series of `TableColumn` elements, which represent the table columns. We can automate this process by right-clicking on the `Table` element in the UI element hierarchy display and selecting the CREATE BINDING context menu option. This will open up the CREATE CONTEXT BINDING wizard shown in Figure 8.25.

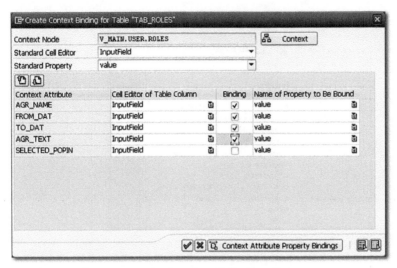

Figure 8.25 Defining Context Bindings for a Table (Part 1)

4. As you can see in Figure 8.25, the CREATE CONTEXT BINDING wizard allows us to define bindings for the context node associated with the Table element's dataSource property. Here, we must apply the following configuration settings for each context attribute we want to display within the Table:

▶ In order for a context attribute to be displayed as a table column, we must activate the checkbox in the BINDING column (see Figure 8.26). If this checkbox isn't checked, a TableColumn element won't be created in reference to that context attribute (though we could always come back and create one later).

▶ To display or edit the contents of the context attribute within a table cell, we must associate the context attribute with a *cell editor*. Conceptually speaking, it's appropriate to think of cell editors as placeholder elements that point to familiar elementary UI elements, such as the InputField, CheckBox, or RadioButton elements. As you can see in Figure 8.26, we're using the InputField element as our cell editor and binding each of the displayed context attributes to the InputField element's value property. To speed things along, we selected the InputField element as the default cell editor for the context binding in the STANDARD CELL EDITOR dropdown list.

5. Finally, once the requisite bindings are in place, we can confirm our changes by clicking on the button with the green checkmark on it.

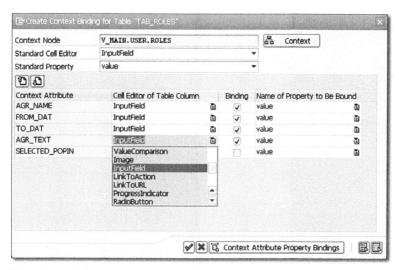

Figure 8.26 Defining Context Bindings for a Table (Part 2)

Figure 8.27 shows what the finished product looks like after the bindings are in place. As you can see, the Table element has been expanded to include a series of TableColumn child elements: one for each column to be displayed within the Table. Each TableColumn element embeds two child elements of its own:

▸ A Caption element to represent the column heading for the TableColumn. By default, the label text displayed will be derived in terms of the data element used to define the context attribute bound to the TableColumn element's cell editor. Of course, we can always override the label text by specifying the text property for the Caption element.

▸ A cell editor element (e.g., an InputField element) is used to represent the contents of a given table cell. The UI elements used to represent these cells are configured as usual. For instance, since we're using the InputField element as the cell editor in our example, the bound context attributes are mapped to the InputField.value property.

Once the requisite bindings are in place, we can configure the look and feel of the Table element using its plethora of design properties. Here, we can specify the background colors of rows and cells, the number of rows that should be displayed at a time, and so on. The Table element can also aggregate child elements such as the ToolBar and Legend elements. See the online help documentation for more information about these features.

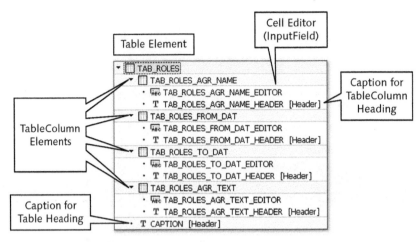

Figure 8.27 Understanding Table Aggregations

Defining Selection Behavior

Though the Table element is primarily used to display (or occasionally edit) data, it can also be used as a selection element since it allows users to select individual rows within the table. For instance, in the user roles table configured in the previous section, we might want to allow users to select an individual row record and display additional details for the role in a popup window. As it turns out, this sort of behavior is quite easy to achieve with the Table element.

If selection is turned on for a Table element, users can make row selections by clicking on the *selection column,* which is rendered on the left-hand side of the Table control (see Figure 8.28). As we mentioned earlier, each row within a Table element corresponds with a context element from the context node bound against the Table.dataSource property. Therefore, whenever users make row selections on the frontend, the Table element can utilize its context binding relationship to update the selection status of the corresponding context elements on the backend. As a result, we can use the IF_WD_CONTEXT_NODE->GET_SELECTED_ELEMENTS() and IF_WD_CONTEXT_ELEMENT->IS_SELECTED() methods to identify selected context elements as usual.

In order to allow for selections to be made within a Table element, we must configure the selectionMode property. Using this property, we can determine whether users can select individual rows or multiple rows, or if they can even make selections at all. Table 8.4 describes the set of values we can choose from when configuring this property. Here, note that the option selected must correspond with the Selection property of the bound context node. For instance, if our USER.ROLES context node had a value of 0..1 configured for its Selection property, it would not be possible to select the multi option.

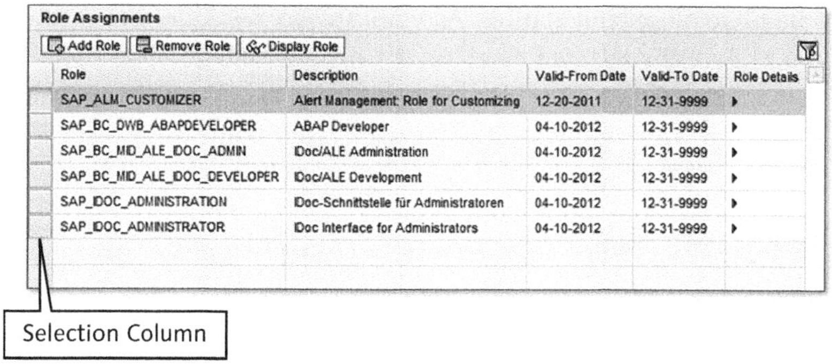

Figure 8.28 Selecting Rows in the Table Element

Mode	Description
auto	Default option that essentially matches the Selection property of the bound context node. When this mode is configured, the lead selection of the context node will be updated whenever selections are made.
single	This option supports the selection of only one row at a time. Whenever users make selections, the lead selection of the context node will be updated accordingly.
multi	This option supports the selection of multiple rows at a time. Whenever users make selections, the lead selection of the context node will be updated accordingly.
none	Whenever this option is set, selections are disabled and the selection column will not be displayed.
singleNoLead	This option is similar to the single option in that it only allows a single row to be selected at a time. However, in this case, selections do not update the lead selection of the context node.
multiNoLead	This option is similar to the multiple option in that it allows multiple rows to be selected at a time. However, in this case, selections do not update the lead selection of the context node.

Table 8.4 Selection Modes for the Table Element

Once the selectionMode property is configured, the Web Dynpro framework will take care of synchronizing user selections on our behalf. In our ZWDC_TABLE_DEMO example, we're exploiting this functionality to enable users to select a role and display it in a popup window, as shown in Figure 8.29. Here, the heavy lifting is implemented within the event handler method tied to the DISPLAY ROLE button. Listing 8.2 contains this implementation. As you can see, we didn't have to do anything special to grab the selected element; it's already queued up as the lead selection element automatically. However, if we'd chosen the singleNoLead value for the selectionMode property, we would have had to obtain the selected element using the IF_WD_CONTEXT_NODE->GET_SELECTED_ELEMENTS( ) method.

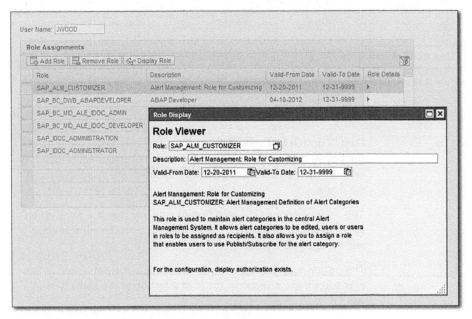

Figure 8.29 Displaying the Selected Role in a Popup Window

```
method ONACTIONDISPLAY_ROLE.
  "Method-Local Data Declarations
  DATA: lo_comp_api   TYPE REF TO if_wd_component,
        lo_window_mgr TYPE REF TO if_wd_window_manager.

  "Obtain a reference to the Web Dynpro window manager:
  lo_comp_api = wd_comp_controller->wd_get_api( ).
  lo_window_mgr = lo_comp_api->get_window_manager( ).
```

```
"Create the window reference:
wd_this->role_display_window =
  lo_window_mgr->create_window(
    window_name = 'W_ROLE_DETAILS'
    title       = `Role Display` ).

"Open up the window:
wd_this->role_display_window->open( ).
endmethod.
```

Listing 8.2 Displaying the Selected Role in a Popup Window

One thing to note about the selection logic implemented in the ZWDC_TABLE_DEMO is that the user selections were not synchronized with the backend until a server roundtrip was triggered (e.g., as a result of a user clicking on a ToolBarButton element in the Table element's ToolBar). In our simple application scenario, this was of no concern since we didn't need to know which row was selected until the user decided to invoke the action to display the role in a popup. However, in some application scenarios, it may not be appropriate to wait that long. In these situations, we have the option of listening for selection events using two different event types defined by the Table element: onLeadSelect and onSelect. Since both of these event types trigger a server roundtrip whenever a user makes a selection, user selections are synchronized in near real time. Though of these event types are similar in nature, the onLeadSelect event is used to track changes to the lead selection while the onSelect event is used to track general selection events.

> **Note**
>
> It's not possible to define event handlers for both event types simultaneously.

Turning On Sorting and Filtering

In the last several years, most users have grown accustomed to working with tables/grids in web applications that emulate features found in desktop spreadsheet applications such as Microsoft Excel. Here, there are two functions in particular that most users have a hard time living without: *sorting* and *filtering*. Though these features can be implemented manually using the provided Table.onSort and Table.onFilter events, it turns out that the Table element comes equipped with standard functionality to provide these services with minimal custom coding effort.

To see how this works, let's first take a look at how filtering can be set up. We can do this by performing the following steps:

1. First of all, we need to define a couple of local context nodes within the view where our Table element is displayed. The first node is a single-element node called TABLE_PROPERTIES that contains a flag called FILTER_ON, which is of type WDY_BOOLEAN. This flag will tell us whether or not filtering is turned on in the user interface. The second node is a single-element node called FILTER that contains context attributes whose names match each of the table columns we want to filter on. Here, note that the type of these context attributes must be STRING since the filter values keyed in by users will be string literals/expressions. Figure 8.30 shows how these context nodes are set up.

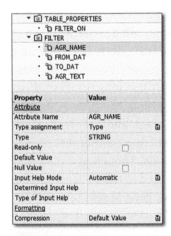

Figure 8.30 Additional Context Nodes Needed for Table Row Filtering

2. Once the requisite context nodes are in place, the next step is to go into each of the TableColumn elements we want to provide filters for and configure the filterValue property. As you can see in Figure 8.31, this value will correspond with the related filter attribute defined within the FILTER node created in the previous step.

3. Next, in order to enlist the default filtering services that come bundled with the Table element, we must tap into its runtime class: CL_WD_TABLE. We can do this via the WDDOMODIFYVIEW() hook method, as demonstrated in Listing 8.3. (We'll take a closer look at this code in a moment.) Figure 8.32 shows the custom attributes we defined to hang onto the runtime class and its method handler, which provides the default sorting/filtering behavior.

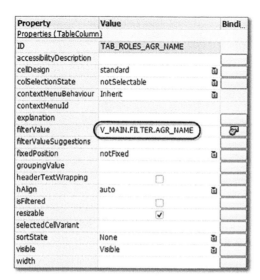

Figure 8.31 Configuring the filterValue Property for TableColumn elements

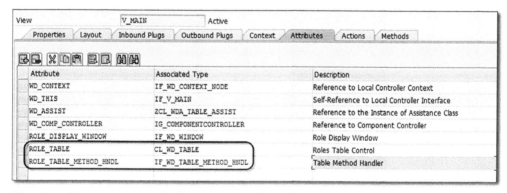

Figure 8.32 Tapping into the Table Element's Method Handler

4. Finally, in order to control when filtering is turned on/off, we've added a ToolBarToggleButton to the Table element's ToolBar, as shown in Figure 8.33. The checked property for the ToolBarToggleButton is bound against the TABLE_PROPERTIES.FILTER_ON context attribute created in step 1. Whenever users click on the ToolBarToggleButton, the button's onToggle event will be fired to invoke the ONACTIONTOGGLE_FILTER() event handler method, whose implementation is shown in Listing 8.5.

383

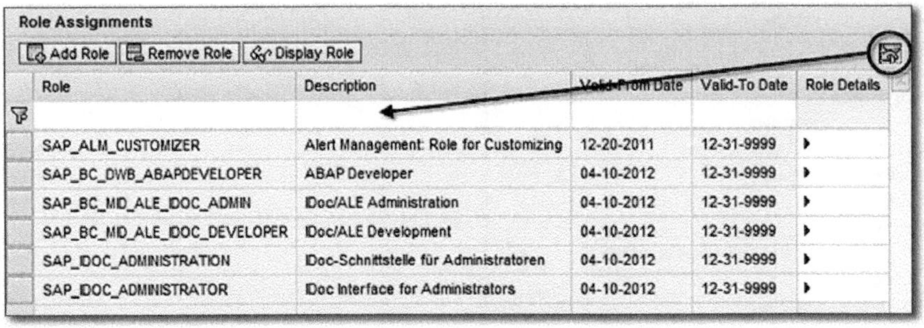

Figure 8.33 Toggling the Filter Row with a ToolBarToggleButton

Once these settings are in place, the standard-delivered filtering functionality will kick in automatically. For the most part, this functionality is carried out by the Table element's method handler, which is made available via the public _method_ handler attribute of the CL_WD_TABLE runtime class. Listing 8.3 shows how we're obtaining a reference to this attribute in the WDDOMODIFYVIEW() hook method. From here, we can trigger the filter operation at any time by calling the APPLY_ FILTER() method of the IF_WD_TABLE_METHOD_HNDL interface.

```
method WDDOMODIFYVIEW.
  "Method-Local Data Declarations:
  DATA lo_nd_table_properties TYPE REF TO if_wd_context_node.
  DATA lo_el_table_properties
    TYPE REF TO if_wd_context_element.
  DATA lv_filter_on
    TYPE wd_this->Element_table_properties-filter_on.

  "Store a reference to the Table element's method handler:
  IF first_time EQ abap_true.
    wd_this->role_table ?= view->get_element( 'TAB_ROLES' ).
    wd_this->role_table_method_hndl ?=
      wd_this->role_table->_method_handler.
  ENDIF.

  "Determine whether or not the role filter is turned on:
  lo_nd_table_properties =
    wd_context->get_child_node(
      name = wd_this->wdctx_table_properties ).
  lo_el_table_properties =
    lo_nd_table_properties->get_element( ).
```

```
lo_el_table_properties->get_attribute(
  EXPORTING
    name =  `FILTER_ON`
  IMPORTING
    value = lv_filter_on ).

  "Turn on filtering as necessary:
  IF lv_filter_on = abap_true.
    wd_this->role_table->set_on_filter( 'FILTER_ROLES' ).
  ELSE.
    wd_this->role_table->set_on_filter( '' ).
  ENDIF.
endmethod.
```

Listing 8.3 Tapping into Standard Filtering Functionality of the Table Element

As you can see in Listing 8.3, we're also using the WDDOMODIFYVIEW() method to dynamically control whether or not the onFilter event of the Table element is turned on by conditionally assigning an action to it (e.g., the FILTER_ROLES action). Listing 8.4 shows how the ONACTIONFILTER_ROLES() event handler method is implemented.

```
method ONACTIONFILTER_ROLES.
  "Apply the role filter:
  wd_this->role_table_method_hndl->apply_filter( ).
endmethod.
```

Listing 8.4 Applying Filtering via the Standard Functionality

As we mentioned earlier, we're using a ToolBarToggleButton to control whether or not filtering is turned on. Listing 8.5 shows how we've implemented the event handler method behind the button's onToggle event. Here, we simply invalidate the FILTER node and call the APPLY_FILTER() method to reset the filter.

```
method ONACTIONTOGGLE_FILTER.
  "Method-Local Data Declarations:
  DATA lo_nd_filter TYPE REF TO if_wd_context_node.

  "Clean up any pre-existing filter settings:
  lo_nd_filter = wd_context->get_child_node(
    name = wd_this->wdctx_filter ).
  lo_nd_filter->invalidate( ).
```

```
   "Toggle the filter settings on the table:
   wd_this->role_table_method_hndl->apply_filter( ).
endmethod.
```

Listing 8.5 Turning Filtering On/Off via a ToolBarToggleButton

Compared to filtering, sorting is quite a bit easier to set up. Basically, once we have a reference to the method handler of the Table element's runtime class, we can invoke its APPLY_SORTING() method to process the sort operation. Listing 8.6 shows how this is being performed within an event handler method for the Table.onSort event. Users can trigger this event by clicking on column headers to sort in ascending or descending order (see Figure 8.34).

```
method ONACTIONSORT_ROLES.
   "Use the default sorting behavior to sort the table:
   wd_this->role_table_method_hndl->apply_sorting( ).
endmethod.
```

Listing 8.6 Sorting the Contents of a Table Element

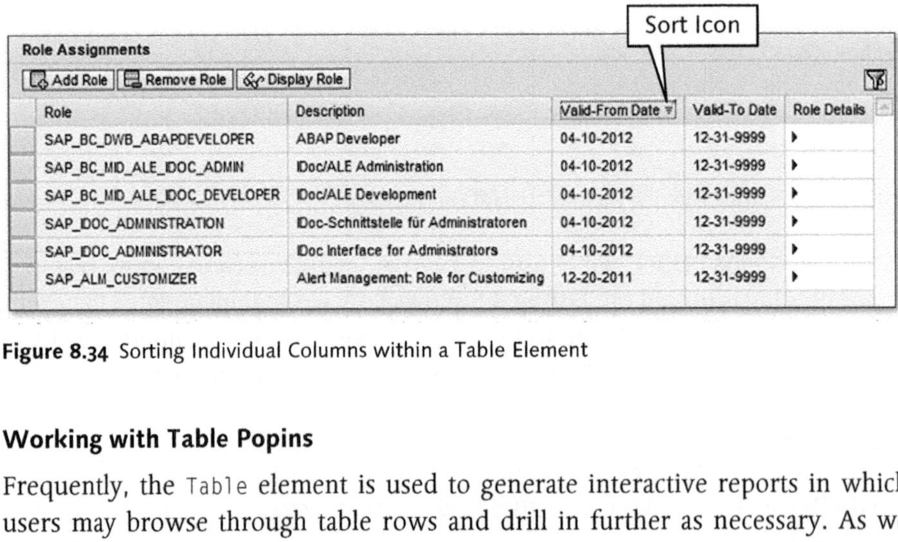

Figure 8.34 Sorting Individual Columns within a Table Element

Working with Table Popins

Frequently, the Table element is used to generate interactive reports in which users may browse through table rows and drill in further as necessary. As we observed earlier, one way of drilling into table rows is to select a row and open a popup window to display further details. Another alternative is to display the additional details in a *popin*.

In the SAP online help documentation, popins are described as follows: "Popins are insertions between the rows of a `Table`, which may refer to a row or individual cells. A popin can be linked to the `Table` for a row popin and to the `TableColumn` for a cell popin." In other words, you can think of popins as being lightweight fly-outs that can be expanded and collapsed as needed to display additional information about a given table row. Figure 8.35 illustrates what popins look like on screen.

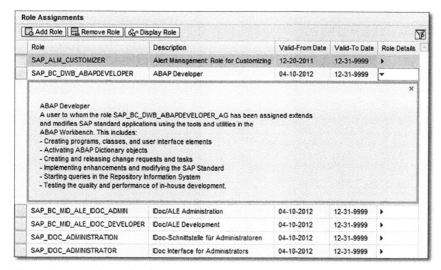

Figure 8.35 Working with Table Popins

To a large degree, the `TablePopin` element is like a layout element, in that it provides a container in which we can embed additional view content relevant for the popin display. Here, for example, we might use the `BusinessGraphics` element to display related information in a chart or elements from the text category to display a subform. For the most part, we have free reign to do here as we please. However, we're restricted from embedding an additional `Table` element within the popin content area.

To understand how table popins are configured, let's see how we implement the role details popin in our `ZWDC_TABLE_DEMO` component (see Figure 8.35). Here, we perform the following steps:

1. First off, we embed a `TablePopin` element into the `Table` by right-clicking on the `Table` element and selecting the Insert Table Popin menu option (see Figure 8.36).

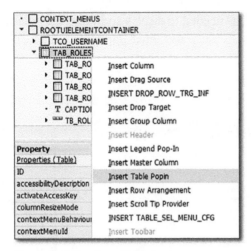

Figure 8.36 Creating a Table Popin

2. Next, we lay out the `TablePopin` content area by right-clicking on the `TablePopin` and selecting the Insert Content menu option. Here, we use the `TransparentContainer` element to define a content area in which we can display a role's long text description in a `TextView` element (see Figure 8.37). As you can see in Figure 8.38, we bind the `TextView.text` property with the `USER.ROLES.ROLE_DETAILS.LONG_DESCRIPTION` attribute. This data is supplied on demand via a supply function called `SUPPLY_ROLE_DETAILS()`, which is defined within the component controller.

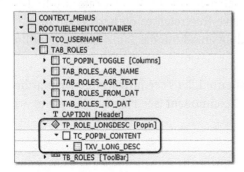

Figure 8.37 Aggregating Content in the TablePopin Element (Part 1)

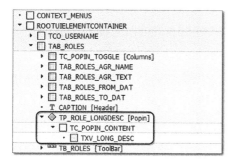

Figure 8.38 Aggregating Content in the TablePopin Element (Part 2)

3. As you can see in Figure 8.35, our sample application includes a close (X) icon in the top right-hand corner of the popin content area. To turn this functionality on, we assign an action called `CLOSE_POPIN` to the `TablePopin.onClose` event as shown in Figure 8.39. We'll see how the event handler method for this action is implemented coming up shortly.

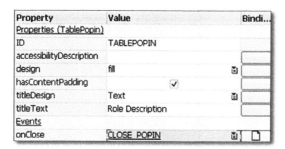

Figure 8.39 Configuring the onClose Event for the TablePopin Element

4. With the `TablePopin` in place, the next step is to provide users with a mechanism for displaying the popin. For this task, we use the `TablePopinToggleCell` element, which is a standard cell variant specifically provided for this purpose. The steps required to set up the toggle cell are as follows:

▸ First, we add a `TableColumn` to the `Table` element as usual by right-clicking on the `Table` and selecting the INSERT COLUMN menu option.

▸ Next, we embed a `TablePopinToggleCell` element into the `TableColumn` by right-clicking on the newly created `TableColumn` element and selecting the INSERT CELL VARIANT menu option. Then, as you can see in the CREATE ELEMENT dialog box shown in Figure 8.40, we create a `TablePopinToggleCell` called `TPTC_POPIN_TOGGLE`.

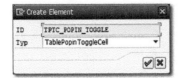

Figure 8.40 Defining a TablePopinToggleCell Element (Part 1)

▶ Figure 8.41 shows how we configure the `TablePopinToggleCell` element. As you can see, we assign the value `POPIN_VARIANT` to the `variantKey` property. This arbitrary value must match the `TableColumn.selectedCellVariant` property, as shown in Figure 8.42, in order for the nested `TablePopinToggleCell` cell variant to be selected.

Property	Value	Binding
Properties (TablePopinToggleCell)		
ID	TPTC_POPIN_TOGGLE	
cellDesign	standard	
hAlign	auto	
variantKey	TOGGLE_CELL	
Events		
onToggle		

Figure 8.41 Defining a TablePopinToggleCell Element (Part 2)

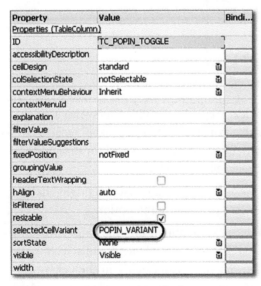

Property	Value	Bindi...
Properties (TableColumn)		
ID	TC_POPIN_TOGGLE	
accessibilityDescription		
cellDesign	standard	
colSelectionState	notSelectable	
contextMenuBehaviour	Inherit	
contextMenuId		
explanation		
filterValue		
filterValueSuggestions		
fixedPosition	notFixed	
groupingValue		
headerTextWrapping		
hAlign	auto	
isFiltered		
resizable	✓	
selectedCellVariant	POPIN_VARIANT	
sortState	None	
visible	Visible	
width		

Figure 8.42 Defining the selectedCellVariant Property of the TableColumn

5. Finally, in order to link the popin with the overarching `Table` element, we bind the `Table.selectedPopin` property with the `USER.ROLES.SELECTED_POPIN` context attribute, as shown in Figure 8.43 and Figure 8.44.

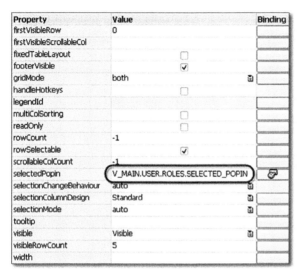

Figure 8.43 Configuring the Table.selectedPopin Property (Part 1)

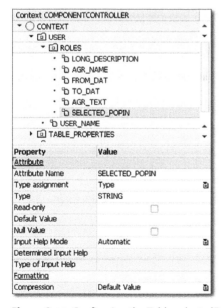

Figure 8.44 Configuring the Table.selectedPopin Property (Part 2)

With the basic configuration in place, the last thing we have to do is implement the event handler method for the `TablePopin.onClose` event. Listing 8.7 shows how we implement this method. As you can see, the only thing required here is to reset the `USER.ROLES.SELECTED_POPIN` attribute. Conveniently, the `TablePopin.onClose` event passes in a reference to the context element for the targeted row in a parameter called `CONTEXT_ELEMENT`. Using this reference, we can reset the `SELECTED_POPIN` context attribute using the `SET_ATTRIBUTE()` method, and the system will take care of closing out the popin from there.

```
method ONACTIONCLOSE_POPIN.
  context_element->set_attribute(
    name = 'SELECTED_POPIN'
    value = '' ).
endmethod.
```

Listing 8.7 Processing the TablePopin.onClose Event

8.3.3 Visualizing Hierarchical Data with the Tree Element

As we observed in the previous section, the `Table` element is great for displaying flat, two-dimensional data structures. However, there are times when the data we're representing is more complex. For example, imagine a requirement in which we need to display the contents of a file directory. Here, the directory may be nested arbitrarily deep to include subfolders, files, and so on. Rather than trying to flatten this data hierarchy to fit inside a `Table` element, we can use the `Tree` element to visualize the data in a more natural and intuitive way.

Figure 8.45 shows what the `Tree` element looks like on the screen. As you can see, it consists of nodes and leaves represented by the `TreeNodeType` and `TreeItemType` elements, respectively. These element types are can be used to define hierarchies in two ways:

▶ If the number of hierarchy levels is known at design time, the `Tree` can be laid out statically by defining a series of `TreeNodeType` and `TreeItemType` elements to match the hierarchy structure.

▶ Otherwise, we can use recursive context nodes to represent hierarchies whose depth is unknown at design time.

Most of the time, the recursive approach makes the most sense because it's much more flexible and extensible.

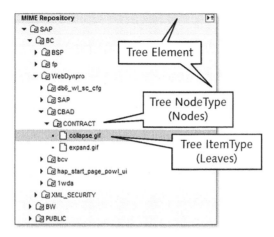

Figure 8.45 Working with the Tree Element

Despite being classified in the complex category, Tree elements are primarily used for selection and navigation. Here, we can use the onAction event defined in the TreeNodeType and TreeItemType elements to respond to user selections and process them accordingly. In this section, we'll explore how all this works by considering how the MIME Repository browser application shown in Figure 8.45 was implemented. You can view this finished product in the ZWDC_TREE_DEMO component provided with the book's source code bundle.

Conceptual Overview

In our example application, we're displaying the contents of the MIME Repository, which was described in Section 8.1.2. As you can see in Figure 8.46, the MIME Repository is organized into a hierarchy with /sap being the top-level root node. Underneath this root node, MIME content is organized into a series of files and folders. So, in our Tree example, we had to differentiate between the two different object types by using the TreeItemType and TreeNodeType elements, respectively. Also, since it would be computationally expensive to load the entire repository into context when the application is first loaded, we're utilizing a lazy loading technique in which subobjects are only loaded whenever a folder is accessed on screen. This was achieved by assigning an event handler method to the TreeNodeType.onLoadChildren event. However, before we get into those details, we first need to take a look at how the MIME Repository data was modeled within the context.

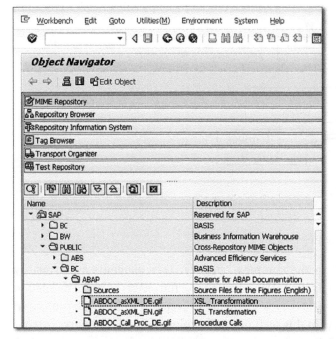

Figure 8.46 Accessing the MIME Repository in the ABAP Workbench

Defining the Context

In order to represent the MIME object data on screen, we had to define a recursive context hierarchy in which MIME content could be nested arbitrarily deep. Figure 8.47 shows how we set this up in our sample application. Here, we have a top-level node called MIME_CONTENT, which has a cardinality of 0..n. This node represents a MIME folder and contains the following attributes:

▶ The NAME attribute is a STRING used to store the object's name.

▶ The PATH attribute is a STRING that refers to the object's path in the MIME Repository hierarchy.

▶ The CONTENT_LOADED attribute is a Boolean (WDY_BOOLEAN) attribute that keeps track of whether or not the folder's content has been loaded already. By storing this information, we can improve the efficiency of the design.

▶ The EXPANDED attribute is a Boolean attribute that keeps track of whether or not the node or folder is expanded on screen.

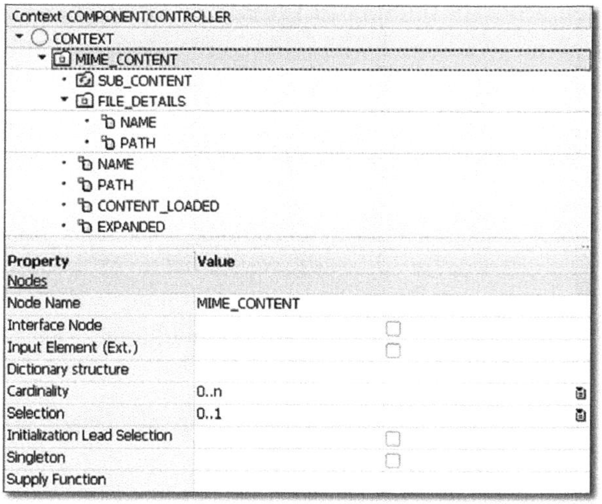

Figure 8.47 Modeling Content from the MIME Repository (Part 1)

In addition to the basic properties used to model a folder in the MIME Repository, the `MIME_CONTENT` node contains a multi-element child node called `FILE_DETAILS` that stores information about each of the files contained within the corresponding folder. As you can see in Figure 8.48, the `FILE_DETAILS` node defines two `STRING` attributes, called `NAME` and `PATH`, that are used to store the file's name and path, respectively.

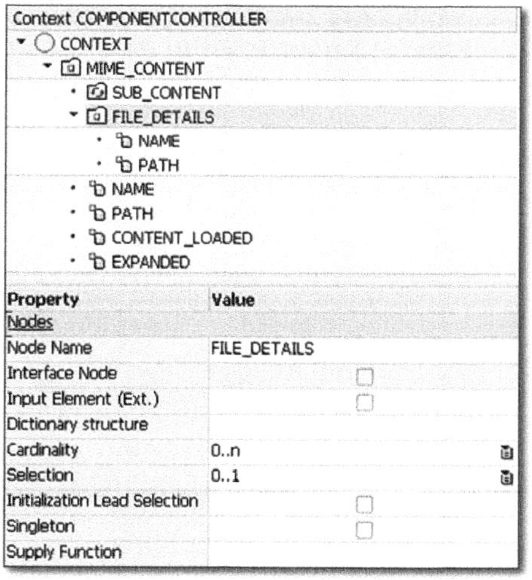

Figure 8.48 Modeling Content from the MIME Repository (Part 2)

Finally, in order to represent an arbitrary number of subfolders within a given folder, the MIME_CONTENT node defines a recursive child node, called SUB_CONTENT, that replicates the MIME_CONTENT folder structure down to the lower hierarchy levels.

UI Element Configuration

Once the context hierarchy was in place, the UI configuration tasks within the View Designer were fairly straightforward. Basically, we had to model the tree itself, and then its nodes and leaves. Figure 8.49 shows how this content is organized within the UI element hierarchy.

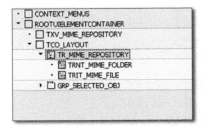

Figure 8.49 Defining the Tree Element Hierarchy

Figure 8.50 shows how we configure the top-level Tree element. The primary thing to note here is the mapping of the Tree.dataSource property to the MIME_CONTENT node, which defines the root of the MIME Repository hierarchy. As you can see, there are a number of other properties to choose from here, most of which are geared toward adjusting the Tree element's look and feel. If you're interested in learning more about the function of these properties, consult the online help documentation.

To represent the MIME folders within the Tree, we use the TreeNodeType element, as shown in Figure 8.51. Here, we mapped the TreeNodeType.dataSource property to the MIME_CONTENT node. This binding causes TreeNodeType elements to be rendered on the screen for each folder element contained within the MIME_CONTENT node—even the recursively defined ones. To visualize the folders on the screen, we mapped the MIME_CONTENT.NAME attribute (used to store the folder name) to the TreeNodeType.text property. We also mapped the iconSource property to a folder icon available for selection within the assigned input help.

Figure 8.50 Configuring the Tree Element

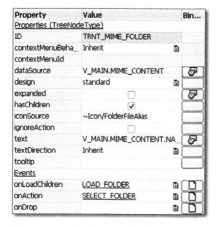

Figure 8.51 Configuring the TreeNodeType Element

Finally, to represent MIME files within the `Tree`, we used the `TreeItemType` element, as shown in Figure 8.52. In this case, we mapped the `MIME_CONTENT.FILE_DETAILS` node to the `TreeItemType.dataSource` property, and the `MIME_CONTENT.FILE_DETAILS.NAME` attribute to the `TreeItemType.text` property. We also mapped the `iconSource` property to a file icon available for selection within the assigned input help.

Property	Value	Bin...
Properties (TreeItemType)		
ID	TRIT_MIME_FILE	
contextMenuBeha...	Inherit	
contextMenuId		
dataSource	V_MAIN.MIME_CONTENT.FIL...	
design	standard	
iconSource	~Icon/File	
ignoreAction	☐	
text	V_MAIN.MIME_CONTENT.FIL...	
textDirection	Inherit	
tooltip		
Events		
onAction	SELECT_FILE	
onDrop		

Figure 8.52 Configuring the TreeItemType Element

Filling the Context

To populate the Tree element with data from the MIME Repository, we used the MIME Repository API provided via the SAP standard IF_MR_API interface. To begin, we statically defined the /sap root node in the WDDOINIT() hook method of the component controller, as shown in Listing 8.8. Then, we passed the newly created context element to an instance method called READ_MIME_FOLDER() to go ahead and preload the contents of the /sap root folder.

```
method WDDOINIT.
  "Method-Local Data Declarations:
  DATA lo_nd_mime_content TYPE REF TO if_wd_context_node.
  DATA lo_el_mime_content TYPE REF TO if_wd_context_element.
  DATA ls_mime_content TYPE wd_this->Element_mime_content.

  "Access the MIME_CONTENT node:
  lo_nd_mime_content =
   wd_context->get_child_node(
      name = wd_this->wdctx_mime_content ).

  "Add the /sap root node to the context:
  ls_mime_content-name = 'SAP'.
  ls_mime_content-path = '/sap'.
  ls_mime_content-expanded = abap_true.

  lo_el_mime_content =
    lo_nd_mime_content->bind_structure(
      new_item = ls_mime_content ).
```

```
    "Go ahead and load the root node's direct descendants:
    read_mime_folder( lo_el_mime_content ).
endmethod.
```

Listing 8.8 Initializing the MIME_CONTENT Context Node

Listing 8.9 shows how we implemented the READ_MIME_FOLDER( ) method. Here, the process flow is defined as follows:

1. First, we query the MIME_CONTENT.CONTENT_LOADED attribute to determine if the selected folder has been read already. If it has, we can skip over the content loading and silently return. Otherwise, we go ahead and mark the flag and move on.

2. Next, we obtain a reference to the MIME Repository API and use it to read the contents of the selected folder.

3. For each found subobject, we perform the following steps:

   ▹ First, we read the properties of the object (e.g., name, URL and so on).

   ▹ If the subobject is a folder, we append the folder as a context element underneath the MIME_CONTENT.SUB_CONTENT node.

   ▹ Otherwise, we append the file as a context element underneath the MIME_CONTENT.FILE_DETAILS node.

The nice thing about the READ_MIME_FOLDER( ) method is that it can also be used to perform the heavy lifting for the TreeNodeType.onLoadChildren event handler method. We'll see how this was achieved in the next section.

```
method READ_MIME_FOLDER.
  "Method-Local Data Declarations:
  DATA lv_loaded TYPE wdy_boolean.
  DATA lv_path TYPE wd_this->Element_mime_content-path.
  DATA lo_mime_api TYPE REF TO if_mr_api.
  DATA ls_io TYPE skwf_io.
  DATA lt_ios TYPE skwf_ios.
  DATA lv_subobj_name TYPE string.
  DATA lv_subobj_url TYPE skwf_url.
  DATA lv_folder_flag TYPE abap_bool.
  DATA lt_path_tokens TYPE string_table.
  DATA lv_name_index TYPE i.
  DATA lo_nd_sub_content TYPE REF TO if_wd_context_node.
  DATA ls_sub_content TYPE wd_this->Element_sub_content.
```

```abap
DATA lo_nd_file_details TYPE REF TO if_wd_context_node.
DATA ls_file_details TYPE wd_this->Element_file_details.
FIELD-SYMBOLS:
  <lfs_io> LIKE LINE OF lt_ios.

"Sanity check - make sure we haven't loaded this
"folder already:
io_folder_elem->get_attribute(
  EXPORTING
    name  = `CONTENT_LOADED`
  IMPORTING
    value = lv_loaded ).

IF lv_loaded EQ abap_true.
  RETURN.
ELSE.
  io_folder_elem->set_attribute(
    EXPORTING
      name  = `CONTENT_LOADED`
      value = abap_true ).
ENDIF.

"Determine the source folder's path:
io_folder_elem->get_attribute(
  EXPORTING
    name =  `PATH`
  IMPORTING
    value = lv_path ).

"Use the MIME/KW Repository APIs to read the objects
"contained within the selected folder:
lo_mime_api = cl_mime_repository_api=>get_api( ).
lo_mime_api->get_io_for_url(
  EXPORTING
    i_url = lv_path
  IMPORTING
    e_loio = ls_io ).

cl_skwf_folder_util=>ios_attach_get(
  EXPORTING
    folder              = ls_io
    iotypeacc           = space
```

```
      x_prefetch_properties = abap_true
    IMPORTING
      ios                   = lt_ios ).

"Add each of the found objects to the context:
LOOP AT lt_ios ASSIGNING <lfs_io>.
  "Lookup the sub-object's URL:
  CALL FUNCTION 'SKWF_NMSPC_IO_ADDRESS_GET'
    EXPORTING
      io  = <lfs_io>
    IMPORTING
      url = lv_subobj_url.

  "Parse out the object name:
  SPLIT lv_subobj_url AT '/'
   INTO TABLE lt_path_tokens.
  lv_name_index = lines( lt_path_tokens ).
  READ TABLE lt_path_tokens INDEX lv_name_index
       INTO lv_subobj_name.

  "Use the URL to read the object properties:
  lo_mime_api->properties(
    EXPORTING
      i_url      = lv_subobj_url
    IMPORTING
      e_is_folder = lv_folder_flag ).

  "Add the subobject to the context:
  IF lv_folder_flag EQ abap_true.
    "If the object is a folder, then we must add it to the
    "recursive SUB_CONTENT node:
    ls_sub_content-name = lv_subobj_name.
    ls_sub_content-path = lv_subobj_url.

    lo_nd_sub_content =
      io_folder_elem->get_child_node( `SUB_CONTENT` ).
    lo_nd_sub_content->bind_structure(
      new_item = ls_sub_content
      set_initial_elements = abap_false ).
  ELSE.
    "Otherwise, we add it to the FILE_DETAILS node:
    lo_nd_file_details =
```

```
        io_folder_elem->get_child_node( `FILE_DETAILS` ).

      ls_file_details-name = lv_subobj_name.
      ls_file_details-path = lv_subobj_url.

      lo_nd_file_details->bind_structure(
        new_item = ls_file_details
        set_initial_elements = abap_false ).
    ENDIF.
  ENDLOOP.
endmethod.
```

Listing 8.9 Loading the Contents of a MIME Folder into the Context

Event Handling

Once the initialization logic outlined in the previous section was in place, we were able to actually see MIME Repository content displayed within the Tree control on screen. However, by default, only the first two levels of data loaded at application startup were visible. To view the contents of additional folders, we had to register an action with the TreeNodeType.onLoadChildren event. Listing 8.10 shows how we defined the event handler method for this action. As you can see, most of the heavy lifting is being performed by the READ_MIME_FOLDER() method described in the previous section. Here, we're using the provided CONTEXT_ELEMENT parameter as a reference to point to the folder the user selected to expand within the Tree.

```
method ONACTIONLOAD_FOLDER.
  wd_comp_controller->read_mime_folder( context_element ).
endmethod.
```

Listing 8.10 Responding to the TreeNodeType.onLoadChildren Event

As users browse through the MIME Repository hierarchy, they can gather more details about a given folder or file by simply clicking on the corresponding node in the Tree. This will cause the onAction event to fire for both the TreeNodeType and TreeItemType elements. Listing 8.11 shows how we implemented the event handler method for the TreeNodeType.onAction event. Here, we're basically just copying the selected folder's metadata into a context node called SELECTED_OBJECT. Figure 8.53 shows how the selected object metadata is displayed on the screen in a Group element.

> **Note**
>
> Since the implementation for the `TreeItemType.onAction` event handler method is almost identical to the one shown in Listing 8.11, we're omitting its implementation here in the text for brevity's sake. Of course, you can find a complete implementation of this method in the `ZWDC_TREE_DEMO` sample component.

```
method ONACTIONSELECT_FOLDER.
  "Method-Local Data Declarations:
  DATA ls_mime_content TYPE wd_this->Element_mime_content.
  DATA lo_nd_selected_object TYPE REF TO if_wd_context_node.
  DATA ls_selected_object
    TYPE wd_this->Element_selected_object.

  "Read the attributes of the selected folder:
  context_element->get_static_attributes(
    IMPORTING
      static_attributes = ls_mime_content ).

  "Update the selection on the screen:
  lo_nd_selected_object =
    wd_context->get_child_node(
      name = wd_this->wdctx_selected_object ).

  MOVE-CORRESPONDING ls_mime_content TO ls_selected_object.

  lo_nd_selected_object->bind_structure(
      new_item = ls_selected_object ).
endmethod.
```

Listing 8.11 Responding to the TreeNodeType.onAction Event

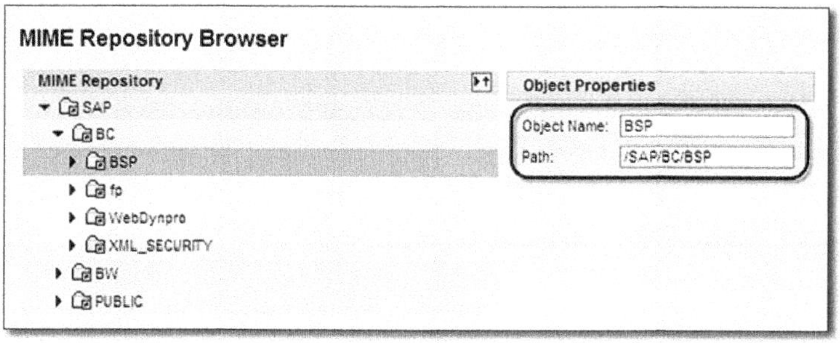

Figure 8.53 Viewing MIME Object Properties

8.3.4 Working with the RoadMap Element

In Section 8.3.1, we observed how the RoadMap element could be used to visualize the steps required in a wizard or guided procedure. For the most part, the Road-Map element is fairly easy to work with in and of itself. However, when developing wizards or guided procedures, you must take special care to synchronize the RoadMap steps with the rest of the elements within the view layout. With this in mind, we'll spend some time in this section reviewing these details so you'll have a better understanding of how the RoadMap element works in conjunction with other UI elements to guide users toward process objectives. To illustrate these concepts, we'll take an in-depth look at a sample wizard delivered by SAP in the DEMO_ROADMAP component.

Getting Started

Before we begin dissecting the DEMO_ROADMAP component, let's briefly take a look at what the application looks like at runtime. As you can see in Figure 8.54, a RoadMap element is being used to guide users through the process of purchasing a book. Each major step within the RoadMap is represented by a square box that contains a meaningful identifier/label to help users understand where they are in the process. The current step is highlighted in orange. As users complete individual steps, they can use the CONTINUE button to move on to the next step. Or, if they need to back up a step, they can click on the BACK button. Alternatively, users can navigate to a particular step in the process by clicking on that step's hyperlink.

Figure 8.54 Defining a Wizard with the RoadMap Element

UI Element Configuration

For the most part, the definition of the user interface shown in Figure 8.54 is pretty straightforward. Figure 8.55 shows the view layout of the MAIN view that users see when they first open the DEMO_ROADMAP application. As you can see, there are three primary elements that dominate the view layout:

▶ At the top of the screen, there's the RoadMap element called ROAD_MAP_1 that's being used to guide users through the purchasing process.

▶ Underneath the RoadMap element, there's a ViewContainerUIElement called VIEW_CONTAINER_UIELEMENT_1, which encapsulates all the different views that will be displayed at specific steps within the RoadMap.

▶ Then, at the bottom of the screen, there are two Button elements called BTN_PREV and BTN_NEXT that are used to move back and forth between steps within the wizard process.

Figure 8.55 Defining a Road Map at Design Time

If we take a closer look at the the ROAD_MAP_1 element definition in Figure 8.56, we can see that it defines five RoadMapStep child elements, one to represent each of the steps shown in Figure 8.54. The currently selected step in the RoadMap is being tracked via the selectedStep property, which is bound to a context attribute of type STRING called ROADMAP.STEP. Figure 8.57 shows how the context is set up for this scenario.

Figure 8.56 Laying out the RoadMap Element

Figure 8.58 illustrates how the individual RoadMapStep elements are configured. Here, key properties to note are the ID, name, and description properties:

▶ The `ID` property is used to uniquely identify each step within the `RoadMap`.

▶ The `name` property can be used to define the text that shows up inside the box that represents a `RoadMapStep` on the screen.

▶ The `description` property can be used to provide a text label that will show up underneath the `RoadMapStep` on screen.

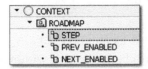

Figure 8.57 Setting up the Context for a RoadMap Implementation

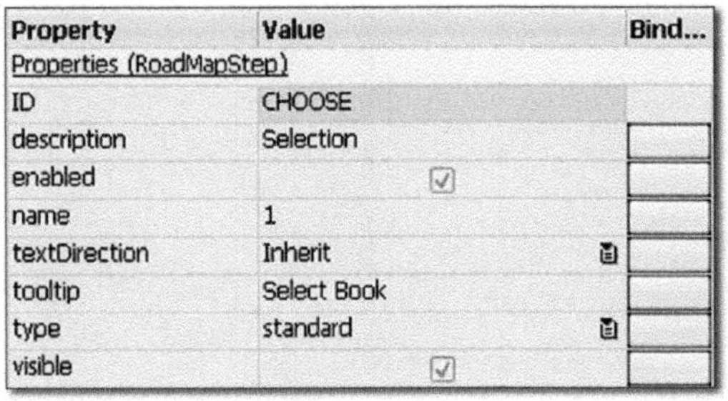

Property	Value	Bind...
Properties (RoadMapStep)		
ID	CHOOSE	
description	Selection	
enabled	☑	
name	1	
textDirection	Inherit	
tooltip	Select Book	
type	standard	
visible	☑	

Figure 8.58 Configuring an Individual RoadMapStep Element

One last thing we should point out is the configuration of the `RoadMap.onSelect` event. As you can see in Figure 8.59, SAP has assigned an action called `SELECT` to this event. Looking carefully at the definition of the event handler method for this action in Figure 8.60, notice how the event handler is set up to receive a parameter called `STEP`. This parameter will be used to adjust the currently selected step within the `RoadMap`. We'll see how this is achieved in the next section.

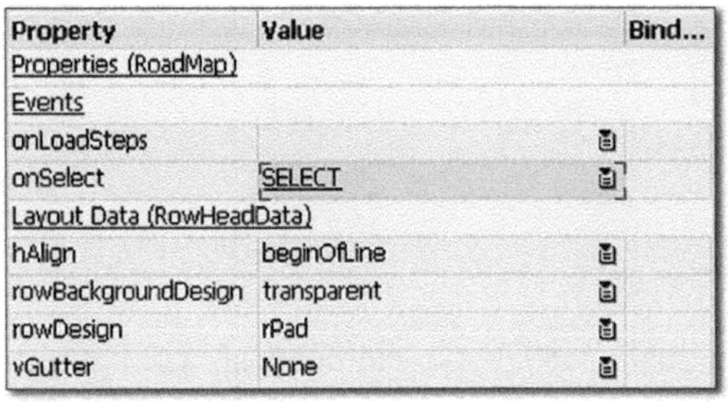

Property	Value	Bind...
Properties (RoadMap)		
Events		
onLoadSteps		
onSelect	SELECT	
Layout Data (RowHeadData)		
hAlign	beginOfLine	
rowBackgroundDesign	transparent	
rowDesign	rPad	
vGutter	None	

Figure 8.59 Wiring up the RoadMap.onSelect Event (Part 1)

Event Handler	ONACTIONSELECT					
Parameter		Type	RefTo	Opt	Associated Type	Sho
WDEVENT		Importi..	☑	☐	CL_WD_CUSTOM_EVENT	
STEP		Importi..	☐	☐	STRING	

Figure 8.60 Wiring up the RoadMap.onSelect Event (Part 2)

Navigation Event Processing

One of the challenges with designing wizard-based processes is that users want the flexibility to move back and forth between steps as they progress through the task flow. This adds complexity to navigation event processing since we must first ascertain where the user is within the process and then determine the proper navigation target from there. To understand how this works, let's trace through a navigation request in the DEMO_ROADMAP application by looking at the navigation flow diagram shown in Figure 8.61.

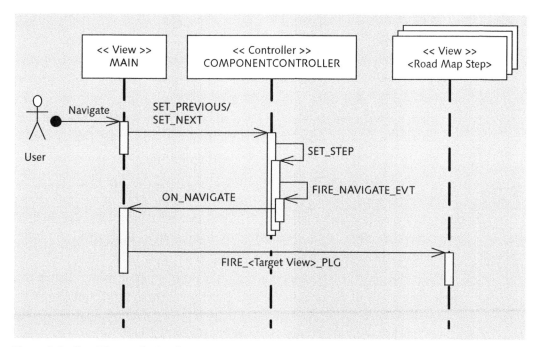

Figure 8.61 Flow Diagram for RoadMap Navigation Processing

As you can see in Figure 8.61, the navigation flow for a selection within the roadmap is implemented as follows:

1. The process begins whenever the user clicks on the BTN_PREV or BTN_NEXT buttons provided for navigation within the MAIN view layout, as shown in Figure 8.54. For the purposes of this flow narrative, we'll assume the user has tried to move to the next step in the process by clicking on the BTN_NEXT button. The process of navigating backwards is essentially the same; the only difference is that the navigation targets are reversed.

2. Next, the event handler method tied to the Button.onAction event forwards the request on to the SET_NEXT() instance method provided by the component controller.

3. The SET_NEXT() method's task is simple: It must query the current RoadMap step from the ROADMAP.STEP context attribute and then determine the appropriate next step for the user. In this simple example, such logic is encoded within a CASE statement.

4. Once the SET_NEXT() method determines the target step, it hands control over to another instance method called SET_STEP(). The SET_STEP() method then performs the following tasks:

   ▶ First, it determines whether or not the BACK and CONTINUE buttons should be enabled for the selected step by adjusting the ROADMAP.PREV_ENABLED and ROADMAP.NEXT_ENABLED context attributes.

   ▶ Then, it updates the ROADMAP.STEP context attribute with the selected step so that the RoadMap element is synchronized with the rest of the process.

   ▶ Finally, it notifies the MAIN view by firing a component controller event called NAVIGATE. Here, it passes the selected step via the defined TARGET parameter.

5. The MAIN view responds to the NAVIGATE event via its ON_NAVIGATE() event handler method. Here, a CASE statement is built around the provided TARGET parameter to determine which view to display.

6. Finally, the ON_NAVIGATE() method refreshes the screen layout to match the selected step by firing an outbound plug that points to the corresponding subview displayed within the ViewContainerUIElement element that makes up the wizard content area (VIEW_CONTAINER_UIELEMENT_1).

For the most part, this process flow is fairly typical of most `RoadMap`-based wizard implementations. As we've observed, the steps illustrated in Figure 8.61 are fairly straightforward to implement in and of themselves. However, since there are so many moving parts, it helps if you take a methodical approach to the task flow design so that all the different pieces fit together seamlessly. When in doubt, you can refer back to the flow diagram in Figure 8.61 to see where the process is breaking down.

8.4   Drag and Drop

Drag and drop support within the Web Dynpro framework was introduced in the SAP NetWeaver 7.01 release. With drag and drop, users can select source UI elements (or embedded element items) by "grabbing" them and dragging them on top of other UI elements. Naturally, this process is much more productive for users than having to manually copy data from one UI element to another.

As of the SAP NetWeaver 7.31 release, only certain UI element types can be used in drag-and-drop operations. This list of supported elements includes the following UI element types:

- `Accordion`
- `CTable`
- `GridLayout` / `MatrixLayout`
- `Image`
- `ItemListBox`
- `PanelStack`
- `Table`
- `Tree`

In the upcoming sections, we'll look at how these elements can be configured to participate in drag-and-drop scenarios.

8.4.1   Conceptual Overview

Since drag and drop is commonly used in many types of GUI applications, its usage requires little introduction on the part of users. However, as a Web Dynpro developer, you may be wondering how these concepts translate to WDA. There-fore, in this section, we'll trace through a drag-and-drop scenario in order to see what's happening behind the scenes.

To guide us through this demonstration, we'll look at how drag and drop works between a pair of ItemListBox elements, as shown in Figure 8.62. Of course, the concepts considered apply equally to drag-and-drop scenarios based on other UI elements such as the Tree or Table elements.

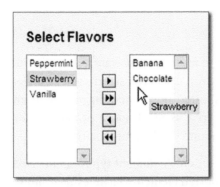

Figure 8.62 Drag and Drop with a Pair of ItemListBox Elements

From a conceptual point of view, the drag-and-drop process can be summarized in three basic steps:

1. The process begins whenever a user begins to drag item(s) from the source ItemListBox element. The drag operation is triggered via the familiar drag ges-ture in which the user clicks on the element(s) and holds down on the mouse button. Behind the scenes, information about the source of the drag-and-drop operation is captured in a DragSourceInfo element embedded within the source ItemListBox element (see Figure 8.63).

2. The user then drags the selected element(s) by holding down the mouse button and moving the mouse pointer over to the target ItemListBox element. As the user drags the element(s), a "ghost" image will appear on the screen to illus-trate that a drag-and-drop operation is being performed. Once the mouse cur-sor is positioned over the target ItemListBox element, the ItemListBox will be highlighted with a dotted line border so that the user has some visual confir-mation that the ItemListBox is a valid drop target (see Figure 8.64). If the user were to hover the mouse cursor over other UI elements, the mouse pointer would be adjusted to display a prohibitive sign (see Figure 8.65).

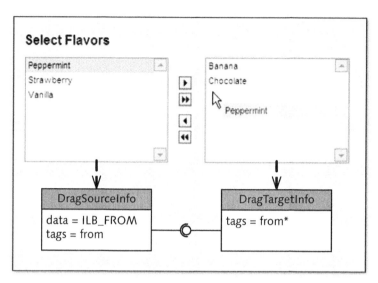

Figure 8.63 Linking the DragSourceInfo and DragTargetInfo Elements

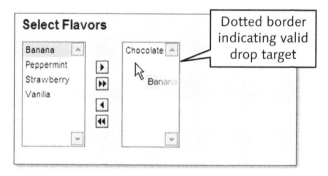

Figure 8.64 Dropping an Object onto a Valid Drop Target

3. Finally, once the user drops the selected item(s), the `onDrop` event on the target `ItemListBox` will be triggered to initiate the data move procedure. The important thing to note here is that drag and drop does not automatically move the data. Instead, developers must use the event parameters passed with the `onDrop` event to determine what the user tried to accomplish on the frontend and then move the data using context API methods as usual.

We'll take a closer look at how these steps are implemented in the next section.

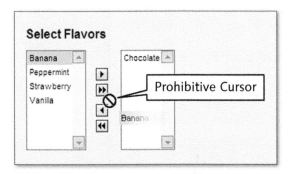

Figure 8.65 Dropping an Object onto an Invalid Drop Target

8.4.2 The Mechanics of Drag and Drop

Having considered the basic concepts of drag and drop in the previous section, let's now turn our attention to the mechanics of drag-and-drop scenarios from a UI element configuration perspective. Here, besides the source/target UI elements, there are three additional element types we need to take into account. Table 8.5 describes each of these UI element types in detail.

UI Element Type	Description
DragSourceInfo	This UI element defines metadata used by the Web Dynpro framework to obtain information about the source UI element participating in a drag-and-drop scenario. The relationship between the source UI element and the DragSourceInfo element is defined by embedding the DragSourceInfo element as a child of the source UI element. Here, we should note that such aggregations are only possible for UI element types that support drag and drop.
	Key metadata for the DragSourceInfo element is contained within the following properties:
	▶ **Data** The data property is like a key that represents the data being transported. Event handler methods can use this property to identify the source context node to pull data from.

Table 8.5 UI Elements Specific to Drag-and-Drop Operations

UI Element Type	Description
DragSourceInfo (Cont.)	▶ **Tags** The tags property contains a text-based token or expression that enables the Web Dynpro framework to identify possible drop targets. Multiple tags can be separated by spaces. In general, the value specified in the tags property represents some kind of meaningful identifier for identifying valid drop targets. Therefore, it's mostly up to developers to come up with a naming convention. However, we're restricted from using the following characters within a tag expression: Colon (:), comma (,), semicolon (;), backslash (\), slash (/), and period (.). ▶ **Scope** When defining a DragSourceInfo element, we also have the option of specifying the scope of the drag source in the source property. Here, we can define component-level scope or global scope depending on whether or not we want the drag source to be included in cross-component scenarios.
DropTargetInfo	This UI element is the analog of the DragSourceInfo element, providing metadata about a potential drop target in a drag-and-drop scenario. Like the DragSourceInfo element, the DropTargetInfo element doesn't stand on its own. Rather, it must be embedded within a UI element that's intended to be a target in a drag-and-drop scenario. From a configuration perspective, the main property to be aware of with the DropTargetInfo element is the tags property. Within this property, we must specify tag values that match corresponding tag values from potential drag sources. However, unlike the DragSourceInfo element, we needn't specify the tag values completely. Instead, we use the asterisk (*) character to define wildcards that match any drag source that meets some basic criteria. For example, we could plug in a value such as from* to enlist a UI element as a potential drop target for any drag-and-drop operation in which the source UI element's DragSourceInfo element contains a value in the tags property that begins with the from prefix (e.g., fromItem1 or fromTable).

Table 8.5 UI Elements Specific to Drag-and-Drop Operations (Cont.)

UI Element Type	Description
DropTarget	The DropTarget element is an invisible element within the layout category used to define a generic target area for a drag-and-drop operation. In effect, this element wraps a target UI element within an invisible frame/container, defining an area for the insertion of data.
	Unlike the DragSourceInfo and DragTargetInfo elements, the use of the DropTarget element is optional in a drag-and-drop scenario. However, it can be useful in situations when we wish to intercept a drop event and perform more sophisticated operations on the target UI element. We'll demonstrate how this works in Section 8.4.3.

Table 8.5 UI Elements Specific to Drag-and-Drop Operations (Cont.)

Now that we have a better grasp on the positioning of the DragSourceInfo and DragTargetInfo elements, let's look at how a drag-and-drop scenario is configured between a pair of UI elements. Here, we must perform the following steps:

1. First, in order to define a drag source, we must embed a DragSourceInfo element within the source UI element that will participate in the scenario. Here, we must assign a data source and drag source identifier in the data and tags properties, respectively (see Figure 8.66).

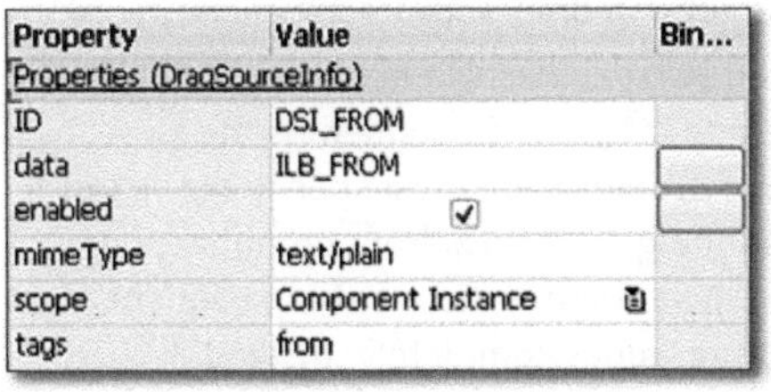

Property	Value	Bin...
Properties (DragSourceInfo)		
ID	DSI_FROM	
data	ILB_FROM	
enabled	☑	
mimeType	text/plain	
scope	Component Instance	
tags	from	

Figure 8.66 Defining a DragSourceInfo Element

2. Next, we need to define a drop target by embedding a DropTargetInfo element into the target UI element. Figure 8.67 shows how this element is configured. Note that in order to receive data from the drag source defined in the previous step, we must configure the DropTargetInfo element's tags property to match the value specified in the DragSourceInfo element. Here, we can use wildcard expressions such as from* to match up the drop target with one or more related drag sources.

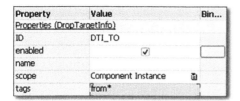

Property	Value	Bin...
Properties (DropTargetInfo)		
ID	DTI_TO	
enabled	☑	
name		
scope	Component Instance	🖺
tags	from*	

Figure 8.67 Defining a DropTargetInfo Element

3. Finally, we must assign an action to the `onDrop` event defined in the target UI element. Within the event handler method for the action, we must implement the logic required to move the data from one UI element to another (or more accurately, from one context node to another).

8.4.3 Case Study: Defining a Drag-and-Drop Scenario

At this point, we're ready to put all the pieces together and see how drag–and-drop scenarios are created within WDA applications. To demonstrate this process, let's take a look at how we might implement the drag-and-drop scenario between a pair of `ItemListBox` elements described earlier in this section. This case study will help us visualize the relationships between the different UI elements that participate in a drag-and-drop scenario, providing a frame of reference that can be applied toward other scenarios based on other UI element types, such as the `Table` element. It will also provide us with an opportunity to see how data gets transfered behind the scenes.

> **Note**
>
> For the purposes of this demonstration, we'll be basing our example on the `ZWDC_DRAGDROP_DEMO` component included with the book's source code bundle. Live demos can also be found in the `WDR_TEST_DRAG_AND_DROP` sample component.

Before we begin looking at specific development tasks, let's briefly go over the functional requirements for our example scenario. As you can see in Figure 8.62, we want to use drag and drop to implement the "browse-and-collect" pattern for a pair of `ItemListBox` elements that contain ice cream flavor choices. Here, the intent is for users to be able to move one or multiple items from one `ItemListBox` to the other by dragging and dropping them onto the target `ItemListBox`. This is straightforward enough. However, to add a slight wrinkle to the process, we also want to maintain the sort order of the flavors regardless of where the user happens to drop the items in the list. So, rather than dropping the selected items directly onto the source/target ItemListBox elements, we're going to wrap up the ItemListBox elements in DropTarget elements. That way, we can intercept the drop operation and organize the contents of the target list box accordingly.

To get things started with our sample application, we need to define the relevant UI elements within the UI element hierarchy. Figure 8.68 shows how we've set this up. As you can see, the UI element hierarchy is organized as follows:

▶ Directly underneath the top-level RootUIElementContainer element, we've defined two DropTarget elements called DT_FROM and DT_TO, respectively.

▶ Each DropTarget element contains two child elements:

  ▶ An ItemListBox element to represent the source/target item list boxes

  ▶ A DropTargetInfo element to define the drop target metadata for the parent DropTarget element

▶ Finally, each ItemListBox element contains a child DragSourceInfo element, which defines the drag source metadata for the parent item list box.

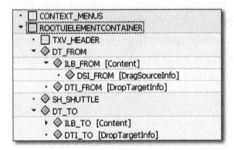

Figure 8.68 Setting up the UI Element Hierarchy

From a configuration perspective, there's nothing special we have to do for the ItemListBox elements. Instead, the bulk of the work goes into defining the drag source/drop target parameters. First, we must set up the DragSourceInfo elements to define the drag source metadata. Figure 8.69 shows how we've set up the DSI_FROM element. As you can see, we have assigned the value from to the tags property and specified the ID of the source ItemListBox element in the data property. These values are arbitrary and can be tailored to suit your preferences.

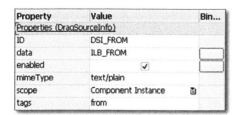

Property	Value	Bin...
Properties (DragSourceInfo)		
ID	DSI_FROM	
data	ILB_FROM	
enabled	☑	
mimeType	text/plain	
scope	Component Instance 🗑	
tags	from	

Figure 8.69 Configuring the DragSourceInfo Element

For the most part, the `DropTargetInfo` elements simply mirror the `DragSourceInfo` element configuration. For example, in Figure 8.70, you can see how we've specified the `tags` property on the `DTI_TO` element to match the `tags` value specified in the `DSI_FROM` element.

Property	Value	Bin...
Properties (DropTargetInfo)		
ID	DTI_TO	
enabled	☑	
name		
scope	Component Instance 🗑	
tags	from*	

Figure 8.70 Configuring the DropTargetInfo Element

Finally, the last step on the configuration side is to go into each `DropTarget` element and assign an event handler method for the `onDrop` event. As you can see in Figure 8.71, we've created an action called `DROP_IT` to process this event. Here, note that we've selected the TRANSFER UI EVENT PARAMETERS checkbox in order to ensure that the event handler method is defined to include all the event parameters needed to process the event.

Create Action		
Component	ZWDC_DRAGDROP_DEMO	
View	V_MAIN	
Action	DROP_IT	👓
Description	Action to Handle the onDrop Event for a DropTarget	
☑ Transfer UI Event Parameters		

Figure 8.71 Creating an Action for the DropTarget.onDrop Event

Once the requisite configuration is completed within the View Designer tool, we can switch over to the Methods tab of the View Editor and provide an implementation for the ONACTIONDROP_IT method. Listing 8.12 provides a sample implementation for this method. For the most part, this is context programming as usual. However, pay attention to the DATA parameter being used to identify the nature of the drag-and-drop operation. Depending on your scenario, this parameter, as well as the other parameters defined for the onDrop event, can be quite useful in determining what sort of drag-and-drop operation a user may have performed on the frontend.

```
method ONACTIONDROP_IT.
  "Method-Local Data Declarations:
  DATA lo_nd_from TYPE REF TO if_wd_context_node.
  DATA lt_from TYPE wd_this->Elements_from.
  DATA ls_from TYPE wd_this->Element_from.
  DATA lo_nd_to TYPE REF TO if_wd_context_node.
  DATA lt_to TYPE wd_this->Elements_to.
  DATA ls_to TYPE wd_this->Element_to.
  DATA lt_selection TYPE wdr_context_element_set.
  DATA lo_element TYPE REF TO if_wd_context_element.

  "Obtain a reference to the from/to context nodes:
  lo_nd_from =
    wd_context->get_child_node( name = wd_this->wdctx_from ).
  lo_nd_to =
    wd_context->get_child_node( name = wd_this->wdctx_to ).

  "Determine the source of the drag-and-drop operation:
  CASE data.
    WHEN 'ILB_FROM'.
      "Fetch the set of items currently in the target:
      lo_nd_to->get_static_attributes_table(
        IMPORTING table = lt_to ).

      "Pull the list of selected items from the source:
      lt_selection =
        lo_nd_from->get_selected_elements( abap_false ).

      "Process each selected item in turn:
      LOOP AT lt_selection INTO lo_element.
        "Copy the selected item over to a buffer that
```

```
    "will be loaded into the target:
    lo_element->get_static_attributes(
      IMPORTING
        static_attributes = ls_from ).

  MOVE-CORRESPONDING ls_from TO ls_to.
  APPEND ls_to TO lt_to.

  "Remove the element from the source:
  lo_nd_from->remove_element( element = lo_element ).
  ENDLOOP.

  "Refresh the target node's contents:
  SORT lt_to BY flavor.

  lo_nd_to->bind_table(
    new_items = lt_to
    set_initial_elements = abap_true ).
WHEN 'ILB_TO'.
  "Fetch the set of items currently in the target:
  lo_nd_from->get_static_attributes_table(
    IMPORTING table = lt_from ).

  "Pull the list of selected items from the source:
  lt_selection =
    lo_nd_to->get_selected_elements( abap_false ).

  "Process each selected item in turn:
  LOOP AT lt_selection INTO lo_element.
    "Copy the selected item over to a buffer that
    "will be loaded into the target:
    lo_element->get_static_attributes(
      IMPORTING
        static_attributes = ls_to ).

  MOVE-CORRESPONDING ls_to TO ls_from.
  APPEND ls_from TO lt_from.

  "Remove the element from the source:
  lo_nd_to->remove_element( element = lo_element ).
  ENDLOOP.
```

```
      "Refresh the target node's contents:
      SORT lt_from BY flavor.

      lo_nd_from->bind_table(
        new_items = lt_from
        set_initial_elements = abap_true ).
  ENDCASE.
endmethod.
```

Listing 8.12 Implementing an Event Handler Method for the onDrop Event

8.5   Summary

In this chapter, we were able to explore some of the more advanced UI elements available within the Web Dynpro framework. Between these elements and the ones considered in Chapter 7, we now have quite a large toolbag to work with when designing view layouts. Now, the biggest problem we'll have is figuring out which element to apply for which application scenario—and that's a good problem to have.

In the next chapter, we'll learn some component-based development techniques that will allow us to mix and match WDA components in various application scenarios. Having an understanding of these concepts is essential for getting the most out of Web Dynpro.

So far, each of the WDA applications we've looked at has been based on a single WDA component. However, in the real world, most WDA applications are composites that combine several WDA components in order to form a workable solution. In this chapter, we'll explore the ways in which such component-based designs are realized.

9 Component-Based Development Concepts

WDA components are positioned as reusable units of code that correspond with atomic steps defined within a business process. Here, for example, we might create a WDA component to encapsulate the process used to maintain an address within the *Business Address Services* (BAS) framework. Once this component is in place, we can reuse it in many WDA applications, such as ones used to maintain business partners, user master records, and so on. In other words, any time we need to maintain addresses, we need only plug in our reusable address component, and our work is done. This is much more effective than trying to piece such solutions together by copying and pasting low-level technical artifacts such as controllers/classes, views, and so on.

In this chapter, we'll learn how to develop composite applications in WDA using component-based development techniques. We get things started by revisiting WDA component interfaces and observing how they define a point of interaction between a pair of WDA components. From there, we delve into the mechanics of component usages from both a design time and runtime perspective. Finally, we will conclude our discussion by looking at some typical component-based development scenarios you'll likely encounter during the course of your day-to-day development work.

9.1 Web Dynpro Component Interfaces: Revisited

The term *component* is used to describe a module that encapsulates a set of related functions (or data). As we read through this definition, the verbal imagery around the word *encapsulate* gives us some insight into the positioning of software components in general and WDA components in particular. Here, it's appropriate to think of WDA components as *black boxes* in the sense that their inner mechanisms are shielded off and hidden away from the outside world.

At first, it may seem overly restrictive for WDA components to be locked down in this way. However, there is a method to this madness. The basic idea here is that clients of WDA components don't need to know how a WDA component works in order to be able to use it. Rather, they simply need to know what services the WDA component provides and how to go about accessing them. WDA components publish such details within a *component interface*.

Figure 9.1 demonstrates how these concepts relate to a pair of WDA components. Here, you can see that in order for WDA component A to leverage services from WDA component B, it must go through B's component interface. This indirection provides several important benefits:

- It effectively decouples the two WDA components, reducing their interaction points to the absolute essentials. This allows the two WDA components to vary independently over time.

- Since WDA component interfaces are designed to be intuitive and easy to use, they reduce the learning curve and make it much easier to tap into a WDA component's resources than trying to figure out how the WDA component works on our own.

- As familiar interface patterns emerge, it may eventually make sense to define standalone component interfaces that can be implemented by multiple WDA components. Such WDA components can then be mixed and matched polymorphically in component usage scenarios.

In the upcoming sections, we'll see how component interfaces are defined for WDA components. We'll also learn how to define and implement standalone component interfaces.

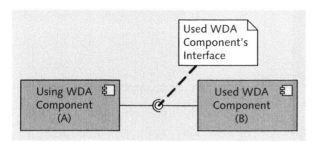

Figure 9.1 Inter-Component Communication via Component Interfaces

9.1.1 Component Interface Overview

As you may recall from Chapter 2, WDA component interfaces are made up of two parts:

▶ **Interface controller**
The interface controller defines the *programmatic portion* of the component interface. It consists of selected elements from the component controller (e.g., methods, events, and context nodes).

▶ **Interface views**
Interface views define the *visual portion* of the component interface, packaging the view layout contained within a window into a reusable, view-like container. Because interface views are cast in the image of views, using components can embed the interface views of external components in places where internal views would normally be embedded.

Figure 9.2 illustrates the positioning of the elements of a WDA component interface in relation to the internal elements that define the component's user interface and behavior. As you can see, the elements of the component interface selectively expose internal elements to the outside world in a controlled manner. Therefore, as component designers, we get to pick and choose which elements should be publicly accessible; everything else remains locked up behind closed doors.

In the next two sections, we'll look at interface controllers and interface views up close.

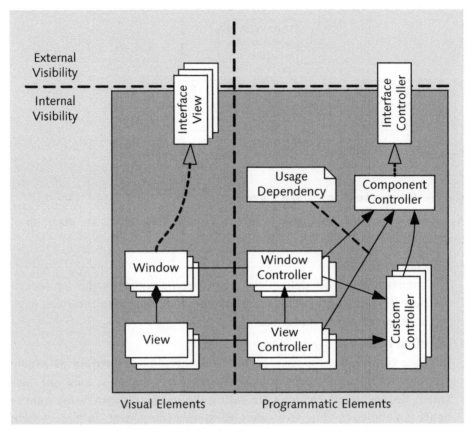

Figure 9.2 WDA Component Interfaces: Revisited

9.1.2 Defining the Interface Controller

Much like the component controllers whose functionality they expose, interface controllers are created automatically whenever a WDA component is created. As mentioned earlier, interface controllers expose a subset of elements from the component controller to the outside world. Therefore, it's appropriate to say that component controllers implement (or provide a realization of) the component interface. The UML class diagram depicted in Figure 9.3 illustrates this relationship.

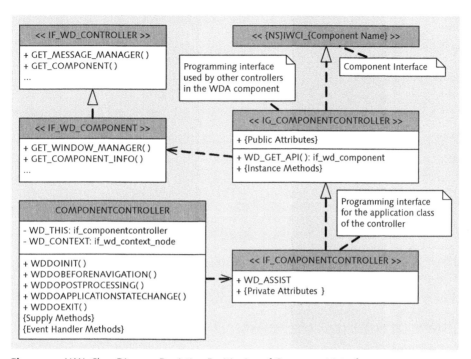

Figure 9.3 UML Class Diagram Depicting Positioning of Component Interface

By default, interface controllers consist of a single method when a WDA component is first created: the WD_GET_API() method, which provides a reference to an object that implements the IF_WD_CONTROLLER interface. In order to expose additional functionality to the interface controller, we must go into the component controller and nominate elements that should be included within the component interface:

▶ **Context nodes**

We can expose context nodes that have been defined directly beneath the top-level root node by selecting the INTERFACE NODE property, as shown in Figure 9.4.

▶ **Methods**

We can expose instance methods of the component controller by selecting the INTERFACE checkbox, as shown in Figure 9.5.

▶ **Events**

We can expose events of the component controller by selecting the INTERFACE checkbox shown in Figure 9.6.

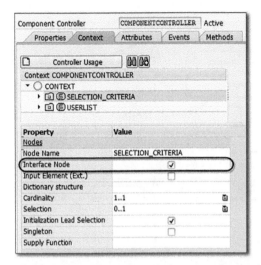

Figure 9.4 Exposing Context Nodes as Interface Nodes

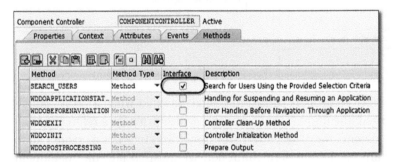

Figure 9.5 Exposing Methods in the Interface Controller

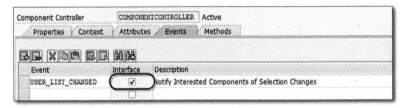

Figure 9.6 Exposing Events in the Interface Controller

Once the relevant interface elements have been defined, we can view the interface controller definition by double-clicking on the INTERFACECONTROLLER node in the left-hand navigation area, as shown in Figure 9.7. This will open the interface controller in the read-only editor view shown in Figure 9.8.

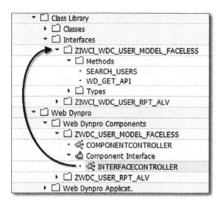

Figure 9.7 Locating the Component Interface in the Web Dynpro Explorer

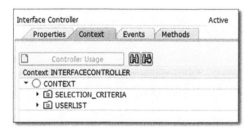

Figure 9.8 Reviewing the Interface Controller Definition

Looking at the PROPERTIES tab of the interface Controller Editor shown in Figure 9.9, you can see that interface controllers reference a separate ABAP-based interface, whose name is of the form `<Namespace>IWCI_<Component Name>`. We can view this interface definition in the Class Builder tool by double-clicking on it. As you can see in Figure 9.10, this generated interface is just like any normal ABAP Objects interface.

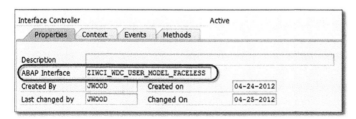

Figure 9.9 Accessing an Interface Controller's ABAP Interface (Part 1)

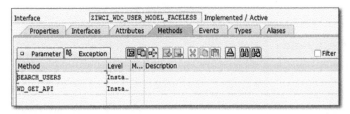

Figure 9.10 Accessing an Interface Controller's ABAP Interface (Part 2)

Given what we learned about controller interfaces in Chapter 4, you might be wondering why a standalone ABAP Objects interface is needed to define the interface controller. Here, the primary difference is that interface controllers extend beyond component boundaries. Consequently, external components don't have visibility to locally defined interfaces such as the IF_COMPONENTCONTROLLER and IG_COMPONENTCONTROLLER interfaces used to access component controller elements internally. Instead, the standalone ABAP Objects interfaces provide external components with something tangible to reference when interfacing with a used component. We'll see how this works in Section 9.2.3.

9.1.3 Configuring Interface Views

In Chapter 6, we briefly described how interface views could be used to embed windows from external components in a window. As you can see in Figure 9.11, from the embedding window's point of view, interface views look just like regular views that are defined locally. This is because interface views define navigation plugs in the same way regular views do.

We can add navigation plugs to an interface view by opening the corresponding window definition and creating plugs that have the INTERFACE property checked (see Figure 9.12). Here, on the inbound side, note that each window will contain a DEFAULT startup plug that is automatically added to the interface view. Though this particular plug is typically used in the definition of WDA applications, it can also be used to embed a window within a view set.

We can display interface view definitions by double-clicking on the corresponding nodes located underneath the COMPONENT INTERFACE • INTERFACE VIEWS folder in the left-hand navigation area of the Web Dynpro Explorer (see Figure 9.13). This will open the interface view in a stripped-down, display-only version of the window editor, as shown in Figure 9.14. Here, we can review the set of navigation plugs exposed via the interface view. We'll see how these navigation plugs are utilized in Section 9.2.5.

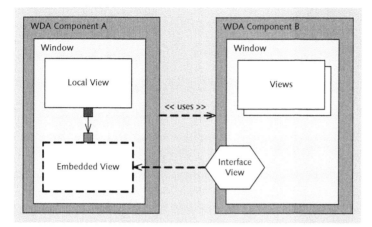

Figure 9.11 Embedding Interface Views in a Window

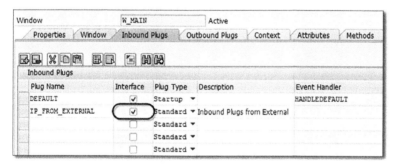

Figure 9.12 Adding Navigation Plugs to an Interface View

Figure 9.13 Displaying an Interface View Definition (Part 1)

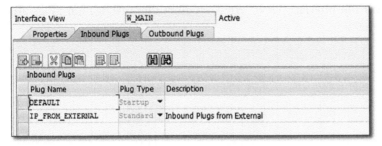

Figure 9.14 Displaying an Interface View Definition (Part 2)

One final thing we should mention about interface views is that, although interface views are created automatically whenever a window is created, we do have the ability to remove a window from the component interface as needed. We do this by navigating to the PROPERTIES tab of the Window Editor tool and deselecting the INTERFACE checkbox, as shown in Figure 9.15. If we wish to add the window back to the component interface later on, we can do so by returning and toggling the checkbox back on.

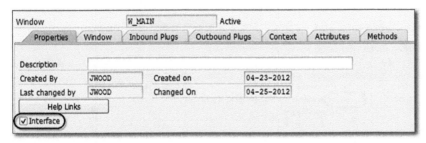

Figure 9.15 Determining the Visibility of a Window

9.1.4 Defining Standalone Web Dynpro Component Interfaces

Occasionally, we may want to create standalone Web Dynpro component interfaces independent from any particular implementation. These component interfaces are particularly useful when it comes to the development of generic application frameworks that assemble multiple WDA components together to form composite applications. Here, standalone component interfaces define a uniform interface that represents the points of interaction between the framework and participating WDA components. We'll see a practical example of this on display in Chapter 14 when we look at the *Floorplan Manager for ABAP* (FPM).

Creating Web Dynpro Component Interfaces

In order to better understand what standalone Web Dynpro component interfaces look like, let's take a look at how they're created. The steps required here are as follows:

1. To begin, we must right-click on the target development package and select the CREATE • WEB DYNPRO • WEB DYNPRO COMPONENT (INTERFACE) menu option (see Figure 9.16).

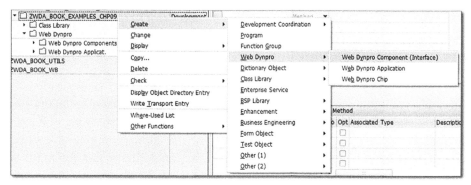

Figure 9.16 Creating a Web Dynpro Component Interface (Part 1)

2. Then, in the WEB DYNPRO: COMPONENT / CREATE INTERFACE dialog box shown in Figure 9.17, we must choose the WEB DYNPRO COMPONENT INTERFACE radio button and provide a name and optional description for the component interface.

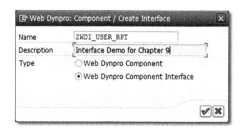

Figure 9.17 Creating a Web Dynpro Component Interface (Part 2)

3. Finally, we can confirm our selections by clicking on the button with the green checkmark on it.

After the Web Dynpro component interface is initially created, it will contain a default interface controller within which we can begin specifying new methods, events, and context nodes (see Figure 9.18). In this case, we must perform these tasks directly inside the interface controller editor since there is no component controller implementation to pull these definitions from.

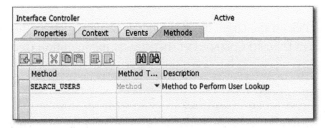

Figure 9.18 Creating a Web Dynpro Component Interface (Part 3)

Also, if we want, we can define one or more interface views by right-clicking on the component interface and selecting the CREATE • INTERFACE VIEW menu option. This will open the CREATE INTERFACE VIEW DEFINITION dialog box shown in Figure 9.19. Here, we can specify the interface view's name and an optional short text description. Once the interface view is created, we can define its navigation plugs within the interface view editor screen shown in Figure 9.20.

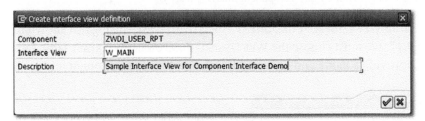

Figure 9.19 Creating a Web Dynpro Component Interface (Part 4)

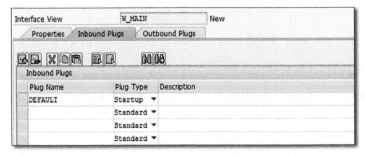

Figure 9.20 Creating a Web Dynpro Component Interface (Part 5)

Implementing Web Dynpro Component Interfaces

Web Dynpro component interfaces are expressions of pure design, containing no implementations of their own. Therefore, in order to make use of them, we must define interface implementations within WDA components. This can be achieved by opening a WDA component in the Component Editor and selecting the IMPLEMENTED INTERFACES tab. Then, in the IMPLEMENTED WEB DYNPRO COMPONENT INTERFACES table shown in Figure 9.21, we can plug in the component interface we want to implement in the NAME column. Once this assignment is established, we can propagate the changes down to the underlying component elements by clicking on the REIMPLEMENT button in the ACTION column.

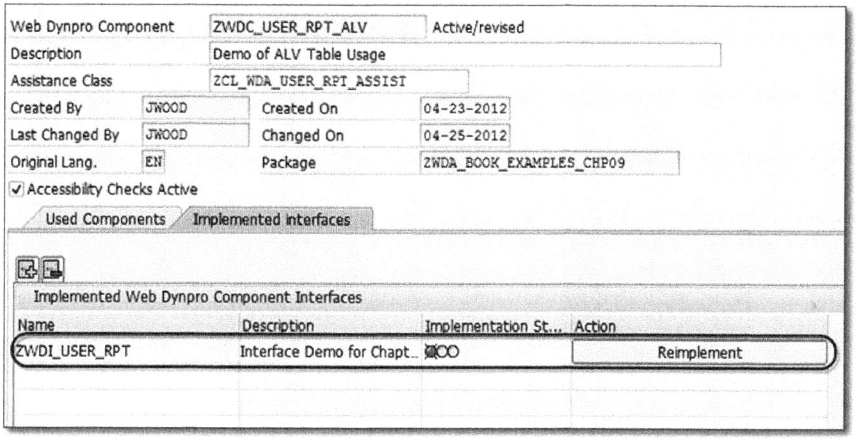

Figure 9.21 Implementing Web Dynpro Component Interfaces (Part 1)

After a component interface has been implemented, you can see its constituent elements carried over into the implementing component's element definitions. For example, in Figure 9.22, you can see how the SEARCH_USERS() method defined in the component interface's interface controller was added to the implementing component's component controller. Of course, it's up to us to define an implementation for the method; the component interface only defines the method signature. The same applies to interface views that are carried over, in the sense that we must lay out the window content just as we would for any normal window.

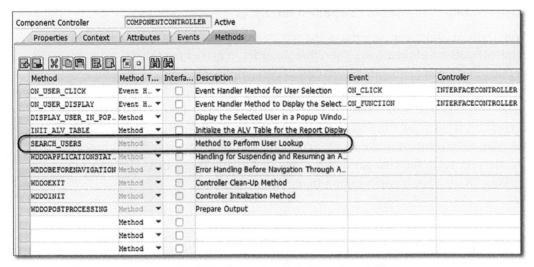

Figure 9.22 Implementing Web Dynpro Component Interfaces (Part 2)

9.2 Component Usage Concepts

Now that we have a better understanding of WDA component interfaces, we're ready to learn how these interfaces are used to implement cross-component usage scenarios. Therefore, in the upcoming sections, we'll see how to define component usages, instantiate components, and access the services of used components.

9.2.1 Defining Component Usages

In order for a component to be able to leverage the services of another component, the using component must declare its usage intentions openly by defining a *component usage*. This can be achieved by performing the following steps:

1. First, we must open the using component in the Component Editor and selecting the USED COMPONENTS tab.

2. Then, in the USED WEB DYNPRO COMPONENTS table shown in Figure 9.23, we can add new rows and define component usages as follows:

   ▹ In the COMPONENT USE column, we must assign a name/key that will be used to reference the component usage throughout the used component.

Here, it makes sense to assign a short, meaningful name to represent the component usage.

▸ In the COMPONENT column, we must plug in the name of the WDA component we want to leverage from.

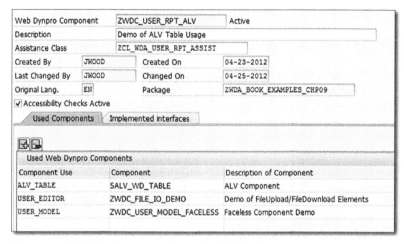

Web Dynpro Component	ZWDC_USER_RPT_ALV	Active
Description	Demo of ALV Table Usage	
Assistance Class	ZCL_WDA_USER_RPT_ASSIST	

Created By	JWOOD	Created On	04-23-2012
Last Changed By	JWOOD	Changed On	04-25-2012
Original Lang.	EN	Package	ZWDA_BOOK_EXAMPLES_CHP09

☑ Accessibility Checks Active

Used Components | Implemented interfaces

Used Web Dynpro Components

Component Use	Component	Description of Component
ALV_TABLE	SALV_WD_TABLE	ALV Component
USER_EDITOR	ZWDC_FILE_IO_DEMO	Demo of FileUpload/FileDownload Elements
USER_MODEL	ZWDC_USER_MODEL_FACELESS	Faceless Component Demo

Figure 9.23 Defining Component Usages in a WDA Component

3. Finally, once the component usage is defined, its definition will be added to the COMPONENT USAGES node in the navigation area of the Web Dynpro Explorer (see Figure 9.24). We'll see how these component usage definitions are used to implement cross-component context mapping scenarios in Section 9.2.4.

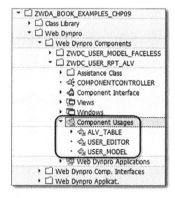

Figure 9.24 Reviewing Component Usages for a WDA Component

9.2.2 Instantiating Used Components

Up until now, we haven't had to worry about instantiating WDA components since the Web Dynpro framework performs this task for us automatically whenever a WDA application is started. However, this default behavior doesn't apply to used components loaded on an ad hoc basis. In these situations, we must manually instantiate those components before we can use them.

> **Note**
>
> The lone exception to this rule is usage scenarios in which we're only embedding interface views from a used component and not accessing data or services of the used component's interface controller.

Used components are instantiated within controller methods of the using component. Which controller is used to perform the initialization largely depends on the scope of the usage scenario. If, for example, a used component is going to be utilized extensively throughout the component, it probably makes sense to instantiate the used component in the WDDOINIT() method of the component controller. Alternatively, if we're using a component just to define an input help for a specific view, then it probably makes sense to simply instantiate the component within a view controller method.

In any case, before we can instantiate a component within a controller method, we must first declare a controller/component usage at the controller level. This process largely mirrors the one described in Section 4.3. Figure 9.25 shows how we're declaring a usage to the interface controller of the SALV_WD_TABLE component.

Once a controller/component usage is established within a controller, two additional methods are added to the controller's local interface:

▶ wd_cpuse_<usage name>()
This method provides a reference to an object that implements the IF_WD_COMPONENT_USAGE interface. This method provides the methods needed to instantiate used components.

▶ wd_cpifc_<usage name>()
This method provides a reference to the used component's interface controller. We'll see how this method is used in Section 9.2.3.

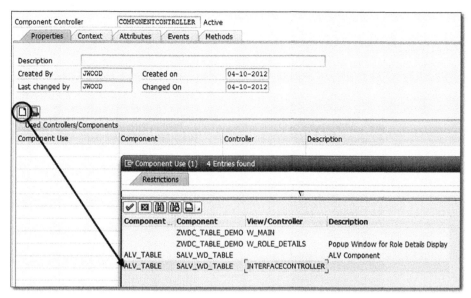

Figure 9.25 Declaring Controller/Component Usages in a Controller

We can use the object reference returned from the WD_CPUSE_<usage name>() method to instantiate a used component by calling the IF_WD_COMPONENT_USAGE ->CREATE_COMPONENT() method. Listing 9.1 demonstrates how this works.

```
method WDDOINIT.
  "Method-Local data Declarations:
  DATA lo_cmp_usage TYPE REF TO if_wd_component_usage.

  "Instantiate the ALV table component:
  lo_cmp_usage = wd_this->wd_cpuse_alv_table( ).
  IF lo_cmp_usage->has_active_component( ) IS INITIAL.
    lo_cmp_usage->create_component( ).
  ENDIF.
endmethod.
```

Listing 9.1 Instantiating a Used Component

As you can see in Listing 9.1, we're calling the HAS_ACTIVE_COMPONENT() method prior to creating the component to ensure that there isn't an existing component instance out there already. Though such a step isn't strictly required whenever a used component is instantiated within the WDDOINIT() method of the component controller, it's nevertheless a good habit to get into since it ensures that the instantiation of a used component (which is computationally expensive) occurs, at most, once.

Rather than having to keep track of the method call signatures and sequence illustrated in Listing 9.1, we can rely on the Web Dynpro code wizard to generate the code for us automatically. As you can see in Figure 9.26, we can do this by selecting the INSTANTIATE USED COMPONENT radio button and plugging in the desired component usage key.

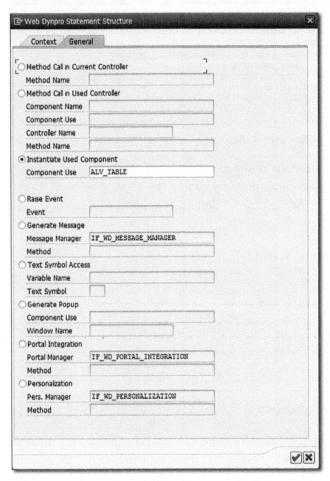

Figure 9.26 Instantiating Used Components via the Code Wizard

9.2.3 Accessing Services of the Interface Controller

Once the requisite component usages are in place and a component is instantiated, we can begin accessing the methods and events of the used component's interface controller. For the most part, this process is very similar to the one used to achieve inter-controller communication within a component (e.g., a view controller calling methods of the component controller).

We can invoke methods of the interface controller by performing the following steps:

- First, we obtain a reference to the interface controller by calling the `WD_CPIFC_<component usage>()` method.
- Then, we use that controller reference to call methods on the controller as usual.

Listing 9.2 demonstrates how this works for a component usage called `USER_MODEL`. If we like, we can use the Web Dynpro code wizard to generate this code for us automatically (see Figure 9.27).

```
method SEARCH_USERS.
  "Method-Local Data Declarations:
  DATA lo_user_ctrl TYPE REF TO ziwci_wdc_user_model_faceless.

  "Delegate the search to the faceless model component:
  lo_user_ctrl = wd_this->wd_cpifc_user_model( ).
  lo_user_ctrl->search_users( ).
endmethod.
```

Listing 9.2 Calling a Method on the Interface Controller

To listen for events triggered by a used component, we simply need to define an event handler method just as we would for events defined by internal controller types. For example, Figure 9.28 shows how we're defining an event handler method called `ON_USER_CLICK()`, which will be invoked on the component controller of a using component whenever the `ON_CLICK` event is triggered in a used component called `SALV_WD_TABLE`. Here, note that the input help will only display events of a used component *if* a component usage is defined for the controller in question.

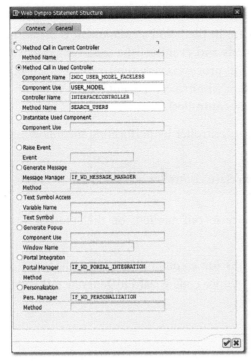

Figure 9.27 Calling Methods of the Interface Controller with the Code Wizard

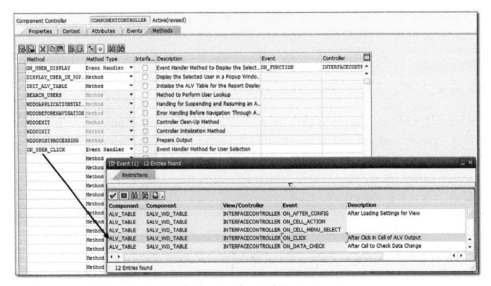

Figure 9.28 Registering to Listen for Events of a Used Component

9.2.4   Cross-Component Context Mapping

As we observed in Section 9.1.2, it's possible to add context nodes from a component's component controller to the component interface by defining such nodes as *interface nodes*. Controllers of using components can then access these interface nodes by implementing *cross-component context mappings*. In this section, we'll see how such mappings are established.

Getting Started

Before we can define cross-component context mappings, there are a few administrative things we must take care of. First of all, in order to access interface nodes exposed via the interface controller of an external component, we must make sure that:

▶ The controller we want to perform the context mapping in has the appropriate usage declaration in place to access the interface controller of the external component.

▶ The external component is instantiated in a method of the using controller, as demonstrated in Section 9.2.2. Ideally, this would occur in the using controller's WDDOINIT() method.

The next thing we have to figure out is *how* we want to map the data. In other words, we need to figure out which component will own the data. On one hand, the external component might be a supplier of data, in which case it should own the context nodes. On the other hand, if the external component is used to consume or display data, it makes sense for the using component to own the data and pass it in to the external component as needed. In the realm of cross-component context mapping, these two scenarios are described as *simple context mappings* and *external context mappings*, respectively. In the upcoming sections, we'll demonstrate both of these mapping types.

Simple Context Mappings

For the most part, simple context mappings work just like the cross-controller mappings we've seen demonstrated in earlier chapters of this book. Figure 9.29 illustrates how simple context mappings work. As you can see, the data contained within the context node(s) flows downstream from the used component to using components. Thus, in this scenario, the used component is the *owner* of the data, in the sense that it supplies the data up front (e.g., via supply functions). Of course, once the context mapping relationship is established, data will flow freely in both directions.

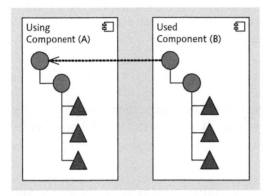

Figure 9.29 Simple Context Mapping Overview

We can set up simple context mappings on the CONTEXT tab of the using controller, as shown in Figure 9.30. Here, notice the panels arranged on the right-hand side of the display. These panels reflect the used components/controllers of the using controller. Within a given panel, we can map the context nodes made visible via the used component's interface controller by dragging and dropping them onto the using controller's context (see Figure 9.30). Once these mappings are in place, we can use the mapped context nodes just as we would any normal context node (e.g., in downstream context mappings, data binding relationships, and so on).

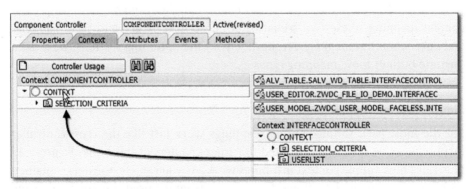

Figure 9.30 Defining a Simple Context Mapping

External Context Mappings

External context mappings work a little differently from any of the cross-controller context mappings we've seen thus far. Here, the data flows in the opposite direction, as demonstrated in Figure 9.31. Thus, in this case, the using component, rather than the used component, is the owner of the data.

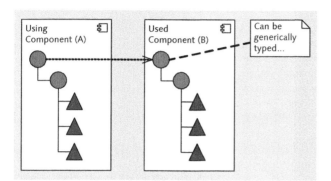

Figure 9.31 External Context Mapping Overview

So why do we care which component owns the data? Well, in many cases, we don't. However, there are certain scenarios in which it makes sense for a WDA component to rely on client components to supply the data. For example, imagine we're developing a generic WDA component that can be used to output reports. Here, in order to maximize reuse, we'd want to define the WDA component in such a way that it could display just about any type of report data. In other words, we'd want the target interface node to be generically typed such that it can be mapped from any type of context node defined in client components. This is where the power of external context mappings comes into play.

With external context mappings, interface nodes are basically positioned as placeholder nodes whose content is defined exclusively via external mappings. As you might expect, the process for setting up external context mappings is slightly more involved than the one used to define simple context mappings. The steps required here are as follows:

1. To get things started, we first need to define the interface node that will be the recipient of the external mapping. For the most part, this can be achieved by creating a context node in the component controller of the external component as usual. However, there are a couple of peculiar aspects of this node configuration we must take into account:

> ▶ In order to maximize flexibility, the node must be generically defined. In other words, it can't contain any child context nodes/attributes of its own. That way, we can map any context node to this node as long as their cardinalities match up.

> ▶ We must turn on external mapping for the context node by selecting the INPUT ELEMENT (EXT.) checkbox for the target interface node, as shown in Figure 9.32.

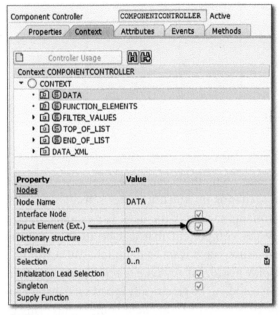

Figure 9.32 Enabling External Mapping for an Interface Node

2. Next, we must define a (reverse) controller usage between the external component's interface controller and the component controller of the using component. We carry out this task within the *using component* by right-clicking on the COMPONENT USAGES • <COMPONENT USAGE> node and selecting the CREATE CONTROLLER USAGE menu option as shown in Figure 9.33.

3. Then, in the CONTROLLER USAGE editor screen shown in Figure 9.34, we can define the (reverse) controller usage by clicking on the CONTROLLER USAGE button and selecting the component controller of the using component (see Figure 9.34).

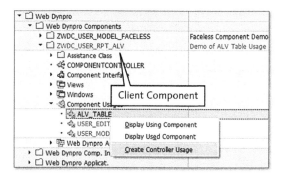

Figure 9.33 Defining an External Context Mapping (Part 1)

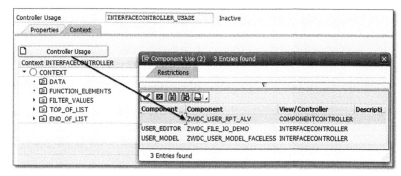

Figure 9.34 Defining an External Context Mapping (Part 2)

4. Finally, we can complete the external context mapping by dragging and dropping the source context node from the using component's component controller to the target node in the external component's interface controller (see Figure 9.35).

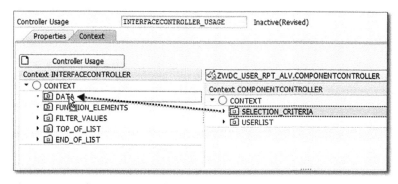

Figure 9.35 Defining an External Context Mapping (Part 3)

At runtime, the externally mapped interface node will assume the type and characteristics of the mapped context node from the client component. Within the external component, we can use methods of the context and the *ABAP Run Time Type Services* (RTTS) APIs to unpack the data and process it as needed. We'll see a practical example of this on display when we look at the standard-delivered SAP List Viewer component in Section 9.4.

9.2.5 Defining Cross-Component Navigation Scenarios

Compared to the steps required to access elements of an external component's interface controller, leveraging windows from an external component is a piece of cake. In general, the only hard part is figuring out where we want to embed the content. Here, we have a couple of options to choose from:

▶ We can embed a portion of the external component's user interface into the view layout of the client component, as with subscreens in classic Dynpro. This amounts to embedding an interface view from the external component in the same place(s) where we'd normally embed a locally defined view.

▶ We can open an interface view of the external component as a popup window using the CREATE_WINDOW_FOR_CMP_USAGE() method of the IF_WD_WINDOW_MAN-AGER interface.

In this section, we'll see how both of these usage scenarios are achieved.

Embedding an Interface View in a Window

For the most part, the process of embedding an interface view from an external component in a window is no different than the one used to embed locally defined views. Here, once a component usage is established within the using component, we can embed interface views from the external component by performing the following steps:

1. In the window of the using component we want to embed the external window into, we can right-click at the desired location within the WINDOW STRUCTURE hierarchy and select the EMBED VIEW menu option (see Figure 9.36).

2. Then, in the WEB DYNPRO: EMBED A VIEW dialog box shown in Figure 9.37, we can select the target interface view in the input help for the VIEW TO BE EMBEDDED input field.

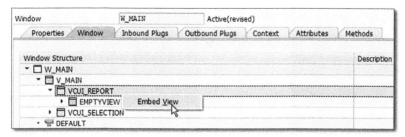

Figure 9.36 Embedding an Interface View into a Window Structure (Part 1)

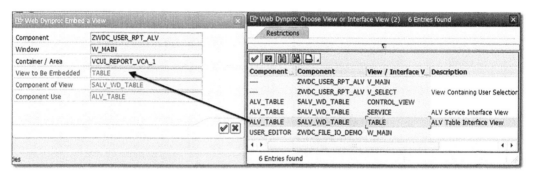

Figure 9.37 Embedding an Interface View into a Window Structure (Part 2)

3. Finally, as necessary, we can define navigation links between local plugs and plugs defined in the target interface view just as we would for local navigation scenarios. Here, as you can see in Figure 9.38, we simply need to select the target inbound plug from the interface view to create the navigation link.

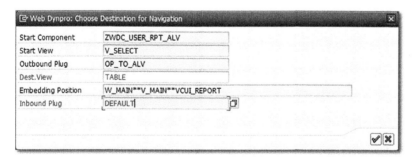

Figure 9.38 Embedding an Interface View into a Window Structure (Part 3)

> **Note**
>
> According to the SAP online help documentation, an interface view can be embedded within a window one time *per component usage*. In other words, if we want to embed the same interface view within a component multiple times, we must declare a separate component usage for each occurrence. Or, if we don't know how many component usages will be needed at design time, we can utilize the dynamic programming capabilities of the Web Dynpro framework to create component usages on the fly. We'll see how dynamic usages are established in Chapter 11.

Opening Interface Views in Popup Windows

To open an interface view in a popup window, we can utilize the CREATE_WINDOW_FOR_CMP_USAGE() method provided via the IF_WD_WINDOW interface. Listing 9.3 demonstrates how this works. As you can see, the call sequence is almost identical to the one used to open regular popup windows (refer back to Section 6.1.4 for more details). However, in this case, the parameters for the CREATE_WINDOW_FOR_CMP_USAGE() method are the component usage name and the interface view name.

```
method DISPLAY_USER_IN_POPUP.
  "Method-Local Data Declarations:
  DATA lo_window_manager TYPE REF TO if_wd_window_manager.
  DATA lo_api_component TYPE REF TO if_wd_component.
  DATA lo_window TYPE REF TO if_wd_window.

  "Use the IF_WD_WINDOW_MANAGER interface to open up the
  "external window in a popup:
  lo_api_component = wd_this->wd_get_api( ).
  lo_window_manager = lo_api_component->get_window_manager( ).
  lo_window =
    lo_window_manager->create_window_for_cmp_usage(
      interface_view_name  = 'W_MAIN'
      component_usage_name = 'USER_EDITOR'
      title                = 'Display User' ).

  lo_window->open( ).
endmethod.
```

Listing 9.3 Opening an Interface View in a Popup Window

Rather than having to code all this from scratch, we can use the Web Dynpro code wizard to generate the code demonstrated in Listing 9.3. As you can see in Figure 9.39, we can do this by selecting the GENERATE POPUP radio button and filling in the component usage and interface view names.

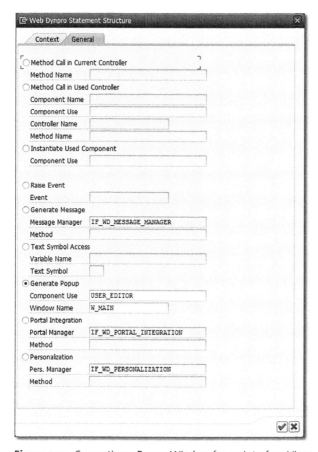

Figure 9.39 Generating a Popup Window for an Interface View

9.3 Case Study: Working with Faceless Components

In the previous sections, we've seen how cross-component integration scenarios are implemented from a nuts-and-bolts perspective. Now, let's switch gears and look at some common use cases for applying componentization techniques. We'll start this analysis by considering the notion of *faceless components*.

As the name suggests, faceless components (or *model components,* as they're sometimes called) are WDA components that don't define any sort of visual interface. Instead, they simply consist of one or more global controllers that encapsulate interactions with complex model objects. Ultimately, this yields a higher level of abstraction for downstream components that need to integrate with the model. Here, rather than having to re-implement these interactions each time, the downstream components can leverage the faceless component to broker communications with the model.

In order to appreciate the value of faceless components, let's look at an example. In this book's source code bundle, we've defined a faceless component called ZWDC_USER_MODEL_FACELESS. This component abstracts the process of performing user lookup queries using the standard BAPI module BAPI_USER_GETLIST. The component interface for the ZWDC_USER_MODEL_FACELESS component consists of two main elements:

▶ Query data is exchanged with client components via a pair of context nodes called SELECTION_CRITERIA and USERLIST (see Figure 9.40).

▶ Queries are initiated via an interface controller method called SEARCH_USERS(). This method assumes the responsibility of converting the selection parameters contained in the SELECTION_CRITERIA node into a format acceptable for the BAPI_USER_GETLIST module.

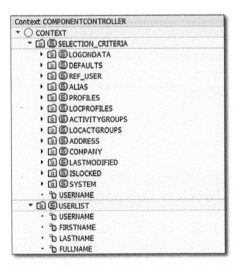

Figure 9.40 Interface Nodes of the Faceless Component

Using the RTTS API, the ZWDC_USER_MODEL_FACELESS component is able to dynamically generate all kinds of user lookup queries. Client components can tap into this functionality to create user queries based on account creation dates, role assignments, or, in the case of the ZWDC_USER_RPT_ALV sample component, address information (see Figure 9.41). Here, all of the heavy lifting is performed by the ZWDC_USER_MODEL_FACELESS component. From a design perspective, all we had to do in the ZWDC_USER_RPT_ALV component was wire up the component usage touch points as follows:

▶ First, we defined a component usage to the ZWDC_USER_MODEL_FACELESS component, as described in Section 9.2.1.

▶ Then, in the WDDOINIT() hook method of the component controller, we instantiated the used component, as described in Section 9.2.2.

▶ Next, we performed simple context mappings to bring over the SELECTION_CRITERIA and USERLIST nodes. Here, we used context attributes from the SELECTION_CRITERIA.ADDRESS node to define the selection screen shown in Figure 9.41. The USERLIST node containing the query results was mapped to an SAP List Viewer control, which displays the found users in a table in the bottom portion of the application screen. We'll see how this works in more detail in the next section.

▶ Finally, in the event handler method for the SEARCH USERS button, we implemented a call to the SEARCH_USERS() method of the faceless component's interface controller.

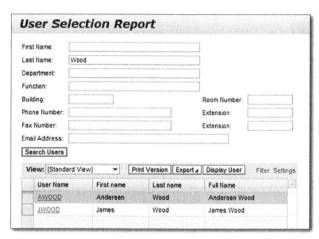

Figure 9.41 A User Query Application Leveraging a Faceless Component

Conceptually speaking, there's nothing special about faceless components; they're just regular WDA components focused on providing application logic. For developers accustomed to working with design patterns, faceless components can be looked at as an extension of the familiar adapter pattern. As such, faceless components should be used in situations when a layer of abstraction is needed to simplify the way controllers interact with the backend data model.

9.4   Case Study: Working with the SAP List Viewer

In Section 9.2.4, we briefly described a scenario in which external context mappings could be used as the basis for building a generic reporting component. As it turns out, SAP provides just such a component with their SAP List Viewer (ALV) component. The ALV component builds upon the Table element introduced in Chapter 8 to render a two-dimensional grid like the one shown at the bottom of the screen in Figure 9.41. In this section, we'll see how the ALV component can be used to implement sophisticated reporting requirements quickly and easily.

Note

The SAP List Viewer component was formerly known as the *ABAP List Viewer* (ALV). It was first introduced as a GUI control for classic Dynpro screens and later adapted for use within WDA applications.

9.4.1   Integrating ALV Content into the View Layout

The ALV component is designed to be both highly flexible and easy to use. In order to achieve this balance, the component comes preconfigured with reasonable default values that make sense for most basic application scenarios. Therefore, in many cases, we can use the component as is out of the box. Or, if nothing else, the defaults get us 75–90% of where we need to go, and then we can tweak the UI from there.

In order to understand how to interface with the ALV component, let's take a look at how the ZWDC_USER_RPT_ALV sample component introduced in the previous section leverages the ALV component to render the user selection report shown in Figure 9.41. Here, we integrated the ALV component by performing the following steps:

1. First, we defined a component usage to the SALV_WD_TABLE component, as shown in Figure 9.42. This WDA component encapsulates the core functionality of the SAP List Viewer.

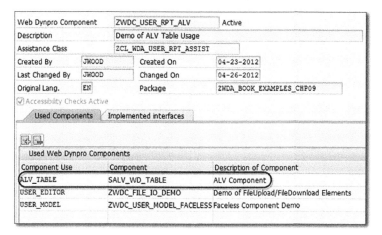

Figure 9.42 Defining a Component Usage for SALV_WD_TABLE

2. Next, we used the Web Dynpro code wizard to generate the component initialization code in the WDDOINIT() method of the ZWDC_USER_RPT_ALV component's component controller as demonstrated in Section 9.2.2.

3. In order to display the report data in the ALV grid, we had to apply an external context mapping to the DATA node of the SALV_WD_TABLE component's interface controller, as shown in Figure 9.43. This process is described at length in Section 9.2.4. As you can see in Figure 9.43, we're mapping the USERLIST node that was mapped from the ZWDC_USER_MODEL_FACELESS component described in the previous section. Here, we see the power of componentization at work as data is generated in one component and displayed in another.

4. Finally, the last step was to embed the ALV table itself into the window structure of the main window of the client ZWDC_USER_RPT_ALV component (which is called W_MAIN). This was achieved by embedding the TABLE interface view of the SALV_WD_TABLE component, as demonstrated in Figure 9.44 and Figure 9.45.

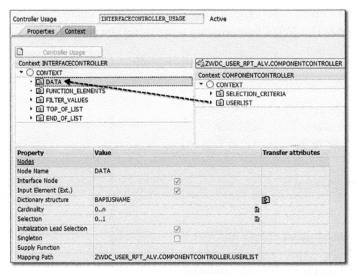

Figure 9.43 Mapping the Report Data to the ALV Component's DATA Node

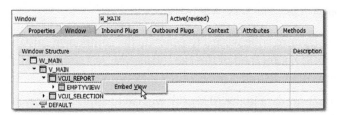

Figure 9.44 Embedding the ALV Table into the Window Structure (Part 1)

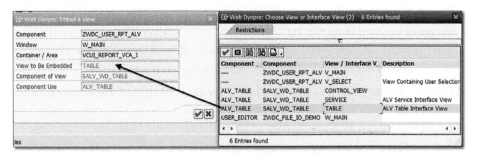

Figure 9.45 Embedding the ALV Table into the Window Structure (Part 2)

Figure 9.41 shows the finished product on the screen. As you can see, we were able to achieve quite a bit in just four easy steps. By default, the ALV component comes equipped with:

► Complex sorting and filtering capabilities

► Export of report data to Microsoft Excel

► Built-in print capabilities

► Personalization controls that allow users to rearrange and hide columns, change sort order, and so on

In the upcoming sections, we'll see how we used other features of the SALV_WD_ TABLE component to expand on this functionality to satisfy custom business requirements.

9.4.2 Accessing the ALV Configuration Model

Once we've integrated the SALV_WD_TABLE component into our custom WDA application, we can tweak its appearance and behavior via an ABAP Objects-based API called the *ALV Configuration Model*. The UML class diagram shown in Figure 9.46 identifies some of the key classes and interfaces that make up the ALV Configuration Model.

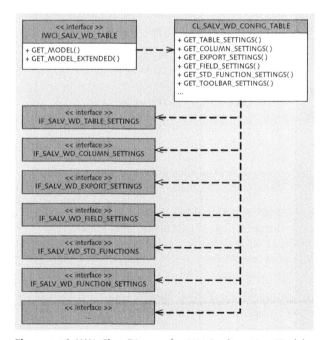

Figure 9.46 UML Class Diagram for ALV Configuration Model

As you can see, we can access this functionality by calling either the `GET_MODEL()` or `GET_MODEL_EXTENDED()` methods of the `IWCI_SALV_WD_TABLE` interface controller.

After we obtain a reference to the ALV Configuration Model, we can use the methods of the `CL_SALV_WD_CONFIG_TABLE` class to access objects that implement the key interfaces depicted in Figure 9.46. Table 9.1 describes these interfaces in further detail.

Interface Name	Usage Description
`IF_SALV_WD_TABLE_SETTINGS`	This interface provides methods that can be used to tweak the ALV output. Here, we can set the visible row count, adjust the `Table` design, and so on.
`IF_SALV_WD_COLUMN_SETTINGS`	This interface can be used to create, adjust, and remove columns from the ALV output. Individual column objects are represented using the `CL_SALV_WD_COLUMN` class.
`IF_SALV_WD_EXPORT_SETTINGS`	This interface provides methods to influence the way the ALV output is exported to external formats such as Microsoft Excel and PDF documents.
`IF_SALV_WD_FIELD_SETTINGS`	This interface provides methods that can be used to maintain fields in the data table used to generate the ALV output. Here, we can add and remove fields, perform aggregations, and so on.
`IF_SALV_WD_STD_FUNCTIONS`	This interface allows us to adjust the settings for the standard ALV functions. Here, for example, we can use the `SET_EXPORT_ALLOWED()` method to determine whether or not the EXPORT button shown in Figure 9.41 is available in the toolbar.
`IF_SALV_WD_FUNCTION_SETTINGS`	This interface provides methods that allow us to add custom functions to the standard toolbar.

Table 9.1 Key Interfaces of the ALV Configuration Model

To demonstrate how the ALV Configuration Model is used, let's look at how we implemented a couple of tweaks to produce the ALV output for our `ZWDC_USER_RPT_ALV` sample component. Here, we had two custom requirements to implement:

- ▶ First, we wanted to adjust the column that contains the user name such that it is rendered using a `LinkToAction` cell editor as opposed to a `TextView`. The goal here is to allow users to display selected user details in a popup window—something we'll see how to accomplish in the next section.

- ▶ Next, we wanted to add a custom DISPLAY USER button to the toolbar as an alternative means for accessing user details.

Listing 9.4 demonstrates how we implemented these features using the ALV Configuration Model. As you can see, the implementation consists of little more than a series of API calls using ABAP Objects classes/interfaces. Thus, we can determine what's going on by simply reading through the code comments.

```
method INIT_ALV_TABLE.
  "Method-Local data Declarations:
  DATA lo_alv_ctrl    TYPE REF TO iwci_salv_wd_table.
  DATA lo_alv_model   TYPE REF TO cl_salv_wd_config_table.
  DATA lo_key_column  TYPE REF TO cl_salv_wd_column.
  DATA lo_cell_editor TYPE REF
    TO cl_salv_wd_uie_link_to_action.
  DATA lo_toolbar_cfg TYPE REF
    TO if_salv_wd_function_settings.
  DATA lo_display_fn  TYPE REF TO cl_salv_wd_function.
  DATA lo_fn_editor   TYPE REF TO cl_salv_wd_fe_button.

  "Obtain a reference to the ALV configuration model:
  lo_alv_ctrl = wd_this->wd_cpifc_alv_table( ).
  lo_alv_model = lo_alv_ctrl->get_model( ).

  "Change the cell editor of the key column to the
  "LinkToAction element:
  lo_key_column =
    lo_alv_model->if_salv_wd_column_settings~get_column(
      id = 'USERNAME' ).

  CREATE OBJECT lo_cell_editor.
  lo_cell_editor->set_text_fieldname( 'USERNAME' ).
  lo_key_column->set_cell_editor( lo_cell_editor ).

  "Also add a new toolbar button to trigger user display:
  CREATE OBJECT lo_fn_editor.
  lo_fn_editor->set_text( 'Display User' ).
```

```
lo_toolbar_cfg =
  lo_alv_model->if_salv_wd_config_table~
    get_toolbar_settings( ).
lo_display_fn =
  lo_toolbar_cfg->create_function( 'DISPLAY_USER' ).
lo_display_fn->set_editor( lo_fn_editor ).
endmethod.
```

Listing 9.4 Using the ALV Configuration Model

As you approach new configuration requirements, we recommend you acquaint yourself with the API by browsing through the class/interface documentation available in the Class Builder tool. You can also find additional information in the online help documentation in the section entitled "SAP List Viewer in Web Dynpro ABAP."

9.4.3 Event Handling Concepts

As we've observed, the SALV_WD_TABLE component is able to operate autonomously, displaying data supplied to it from client components. This is as it should be since the ALV component should be effectively decoupled from its clients. However, that's not to say that client components shouldn't occasionally receive updates from the ALV layer. Here, for example, we might want to be notified whenever the user selects a record, clicks on a cell, or presses a button in the toolbar. In these situations, we can register to listen for events from the interface controller of the SALV_WD_TABLE component as described in Section 9.2.3.

In our ZWDC_USER_RPT_ALV sample component, we're listening for two events:

▶ ON_CLICK
This event will be triggered whenever a user clicks on a cell within the ALV grid. Thus, we'll use it in our sample application to respond to click events triggered against the LinkToAction element that was defined as a cell editor for the USERNAME column in the previous section.

▶ ON_FUNCTION
This event is triggered whenever custom functions are triggered in the toolbar. Thus, we'll use it to respond to the click event of the DISPLAY USER button added in the previous section.

Figure 9.47 shows how we've defined two event methods called ON_USER_ CLICK() and ON_USER_DISPLAY() to handle these two event types.

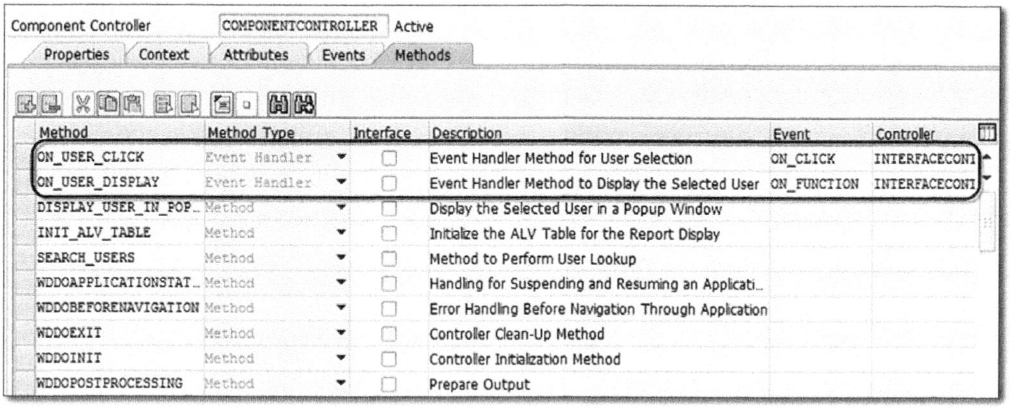

Figure 9.47 Defining Event Handler Methods for the ALV Component

For the most part, there's nothing special about these event handler methods. For instance, as you can see in Listing 9.5, almost all we're doing is using the provided R_PARAM parameter to extract the user name that was clicked on in the USER-NAME column. Once we have this value in hand, we're handing it off to a method called DISPLAY_USER_IN_POPUP() to display the user details.

```
method ON_USER_CLICK.
  "Method-Local Data Declarations:
  DATA lv_username TYPE xubname.
  FIELD-SYMBOLS <lfs_username> TYPE ANY.

  "Grab the selected user name from the event parameters:
  ASSIGN r_param->value->* TO <lfs_username>.
  IF NOT <lfs_username> IS ASSIGNED.
    RETURN.
  ELSE.
    lv_username = <lfs_username>.
  ENDIF.

  "Display the user in a popup window:
  wd_this->display_user_in_popup( lv_username ).
endmethod.
```

Listing 9.5 Responding to the ALV Component's ON_CLICK Event

Listing 9.6 shows how we've implemented the DISPLAY_USER_IN_POPUP() method. Here, we're leveraging the ZWDC_FILE_IO_DEMO component developed in Chapter 8 to display the selected user's information in a popup window. As you can see, we do this by calling the CREATE_WINDOW_FOR_CMP_USAGE() method described in Section 9.2.5.

```
method DISPLAY_USER_IN_POPUP.
  "Method-Local Data Declarations:
  DATA lo_cmp_usage TYPE REF TO if_wd_component_usage.
  DATA lo_user_ctrl TYPE REF TO ziwci_wdc_file_io_demo.
  DATA lo_window_manager TYPE REF TO if_wd_window_manager.
  DATA lo_api_component TYPE REF TO if_wd_component.
  DATA lo_window TYPE REF TO if_wd_window.

  "Display the user in the user display component developed in
  "Chapters 7 and 8.
  "First, we must pre-select the provided user:
  lo_cmp_usage = wd_this->wd_cpuse_user_editor( ).
  IF lo_cmp_usage->has_active_component( ) IS INITIAL.
    lo_cmp_usage->create_component( ).
  ENDIF.

  lo_user_ctrl = wd_this->wd_cpifc_user_editor( ).
  lo_user_ctrl->set_user( iv_username ).

  "Then, we can use the IF_WD_WINDOW_MANAGER interface to open
  "up the window in a popup:
  lo_api_component  = wd_this->wd_get_api( ).
  lo_window_manager = lo_api_component->get_window_manager( ).
  lo_window =
    lo_window_manager->create_window_for_cmp_usage(
      interface_view_name  = 'W_MAIN'
      component_usage_name = 'USER_EDITOR'
      title                = 'Display User' ).

  lo_window->open( ).
endmethod.
```

Listing 9.6 Displaying the Selected User in an External Popup Window

Finally, Listing 9.7 shows how we implemented the `ON_USER_DISPLAY()` method. Here, we're obtaining the selected user via the lead selection of the `USERLIST` node mapped to the ALV component. Then, we once again leverage the `DISPLAY_ USER_IN_POPUP()` method to display the user details.

```
method ON_USER_DISPLAY.
  "Method-Local Data Declarations:
  DATA lo_nd_users TYPE REF TO if_wd_context_node.
  DATA lo_el_users TYPE REF TO if_wd_context_element.
  DATA lv_username TYPE wd_this->Element_userlist-username.

  "Obtain the currently selected user record:
  lo_nd_users =
    wd_context->get_child_node(
      name = wd_this->wdctx_userlist ).
  lo_el_users = lo_nd_users->get_element( ).
  IF lo_el_users IS INITIAL.
    RETURN.
  ENDIF.

  lo_el_users->get_attribute(
    EXPORTING
      name =  `USERNAME`
    IMPORTING
      value = lv_username ).

  "Display the user in a popup window:
  wd_this->display_user_in_popup( lv_username ).
endmethod.
```

Listing 9.7 Responding to the ALV Component's ON_FUNCTION Event

Figure 9.48 shows the finished product, with the user details displayed in a popup window rendered via the `ZWDC_FILE_IO_DEMO` component. This is an excellent demonstration of how components can be stacked on top of one another in layered fashion. As we continue to expand our WDA skills in the upcoming chapters, we'll see this sort of design approach on display again and again.

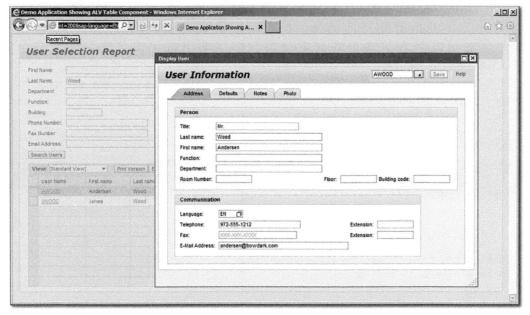

Figure 9.48 Displaying the Selected User in an External Popup Window

9.5 Guidelines for Applying Multi-Component Designs

Now that we've seen how to implement cross-component integration scenarios, you might be wondering how these concepts should be applied toward the creation of new WDA applications. To address any questions you might have, we've put together a Q&A list in Table 9.2 to help guide you through this design process.

Question	Answer
Should every WDA application be based on a multi-component architecture?	No. There are many application scenarios that can be implemented using a single WDA component. Here, there's no point in forcing a multi-component design where it's not needed.

Table 9.2 Guidelines for Applying Multi-Component Designs

Question	Answer
How granular should individual WDA components be defined?	WDA components are intended to be positioned as reusable units of code that correspond with atomic steps of a business process. Recognizing that such criteria can be rather subjective, our recommendation is to use your best judgment to identify where these process boundaries begin and end. Perhaps the best piece of advice we can offer is to periodically evaluate the makeup of a WDA component to make sure all its features are strongly related. If they're not, the component probably needs to be split apart into smaller components that specialize in performing specific tasks.
How do we achieve/maximize reuse with WDA components?	One of the primary challenges of maximizing the reuse of a WDA component is in determining exactly where and how the component may be leveraged by other client components. Short of having this information in hand at design time, the next best thing is to make sure the WDA component is well organized internally. Here, we can offer several basic tips: ▸ Avoid defaulting or hard-coding values that influence the component display or behavior. Instead, provide a parameterization mechanism via inbound plugs of the interface view or methods of the interface controller to define these values. ▸ Build flexible view layouts using small granular views that can be mixed and matched as needed using the `ViewContainerUIElement` element. ▸ If the business process represented by the WDA component consists of multiple substeps, encapsulate each step such that it can be accessed directly (e.g., using parameterization techniques). ▸ If a view is likely to be reused in multiple scenarios, wrap it up in its own window or interface view so we can easily display it using a popup window.

Table 9.2 Guidelines for Applying Multi-Component Designs (Cont.)

Question	Answer
How do we achieve/maximize reuse with WDA components? (Cont.)	▶ If the component maintains an operation mode (e.g., *Create* vs. *Change* vs. *Display*), define the state transition logic centrally within the component controller/context. This makes it easier for external components to tap into this functionality in an ad hoc manner. ▶ Use supply functions and lazy loading techniques to load pertinent data on demand.
Are there any potential performance issues to be aware of when implementing multi-component architectures?	Yes. In general, there is some overhead associated with instantiating WDA components. The amount of overhead introduced varies from component to component. For example, if a component preloads lots of resources using the WDDOINIT() hook method of the component controller, that component will take longer to load than a component that utilizes lazy loading techniques. The amount of overhead introduced with component usages shouldn't be a deterrent for implementing multi-component designs as long as the components are designed properly. The potential performance issues only manifest themselves whenever there are too many components in play as a result of a poor design.

Table 9.2 Guidelines for Applying Multi-Component Designs (Cont.)

As you read through the Q&A list in Table 9.2, keep in mind that the recommendations offered are meant to be guidelines rather than hard and fast rules. Often, there may be extenuating circumstances that may influence your design approach one way or another. You will also no doubt come up with your own design preferences as you gain additional experience working with multi-component architectures. We'll have plenty of opportunities to do just that as we progress through the remainder of this book. In particular, we'll see these concepts come into play when we look at input help in Chapter 10 and the Floorplan Manager for WDA (FPM) in Chapter 14.

9.6   Summary

In this chapter, we learned how to implement multi-component designs using WDA. We began this journey by reviewing the definition of component interfaces and their relationships with internal component elements. From there, we explored the notion of component usages by looking at particular ways of tapping into the various resources of external components. Finally, we concluded our analysis by reviewing a couple of case studies that highlighted scenarios when componentization makes sense.

Ultimately, one of the primary goals of component-based development is *reuse*. With just a little bit of careful consideration up front, we can design autonomous components that can be utilized in many different application scenarios. In the next chapter, we'll see some of these concepts on display as we investigate various options for providing input help for users.

As the saying goes, "The customer is king." Therefore, as we design new WDA applications, we should take care to make sure users are provided with the appropriate input helps, feedback, and so on to ensure a worthwhile experience. In this chapter, we'll look at ways of achieving these qualities in our applications.

10 User Interaction

Despite our best efforts to design WDA applications that are intuitive and easy to use, some users may need some additional guidance to determine how to proceed when entering data, making selection choices, and so on. This is particularly the case for casual users who rarely access the system. However, that's not to say that even the most advanced users won't need some direction from time to time.

We can avoid a lot of user frustration (not to mention angry help desk calls) by developing WDA applications that are more interactive. Here, we're talking about adding those little bells and whistles that provide feedback to users and make it easier to enter data, locate help documentation, and so on. In this section, we'll survey some of the built-in tools you have at your disposal to implement these kinds of requirements. These tools supplement and round out the UI elements described in Chapters 7 and 8 to improve the overall user experience.

10.1 Defining Input Helps

In Chapters 7 and 8, we looked at a number of UI element types that could be used to build input forms. However, by and large, most input forms tend to be built primarily around the `InputField` element. As we learned in Chapter 7, this element can be used to input strings, numbers, dates, and so on. Here, the built-in capabilities of the backend runtime class (`CL_WD_INPUT_FIELD`) automatically take care of:

- Converting user input into the internal data type (as defined by the context attribute bound against the `InputField.value` property) and vice versa.
- Validating user input to make sure users enter data that fits within the parameters of the field's data type. For example, such checks ensure that users can't enter invalid date values such as 2/31/2013.

Collectively, these features make it possible to define an input field that ensures that user input fits within the confines of a particular data type (or *lexical space*). However, as useful as these features are, what users really need help with is figuring out the semantic meaning of a particular field (i.e., what's the field's *value space*?). For example, if we have an `InputField` element being used to enter a plant code in an SAP ERP system, how does the user know which plant codes are valid?

Sometimes we can address these kinds of problems by using a dropdown list, radio button group, or checkbox group element instead. However, if the list of possible values continues to grow, these options become less and less viable for performance/usability reasons. In these situations, a better alternative is to provide users with *input helps* that can be used to lookup the proper set of input values. In this section, we'll consider the various options available for defining input helps in WDA.

10.1.1 ABAP Dictionary Search Helps

WDA was built from the ground up to tightly integrate with the ABAP Dictionary. As we've seen at several points throughout this book, ABAP Dictionary objects are used extensively in the definition of context node hierarchies, UI element definitions, and so on. Another area where this integration comes into play is in the definition of input helps. Here, we can leverage existing search helps from the ABAP Dictionary to provide input helps that have a similar look and feel to the ones users are accustomed to working with in the SAP GUI. In this section, we'll see how this is achieved.

Introduction to Search Helps

Even if you've never had the opportunity to work with search helps in the ABAP Dictionary, you've probably come into contact with them at one point or another while working in the SAP GUI. Here, you may have heard several different terms used to describe search helps: input helps, F4 helps, and so on. In any case, regardless of what we call them, search helps provide a mechanism for displaying the set of all possible input values for a screen field.

In order to understand how search helps work, let's consider an example. Figure 10.1 demonstrates how a search help called DD_TYPES is used to look up data types within the ABAP Dictionary (Transaction SE11). As you can see in the figure, we can utilize this search help to locate data elements that match a particular criterion by performing the following steps:

1. To access the search help, we can click on the highlighted search help symbol displayed adjacent to the DATA TYPE input field (❶), as shown in Figure 10.1.

2. Though not shown in the figure, this opens a dialog box in which we can select the type of search we want to conduct. For the purposes of this example, we chose the SEARCH FOR DATA ELEMENTS option.

3. In the REPOSITORY INFO. SYSTEM: FIND DATA ELEMENTS dialog box, we can key in search criteria to help direct the search (❷). For instance, in the example shown in Figure 10.1, we're looking for character-type data elements with a length of 241. We also have the option of using the other functions in the toolbar to expand the search as needed. In any case, once we confirm our selection criteria, we can initiate the search by clicking on the button with the green checkmark on it.

4. Finally, the matching search results will be presented to us in a list. Once we find the data element we want, we can double-click on it to copy the value directly into the input field (❸).

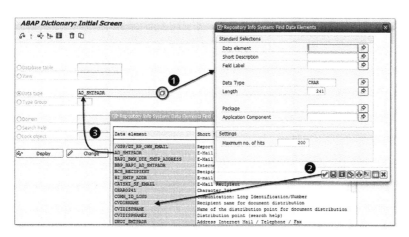

Figure 10.1 Interacting with Search Helps in the SAP GUI

Depending on the way a particular search help is defined, you may find that the search experience varies somewhat. For instance, if there is only one search path, the value restriction dialog box from step 2 will be omitted. Conversely, if there are many possible search paths, the dialog box will present an initial dialog box in which you can choose among several alternative paths. At the end of the day, though, all search helps essentially perform the same function: provide users with a convenient way of locating the proper input value for a given field.

Defining Search Helps in the ABAP Dictionary

Having looked at how search helps function in the previous section, let's now turn our attention to how search helps are defined. Here, we must differentiate between the following types of search helps:

▶ **Elementary search helps**
Elementary search helps describe a single search path. The data element search path that was selected in Figure 10.1 is an example of an elementary search help (DD_DTEL).

▶ **Collective search helps**
Collective search helps combine several elementary search helps in order to offer users several alternative search paths. We encountered this in the previous section when we observed the behavior of the search help tied to the DATA TYPE field on the initial screen of the ABAP Dictionary transaction. This field is linked with a collective search help called DD_TYPES, which includes elementary search helps that can be used to search for data elements, structures, table types, and so on (see Figure 10.2).

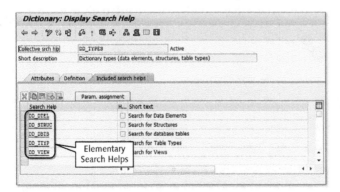

Figure 10.2 Definition of a Collective Search Help

As ABAP Dictionary objects, search helps are maintained within the ABAP Dictionary (Transaction SE11) or in the ABAP Workbench (Transaction SE80). Figure 10.2 provides an example of what a collective search help looks like within this editor. Of course, since collective search helps simply aggregate one or more elementary search helps, their definition is rather straightforward. The core search logic is encoded within the individual elementary search helps

To see what all goes into an elementary search help definition, let's take a look at the H_SPFLI search help example included as part of the class ABAP flight training model shipped with every SAP NetWeaver system. Figure 10.3 shows how this search help is being used to look up flight connection numbers within the SPFLI table in the ABAP Dictionary.

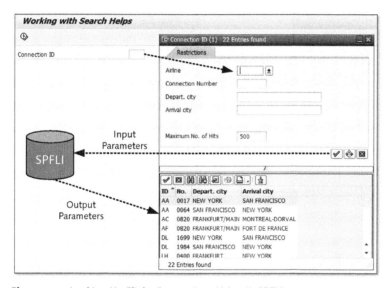

Figure 10.3 Looking Up Flight Connections Using H_SPFLI

In order to implement the selection path illustrated in Figure 10.3, there are several selection attributes we need to configure. In particular, as you can see in Figure 10.4, there are essentially three key attributes that influence a search help's behavior:

- **Selection method**

  In this field, we can select the source table or view from the ABAP Dictionary that the data will be extracted from. For example, with the H_SPFLI search help, the selection method points to the SPFLI table.

▶ **Search help parameters**

Search help parameters make up the search help's interface. In other words, they define the fields from the table or view selected in the SELECTION METHOD field that are used within the input help. There are two different types of search help parameters: *input parameters* and *output parameters*. Input parameters are used as inputs to the selection process, while output parameters make up the result set displayed within the hit list. Note that it's possible to make a given parameter both an importing and exporting parameter by simply selecting the corresponding checkboxes in the IMP and EXP columns shown in Figure 10.4.

▶ **Search help exits**

Search help exits are function modules that make it possible to override the standard behavior of the search help. Here, we simply plug in a function module whose interface matches that of the SAP standard function F4IF_SHLP_EXIT_EXAMPLE. Within this function, we can define custom logic to enhance the selection process as needed.

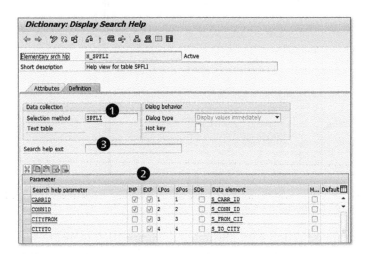

Figure 10.4 Defining a Search Help

Since this is a book on WDA programming, we'll limit our description of search help definitions here to the basics. You can find detailed information about search helps in the SAP online help documentation, in the section entitled "Search Helps." Alternatively, if you're looking for something with a more hands-on approach, you can check out *ABAP Data Dictionary* (Gupta, SAP PRESS, 2011).

Integrating Search Helps with Web Dynpro

From a design perspective, the process of integrating search helps into `Input-Field` elements requires little effort on the part of developers. Basically, all we have to do is make sure the INPUT HELP MODE property for the context attribute bound against the `InputField.value` property is properly maintained; the Web Dynpro framework assumes the responsibility of generating and rendering the search help at runtime. Figure 10.5 illustrates the relationship between an `Input-Field` and the context attribute bound against its `value` property.

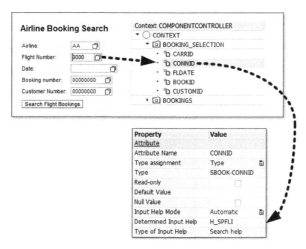

Figure 10.5 Integrating Search Helps via Context Attributes

As you can see in Figure 10.5, the INPUT HELP MODE for the `BOOKING_SELECTION` `.CONNID` attribute was derived automatically in reference to the attribute's data type (`SBOOK-CONNID`). Here, the system was able to resolve the `H_SPFLI` search help from the search help assigned to the `CONNID` field in table `SBOOK` (see Figure 10.6). You can find more information about how the system performs this search help resolution process in the online help documentation, in the section entitled "Assignment of Search Helps to Screen Fields."

In some cases, the system may not be able to locate a search help for the data type specified. Or, we may wish to override the default search help selection with another search help of our own choosing. In either case, we can manually assign a search help to a context attribute by selecting the `Dictionary Search Help` value in the INPUT HELP MODE property and plugging in a search help in the DICTIONARY SEARCH HELP property (see Figure 10.7).

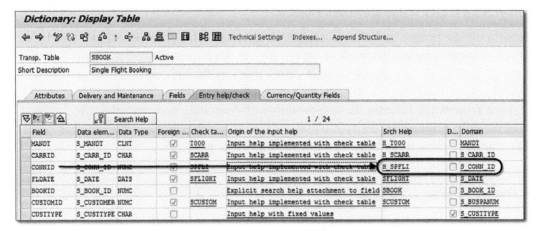

Figure 10.6 Deriving the Search Help for an ABAP Dictionary Type

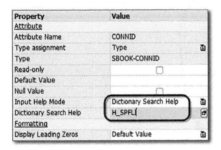

Figure 10.7 Manually Assigning a Search Help to a Context Attribute

Features of Search Helps in WDA Applications

For the most part, users will find that search helps in WDA applications operate pretty much like the ones they're accustomed to working with in classic Dynpro transactions. Figure 10.8 demonstrates this by showing what the H_SPFLI search help looks like in a custom WDA application. As you can see, the popup dialog box for the search help has a similar look and feel to the one we observed in the SAP GUI in Figure 10.3. Some features to note here:

▶ InputField elements with search help assignments are automatically rendered with the familiar search help symbol adjacent to the input field.

▶ The Web Dynpro framework automatically renders the search help dialog box based on the underlying search help definition. Here, the system takes the liberty of generating filter criteria fields using select options and so on.

▶ If the linked search help is a collective search help, the dialog box will include a dropdown list that allows users to toggle between different search paths.

▶ Input and output parameters for the search help are automatically mapped for context attributes within the same context node. For example, in Figure 10.8, the fields in the AIRLINE BOOKING SEARCH selection screen are all defined in terms of a context node assigned to the dictionary structure SBOOK. This makes it possible for the framework to automatically map the value in the AIRLINE field (AA) to the corresponding input parameter of the H_SPFLI search help. Similarly, if the search help defines multiple output parameters, those values will be automatically copied as well.

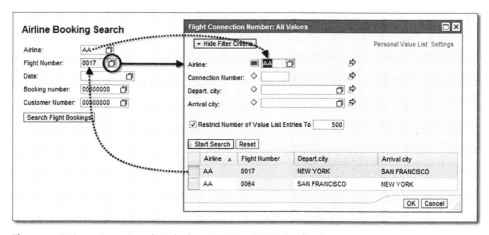

Figure 10.8 Accessing a Search Help from Within a WDA Application

Another useful feature of search helps in WDA applications is the *personal value list*. As the name suggests, this feature allows users to store particular hit list entries in a personalized cache that can be used to bypass the data lookup process in the future. You can maintain personal value lists by performing the following steps:

1. First, in the search help dialog box, click on the PERSONAL VALUE LIST link (see Figure 10.9).

2. Then, in the MAINTENANCE OF PERSONAL VALUE LIST dialog box shown in Figure 10.10, you can copy relevant hit list values over to the personal value list by selecting the entries and clicking on the ADD ITEM button.

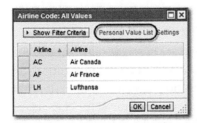

Figure 10.9 Maintaining a Personal Value List (Part 1)

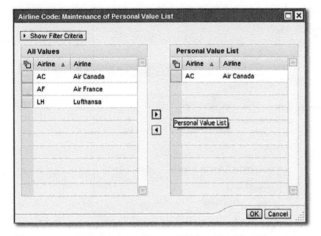

Figure 10.10 Maintaining a Personal Value List (Part 2)

3. Finally, once the personal value list is maintained, the pertinent values will show up automatically in a dropdown list when the search help is accessed at runtime (see Figure 10.11). As necessary, users can maintain this list of values further by clicking on the MAINTAIN PERSONAL VALUE LIST link that shows up in the dropdown list. Or, they can bypass this list altogether by clicking on the ALL VALUES link.

Figure 10.11 Utilizing the Personal Value List at Runtime

10.1.2 OVS Value Helps

Occasionally, we may run into complex input help scenarios in which ABAP Dictionary search helps cannot meet the business requirements. For example, imagine a case for which the set of possible input values must be obtained via an external lookup (e.g., a web service call) rather than an ABAP Dictionary table. In these situations, we can utilize the *OVS value help* component (where OVS stands for *Object Value Selection*).

OVS Value Help Overview

OVS value helps are implemented via a standard WDA component called WDR_OVS. This generic component works in conjunction with components to define input help solutions. In and of itself, the WDR_OVS component doesn't know what you want to search for or how you want to search for it. Therefore, it's up to using components to supply this information on demand by registering an event handler method to listen for the OVS event (which is defined in the interface controller of the WDR_OVS component). Then, at specific points within the search lifecycle, the WDR_OVS component will raise the OVS event, allowing registered event handler methods to respond accordingly. This can be achieved by calling methods on the provided OVS_CALLBACK_OBJECT object parameter, which is of type IF_WD_OVS. Figure 10.12 illustrates how this event lifecycle plays out at runtime.

As you can see in Figure 10.12, the OVS event is raised at four different phases within the search lifecycle:

▶ **Phase ❶**
This phase is initiated before the search dialog is displayed whenever the user clicks on the input help symbol. At this stage, we can preconfigure the OVS behavior by calling the SET_CONFIGURATION() method on the OVS_CALLBACK_OBJECT object parameter. Here, we can define the title of the dialog window, column headings, and so on. We can also specify whether or not one or several rows from the hit list can be selected by the user.

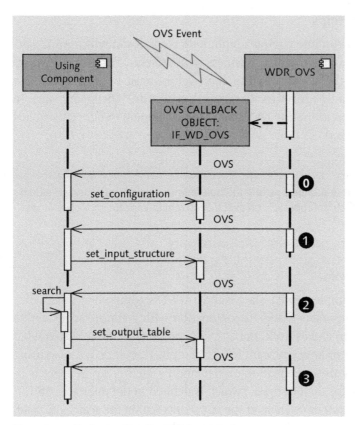

Figure 10.12 Understanding the OVS Event Cycle

▶ **Phase ❶**

If we want the OVS to display the optional selection view, this phase can be used to specify the selection fields that are to be provided on the screen. We can do this using the SET_INPUT_STRUCTURE() method of the OVS_CALLBACK_ OBJECT object parameter.

▶ **Phase ❷**

In this phase, we perform the actual lookup using whichever model object we deem appropriate. Here, we can use the selection parameters defined in Phase 1 to guide the search as needed. Once the search is complete, the result list can be sent back to the OVS component using the SET_OUTPUT_TABLE() method of the OVS_CALLBACK_OBJECT object parameter.

► **Phase ❸**

In this phase, we can access the selected search results and process them accordingly (e.g., using the context API and so on). The search results can be accessed via the SELECTION attribute of the OVS_CALLBACK_OBJECT object parameter.

The code excerpt in Listing 10.1 illustrates how these events are processed programmatically within an event handler method.

```
method on_ovs.
  CASE ovs_callback_object->phase_indicator.
    WHEN if_wd_ovs=>co_phase_0.
      "Configure the Object Value Selector:
      ovs_callback_object->set_configuration( ... ).
    WHEN if_wd_ovs=>co_phase_1.
      "Define the selection screen parameters - as necessary:
      ovs_callback_object->set_input_structure( input = ... ).
    WHEN if_wd_ovs=>co_phase_2.
      "Use the ovs_callback_object->query_parameters
      "instance attribute to obtain user selection criteria...
      ASSIGN ovs_callback_object->query_parameters->* TO ...

      "Perform the lookup using some kind of model object:
      CALL METHOD wd_comp_controller->...

      "Pass the results table on to the WDR_OVS component:
      ovs_callback_object->set_output_table( output = ... ).
    WHEN if_wd_ovs=>co_phase_3.
      "Process the selection results as needed:
      ASSIGN ovs_callback_object->selection->* TO ...
  ENDCASE.
endmethod.
```

Listing 10.1 Defining an Event Handler for the OVS Event

Defining OVS Value Helps: Step-by-Step

Now that we have a basic feel for how OVS value helps work, let's take a look at how they're integrated into WDA components. To guide us through this discussion, we'll consider how the OVS component is integrated into the DEMO_VALUE_HELP sample component provided by SAP (see Figure 10.13).

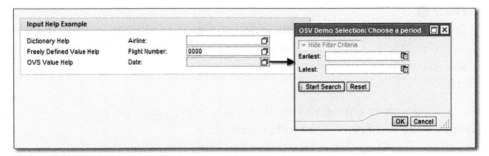

Figure 10.13 Working with OVS Value Helps

In general, the steps required to define an OVS value help within a WDA component are as follows:

1. First of all, as you would expect, we must define a component usage to the WDR_OVS component within our using component. Figure 10.14 shows how SAP has defined a component usage called OVS_USAGE in the DEMO_VALUE_HELP component.

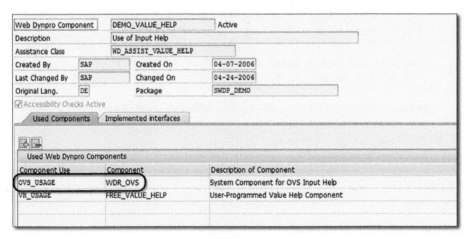

Figure 10.14 Defining OVS Value Helps in a WDA Component (Part 1)

2. Next, we must define a component/controller usage within the view that will be integrating the OVS value help. Figure 10.15 shows how this usage was established for the V1 main view of the DEMO_VALUE_HELP component.

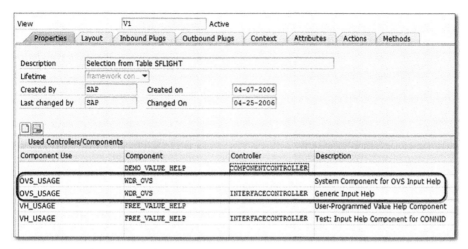

Figure 10.15 Defining OVS Value Helps in a WDA Component (Part 2)

3. Once the component usage(s) are in place, the next step is to define an event handler method to respond to the OVS event raised at specific milestones within the search lifecycle. As you can see in Figure 10.16, the V1 view defines a method called ON_OVS() for this purpose. This basic outline for this method mirrors that of the code excerpt in Listing 10.1.

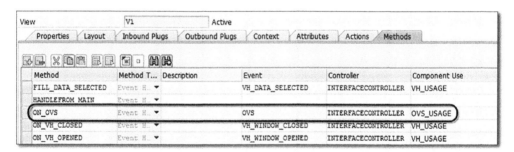

Figure 10.16 Defining OVS Value Helps in a WDA Component (Part 3)

4. Finally, in order to integrate the OVS value help into the view layout, we must assign it to a context attribute, as demonstrated in Figure 10.17. Here, we simply assign the value Object Value Selector to the INPUT HELP MODE property and plug in the component usage in the OVS COMPONENT USAGE property.

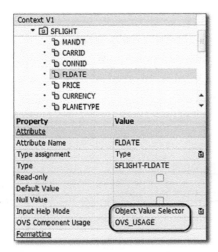

Figure 10.17 Defining OVS Value Helps in a WDA Component (Part 4)

Once these configuration items are in place, the Web Dynpro framework will take care of launching the OVS value help whenever users trigger the input help. Here, the framework will assume the responsibility of instantiating the WDR_OVS component, opening the search help dialog box, and so on. As developers, our only role in this process is to make sure we supply the proper information to the OVS_CALLBACK_OBJECT object parameter when the OVS event is triggered at run-time.

10.1.3 Freely Programmed Input Helps

As we observed in the previous section, OVS value helps provide us with quite a bit of flexibility when it comes to defining custom input helps. However, one thing we don't have a lot of control over is the layout of the various input help screens. Here, we're forced to work within the confines of the framework laid out by the WDR_OVS component.

Most of the time, this is a good thing because OVS value helps present a uniform interface that mirrors that of input helps developed using search helps from the ABAP Dictionary. However, there are those select occasions when we may want to come up with our own design for one reason or another. In these situations, we have the option of creating our own input help components. In this section, we'll see how this is accomplished.

Defining a Custom Input Help Component

Custom input help components must implement the IWD_VALUE_HELP component interface. This interface is minimalistic, providing us with the freedom to develop input help screens in whatever way we deem appropriate. However, before we head down that path, there are several configuration items we must take care of:

1. First of all, as you can see in Figure 10.18, custom input help components must implement the aforementioned IWD_VALUE_HELP component interface.

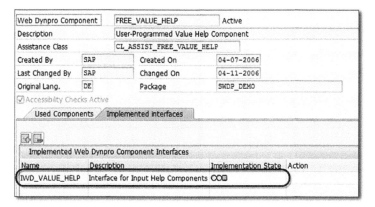

Figure 10.18 Implementing the IWD_VALUE_HELP Component Interface

2. Secondly, as a result of implementing the IWD_VALUE_HELP interface, custom input help components inherit a window called WD_VALUE_HELP (see Figure 10.19). The view layout for the input help must be contained within this window.

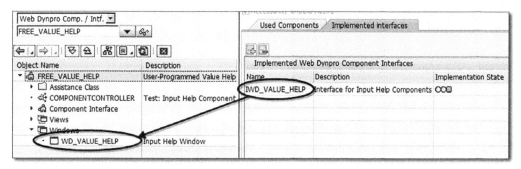

Figure 10.19 Inheritance of the WD_VALUE_HELP Window

3. Finally, custom input help components must implement the SET_VALUE_HELP_ LISTENER() method inherited from the IWD_VALUE_HELP component interface (see Figure 10.20). This callback method is automatically called by the Web Dynpro framework early in the initialization process, providing a reference to an object of type IF_WD_VALUE_HELP_LISTENER. As you can see in Figure 10.20, this object reference is cached in a controller attribute so it can be accessed later on—more on this in a moment.

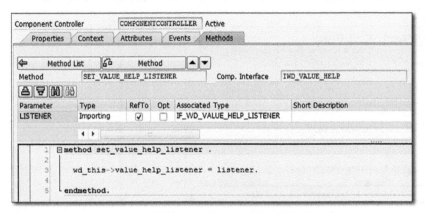

Figure 10.20 Implementing the SET_VALUE_HELP_LISTENER() Method

Aside from these basic settings, the Web Dynpro framework places no restrictions on how the input help screens should be laid out, how the input data should be obtained, etc. Perhaps more importantly, it also doesn't specify how the selected hit list values should be returned to using components. Therefore, we're free to utilize all the cross-component design techniques detailed in Chapter 9 to exchange the data back and forth (e.g., cross-component context mappings, events, and so on). This data exchange can be synchronized with using components via the VH_WINDOW_CLOSED and VH_WINDOW_OPENED events inherited from the IWD_VALUE_HELP component.

Once the selected hit list items are copied into the using component, we must notify the Web Dynpro framework that the input help dialog box is ready to be closed. We can do this by invoking the CLOSE_WINDOW() method of the IF_WD_ VALUE_HELP_LISTENER object reference passed to the component via the afore-mentioned SET_VALUE_HELP_LISTENER() method. This method should also be called if the user cancels the selection process or an error occurs.

Integrating Custom Input Help Components as Input Helps

Once a custom input help component is defined, we can integrate it into other WDA components in much the same way that the standard WDR_OVS component is integrated for OVS value helps:

1. First, we must define a component usage for the custom component, as demonstrated in Figure 10.21.

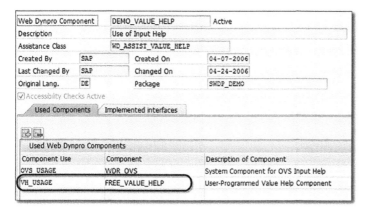

Figure 10.21 Defining Custom Input Helps in a WDA Component (Part 1)

2. Next, we need to define a component/controller usage for the custom input help component on the target view, as demonstrated in Figure 10.22.

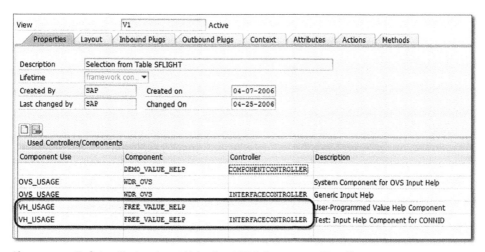

Figure 10.22 Defining Custom Input Helps in a WDA Component (Part 2)

3. Finally, in order to attach the input help to an `InputField` element, we must assign the custom input help component to a context attribute, as demonstrated in Figure 10.23. Here, we set the INPUT HELP MODE property to `Freely Programmed` and plug in the component usage in the INPUT HELP COMPONENT USAGE property.

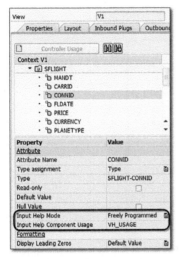

Figure 10.23 Defining Custom Input Helps in a WDA Component (Part 3)

Figure 10.24 demonstrates the integration of a custom input help component called `FREE_VALUE_HELP` with the `DEMO_VALUE_HELP` sample component introduced in Section 10.1.2. Here, notice how the hit list is being rendered using a `Table` element. Of course, SAP could have just as easily rendered the hit list using an ALV component, `CTable`, `RowRepeater`, etc.

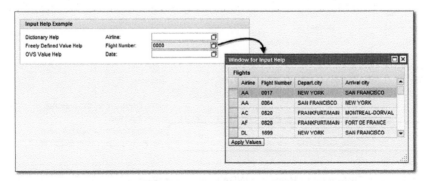

Figure 10.24 Working with Freely Programmed Input Helps

> **Note**
>
> Despite all the power afforded by freely programmed input helps, we recommend you use this input help option as a last resort in situations when ABAP Dictionary search helps and OVS value helps can't fulfill the business requirements at hand. There are several reasons for this:
>
> ▶ First of all, quite a bit more development effort is required to design and maintain freely programmed input helps.
>
> ▶ Secondly, the other two standard options present a uniform interface that users are accustomed to working with.
>
> ▶ Finally, as we learned in Section 10.1.1, ABAP Dictionary Search Helps search helps allow users to maintain personal value lists, which speed up the data entry process quite a bit.
>
> The bottom line is that there's no point in reinventing the wheel if we don't have to.

10.1.4   Select Options

Each of the input help options we've considered so far have been geared toward the selection of a single input value. However, if we're building selection screens and the like, users may need additional help in specifying complex selection criteria. Recognizing this, SAP decided to bring over a tried and true input help concept from the classic Dynpro environment: *select options*. In this section, we'll see how to integrate select options into WDA applications.

Select Options Introduction

As we mentioned previously, the notion of select options is a carryover from classic Dynpro screen programming. In this environment, select options are added to the selection screen of ABAP report programs using the SELECT-OPTIONS statement, which is demonstrated in Listing 10.2. Here, we've defined two select options, called S_CARRID and S_CONNID, to allow users to specify selection criteria for looking up flight connections.

```
REPORT zselopt_test.
TABLES: spfli.
DATA: gt_spfli TYPE STANDARD TABLE OF spfli.

SELECT-OPTIONS:
```

```
  s_carrid FOR spfli-carrid,
  s_connid FOR spfli-connid.

START-OF-SELECTION.
  "Use select options to drive a query against SPFLI:
  SELECT *
    INTO TABLE gt_spfli
    FROM spfli
   WHERE carrid IN s_carrid
     AND connid IN s_connid.
  ...
```

Listing 10.2 Using Select Options in a Database Query

Figure 10.25 shows what the two select options from Listing 10.2 look like on screen. As you can see, the provided input mask allows users to enter a range of values using the various tab pages:

▶ **Select single values**
On this tab, users can enter single values they want to include in the search criteria. Here, they can use the provided operators to define conditional expressions, such as *equal to*, *less than*, and so on.

▶ **Select ranges**
On this tab, users can enter ranges of values they want to search within. An example of a search range might be all documents with a number between 6000000100 and 6000000200.

▶ **Exclude single values**
This tab is the analog of the SELECT SINGLE VALUES tab in that value expressions specified here are used to filter out records from the selection.

▶ **Exclude ranges**
This tab is the analog of the SELECT RANGES tab, allowing users to exclude various ranges of values from the selection.

Behind the scenes, the selection criterion specified within select options is captured in a special kind of internal table called a *range table*. These range tables make it easy to encode complex selection criteria within the WHERE clause of an Open SQL SELECT statement, as demonstrated in Listing 10.2. Here, the Open SQL interpreter assumes the responsibility of unpacking the range table selection criteria and processing the query accordingly.

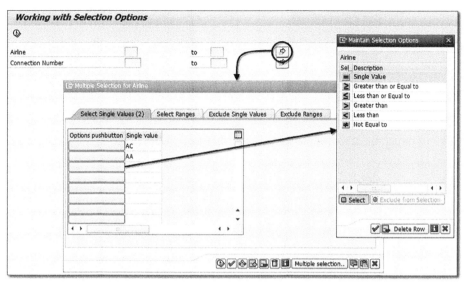

Figure 10.25 Working with Select Options in the SAP GUI

Table 10.1 describes the fields that make up the rows within a range table in detail. Though it's useful to understand how these fields work, keep in mind that the population of these fields will be taken care of by users working within the select option dialog window (see Figure 10.25).

Field Name	Description
SIGN	This field determines whether or not the records matching the selection criteria encoded in the current row should be included or excluded from the selection. Valid values for the SIGN field include: ▶ I (Include) ▶ E (Exclude) See the BAPISIGN data element for more information about this field.
OPTION	This field allows users to choose different selection operators to specify selection criteria. The list of possible values is included below. ▶ EQ (Equal) ▶ NE (Not Equal) ▶ BT (Between)

Table 10.1 Fields within a Range Table

Field Name	Description
OPTION (Cont.)	▶ NB (Not Between)
	▶ LT (Less Than)
	▶ LE (Less Than or Equal To)
	▶ GT (Greater Than)
	▶ GE (Greater Than or Equal To)
	▶ CP (Contains Pattern)
	▶ NP (Does Not Contain Pattern)
	The operator specified in the OPTION field works in conjunction with the other three fields to build complex selection expressions. For example, if a user chooses to search for objects in a given date range, a selection row is created within the range table like this:
	▶ SIGN = I
	▶ OPTION = BT
	▶ LOW = (From Date)
	▶ HIGH = (To Date)
	Such criteria is maintained using the various toolbar buttons and input fields provided in the select option dialog box shown in Figure 10.25.
LOW	This field contains the *low* operand for the selection expression. Or, in the case of unary operators such as EQ, the LOW field contains the lone operand used in the evaluation process.
HIGH	If the BT or NB operators are selected in the OPTION field, then the HIGH field can be used to specify the high end of the range expression.

Table 10.1 Fields within a Range Table (Cont.)

Since this is a book about WDA programming, we'll limit our introduction to select options to the concepts considered in this section. You can find more information about select options in the online help documentation and in the ABAP keyword documentation for the SELECT-OPTIONS statement. For now, we'll turn our attention to how select options are integrated into WDA applications.

Integrating Select Options with Web Dynpro

Much like OVS value helps and freely programmed input helps, select options in WDA are realized via a standalone WDA component called WDR_SELECT_OPTIONS. This component takes care of rendering select options, presenting users with an experience roughly equivalent to that of select options created via the SELECT-OPTIONS statement in classic Dynpro report programming.

> **Note**
>
> In the SAP NetWeaver 7.31 release, the WDR_SELECT_OPTIONS component will be deprecated in favor of a new component called WD_SELECT_OPTIONS_20. This component will provide even more options for adjusting the look, feel, and behavior of the select options on screen.

Unlike the other input help–based components we've looked at so far, the process of integrating select options based on the WDR_SELECT_OPTIONS component into WDA applications is more involved. Therefore, to demonstrate this process, let's look at an example component from this book's code bundle: ZWDC_SELOPT_DEMO. This component uses select options to allow users to search for flight connections from the default flight data model used in many SAP demonstrations. The steps required to set this up were as follows:

1. As you might expect, the first step for integration was to define a component usage to the WDR_SELECT_OPTIONS component, as demonstrated in Figure 10.26.

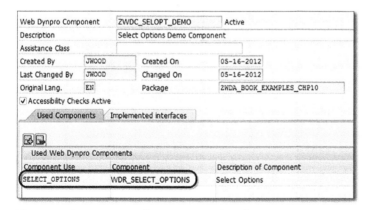

Figure 10.26 Integrating Select Options with Web Dynpro (Part 1)

2. Next, we needed to define a context node to store the selection criteria specified within the select option. Figure 10.27 shows how we created a node called CONNID_SELECTION for this purpose. This multi-element node contains four context attributes matching the range table row type, as described in Table 10.1. Here, the context attributes are typed as follows:

- ▶ SIGN: BAPISIGN

- ▶ OPTION: BAPIOPTION

- ▶ LOW: S_CONN_ID

- ▶ HIGH: S_CONN_ID

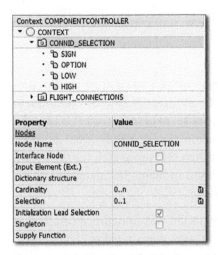

Figure 10.27 Integrating Select Options with Web Dynpro (Part 2)

3. On the presentation side of things, we had to define a usage to the component/controller in the view where the select options is displayed: V_MAIN (see Figure 10.28).

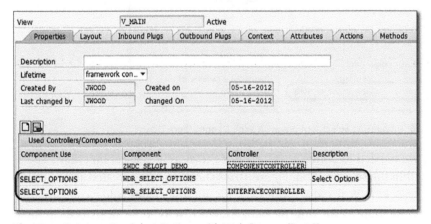

Figure 10.28 Integrating Select Options with Web Dynpro (Part 3)

4. Within the layout for V_MAIN, several configuration steps were required. First, we had to embed a ViewContainerUIElement into the view layout as a placeholder for the embedded select options interface view (see Figure 10.29).

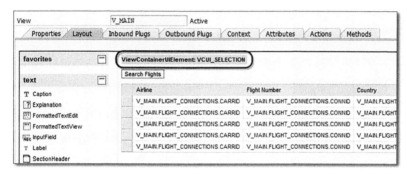

Figure 10.29 Integrating Select Options with Web Dynpro (Part 4)

5. Then, we had to embed the WND_SELECTION_SCREEN interface view from the WDR_SELECT_OPTIONS component into the window layout, as demonstrated in Figure 10.30.

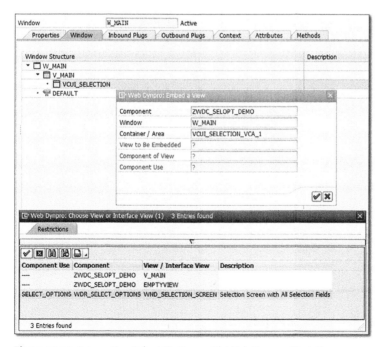

Figure 10.30 Integrating Select Options with Web Dynpro (Part 5)

6. Finally, once those integration steps were complete, the only remaining steps were to plug in the source code necessary to initialize and interact with the select option component at runtime. We'll see how this code was implemented in just a moment.

As a generic component, the WDR_SELECT_OPTIONS component must be initialized for display based on the selection criteria you want to provide on screen. Therefore, in order to allow users to search for flight connections in our flight example, we had to initialize the WDR_SELECT_OPTIONS component to produce a range table based on the S_CONN_ID (*Flight Connection Number*) data type. This initialization logic was performed within the WDDOINIT() method of the V_MAIN view controller, as demonstrated in Listing 10.3.

```
method WDDOINIT.
  "Method-Local Data Declarations:
  DATA lo_cmp_usage    TYPE REF TO if_wd_component_usage.
  DATA lo_selopt_ctrl  TYPE REF TO iwci_wdr_select_options.
  DATA lr_connid_range TYPE REF TO data.

  "Instantiate the WDR_SELECT_OPTIONS component:
  lo_cmp_usage = wd_this->wd_cpuse_select_options( ).
  IF lo_cmp_usage->has_active_component( ) IS INITIAL.
    lo_cmp_usage->create_component( ).
  ENDIF.

  "Call the INIT_SELECTION_SCREEN method in the component
  "interface controller to initialize the select option:
  lo_selopt_ctrl = wd_this->wd_cpifc_select_options( ).
  wd_comp_controller->mo_selopt_helper =
    lo_selopt_ctrl->init_selection_screen( ).

  lr_connid_range =
    wd_comp_controller->mo_selopt_helper->create_range_table(
      i_typename = 'S_CONN_ID' ).

  wd_comp_controller->mo_selopt_helper->add_selection_field(
    i_id = 'S_CONN_ID'
    it_result = lr_connid_range ).
endmethod.
```

Listing 10.3 Initializing the Select Option on the Screen

As you can see in Listing 10.3, much of the select options setup process is cross-component initialization code as usual. However, pay attention to the INIT_SELECTION_SCREEN() method of the interface controller because this method provides access to the configuration object needed to set up the select option. The returned object, which is of type IF_WD_SELECT_OPTIONS, offers a number of methods that can be used to dynamically create range tables, add selection fields to the screen, adjust the layout, and more. In Listing 10.3, we're using the CREATE_RANGE_TABLE() and ADD_SELECTION_FIELD() methods to dynamically create a range table and add it as a selection field within the select options view layout. For the purposes of our simple example, this was all the customization that was required.

Listing 10.4 contains the event handler code used to process search requests when users click on the SEARCH FLIGHTS button shown in Figure 10.31. Within this method, we're once again enlisting the services of the IF_WD_SELECT_OPTIONS interface, using its GET_SELECTION_SCREEN_ITEMS() method to obtain a reference to the dynamically generated range table populated by users in the selection screen. Then, we were able to use the range table in the WHERE clause of the SELECT statement used to look up flights from table SPFLI.

Figure 10.31 Visualization of Select Options in WDA Applications

```
method SEARCH_FLIGHTS.
  "Method-Local Data Declarations:
  DATA lt_items TYPE
    if_wd_select_options=>tt_selection_screen_item.
  DATA lo_nd_connid_selection TYPE REF TO if_wd_context_node.
  DATA lo_nd_flight_connections TYPE REF TO
    if_wd_context_node.
```

495

```
DATA lt_flight_connections TYPE
  wd_this->Elements_flight_connections.
FIELD-SYMBOLS:
  <lfs_item> LIKE LINE OF lt_items,
  <lfs_range_tab> TYPE wd_this->Elements_connid_selection.

"Copy the contents of the range table into context:
wd_this->mo_selopt_helper->get_selection_screen_items(
  IMPORTING et_selection_screen_items = lt_items ).
READ TABLE lt_items INDEX 1 ASSIGNING <lfs_item>.
ASSIGN <lfs_item>-mt_range_table->* TO <lfs_range_tab>.

lo_nd_connid_selection =
  wd_context->get_child_node(
    name = wd_this->wdctx_connid_selection ).
lo_nd_connid_selection->bind_table(
  new_items = <lfs_range_tab>
  set_initial_elements = abap_true ).

"Perform the flight query:
SELECT *
  INTO TABLE lt_flight_connections
  FROM spfli
 WHERE connid IN <lfs_range_tab>.

"Store the results in context:
lo_nd_flight_connections =
  wd_context->get_child_node(
    name = wd_this->wdctx_flight_connections ).
lo_nd_flight_connections->bind_table(
  new_items = lt_flight_connections
  set_initial_elements = abap_true ).
endmethod.
```

Listing 10.4 Using Select Options to Build Dynamic Queries

As we've seen in this section, the WDR_SELECT_OPTIONS component makes it very easy to generate complex selection fields on the screen. When we look at dynamic programming concepts in Chapter 11, we'll see that this functionality can be exploited on a larger scale.

10.1.5 Suggested Values for Input Fields

A common feature in many Web 2.0 applications is the so-called *suggested values* function. This function is designed to save users valuable keystrokes by suggesting appropriate values based on the data keyed in thus far. Figure 10.32 demonstrates how this feature works for Google's web search tool (*http://www.google.com*). Here, notice that Google is providing a list of possible values matching the expression "SAP Web D". Naturally, the list of matching values will be continually refined as more characters are entered into the input field.

Figure 10.32 Suggested Values for the Google Search Screen

As you might expect, implementing the suggested values function from scratch is no trivial matter. Fortunately, as of the SAP NetWeaver 7.02 release, we now have the option of turning on the suggested values feature for InputField elements through configuration rather than custom development. Here, there are several prerequisites we must account for in order to turn on the feature:

▶ First of all, the InputField.value property must be bound to a context attribute whose input help settings point to an ABAP Dictionary search help. None of the other input help options are supported.

▶ Secondly, the InputField.suggestValues property must be checked. (It's unchecked by default.) This property determines whether or not the suggested values feature will be active at runtime.

▶ The WDA application parameter WDALLOWVALUESUGGEST must be turned on.

▶ Accessibility mode for the WDA application must be deactivated.

Once these prerequisites are accounted for, the Web Dynpro framework will take care of generating the suggested values list at runtime. Figure 10.33 shows how the value list is rendered for the DEMO_VALUE_SUGGEST sample component provided by SAP.

Figure 10.33 Suggested Values for an InputField in a WDA Application

10.2   Providing Help Texts

Occasionally, users may need assistance navigating through WDA applications. For example, explanation texts may be needed to describe the purpose of a particular screen. Or, when filling in a form, users may require some help figuring out what certain input fields are used for. In this section, we'll look at some standard features that can be used to annotate screens in WDA applications.

10.2.1   Working with the Explanation UI Element

In Chapter 7, we briefly introduced the Explanation UI element, which is a member of the text category of UI elements. This UI element type is used to display explanatory texts on screen (see Figure 10.34).

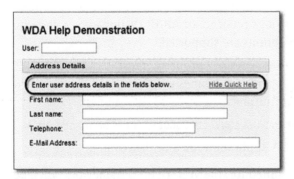

Figure 10.34 Working with the Explanation UI Element

Conceptually speaking, the Explanation element is similar to the TextView element in that it can be used to display blocks of text on screen. This text can be provided via the Explanation.text property in several different ways:

- ▸ Statically within the View Designer tool
- ▸ Dynamically through context data binding
- ▸ Via translatable texts from the *Online Text Repository* (OTR)
- ▸ Via SAPScript texts

Given the similarities to the `TextView` element, you might be wondering what sets the `Explanation` element apart. The primary difference is in the way the `Explanation` element integrates with the built-in help text capabilities of the Web Dynpro framework. This integration allows users to show and hide help texts as needed by:

- ▸ Using the standard DISPLAY QUICK HELP and HIDE QUICK HELP context menu options (see Figure 10.35).
- ▸ By clicking on the HIDE QUICK HELP link displayed within the `Explanation` element's content area (see Figure 10.34). Here, note that this link is only displayed when the `Explanation.design` property is set to `emphasized`.
- ▸ Configuring the `WDHIDEMOREFIELDHELPASDEFAULT` application parameter, which is of type `WDY_BOOLEAN`.

Overall, this flexibility makes it easy to provide users with explanatory text in an unobtrusive manner based on their needs and preferences.

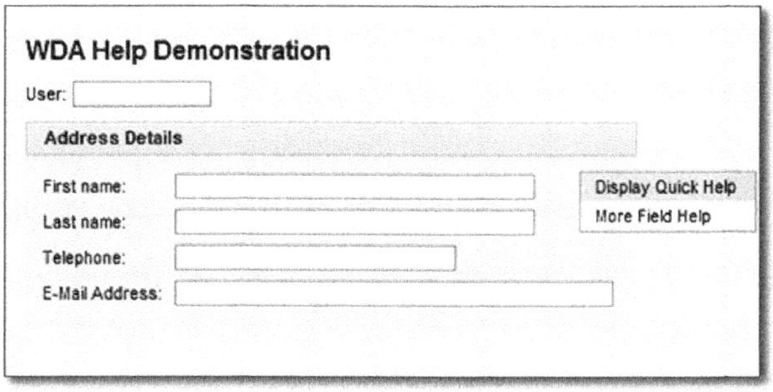

Figure 10.35 Enabling and Disabling Quick Help in a WDA Application

10.2.2 Explanation Property for UI Elements

A number of UI elements come equipped with an `explanation` property, which provides a sort of expanded tooltip text that users can access to display more information about a field. For example, Figure 10.36 shows the `explanation` property at work for an `InputField` element. Users can access this text by clicking on the hyperlink highlighted in green for the corresponding `Label` element.

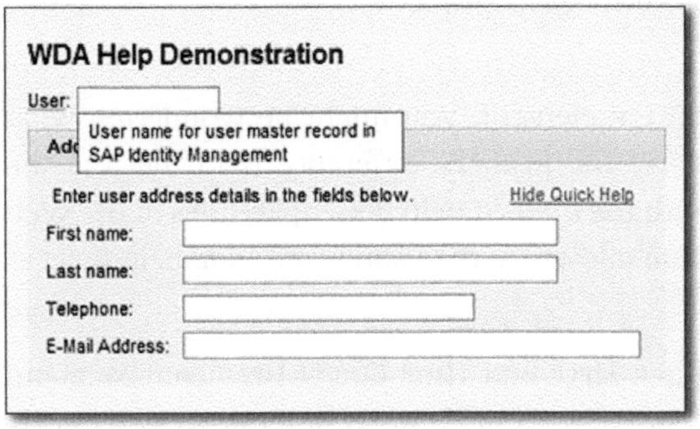

Figure 10.36 Demonstration of the Explanation Text on the Screen

The contents of the `explanation` text property can be supplied in a number of different ways:

▸ Statically via the View Designer tool
▸ Via context data binding
▸ Via OTR texts
▸ Via data elements from the ABAP Dictionary

Figure 10.37 shows the editor screen accessed via the input help for the `explanation` property. Within this screen, we can access various help texts from data elements in the ABAP Dictionary, OTR texts, and so on.

For a complete listing of UI elements that support the `explanation` property, check out the online help documentation, in the "Explanation Property" section, which is contained within "Help Texts for Web Dynpro Applications."

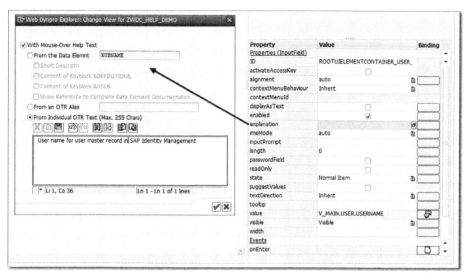

Figure 10.37 Filling in the Explanation Property for an InputField Element

10.2.3 Integrating Classic F1 Help from the ABAP Dictionary

Besides the explanatory text made available via the `explanation` property described in the previous section, the Web Dynpro framework also allows us to integrate classic F1 helps from the ABAP Dictionary. Figure 10.38 shows an example of the classic F1 help in the SAP GUI. Here, the user can access this help by placing the cursor in an input field and hitting the F1 key.

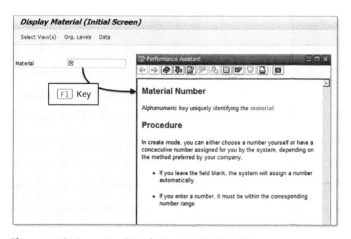

Figure 10.38 Accessing F1 Help Text in the SAP GUI

The help text contained in F1 helps is supplied via data element definitions from the ABAP Dictionary (see Figure 10.39). Therefore, in order to tap into this functionality in WDA, we need only bind `InputField` elements with context attributes whose type is defined in terms of data elements. Then, at runtime, the Web Dynpro framework can inspect the data element definition and dynamically render the help text.

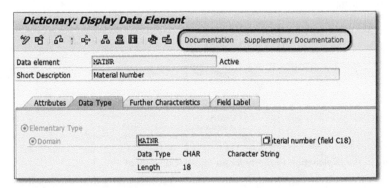

Figure 10.39 Providing Documentation for Data Elements

To access the F1 help text in WDA applications, users can right-click on the field they want to read about and select the MORE FIELD HELP context menu option. This will bring up the MORE FIELD HELP dialog box shown in Figure 10.40. As you can see, the dialog box has a similar look and feel to the one rendered in the SAP GUI (see Figure 10.38).

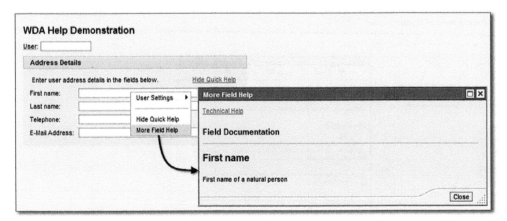

Figure 10.40 Accessing F1 Help Text in a WDA Application

10.3   Confirmation Dialog Boxes

When interacting with users, there are occasions when we need to prompt users to confirm a particular selection. For example, if a user clicks on a button to close the application, we might want to display a confirmation dialog box asking them if they want to discard any changes they may have made. Or, we might just want to display a modal dialog box to get the user's attention.

Though it would be possible to create custom windows or views to display such prompts, it turns out there is a quicker way. If you recall from Chapter 6, dialog boxes are created using the IF_WD_WINDOW_MANAGER interface. This interface also provides a method called CREATE_POPUP_TO_CONFIRM() that can be used to dynamically generate confirmation dialog boxes without having to create a custom window beforehand. Figure 10.41 provides an example of a dialog box created using this method.

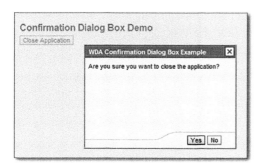

Figure 10.41 A Confirmation Dialog Box Example

For the most part, the Web Dynpro framework takes care of all the heavy lifting when it comes to rendering confirmation dialog boxes. From a development perspective, we need only supply a few pieces of information to the CREATE_POPUP_TO_CONFIRM() method in order for it to do its job. This information comes in the form of the following parameters:

▶ MESSAGE_TYPE
The type of the dialog box (e.g., question, information, error, and so on).

▶ WINDOW_TITLE
The text displayed in the title bar of the dialog box.

▶ TEXT
The text displayed in the content area of the dialog box.

▶ BUTTON_KIND

A numeric value used to determine the types of buttons displayed in the dialog box (e.g., Yes/No/Cancel, OK/Close, and so on).

Parameters are also provided to adjust the dimensions and orientation of the dialog box on screen.

Listing 10.5 provides the code excerpt used to create the dialog box shown in Figure 10.41. In this scenario, the OPEN_CONF_DIALOG() method is being invoked via the event handler method associated with the CLOSE APPLICATION button in the source view. Here, note that the positioning of this method within a view controller method was more than just coincidence. Indeed, if you look at the calls to the IF_WD_WINDOW->SUBSCRIBE_TO_BUTTON_EVENT() method, you can see that we must register the onAction events of the buttons from the dialog box (i.e., the YES and No buttons) with actions defined within a view (e.g., the CONF_YES and CONF_NO actions in Listing 10.5). Therefore, when a user clicks on one of these buttons at runtime, the corresponding event handler methods tied to these actions is triggered within the view controller. Naturally, the Web Dynpro framework takes care of firing the events, closing the dialog window, and so on.

> **Note**
>
> This example is provided via the ZWDC_DIALOG_DEMO component provided with this book's source code bundle.

```
method OPEN_CONF_DIALOG.
  "Method-Local Data Declarations:
  DATA: lo_comp_api   TYPE REF TO if_wd_component,
        lo_window_mgr TYPE REF TO if_wd_window_manager,
        lo_popup      TYPE REF TO if_wd_window,
        lt_text       TYPE string_table,
        lo_view_api   TYPE REF TO if_wd_view_controller.

  "Obtain a reference to the window manager for the component:
  lo_comp_api = wd_comp_controller->wd_get_api( ).
  lo_window_mgr = lo_comp_api->get_window_manager( ).

  "Create the confirmation dialog box:
  APPEND `Are you sure you want to close the application?`
      TO lt_text.
  lo_popup =
```

```
lo_window_mgr->create_popup_to_confirm(
  text            = lt_text
  button_kind     = if_wd_window=>co_buttons_yesno
  message_type    = if_wd_window=>co_msg_type_question
  window_title    = 'WDA Confirmation Dialog Box Example'
  window_position = if_wd_window=>co_center ).

lo_view_api = wd_this->wd_get_api( ).
lo_popup->subscribe_to_button_event(
  button            = if_wd_window=>co_button_yes
  action_name       = 'CONF_YES'
  action_view       = lo_view_api
  is_default_button = abap_true ).

lo_popup->subscribe_to_button_event(
  button            = if_wd_window=>co_button_no
  action_name       = 'CONF_NO'
  action_view       = lo_view_api
  is_default_button = abap_false ).

  "Open the dialog box:
  lo_popup->open( ).
endmethod.
```

Listing 10.5 Opening a Confirmation Dialog Box

> **Note**
>
> The IF_WD_WINDOW interface provides an attribute called POPUP_TO_CONFIRM (which is of type IF_WD_POPUP_TO_CONFIRM_N) that can be used to link the button events from the confirmation dialog box with event handler methods of global controller types. So, if you have a scenario in which you want to centralize the handling of a confirmation dialog box, this attribute can provide the necessary functionality.

10.4 Displaying Messages

During the course of an application session, there are many situations in which we need to display messages on screen. For example, if a user makes an invalid selection on screen, we should issue an error message that provides details about the error and how to correct it. In WDA applications, this can be achieved using the Message Manager. In this section, we'll learn how to work with the Message Manager and customize the display of messages on the screen.

10.4.1 Creating Messages with the Message Manager

As we mentioned earlier, messages in WDA applications are created via the *Message Manager*, which is essentially an object-oriented API based on the IF_WD_MESSAGE_MANAGER interface. We can obtain an object reference based on this interface from any controller method using the GET_MESSAGE_MANAGER() method of the IF_WD_CONTROLLER interface. Then, once we have this object reference in hand, we can create messages using one of the various REPORT_*() methods defined within the IF_WD_MESSAGE_MANAGER interface. Listing 10.6 demonstrates how this works.

```
DATA lo_api_controller  TYPE REF TO if_wd_controller.
DATA lo_message_manager TYPE REF TO if_wd_message_manager.
DATA lt_msg_params       TYPE wdr_name_value_list.
FIELD-SYMBOLS:
  <lfs_msg_param> LIKE LINE OF lt_msg_params.

lo_api_controller ?= wd_this->wd_get_api( ).
lo_message_manager =
  lo_api_controller->get_message_manager( ).

APPEND INITIAL LINE TO lt_msg_params
            ASSIGNING <lfs_msg_param>.
<lfs_msg_param>-name  = 'USER'.
<lfs_msg_param>-value = 'XWOOD'.

CALL METHOD lo_message_manager->report_success
   EXPORTING
     message_text = `User &USER was created successfully.`
     params       = lt_msg_params.
```

Listing 10.6 Displaying Messages Using the Message Manager API

Figure 10.42 shows what the success message generated using the code from Listing 10.6 looks like on screen. We'll look at ways of customizing the location and rendering of messages in Section 10.4.3.

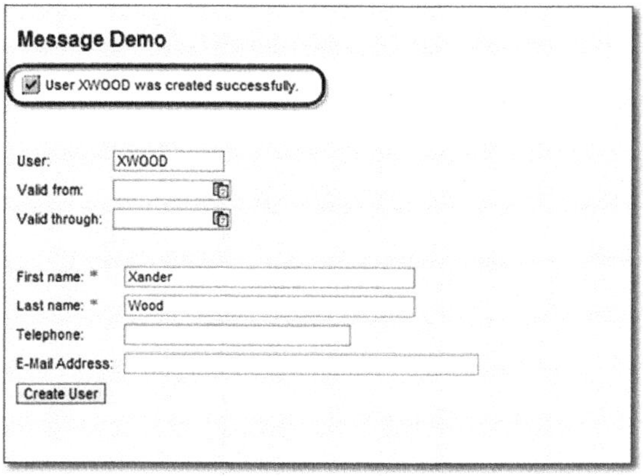

Figure 10.42 Displaying a Success Message on the Screen

Table 10.2 contains a list of some of the more commonly used methods within the IF_WD_MESSAGE_MANAGER interface. As you can see, the method names are quite intuitive and easy to follow. You can also find detailed documentation for each method within the Class Builder tool.

Method Name	Description
report_exception	This method creates a message based on an ABAP Objects exception class (which implements the IF_MES-SAGE interface).
report_success	This method is used to display a plain text success message on the screen.
report_warning	This method is used to display a plain text warning message on the screen.
report_error_message	This method is used to display a plain text error message on the screen.
report_t100_message	This method is used to display T100-style messages on the screen. Such messages are maintained in message classes using Transaction SE91.
report_element_*	These methods can be used to display error messages that are linked to context elements. Such linkages make it possible for users to navigate from the message to the UI element that is bound to the context element.

Table 10.2 Selected Methods of the IF_WD_MESSAGE_MANAGER Interface

Method Name	Description
report_attribute_*	These methods can be used to display error messages that are linked to context attributes. Such linkages make it possible for users to navigate from the message to the UI element that is bound to the context attribute.
is_empty	This Boolean method can be used to determine whether or not any messages exist within the Message Manager collection.
clear_messages	This method can be used to remove any pre-existing messages from the collection.
get_messages	This method can be used to obtain the complete list of messages currently contained in the collection.

Table 10.2 Selected Methods of the IF_WD_MESSAGE_MANAGER Interface (Cont.)

Linking Messages with UI Elements

As noted in Table 10.2, the IF_WD_MESSAGE_MANAGER interface defines a number of methods that make it possible to link messages with context elements/attributes. By extension, this implies that we can link messages with UI elements that are bound against those context elements/attributes. This feature comes in handy whenever we need to perform field validations and so on.

In order to understand how message linkages work, let's look at an example from this book's source code bundle: the ZWDC_MESSAGE_DEMO sample component. As you can see in Figure 10.43, this simple component defines an input form that simulates the creation of user master records. During the course of the data input process, error messages are raised to alert users to input errors and guide them to resolution.

Before we look into the mechanics of message linking from a code perspective, let's briefly consider what it is we're trying to achieve functionally. Here, the goal is to provide users with additional context about an error situation. For instance, in the screenshot shown in Figure 10.43, notice that the error message is rendered as a hyperlink. Users can click on this hyperlink to determine which field contained the invalid input that caused the error to occur. As you can imagine, this feature can come in quite handy for users trying to navigate through a myriad of error messages.

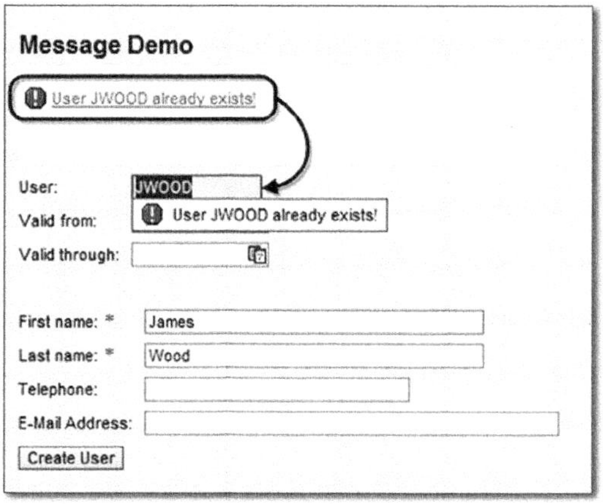

Figure 10.43 Linking an Error Message with a Context Attribute

Listing 10.7 demonstrates the code required to generate the linked message depicted in Figure 10.43. As you can see, there's not too much we have to do, code-wise, to establish this linkage. Basically, we just passed in the target context attribute (USER.USERNAME) to the REPORT_ATTRIBUTE_ERROR_MESSAGE() method and the Web Dynpro framework took over from there.

```
method ONACTIONCREATE.
  "Method-Local Data Declarations:
  DATA lo_api_controller  TYPE REF TO if_wd_controller.
  DATA lo_msg_mgr          TYPE REF TO if_wd_message_manager.
  DATA lt_msg_params       TYPE wdr_name_value_list.
  DATA lo_nd_user TYPE REF TO if_wd_context_node.
  DATA lo_el_user TYPE REF TO if_wd_context_element.
  DATA lv_username TYPE wd_this->Element_user-username.

  FIELD-SYMBOLS:
    <lfs_msg_param> LIKE LINE OF lt_msg_params.

  "Obtain a reference to the message manager:
  lo_api_controller ?= wd_this->wd_get_api( ).
  lo_msg_mgr =
    lo_api_controller->get_message_manager( ).

  "Retrieve the selected user name via the context:
  lo_nd_user =
    wd_context->get_child_node( name = wd_this->wdctx_user ).
```

```
  lo_el_user = lo_nd_user->get_element( ).

  lo_el_user->get_attribute(
    EXPORTING name  = `USERNAME`
    IMPORTING value = lv_username ).

  "Build a parameters table for messages using the user name:
  APPEND INITIAL LINE TO lt_msg_params
              ASSIGNING <lfs_msg_param>.
  <lfs_msg_param>-name  = 'USER'.
  <lfs_msg_param>-value = lv_username.

  "Check to see if the user already exists:
  SELECT SINGLE bname
    INTO lv_username
    FROM usr01
   WHERE bname EQ lv_username.

  IF sy-subrc EQ 0.
    "If it does, then issue an error message and halt
    "processing:
    CALL METHOD lo_msg_mgr->report_attribute_error_message
      EXPORTING
        message_text   = `User &USER already exists!`
        element        = lo_el_user
        attribute_name = 'USERNAME'
        params         = lt_msg_params.

    RETURN.
  ENDIF.
  ...
endmethod.
```

Listing 10.7 Linking an Error Message to a Context Attribute

In addition to the context attribute–based methods, the IF_WD_MESSAGE_MANAGER interface provides methods for linking to entire context elements. This feature is useful when node collections are being edited en masse (e.g., in a Table element) and we need to draw attention to an error in a specific record.

Using the Web Dynpro Code Wizard and Assistance Classes

As we've observed throughout this section, the Message Manager API makes it relatively painless to display messages on screen. However, if we're building a large application with many messages, it helps to automate this process as much as possible. Here, we have a couple of options to speed things along.

The first and most obvious option is to use the GENERATE MESSAGE option of the Web Dynpro code wizard, as demonstrated in Figure 10.44. Here, the wizard assumes the responsibility of generating the message display code illustrated in Listing 10.6. As is the case with most auto-generated code, though, we may have to tweak the code a little bit after the fact to get it to do exactly what we want.

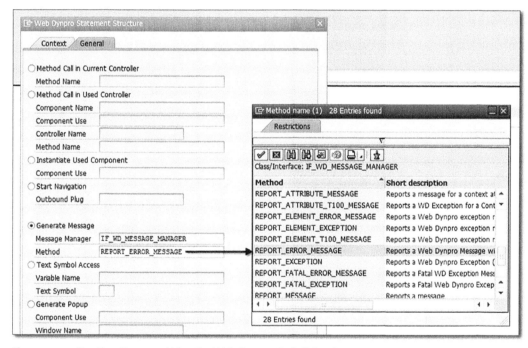

Figure 10.44 Creating Messages Using the Web Dynpro Code Wizard

The other option is to employ a tried and true OOP technique called *composition*. With this method, we define a base-level assistance class that implements the IF_WD_MESSAGE_MANAGER interface, deferring the individual method calls to a message manager instance passed in sometime during component creation (e.g., in the WDDOINIT() method of the component controller). In this book's code bundle, we've defined a class called ZCL_WDA_BASE_ASSISTANCE that can be used for this purpose. Figure 10.45 shows a UML class diagram, which illustrates how this assistance class is constructed.

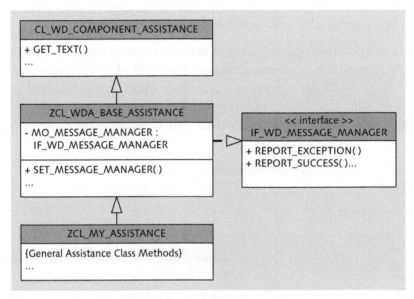

Figure 10.45 UML Class Diagram for Custom Assistance Class

Using the ZCL_WDA_BASE_ASSISTANCE class (or a subclass), we can create messages within any controller method on the fly using the WD_ASSIST controller attribute. Listing 10.8 demonstrates how this works. Here, notice that we don't have to obtain a reference to the Message Manager before creating the message. Instead, this reference is obtained once within the WDDOINIT() method of the component controller and passed into the assistance class using the SET_MESSAGE_MANAGER() instance method (see Figure 10.45). Naturally, we can generate the method calls using the PATTERN button of the controller method editor as we would any other method.

```
DATA lt_msg_params TYPE wdr_name_value_list.
FIELD-SYMBOLS:
  <lfs_msg_param> LIKE LINE OF lt_msg_params.

APPEND INITIAL LINE TO lt_msg_params
          ASSIGNING <lfs_msg_param>.
<lfs_msg_param>-name  = 'USER'.
```

```
<lfs_msg_param>-value = 'XWOOD'.

CALL METHOD wd_assist->report_success
  EXPORTING
    message_text = `User &USER was created successfully.`
    params       = lt_msg_params.
```

Listing 10.8 Creating Messages Using a Custom Assistance Class

10.4.2   Automatic Message Generation

In the previous section, we learned how to use the Message Manager API to strategically create messages of different varieties (e.g., success messages, error messages, and so on). However, in some cases, the Web Dynpro framework will take care of issuing messages for us automatically. For example, we didn't have to do anything special to create the error messages depicted in Figure 10.46. Instead, the Web Dynpro framework created these messages automatically as a result of conversion errors detected within the corresponding InputField elements.

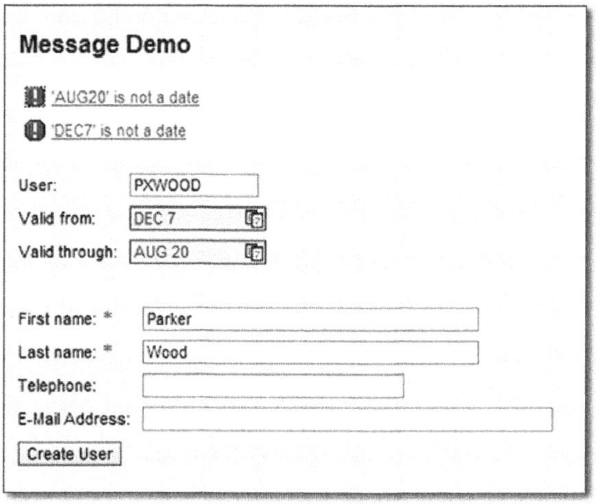

Figure 10.46 Example of Automatically Generated Error Messages

Back in Chapter 3, we also briefly introduced another way to automatically generate error messages when we looked at the CHECK_MANDATORY_ATTR_ON_VIEW() method of class CL_WD_DYNAMIC_TOOL. As you may recall, we invoked this method within the WDDOBEFOREACTION method, as illustrated in Listing 10.9. At runtime, this code will check to see if users entered data in all the required fields in the source view (i.e., the fields marked with the red asterisk) and display error messages if they haven't. Figure 10.47 shows what these error messages look like on screen. Here, notice how each of the error messages is linked to the corresponding InputField elements that are in error.

```
method WDDOBEFOREACTION.
  "Method-Local Data Declarations:
  DATA lo_api_controller TYPE REF TO if_wd_view_controller.
  DATA lo_action         TYPE REF TO if_wd_action.

  lo_api_controller = wd_this->wd_get_api( ).
  lo_action = lo_api_controller->get_current_action( ).

  IF lo_action IS BOUND.
    CASE lo_action->name.
      WHEN 'CREATE'.
        cl_wd_dynamic_tool=>check_mandatory_attr_on_view(
          EXPORTING
            view_controller = lo_api_controller ).
    ENDCASE.
  ENDIF.
endmethod.
```

Listing 10.9 Checking Mandatory Attributes for a View at Runtime

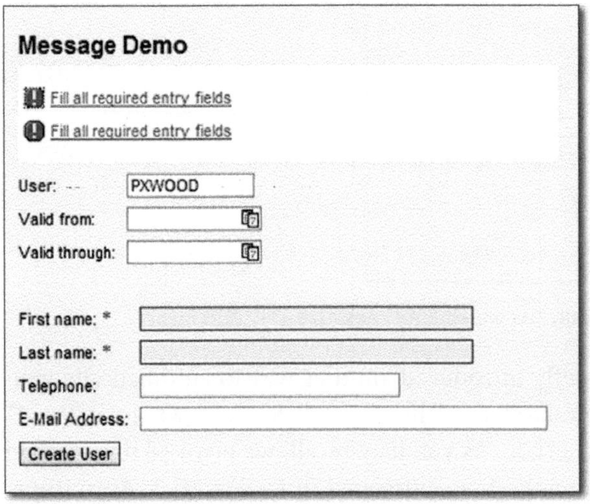

Figure 10.47 Verifying Input in Required Fields

10.4.3 Customizing the Message Area

Messages created via the Message Manager are displayed in a special area of the screen called the *message area*. From a configuration perspective, we have several options for customizing the look and feel of the message area:

▶ Within a WDA application definition, we can determine whether or not the message area should be visible all the time or on demand (see Figure 10.48).

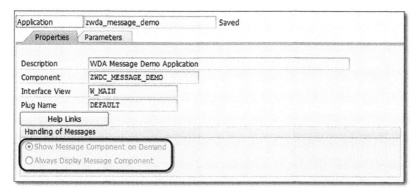

Figure 10.48 Controlling the Handling of Messages in WDA Applications

▶ If we want to control the placement of messages on screen, we can add the MessageArea UI element to the view layout. However, before using this element, we recommend you read through the online help documentation, in the section entitled "Reusable Components and the Message Area." Here, you'll find that there are certain limitations to using the MessageArea element in multi-component designs. For this reason, we recommend you avoid using this element unless you have a really good reason for using it.

▶ We can use the SET_DISPLAY_ATTRIBUTES() method of the IF_WD_MESSAGE_AREA interface to adjust the look and feel of the message area. This method supports the following parameters:

  ▷ I_SHOW_ONLY_CURRENT
  This Boolean parameter can be used to determine whether or not only current messages should be displayed.

  ▷ I_MSG_LINES_VISIBLE
  This parameter allows us to select the number of simultaneously displayed messages whenever the message log is expanded.

▶ **I_USE_TOGGLE_AREA**
This parameter can be used to enable the message area to be toggled between text line and list mode.

▶ **I_FOR_ALL_INSTANCE**
This Boolean parameter can be used to push the configured settings down to all message area instances.

▶ **I_DISPLAY_EMPTY_LINES**
This parameter can be used to statically define the size of the message area.

In order for the changes made via the SET_DISPLAY_ATTRIBUTES() method to be picked up by views at runtime, we recommend that this method be called within the WDDOINIT() method of the overarching window element, as demonstrated in Listing 10.10.

```
method WDDOINIT.
  "Method-Local Data Declarations:
  DATA lo_api TYPE REF TO if_wd_window_controller.
  DATA lo_msg_area TYPE REF TO if_wd_message_area.

  "Obtain a refence to the message area:
  lo_api ?= wd_this->wd_get_api( ).
  lo_msg_area = lo_api->get_message_area( ).

  "Adjust the display attributes:
  lo_msg_area->set_display_attributes(
    i_for_all_instances = abap_false
    i_msg_lines_visible = '3'
    i_use_toggle_area   = abap_true
    i_show_only_current = abap_false ).
endmethod.
```

Listing 10.10 Customizing the Message Area Display

Figure 10.49 and Figure 10.50 demonstrate the look and feel of the message area after the customization settings from Listing 10.10 were applied. As you can see, the customized message area offers quite a bit more features than the standard out-of-the-box message area we've seen throughout the course of this section. Specific features of note include:

- The ability to group messages together to conserve space on the screen
- The ability to show and hide the full list of messages
- The ability to display messages in a table with sort/filter capabilities
- Access to a message log that allows users to track the progression of messages
- The RESET LOG button, which can be used to clear out existing messages

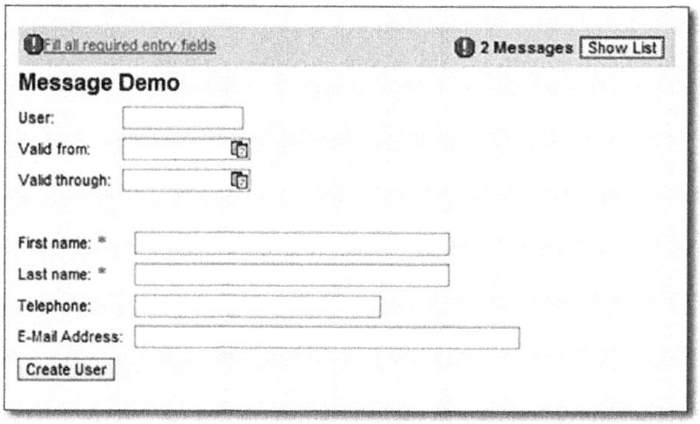

Figure 10.49 Example of a Customized Message Area (Part 1)

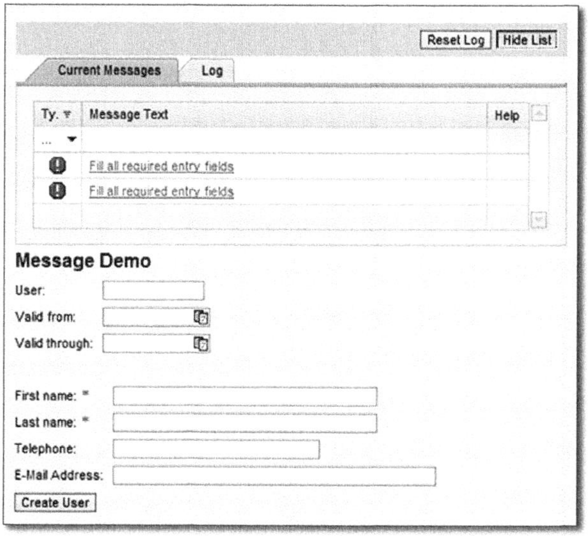

Figure 10.50 Example of a Customized Message Area (Part 2)

517

10.5 Summary

In this chapter, we surveyed the various built-in tools that can be used to interact with users. Here, we looked at different options for providing input helps, help texts, confirmation dialog boxes, messages, and more. Collectively, these features go a long way toward making WDA applications more user friendly. In Chapter 11, we'll take a look at some dynamic programming techniques that can be used to customize and enhance the user experience even more.

One of the prerequisites for leveraging the declarative programming features of the Web Dynpro framework is having all the application requirements in place at design time. Recognizing that this may not always be feasible, SAP also provides a number of dynamic programming capabilities within the Web Dynpro framework. In this chapter, we'll learn how to utilize these features.

11 Dynamic Programming

As we've seen throughout the course of this book, the declarative programming model employed by Web Dynpro is flexible enough to support most of the typical application requirements that come our way. However, we may occasionally run into application scenarios that don't quite fit within the confines of the framework. For example, imagine an application in which the entire view layout is predicated upon user input collected in a selection screen. Here, since we can make no assumptions ahead of time regarding the view layout, we can't use declarative techniques to lay out the user interface. Instead, we must rely on dynamic programming techniques to construct the user interface on the fly.

In this chapter, we'll explore some of the dynamic programming capabilities supported by the Web Dynpro framework. During the course of our analysis, we'll learn how to manipulate the context, adjust the view layout, and dynamically integrate other WDA components. Then, in Section 11.4, we'll see how these features work in tandem to create a flexible data browser tool similar to the standard ABAP Browser tool provided with the ABAP Dictionary (Transaction SE16).

11.1 Manipulating the Context

For the most part, dynamic programming techniques are used in situations when we need to augment the view layout in an ad hoc fashion. Of course, if we're going to create a bunch of new UI elements, we'll need a way to supply them with data. For this, we'll need to be able to dynamically manipulate controller contexts at runtime—a task that can be achieved using the context API.

11.1.1 Working with the IF_WD_CONTEXT_NODE_INFO Interface

To modify controller contexts at runtime, we must engage the services of the IF_WD_CONTEXT_NODE_INFO interface. This interface is described in the interface documentation as being the "[i]nterface for the metadata of a node." In other words, it provides an assortment of methods for displaying context node metadata, modifying context nodes, and more. We caught a little glimpse of this when we looked at the maintenance of attribute value sets and the DropDownByKey UI element in Chapter 7. In this section, we'll broaden our scope and look more closely at some of the advanced features of the IF_WD_CONTEXT_NODE_INFO interface.

Accessing the IF_WD_CONTEXT_NODE_INFO Interface

As we observed in Chapter 7, we can obtain a reference to a context node's metadata by calling the GET_NODE_INFO( ) method of the IF_WD_CONTEXT_NODE interface, as demonstrated in Listing 11.1. The GET_NODE_INFO( ) method returns an object reference that implements the IF_WD_CONTEXT_NODE_INFO interface. In the upcoming sections, we'll learn how to use this object reference to introspect the context node's metadata, add child nodes/attributes, and so on.

```
METHOD some_controller_method.
  DATA lo_node_info TYPE REF TO if_wd_context_node_info.

  lo_node_info = wd_context->get_node_info( ).
  ...
ENDMETHOD.
```

Listing 11.1 Obtaining a Reference to a Context Node's Metadata

Interface Method Overview

Once we obtain a reference to a context node's metadata using the IF_WD_CONTEXT_NODE->GET_NODE_INFO( ) method, we can use the provided IF_WD_CONTEXT_NODE_INFO object reference to perform a number of useful tasks. Table 11.1 provides a general overview of some of the more commonly used methods provided with this interface. For the most part, the methods are intuitive and easy to use since they reflect tasks normally performed statically within the Context Editor tool. We'll see some of this on display in the upcoming sections when we look at dynamic context node and context attribute manipulation.

Method Name	Description
add_attribute( )	This method is used to add a new context attribute to the context node. It receives an input structure of type WDR_CONTEXT_ATTRIBUTE_INFO, which provides a number of fields that correspond with those used to define context attributes statically.
add_new_child_node( )	This method can be used to dynamically create a new child node underneath the context node. We'll see how this method works in Section 11.1.2.
get_attribute( ) get_attributes( )	These methods can be used to obtain the metadata for context attributes. Here, note that the methods work for context attributes created statically and dynamically.
get_child_node( ) get_child_nodes( )	These methods can be used to obtain the metadata of child context nodes. Naturally, the metadata is represented via object references that implement the IF_WD_CONTEXT_NODE_INFO interface.
get_name( )	This method provides the current context node's name. This method can come in handy when we're using the get_child_node*( ) or get_parent( ) methods to traverse the node hierarchy and need to determine our current location.
get_parent( )	This method returns a reference to the metadata of the context node's parent node. As you'd expect, the returned object reference implements the IF_WD_CONTEXT_NODE_INFO interface.
get_static_attributes_type( )	This method returns the runtime type information (RTTI) of the context node's element structure. The RTTI information is provided in the form of a CL_ABAP_STRUCTDESCR object reference.

Table 11.1 Selected Methods of IF_WD_CONTEXT_NODE_INFO

Method Name	Description
is_...( )	The IF_WD_CONTEXT_NODE_INFO interface provides a number of Boolean methods of the form IS_...( ). These methods can be used to determine the context node's cardinality, whether or not the context node is a singleton, and so on.
remove_attribute( )	This method can be used to delete a context attribute from the context node definition. The attribute in question is specified via the NAME parameter, which is of type STRING.
remove_child_node( )	This method can be used to remove a child node from the context node. The child node is specified via the NAME parameter, which is of type STRING. Here, we should point out that only dynamically created nodes can be removed.
remove_dynamic_attributes( )	This method removes all the dynamically created context attributes from a context node definition.

Table 11.1 Selected Methods of IF_WD_CONTEXT_NODE_INFO (Cont.)

11.1.2 Adding Context Nodes to the Node Hierarchy

As described in Table 11.1, we can add new child context nodes to the node hierarchy using the ADD_NEW_CHILD_NODE( ) method of the IF_WD_CONTEXT_NODE_INFO interface. To demonstrate the use of this method, we'll consider the creation of the context node hierarchy depicted in Figure 11.1. This context node hierarchy is utilized within the data browser tool described in Section 11.4. In this scenario, the selection criteria underneath the statically defined QUERY_PARAMETERS node will change to correspond with the table the user has selected to browse from. In other words, the node called {Field 1} represents the first field in the table, {Field 2} represents the second field, and so on.

Before we begin reviewing how the ADD_NEW_CHILD_NODE( ) was used to implement our sample application requirements, let's take a closer look at the method's signature. Table 11.2 describes some of the more commonly used parameters for the ADD_NEW_CHILD_NODE( ) method. As we create new child nodes, we can use these parameters to specify node properties in much the same way we configure them statically within the Context Editor tool.

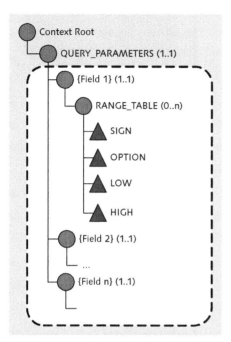

Figure 11.1 Dynamically Adding Context Nodes to the Node Hierarchy

Parameter Name	Description
STATIC_ELEMENT_TYPE	This parameter can be used to predefine the context attributes for the node in reference to a structure type from the ABAP Dictionary.
NAME	This parameter is used to specify the name of the newly created context node.
IS_MANDATORY	This Boolean parameter determines whether or not at least one context element must exist within the node element collection at all times (e.g., cardinality 1..*).
IS_MANDATORY_SELECTION	This Boolean parameter determines if at least one context element is selected within the node element collection at all times.
IS_MULTIPLE	This Boolean parameter determines if more than one element can exist within the node element collection.

Table 11.2 Selected Parameters of the ADD_NEW_CHILD_NODE( ) Method

Parameter Name	Description
IS_MULTIPLE_SELECTION	This Boolean parameter determines if more than one element can be selected within the node element collection at a time.
IS_SINGLETON	This Boolean parameter determines if the newly created context node will be a singleton.
IS_INITIALIZE_LEAD_ SELECTION	This Boolean parameter determines if the lead selection of the node element collection should be selected at all times.
STATIC_ELEMENT_RTTI	This parameter provides a dynamic alternative to the STATIC_ELEMENT_TYPE parameter used to define context attributes. Here, a reference to an object of type CL_ABAP_ STRUCTDESCR can be provided to define the context attributes.
IS_STATIC	This Boolean parameter determines whether or not the newly created node is statically defined. If this parameter is set to abap_true (which is the default behavior), the node is treated like a statically-defined node and cannot be deleted. So, if you have designs on deleting/recreating a context node hierarchy within your application, this parameter should be set to abap_false.
ATTRIBUTES	This parameter provides a third alternative to predetermining the context attributes for the newly created node. Here, the properties for the context attributes are specified within an internal table of type WDR_CONTEXT_ATTR_INFO_MAP.

Table 11.2 Selected Parameters of the ADD_NEW_CHILD_NODE( ) Method (Cont.)

Listing 11.2 contains an excerpt of the method used to build the node hierarchy depicted in Figure 11.1. Here, the node hierarchy is being constructed as follows:

1. First, we obtain a reference to the metadata for the statically defined QUERY_ PARAMETERS node (see Figure 11.1). This is achieved by calling the GET_NODE_ INFO() method of the IF_WD_CONTEXT_NODE interface.

2. Then, the method loops through the fields from the selection screen of the data browser tool and creates a new child node underneath the QUERY_PARAMETERS node for each selection parameter/select option that has data in it. Here, the newly created context node is named in reference to the selection parameter

and has a cardinality of 1..1. As you can see in Listing 11.2, these properties were defined as follows:

▷ The context node name was specified in the NAME parameter.

▷ To define a cardinality of 1..1, we set the IS_MANDATORY Boolean parameter to abap_true.

▷ Finally, since the query parameter list can change as users adjust their selections, we set the IS_STATIC parameter to abap_true so that we can delete the newly created node later, during the application session.

3. Finally, underneath the newly created query parameter node, we are calling the ADD_NEW_CHILD_NODE() method again to create another child node called RANGE_TABLE to store the range table from the selection parameter's select option definition. (See Section 10.1.4 for a refresher on selection options in WDA.) Here, note the use of the STATIC_ELEMENT_RTTI parameter to specify the line type of the range table from the selection option.

> **Note**
>
> You can find a full implementation for this method in the component controller of the ZWDC_DYNAMIC_DEMO component provided with this book's source code bundle.

```
method COPY_SELECTION_CRITERIA.
  ...
  "Obtain a reference to the metadata for the
  "QUERY_PARAMETERS node:
  lo_nd_query_parameters =
    wd_context->get_child_node(
      name = wd_this->wdctx_query_parameters ).
  lo_nd_query_parameters_info =
    lo_nd_query_parameters->get_node_info( ).

  "Loop through the selection screen items:
  LOOP AT lt_selopt_items ASSIGNING <lfs_selopt_item>.
    "De-reference the select option range table:
    ASSIGN <lfs_selopt_item>-mt_range_table->*
        TO <lfs_range_tab>.
    IF lines( <lfs_range_tab> ) EQ 0.
      CONTINUE.
    ENDIF.
```

```abap
"Create a new query parameter for the selection screen
"field:
lo_nd_query_parameter_info =
  lo_nd_query_parameters_info->add_new_child_node(
    name         = <lfs_selopt_item>-m_id
    is_mandatory = abap_true
    is_static    = abap_false ).

"Derive the RTTI metadata for the select option line:
lo_range_tab_meta ?=
  cl_abap_tabledescr=>describe_by_data_ref(
    <lfs_selopt_item>-mt_range_table ).

lo_range_tab_line_meta ?=
  lo_range_tab_meta->get_table_line_type( ).

"Create a RANGE_TABLE child node based upon the select
"option metadata:
lo_nd_query_parameter_info->add_new_child_node(
  name               = 'RANGE_TABLE'
  is_mandatory       = abap_true
  static_element_rtti = lo_range_tab_line_meta
  is_static          = abap_false ).

lo_nd_query_parameter =
  lo_nd_query_parameters->get_child_node(
    <lfs_selopt_item>-m_id ).

lo_nd_query_parameter_range =
  lo_nd_query_parameter->get_child_node( 'RANGE_TABLE' ).
lo_nd_query_parameter_range->bind_table(
  <lfs_range_tab> ).
ENDLOOP.
...
endmethod.
```

Listing 11.2 Dynamically Creating a Context Node Hierarchy

As you can see in Listing 11.2, once dynamic context nodes are created, we can access them as usual (e.g., using the GET_CHILD_NODE() method of the IF_WD_CONTEXT_NODE interface). This is possible since, from an API perspective, there's really no difference between statically defined and dynamically defined context nodes. So, once we get past the administrative setup, we can manipulate the dynamically generated context nodes using the context API methods described in Chapter 5. Furthermore, we can also bind the newly created context nodes to dynamically generated UI elements. We'll see how to achieve this in Section 11.2.4.

11.1.3   Adding Context Attributes to a Context Node

In the previous section, we learned that the ADD_NEW_CHILD_NODE() method of the IF_WD_CONTEXT_NODE_INFO interface provides several parameters that can be used to define the context attributes for a context node up front. In some cases, though, we may want to create new context attributes on the fly. In these situations, we can use the ADD_ATTRIBUTE() method of the IF_WD_CONTEXT_NODE_INFO interface.

The ADD_ATTRIBUTE() method defines a single importing parameter called ATTRIBUTE_INFO, which is of type WDR_CONTEXT_ATTRIBUTE_INFO. Within this structure, we can specify the same sorts of properties we would configure for a context attribute declaratively defined in the Context Editor tool.

Listing 11.3 demonstrates how the ADD_ATTRIBUTE() method is used to create a context attribute called USER.USER_NAME. Here, we're using fields of the WDR_CONTEXT_ATTRIBUTE_INFO structure to specify the attribute's type (XUBNAME) and its value help mode. If we'd wanted to, we could have specified other properties for the context attribute, such as the default value (using the DEFAULT_VALUE field), its attribute value set (using the VALUE_SET field), and so on.

```
DATA lo_nd_user TYPE REF TO if_wd_context_node.
DATA lo_nd_user_info TYPE REF TO if_wd_context_node_info.
DATA ls_attr_info TYPE wdr_context_attribute_info.

"Obtain a reference to the USER node's metadata:
lo_nd_user =
  wd_context->get_child_node(
    wd_this->wdctx_query_parameters ).
lo_nd_user_info = lo_nd_user->get_node_info( ).

"Create an attribute called USER_NAME:
ls_attr_info-name = 'USER_NAME'.
ls_attr_info-type_name = 'XUBNAME'.
```

```
ls_attr_info-value_help_mode = '0'.  "Automatic
lo_nd_user_info->add_attribute( ls_attr_info ).
```

Listing 11.3 Dynamically Adding a Context Attribute to a Context Node

11.1.4 Dynamic Context Programming Dos and Don'ts

Having seen the power of dynamic context programming up close in this section, it can be tempting to get carried away thinking of the ways custom coding could save us a few of the tedious key strokes and/or button clicks it takes to statically define a context node hierarchy. However, before you head down this path, we urge you to think in terms of the overall picture. While it may be possible to automate a step or two by defining a context dynamically, there are repercussions to doing so. Most notably, the task of data binding with UI elements in the view layer changes considerably since we now also have to apply dynamic programming techniques in order to link the dynamic nodes/attributes with UI elements.

Because of these ripple effects, we recommend you limit the use of dynamic context programming techniques to those scenarios in which there is no other alternative. For most applications, the static approach will work just fine. Plus, it adds more transparency to the application design since everything is laid out statically for all to see at design time.

11.2 Modifying the View Layout at Runtime

Sometimes, application requirements dictate that we step outside the comfy confines of Web Dynpro's declarative programming model and generate or adjust view layouts by hand using custom ABAP Objects code. For the most part, this process is fairly straightforward and easy to learn once you understand how to locate and work with the relevant runtime classes for UI elements. From there, it's basically object-oriented ABAP as usual.

In this section, we'll learn how to interject custom view generation logic into the Web Dynpro phase model. Along the way, we'll learn how to modify the UI element hierarchy, adjust the properties of UI elements, and more. Finally, we'll conclude by looking at some declarative-based design alternatives that should be considered before you head down the dynamic programming path.

11.2.1 Getting Started with the WDDOMODIFYVIEW( ) Hook Method

Back in Chapter 4, we briefly introduced the WDDOMODIFYVIEW() hook method and its positioning within the Web Dynpro phase model. As you may recall, this hook method is called just before the Web Dynpro framework begins to render a view at runtime. Within this method, we're free to modify the view layout in any way we like. The scope of the changes could be as small as tweaking a handful of fields or as extensive as constructing the entire view layout from scratch.

The UML class diagram in Figure 11.2 illustrates the signature of the WDDOMODIFY-VIEW() method. As you can see, this method receives two importing parameters that are provided courtesy of the Web Dynpro framework:

▶ FIRST_TIME

This Boolean parameter provides an indicator that tells us whether or not the view is being rendered for the first time. This parameter can come in handy when we need to make sure UI element changes are only performed before the view is rendered for the first time.

▶ VIEW

The VIEW parameter provides a reference to an object that implements the IF_WD_VIEW interface shown in Figure 11.2. We can use this object reference to tap into the UI element hierarchy and begin making changes.

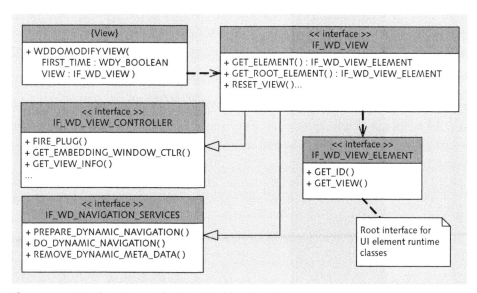

Figure 11.2 UML Class Diagram for View Modification API

Listing 11.4 shows a sample implementation of the WDDOMODIFYVIEW() method. As you can see, we're using the GET_ROOT_ELEMENT() method of the VIEW parameter to obtain a reference to the top-level RootUIElementContainer element. Here, notice how we're performing a downcast on the ROOT_VIEW_ELEMENT returning parameter, casting it into an object reference of type CL_WD_UIELEMENT_CONTAINER. This indirection is necessary since we want to be able to access methods of the CL_WD_ UIELEMENT_CONTAINER runtime class to add and remove elements from the UI element hierarchy. We'll have more to say about the relationship between these class/ interface types in Section 11.2.2.

```
method WDDOMODIFYVIEW.
  DATA lo_root_element TYPE REF TO cl_wd_uielement_container.

  "Check to see if the view has been rendered already:
  IF first_time NE abap_true.
    RETURN.
  ENDIF.

  "Obtain a reference to the root UI element container:
  lo_root_element ?= view->get_root_element( ).

  "Add, update, and remove UI elements from the UI element
  "hierarchy as needed:
  lo_root_element->remove_all_children( ).
  ...
endmethod.
```

Listing 11.4 Working with the WDDOMODIFYVIEW() Hook Method

Once we obtain the reference to the RootUIElementContainer element, we can use the methods of the CL_WD_UIELEMENT_CONTAINER runtime class to begin traversing the UI element hierarchy and make changes. To some degree, this is analogous to the way we use the WD_CONTEXT controller attribute to access the context node hierarchy. From here, we can use API methods to traverse the UI element hierarchy, add and remove UI elements, and so on. We'll see how this is achieved in the upcoming sections.

11.2.2 Navigating the Class Hierarchy for UI Elements

One of the prerequisites for dynamic UI programming in WDA is being able to identify all the UI element runtime classes that will be needed to produce the desired effects on the screen. Therefore, in this section, we'll briefly introduce you to the UI element class hierarchy and show you how to assemble your own piece lists to satisfy specific application requirements.

Looking at the UML class diagram depicted in Figure 11.2, you can see that the IF_WD_VIEW interface defines two getter methods we can use to obtain references to UI elements at runtime: GET_ROOT_ELEMENT() and GET_ELEMENT(). As we observed in Listing 11.4, the GET_ROOT_ELEMENT() method provides us with a reference to the top-level RootUIElementContainer element. We can use this object reference to traverse through the rest of the UI element hierarchy step by step. Alternatively, if we know which UI element we're looking for, we can access it directly using the IF_WD_VIEW->GET_ELEMENT() method. This method allows us to access UI elements directly using their ID property. Regardless of the approach we take, though, we'll end up with an object reference that implements the IF_WD_VIEW_ELEMENT interface (see Figure 11.2).

The IF_WD_VIEW_ELEMENT interface represents the foundation of the UI element class hierarchy. As you can see in the UML class diagram shown in Figure 11.3, all UI element runtime classes implement this interface either directly or indirectly. Therefore, you'll find that the IF_WD_VIEW_ELEMENT interface is used extensively within the dynamic view programming APIs since it allows for polymorphic calls using interchangeable UI element runtime classes.

> **Note**
>
> If you're not familiar with polymorphism as it relates to ABAP Objects, you might want to check out *Object-Oriented Programming with ABAP Objects* (Wood, SAP PRESS, 2009).

As we work our way down the inheritance tree depicted in Figure 11.3, you can see that the runtime classes become more and more specialized. For instance, underneath the abstract CL_WD_UI_ELEMENT class, you'll notice a number of UI element runtime classes whose names may look familiar: CL_WD_LABEL, CL_WD_TABLE, and so on. These classes correspond with familiar UI elements such as the Label and Table elements. Each of these classes provide getter and setter methods that match up with the properties defined by the UI element. For example, the CL_WD_LABEL class provides methods such as SET_TEXT() and SET_LABEL_FOR() to specify the text and labelFor properties for the Label element, respectively.

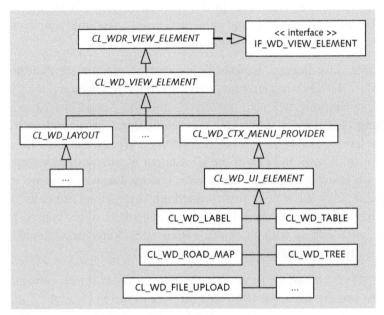

Figure 11.3 UML Class Diagram for UI Element Runtime Classes

Overall, you'll find that there's a runtime class defined for each UI element type provided with the Web Dynpro framework. In addition, there are a number of abstract base classes that define common functionality shared by several UI elements (e.g., CL_WD_ABSTRACT_DROPDOWN for the various DropDownBy* element flavors).

We can determine the name of the runtime class that corresponds with a specific UI element type by looking at the UI element reference documentation provided via the SAP Help Portal (*http://help.sap.com*). You can locate this documentation by performing a search for the term "Web Dynpro user interface elements." Once you locate the UI element you're looking for, you can search within the page for the term "runtime class" to find the name of the ABAP Objects class used to represent the UI element at runtime.

Another useful tool we can use to traverse the class hierarchy for UI elements is the Class Browser integrated into the ABAP Workbench. As you can see in Figure

11.4, this tool allows us to navigate inheritance relationships visually within a tree control.

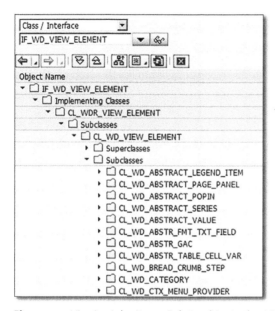

Figure 11.4 Viewing Inheritance Relationships in the ABAP Workbench

11.2.3 Adding UI Elements to the UI Element Hierarchy

In general, the process of adding new elements to the UI element hierarchy is pretty much the same regardless of which UI element is being added. Here, the steps required are as follows:

1. First, we must obtain a reference to the container element that will store the newly created UI element. We caught a glimpse of this in Listing 11.4 when we obtained a reference to the RootUIElementContainer element. Alternatively, we can use the IF_WD_VIEW->GET_ELEMENT() method to access a particular container element within the hierarchy. A third option is to create our own container element using this same process.

2. Next, we have to manually create the new UI element using the NEW_<element>() factory method provided with the UI element's runtime class. For example, to create a new InputField element, we would call the static NEW_INPUT_FIELD() method of class CL_WD_INPUT_FIELD.

3. Depending on the layout being used within the parent container, we may need to define the layout data for the newly created UI element. We can do this by calling the NEW_*() factory method from one of the layout data runtime classes (i.e., a subclass of CL_WD_LAYOUT_DATA).

4. Finally, we can add the newly created element to the container by calling the container element's ADD_CHILD() method, which accepts any UI element that inherits from the abstract base class CL_WD_UIELEMENT.

To demonstrate how this process is realized programmatically, let's consider an example based on the ZWDC_DYNAMIC_LAYOUT sample component provided with this book's source code bundle. The main view of this component (V_MAIN) is shown in Figure 11.5. Here, you can see that we've dynamically added three UI elements to the layout: a Label element, an InputField element, and a Button element. In addition, we've wired up the onEnter and onAction events of the Input-Field and Button elements to trigger an action called NAME_SELECTED. The event handler method associated with this action displays the popup window shown in Figure 11.5.

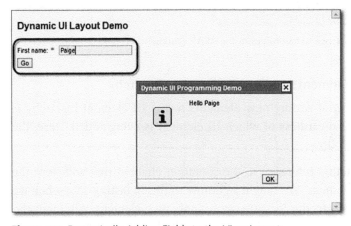

Figure 11.5 Dynamically Adding Fields to the View Layout

Listing 11.5 contains the implementation of the WDDOMODIFYVIEW() method of the V_MAIN view shown in Figure 11.5. Though the code itself is relatively straightforward, there are a few highlights worth mentioning:

▶ The newly-created UI elements are being added directly beneath the RootContainerUIElement, which is obtained via the GET_ROOT_ELEMENT() method of the IF_WD_VIEW interface.

▶ Each of the UI elements was created using the NEW_<element>() method of its respective runtime class. As you can see, each of these methods provides a number of importing parameters that can be used to pre-initialize the element's properties. Here, we can pass in the values directly or bind the property to context nodes/context attributes. In the case of the InputField element, you can see that we chose the latter approach to bind the InputField.value property to a context attribute called USER_INFO.FIRST_NAME.

▶ Since the Layout property of the RootContainerUIElement element in the V_MAIN view was configured to use the MatrixLayout, we had to assign layout data to each of the newly-created UI elements using the CL_WD_MATRIX_HEAD_DATA and CL_WD_MATRIX_DATA classes.

```
method WDDOMODIFYVIEW.
  "Method-Local Data Declarations:
  DATA lo_root_element TYPE REF TO cl_wd_uielement_container.
  DATA lo_label TYPE REF TO cl_wd_label.
  DATA lo_input_field TYPE REF TO cl_wd_input_field.
  DATA lo_button TYPE REF TO cl_wd_button.
  DATA lo_matrix_data TYPE REF TO cl_wd_matrix_data.
  DATA lo_matrix_head_data TYPE REF TO cl_wd_matrix_head_data.

  "Check to see if the view has been rendered already:
  IF first_time NE abap_true.
    RETURN.
  ENDIF.

  "Obtain a reference to the root UI element container:
  lo_root_element ?= view->get_root_element( ).

  "Create the UI elements to be added to the layout:
  lo_input_field =
    cl_wd_input_field=>new_input_field(
      bind_value = 'USER_INFO.FIRST_NAME'
      id         = 'INP_NAME'
      on_enter   = 'NAME_SELECTED'
      state      = cl_wd_input_field=>e_state-required
      view       = view ).

  lo_label =
    cl_wd_label=>new_label(
      id         = 'LBL_NAME'
```

```
          label_for = 'INP_NAME' ).

  lo_button =
    cl_wd_button=>new_button(
      id        = 'BTN_GO'
      on_action = 'NAME_SELECTED'
      text      = 'Go' ).

  "Add the new UI elements to the view layout:
  lo_matrix_head_data =
    cl_wd_matrix_head_data=>new_matrix_head_data(
      element = lo_label ).
  lo_root_element->add_child( lo_label ).

  lo_matrix_data =
    cl_wd_matrix_data=>new_matrix_data(
      element = lo_input_field ).
  lo_root_element->add_child( lo_input_field ).

  lo_matrix_head_data =
    cl_wd_matrix_head_data=>new_matrix_head_data(
      element = lo_button ).
  lo_root_element->add_child( lo_button ).
endmethod.
```

Listing 11.5 Dynamically Adding Fields to the View Layout

For the most part, the code excerpt in Listing 11.5 is representative of the kind of logic required to dynamically construct view layouts. Naturally, it may take more work to configure some of the more complex UI elements, but the same process applies nonetheless. In the next section, we'll look more closely at ways of configuring UI elements once they're created.

11.2.4 Manipulating UI Elements Programmatically

Once a UI element has been created (either statically or dynamically), we can manipulate its properties at runtime using methods provided in the element's runtime class. Here, we have three basic types of methods at our disposal:

▶ **Getter and setter methods**
The GET_<property>() and SET_<property>() methods can be used to query and specify, respectively, the value of a given UI element property,. For exam-

ple, we can use the GET_ENABLED() method to query a UI element's enabled property, and the SET_ENABLED() method to specify its value.

In addition to getting/setting the values of standard properties, getter and setter methods can also be used to link events with actions in the view. For instance, we can use the SET_ON_ACTION() method of the CL_WD_BUTTON class to link on the onAction event of a Button element with an action.

▶ **Data binding methods**
These methods can be used to work with properties that can (or must) be bound to the context. To bind a property with a context attribute, we can use the BIND_<property>() method. This method receives a parameter called PATH (of type STRING), which contains the path to the target context node or context attribute using the familiar dot notation: e.g., UI_PROPERTIES.READ_ONLY. The BOUND_<property>() methods can be used to determine the node path currently bound to a given property (if any).

▶ **Aggregation methods**
These methods are provided with the runtime classes for complex UI element types which may aggregate one or more child elements. Here, we can use the ADD_*() and REMOVE_*() methods to maintain the element collection. We saw an example of this with the CL_WD_UIELEMENT_CONTAINER class in Listing 11.5 whenever we added UI elements using the ADD_CHILD() method.

To demonstrate how these methods are used, let's see how we might rework the example from Listing 11.5 to use methods of the UI element runtime classes to configure the newly-created elements. Listing 11.6 provides an excerpt that shows what these changes look like. Here, notice how we're using methods of the CL_WD_INPUT_FIELD class to specify its properties rather than providing these property values up front whenever the InputField element is created in the NEW_INPUT_FIELD() method. As you can see, there's nothing particularly complex going on here, just method calls as per usual.

```
method WDDOMODIFYVIEW.
  "Method-Local Data Declarations:
  DATA lo_input_field TYPE REF TO cl_wd_input_field.
  ...
  "Obtain a reference to the root UI element container:
  lo_root_element ?= view->get_root_element( ).

  "Create the UI elements to be added to the layout:
```

```
lo_input_field =
  cl_wd_input_field=>new_input_field(
    id        = 'INP_NAME'
    view      = view ).

lo_input_field->bind_value( 'USER_INFO.FIRST_NAME' ).
lo_input_field->set_on_enter( 'NAME_SELECTED' ).
lo_input_field->set_state(
  cl_wd_input_field=>e_state-required ).
...
endmethod.
```

Listing 11.6 Working with Methods of the UI Element Runtime Classes

11.2.5 Declarative Alternatives

Having now been exposed to some techniques for dynamically manipulating the view layout, it can be easy to get carried away and start using this approach all over the place. However, before you head down this path, we urge you to exercise some restraint and make sure a dynamic approach is truly warranted. After all, it kind of defeats the purpose of using a declarative programming model if we constantly circumvent it by writing a lot of custom code that's costly to maintain.

Often, if we think about a UI programming requirement a little bit harder, we may be able to come up with an alternative approach based on declarative programming techniques. Some potential workarounds to consider include the following:

- ▶ As we learned in Chapters 7 and 8, the Web Dynpro framework provides a number of complex UI element types that can be used to flexibly create view layouts. So, before we head down the dynamic programming path, it makes sense to take another sweep through the UI element catalog and make sure there aren't any existing UI elements that might satisfy the requirements at hand. For example, if our requirement is to repeat a portion of the view layout a number of times, we can use the RowRepeater element to replicate the content rather than encoding this output in a loop in the WDDOMODIFYVIEW() method.

- ▶ If all we need to do is modify the properties of a UI element, it makes sense to see if we can modify these property values via context attributes instead of writing custom code to call setter methods on the UI element's runtime class.

▸ Finally, if the same set of dynamic requirements pops up over and over again, we can encapsulate these requirements in a standalone WDA component that can be leveraged using declarative techniques. That way, we minimize the scope of the dynamic coding to a single component. The `SALV_WD_TABLE` component provides an example of this as it encapsulates all the logic required to generate an ALV table using externally provided data.

11.3 Working with Dynamic Component Usages

So far, the scope of the dynamic programming techniques we've considered has been limited to a single WDA component. While these techniques are powerful in and of themselves, we can really take things to the next level if we can figure out ways to leverage the services of external components on demand. In this section, we'll see how such economies of scale can be achieved.

11.3.1 Dynamically Creating Component Usages

In Chapter 9, we learned how to statically define component usages using the Component/Controller Editor tools. As you may recall, these usage definitions consisted of little more than a name and a reference to the component being leveraged. Given the relative straightforwardness of this task, it's not a stretch to imagine that the same thing can be achieved dynamically using the Web Dynpro runtime API. Here, we have a couple of different options to choose from:

▸ We can clone an existing component usage at runtime using the `CREATE_COMP_USAGE_OF_SAME_TYPE()` method of the `IF_WD_COMPONENT_USAGE` interface.

▸ We can define *component usage groups*, which manage component usages via a separate API.

In the upcoming sections, we'll take a look at both of these approaches in turn.

Cloning Component Usages

More often than not, we probably know which WDA component we want to utilize at design time. The problem is that we don't know how many instances of it will be needed at runtime. In these situations, we can define a *template* component usage and then clone it as many times as we need to at runtime. To demonstrate how this works, let's take a look at an example using the `WDR_TEST_DYNAMIC` component provided by SAP. As you can see in Figure 11.6, this component has defined a template component usage called USAGE1. We can access this usage at runtime using the generated WD_CPUSE_<usage name>() method of the controller that defines the usage (e.g., the WD_CPUSE_USAGE1() method). This method will return an object reference that implements the IF_WD_COMPONENT_USAGE interface.

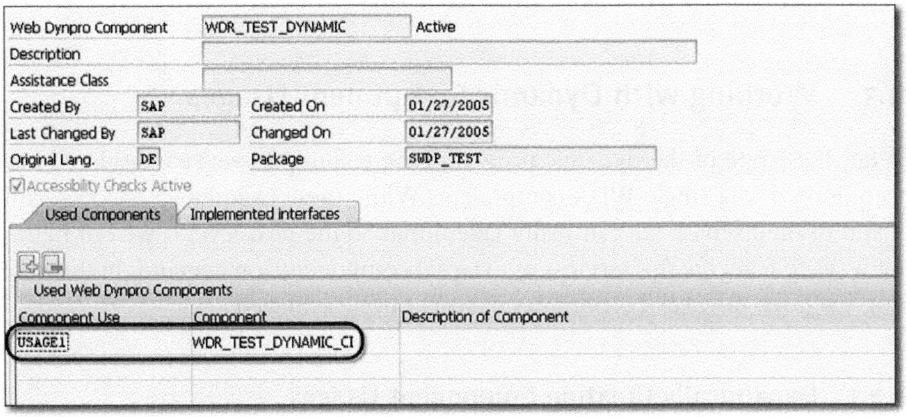

Figure 11.6 Defining a Template Component Usage for Cloning Purposes

Once we have the component usage reference in hand, we can use the CREATE_COMP_USAGE_OF_SAME_TYPE() method of the IF_WD_COMPONENT_USAGE interface to basically clone the component usage. This is demonstrated in Listing 11.7.

```
method SOME_CONTROLLER_METHOD.
  DATA lo_template_usage TYPE REF TO if_wd_component_usage.
  DATA lo_cloned_usage TYPE REF TO if_wd_component_usage.

  lo_template_usage = wd_this->wd_cpuse_usage1( ).
  lo_cloned_usage =
    lo_template_usage->create_comp_usage_of_same_type(
      'MY_USAGE' ).
  ...
endmethod.
```

Listing 11.7 Cloning a Component Usage at Runtime

> **Note**
>
> When dynamic component usages of this type are created, it's a good idea to store them somewhere in a global controller (e.g., a context node or controller attribute) so you can keep track of them within the application session. SAP provides the WDAPI_COMPONENT_USAGE structure type for this purpose.

Working with Component Usage Groups

Another alternative for dynamically creating component usages is to utilize *component usage groups*. Component usage groups are based on the IF_WD_COMPONENT_USAGE_GROUP interface and offer quite a bit more flexibility than the cloning approach described in the previous section since they don't lock us into having to specify a template component at design time.

Listing 11.8 demonstrates how component usage groups are created. In this example, we're using the WDDOINIT() method of the component controller to create a usage group called SELOPT_USAGE_GRP and store its reference in a controller attribute. For the purposes of this example, we've arbitrarily chosen the WDR_SELECT_OPTIONS component as the type of component contained within the usage group. Another option would have been to use a variable to dynamically specify the name of the WDA component we want to use to define this group.

```
method WDDOINIT.
  "Method-Local Data Declarations:
  DATA lo_comp_api TYPE REF TO if_wd_component.

  "Initialize the component usage group:
  lo_comp_api = wd_this->wd_get_api( ).

  IF lo_comp_api->has_cmp_usage_group( 'SELOPT_USAGE_GRP' )
    EQ abap_false.
    wd_this->selopt_comp_usages =
      lo_comp_api->create_cmp_usage_group(
        name          = 'SELOPT_USAGE_GRP'
        used_component = 'WDR_SELECT_OPTIONS' ).
  ENDIF.
endmethod.
```

Listing 11.8 Defining Component Usage Groups

Once a component usage group is established, we can use it to create a component usage using the ADD_COMPONENT_USAGE() method of the IF_WD_COMPONENT_USAGE_GROUP interface. As you can see in Listing 11.9, the ADD_COMPONENT_USAGE() method returns an object reference of type IF_WD_COMPONENT_USAGE. Once this reference is obtained, we can use it to utilize the component usage as usual. However, as opposed the cloning approach above, we don't have to keep track of the component usage for the long term. Instead, we can let the component usage group keep track of it and retrieve it on demand using the GET_COMPONENT_USAGE() method of the IF_WD_COMPONENT_USAGE_GROUP interface.

```
method ADD_COMPONENT_USAGE.
  DATA lo_comp_usage TYPE REF TO if_wd_component_usage.

  lo_comp_usage =
    wd_this->selopt_comp_usages->add_component_usage(
      name = 'USAGE_1' ).
endmethod.
```

Listing 11.9 Adding a Component Usage to a Component Usage Group

11.3.2 Dynamically Embedding Interface Views

As we learned in Chapter 9, an interface view from a used component can only be embedded within a using component one time per component usage. So, in other words, if we want to embed the interface view of a used component multiple times, we must define a separate component usage for each occurrence to do so. While this limitation usually doesn't present a problem for most typical cross-component design scenarios, there are times when it would be nice to be able to embed an arbitrary number of instances of an interface view into the view layout. Fortunately, we can get around this limitation by dynamically creating component usages and embedding the interface views from there. This is achieved by dynamically including the interface view of the used component into the navigation structure of a window in the using component.

Interface views of used components are integrated into the navigation structure of a window via dynamically generated navigation links. These links must be created within a method of the view controller that embeds the target interface view. The steps required to create these dynamic navigation links are as follows:

1. First, we need to determine the positioning of the interface view within the using component. Here, we have two options to choose from:

   ▷ We can embed the interface view directly within a window of the used component, as illustrated in Figure 11.7.

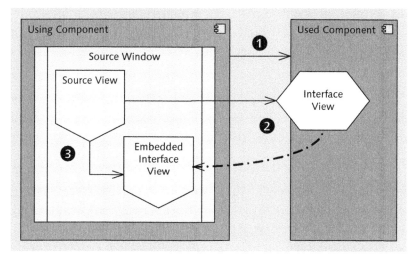

Figure 11.7 Determining the Embedding Position of Interface Views (Part 1)

   ▷ Or, we can nest the interface view within a view of the using component using the `ViewContainerUIElement` element type, as illustrated in Figure 11.8.

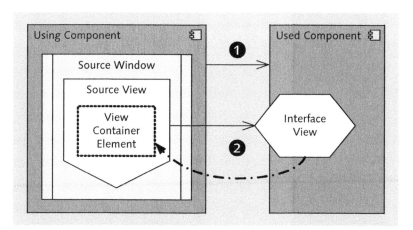

Figure 11.8 Determining the Embedding Position of Interface Views (Part 2)

2. Then, once we figure out where the interface view is going to go, we can use the PREPARE_DYNAMIC_NAVIGATION() method of the IF_WD_VIEW_CONTROLLER interface to implant the interface view at the selected position. Normally, this method is called within an event handler method of the source view. However, the method can be invoked elsewhere, provided that the call occurs before the WDDOBEFORENAVIGATION() method of the phase model completes.

3. Finally, the embedding process is completed by firing the dynamically generated navigation link established in the call to the PREPARE_DYNAMIC_NAVIGATION() method.

Listing 11.10 demonstrates how this process flow is implemented within a view controller method called ONACTIONEMBED_VIEW(). Looking at the code, you'll observe that we didn't dynamically create a component usage beforehand in order for the linkage to work. Instead, we chose to let the PREPARE_DYNAMIC_ NAVIGATION() method of the IF_WD_VIEW_CONTROLLER interface create the requisite component usage on our behalf. Then, after the call to PREPARE_DYNAMIC_ NAVIGATION(), we're triggering the dynamically created navigation link by firing the outbound plug of the source view (e.g., OP_TO_INTVIEW).

> **Note**
>
> This method is provided in the V_MAIN view of the ZWDC_DYNAMIC_COMP component provided with this book's source code bundle.

```
method ONACTIONEMBED_VIEW.
  "Method-Local Data Declarations:
  DATA lo_view_ctrl_api TYPE REF TO if_wd_view_controller.
  DATA lo_comp_usage TYPE REF TO if_wd_component_usage.

  "Obtain a reference to the view controller API:
  lo_view_ctrl_api = wd_this->wd_get_api( ).

  "Set up the dynamic navigation to the target interface view:
  lo_comp_usage =
    lo_view_ctrl_api->prepare_dynamic_navigation(
      source_window_name       = 'W_MAIN'
      source_vusage_name       = 'V_MAIN_USAGE_0'
      source_plug_name         = 'OP_TO_INTVIEW'
      target_component_name    = 'WDR_TEST_DYNAMIC_1'
      target_component_usage   = 'FLIGHT_RPT_USAGE'
```

```
    target_view_name          = 'WO'
    target_plug_name          = 'DEFAULT'
    target_embedding_position = '' ).

  "Fire an outbound plug to dynamically embed the
  "interface view:
  wd_this->fire_op_to_intview_plg( ).
endmethod.
```

Listing 11.10 Dynamically Embedding an Interface View

Perhaps the biggest challenge with dynamically embedding interface views is figuring out how to specify all the parameters defined within the PREPARE_DYNAMIC_ NAVIGATION() method. Table 11.3 describes the purpose of each of these parameters so you have a clearer sense of what goes where.

Parameter Name	Description
SOURCE_WINDOW_NAME	This parameter contains the name of the source window that will embed the interface view.
SOURCE_VUSAGE_NAME	This parameter refers to the *source view usage name* for the source view that's triggering the navigation. This value can be located in the window structure of the source window using the VIEW USE property, as shown in Figure 11.9.
SOURCE_PLUG_NAME	This parameter contains the name of the outbound plug in the source view that will trigger the dynamic navigation.
TARGET_COMPONENT_NAME	This parameter refers to the name of the component being leveraged.
TARGET_COMPONENT_USAGE	This parameter specifies the name of the component usage for the target component. Note that if the component usage doesn't already exist, a new one will be created automatically via this method.
TARGET_VIEW_NAME	This parameter refers to the name of the interface view being embedded from the used component.

Table 11.3 Parameters of the PREPARE_DYNAMIC_NAVIGATION() Method

Parameter Name	Description
TARGET_PLUG_NAME	This parameter refers to an inbound plug that's part of the component interface for the selected interface view.
TARGET_EMBEDDING_POSITION	This parameter allows us to specify the embedding position for the target interface view. Note that if we leave this parameter blank, the interface view will be embedded directly within the source window (see Figure 11.7). If we wish to place the target interface view inside a ViewContainerUIElement element, we must provide the path to the target element. See the method documentation for the IF_WD_NAVIGATION_SERVICES interface in the Class Builder tool for more information about the syntax required to achieve this.

Table 11.3 Parameters of the PREPARE_DYNAMIC_NAVIGATION( ) Method (Cont.)

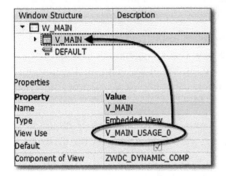

Figure 11.9 Determining the Source View Usage Name

11.3.3 Calling Methods of the Interface Controller

Once a dynamic component usage is established, it's a relatively simple matter to access methods of a used component's interface controller. As you can see in Listing 11.11, all we really have to do is call the GET_INTERFACE_CONTROLLER( ) method of the IF_WD_COMPONENT_USAGE interface, and it will take care of providing us with an interface controller object reference. From here, we can begin calling methods of the controller interface as usual.

```
method SOME_CONTROLLER_METHOD.
  "Method-Local Data Declarations:
  DATA lo_iface_ctrl TYPE REF TO ziwci_wdi_user_rpt.
  DATA lo_comp_usage TYPE REF TO if_wd_component_usage.

  "Create a component usage as described in Section 11.3.1:
  lo_comp_usage = ...

  "Obtain a reference to the leveraged component's interface
  "controller:
  lo_iface_ctrl ?= lo_comp_usage->get_interface_controller( ).

  "Call the controller methods as per usual:
  lo_iface_ctrl->search_users( ).
endmethod.
```

Listing 11.11 Calling Methods of the Interface Controller

11.3.4 Registering Event Handler Methods

To listen to events raised by dynamically created components, we must enlist the services of the ADD_EVENT_HANDLER() method provided with the IF_WD_COMPONENT_USAGE interface. The sample controller method in Listing 11.12 demonstrates how this works. As you can see, the method call is straightforward, linking an event from the used component's interface controller with a handler method provided from the using component. At runtime, the Web Dynpro framework will take care of routing the event to the event handler method as needed.

```
method SOME_CONTROLLER_METHOD.
  "Method-Local Data Declarations:
  DATA lo_comp_api   TYPE REF TO if_wd_component.
  DATA lo_comp_usage TYPE REF TO if_wd_component_usage.

  "Create a component usage as described in Section 11.3.1:
  lo_comp_usage = ...

  "Obtain a reference to the Web Dynpro component API:
  lo_comp_api = wd_comp_controller->wd_get_api( ).

  "Register an event handler method to listen for an event
```

```
  "triggered by the used component:
  lo_comp_usage->add_event_handler(
    listener        = lo_comp_api
    handler_name    = 'SOME_HANDLER_METHOD'
    controller_name = 'INTERFACECONTROLLER'
    event_name      = 'SOME_EVENT' ).
endmethod.
```

Listing 11.12 Dynamically Registering Event Handler Methods

11.3.5 Programming against Component Interfaces

In Chapter 9, we learned how Web Dynpro component interfaces could be used to define the interface of a WDA component independently from its implementation. To some extent, it's appropriate to think of these Web Dynpro component interfaces as being like a template or contract in that they specify the data and services that will be provided by implementing components. Looking at this relationship from the perspective of the implementing WDA component, we can say that the component *inherits* these characteristics from the component interface. If you're familiar with object-oriented programming (OOP) concepts, you may see where we're going with this: Web Dynpro component interfaces allow us to create inheritance hierarchies with WDA components.

Conceptually speaking, this sort of inheritance gives rise to a family of WDA components that can be used interchangeably. Of course, in order for this to work, clients must be able to program against the Web Dynpro component interface rather than a specific WDA component implementation. Here, the primary challenge lies in the fact that we cannot instantiate component interfaces (since they have no implementation of their own). Fortunately, we can get around this limitation by using dynamically created component usages to substitute concrete WDA component implementations at runtime.

To understand how this works, let's take a look at an example provided with the WDR_TEST_DYNAMIC sample component provided by SAP. This component provides a user interface that allows users to embed the interface view of a family of WDA components into a TabStrip element, as demonstrated in Figure 11.10. Here, the only prerequisite is that the embedded components implement the WDR_TEST_DYNAMIC_CI component interface.

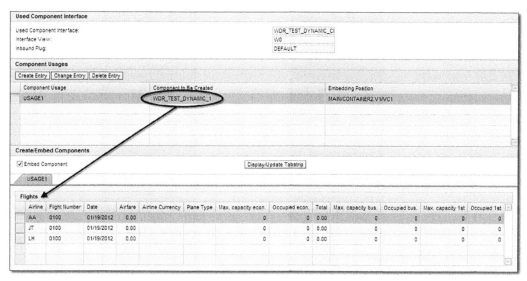

Figure 11.10 UI for the WDR_TEST_DYNAMIC Component

Figure 11.11 shows how the WDR_TEST_DYNAMIC component has defined a template component usage against the WDR_TEST_DYNAMIC_CI component interface. Since it's not possible to directly instantiate an abstract component interface, the WDR_TEST_DYNAMIC component relies on the *late binding* mechanism of the Web Dynpro runtime environment to substitute concrete WDA components at runtime. With late binding, the connection between the component usage reference and the target component is established based on the target component's *type*. This sleight of hand is made possible by the target component's providing all the same features as the selected component interface (e.g., methods, context nodes, interface views, and so on). From the perspective of the runtime environment, the target component fits the profile of the component interface, so it implicitly casts the component reference behind the scenes.

If we trace through the logic of the WDR_TEST_DYNAMIC component, we can see that the dynamic component references are established in three stages. The first step is carried out in the WDDOINIT() method of the component controller, as illustrated in the code excerpt in Listing 11.13. Here, an object reference of type IF_WD_COMPONENT_USAGE is generated from the USAGE1 template usage depicted in Figure 11.11.

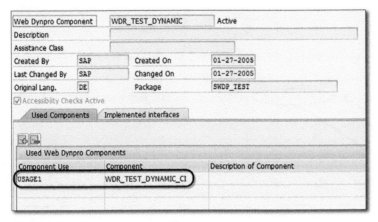

Figure 11.11 Defining a Component Usage against a Component Interface

```
method WDDONIT.
  ...
  wd_this->usage1 = wd_this->wd_cpuse_usage1( ).
  ...
endmethod.
```

Listing 11.13 Polymorphic WDA Component References (Part 1)

Then, as users propose new component usages via the UI, the ADD_COMPONENT_USAGE() method of the component controller is called to dynamically create a new component usage (see Listing 11.14).

```
method add_component_usage.
  ...
  l_cmp_usage-component_usage =
    wd_this->usage1->create_comp_usage_of_same_type(
      l_cmp_usage-component_usage_name ).
endmethod.
```

Listing 11.14 Polymorphic WDA Component References (Part 2)

Finally, whenever users choose to display the selected components in the Tab-Strip control, the ONACTIONSHOW_TABSTRIP() method shown in Listing 11.15 is invoked. The dynamic type substitution occurs during the call to the PREPARE_DYNAMIC_NAVIGATION() method. Here, the name of the implementing component is proposed via the TARGET_COMPONENT_NAME parameter. As long as the selected component implements the WDR_TEST_DYNAMIC_CI component interface, the component usage will be dynamically established within this method call. From here, we can instantiate the used component and leverage its services as usual.

```
method onactionshow_tabstrip.
  ...
  try.
    wa_cmp_usage-component_usage =
      l_view_controller_api->prepare_dynamic_navigation(
        source_window_name = 'W0'
        source_vusage_name = 'MAIN_USAGE_1'
        source_plug_name   = 'TO_V1'
        target_component_name =
          wa_cmp_usage-used_component
        target_component_usage =
          wa_cmp_usage-component_usage_name
        target_view_name =
          l_usage_group-interface_view
        target_plug_name =
          l_usage_group-inbound_plug
        target_embedding_position =
          wa_cmp_usage-embedding_position ).
  catch cx_wd_runtime_repository.
    raise exception type cx_wdr_rt_exception.
  endtry.

  if wa_cmp_usage-component_usage->has_active_component( )
     is not initial.
    wa_cmp_usage-component_usage->delete_component( ).
  endif.
  wa_cmp_usage-component_usage->create_component(
    wa_cmp_usage-used_component ).
  ...
endmethod.
```

Listing 11.15 Polymorphic WDA Component References (Part 3)

If you're familiar with OOP concepts, you know that the functionality described within this section can be summed up in a single word: *polymorphism*. Polymorphism is one of the main pillars of OOP, building on top of inheritance trees to introduce a form of "plug and play" to software designs. This feature opens the doors to all sorts of interesting possibilities. For example, when developing internationalized applications, we can use component interfaces to define core behavior and then plug in country-specific solutions at runtime. When you think about it, the possibilities are endless.

11.4 Case Study: Creating a Data Browser Tool

Before we wrap things up, we thought it would be a worthwhile exercise to look into the creation of a full-scale application built on dynamic programming techniques: a data browser tool similar to the Data Browser transaction included with the ABAP Dictionary (Transaction SE16). The peculiarities of this application require that we utilize all the dynamic programming techniques we've learned throughout the course of this chapter. Therefore, it provides an excellent point of reference for reviewing how these techniques fit together in real-world application scenarios.

11.4.1 Requirements Overview

From a functional perspective, we chose to implement our data browser application using a road map–based approach. Here, the step flow is as follows:

1. First, the user must select a table from the ABAP Dictionary in the TABLE NAME input field, as shown in Figure 11.12.

Figure 11.12 Road Map for Browsing Table Contents (Part 1)

2. Then, based on the table selected in step 1, users will be taken to a selection screen that will allow them to specify selection criteria for browsing the selected table. As you can see in Figure 11.13, the selection fields are rendered as selection options using the WDR_SELECT_OPTIONS component introduced in Chapter 10.

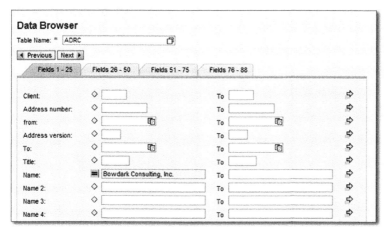

Figure 11.13 Road Map for Browsing Table Contents (Part 2)

3. Finally, the selection results are displayed in a `Table` element, as shown in Figure 11.14. Had we been more ambitious, we could have displayed the result set using an ALV table, but we'll leave this as a reader exercise.

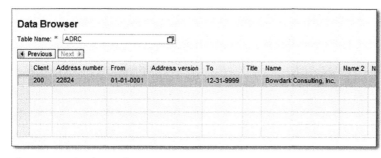

Figure 11.14 Road Map for Browsing Table Contents (Part 3)

Looking over the application requirements outlined above, we can see that this application presents several unique challenges:

- First of all, since the layout of the selection screen view is 100% dependent upon the table selected in step 1, we must construct the view layout dynamically. Here, we must use the selected table metadata to derive the selection fields on the screen.

- Secondly, since the selection screen is dynamic, we can't model the selection criteria input using a statically defined context node. Instead, we must create a context node on the fly using the RTTI and context APIs. Then, when we want to perform the actual database query, we must extract the data from this dynamically generated node and build a dynamic WHERE clause for the Open SQL SELECT statement.

► Finally, in order to display the query results, we must come up with a way to dynamically create a Table element and display it on screen.

In the upcoming sections, we'll see how these requirements were met within the ZWDC_DATA_BROWSER sample component provided within this book's source code bundle.

11.4.2 Generating a Selection Screen Using Selection Options

The generation of the selection screen for the data browser application was split into two separate steps:

► First, we generated the requisite component usages to the WDR_SELECT_OPTIONS component used to render all the selection fields. This task was carried out in the GENERATE_SEL_SCREEN() method of the V_MAIN view controller.

► Then, in the WDDOMODIFYVIEW() method of the V_QUERY view, we embedded the selection options within a TabStrip control as shown in Figure 11.13.

For brevity's sake, we won't include the entire code listing for the GENERATE_SEL_SCREEN() method here within the text because it's too complex. However, the following process narrative touches on the high points:

1. **Lines 22-39**
   The first step is to clean up any existing component references utilized in a previous query. To simplify matters, we're storing the WDR_SELECT_OPTIONS component references in a component usage group called MO_SELOPT_COMP_USAGES (which is initialized within the WDDOINIT() method of the component controller). The cleanup process requires that we:

   ▹ Remove the generated components from the navigation structure of the source window using the REMOVE_DYNAMIC_META_DATA() method of the IF_WD_VIEW_CONTROLLER interface.

   ▹ Remove the component usages themselves using the REMOVE_ALL_CMP_USAGES() method of the IF_WD_COMPONENT_USAGE_GROUP interface.

2. **Line 42**

    Next, we call a helper method called GET_TABLE_FIELDS() to look up the table metadata for the selected table. This information is obtained via the RTTI class CL_ABAP_STRUCTDESCR.

3. **Line 44-116**

    Finally, within this section of the code, we implement a loop to create selection options for each of the table fields derived in step 2. Here, we're grouping the selection fields into groups of twenty-five fields in order to reduce the amount of vertical scrolling required for tables with many fields. This logic yields a separate WDR_SELECT_OPTIONS component usage for group. The individual selection fields within this group are added to the view layout of the WDR_SELECT_OPTIONS component using the ADD_SELECTION_FIELD() method provided via the used component's interface controller.

    In order to create the component usages, we're using the ADD_COMPONENT_USAGE() method of the IF_WD_COMPONENT_USAGE_GROUP interface, as demonstrated in Section 11.3.1.

    After each selection field group is created, we call a helper method called ADD_SELECT_OPTION() to add the newly created selection option to the navigation structure. This step puts us in a position to add the selection options to the custom TabStrip control when we go to render the V_QUERY view. Here, notice at line sixty-nine how we're defining embedding position for the selection options: V_MAIN/VCUI_CONTENT_AREA.V_QUERY/VCUI_# (where the # token refers to a sequential number representing the index of the current component usage). We'll see how this nomenclature is used to dynamically generate the V_QUERY view layout in just a moment.

After the selection options components are created and initialized, the process of adding them to the screen is relatively straightforward. Listing 11.16 contains an excerpt of the WDDOMODIFYVIEW() method for the V_QUERY view. Here, we're creating a separate Tab element for each WDR_SELECT_OPTIONS component usage. Within each Tab element, UI elements are organized as follows:

▶ We define the Tab element's label by dynamically creating a Caption element using the CL_WD_CAPTION runtime class.

▶ The selection option itself will be embedded within a ViewContainerUIElement element. Here, notice how the ID property of the ViewContainerUIElement

element is being defined in reference to the embedding position defined previously. This linkage is all that's required to cause the selection options to be embedded within the view layout.

▶ After the `ViewContainerUIElement` element is created, we're assigning its layout property using the `CL_WD_MATRIX_HEAD_DATA` runtime class.

```
method WDDOMODIFYVIEW.
  ..
  "Obtain a reference to the root UI element container:
  lo_tabstrip ?= view->get_element( 'TS_QUERY_FLDGROUPS' ).
  lo_tabstrip->remove_all_tabs( ).
  ...
  LOOP AT lt_selopt_comp_usages
    ASSIGNING <lfs_selopt_comp_usage>.
    ...
    "Determine where to attach the selection option:
    SPLIT <lfs_selopt_comp_usage>-embedding_position AT '.'
     INTO TABLE lt_embedding_pos_tokens.
    lv_token_count = lines( lt_embedding_pos_tokens ).
    READ TABLE lt_embedding_pos_tokens INDEX lv_token_count
     ASSIGNING <lfs_embedding_pos_token>.
    SPLIT <lfs_embedding_pos_token> AT '/'
     INTO lv_view_name lv_container_name.

    CONCATENATE 'TAB_'
             <lfs_selopt_comp_usage>-component_usage_name
        INTO lv_element_id.
    lo_tab =
      cl_wd_tab=>new_tab( id = lv_element_id view = view ).
    CONCATENATE 'Fields' lv_from_index_str '-' lv_to_index_str
        INTO lv_label_text
      SEPARATED BY space.

    CONCATENATE 'CAP_'
             <lfs_selopt_comp_usage>-component_usage_name
        INTO lv_element_id.
    lo_caption =
      cl_wd_caption=>new_caption( id = lv_element_id
                                  view = view
                                  text = lv_label_text ).
    lo_tab->set_header( lo_caption ).
```

```
      lo_selopt_container =
        cl_wd_view_container_uielement=>
          new_view_container_uielement(
            id = lv_container_name
            view = view ).

      lo_matrix_data =
        cl_wd_matrix_head_data=>new_matrix_head_data(
          element = lo_selopt_container
          width = '100%' ).

      lo_tab->set_content( lo_selopt_container ).
      lo_tabstrip->add_tab( lo_tab ).
      ...
    ENDLOOP.
  endmethod.
```

Listing 11.16 Dynamically Rendering the V_QUERY View

11.4.3 Dynamic Context Manipulation

After users enter their selection criteria on the V_QUERY view, they can execute the query by clicking the Next button (see Figure 11.13). At this point in the process, we have to extract the selection criteria from the selection options and use them build our dynamic SELECT statement. Given the complexity of this task, it makes sense to store the selection criteria within an intermediate data structure. Though we could have potentially used a controller attribute for this, there are certain efficiencies to be gained by using a context node to store the data. And, if nothing else, it provides us with an opportunity to review dynamic context manipulation.

Figure 11.15 shows the statically defined context node that will serve as the basis for storing the selection criteria. At runtime, we'll modify this node to define subnodes to capture the selection criteria entered within the individual selection fields. Figure 11.16 provides a rendering of what the dynamic node structure will look like.

The logic required to build the QUERY_PARAMETERS node hierarchy depicted in Figure 11.16 is encapsulated within an instance method in the component controller called COPY_SELECTION_CRITERIA(). Listing 11.17 provides an excerpt of this method, highlighting the key points related to dynamic context manipulation. As you can see, the steps carried out here are as follows:

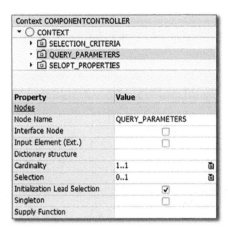

Figure 11.15 Baseline Configuration of the QUERY_PARAMETERS Node

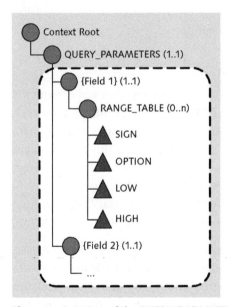

Figure 11.16 A View of the QUERY_PARAMETERS Node at Runtime

1. The first step, though not depicted in Listing 11.17 for brevity's sake, is to remove any pre-existing child nodes underneath the QUERY_PARAMETERS node. This is achieved by obtaining a reference to the QUERY_PARAMETERS node's metadata and invoking the REMOVE_CHILD_NODE() method provided with the IF_WD_CONTEXT_NODE_INFO interface.

2. Then, we loop through the provided component usages/selection option references to process each of the field groups.

3. For each `WDR_SELECT_OPTIONS` component reference, we obtain a reference to the interface controller and use the companion helper class to obtain a listing of selection screen items using its `GET_SELECTION_SCREEN_ITEMS()` method.

4. For each selection screen item/field, we copy the selection criteria by performing the following steps:

   ▷ First, we obtain a reference to the selection item's range table. If it is empty (i.e., the user didn't enter any selection criteria in that field), we move on.

   ▷ Otherwise, we create a new child node underneath the `QUERY_PARAMETERS` node to store the selection criteria. This node is created by calling the `ADD_NEW_CHILD_NODE()` method of the `IF_WD_CONTEXT_NODE_INFO` interface as described in Section 11.1.2. Here, the node's name matches the field name.

   ▷ Underneath the newly created child node, we need to attach the selection item's range table. For this task, we're using the RTTI API to introspect the range table's metadata so the newly created `RANGE_TABLE` node is type compatible. This metadata is passed as a parameter to the call to `ADD_NEW_CHILD_NODE()`.

   ▷ Finally, once the dynamic context manipulation is complete, we use the context APIs as usual to copy the data and move on to the next field.

```
method COPY_SELECTION_CRITERIA.
  ...
  "Loop through the select options to see if the users
  "provided any input. If so, add it to the QUERY_PARAMETERS
  "node dynamically:
  lt_selopt_comp_usages =
    wd_this->mo_selopt_comp_usages->get_component_usages( ).
  LOOP AT lt_selopt_comp_usages
    ASSIGNING <lfs_selopt_comp_usage>.
    "Read the user selection option input:
    lo_selopt_ctrl ?=
      <lfs_selopt_comp_usage>-component_usage->
        get_interface_controller( ).
    lo_selopt_helper =
      lo_selopt_ctrl->init_selection_screen( ).
    lo_selopt_helper->get_selection_screen_items(
      IMPORTING et_selection_screen_items = lt_selopt_items ).
```

```abap
"Loop through each of the select options in turn:
LOOP AT lt_selopt_items ASSIGNING <lfs_selopt_item>.
  "De-reference the select option range table:
  ASSIGN <lfs_selopt_item>-mt_range_table->*
      TO <lfs_range_tab>.
  "If the range table is empty, move on:
  IF lines( <lfs_range_tab> ) EQ 0.
    CONTINUE.
  ENDIF.

  "Create a new query parameter for the selection field:
  lo_nd_query_parameter_info =
    lo_nd_query_parameters_info->add_new_child_node(
      name        = <lfs_selopt_item>-m_id
      is_mandatory = abap_true
      is_static   = abap_false ).

  "Derive the RTTI metadata for the select option line:
  lo_range_tab_meta ?=
    cl_abap_tabledescr=>describe_by_data_ref(
      <lfs_selopt_item>-mt_range_table ).
  lo_range_tab_line_meta ?=
    lo_range_tab_meta->get_table_line_type( ).

  "Create a RANGE_TABLE child node based upon the select
  "option metadata:
  lo_nd_query_parameter_info->add_new_child_node(
    name = 'RANGE_TABLE'
    is_mandatory        = abap_true
    static_element_rtti = lo_range_tab_line_meta
    is_static           = abap_false ).

  lo_nd_query_parameter =
    lo_nd_query_parameters->get_child_node(
      <lfs_selopt_item>-m_id ).
  lo_nd_query_parameter_range =
    lo_nd_query_parameter->get_child_node(
      'RANGE_TABLE' ).
  lo_nd_query_parameter_range->bind_table(
    <lfs_range_tab> ).
ENDLOOP.
```

```
  ENDLOOP.
endmethod.
```

Listing 11.17 Implementation of Method COPY_SELECTION_CRITERIA( )

After all the selection data is copied into context, we use it to build the dynamic SELECT statement in a component controller instance method called BUILD_ DYNAMIC_QUERY(). Since this is plain ABAP programming as usual, we won't review the implementation of this method here.

11.4.4 Generating the Results Screen

After the user's selection criterion is captured, the last step in the process is to perform the SQL query and display the result set on screen. The query is triggered within the HANDLEDEFAULT() inbound plug event handler method of the V_ RESULTS view controller, as shown in Listing 11.18. As you can see, the results of the query are stored in a dynamically generated context node called QUERY_ RESULTS.

```
method HANDLEDEFAULT.
  ...
  "Retrieve the name of the table we're querying from the
  "context:
  lo_nd_selection_criteria =
    wd_context->get_child_node(
      name = wd_this->wdctx_selection_criteria ).
  lo_el_selection_criteria =
    lo_nd_selection_criteria->get_element( ).

  lo_el_selection_criteria->get_attribute(
    EXPORTING
      name =  `TABLE_NAME`
    IMPORTING
      value = lv_table_name ).

  "Build an internal table to store its contents:
  lo_table_line ?=
    cl_abap_structdescr=>describe_by_name( lv_table_name ).
  lo_table_type =
    cl_abap_tabledescr=>create( p_line_type = lo_table_line ).
  CREATE DATA lr_query_results TYPE HANDLE lo_table_type.
```

```
ASSIGN lr_query_results->* TO <lfs_query_results>.

"Perform the query:
wd_comp_controller->get_query_results(
  IMPORTING et_query_results = <lfs_query_results> ).

"Copy the results into context:
lo_nd_root_info = wd_context->get_node_info( ).
lt_root_child_nodes = lo_nd_root_info->get_child_nodes( ).

LOOP AT lt_root_child_nodes ASSIGNING <lfs_root_child_node>
  WHERE name EQ 'QUERY_RESULTS'.
  lo_nd_root_info->remove_child_node( 'QUERY_RESULTS' ).
  EXIT.
ENDLOOP.

CALL METHOD lo_nd_root_info->add_new_child_node
  EXPORTING
    name                = 'QUERY_RESULTS'
    static_element_rtti = lo_table_line
    is_static           = abap_false
  RECEIVING
    child_node_info     = lo_nd_query_results_info.

lo_nd_query_results =
  wd_context->get_child_node( name = 'QUERY_RESULTS' ).
lo_nd_query_results->bind_table( <lfs_query_results> ).
endmethod.
```

Listing 11.18 Performing the Dynamic SQL Query (Part 1)

Listing 11.19 contains an excerpt of the GET_QUERY_RESULTS( ) instance method used to perform the actual query. This method returns a generic table reference that gets copied into the QUERY_RESULTS node, as illustrated in Listing 11.18.

```
method GET_QUERY_RESULTS.
  ...
  "Retrieve the name of the table we're querying from the
  "context:
  lo_nd_selection_criteria =
    wd_context->get_child_node(
      name = wd_this->wdctx_selection_criteria ).
```

```
lo_el_selection_criteria =
  lo_nd_selection_criteria->get_element( ).

lo_el_selection_criteria->get_attribute(
  EXPORTING
    name =  `TABLE_NAME`
  IMPORTING
    value = lv_table_name ).

"Build an internal table using the table's metadata:
lo_table_line ?=
  cl_abap_structdescr=>describe_by_name( lv_table_name ).
lo_table_type =
  cl_abap_tabledescr=>create( p_line_type = lo_table_line ).

CREATE DATA lr_query_results TYPE HANDLE lo_table_type.
ASSIGN lr_query_results->* TO <lfs_query_results>.

"Perform the dynamic query:
SELECT *
  INTO TABLE <lfs_query_results>
  FROM (lv_table_name)
  WHERE (wd_this->mt_where_clause).

et_query_results = <lfs_query_results>.
endmethod.
```

Listing 11.19 Performing the Dynamic SQL Query (Part 2)

Despite what you might expect, the chore of rendering the query result set within the V_RESULTS view was perhaps the simplest part of this entire process. This simplicity was due in no small part to a powerful helper method provided with the CL_WD_DYNAMIC_TOOL class: CREATE_TABLE_FROM_NODE(). As the name suggests, this method creates a Table element in reference to a context node. One of the beauties of this method is that it doesn't care where the context node came from; it just unpacks the context node and renders the Table element accordingly. Thus, as you can see in Listing 11.20, the implementation of the WDDOMODIFYVIEW() method for the V_RESULTS view is fairly minimalistic.

```
method WDDOMODIFYVIEW.
  "Method-Local Data Declarations:
```

```
DATA lo_ui_root TYPE REF TO cl_wd_uielement_container.
DATA lo_query_results_node TYPE REF TO if_wd_context_node.
DATA lo_table TYPE REF TO cl_wd_table.

"Obtain a reference to the root UI element container:
lo_ui_root ?= view->get_root_element( ).
lo_ui_root->remove_all_children( ).

"Retrieve the dynamically generated query results node:
lo_query_results_node =
  wd_context->get_child_node( 'QUERY_RESULTS' ).

"Create the Table element that will display the results:
lo_table = cl_wd_dynamic_tool=>create_table_from_node(
  ui_parent = lo_ui_root
  table_id  = 'TAB_QUERY_RESULTS'
  node      = lo_query_results_node ).
endmethod.
```

Listing 11.20 Displaying the Query Results in a Table Element

As we mentioned earlier, another option for rendering the query results would have been to enlist the services of the SALV_WD_TABLE component to display the results in an ALV table. In this scenario, we would have to work with dynamic component usages in order to copy over the result data and display the table on the screen.

11.5 Summary

In this chapter, we learned how to harness the power of the dynamic programming capabilities of the Web Dynpro framework. In particular, we learned how to manipulate the context at runtime, modify the view layout, and even leverage external component resources on the fly. Collectively, these techniques provide us with the flexibility to handle those oddball requirements that just don't quite fit within the confines of Web Dynpro's declarative programming model.

In this next chapter, we'll look at some other techniques for customizing and personalizing WDA applications. As we'll see, many of these techniques can be used to tweak the look and feel of a WDA component without requiring any custom coding.

Applications are often built to support multiple use cases, which they typically achieve by supporting configurable options in their design. In this chapter we'll explore WDA's configuration framework and demonstrate how to build the same kind of flexibility into your applications.

12 Configuration and Adaptation

Now that you've spent some time learning about the fundamentals of WDA development, it's time to learn about some of the finer features the framework has to offer. Specifically, we'll be taking a look some of the configuration options WDA possesses and how to incorporate them into your applications. Each of these options or features is designed to provide a foundation from which to enhance the well-roundedness of your applications and to give them flexibility in their development and deployment.

Web Dynpro's configuration and adaptation features come in two flavors, which are surprisingly not "configuration" and "adaptation"—at least not directly. On the one hand, you have a set of built-in features that are native to WDA as a whole. These features tend to focus on manipulating UI elements, whether by changing their visibility and layout or by defaulting the values that they may hold. Essentially, they give you a chance to change a view's content outside the confines of development. On the other hand, you have your component-defined configuration options, which are restricted to use in a specific component. These options are created explicitly by the developer for their WDA component and are used to govern its configurable functionality. Ultimately, they provide you with the means to generalize and abstract the behavior of your components for use over multiple business scenarios.

In this chapter, we'll examine the specifics of these configuration and adaptation features and the methodologies by which to employ them. We'll also take a look at how WDA integrates the concepts of internationalization, accessibility, and themes into its framework. Each of these concepts provides a slightly different dimension on configuration and adaptation, but they are equally designed to provide your applications flexibility in their employment.

12.1 The Adaptation Concept

When it comes to modifying existing applications, the WDA framework provides two major methodologies. The first of these methodologies is the process of *enhancement*, which allows you to make changes to an application's underlying development objects. We'll talk about enhancement at greater length in Chapter 13. The other of these methodologies is the process of *adaptation*, which encompasses all the ways to make configuration changes to an application that don't involve making any changes to code.

12.1.1 Adaptation Layers

The first thing that you have to understand about adaptation is that it isn't just an activity for developers. Adaptation may occur in the development cycle, during deployment, or even during an application's use by its end users. Consequently, the concept of adaptation is broken down into three activity layers, as depicted in Figure 12.1.

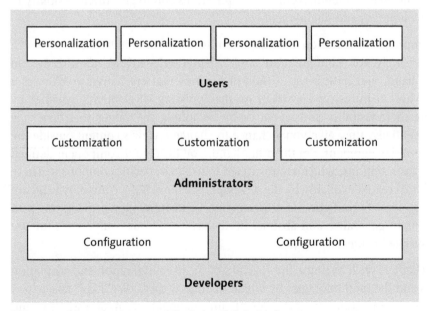

Figure 12.1 Adaptation Layers and the Roles of their Configurators

These layers are defined as follows:

- **Configuration**

  Configuration encompasses base-level settings made to components and applications by developers. For components, these settings are stored in a *component configuration* development object, whereas for applications, these settings are stored in an *application configuration*. Since both configuration products yield development objects, configuration tasks appropriately occur during application or component design and are thus considered modifications. Configuration objects may be transported via workbench requests.

- **Customization**

  Customization refers to client-wide settings made to a component by an application's administrator. Unlike with configuration, customization may only apply to component adaptations and are created after the design process, during the application's runtime. Customizations may be transported via customizing requests and are considered modification-free enhancements.

- **Personalization**

  Personalization is the topmost adaptation layer and has the smallest configuration footprint of all three layers, since it only pertains to configuration made by users for themselves on a user-by-user basis. Personalization settings may be enacted by all users who have access to a given application or view as long as the personalization is allowed.

> **Note**
>
> The terms *developers*, *administrators*, and *users* can take on different meanings in the context of a given organization. For the purposes of this discussion, developers are considered users who possess the S_DEVELOP authorization object, administrators are users who possess the S_WDR_P13N object for a given application, and *users* refers to lay users who possess neither authorization object.

12.1.2 Adaptation Multiplicity and Processing

As you may have inferred from Figure 12.1, components may have multiple configurations associated with them. In order to select and process the appropriate configuration, the following rules are adhered to when reading configuration data:

▶ If a configuration ID is specified when the component is generated (i.e., by means of the `SAP-WD-CONFIG URL` parameter), this configuration is used.

▶ If a component configuration is specified in an application configuration (by means of the `WDCONFIGURATIONID parameter), that configuration is read.`

▶ Otherwise, SAP forms and supplies a configuration ID behind the scenes, creating a hash value determined by the application name and the component usage.

These rules ensure that adaptation data is shared between components only if it is explicitly specified. The data is only shared if two component usages reference the same configuration ID.

12.2   Component Configuration with the Configuration Editor

In this section, we'll cover the basics of configuring and customizing WDA components in the *Configuration Editor*, which allows you to adjust both component-defined and built-in component properties. When you configure a component, you create a development object known as a *component configuration*. If you were to customize the same component, you would still create a component configuration, only it would be stored in your ABAP system's customization layer as opposed to within the development repository.

12.2.1   Accessing the Configuration Editor

In order to configure a component, you must work with the Configuration Editor, whose initial screen is shown in Figure 12.2.

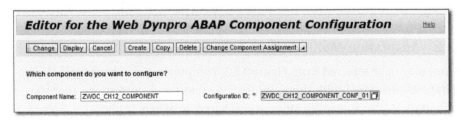

Figure 12.2 Initial View of the WDA Component Configuration Editor

You can access it in any of the following ways:

▶ In the Object Navigator (Transaction SE80), by opening the context menu of your component in the object browser and selecting CREATE/CHANGE CONFIGURATION.

▶ By launching Web Dynpro application CONFIGURE_COMPONENT directly. As with all WDA applications, you can do this by testing it from SE80, testing its service from SICF, or running it directly from the browser, in this case with the URI */sap/bc/webdynpro/sap/configure_component*.

▶ If you already have a component configuration to work with, you may browse and display it in the Web Dynpro Explorer and click the START CONFIGURATOR push button to launch the editor. It should reside in the COMPONENT CONFIGURATIONS folder of your Web Dynpro component.

However you decide to access the Configuration Editor, it will launch in a browser window as a WDA application. Once open, you may change, display, create, copy, or delete component configurations by selecting the appropriate option from its toolbar. Additionally, you may rename existing configurations, create enhancements to a component configuration (remember, configurations are development objects), or change a component configuration's component assignment.

12.2.2 Accessing the Customization Editor

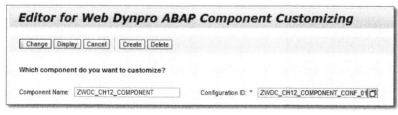

Figure 12.3 Initial View of the WDA Component Customization Editor

In order to customize a Web Dynpro component, you may call on the Customization Editor, whose initial screen is depicted in Figure 12.3. The Customization Editor is accessed by one of the following means:

► By opening the Configuration Editor and specifying URL parameter `ADMIN_MODE=X`.

► By launching Web Dynpro application `CUSTOMIZE_COMPONENT` directly. Like with the Configuration Editor, you may do this by testing it from SE80, testing its service from SICF, or running it directly from the browser (URI path */sap/bc/webdynpro/sap/customize_component*).

Like with the Configuration Editor, the Customization Editor is a WDA application itself and will launch in its own browser window. You have the options of changing, displaying, creating, and deleting component customizations from the editor.

Customizing vs. Configuring Components

When you configure a component in WDA, you generate a development object that contains that configuration. As a result, configuration is considered a modification task. If you were to customize the same component, you'd generate adaptation data stored in the customization layer as a delta change. Thus, customization is a modification-free enhancement process and will allow you to upgrade your system without the fear of overwriting your configuration objects. This distinction may have less impact when you're creating and configuring a component from scratch, but it has significant implications for when you adapt SAP or third-party components.

12.2.3 Creating a Component Configuration

Creating a component configuration is a rather simple process once you've accessed the Configuration Editor or Customization Editor:

1. From the editor's intial screen, enter the name of the component you wish to configure and an ID for your component configuration.

2. Click the CREATE button.

3. You will be prompted to supply a description for your configuration object (as well as specify a package). Click OK to continue.

4. You will be prompted to add your configuration to a development or customization request (if you did not create it as a local object). Enter the information the dialog requests and click the SAVE button.

5. The application will create and save your new component configuration and open it in change mode for editing.

> **Note**
>
> When specifying a component ID for your configurations or customizations, be aware that they should possess globally unique IDs to differentiate them from each other. Configurations and customizations, however, may share the same ID, establishing an enhancement relationship between the two objects. The customization will then base its content on that of the configuration.

12.2.4 Configuring Component-Defined Properties

Component-defined properties are unique to each component, and you may adapt them in the Configuration Editor by selecting the COMPONENT-DEFINED tab after displaying your adaptation object, as seen in Figure 12.4. Component-defined properties are based on context nodes that you specify in your component's *configuration controller*. Therefore, the actions you may take in configuring component-defined data are akin to manipulating data within a context structure (albeit by a graphical interface as opposed to in code).

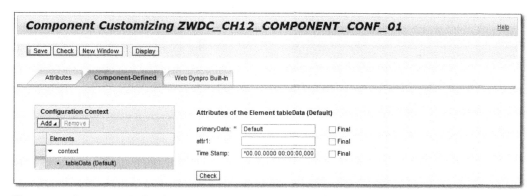

Figure 12.4 Component-Defined Properties in the Configuration Editor

In the Configuration Editor, you may perform any of the following activities with component-defined data:

- If an element in the CONFIGURATION CONTEXT can contain subelements (i.e., if it's a node), additional subelements may be added to it.
- If an element in the configuration context is part of a multiple node (a node with cardinality $0..n$ or $1..n$), you can change its position within the node via its context menu.
- Remove subelements from a node if its cardinality permits it.

- ▸ Set and check the uniqueness of the primary attribute value of a subelement.
- ▸ Adjust the attributes of a given data element or node.
- ▸ Mark attributes within data elements or nodes as final.

12.2.5 Configuring Built-In Properties

Web Dynpro's built-in adaptation properties are modeled on the UI element properties contained in your components' views. This adaptation feature allows you to manipulate these properties after your views have been designed and activated in the Web Dynpro Explorer. Please note that this activity is not a replacement for the view design process: you can't add or remove elements from a view, only manipulate existing elements or render them invisible.

You can adapt built-in properties in the Configuration Editor by selecting the WEB DYNPRO BUILT-IN tab and adjusting the settings therein. Figure 12.5 displays an example of built-in properties being viewed from the tab.

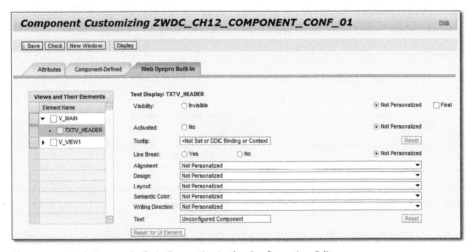

Figure 12.5 Web Dynpro Built-In Properties in the Configuration Editor

12.3 Application Configuration

Application configurations are designed to tie the components you use in an application (i.e., the main component and all of its used components) to the component configurations you've created. Table 12.1 illustrates this concept:

Application Component	Component Configuration
WDC_MAIN	WDC_MAIN_CONFIG
WDC_USED1	WDC_USED1_CONFIG
WDC_USED2	N/A
WDC_USED3	WDC_USED3_CONFIG

Table 12.1 An Example of an Application Configuration Tying Multiple Used Components to Their Component Configurations

> **Note**
>
> Some of the components used in your application may not have a component configuration associated with them. They will still appear in the Application Editor alongside your other components, but will be devoid of a component configuration entry.

12.3.1 Accessing the Application Configurator

Application configurations are created and maintained in the *application configurator*. Like the configuration and customization editors for components, this is a Web Dynpro application you may call in any of the following ways:

▶ In the Object Navigator (Transaction SE80), open the context menu of your WDA application in the object browser and select CREATE/CHANGE CONFIGURATION.

▶ Launch the Web Dynpro application CONFIGURE_APPLICATION directly. Like with the Configuration Editor, you can do this by testing it from SE80, testing its service from SICF, or running it directly from the browser (URI path */sap/bc/webdynpro/sap/configure_application*).

▶ If you already have an application configuration to work with, you may browse and display it in the Web Dynpro Explorer and click the START CONFIGURATOR push button to launch the editor. It should reside in the APPLIC. CONFIGURATIONS folder of your Web Dynpro application.

As with the component configuration editors, the Application Editor will launch in a new browser window when you call on it.

12.3.2 Creating an Application Configuration

Creating an application configuration is quite similar to the process of creating a component configuration:

1. From the editor's intial screen, enter the name of the application you wish to configure and an ID.

2. Click the CREATE button.

3. You will be prompted to supply a description for your application object (as well as specify a package). Click OK to continue.

4. You will be prompted to add your configuration to a workbench request (if you did not create it as a local object). Enter the information the dialog requests andclick the SAVE button.

5. The application will create and save your new application configuration and open it in change mode for editing.

> **Note**
>
> Unlike with components, application configurations may not be customized or personalized. These are TADIR objects, and you must have developer authorizations in order to create them.

12.3.3 Assigning Component Configurations

On the STRUCTURE tab of your application configuration, you may assign components to specific configurations by either entering in their configuration IDs or using the search help. Each component used in your application will display according to its usage inheritance in the ASSIGNMENT OF COMPONENT CONFIGURATIONS table, to which you may then make a component assignment.

12.3.4 Specifying Application Parameters

Application configurations may also define default parameters that should be called with your application. These settings are specified on the APPLICATION PARAMETERS tab in the editor. Application parameters take on two different variants: those native to WDA and custom parameters you define in your component's inbound startup plug. The editor will automatically pick up on any custom parameters you define and display them on the tab (Figure 12.6).

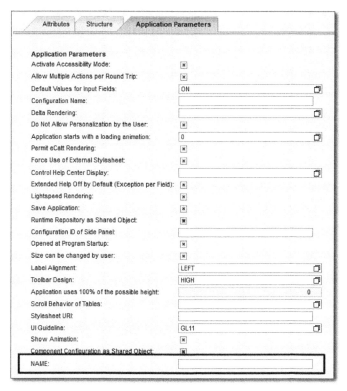

Figure 12.6 A Custom Parameter Displaying on the Application Parameters Tab

12.3.5 Assigning Application Configurations

Application configurations are assigned to applications by means of application parameter WDCONFIGURATIONID. This parameter must either be configured in your application object definition on the PARAMETERS tab or supplied as URL parameter SAP-WD-CONFIGID (e.g., from SAP NetWeaver Portal).

12.4 Personalization and Customization

Web Dynpro applications may be adapted at runtime by both end users and administrators. This is a built-in adaptation concept for all WDA applications. End users may make personalizations against their user names in a system, which will persist in the system even after their session ends. In turn, administrators may make customizations that affect all users in a specific client.

12.4.1 Personalizing Applications

If personalization is enabled, end users may individually adapt an application to their own needs. Typically, this is in the form of making UI modifications such as setting preferred default values for fields, hiding tabs and table columns, or specifying a default number of table rows to view, to an application. Personalization settings are accessed by right-clicking on a UI element in an application and enacting one of the available options from the USER SETTINGS folder of the element's context menu, as depicted in Figure 12.7.

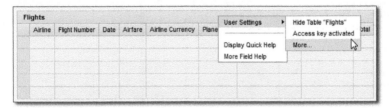

Figure 12.7 Displaying the Personalization Menu of a Table

Note
Unlike configuration and customization adaptations, personalization settings cannot be transported, even if the user exists across systems. These settings must be manually set by the end user in each application of each client of each system.

12.4.2 Embedding Built-In Configuration Options in a Custom Personalization Dialog

As a developer, you may want to create your own personalization dialog for an application. For example, you might like a dialog that captures all the personalization options for the application so you don't have to view them element by element. As a part of your development, you may want to embed some of the built-in Web Dynpro personalization functionality; for example, on a tabstrip. SAP fortunately supplies this functionality as a part of component interface IWD_PERSONALIZATION; all you need to do is implement it.

The key method to call in this interface is the INIT_PERSONALIZATION method, which initializes the component interface to construct the appropriate built-in view for your specified view element.

12.4.3 Customizing Applications

In addition to using the Customization Editor, administrators may customize an application's built-in UI settings by calling on it in *administration mode*. Administration mode may be enabled by any one of the following means:

▸ Calling the application with the `sap-config-mode` URL parameter set to X

▸ Displaying the application definition in the Web Dynpro Explorer in Transaction SE80 and selecting WEB DYNPRO APPLICATION • TEST • IN BROWSER—ADMIN MODE from the GUI menus

▸ Calling the application from SAP NetWeaver Portal in preview mode

When the application displays, the administrator may then right-click on a UI element and choose SETTINGS FOR CURRENT CONFIGURATION from the context menu to open the application's customization dialog. Figure 12.8 displays an example of a customization dialog in action.

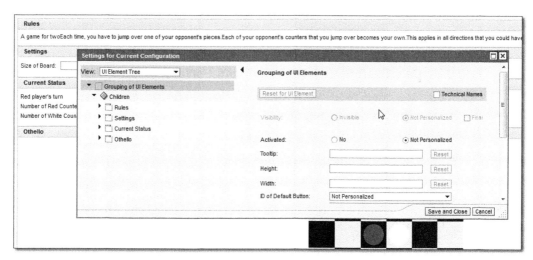

Figure 12.8 Displaying the Customization Dialog in an Application

Decorative UI Elements

You may add *decorative UI elements* to an application from this same application customization screen. Decorative UI elements may be added to container UI elements (i.e., `Group`, `Tray`, `TransparentContainer`, and `ScrollContainer`) by selecting the Decorative Element: Add link while viewing the element's attributes. The elements types that you may add are as follows:

- Caption
- Explanation
- FormattedTextView
- HorizontalGutter
- Image
- LinkToURL
- TextView

Transporting Application Customizations

As with component customizations, you may transport application customizations between environments by attaching them to a customizing transport request. You should be automatically prompted to add your customization to a transport when you try to save it, unless you have system settings enabled that bar customizing transports.

12.4.4 Deactivating Customization and Personalization

You may have circumstances in which you want to restrict end users' or administrators' ability to adapt components or applications. There are two methods of doing this:

- **Restriction by application parameter**

  You may deactivate personalization for end users in a given application by means of the WDDISABLEUSERPERSONALIZATION application parameter. This parameter is set when X is passed as the parameter's value.

  This parameter does not restrict an administrator's ability to customize the application.

- **Restriction by component configuration data**

  You can control component customization and personalization by means of a component's configuration data. Open the desired component definition in the Web Dynpro Explorer and select Edit • Configuration Data from the GUI menu. You may set options for both component-defined and built-in personalization from the dialog that appears.

12.4.5 Managing Personalization and Customization Data

Managing a component's adaptation data and its transport can be a tricky problem, especially in long or repetitive implementation cycles or in a production scenario when the number of end user personalizations can increase dramatically. Fortunately, SAP provides a tool in the form of Web Dynpro application WD_ANALYZE_CONFIG_USER that assists in the analysis of this data.

With this tool, you may do the following:

- ▶ View customization and personalization data for a given component
- ▶ Launch the component configuration and customization tools in order to further examine or change the relevant adaptation
- ▶ Manually initiate the transport of configuration and customization data
- ▶ Delete selected adaptation data

An example of this tool in action can be seen in Figure 12.9.

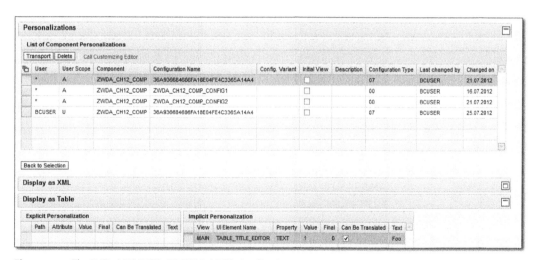

Figure 12.9 The WD_ANALYZE_CONFIG_USER Application

12.5 Component-Defined Adaptation

Component-defined adaptations are a class of adaptations whose configuration schemas are defined by the developer. These adaptations may support any custom functionality the developer makes configurable in a WDA component. For example, you could incorporate configurable threshold values for an input field into your application by this type of adaptation. Or, on the other hand, you could toggle an element's UI properties in lieu of using the built-in features. The scope of how you use component-defined adaptation is limited only by technical feasibility and the developer's imagination.

12.5.1 Configuration Controllers

Central to the component-defined adaptation methodology is a development object known as the *configuration controller*. This controller is nothing more than a uniquely identified custom controller belonging to the component in question. Components may have, at most, one configuration controller (though they may have as many custom controllers as is practical).

Defining a component controller is a fairly simple process:

1. Browse to your component in the Web Dynpro Explorer.

2. Identify a custom controller you want to use as your configuration controller. If you want to create a new custom controller, you may initiate this process by opening the context menu of your component and selecting CREATE • CUSTOM CONTROLLER from the menu options.

3. Once your controller is identified, display its context menu by right-clicking on it in the explorer. Select the option (RE)SET AS CONFIG. CONTROLLER from the menu to set this controller as your component controller, as seen in Figure 12.10.

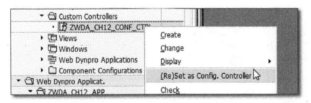

Figure 12.10 Defining a Configuration Controller

> **Note**
>
> If you want to swap to a different configuration controller for your component during the course of development, you may repeat this process. Please be aware that this is a swapping process; you can't have more than one configuration controller in a component.

12.5.2 Component-Defined Adaptation Data

Component-defined adaptation data is stored in the context of the configuration controller, whose structure is defined at design time like other controller contexts in WDA. When the application runs, data from the three adaptation layers is combined, applied to this context, and made available for the lifetime of the component.

As with all contexts, the configuration controller context may contain nodes defined to contain multiple subelements (i.e., they have cardinalities of 0..n or 1..n). In the Configuration Editor, to distinguish among elements belonging to these nodes, you should specify one of the element's attributes to be the *primary attribute*. This attribute will serve as a unique key by which to identify the element in the configuration. If you want, you may even configure a *generic primary attribute* to take this role, which will automatically generate an ID for itself in the Configuration Editor. This is done by creating a primary attribute in your context and setting its type to a data element from the WDY_CONF_GEN_PRIMARY domain. Primary attributes are denoted with a red asterisk in the Configuration Editor.

If you examine Figure 12.11, you can see the relationship between a configuration controller context and the settings that you define in the Configuration Editor. Note how the primary attribute defined for the context node becomes a node identifier in the CONFIGURATION CONTEXT tree.

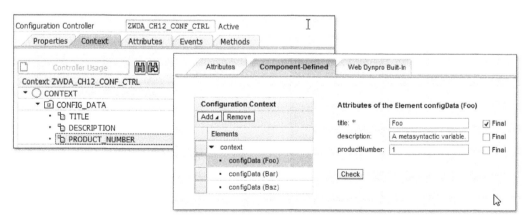

Figure 12.11 Component-Defined Adaptation Data Definition and Configuration

When defining your configuration controller's context, keep the following principles in mind:

▶ The context attributes must have simple data types; i.e., they must not be tables, structures, or references.

▶ The context structure should not be changed at runtime.

▶ The context must not contain any recursive nodes.

▶ The context should not contain any singleton nodes.

▶ The context should specify a primary attribute for every multiple node (cardinalities of 0..n or 1..n).

▶ If you wish to be able to translate the value of your attribute, you should assign it a data type from the WDY_CONF_TRANSL_TEXT domain.

▶ Primary attributes should not be translatable.

▶ For Boolean values, use a data type with the domain WDY_BOOLEAN in order to display a checkbox within the Configuration Editor.

12.5.3 Mandating and Deactivating Component-Defined Configuration Data

Being able to set component-defined configuration data may be mandated or deactivated in your component's configuration data options. You may specify these settings by following the procedure below:

1. Select and display your component in the Web Dynpro Explorer.

2. Select EDIT • CONFIGURATION DATA from the GUI menu.

3. A dialog will display presenting you with options to mandate or disallow the use of component-defined configuration data in the following two fields:

   ▶ COMPONENT-DEFINED CONFIGURATION

   ▶ COMPONENT-DEFINED PERSONALIZATION

4. Click the CONTINUE button to apply your changes.

5. Save the changes to your component definition.

> **Note**
>
> Component-defined configuration data may also be set at the personalization level. Unlike with configuration and customization, though, SAP doesn't provide a native UI from which to do this. If you want to allow this sort of personalization, you'll have to provide the means to do it as part of your development. The IF_WD_PERSONALIZATION interface may be used in order to persist your personalization data.

12.6   Parameterization

Beyond adaptation, a developer may make use of *application parameters* to influence the functionality of a WDA application. Application parameters—specifically URL parameters—are a carryover from the world of HTTP GET and POST parameters, in which you pass forms and other data to a remote web server, ostensibly in order to be processed. In an HTTP GET request, these parameters are passed via the web application's URI query string—everything in the URL past the '?' delimiter. An example of a parameter being passed via an HTTP GET request would be your enabling application customization in a WDA application (by supplying the `sap-config-mode` parameter). In an HTTP POST request, these parameters are sent within the body of the request and aren't immediately visible to the end user.

In truth, anything that can be passed as an application parameter can probably be developed as an input or selection on a view controller or component-defined configuration option, but sometimes there's a need to provide handy manual switching in your applications—at a framework level, for instance.

> **Built-In WDA Application Parameters**
>
> SAP already provides many WDA framework-level application parameters, some of which you may already be familiar with. You may peruse the full published extent of these parameters on the SAP Help website (*http://help.sap.com*) under the help topic Web Dynpro ABAP • Reference • Application Parameters and URL Parameters.

12.6.1   Setting Parameters

Application parameters may be set in a variety of places within the system:

▶ You may set the parameters by editing the Parameters tab of an application definition in the Web Dynpro Explorer.

▶ You may set parameters in an application configuration on the Parameters tab of the `CONFIGURE_APPLICATION` application.

▶ You may specify client-wide Web Dynpro parameters in the `WD_GLOBAL_SETTING` application.

▶ You may set certain parameters on a per-user basis in Transaction SU01 (e.g., the `ACCESSIBILITY_MODE` parameter).

► You may set parameters in the application's URL by supplying them in the URL's query string as the following syntax indicates:

```
<protocol>://<host>:<port>/<application-uri>
?<param1-name>=<param1-value>
&<param2-name>=<param2-value>
&<...>
```

> **Note**
>
> URL parameters are always evaluated before application parameters are enacted and always override the application parameters' settings. The sole exception to this case is if mandatory logon data is set for an application in Transaction SICF.

12.6.2 Processing Parameters

Application parameters are processed in the window controller of a WDA component. Parameters are automatically passed to the event handler of the window's inbound plug, as specified in the application definition.

For example, in Figure 12.12, the NAME parameter is defined in event handler HANDLEDEFAULT, which handles calls to the inbound plug DEFAULT. In the application definition that calls this window by this plug, we could specify NAME as an application parameter, or dynamically set it in the application's URL. Furthermore, since NAME is a parameter for the event handler call, we have a method where we can designate how to process the parameter's value.

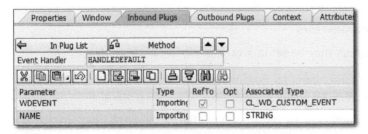

Figure 12.12 A Custom Parameter Defined in an Inbound Plug Handler

> **Note**
>
> Application parameters must be specified as type STRING. This type corresponds to the IHTTPVAL type, which is used by the framework to process parameters.

12.6.3 Parameter Security

When processing URL parameters in your code, you absolutely must validate the contents of the parameter and take precautions against potential malicious attacks. Unlike data passed in a WDA form, parameter data has none of the protections that are built into the WDA framework. Be aware of how a malicious user might attempt to use your parameters and keep an eye on the potential hazards of cross-site scripting (XSS) and SQL injection attacks.

> **Note**
>
> A great set of tools in your arsenal are the methods of class `CL_HTTP_UTILITY`, which provide a variety of ways to encode and decode HTTP data, as well as some other helpful tools.

12.7 Accessibility

When it comes to the well-roundedness of your applications, at some point you have to take into account the potential physical limitations of your user base. Users with physical disabilities may rely on specialized technology in order to interact with a given application, and often that technology requires that certain *accessibility* standards be met to ensure its smooth operation.

For the most part, Web Dynpro addresses this issue by incorporating certain accessibility properties into its UI elements. These UI properties may then be consumed by screen reader programs and the like in order to better present visual information to users. The primary UI properties Web Dynpro uses for this purpose are the `tooltip` and the `accessibilityDescription`, which are shown in Figure 12.13 and described below:

- Tooltips are used to provide semantic information about a UI element, e.g., to denote the purpose of a button or a field. Tooltips should be maintained for an element whenever:
    - The UI element doesn't have a heading.
    - No label is assigned to the UI element.
    - Elements with a text property don't have the text set, for example, when a button or link is missing its text. (This doesn't apply to the `caption` element, which is never checked for a tooltip.)

▶ Accessibility descriptions are designed to provide short, title-like descriptions of a UI element. They're often used to provide alternative titles to elements that typically don't carry a visible title themselves.

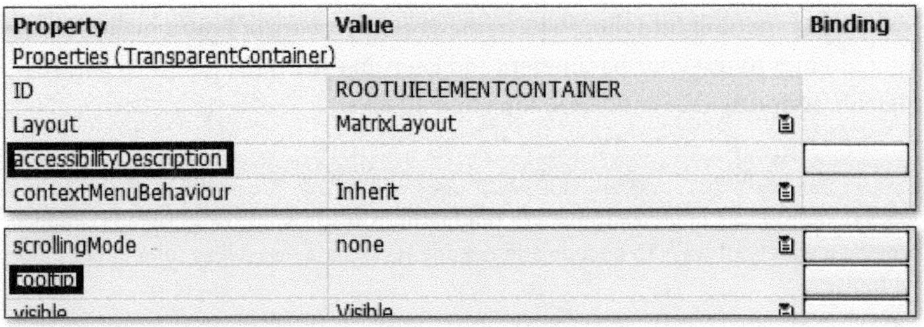

Property	Value	Binding
Properties (TransparentContainer)		
ID	ROOTUIELEMENTCONTAINER	
Layout	MatrixLayout	
accessibilityDescription		
contextMenuBehaviour	Inherit	
scrollingMode	none	
tooltip		
visible	Visible	

Figure 12.13 Accessibility Properties of a TransparentContainer

Web Dynpro actually checks at design time whether your development is compliant with its accessibility features. This is done as a part of the syntax check. If you want to disable accessibility checks, you may instruct the system to ignore them for a given component by unchecking the ACCESSIBILITY CHECKS ACTIVE flag in your component's attributes. It is, however, not recommended to disable this permanently, as you will more likely than not forget to incorporate accessibility altogether.

Note

For description of how WDA validates accessibility in its syntax checks, please refer to help topic WEB DYNPRO ABAP • WEB DYNPRO ABAP: DEVELOPMENT IN DETAIL • ADVANCED CONCEPTS • ACCESSIBILITY IN WEB DYNPRO ABAP APPLICATIONS on the SAP Help website (*http://help.sap.com*). This help topic gives you a complete breakdown of checks carried out per UI element type.

12.8 Style Sheets

Style sheets are a means of providing your applications with a common look and feel by establishing a common design specification that all elements on screen should adhere to. In the HTML world, you're given considerable flexibility in how you use and implement style sheets in your applications and pages and can reference multiple style sheets almost at will. In WDA, things are a little more structured.

For the most part, you can't use your own style sheets in WDA applications. In fact, the style of a UI element—as you well know—is typically adjusted by the setting of the element's properties in the view layout designer. These properties include things like `design` and `semanticColor`. And there is a method to SAP's madness. By explicitly defining properties by which you can control your element's style, you make those style options well known, which means you can build *themes* out of them.

12.8.1 WDA Integration with Themes

SAP systems already ship with a number of themes loaded in them. These themes may be viewed in the MIME Repository under the path */SAP/PUBLIC/BC/UR/ nw5/themes*. Here, you'll find a number of theme folders containing an extensive number of Cascading Style Sheet (CSS) files and images designed to integrate with a variety of web browsers. To apply one of these themes to your WDA application, use the `WDTHEMEROOT` application parameter or `SAP-THEME` URL parameter with one of the predelivered theme values, as defined in Table 12.2.

Theme Name	Parameter Value
Chrome	`sap_chrome`
High Contrast	`sap_highcont`
High Contrast Black	`sap_hcb`
Standard	`sap_standard`
Tradeshow	`sap_tradeshow`
Tradeshow Plus	`sap_tradeshow_plus`

Table 12.2 Themes Shipped with AS ABAP and Their Parameter Values

If your application is integrated in SAP NetWeaver Portal, the portal will typically specify what theme your application should use. This is done by means of the `SAP-EP-THEMEROOT` URL parameter.

12.8.2 Integrating a Custom Theme into WDA

You may specify that WDA use a custom theme at an arbitrary location by use of the `SAP-CSSURL` URL parameter with a value describing the URL location of your theme (e.g., */sap/public/mytheme*).

In order to create a custom theme, we recommend you download a copy of one of the themes (using a program like `BSP_UPDATE_MIMEREPOS`) and modify it. You may then upload it back into the MIME Repository under a public folder (using the same program) and configure your WDA application to reference it.

12.8.3 Setting a Global Theme for WDA

You may specify that your system use a global theme for all your WDA application. This is done by setting the STYLESHEET URI field in WDA application `WD_GLOBAL_SETTING`.

> **Note**
>
> For full documentation on the decision tree for selecting a theme, please refer to help topic WEB DYNPRO ABAP • WEB DYNPRO ABAP: DEVELOPMENT IN DETAIL • ADVANCED CONCEPTS • STYLESHEETS IN WEB DYNPRO ABAP on the SAP Help website (*http://help.sap.com*).

12.9 Internationalization and Translation

Internationalization is the process by which the language-specific components of an application (i.e., UI labels, messages, and texts in general) are designed to be adaptable so that the application may be translated to suit the needs of its users. SAP, with its global reach, has long regarded the need for internationalization to be a core component of its technology platforms, and WDA is no different. Consequently, it's designed to integrate with many of the ABAP's already proven translation tools—the *Online Text Repository (OTR)*, *text symbols*, and *SE63 translation*.

Texts take on a variety of forms in web applications, but they generally fall into three categories:

- Static texts
- Dynamic texts
- Long texts

The remainder of this section will discuss some of the most common methodologies for internationalizing these texts.

12.9.1 Static Texts

Static texts, as their name indicates, are texts that don't possess any dynamic qualities and are typically defined at design time. On-screen titles, button texts, and field labels are all common examples of these texts that may occur in your applications. The recommended approach to internationalizing and translating these texts is to use *OTR short texts*, which are texts up to 255 characters in length that are stored in ABAP's Online Text Repository.

The process for applying OTR short texts to WDA screen elements is an almost trivial event. The developer need only do the following:

1. Display the LAYOUT tab in change mode for the component view in which you want to apply the text and navigate to the UI element that will contain the text.

2. Locate and select the element property on which you want to set the OTR text:

   - If you wish to use an existing OTR text, simply click on the TEXT SELECTION button to the right of the property and select the appropriate OTR alias from the selection list that displays.

   - If you want to create a new OTR text, type in the character string `$OTR:<aliasname>` in the value field of the property, where `<aliasname>` is the name of the new OTR alias you want to create. A dialog prompts you to create this new alias, which is assigned to the package of your WDA application.

   Figure 12.14 displays an example of this step when complete.

3. Save your entries.

Figure 12.14 Setting an OTR Alias for a Text Property

12.9.2 Dynamic Texts

Dynamic texts are texts generated dynamically at runtime. They may be user-interface texts that change depending on the state of your application. They may contain variables, such as return messages containing information on submitted data. In general, these are algorithmically constructed and displayed.

The general recommendation for creating dynamic texts is to use *text symbols* in your WDA component's assistance class. These text symbols may then be programmatically accessed by your component or view controllers by use of the IF_WD_COMPONENT_ASSITANCE~GET_TEXT() method of your WD_ASSIST attribute, as in Listing 12.1. Here, we are loading the text symbol into one of our component's context elements, where it may later be tied to a UI element's text property in one of the component's views.

```
method WDDOINIT .
  DATA: l_i13n_node TYPE REF TO if_wd_context_node,
        l_dyntext_val TYPE string.

  " Retrieve the text symbol from the assitance class. Text
  " symbol 000 is parameterized as '&PARA1& Text'.
  l_dyntext_val =
    wd_assist->if_wd_component_assistance~get_text(
      key = '000'
      para1 = 'Dynamic'
    ).

  " Get the current node from the context.
  l_i13n_node = wd_context->get_child_node(
    wd_this->wdctx_i13n
  ).

  " Set the current node's DYNAMIC_TEXT attribute.
  l_i13n_node->set_attribute(
```

```
   name = 'DYNAMIC_TEXT'
   value = l_dyntext_val
 ).
endmethod.
```

Listing 12.1 Loading a Text Symbol from an Assistance Class into a Context Attribute Translating Text Symbols

> **Note**
>
> You may translate text symbols by viewing the text elements in the assistance class (GOTO • TEXT ELEMENTS) and then selecting GOTO • TRANSLATION from the subsequent screen that appears.

12.9.3 Long Texts

Long texts are texts with no set length and that are typically used to present long-form descriptive data. This data could include anything from part or product descriptions to broadcast messages made to end users.

While multiple ABAP technologies exist to deal with these long texts, SAP specifically recommends that WDA applications utilize the `FormattedTextView` element in their display and the use of SAPScript to assist in their translation. In-depth documentation on both of these technologies is available on the SAP Help website (*http://help.sap.com*).

12.10 Summary

In this chapter, we delved deeply into the world of adaption, a WDA application's primary means of being configured. We learned that adaptation occurs in layers that stretch from the developer to the end user and about the different types of configuration features that Web Dynpro has to offer. We learned how to configure, customize, and personalize components and applications and how to define configuration parameters in our own components. Additionally, we took a look at some of the configurable options the framework has to offer that allow us to round out our applications.

Overall, Web Dynpro supports a powerful and robust framework for configuration. Understanding this framework is a key ingredient in developing and implementing WDA applications in your landscape and provides valuable insight into the mechanics of many of the applications that may be deployed to your system(s) by third parties, especially if you need to address functionality gaps.

In the next chapter, we'll shift our attention away from configuring applications to how to modify and enhance them. This presents the other side of the coin—how to address the modification of existing applications—where we'll adjust the development objects themselves.

Modifications and enhancements occupy that space in your development toolkit for when an application doesn't quite give you the functionality you need but could mold into your business process if you just tweaked it. In this chapter, we'll examine how you can use these tools with WDA.

13 Modifications and Enhancements

One of the greatest strengths of ABAP technology has always been in the innate accessibility customers have had in modifying applications and code delivered on the ABAP platform. And it's readily apparent why SAP might focus so much on that ability—no two companies and no two customers have identical business processes. This means that when you deliver a business application to a customer, it has to be malleable enough that they can adjust it to their needs. In Web Dynpro, some of that malleability comes in the form of customization and configuration, which we discussed in the last chapter, but some of it also comes from how WDA integrates into the *Enhancement Framework.*

In the previous chapters of this book, you were introduced to the building blocks of Web Dynpro and how to use them to create new applications to suit your business requirements. In this chapter, we'll focus on an equally important task: modifying existing WDA applications to suit those same needs. In fact, as WDA development gains steam in terms of both SAP-delivered code and what is delivered by third parties, *enhancement* will become a more frequent part of the implementation process (just as it has in classic ABAP technologies). This chapter will therefore delve into tools, features, and concepts you can use to complete your enhancement tasks using the WDA framework.

13.1 WDA Integration with the Enhancement Framework

Web Dynpro is designed to integrate directly into ABAP's Enhancement Framework. Just as with classic ABAP development, the framework enables you to make changes to development objects without changing the original repository object. This is important because it allows you the opportunity to manage WDA enhancements during the patching or upgrade of a system by identifying potential collisions in the two change sets. Changes made to an object without the use of enhancements (i.e., unstructured changes made directly on the objects themselves) are called *modifications*. Modifications don't provide any guided conflict resolution in the upgrade of an application and may result in a loss code. Therefore, we recommend that you almost exclusively use enhancements to make changes to existing applications.

The Enhancement Framework supports two basic types of enhancement: *explicit* enhancements and *implicit* enhancements. Explicit enhancement options consist of explicitly defined enhancement spots in your source code where custom processing may be carried out, including the use and implementation of *Business Add-Ins (BAdIs)*. Implicit enhancement options consist of predefined places in the code where ABAP expects customer changes to be implemented, such as creating new parameters for function modules, extending the attributes of a class, and enacting custom processing at the end of a program. Implicit enhancement options also include the various types of enhancements you can make to Web Dynpro objects. In this chapter, we'll discuss both types of enhancement because, while changing existing WDA applications is typically an act of implicit enhancement, you may find cases where specifying an explicit enhancement is your best design option.

13.1.1 Enhancement Spots

When an explicit enhancement is specified, it's assigned to an *enhancement spot*. Enhancement spots may contain multiple enhancement options of the same type, either source code options defined with the ENHANCEMENT-POINT keyword or BAdI calls using the GET BADI and CALL BADI calls. These spots may then be assigned to *composite enhancement spots*, which exist to provide logical grouping containers for your simple spots. Figure 13.1 depicts the relationship of these objects in the Enhancement Framework.

In Web Dynpro, enhancement spots are typically created and called in the backing controller or assistance classes that provide WDA applications with their dynamic functionality.

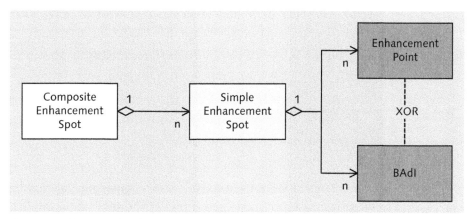

Figure 13.1 The Hierarchy of Enhancement Spot Objects

13.1.2 Enhancement Implementations

The key development object for enhancements is the *enhancement implementation*. Enhancement implementations, as the name suggests, contain the actual coding artifacts used to implement the enhancement, whether they are source code, BAdI implementations, methods, parameters, attributes, etc. For Web Dynpro enhancements, these may contain any of the artifacts that belong to a WDA component: views, controllers, windows, and the elements contained within.

Enhancement implementations, like enhancement spots, can be organized into larger composite containers known as *composite enhancement implementations*. These groupings are largely made for organizational purposes. The packaging of a simple or composite implementation is what really matters because the switches for hooking into the *Switch Framework* are defined there.

13.1.3 Creating an Enhancement Implementation

Before we go any further, let's take a look at how to create an enhancement implementation for a Web Dynpro component:

1. Browse to your component in the Object Navigator (Transaction SE80) and make sure you're in display mode. (If you're not in display mode, options for enhancing a component will be disabled since you may either change or enhance a component, but not both.)

2. Open the view or controller definition in which you wish to make your enhancement.

3. Click the ENHANCE button in the Web Dynpro Explorer toolbar, as shown in Figure 13.2.

Web Dynpro Explorer: Display Component

Figure 13.2 Location of the Enhance Button on the WD Explorer Toolbar

4. If enhancement implementation already exist for your component, you may be prompted to select from a list of implementations. If you select from this list, you may skip the rest of the creation process. Otherwise, you may select the CREATE ENHANCEMENT IMPLEMENTATION button on this dialog and continue.

5. A dialog displays, prompting you to identify a name and description for your enhancement. You also may optionally specify a composite enhancement implementation to assign your new implementation to. Fill out the required fields and click the checkmark button to continue.

6. The standard package and transport assignment dialogs should appear. Assign a package and transport for the enhancement implementation and save your changes.

7. In your component, a folder for ENHANCEMENT IMPLEMENTATIONS will display. Likewise, in the package to which you assigned your enhancement implementation, an ENHANCEMENTS folder will appear containing your enhancement implementation and a copy of the component you want to enhance. You may work with your enhancements in either of these folder structures. They are shown in Figure 13.3.

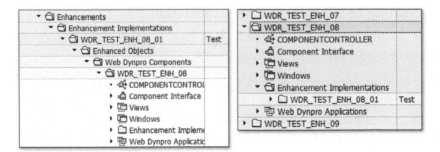

Figure 13.3 The Enhancement Implementations Folder at the Package and Component Levels

> **Namespace Prefixes for Enhancement Implementations**
>
> By appending a namespace prefix to the name of your enhancement implementation and all its implementation elements, you can avoid potential name conflicts with objects in the original component. More information on namespaces can be found on the SAP Help website (*http://help.sap.com*) under the CHANGE AND TRANSPORT SYSTEM • NAMESPACES AND NAMING CONVENTIONS (BC-CTS-NAM) help topic.

13.1.4 Switch Framework Integration

As with other ABAP enhancement implementations, WDA enhancement implementations may also integrate with the *Switch Framework*. This framework allows you to control which add-ons and enhancement implementations are enabled on a given system. Activities for working with the Switch Framework for WDA enhancements are consistent with those of non-WDA objects, so please refer to the help topic SWITCH FRAMEWORK on the SAP Help website (*http://help.sap.com*) for more information.

13.2 Enhancing Web Dynpro Components

Most Web Dynpro development objects are enhanced by means of implicit enhancements. These include enhancements made to views, windows, and controllers, and in the component definition itself. In the few occasions when an explicit enhancement is made, the enhancements are typically attributed to the source text of a controller or assistance class. This section focuses on what implicit enhancements are at your disposal in WDA objects.

13.2.1 Creating New Views

One of the simplest enhancements you can make to a WDA component is to create a new view. Since new views are essentially add-on development objects for the component, you start off with about as blank a slate as possible in the enhancement process. Still, depending on the complexity of the new view's integration, it may require you to make further adjustments to other objects within your WDA component in order to enable its use. For example, if you plan on actually displaying your new view, you'll almost certainly have to enhance one of your component's windows to accommodate this.

One of the few places in which you don't use the Web Dynpro Explorer toolbar's ENHANCE button is in the creation of new views. Instead, use the CREATE AS ENHANCEMENT functionality of the VIEWS folder's context menu to initiate the process of creating a new view, as depicted in Figure 13.4.

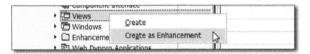

Figure 13.4 The Create-as-Enhancement Option for Creating New Views

New view enhancements are developed in much the same way as a non-enhancement views: develop your context, set your layouts, and bind data elements as you would in the creation of any other view.

> **Note**
>
> The view you create will be maintained under the ENHANCEMENT IMPLEMENTATIONS folder of your component. It will not display in your VIEWS folder.

13.2.2 Enhancing Existing Views

Views may be enhanced in both their layout and controller layers. This section largely covers enhancement to the layout layer. Information on controller-based enhancements (i.e., for views, windows, and components) can be found in the next section.

The enhancement process for existing views starts with displaying the view definition and clicking the ENHANCE button in the Web Dynpro toolbar. As with standard WDA development, enhancements to the layout of a view are performed on the view's LAYOUT tab. However, there are a couple of key differences you must be aware of that pertain to making enhancements:

▶ You may not make changes to the properties of existing UI elements in the view. The elements' properties will be grayed out as read only. Please refer to Chapter 12 for more on how to adjust these properties by component configuration.

▶ You may not delete existing UI elements from the view; however, you may suppress them, which we will examine further in this section.

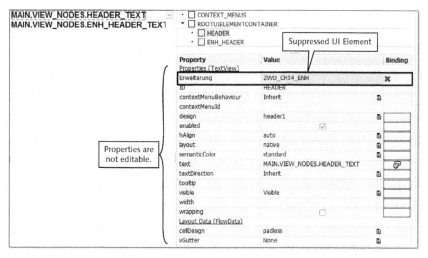

Figure 13.5 Differences in the Layout Tab of a View in Enhancement Mode

Creating New UI Elements

New UI elements may be created and added to a view much as if you were making a change to one of your own custom components.

Suppressing Existing UI Elements

As we mentioned earlier, existing UI elements may not be deleted, but they may be suppressed. In order to do so, select the UI element and choose REMOVE ELEMENT from its context menu. A new property appears for the element, as shown (in German) in Figure 13.5. This property indicates that the element is no longer bound to the view in your enhancement and subsequently won't be displayed. In fact, the element won't even be processed when the page is generated, which has implications on any dynamic programming the element may participate in. No one wants a dreaded shortdump over a null pointer.

Creating New Actions and Plugs

You may create new actions and plugs (inbound and outbound) for views as part of the enhancement process. Their inclusion, of course, is designed to support the creation of new Buttons and other UI elements that provoke events.

13.2.3 Enhancing Controllers

All the different types of Web Dynpro controller parts may be enhanced in an enhancement implementation. However, the following caveats also apply:

▶ Existing controller parts may not be changed or deleted in the enhancement implementation.

▶ Enhanced objects in the component controller can't be included in the interface controller for external access.

▶ Additional attributes added to one of the controller's context nodes must be dynamically referenced at runtime because they won't become statically available in the interface controller as usual.

As with views, you initiate the controller enhancement process by displaying the relevant controller and clicking the ENHANCE button in the Web Dynpro Explorer toolbar.

Enhancing a Controller's Context

Additional nodes and attributes may be added to a controller's context at will in an enhancement implementation. We recommend, however, that you use the CREATE USING WIZARD • ATTRIBUTES FROM COMPONENTS OF A STRUCTURE functionality of the context menu when it comes to creating nodes bound to a dictionary structure. Context nodes and attributes created in this manner will have the additional `Enhancement Implementation` property included in their definition.

Enhancing Controller Methods

New methods may be added to a controller at will. However, as existing methods may not be changed or deleted, special method exits may be implemented to handle changes in their processing. These exits are defined as in Table 13.1.

You may create an implementation stub for any of these exit methods by selecting the appropriate push button on the METHODS tab in your component definition, as indicated in Figure 13.6. You may also remove exit method implementations by selecting the appropriate method on the METHODS tab and clicking one of the three delete buttons available on the methods listing's toolbar.

Exit Type	Description
Pre-Exit	A pre-exit method allows you to append additional processing to the beginning of a method call. It automatically provides all the importing and changing parameters of the original method in its method signature.
Post-Exit	A post-exit method allows you to append additional processing to the end of a method call. It provides all the importing parameters of the original method in its signature as well as all the other declared parameters (exporting, changing, and returning) as changing parameters.
Overwrite Exit	An overwrite exit method adopts the method signature of the original method and is executed in lieu of it. Only one overwrite exit may be active per method.

Table 13.1 A Breakdown of the Various Method Exits Provided in Order to Enhance Existing WDA Controller Methods

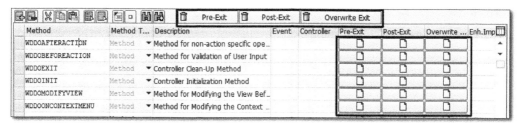

Figure 13.6 The Methods Tab in a Controller Enhancement

Note
In order for the method exits' functionality to properly invoke, references to the local controller interface in your controller's source text should use the WD_THIS convention, as opposed to directly referencing the interface using the ME keyword.

Adding New Attributes

New attributes may be added to a controller with no issue.

Adding Events

New events and their event handlers may be added to a controller via an enhancement implementation. This functionality is designed to support any eventing UI elements that you may have added to your component.

13.2.4 Adding New Windows

New windows may be added to your component by means of the WINDOWS folder's context menu. Simply select the CREATE AS ENHANCEMENT option from the menu to initiate the process, as shown in Figure 13.7. As with newly created views, your new window will be available under the ENHANCEMENT IMPLEMENTATIONS folder for you to edit.

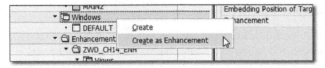

Figure 13.7 Creating a New Window as an Enhancement

13.2.5 Enhancing Existing Windows

Windows may be enhanced by embedding new views within them or creating new navigation links. As with other enhancements to Web Dynpro objects, existing window content may not be changed or deleted but, in some instances, may be suppressed. Windows are enhanced via the ENHANCE button in the Web Dynpro Explorer toolbar.

Adding Views

You may embed additional views in an enhanced window by right-clicking on the appropriate window on the WINDOW tab and selecting the EMBED VIEW or EMBED EMPTY VIEW option from the context menu (much like you would in change mode).

> **Note**
>
> Since enhancement doesn't allow you to change the properties of existing views, you won't be allowed to set a newly embedded view as the default view for a window. If you want to embed a new default view, we recommend you enhance your component with a new window and create a new subsequent application.

Enhancing Navigation Links

As with views, new navigation links may be added to a window in order to support newly embedded views or to create new navigation options between existing views. You may also remove links by suppression and define new navigation targets for links, which combines the suppression of an existing link and the addition of a new one in a single step. All these options are available via the context menu for your outbound plugs or for the navigation links themselves.

13.2.6 Enhancing Components

A component itself may also be the target of enhancement. We've already discussed two cases in which this is done, in the adding of views and in the adding of windows. You may also add additional component usages to your component. These new usages may be used throughout the component in order to support your other enhancements.

13.3 Explicit Enhancements in Web Dynpro

While the vast majority of enhancements in Web Dynpro are enacted by implicit means, there may be some instances in which either you or a component's author may wish to specify the use of explicit enhancements. Typical use cases for this might be in the marshaling of data for your application or in how you generate dynamic content for your component (either in the context or in the UI).

The good news about using explicit enhancements in WDA is that their use and implementation is not very far from how they're used in standard ABAP.

13.3.1 Working with BAdIs

BAdIs may be called from the source text of your WDA applications. Their definitions, implementations, and invocations are executed in the same manner as in standard ABAP. For example, if you examine the sample code in Listing 13.1, there is no discernible difference between how you'd invoke a BAdI from within a WDA method and how you'd invoke it from anyplace else using the ABAP language.

```
method WDDOINIT .

  DATA: bd_handler TYPE REF TO z_badi_ch13_data,
        desc_key TYPE char10,
        description TYPE string.
```

```
GET BADI bd_handler.
CALL BADI bd_handler->get_description
EXPORTING
  key = desc_key
IMPORTING
  desc = description.
...

endmethod.
```

Listing 13.1 Calling a BAdI from within a Component Method

Additionally, as in standard ABAP, the usage of BAdIs goes essentially unrestricted. You may make a BAdI call from any piece of source text, whether it's in a controller or in an assistance class. Given this freedom, it's important to consider where you want to place your BAdI calls for maximum maintainability and how that fits into Web Dynpro's MVC design pattern.

For BAdIs that take the role of data access objects, you should generally consider placing those calls in either your WDA application's assistance class or component controller methods. As with other component data, this provides for a good separation of your data model from your UI functionality.

For BAdIs that take on other roles, such as generic event handling, placing where a call is made becomes much more a matter of the developer's discretion. By placing all your BAdI calls in a centralized code object, though, you can again provide a good separation between UI-relevant functionality and deeper processing.

> **Note**
>
> For more information of BAdIs, please refer to the ENHANCEMENT FRAMEWORK • ENHANCEMENT TECHNOLOGIES • BUSINESS ADD-INS (BADIS) help topic on the SAP Help website (*http://help.sap.com*).

13.3.2 Working with Enhancement Options

Because WDA controller methods may not be changed or deleted, enhancement options (implemented by using the `enhancement-point`, `enhancement-section`, and `enhancement` keywords) may not be implemented within a component's code artifacts. Instead, you must use the implicit exits supplied to your methods by the

WDA framework that were discussed in Section 13.2.3. This restriction, however, doesn't apply to your assistance classes because they adhere to the enhancement behavior of global classes in ABAP.

13.4   Adjustments after an Upgrade

As we mentioned at the beginning of this chapter, the key benefit of using the Enhancement Framework comes during your system's upgrade process. If an enhanced component is changed in its original system, a conflict could result when you import the change into the system where your enhancement is located. The Enhancement Framework tracks these conflicts against your enhancements and displays them in the Enhancement Information System, which also provides you with a centralized user interface from which to make adjustments to your enhancements.

13.4.1   Types of Web Dynpro Conflicts

Due to the nature of the enhancements you're allowed to make to Web Dynpro objects—you can't change or delete items—only two major types of conflict are expected as part of the upgrade processes:

▶ *Name collisions* occur when an object in your enhancement shares its name with an object introduced in the change. If you practice using a customer namespace in the naming of your enhancement objects, this type of conflict should never occur (at least when upgrading an SAP-delivered component).

▶ *Invalid references* occur when the object that was enhanced no longer exists as of the change (i.e., it was renamed or deleted).

13.4.2   Making Adjustments to Your Enhancements

In order to make adjustments to your WDA enhancements after an upgrade, follow this procedure:

1. Start the Enhancement Information System from either the Object Navigator (Transaction SE80) or Transaction SPAU_ENH. You may have to change your Object Navigator settings in order to view the Enterprise Information System. You may do this by selecting SETTINGS... from the UTILITIES(M) menu in Transaction SE80.

2. Choose ENHANCEMENTS (UPGRADE VIEW) in the object list to display the enhancements that need to be adjusted.

3. Select the applicable adjustment you want to make from the list that displays and click on its ADJUSTMENT tab.

4. Double-click the entries in the ALV grid that displays to view each individual conflict.

5. Resolve all name conflicts by renaming or deleting the appropriate enhancement implementation element.

6. Apply your adjustments by clicking the ADJUST ENHANCEMENT IMPLEMENTATION button.

7. Save and activate your work.

13.5 Summary

In this chapter, we explored the concept of enhancement and how Web Dynpro fits into the Enhancement Framework. We learned the benefits of using the framework and taking advantage of its robust methodology for managing and adjusting enhancements in an upgrade scenario—benefits that wouldn't be available if we were to simply modify existing components. We also learned that WDA is designed from the ground up to integrate into this framework by the implicit enhancement of its component elements, and how it provides this in a manner intuitive to those already familiar with Web Dynpro development. Though implicit enhancement is the norm in WDA applications, we know we can also explicitly enhance WDA source text in some areas, but we should give consideration to where those enhancement options should be placed in order to enforce good MVC design.

In the next chapter, we'll take a look at the Floorplan Manager framework and how costly development can be avoided by adapting its components.

Developing uniformity and consistency in your applications' user interfaces can be an equally challenging and tedious task to perform. To that end, WDA's Floorplan Manager provides us with a framework that simplifies those tasks by delivering common and configurable UI design patterns.

14   Working with the Floorplan Manager

One of the things you may have noticed about Web Dynpro is just how open a canvas you have when it comes to developing your user interfaces. Of course, this freedom comes with a price—namely that unless you're in the business of developing your own framework, you'll find that building cohesiveness into your WDA applications and between your components can be something of a haphazard task. For instance, how do you integrate several components into a single application governed and accessed through a single URL? You could integrate them through SAP NetWeaver Portal, but if the components represent steps A, B, and C in some kind of process flow, wouldn't you want that to be a guided activity instead of giving the user the freedom to run the steps out of order? You could choose to integrate them via component usages, but how reusable is that solution the next time you find yourself with a similar requirement? Furthermore, consider the amount of labor involved in just stringing together the navigation for such a component—you'd need plugs for every view, buttons for every plug, events for every button, and the backing code to link them all together. Fortunately, SAP also realizes how these kinds of requirements can bog down development and seeks to address the problem with a framework called the *Floorplan Manager (FPM)*.

The Floorplan Manager is an application framework that allows you to develop composite WDA applications based on SAP-delivered design patterns. Floorplans themselves are Web Dynpro applications that integrate with your components and provide them with common design elements, such as identification areas, message areas, navigation regions, and toolbars, similar to the layout and features provided in many SAP applications. Combined, the use of these features is designed to reduce the overhead cost of developing similar functionality in your components and to convert their implementation into a configuration task.

In this chapter, we'll explore the FPM framework and how it may be used to enhance or even provide an alternative to some WDA development. In addition, we'll take a look at the WDA Page Builder, which provides a different style of application integration, though it shares many similarities with the FPM model.

14.1 Floorplan Architecture

Before we continue into how to actually construct a floorplan application, you need to learn a little bit about how the framework is designed and what objects comprise a floorplan application.

14.1.1 Design of a Floorplan Manager Application

Floorplan Manager applications are structured to implement standard SAP design patterns. These design patterns include standard UI designs for managing and displaying business object data and facilitating complex business activities with the use of wizards. Additionally, FPM applications are designed to adopt many of the UI features found in your typical SAP application, including all of the features shown in Figure 14.1, which comprise the layout and design areas of an FPM application:

▶ **Identification area**
This area identifies the application and provides links to application help and other application-wide features. The content of this area is largely set by configuration properties.

▶ **Message area**
This area returns feedback to the user based on their actions within the application. Typically, no customization is required for this area of the application.

▶ **Navigation area**
This area displays navigation options within the application (e.g., buttons to change what a user is viewing), as well as commands to be executed that are relevant to the data presented in the content area. The developer or configurator usually determines what is displayed here.

▶ **Content area**

This area contains the main content of an FPM application, displaying business data, input options, and whatever else that you wish to present to the application's user. The content of this section is chiefly comprised of *User Interface Building Blocks (UIBBs)* which are configured for use by the developer.

Figure 14.1 Design Areas of a Floorplan Manager Application

14.1.2 Implementation Architecture of a Floorplan Manager Application

Floorplan applications are comprised of several interrelating component and configuration objects that must be strung together. Figure 14.2 gives an overview of what artifacts are required to implement a floorplan application.

The first thing you have to understand about floorplan applications is that unlike with most of the Web Dynpro applications you've created so far, you won't be referencing your own component in the application's definition. The navigation target of your floorplan application will instead be one of the floorplan components SAP provides. In turn, the floorplan component will call on your components by the references you provide in its configuration. Component configuration, you'll find, is an integral part of working with floorplan applications and most of your implementation tasks will take place in the Configuration Editor for the Floorplan Manager.

But before we get too deeply into that, let's take a closer look at some of the objects that a floorplan implementation contains and the roles that they play.

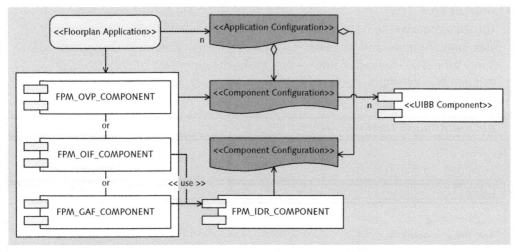

Figure 14.2 Implementation Architecture of a Floorplan Application

14.1.3 Floorplan Components

Floorplan components, as mentioned, are SAP-delivered components that serve as the entry point into a floorplan application. Each of these components defines a *floorplan*, which model common UI design patterns that you may find across SAP's technology platforms. Currently, four types of floorplans are provided that are implemented in three WDA components, as defined in Table 14.1.

Floorplan Name	Component
Object Instance Floorplan (OIF)	FPM_OIF_COMPONENT
Guided Activity Floorplan (GAF)	FPM_GAF_COMPONENT
Quick Activity Floorplan (QAF)	FPM_OIF_COMPONENT
Overview Page Floorplan (OVP)	FPM_OVP_COMPONENT

Table 14.1 The Available Floorplan Types and the Components That Implement Them

Each of these floorplans is configured using the Floorplan Manager's Configuration Editor. As part of this configuration, you may integrate other WDA components into your floorplan as long as they're defined as UIBBs.

Object Instance Floorplans

The Object Instance Floorplan (OIF) provides a template for displaying and manipulating the data, attributes, and associations of business objects within your system. These business objects roughly equate to all the data you may associate with a given business process. Figure 14.3 shows a sample OIF application.

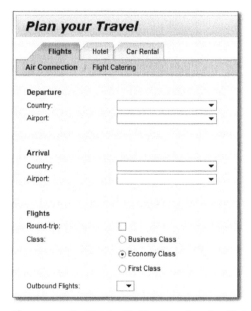

Figure 14.3 An OIF Application Based on the Flight Demo Scenario

Guided Activity Floorplans

The Guided Activity Floorplan (GAF) provides a template for conducting a user through a step-by-step activity—it allows you to create a wizard application, in essence, for the creation and management of business data. One of the hallmarks of this design pattern is the roadmap UI element, which supplies the user with information about where exactly they are in the activity and how many steps remain to be completed. Figure 14.4 shows an example GAF application.

Figure 14.4 A GAF Application Based on the Flight Demo Scenario

Quick Activity Floorplans

The Quick Activity Floorplan (QAF) provides you with a template to display or manipulate specific data in a business object. While QAF applications use the same underlying component as OIF applications, their major distinction is scope. Where an OIF application is typically designed to provide a user with complete information about a business object, QAF applications are designed to implement a specific task and usually show no more data than necessary. Typically, the difference between an OIF application and a QAF application is the presence or absence of tab controls. Figure 14.5 shows an example QAF application.

Figure 14.5 A QAF Application Based on the Flight Demo Scenario

Overview Page Floorplans

The Overview Page Floorplan (OVP) provides a template for creating overview pages that display and link to information or tasks about given business objects or scenarios. OVP applications distinguish themselves from other floorplan applications in that they follow a pattern of displaying generic data on the overview page and then supply you with functionality to delve deeper into that data and perform tasks on it. They may also aggregate many pieces of data on one screen as they provide a liberal use of sections on the screen. Figure 14.6 shows an example OVP application.

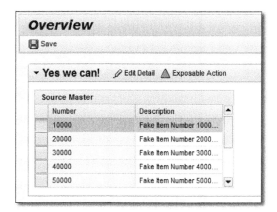

Figure 14.6 An OVP Application Displaying Business Object Data in a Section

14.1.4 User Interface Building Blocks

User Interface Building Blocks (UIBBs) are Web Dynpro components that implement the IF_FPM_UI_BUILDING_BLOCK interface. This is a special interface that allows a WDA component to integrate into a floorplan application by providing a method framework to the component that the FPM application framework can call on. If you intend to integrate a custom component into a floorplan application, you'll need to implement this interface in your component. SAP already provides a number of UIBBs, both those that are application specific and special *Generic User Interface Building Blocks (GUIBBs)*, which may be configured to work in your floorplan applications and provide common UI elements (composite forms, lists, tabs, etc.) as opposed to component views providing specific business functionality.

IF_FPM_UI_BUILDING_BLOCK

The Web Dynpro interface IF_FPM_UI_BUILDING_BLOCK contains five methods that the UIBB must implement. These methods occur in an event cycle carried out by the Floorplan Manager framework and are described in Table 14.2 in the order that they are executed.

Method Name	Description
FLUSH	The first method called in the FPM event loop.
NEEDS_CONFIRMATION	This method provides an opportunity for the UIBB to display a confirmation dialog box before the FPM event processes.
PROCESS_EVENT	In this method, the UIBB processes the FPM event.
AFTER_FAILED_EVENT	This method is called if the FPM event fails to process correctly.
PROCESS_BEFORE_OUTPUT	The last method called in the FPM event loop.

Table 14.2 List of Interface Methods Defined in IF_FPM_UI_BUILDING_BLOCK

14.1.5 Floorplan Configuration Objects

An integral part of any floorplan application implementation is its configuration objects. These include a component configuration for your floorplan component, component configurations for any used components (including UIBBs), and an application configuration.

In the component configuration of a floorplan component, you essentially define your floorplan application's implementation—how you want to format and style your application, which UIBBs go where, and if they interact with one another. These configurations are managed by the Floorplan Manager's Configuration Editor, a custom editor built to service a floorplan component's component-defined adaptation parameters.

In keeping with adaptation principles, for each used component in a Floorplan Manager application, you may define a component configuration object. For components that have an explicit usage defined in the Floorplan Manager component's definition (i.e. FPM_IDR_COMPONENT), the floorplan application configuration manages which configuration is linked to the component. For UIBB components, since they're tied to a floorplan dynamically, you link to their component configuration in the Floorplan Manager's Configuration Editor.

Finally, every floorplan application has an application configuration, which assumes the same role it would play in any other Web Dynpro application, grouping and assigning component configurations to components for use in your application.

14.2 Getting Started with Floorplans

Now that you know a little bit more about what constitutes a floorplan application, let's get into the mechanics of how to build one. To do so, we'll need to use or create each of the development or configuration objects we discussed in the last section. We'll start by creating our own UIBB.

14.2.1 Implementing a UIBB

In order to implement a UIBB, we'll have to implement the `IF_FPM_UI_BUILDING_BLOCK` interface in one of our Web Dynpro components. This is carried out in the same way you'd implement any other Web Dynpro interface into a component:

1. In the Object Navigator (Transaction SE80), browse to your component and display its component definition in change mode.
2. Display the IMPLEMENTED INTERFACES tab by selecting it.
3. On the IMPLEMENTED WEB DYNPRO COMPONENT INTERFACES table, enter `IF_FPM_UI_BUILDING_BLOCK` as an entry and hit [Enter]. The other values in table entry will automatically populate with information about the interface.
4. Click the REIMPLEMENT push button for your entry in the ACTION column of the table. This will automatically generate method stubs for the interface in your component controller. (In a real-world application, you'd obviously implement these methods as you see fit, but here we're only interested in a simple integration scenario.)
5. Save and activate your changes in both the component definition and in the component controller.

14.2.2 Creating a Floorplan Application

In order to create our floorplan application, we have a multitude of configuration objects to create: an application, an application configuration, and each component configuration. While you're certainly welcome to create each of these objects manually, an easier way to do so would be by using the *Application Creation Tool* for FPM, as shown in Figure 14.7. This tool creates all the development objects you need for a new floorplan application:

1. Start Web Dynpro application `FPM_CFG_APPL_CREATION_TOOL` through any of the usual means (testing it from the Object Navigator or Transaction SICF, or running it directly from your browser).

2. Enter an application name and description for your new FPM application in their respective fields. Choose which floorplan you want to use by selecting it from the dropdown menu.

3. Click the PROPOSE button. This will propose and display configuration names for each of the configuration objects you'll need as a part of your application, including a header component configuration (for `FPM_IDR_COMPONENT`) if it's used by the floorplan that you selected.

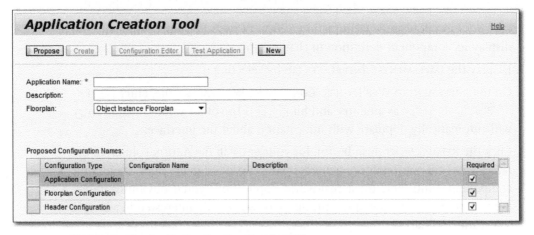

Figure 14.7 The Application Creation Tool for FPM

4. If you're satisfied with the proposed values, click the CREATE button in order to create each configuration object. Otherwise, you may edit the name and description of each configuration and then click CREATE.

5. The system will create each object. You may additionally perform any of the following options from this screen:

   ▸ Click TEST to run your newly created application.

   ▸ Select a component and click CONFIGURATION EDITOR to edit its configuration. This will open in a new window.

   ▸ Click NEW to create another FPM application using the tool.

> **Note**
>
> In addition to the Application Creation Tool, you may copy and browse existing FPM configurations using the *Application Hierarchy Browser*. This application displays the configuration object structure of an FPM application configuration in a tree format and allows you to copy individual component and application configurations for implementations in which you only want to make small changes in an existing application. This tool may be executed by calling on Web Dynpro application `FPM_CFG_HIERARCHY_BROWSER`.

14.2.3 Configuring a Floorplan Application

Now that you have each of your configuration objects, you may finally configure your FPM application. For the purposes of this section, we'll be adding the UIBB component you created earlier to your FPM application:

1. Launch the Configuration Editor for the floorplan component you selected. You may do so by any of the following methods:

   ▷ If you're still in the Application Creation Tool, select the FLOORPLAN CONFIGURATION row of the configuration table and click the CONFIGURATION EDITOR button.

   ▷ Locate the floorplan component's configuration object in the Object Navigator (SE80) and click the START CONFIGURATOR button you see when you display its attributes.

   ▷ Start the `CONFIGURE_COMPONENT` application and enter the name of the configuration to edit.

2. Enter into change mode for the FPM component configration. A custom Configuration Editor will display, similar to the one shown in Figure 14.8.

3. An empty UIBB component should already be populated in the content section of your floorplan. Click the ATTRIBUTES button for this UIBB.

4. Change the attributes of the UIBB to define a usage to the component you created in Section 14.2.1.

5. Save your changes and test your FPM application. You may call it from the Application Creation Tool or by looking up the application in the Object Navigator (SE80) and testing it. Your component should display within the framework of the FPM application. Figure 14.9 shows a very simple example of this.

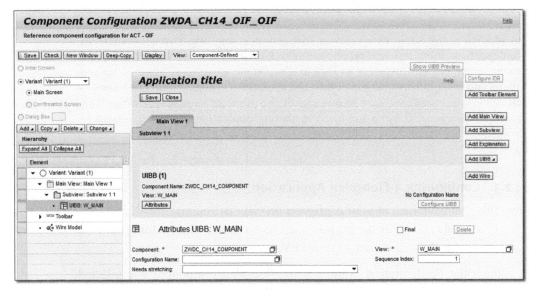

Figure 14.8 The Configuration Editor for an OIF Component

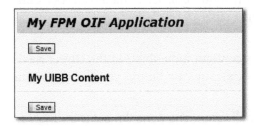

Figure 14.9 A Custom UIBB Displaying within an FPM Application

The FPM component editor allows more than just changing the type of UIBB you use in your application. The editor also integrates options for configuring toolbars, adding views, configuring decorative elements, adding wires, etc. These options will be discussed at greater length in during the course of the chapter.

14.3 Working with the Configuration Editor

The FPM Configuration Editor is a custom component-defined adaptation data editor. As such, it integrates into Web Dynpro's adaptation framework and may be called on using many of the means available to call on the standard Configuration Editor. Additionally, the Configuration Editor may be called in either the development mode or customization mode, depending on how you want to define or implement changes to your FPM applications. If you plan to modify an existing or delivered application, we recommend you customize these applications so that you will have made a modification-free change that won't be overwritten during an upgrade. For custom applications, how you implement the configuration is at your discretion.

14.3.1 Accessing the Configuration Editor

The Configuration Editor may be accessed through any of the means you use in order to change component-defined adaptation data.

Customizing Configurations as an Administrator

As an administrator, you may launch the editor by use of the CUSTOMIZE_COMPONENT application. If you were to run your FPM application in administrator mode (i.e., with the sap-config-mode=X parameter specified), an ADAPT CONFIGURATION link would display in the application's identification region (as shown in Figure 14.10), also taking you to the tool.

Figure 14.10 An Application Running in Administrator Mode

Developing Configurations

As a developer, you may launch the editor by use of the CONFIGURE_COMPONENT application. This may be launched in multiple places in the Object Navigator (Transaction SE80) or by running your application in expert mode. Expert mode is enabled by setting parameter FPM_CONFIG_EXPERT=X in a user's parameter data. As a result, a CHANGE CONFIGURATION link will appear in your FPM application's identification region, as shown in Figure 14.11. (Optionally, an APPLICATION HIERARCHY link may also appear and will direct you to the Application Hierarchy tool.)

Figure 14.11 An Application Running in Expert Mode

> **Note**
>
> As with the adaptation concept in general, if you want to customize FPM configurations, your user ID will require at least the S_WDR_P13N authorization. On the other hand, if you want to develop configuration objects, your user ID will require the S_DEVELOP authorization.

14.3.2 Features of the Configuration Editor

When you open the Configuration Editor, you're presented with a feature-rich screen similar to Figure 14.12, containing the following work areas:

▶ **Message area**
This area displays feedback to the developer or administrator about the actions they've taken in the editor (e.g., success and error messages, warnings, etc.).

▶ **Navigation region**
The navigation region is composed of two parts, as indicated below. You use these areas to browse and navigate through the pieces of your application.

  ▷ The *control area* allows you to select which screen you want to configure in the application. You may select among the initial screen, variant screens, and the dialog boxes tied to the application.

  ▷ The *hierarchy* area provides a hierarchy tree of all the elements you may configure. By selecting an element in the tree, you'll be able to manipulate its attributes and manage its contents.

▶ **Preview**
The preview area of the editor displays a preivew of your application. Only components that have implemented the IF_FPM_CFG_PREVIEW interface will display in this area. Otherwise, the editor will present a stand-in box to represent the element.

▶ **Action area**

This area contains push buttons and links to actions you may carry out in the editor for the given application. The actions available in this area vary among floorplans.

▶ **Attribute view**

The attribute view allows you to manipulate the attributes of a configurable element on the screen. Additionally, this is where the delete functionality for many elements resides.

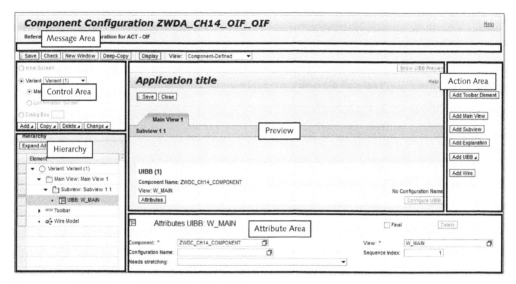

Figure 14.12 Work Areas of the Configuration Editor

14.3.3 Assigning a UIBB to the Page

UIBBs are added to your floorplan application by use of the Add UIBB button located in the action area of the Configuration Editor. Its use is demonstrated in the following procedure:

1. In the Configuration Editor, navigate to where you want to place the UIBB in the application.

2. If an unconfigured UIBB already exists in the page or section you're working in, click the Attributes button of the previewed UIBB to display its configuration. Otherwise, click the Add UIBB button in the action area of the editor to add a UIBB to the screen.

3. In the attributes area, specify the UIBB's component type, the view of the component you want to use, and a configuration name for the UIBB's component configuration.

4. Click SAVE to save your changes. A warning message may appear if the component configuration you specified doesn't exist.

5. Having specified a component configuration for your UIBB, the CONFIGURE UIBB button should activate for your UIBB in the preview section of the screen. Click it to launch the Configuration Editor for the component.

6. In the Configuration Editor, create your new configuration object if it doesn't exist or switch to change mode in order to configure the UIBB. Select the appropriate package and transport as necessary when making this transition.

7. If your UIBB requires a feeder class (i.e., is a data-consuming GUIBB), you may be prompted to specify it upon entering the editor.

8. Edit the UIBB's parameters on the component configuration screen and click the SAVE button.

14.4   Working with GUIBBs

In addition adding UIBBs to a floorplan, you may also add *Generic User Interface Building Blocks (GUIBBs)*. GUIBBs are types of building blocks that are supplied by SAP. These building blocks take on the form of common user interface structures a user might see, such as forms, tab controls, and trees. While you could create any of these UI elements in your own WDA components, the goal is to improve the uniformity of these types of views across your applications by providing common components from which they're constructed. For example, by using a search GUIBB in your application, you provide a selection screen similar to what is found in an SAP GUI application. This is all meant, of course, to enhance the familiarity of and adoption rate of your applications.

Some GUIBBs contain data, while some don't. For instance, a tab control contains no data—it's entirely a presentation-layer artifact. On the other hand, a form or list GUIBB is designed to present you with data marshaled by means of a *feeder class*. These feeder classes implement GUIBB-specific interfaces whose methods are called on to supply data to the GUIBB. A breakdown of the available GUIBBs on the system, their underlying WDA components, and their feeder class interfaces (if applicable) are listed in Table 14.3.

GUIBB	Component	Feeder Class Interface
Form	FPM_FORM_UIBB	IF_FPM_GUIBB_FORM
List	FPM_LIST_UIBB	IF_FPM_GUIBB_LIST
Tab Control	FPM_TABBED_UIBB	N/A
Search	FPM_SEARCH_UIBB	IF_FPM_GUIBB_SEARCH
Launchpad	FPM_LAUNCHPAD_UIBB	N/A
Confirmation Screen	GUIBB_CONFIGURABLE_CONF	N/A
Hierarchical List	FPM_TREE_UIBB	IF_FPM_GUIBB_TREE

Table 14.3 GUIBB Components and their Feeder Classes

Since GUIBBs are a type of UIBB, they may be incorporated into your floorplan applications from the Configuration Editor, just as you'd incorporate any other UIBB.

Many of the GUIBB elements come with their own editors, which may be launched from either the FPM editor or the standard component editor. If the GUIBB incorporates data from a feeder class, this data is automatically integrated into the editor for you to manipulate its look and feel.

14.5   Configuring Wires

The Floorplan Manager offers the ability to link and transfer data between two UIBBs by *wiring* the components together. Wires in FPM are declared globally within your application and enact a one-way data transfer between components from a source to a target as long as the requisite interfaces are implemented.

Specifically, both UIBB components must implement the IF_FPM_UIBB_MODEL Web Dynpro interface, which supplies a reference to a class implementing the IF_FPM_FEEDER_MODEL interface via the GET_MODEL_API method. These interfaces are further governed by a *connector class (of type* IF_FPM_CONNECTOR*)*, which serves to transfer data between interfaces based on the specified *output type*: lead selection, selection, or collection data.

Even further adding to the interface requirements, in an FPM application, a component may only be the target of a single wire. This is due in part to how the FPM framework determines wires sources and targets in an application. Source components, on the other hand, may supply data to multiple targets.

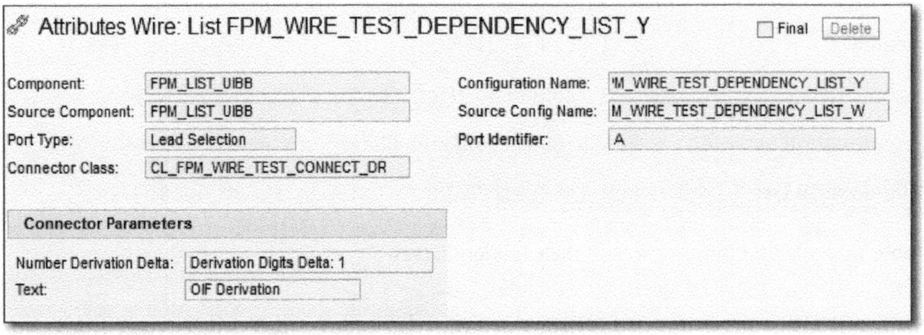

Figure 14.13 Attributes of a Wire Configuration

Each of these pieces is defined in the wiring's attributes during its configuration, as shown in Figure 14.13. In many cases, this may seem a bit much to develop, and there are perhaps more elegant ways of sharing data between UIBB components (e.g., implementing component usages to an IF_FPM_SHARED_DATA component or proxying data transfers through standard ABAP classes or function groups), but for GUIBB integration with your applications, wiring is essential.

14.6 Working with Dialog Boxes

Floorplan Manager applications may incorporate dialog boxes in order to inform users of system actions, provide missing data, or confirm an action they perform. Dialog boxes are flexible components that may contain one or many UIBBs.

14.6.1 Creating an FPM Dialog Box

To create an FPM dialog, follow these steps:

1. In the Configuration Editor, click the ADD push button and select DIALOG BOX, as depicted in Figure 14.14.

2. Specify the name and object ID of your dialog box in the popup that appears and click the ADD button to add it to your FPM application.

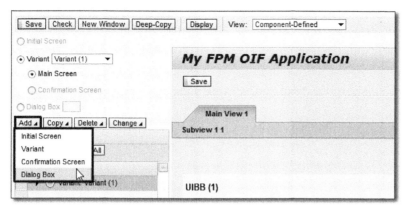

Figure 14.14 Adding a Dialog Box in the Configuration Editor

3. An editor view for the dialog box diplays. Modify the attributes of the dialog box as you see fit. You may perform any of the following operations:

▸ Select which standard dialog box buttons to display.

▸ Configure tooltips for each button that displays.

▸ Define a title for the dialog box.

▸ Select a layout type for any UIBBs contained with the dialog box.

4. Modify the default UIBB's attributes so that they refer to a component. You may additionally add other UIBBs to the dialog box as you see fit.

5. Save your changes by clicking the SAVE button.

14.6.2 Assigning a Dialog Box to a Toolbar Button

To assign a dialog box to a toolbar button, follow these steps:

1. Switch to the Configuration Editor for your FPM application.

2. Select the ADD ELEMENT TO TOOLBAR push button on the screen to create a new toolbar button.

3. A dialog box appears, asking you to select a toolbar element to create. Select OTHER FUNCTION under the APPLICATION SPECIFIC FUNCTION BUTTONS (OPTION) section of the popup.

4. Enter attributes for the button's standard attributes (e.g., label, explanation text, and tooltip).

5. For the FPM EVENT ID field, enter `FPM_OPEN_DIALOG`.

6. In the MAINTAIN EVENT PARAMETERS table, add `DIALOG_BOX_ID` and the ID you gave your dialog box as a parameter by clicking the ADD PARAMETER button and entering each value as the PARAMETER NAME and PARAMETER VALUE, respectively (Figure 14.15).

7. Save your changes and test the button's functionality by launching the application.

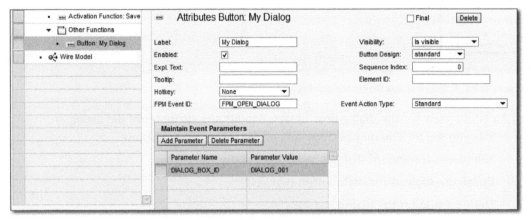

Figure 14.15 Assigning a Dialog Box to a Toolbar Button

14.6.3 Calling Dialog Boxes Programmatically

You may additionally call on dialog boxes programmatically from your UIBB's code. This is done by a method call to `IF_FPM~OPEN_DIALOG_BOX` or by manually triggering event `FPM_OPEN_DIALOG` with its requisite parameters by using method `IF_FPM~RAISE_EVENT_BY_ID`.

14.7 Web Dynpro Page Builder

Strictly speaking, the Web Dynpro Page Builder is not a part of the FPM framework, but it does represent a similar technology with similar integration goals. Like FPM, the Page Builder is a Web Dynpro component through which you configure and expose other Web Dynpro content. Unlike FPM, though, you aren't restricted to the floorplans provided by SAP to determine the layout of your application, and in the case of *side panels*, you can actually embed a Page Builder application within your WDA application, making their integration more than a one-way consumer relationship.

Page Builder applications consist of *Pages* and *Collaborative Human Interface Parts (CHIPs)*. Each page has a *canvas* onto which you place your CHIPs in the layout of your choice. Each CHIP, in the meantime, may expose web pages contained within IFrames, links and favorites, or even a WDA component, which is where our primary interest lies. Figure 14.16 shows an example of a Page Builder application. As you can see, the application is split into tray-based sections, each representing a CHIP.

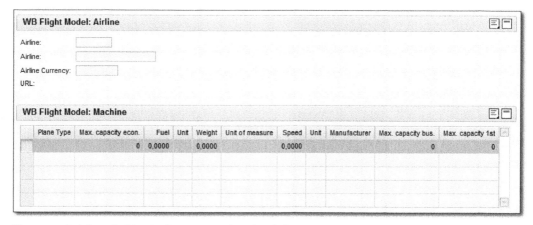

Figure 14.16 A Page Builder Application Based on the Flight Demo Scenario

14.7.1 Creating Pages

Pages are instantiations of the WDR_CHIP_PAGE WDA application, which is an implementation of component WDR_CHIP_PAGE. In order to create your own page, you should create an application configuration for it by selecting the CREATE/ CHANGE CONFIGURATION option from the **WDR_CHIP_PAGE** application's context menu in Transaction SE80. For this application configuration, you'll have to set component configurations for the WDR_CHIP_PAGE component and its CHIP_CATA- LOG usage.

14.7.2 Accessing the Page Builder

The Page Builder is implemented as a runtime authoring environment executed from your application. To do this, append URL parameter `sap-config-mode` with value `config` to your application's URL. For example:

https://<hostname:port>/sap/bc/webdynpro/sap/WDR_CHIP_PAGE?sap-wd-configid= <app-config-id>&sap-config-mode=config

---

Note

In order to run the Page Builder, you'll need authorization S_PB_PAGE.

Once inside the page builder, you can define the page's layout and containers and add, remove, or configure CHIPs in those containers, including wiring them together for integration and navigation. The following CHIPs are provided to you by default:

▶ Web CHIPs, which display web pages you may specify by URL

▶ Favorites lists, which allow you to display a list of CHIPs as links that may either be opened in a new window (default behavior) or displayed on the page using a *display area*

▶ Display areas, which integrate with favorites lists to display CHIP content

In addition to these CHIP content options, you may define CHIPs that refer to Web Dynpro components, whose creation is discussed in the next section.

14.7.3 Creating Web Dynpro CHIPs

You may expose WDA components as Page Builder CHIPs by defining a Web Dynpro CHIP in the Web Dynpro Explorer. To do this, simply select a Web Dynpro component in the Object Navigator (Transaction SE80) and select CREATE • WEB DYNPRO CHIP from its context menu. This will display an object definition for your CHIP similar to Figure 14.17, which you configure to expose your component.

For your CHIP, you may additionally configure *inports* and *outports*, which allow you to transfer data between CHIPs.

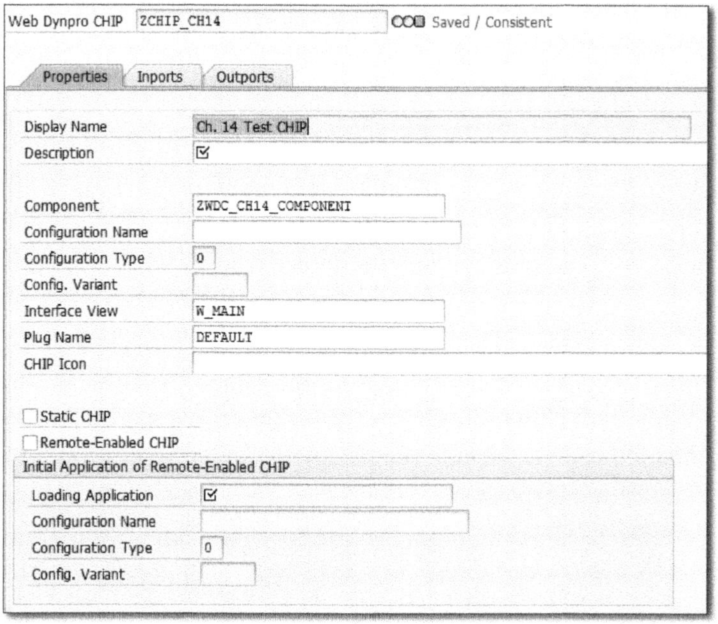

Figure 14.17 Object Definition for a Page Builder CHIP

Defining a CHIP Inport

Inports allow you to send data to your WDA component from other CHIPs. An inport in your component takes the form of an interface method defined in your component controller. To define a CHIP inport:

1. Open the Methods tab of the component controller in your component.

2. Create a method on this tab and set the Interface flag.

3. Create importing parameters for this method and set their types. You must have at least one parameter in your method for it to serve as an inport.

4. This method may be referenced as an inport on the Inports tab of your CHIP object definition.

Defining a CHIP Outport

Outports allow you to send data from your WDA component to other CHIPs. These are defined as events in the component controller of your WDA component. To define a CHIP outport:

1. Open the Events tab of the component controller in your component.

2. Create an event on this tab and set the Interface flag.

3. Create a parameter for this event.

4. Go to the action handler from where the event is to be fired in your component. This will likely be in an action definition in one of your components views.

5. Add suitable statements to your action handler in order to fire the event you created.

   You may use the Web Dynpro code wizard to generate these statements by selecting the Method Call in Used Controller option on the General tab and specifying your component controller and the appropriate event. You'll have to modify the generated code to include the parameter(s) you want to pass to another CHIP.

6. This event may be referenced as an outport on the Outports tab of your CHIP object definition.

14.7.4 Adding a Side Panel to WDA Applications

One of the key features Page Builder brings with it is the ability to integrate a side panel into your Web Dynpro applications. In order to do this, you must prepare your component's view by doing the following:

1. On the Layout tab of your view, add a `PageHeader` UI element to your view with the element ID `PAGE_HEADER`. You must use this name and not deviate from it.

2. Add a `TransparentContainer` UI element as the title content of your `Page-Header` and set its layout to either `MatrixLayout` or `FlowLayout` as shown in Figure 14.18.

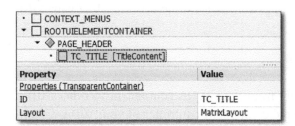

Figure 14.18 Defining Elements in a View to Enable a Side Panel

3. On the ACTIONS tab of your view, define an event named OPEN_SIDE_PANEL and save it. Again, you shouldn't deviate from this name.

4. In the action handler for the action you just created, add the following code:

```
cl_wd_side_panel_api=>get_api( )->open( ).
```

5. On the METHODS tab of your view, you'll also need to define the following in the view's WDDOINIT method:

```
cl_wd_side_panel_api=>get_api( )->init(
    view_controller = wd_this->wd_get_api( )
    open_action_name = 'OPEN_SIDE_PANEL'
).
```

6. Finally, you need to open your application in configuration mode (e.g., using the sap-config-mode=x parameter) and specify your side panel configuration by clicking the SET ADDITIONAL INFORMATION link in the PageHeader element you created in your view, as shown in Figure 14.19.

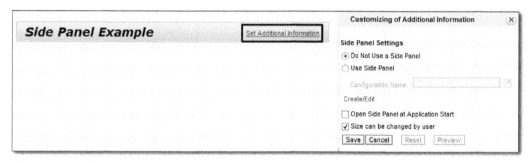

Figure 14.19 Configuration Options for a Side Panel

Side panels exist as special implementations of Page Builder pages. You may create a side panel by launching the Page Builder Configuration Editor with the following additional parameters:

▶ page_type=SIDE_PANEL

▶ side_panel_editor_enabled=x

Your editor URL might then be extended to:

https://<hostname:port>/sap/bc/webdynpro/sap/WDR_CHIP_PAGE?sap-wd-configid=<app-config-id>&sap-config-mode=config&page_type=SIDE_PANEL&side_panel_editor_enabled=X

14.8   Summary

In this chapter, we took a tour of the Floorplan Manager and an accompanying framework, the Web Dynpro Page Builder. Each of these technologies is designed to accelerate development and provide you with a common framework from which to construct your applications. In the long run, even if you choose not to use these technologies in your own WDA applications, be aware that applications based on these frameworks are already being delivered. At the very least, an awareness of what they bring to the table and how they're used will serve you when it comes to adapting and modifying such content.

A fair question to ask about any technology platform is how well it integrates with other technologies and what you must do to make that integration work. In this chapter, we'll answer that question by exploring some of the options you have to integrate WDA with other technologies.

15 WDA Integration

Integration has always been a keen topic of discussion for developers. Sometimes the offerings of one technology make it a better medium in which to develop functionality over others. Web Dynpro, like all technologies, has its warts and cannot or should not—by limitation or scope—be the sole implementing technology of your solution. Of course, this means you'll have to find some way to integrate your technologies.

This chapter is designed to provide you with a sample of the technologies Web Dynpro is designed to integrate with and how to make that integration happen. In this chapter, we'll take a look at integrating with *Rich Internet Applications* such as Adobe Flex and Microsoft Silverlight, technologies that already integrate into SAP GUIs such as Adobe Interactive Forms. We'll also look at how to integrate WDA applications into SAP NetWeaver Portal and call other applications and services.

> **Note**
>
> When integrating between different technology platforms, it's almost a given that certain limitations exist for their interoperability and support. As you embark on integrating WDA with any of the technologies discussed in this chapter, be sure to keep aware of the officially supported software levels for each platform. While SAP Notes (*http://service.sap.com/notes*) often provide the final word on version compatibility, good references also exist in each of the technology's individual help topics at the SAP Help website (*http://help.sap.com*) and within in the SAP Product Availability Matrix (*http://service.sap.com/pam*).

15.1   RIA Integration with Web Dynpro Islands

In SAP NetWeaver 7.01 (EHP 1), Web Dynpro began offering integration support for Adobe Flash applications using Adobe Flash Islands built in the Adobe Flex framework. As of SAP NetWeaver 7.02 (EHP 2), Web Dynpro has been expanded to support additional features in Flash applications and integration with Microsoft Silverlight applications using Microsoft Silverlight Islands. Both Adobe Flash and Microsoft Silverlight are web application frameworks that belong to the Rich Internet Application (RIA) paradigm. That is, they're designed to create highly interactive, often highly graphical applications and widgets for the web and mobile devices. They achieve this high level of interactivity by running entirely on the client side through the use of browser and operating system plugins. In a web browser context, RIA technologies are not typically designed to display all elements of a page—they rely on HTML containers to embed and specify their use and are typically regulated to bringing specific and limited functionality to a web page. (In the device context, this is different, and RIA technologies often take on all aspects of an application.) Web Dynpro, being a web technology platform designed to generate HTML, therefore seeks to follow this same pattern of integration as well as provide tools through which both technologies may communicate with one another on a page and influence each other's data. In general, we refer to this Web Dynpro integration pattern as the *Islands Framework*.

15.1.1   View Concepts in the Islands Framework

Islands are UI element types designed to contain and interface with Rich Internet Applications. Currently, Web Dynpro supports two types of Islands: the FlashIsland element and the SilverlightIsland element, which in turn support Flash and Silverlight applications, respectively. Unlike most UI elements, these elements aren't designed to be added to a view, but to replace the root element of a view in its entirety. You may do this by following the procedure below:

1. Navigate to your component in the Object Navigator (Transaction SE80) and display your view in change mode in the Web Dynpro Explorer.

2. In the layout editor of your view (i.e., on the LAYOUT tab), select and open the context menu of your view's ROOTUIELEMENTCONTAINER and select the SWAP ROOT ELEMENT option from the menu, as shown in Figure 15.1.

3. A dialog will appear in which you may select to swap the element's type for a `FlashIsland` or `SilverlightIsland` element, which is again shown in Figure 15.1.

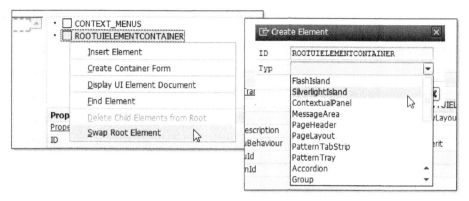

Figure 15.1 Swapping the Root Element of a View

Once these elements are swapped, you'll no longer be able to add the majority of Web Dynpro UI elements to the view—it will be entirely dedicated to the RIA application you want to expose. In turn, if you want to mix WDA and Islands content on a page, we recommend you adopt the "view-within-a-view" concept and embed your Islands within a `ViewContainerUIElement` in the WDA view.

15.1.2 Data Transfer Concepts in the Islands Framework

While you may no longer be able to insert your typical UI elements within your Islands view, you're now offered the opportunity to add some Islands-specific elements to the view. Options to insert these elements should appear on the context menu of your `ROOTUIELEMENTCONTAINER`, as indicated in Figure 15.2.

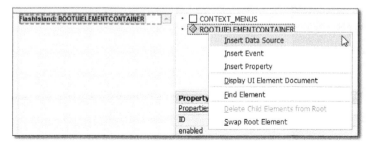

Figure 15.2 New Elements that May Be Added to an Islands View

Among these options are the INSERT DATA SOURCE and INSERT PROPERTY choices, which allow you to add GACDataSource and GACProperty elements, respectively, to your Island. What these elements represent are data transfer objects analogous to the nodes and attributes in your context. You use these elements to construct a context by which to send and receive data from your Islands application. Please keep the following in mind while constructing this context:

▶ GACDataSource elements represent nodes of multiplicity (cardinality x..n) in a context. These may, in turn, contain further GACDataSource elements (i.e., child nodes) or GACProperty elements.

▶ GACProperty elements represent attribute data in a context.

▶ For performance reasons, you shouldn't transfer all your view context data to the Island; send only what you need.

▶ The integration of GAC controls in WDA dialog boxes (i.e., popups) is not supported.

GAC control properties, which are the key to how WDA components integrate with their Islands applications, possess the properties shown in Table 15.1 and Table 15.2.

Property Name	Type	Description
id	STRING	The element's ID in Web Dynpro.
dataSource	Context Node	A context node in the view controller your data binds to.
name	STRING	The name of the list object to fill in your Islands application. This name must be identical to what you've coded in your application.

Table 15.1 GACDataSource Properties

Property Name	Type	Description
id	STRING	The element's ID in Web Dynpro.
name	STRING	The name of the variable to fill in your Islands application. This name must be identical to what you've coded in your application.

Table 15.2 GACProperty Properties

Property Name	Type	Description
readOnly	WDY_BOOLEAN	Indicates whether the Islands application may write to this property.
value	STRING	The value of the property to transfer as a STRING.

Table 15.2 GACProperty Properties (Cont.)

The absolutely essential property each of these controls has is the name property, which must be identical to the bound variable names defined in the Islands application's code.

15.1.3 Eventing Concepts in the Islands Framework

In addition to GAC data control elements, you may also define event control elements for an Islands view. These elements allow you to handle events triggered in an Islands-enabled RIA component within your WDA application. Specifically, the GACEvent and GACEventParameter controls are designed to assist you with this and may be added to your Islands view in a similar fashion to the data controls (i.e., from the ROOTUIELEMENTCONTAINER's context menu).

GAC event controls similarly have key properties that must be defined as shown in Table 15.3 and Table 15.4.

Property Name	Type	Description
id	STRING	The element's ID in Web Dynpro.
name	STRING	The name of the event as defined in your Islands application code.
onAction	WD Event	The event to trigger on the Web Dynpro side.

Table 15.3 GACEvent Properties

Property Name	Type	Description
id	STRING	The element's ID in Web Dynpro.

Table 15.4 GACEventParameter Properties

637

Property Name	Type	Description
name	STRING	The name of the event parameter as defined in your Islands application's code.
type	WDUI_GAC_DATA_TYPE	The parameter's data type.

Table 15.4 GACEventParameter Properties (Cont.)

Again, it's absolutely essential to match the name properties defined in these controls to the parameter names you use in your Islands application's code.

15.2 Adobe Flash Islands Integration

Adobe Flex (*http://adobe.com/flex*) is an RIA framework that's compatible with Adobe Flash Player technology. As we discussed above, Web Dynpro integrates with this technology by means of the FlashIsland UI element. This section will delve further into how to make this integration occur.

15.2.1 Preparing Adobe Flash Builder to Work with Web Dynpro

Adobe Flex integrates with WDA via SAP Web Dynpro Island Library for Flex. As an initial step in your Adobe Flex development, you'll need to obtain and reference these libraries in your Flex application project. To prepare Adobe Flash Builder to work with Web Dynpro, follow these steps:

1. SAP distributes the Web Dynpro Island Library for Flex files within its MIME Repository on ABAP servers. In the ABAP Workbench Object Navigator (Transaction SE80), select the MIME REPOSITORY browser and navigate to the path *SAP/PUBLIC/BC/UR/nw7/FlashIslands*.

2. Locate the two files *WDIslandLibrary.swc* and *WDIslandLibrary-debug.swc* and download them to your local file system via their right-click context menus.

3. Switch to Adobe Flash Builder and open your Flex project.

4. Right-click on your project in the Package Explorer and select PROPERTIES.

5. In the dialog that appears, select FLEX BUILD PATH from the properties navigator and define references to the downloaded libary files either by adding them

individually with the ADD SWC... button or by a common folder you may have saved them to with the ADD SWC FOLDER... button.

6. The Web Dynpro Island Library for Flex should now be available to your project, as shown in Figure 15.3.

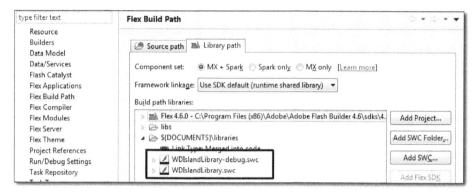

Figure 15.3 Referencing the WD Island Library for Flex in a Project's Build Properties

15.2.2 Integrating Flash Islands in Web Dynpro

You learned how to prepare a WDA view in order to embed a FlashIsland element back in Section 15.1.1. However, that discussion didn't delve into the individual properties you must set in your element in order to actually expose a Flash application. That procedure is defined below:

1. Build and export your Adobe Flex application.

2. Import the application into your WDA component as a new MIME object. (You may alternatively import the application into the MIME Repository and reference it from there.)

3. Open your FlashIsland view in change mode.

4. Set the swfFile property in your FlashIsland container to reference the MIME object you just uploaded. Figure 15.4 depicts an example of this.

5. Additionally, provide appropriate height and width properties for the Flash-Island. Views that don't provide a height value will render with zero height, which will prevent you from seeing your content.

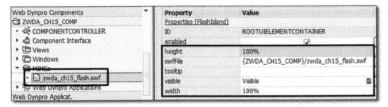

Figure 15.4 A FlashIsland Referencing a Flex Application in a WDA Component's MIMEs Folder

15.2.3 Data Transfer

As we discussed in Section 15.1.2, data transfer between a `FlashIsland` and a Flex application is conducted by defining GAC data controls for each data property you want to share between applications. On the Flex side of the house, in order to bind your data, you must first register your Flex component in the Adobe Flex `FlashIsland` framework and then create and bind variable names for each of the GAC controls you created.

Figure 15.5 illustrates this concept. For each of the bound variables defined in the Flex application code, a `GACDataSource` or `GACDataProperty` is created in the WDA application to match. The `name` property of each of these GAC data controls is then set to hold the name of the Flex application variable it represents.

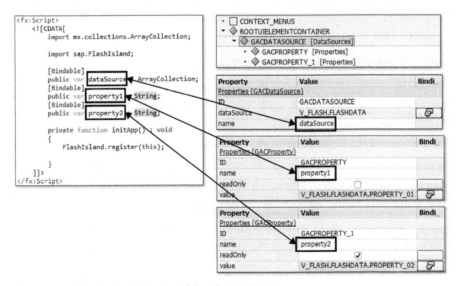

Figure 15.5 Data Binding between Adobe Flex and WDA

15.2.4 Event Integration

You may fire an event in your Web Dynpro application from within a Flash Islands application. You implement this by adding GAC event controls to your `FlashIsland` element and calling the `FlashIsland.fireEvent` method from within your Adobe Flex application. Your `GACEvent` controller will in turn call on the Web Dynpro action it's bound to.

Figure 15.6 illustrates this concept. `GACEvent` and child `GACEventParameter` controls are defined in the WDA application in order to handle the event fired from the Flex application. Similar to GAC data controls, the `name` property of each of these controls is defined to match the event and parameter names that were used in the Flex application.

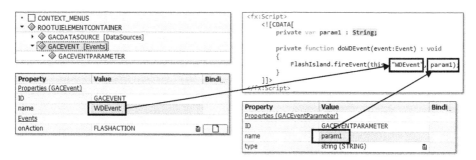

Figure 15.6 Event Binding between Adobe Flex and WDA

You may retrieve parameter data passed to your WDA application during the event call by using the `GET_DATA` method of your `WDEVENT` parameter in your action handler method.

15.2.5 Theme Integration

As of SAP NetWeaver 7.02 (EHP 2), the Adobe Flash Islands framework offers integrated support for the use of standard and customer themes within Flex applications. In order to support this functionality, you need to register the `FlashIslandTheme` object along with your component when you initialize your Flex application:

```
private function initApp() : void {
    FlashIsland.register(this, new FlashIslandTheme());
}
```

15.2.6 Drag and Drop Integration

Additionally, as of SAP NetWeaver 7.02 (EHP 2), you may drag and drop between WDA and Adobe Flex components.

15.3 Microsoft Silverlight Islands Integration

Microsoft Silverlight (*http://www.microsoft.com/silverlight*) may integrate with your Web Dynpro applications using many of the same features of Islands Framework available to Adobe Flash applications. They accomplish this by incorporating the `SilverlightIsland` UI element in a Web Dynpro component view and using many of the same GAC controls to enact data transfer and fire events between your Silverlight and WDA applications.

15.3.1 Preparing Microsoft Visual Studio to Work with Web Dynpro

Microsoft Silverlight integrates with WDA via SAP Web Dynpro Island Library for Silverlight. As an initial step in your Microsoft Silverlight development, you'll need to obtain and reference these libraries in your Silverlight application project. To prepare Microsoft Visual Studio to work with Web Dynpro, follow these steps:

1. SAP distributes the Web Dynpro Island Library for Silverlight file within its MIME Repository on ABAP servers. In the ABAP Workbench Object Navigator (Transaction SE80), select the MIME REPOSITORY browser and navigate to the path *SAP/PUBLIC/BC/UR/nw7/SilverIslands*.

2. Locate the file *WDSilverlightIslandLibrary.dll* and download it to your local file system via its context menu.

3. Switch to Microsoft Visual Studio and open your Silverlight project.

4. In the Solution Explorer, open the context menu of the REFERENCES folder and select ADD REFERENCE.

5. In the dialog that appears, find the file you downloaded by browsing to it.

6. Select it and click the OK button to add the reference to your project.

7. The Web Dynpro Island Library for Silverlight should now be available to your project.

15.3.2 Integrating Silverlight Islands in Web Dynpro

Similar to the way Adobe Flash applications work, Silverlight applications are integrated into Web Dynpro by storing the application file in the MIME Repository and referencing it from your `SilverlightIsland` element. To do this, follow the procedure below:

1. Build and export your Silverlight application.

2. Import the application into your WDA component as a new MIME object. (You may alternatively import the application into the MIME Repository and reference it from there.)

3. Open your `SilverlightIsland` view in change mode.

4. Set the `source` property in your `SilverlightIsland` container to reference the MIME object you just uploaded.

5. Additionally, provide appropriate `height` and `width` properties for the `SilverlightIsland`. Views that don't provide a `height` value will render with zero height, which will prevent you from seeing your content.

15.3.3 Data Transfer

In order to enable a Silverlight application to transfer data to Web Dynpro, you need to register your Silverlight component with the Silverlight Island framework by means of the `SilverlightIsland.Register` method. An example of this is illustrated in Figure 15.7.

```
namespace ZWDC_CH15_COMP
{
    public partial class MainPage : UserControl
    {
        private SilverlightIsland silverlightFramework = new SilverlightIsland();

        public MainPage(StartupEventArgs e)
        {
            InitializeComponent();

            // Register with Web Dynpro
            silverlightFramework.Register(this, e);
```

Figure 15.7 Registering a Component with the Silverlight Framework

For `GACProperty` controls that aren't associated with a data source (i.e., are direct properties of the `SilverlightIsland` element), you may bind them to the `IslandPropertyAttribute` class in Silverlight, as shown in Figure 15.8.

```
[IslandPropertyAttribute(typeof(string))]
public string nonDSProperty { get; set; }
```

Figure 15.8 Binding a GACProperty That Is Not a Child of a GACDataSource

For `GACDataSource` controls, the data is set by defining variables for `IIslandData-sourceObject` and `IIslandDatasourceProperty` interfaces, as shown in Figure 15.9.

```
// A SilverlightIsland DataSource
public IIslandDatasourceObject dataSource { get; set; }

// SilverlightIsland DataSource Attributes
public IIslandDatasourceProperty property1 { get; set; }
public IIslandDatasourceProperty property2 { get; set; }
```

Figure 15.9 Binding to a GACDataSourceEvent Integration

`GACEvent` controls for Silverlight may be fired by use of the `SilverlightIsland.FireEvent` method. Event parameters are supplied to this method by means of a dictionary object, as shown in Figure 15.10.

```
IDictionary<string, object> eventParam = new Dictionary<string, object>();
eventParam.Add("parameter1", param1);
eventParam.Add("parameter2", param2);

silverlightFramework.FireEvent(this, "SilverlightEvent", eventParam);
```

Figure 15.10 Firing a Web Dynpro Event in Silverlight

15.4 SAP Interactive Forms by Adobe Integration

Aside from Rich Internet Applications, you also have the ability to integrate certain business document technologies within your Web Dynpro applications. One such type of business document is the Portable Document Format (PDF), which is integrated into Web Dynpro using SAP Interactive Forms by Adobe®.

The SAP Interactive Forms technology suite has been around for some time in ABAP systems, integrating directly into SAP GUI applications and performing tasks like outputting data for printing or archiving and serving as an online or offline data input mechanism. Web Dynpro use cases for forms sharply align with these tasks, allowing you to perform any of the following integration scenarios:

- Providing an input mechanism for online data input
- Providing print documents
- Providing an offline input mechanism

Forms integration with WDA is enabled by use of the `InteractiveForm` UI element. In the next few subsections, we'll explore how to use and integrate this element into your WDA applications.

Note

A whole host of prerequisites exist for integrating SAP Interactive Forms with Web Dynpro, including special software components and usage types. For a full list of these prerequisites, please consult the help topic WEB DYNPRO ABAP • WEB DYNPRO ABAP: DEVELOPMENT IN DETAIL • INTEGRATION • INTEGRATING FORMS • PREREQUISITES FOR FORM INTEGRATION on the SAP Help website (*http://help.sap.com*).

15.4.1 Creating a New Form from Web Dynpro

You can create new forms for your application directly in the Web Dynpro Explorer of the Development Workbench. The data structure of these forms is created by conforming to a specified node structure in your view's context. To create a new form from Web Dynpro, follow these steps:

1. Browse to and display a view in your Web Dynpro component in which you want to embed your form. (You may also choose to create a new view.)

2. In the view's context, create the data structure you intend to use in your form under a new node by supplying it with attributes.

3. Switch to the LAYOUT tab of your view and insert an `InteractiveForm` UI element on the page.

4. Select the `templateSource` property and insert a name for your new form. This name should be globally unique in the system (among all forms, WDA-based or otherwise). A dialog appears, asking you to specify a form interface.

5. Enter a name for the form interface in the INTERFACE NAME field of the dialog. Again, this name should be globally unique in the system.

6. Click the CONTEXT button on the dialog. A second dialog appears, displaying your view's context.

7. Select the context node you created earlier to represent the data structure of the form and click Continue. The selection you make here will bind to the dataSource property of your InteractiveForm UI element.

   The system creates your form objects and launches the Form Builder.

8. On the Properties tab of the Form Builder, choose ZCI Layout as the Layout Type and press Enter.

9. Insert the *ZCI-Skript* script that pairs with your layout type by selecting Utilities • Insert Web Dynpro Script from the GUI menu.

   As of SAP NetWeaver 7.01 (EHP 1), this is performed automatically.

10. Construct and compile your form using controls from the Web Dynpro Native library.

11. Compile your form using the UI controls from the Web Dynpro Native library.

12. Save your form and activate it.

13. Back in the Web Dynpro Explorer, specify whether your form is interactive or a print form by setting the enabled property of your InteractiveForm element. Interactive forms are enabled, and print forms are not.

15.4.2 Integrating Existing Forms

If you already have a form created that you want to expose in Web Dynpro, you may opt to specify the form name in your InteractiveForm element's template-Source property. Web Dynpro, in turn, will generate a context node modeled on the form's data structure in your view.

> **Note**
>
> When integrating an existing form into Web Dynpro, you may have to update the form to use the ZCI layout as its template. For more information on how to accomplish this, please refer to help topic Enabling Form-Based Processing of Business Data • Providing Output Forms and Interactive Offline Forms • Defining Form Templates • Defining the Layout of a Form Template • Checking and Updating Adobe Form Layouts on the SAP Help website (*http://help.sap.com*).

15.5   SAP NetWeaver Portal Integration

One of the technologies you've probably heard a good bit about in conjunction with WDA is SAP NetWeaver Portal. Portals are essentially content management systems for web applications. They catalog and aggregate web applications, often from disparate systems, and present them in a unified manner on a single web page. Very often they also provide authentication services to these web applications by establishing single sign-on relationships with the hosts of the web applications. Even more, they can also provide their own web applications and services, such as document management and collaborative workspace areas for teams. SAP NetWeaver Portal incorporates all these features.

> **Note**
>
> Obviously, this section focuses on only a small element of SAP NetWeaver Portal. For more information, you can consult *The Complete Guide to SAP NetWeaver Portal* (Chaitanya, SAP PRESS, 2012).

15.5.1   Preparing SAP NetWeaver Portal to Work with WDA

The portal displays your WDA application to end users through objects called *iViews*. These iViews use the IFRAME HTML tag in order to present your application as a piece of a portal page. On a portal system that connects to an ABAP backend system, these iViews generate the URL to your application dynamically. This is done so that when you move an iView through your landscape from development to production, you only have to change your AS ABAP system's server address in order for it to operate in the new environment. (This is a similar principle to maintaining ports on an ABAP system.) In order to enable this functionality, your iView is reliant on a portal configuration object known as a *system object*.

Figure 15.11 illustrates how system object data is referenced when a request is made to an iView on your SAP NetWeaver Portal system. The iView essentially reads the connection data from the system object, and constructs and returns an embedded URL to your browser that instructs it to access your WDA application on the Web AS ABAP system.

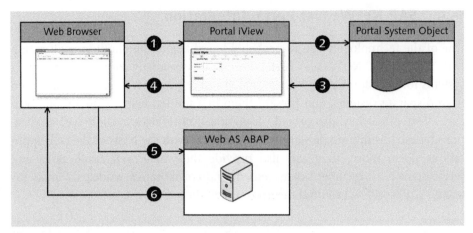

Figure 15.11 Portal Processing Sequence for a WDA iView Request

System objects are created as follows on an SAP NetWeaver 7.0–based portal system:

1. Log on to your portal system with administration rights.

2. Navigate to SYSTEM ADMINISTRATION • SYSTEM CONFIGURATION • SYSTEM LANDSCAPE using the tab navigation structure in the portal.

3. Browse in the Portal Content Directory to the folder in which you want to place your new system object and open its context menu.

4. Select NEW • SYSTEM (FROM TEMPLATE) from the menu options.

5. The system object creation wizard appears. Select the appropriate template that describes your AS ABAP system in your landscape (e.g., SAP SYSTEM USING DEDICATED APPLICATION SERVER or SAP SYSTEM WITH LOAD BALANCING) and click NEXT.

6. Fill out the properties on the screen that appears. These uniquely define your system object in the portal's content directory. Click NEXT to continue.

7. Click FINISH to create the system object and then click OK to start its editor.

8. For a connection to an AS ABAP system to work, you'll have to define the properties listed under WEB APPLICATION SERVER (WEB AS). When entering in your host name, please be sure to include the server's port as part of the name if it's non-standard, as shown in Figure 15.12.

9. Save the changes to your system object when your changes are complete.

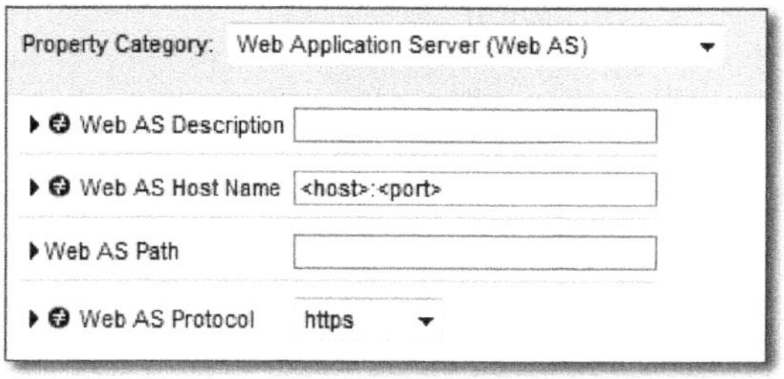

Figure 15.12 Web AS Properties in the System Object Definition

At this point, you may also need to set up a single sign-on between your portal and your AS ABAP system. How to do this and the options you have in its implementation are discussed at length in Chapter 16.

> **Note**
>
> On an SAP NetWeaver 7.3-based system, you initiate the wizard by navigating to System Administration • System Landscape on your portal and using the New button on the System Landscape Overview page to create your system object. Some small idiosyncrasies exist between each version of the wizard, but the procedure remains mostly the same.

15.5.2   Creating Web Dynpro ABAP iViews

After creating your system object, you'll need to create an iView to connect to your WDA application. You may do this as follows on an SAP NetWeaver 7.0–based portal system:

1. Log on to your portal system and select the Content Administration tab.

2. Browse to the Portal Content Directory folder in which you want to create your iView and launch the iView creation wizard by selecting New • iView from the context menu of your folder of choice.

3. A wizard launches. Select the Web Dynpro ABAP Application option for your WDA iView and click Next.

4. Enter the iView object properties on the screen that appears. This will uniquely identify your iView on the portal.

5. Enter the following information on the page that appears and click Next.

   ▹ Select the system object name (or its alias) that you created earlier for the System field.

- ▶ Enter the NAMESPACE for your WDA application.

- ▶ Enter the APPLICATION NAME for your WDA Application.

- ▶ You may additionally specify a CONFIGURATION NAME tying to an application configuration here and/or any application parameters for the WDA application.

6. Click FINISH to complete the creation of your view.

You may preview your WDA application by opening the context menu of the object you just created and selecting the PREVIEW option.

Note
At this point, your WDA application will still not be available to a portal user. In order to expose it to the end user, you'll have to add it to a portal role. For information on how perform this task, please examine the help topic PORTAL • PORTAL ADMINISTRATION GUIDE • CONTENT ADMINISTRATION • ROLES AND WORKSETS on the SAP Help website (*http://help.sap.com*).

15.5.3 Portal Event Integration

You may trigger and register for events that occur in the portal, allowing you WDA application to respond to occurrences in other iViews on your portal page. In order to manage portal events in WDA, use the methods of interface IF_WD_ PORTAL_INTEGRATION. For example, in order to trigger an event in the portal, use the FIRE method defined therein. Conversely, in order to listen and handle an event coming from the portal, you must define an action and handler for the event in your controller and then register your WDA application as an event subscriber using the SUBSCRIBE_EVENT method.

15.5.4 Portal Navigation

You may additionally tap into the portal's navigation framework using the methods of IF_WD_PORTAL_INTEGRATION. There are a number of scenarios for this, each using different portal navigation technologies:

- ▶ Object-based navigation (OBN)

- ▶ Absolute navigation

- ▶ Relative navigation

For more information on how to use these technologies, please refer to help topic WEB DYNPRO ABAP • WEB DYNPRO ABAP: DEVELOPMENT IN DETAIL • INTEGRATION • PORTAL INTEGRATION • PORTAL NAVIGATION on the SAP Help website (*http://help.sap.com*).

15.6   Consuming Web Services in WDA

Web Dynpro ABAP can't directly consume web services. Instead, you may broker a connection to a web service by means of an ABAP proxy object and a governing component controller, as depicted in Figure 15.13. A wizard to create your Web Dynpro component controller for the web service may be found in the context menu of your component in the Object Navigator (Transaction SE80). In order to initiate this wizard, you should select CREATE • SERVICE CALL from the list of options and select WEB SERVICE PROXY as your controller's service type at the appropriate place in the wizard.

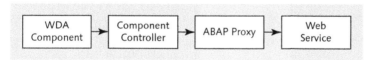

Figure 15.13 Development Pattern for Consuming Web Services in WDA

15.7   Summary

Web Dynpro offers to an application developer a considerable number of integration options that run the gamut from supplying embedded content to being consumed and presented by an SAP NetWeaver Portal system. There is no doubt that as the technology matures, the number of options available to you will increase significantly. Additionally, as the way we use web technology shifts, WDA has poised itself to integrate with these shifts by supplying generic frameworks that may be reused in order to accomodate new technologies. The future of WDA integration will be an interesting one, to say the least.

In the next chapter, we'll discuss a different type of integration topic: how to integrate security into your applications and the Web Dynpro framework. Just as with the feature and functionality integration we discussed in this chapter, security is a broad topic but essential for you to get the most out of WDA.

An ever-increasingly important part of development is to consider the security issues your applications may have. In this chapter, we'll examine security concepts in both WDA programming and the AS ABAP infrastructure to better enable the security and usage of your applications.

16   Security Concepts

Security can be a broad topic of conversation when it comes to the IT landscape. It permeates at all levels, and each level brings its own considerations to the table: physical infrastructure, networks, systems, applications, etc. Web Dynpro is no different in this regard, and it has its own unique concerns to think about. It is, after all, a web application framework, which implies that your applications will have a greater reach and promote greater connectivity between parties over the web. And in casting this wider web, adequately securing your WDA applications becomes an imperative task.

In this chapter, we'll examine some of the security and authentication practices you may employ to secure your WDA applications. This is by no means a comprehensive guide to AS ABAP security, but is designed to give you some helpful guidance in where to start and the considerations you may need to be aware of when developing your applications.

> **Note**
>
> We strongly encourage you to keep your system(s) up to date with the latest security updates and patches provided by SAP. You should also keep regular track of emerging security threats and how they should be mitigated by referring to any new SAP Security Notes that are published. A good resource for this information can be found in the Security Portal of the SAP Service Marketplace at *http://service.sap.com/security*.

16.1　System Logon

The first layer of security in connecting to a Web Dynpro application is the authentication process governing access to your AS ABAP system. As Figure 16.1 shows, there are multiple use cases on how a user may gain access to your WDA applications.

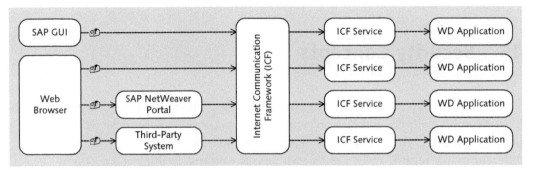

Figure 16.1 Use Cases for Access to a Web Dynpro Application

Provided that the appropriate configuration is set up, a user may access your applications in any of the following ways:

▶ From SAP GUI

▶ Directly from a web browser

▶ Via an SAP Portal

▶ Through a third-party system

That is how the users see it, though. Under the covers, each of these use cases relies on the user authentication mechanism defined for your application (either globally for your system or in the individual ICF service catering to your application). We'll be taking a look at a few of these authentication mechanisms in the rest of this section.

16.1.1　Customizing the Logon Screen for Your Applications

By default, Web Dynpro applications are set to present you with a logon screen if they need to authenticate you into the system. The configuration for this may be found by using the following procedure:

1. Open Transaction SICF in your GUI and navigate to service node */default_host/ sap/bc/webdynpro*, either by filling in the appropriate fields on the form or by browsing there after running the form without any filter criteria.

2. Select the ERROR PAGES tab of the service definition and then select the LOGON ERRORS subtab.

3. Click on the CONFIGURATION push button that corresponds to the SYSTEM LOGON radio button option.

4. A popup indicates the default settings for the logon screen, as shown in Figure 16.2.

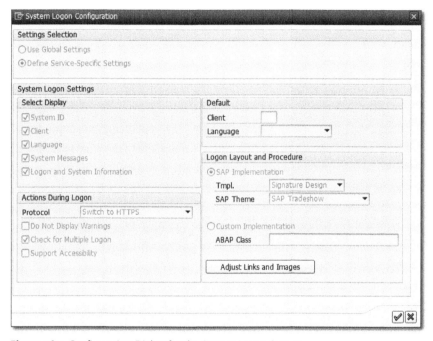

Figure 16.2 Configuration Dialog for the System Logon Screen

If the configuration of this screen is unsatisfactory to you or you want to change its presentation, you may reconfigure the screen for all Web Dynpro applications at this service node, or for an individual application at its own service node (thus breaking its system logon inheritance).

Most of the settings on the configuration dialog are self-explanatory; you can turn on and off fields to display on the logon screen by selecting the appropriate option. Or, you can mandate connection protocols and the default client and language to use. However, one peculiarity of the configuration options available to you is the ability to customize your logon implementation by selecting an ABAP class. This class must implement CL_IFC_SYSTEM_LOGON, which provides methods that write the logon and change password forms to the logon screen (i.e., HTM_LOGIN and HTM_CHANGE_PASSWD, respectively).

Logon screens work best the less you have to use them. End users don't want to have to re-enter their credentials every time they try to access a Web Dynpro application on your system. In order to provide this functionality, you should set your system to create and accept *SSO tickets*, which we'll discuss in the next section.

Logon Data and HTTPS

If you examine the logon screen configuration dialog in Figure 16.2, it provides an option for you to select the protocol used during logon. We highly recommend you log on to your system using one of the two HTTPS options. HTTPS ensures that the data (e.g., your username and password) passed to the logon screen is transmitted in an encrypted format. To send logon data in plain text (over HTTP) presents a hypothetical attacker on your network with the opportunity to glean this information and gain access to your system.

HTTPS is enabled only after you set up SSL on your system. For a guide on setting up SSL on your system, please consult help topic NETWORK AND TRANSPORT LAYER SECURITY • TRANSPORT LAYER SECURITY ON THE AS ABAP • CONFIGURING THE AS ABAP FOR SUPPORTING SSL on the SAP Help website (*http://help.sap.com*).

16.1.2 Logon Using SSO Tickets

Provided that your system is set up to accept them, you may authenticate into your WDA applications using *SSO tickets*. SSO tickets take the form of either *logon tickets* or *assertion tickets*:

▶ A logon ticket is a cookie issued to your browser or device from your AS ABAP system with the name MYSAPSSO2.

▶ An assertion ticket is transferred as an HTTP header variable with the name MYSAPSSO2.

The content of your MYSAPSSO2 cookie or header contains an encrypted logon string issued by your system that allows you to log over the validity period of the ticket without having to re-enter your username and password. Additionally, if you establish a trust between your system and another SAP system, portal, or even third-party system, you'll be able to log on to one system and *single sign-on* into your WDA applications.

To enable this functionality, you'll have to adjust certain system parameters via Transaction RZ11:

Parameter Name	Value	Description
login/accept_sso2_ticket	1	Instructs the server to permit logons using an SSO ticket.
login/create_sso2_ticket	1 or 2	Instructs the server to issue SSO tickets upon a successful login.
login/ticket_expiration_time	[h]h[:mm]	Sets the validity period of a logon ticket before a user must be issued a new one, in hours and (optionally) minutes.

Table 16.1 System Parameters in Order to Enable SSO Logon

Logon Tickets and Fully Qualified Domain Names (FQDN)

The issuance of a logon ticket and whether it may be accepted by your AS ABAP system are dependent on the domain name you've set for your server. Per the cookie handling rules that have been established for web browsers, cookies that are not issued against your server's host name or one of its domains won't be sent to your server. In order to ensure that this hand-off occurs, particularly between systems that are utilizing single sign-on, make sure your AS ABAP system is configured to use a *fully qualified domain name*.

For information on how to set parameters for this, please examine the help topic Web Dynpro ABAP • Web Dynpro ABAP Configuration • Fully Qualified Domain Names (FQDN) on the SAP Help website (*http://help.sap.com*).

16.1.3 Establishing a Single Sign-On Between Systems Using SSO Tickets

As we mentioned in the last section, you may establish single sign-on into your system through the use of SSO tickets. In order for this to occur, the following requirements must be met:

▶ Usernames must match between the foreign system and your own. This allows the user logging on to the foreign system to access his user profile on your system.

▶ The foreign system must be capable of producting an SSO ticket. If the system is an SAP AS ABAP or AS JAVA system, this functionality should be provided as part of its core implementation. If the foreign system is a non-SAP system, you'll have to search for a third-party solution that bridges this gap—SAP working with larger software partners will sometimes provide guidance on this.

▶ Per cookie handling rules, the SSO ticket the foreign system produces must be capable of being issued on one of the network domains your system resides on. For foreign systems on a different subnet that share the same root domain as your AS ABAP system, you may apply the principle of *domain-relaxing* on your cookie in order to enable this. For foreign systems that don't share your root domain, you'll have to proxy the creation of your cookie through a host that shares your system's domain by either a custom cookie-rewriting web application or by using the MDC host application provided on SAP NetWeaver Portal systems.

▶ You must import the system *personal security environment (PSE)* certificate of the foreign system into your system's trust manager. This certificate is used to decrypt the MYSAPSSO2 ticket issued by the foreign system in order to read the user information contained therein.

Importing a PSE into Your System

A foreign system's PSE certificate may be imported into your system by means of Transaction STRUSTSSO2. Follow these steps:

1. Obtain a copy of the foreign system's PSE certificate. This is typically located in the system's keystore. The base64-encoded DER certificate format is recognizable by AS ABAP and should be sufficient to transfer the certificate.

2. Open Transaction STRUSTSSO2 in SAP GUI on the client you want to establish a trust to. Users are stored by client, so you'll have to enact this procedure multiple times in order to provide single sign-on to multiple clients.

3. Select the SYSTEM PSE folder in the keystore navigation tree.

4. Upload the foreign key certificate by selecting the IMPORT button on the CERTIF-ICATE section of the screen.

5. A dialog appears, giving you options about how to import the certificate. When you click the INPUT button on the dialog, it closes, and information contained in the certificate should populate to the screen.

6. Click the ADD TO CERTIFICATE LIST push button in the CERTIFICATE section to upload the certificate to your keystore.

7. Click the ADD TO ACL push button in the same section to enable single sign-on into the current client.

8. Save your changes. Single sign-on via SSO ticket should now be enabled between your systems.

16.1.4 Logon Using an Identity Provider (IdP)

A good alternative to using SSO tickets to log on to your system is to use an *identity provider (IdP)* service that provides a common authentication mechanism for use throughout your organization. Identity providers operate on the principle that authentication into any system in a landscape should be centralized as opposed to unique to a system or negotiated via system-to-system single sign-on, as depicted in Figure 16.3. A major benefit of this approach is having a much cleaner system landscape where your systems need only be configured to trust the IdP in order to engage single sign-on, as opposed to potentially having to configure trusts for several systems (and then having to carry that configuration every time you stand up a new landscape). Additionally, many third-party systems are designed to integrate with IdPs, since they're often based on non-proprietary standards and could eliminate the need to engage in custom authentication module development.

SAP itself supports the use of *X.509 client certificates* and *SAML 2.0* as IdP technologies. For more information about using these technologies in an IdP configuration, consult help topic USER AUTHENTICATION AND SINGLE SIGN-ON • AUTHENTICATION ON THE AS ABAP on the SAP Help website (*http://help.sap.com*).

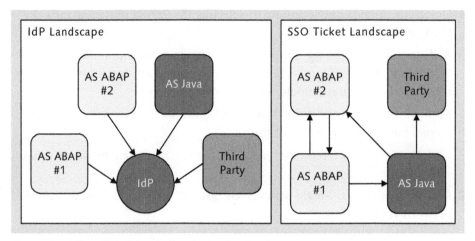

Figure 16.3 IdP vs. SSO Ticket Authentication in a Landscape

16.2 System Logoff and Error Pages

In addition to being able to specify a customized logon screen for your WDA application, you may customize logoff and error pages for the application. By employing these customized pages, you can prevent sending system or error information that you would rather not disclose to an end user (or potential attacker). You're also granted the opportunity to gracefully handle the user experience in these situations.

16.2.1 Application Logoff Page

When a WDA application exits and no other application is subsequently called, the Web Dynpro framework is designed to send you to a standard logoff page. This logoff page, like the logon screen, is configured in the Internet Communication Framework, which may be configured from Transaction SICF. In order to configure a logoff page for your application, perform the following steps:

1. Open Transaction SICF and navigate to your WDA application's service node (or parent node if you want to apply your changes in a hierarchical manner).

2. Select the ERROR PAGES tab on the service configuration screen.

3. Select the LOGOFF PAGE subtab.

4. Using the Explicit Response Page Header and Explicit Response Page Body screen segments, you can create an HTML page that will be sent back to the user, as shown in Figure 16.4. Alternatively, you may redirect the user to a specifield URL upon logout by using the Redirect to URL screen segment and radio option.

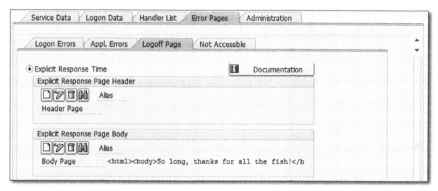

Figure 16.4 A Modified Logoff Page

16.2.2 Application Error Page

In an unmodified system, if an application error occurs, you'll receive an error message very much like the one shown in Figure 16.5. This error message contains such information such as hostnames, system IDs, logical system names, and user IDs—none of which you want to share with your user base or any potential attackers out there.

In order to mitigate the risk of someone maliciously using this information, you may create a separate error page for your application, in much the same way as you created your own logoff page in the last section.

To do this, you should follow the below procedure:

1. Open Transaction SICF and navigate to your WDA application's service node (or parent node if you want to apply your changes in a hierarchical manner).

2. Select the Error Pages tab on the service configuration screen.

3. Select the Appl. Errors subtab.

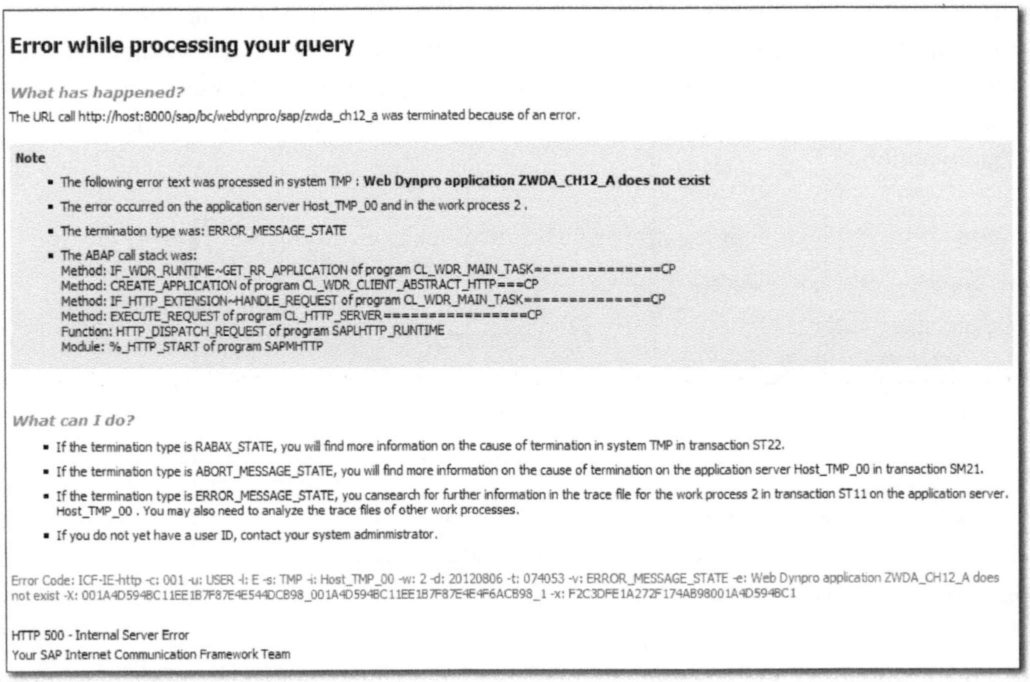

Error while processing your query

What has happened?

The URL call http://host:8000/sap/bc/webdynpro/sap/zwda_ch12_a was terminated because of an error.

Note

- The following error text was processed in system TMP : **Web Dynpro application ZWDA_CH12_A does not exist**
- The error occurred on the application server Host_TMP_00 and in the work process 2 .
- The termination type was: ERROR_MESSAGE_STATE
- The ABAP call stack was:
  Method: IF_WDR_RUNTIME~GET_RR_APPLICATION of program CL_WDR_MAIN_TASK==============CP
  Method: CREATE_APPLICATION of program CL_WDR_CLIENT_ABSTRACT_HTTP===CP
  Method: IF_HTTP_EXTENSION~HANDLE_REQUEST of program CL_WDR_MAIN_TASK==============CP
  Method: EXECUTE_REQUEST of program CL_HTTP_SERVER=================CP
  Function: HTTP_DISPATCH_REQUEST of program SAPLHTTP_RUNTIME
  Module: %_HTTP_START of program SAPMHTTP

What can I do?

- If the termination type is RABAX_STATE, you will find more information on the cause of termination in system TMP in transaction ST22.
- If the termination type is ABORT_MESSAGE_STATE, you will find more information on the cause of termination on the application server Host_TMP_00 in transaction SM21.
- If the termination type is ERROR_MESSAGE_STATE, you cansearch for further information in the trace file for the work process 2 in transaction ST11 on the application server. Host_TMP_00 . You may also need to analyze the trace files of other work processes.
- If you do not yet have a user ID, contact your system adminmistrator.

Error Code: ICF-IE-http -c: 001 -u: USER -l: E -s: TMP -i: Host_TMP_00 -w: 2 -d: 20120806 -t: 074053 -v: ERROR_MESSAGE_STATE -e: Web Dynpro application ZWDA_CH12_A does not exist -X: 001A4D5948C11EE1B7F87E4E544DCB98_001A4D5948C11EE1B7F87E4E4F6ACB98_1 -x: F2C3DFE1A272F174AB98001A4D5948C1

HTTP 500 - Internal Server Error
Your SAP Internet Communication Framework Team

Figure 16.5 A Standard Error Page Containing System Information

4. Using the EXPLICIT RESPONSE PAGE HEADER and EXPLICIT RESPONSE PAGE BODY screen segments, you can create an HTML page that will be sent back to the user.

Alternatively, you may redirect the user a specifield URL upon logout by using the REDIRECT TO URL screen segment and radio option.

> **Note**
>
> If you click the DOCUMENTATION button, it supplies you with a list of parameters you may use in your error message to denote specific information about the error.

16.2.3 External Aliases

If you want to separate which logon, logoff, and error pages different user bases see when they view your application, you may do so by creating an *external alias* for your application. An external alias provides an additional service path through which you may call your application. For example, you may have the following WDA application service on your system:

https://<host:port>/sap/bc/webdynpro/sap/ZWDA_TEST_APP

You could define an external alias through which to call this application as:

https://<host:port>/mycompany/external/ZWDA_TEST_APP

This new service node would have its own service configuration you could modify at will, specifying new logon criteria, new error pages, and other service properties. You could then supply one URL to one set of users (e.g., your internal users), and the other to another set of users.

In order to create an external alias, you must do the following:

1. Call Transaction SICF and browse the service directory by running your filter wide open.
2. Click the EXTERNAL ALIASES button on the MAINTAIN SERVICE toolbar at the top of the screen.
3. Select a host (e.g., default_host) in the service tree and click the CREATE NEW EXTERNAL ALIAS button on that same toolbar.
4. Specify an alias name for your service and provide it with a description. Alias names take the form of paths, such as */mycompany/external/ZWDA_TEST_APP*.
5. On the TRG. ELEMENT tab, browse to your WDA application and double-click it to set it as your external alias's target service.
6. Edit any additional service properties you want to change (e.g., logoff or error pages) and save your changes.
7. You should be able to access your application from the external alias path you defined.

16.3   Authorizations

Authorizations provide an important second layer of security to your Web Dynpro applications and may be used to block access to an application or its features. Access to Web Dynpro applications is restricted by the use of authorization object S_ICF. Authorization checks for this object are specified at the ICF service level for your application and may be configured using the following procedure:

1. Open Transaction SICF in SAP GUI and navigate to your Web Dynpro application's service.

2. Display the service in edit mode.

3. On the SERVICE DATA tab, you may specify an arbitrary value in the SAP AUTHORIZATION field, as shown in Figure 16.6. This value may then be specified in conjunction with one of S_IFC's field values in a role in order to restrict access to the application.

4. Save your changes when you're finished.

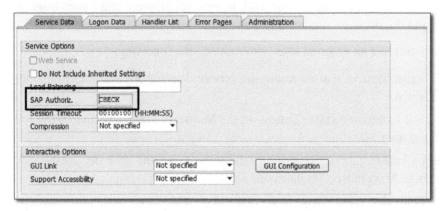

Figure 16.6 Specifying an Authorization Value for Your WDA Application

The structure of the S_ICF authorization object pairs predefined field values against the check value you specify in the service. The principal field value you need to be concerned with is the SERVICE field, which protects calls made to an ICF service. An authorization in a role might therefore look like Figure 16.7.

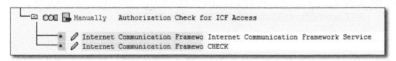

Figure 16.7 An ICF Service Authorization Check in a Role for the Authorization Value of CHECK

Aside from checking authorizations at the service level, you may also carry out authorization checks in your WDA component code. You may use these authorizations as you would in standard ABAP code to restrict access to data and functionality. These checks are carried out using the standard authorization check keyword of AUTHORITY-CHECK.

16.4 Application Data Security

When it comes to security, you must be consistently aware that Web Dynpro applications are web applications and therefore vulnerable to the data exploits every web application faces:

- All data sent to the client via an HTTP response can be accessed and manipulated by the user. This means that hiding data on a page doesn't guarantee its security, so be careful of what you send to your users.
- All data sent from the client to a web application via an HTTP request can be manipulated. This means that all data sent to your web application should be validated.

You should keep these principles in mind as you design and implement your applications:

- **URL and application parameter security**
  If you recall from Chapter 12, the processing of URL parameters is such that, with few exceptions, URL parameters always override the application parameters you set in your Web Dynpro application. As a result, you must always check the values of your URL parameters so you don't enact functionality you'd rather not process.

- **Exit plugs and portal navigation**
  Parameters sent when an exit plug is called, or in a portal navigation, are sent to your application from the client. Therefore, you shouldn't set any data in these parameters that shouldn't be visible to the user.

- **Portal eventing**
  Portal eventing is captured on the client side of an application's processing (in JavaScript). Since this is all occurring on the client side, you must both validate any incoming data sent from a portal event and prevent the client from receiving any sensitive outbound data from your server.

- **CHIP inports and outputs**
  CHIP inport and output parameters are also sent to and received from the client. Again, you must validate your inbound data and prevent sensitive data from being processed via these parameters.

16.5   Security of Context Data in a View

Any data supplied to a view's context carries the risk of mistakenly being exposed to an end user. As a development practice, then, SAP recommends that you populate your view's context with only the data it needs to function. This has two effects: you automatically reduce your data's risk of exposure by not making it available to the UI elements of your view, and you can improve the runtime performance of your application by consuming less memory.

The Web Dynpro framework doesn't, however, come without its own protections for context data. The following behaviors are adhered to when a client attempts to work with data in the context:

▶ If the client attempts to access context data that's not currently visible from a UI element, the system will short dump.

▶ If the client attempts to change context data that doesn't exist or is read only, the system will short dump.

▶ If a client attempts to set data that's invalid for a data type, the system will return a validation error message.

▶ The system will only send data to the client that's bound to a UI element and to which that UI element is visible.

▶ The system will allow changes only to context data that's allowed to be modified (i.e., the bound UI element's `enabled` and `readonly` properties are appropriately set).

Otherwise, if a client sends valid data that changes the contents of the context, it's the developer's responsibility to do the following:

▶ Validate the correctness of the data.

▶ Examine the data for specific types of attacks, such as SQL-injection attacks.

▶ Validate that the data should be changed based on user permissions and business logic.

16.6   File Upload Security

The ability to upload files to your system can present some unique security and performance risks. Too large a file will cause the system's work process that's handling your request to use heap memory to read the file. Additionally, there's the security of the file's content itself to consider. While your system may be immune to the effects of a virus attached to the file, if that file is meant to be shared in any manner with other users, you've just created a vector in your IT landscape for virus dispersal.

In order to protect your system's performance, you may restrict the maximum possible size of a file upload by setting the `icm/HTTP/max_request_size_KB` parameter in your systems profile (RZ11).

The `FileUpload` UI element is automatically configured to use the SAP virus scan infrastructure if it's configured to handle HTTP requests. If a virus is detected during the upload, the system issues an error message. It doesn't write the file data or information to the context.

16.7   Whitelist Infrastructure

If your WDA application integrates with an external resource such as an external CSS file (e.g., one provided by the portal), you may use the whitelist functionality found in class `CL_HTTP_UTILITY` in order to validate that the URL of the resource passed to your application may be legitimately used on your system. The whitelist functionality operates on a rather simple premise. You define whitelist entries in a table that indicates which protocol, host, port, and URI may be permissibly accessed on a remote system and then perform checks against those entries whenever you're supplied a potentially harmful external resource. Using SAP's whitelist infrastructure, you make checks against the whitelist table using the following method, which will throw an exception if the check fails:

```
CL_HTTP_UTILITY=>IF_HTTP_UTILITY~CHECK_HTTP_WHITELIST
```

Whitelist entries are stored on your system in table `HTTP_WHITELIST`, which, like many tables, may be maintained from Transaction SE16. The structure of table entries is as shown in Table 16.2.

Table Field	Description
ENTRY_TYPE	The URL type to be compared when using this entry. This field is primarily used as a filter device to protect table performance if you have an especially large table.
HOST	A hostname to validate against.
PROTOCOL	A protocol to validate against (e.g., HTTP or HTTPS).
PORT	A port to validate against.
URL	A URL to validate against.

Table 16.2 Structure of the HTTP_WHITELIST Table

Some of the entries in this table may contain wildcards (*), such as the host and URL. Some entries may also be blank, which means that the characteristic will not be checked when you validate the resource. It's assumed that you'll typically use this functionality when validating raw data, such as URL parameter values that are passed to your application.

16.8   Summary

In this chapter, we gave an overview of some of the security and authentication features of Web Dynpro and the AS ABAP stack. With the greater level of access WDA and other web application technologies bring to your SAP system, you as a developer have to be much more aware of the vulnerabilities and cognizant of your responsibilities to secure your system and applications. Security is one of those never-ending battles in an IT deployment, since new threats are always keen to present themselves. Hopefully you've found some guidance in this chapter on what risks and options you need to be aware of. Please remember that knowledge and vigilance are the ultimate weapons against security threats, and those must continually evolve to ensure your success.

The successful adoption of a WDA application can often depend on how well it runs. In this chapter, we'll examine some of the tools and techniques you can use to enhance your WDA application's performance.

17   Performance Tuning

In the early days of web application development, a common complaint raised by users was that web applications were slower and less responsive than the mainframe terminals or rich client applications they were accustomed to working with. For the most part, this lack of responsiveness can be traced back to limitations of the underlying HTTP protocol, which wasn't really designed with web application programming in mind. Over time, web developers were able to overcome most of these limitations through the introduction of clever workarounds such as AJAX, advanced JavaScript libraries, and so on. Collectively, these methods, combined with advances in browser technology and Internet standards, have helped speed things up quite a bit.

As we've seen, the Web Dynpro framework incorporates many of these latest features out of the box; all we have to do as developers is turn them on. However, from a practical perspective, the performance tuning of WDA applications involves more than just flipping a switch here and there. Rather, we must adopt a more holistic approach that addresses all the areas of a WDA application, which can affect performance.

In this chapter, we'll consider just such an approach to performance tuning. To get things started, we'll look at WDA applications through a wide lens and try to identify specific areas of an application that may require tuning. From there, we'll segue into a discussion on best practices and offer up some practical design tips. Then, after surveying some of the profiling tools provided by SAP, we'll point you in the direction of a performance tuning checklist you can use to double-check your day-to-day development work.

17.1 Formulating an Approach

Most of the time, performance problems with WDA applications (and, indeed, applications in general) are reported using vague expressions such as, "It's slow." Since these kinds of defect reports don't give us much to go on, the task of performance tuning can feel overwhelming at first. After all, the root cause of the problem could be coming from just about anywhere. Of course, with time and experience, you'll find that your hunches will serve you well as you approach these problems.

In the absence of clairvoyance, though, we must adopt a methodical approach that systematically traces through the various layers of a WDA application. Here, it makes sense to align our process with the MVC paradigm, which lies at the heart of the Web Dynpro framework. That way, we can quickly eliminate various layers and narrow in on the heart of the problem.

Figure 17.1 illustrates the handoffs between each of the layers that exist within a WDA application. As you can see, data flows upward from the model layer and through the controller and view layers and is ultimately transmitted to the client via the HTTP protocol. Then, whenever users trigger events on the frontend, data is transmitted along the same path in the opposite direction. So, depending on the nature of the performance problem in question, our basic approach is to pick up at the appropriate step in the data flow and trace our way through the application until we arrive at the source of the bottleneck.

To demonstrate how this process works, let's imagine we receive a report that indicates that a WDA application is taking a long time to load at startup. To troubleshoot this error, we'd start with the model layer and work our way upwards:

1. At the model layer, we'd look at the classes or function modules to determine if any of these objects are bogging down for some reason. Here, for example, we might find a SQL query statement that needs to be tuned or a logic routine that needs to be reworked.

2. If the model layer is running smoothly, the next step is to look at the controller layer and see if any of the hook methods involved in the initialization process (e.g., the WDDOINIT() method, supply function methods, and so on) are running slowly. Questions we might ask ourselves here include:

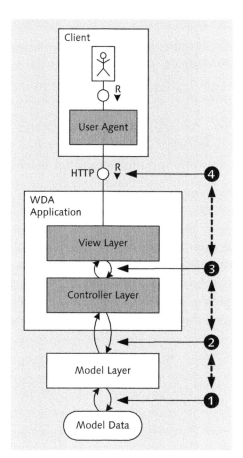

Figure 17.1 Tracing the Performance of WDA Applications

▷ Are any of the methods performing tasks that belong to the model layer (e.g., executing SELECT statements)?

▷ Are we pulling too much data back from the model layer? Do we need to apply filters to reduce the amount of data being extracted?

▷ Can some of the initialization tasks be deferred such that they're only executed on demand?

3. Moving along to the view layer, our next task is to look at how the view layout is constructed to see if it's too complex. Examples of common performance problems here include:

▶ The UI element hierarchy contains deeply nested UI element containers.

▶ Some dynamic layout generation logic has spun out of control in the WDDO-MODIFYVIEW() hook method of one of the views.

▶ One or more views are performing tasks that should be relegated to the controller or model layers.

4. Lastly, if everything seems to be running smoothly within the application itself, it could be that there are issues with the HTTP transmission layer. However, before pointing the finger at the network operations team, we should check to see whether or not the latency is due to our transmitting too much data over the wire. This can sometimes happen with report applications that pull back large amounts of data.

As we worked through this troubleshooting exercise, did you notice how we systematically eliminated potential error sources? When dealing with complex performance issues, we can't stress enough how important this process of elimination can be. If nothing else, isolating the problem(s) helps us determine where to go get help—either internally within the project team or externally via a customer message to SAP.

In the upcoming sections, we'll look more closely at some of the issues described in this example exercise, as well as many others. We'll also demonstrate several tools you can use to speed along the analysis process.

17.2 Best Practices and Design Tips

Most performance problems can be traced back to poor design decisions. Therefore, in this section, we'll consider some best practices and design tips that should help you avoid running into performance problems in your own WDA applications. Additionally, these principles can be used as a guide for refactoring poorly performing WDA applications after the fact.

17.2.1 Separation of Concerns

One of the biggest mistakes we see novice WDA developers make is the violation of basic MVC design principles. Here, it's not uncommon to find SQL statements nested within controller methods, heavyweight operations being performed at the view layer, and so on. Alas, no matter how strongly SAP warns against such practices in the help documentation, there is a limit to what can be enforced within the syntax check. Therefore, it's up to us as developers to make sure such rules are followed.

While we hope you understand by now the value of doing things this way from a design perspective, you might be wondering what this design practice has to do with performance tuning. As it turns out, it matters a great deal. This is because WDA components run inside a specialized container rather than directly within the ABAP runtime environment. Consequently, ABAP code running within a controller method runs slower than the same piece of ABAP code contained within an ABAP Objects class or function module.

So, while it may be tempting to cut a few corners and plug in some model logic within a controller method, it will be worthwhile in the long run to take the time to do things correctly by keeping model logic separate. Of course, if you need to simplify access to the model layer from your controller methods, you can do so by utilizing the assistance class, as described in Chapter 4.

Another advantage of keeping the model layer separate is that it makes it possible to profile and tune the model classes separately outside the context of a WDA application. In this scenario, the model code can be tested and tuned using familiar ABAP performance tuning tools, such as ABAP Unit, ABAP Runtime Analysis, and the Code Inspector tool. Plus, it opens up the model code for development and maintenance from a wider audience of ABAP developers—including those who don't know WDA.

17.2.2 Context Management

As we learned in Chapter 5, controller contexts are used to facilitate the transfer of data between the model and view layers. For the most part, we don't have to worry too much about this transfer process, provided that we remember to abide by the following basic rules:

▶ First of all, it's important to remember that controller contexts should be used only to store data that will be displayed within the UI. All other application-state data should be stored elsewhere (either in the model layer or in controller attributes).

▶ Wherever possible, we should strive to keep the context node hierarchy small and manageable. For example, if defining context nodes in terms of an ABAP Dictionary structure, we should eliminate any unneeded context attributes.

▶ We should use singleton nodes wherever possible in order to reduce the overall memory footprint of our WDA applications.

▶ We should avoid the definition of long-spanning context mapping chains where we can. For example, if context data is needed only in a specific view, we should define the context nodes locally within the view rather than within a global controller.

In addition to the design rules outlined above, we also need to pay close attention to the ways we're reading from and writing to the context. Here, it really pays to take the time to ensure that context updates are being performed judiciously. Some basic design tips here include:

▶ Avoiding the use of the "kill-and-fill" technique to update a context node's element collection. Here, we're talking about invalidating a context node and simply letting a supply function reload its contents, rather than taking the time to update individual records using API methods.

▶ Wherever possible, it's a good idea to use API methods that bundle operations together in a single method invocation. For example, when copying the contents of an internal table to a context node, it's preferable to utilize the BIND_TABLE() method of the IF_WD_CONTEXT_NODE interface to copy the data, rather than looping through the table and adding the records one by one.

▶ If memory consumption is a problem, it's a good idea to utilize the *_REF() methods of the IF_WD_CONTEXT_NODE and IF_WD_CONTEXT_ELEMENT interfaces (e.g., the GET_ATTRIBUTE_REF() method) because these methods pass the data by reference and avoid unnecessary copy operations.

17.2.3 Managing Resources

The overall memory footprint of a WDA application at a given point in time can be computed by adding up the resources utilized by the main WDA component as well as any used components that are currently in scope. While the data stored in controller contexts usually represents the largest piece of this pie percentage-wise, there are other resource types we must take into account if we are to properly tune our WDA applications. Therefore, in this section, we'll take a look at several of these resource types up close.

Data Used to Maintain the Application State

Besides the data that gets loaded into the context, a given WDA application may need to keep track of various other data objects behind the scenes in order to maintain the application state. Examples of such data objects include model object references, indexes used for the purposes of pagination, and so on.

While it's perfectly valid to store such data objects within controller attributes, the memory footprint of a WDA application can swell to unmanageable proportions in a hurry if we're not careful. Therefore, when storing data in controller attributes, it's important to bear in mind the following:

► Controller attributes shouldn't be used as a substitute for a model layer. Therefore, if you find yourself having to create a large number of controller attributes to maintain the application state, it's likely that the model layer of your application needs work.

► The data stored in controller attributes should be pared down to just the essentials. In other words, rather than storing a large data object in memory for a long period of time, can we achieve the same results by simply storing the object's key and loading the object on demand?

► As is the case with most global variables, we should always clean up the data in controller attributes once we're finished with them.

Used Components

Since used components are logically positioned as black boxes from a development perspective, it can be easy to lose sight of the fact that these components may have a fairly sizeable memory footprint at runtime. Therefore, we should take care to ensure that the lifespan of such used components is as short as possible. This implies that:

► We prefer to instantiate components on an as-needed basis rather than preloading them at startup (e.g., in the WDDOINIT() method of the component controller).

► We delete used component instances when we're finished with them, using the DELETE_COMPONENT() method of the IF_WD_COMPONENT_USAGE interface.

Defining the Lifespan of Embedded Views

In some cases, we may be able to trim some extra fat off WDA components by adjusting the lifespan of embedded views. This can be achieved by selecting the when visible option in the LIFETIME property of views, as shown in Figure 17.2. Whenever this option is selected, a given view will be loaded into context only if it's *visible* within the view assembly. Here, it's important to realize that there's a fundamental difference between a view being visible within the view assembly and being visible on screen.

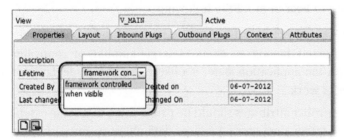

Figure 17.2 Controlling the Lifespan of Views

To put this into perspective, consider the user maintenance application shown in Figure 17.3. Here, the view layout is defined in terms of a TabStrip element with four tabs, and the content area of each of the tabs is defined by a separate view embedded within a ViewContainerUIElement (see Figure 17.4). By default, when this application loads at runtime, each of the embedded views (e.g., V_ADDRESS, V_DEFAULTS, and so on) will be loaded into context—regardless of whether they're visible on screen. This is because the views are part of the overall view assembly.

As you can imagine, this default behavior can prove problematic for complex screens that embed a number of views within the view assembly. Fortunately, we can avoid such overhead by utilizing the aforementioned LIFETIME property of views as follows:

1. First of all, we must go into each of the embedded views and set the LIFETIME property to when visible. We also need to define an inbound plug that will be used to load the view into context on demand.

2. Next, we must adjust the view assembly such that the default view for each of the ViewContainerUIElement elements is the EmptyView (see Figure 17.5). That way, the target views won't be part of the view assembly at startup.

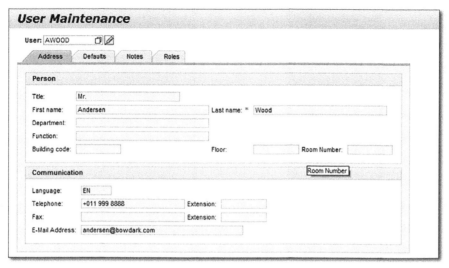

Figure 17.3 Understanding the Visibility of Embedded Views (Part 1)

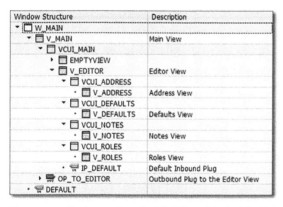

Figure 17.4 Understanding the Visibility of Embedded Views (Part 2)

3. After the view assembly is updated, we also need to define navigation links between the parent view (V_EDITOR) and the embedded views within the Tab-Strip element. These navigation links will be used to load the views on demand.

4. Finally, the last step is to configure the onSelect event of the TabStrip element so we can react to tab selections and display the target views. We achieve the latter by firing the navigation links created in the previous step.

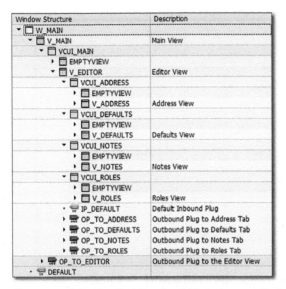

Figure 17.5 Adjusting the View Assembly to Improve Performance

Once this configuration is in place, each of the embedded views will be loaded only when users click the corresponding tab. We can verify this behavior by setting a breakpoint in the WDDOINIT() method of each of the view controllers. In this case, the method will be invoked only when the view is directly accessed the first time.

Performance Trade-offs

Given the performance benefits demonstrated in this section, it might seem like it's always a good idea to set the LIFETIME property of a view to when visible. However, there's a trade-off to consider here. Whenever this property is set, a view must be initialized each time it's displayed. Therefore, if it takes a long time to initialize a view, it may not be a good idea to have the framework load it on demand. Instead, it's best to accept the default framework controlled value so the initialization cost is minimized.

Managing Interface Views of External Components

Unlike views, interface views don't provide us with a LIFETIME property that can be used to control the lifespan of embedded interface views. Nevertheless, we can still influence when such interface views (and by extension, their overarching components) are loaded into a using WDA component. Here, we can apply the same basic methodology demonstrated in the previous section.

For instance, imagine we reworked the user maintenance application shown in Figure 17.3 such that the contents' ROLES tab were defined using an ALV table. Now, if we were to embed the TABLE interface view of the SALV_WD_TABLE component as the default view underneath the VCUI_ROLES element, the framework would take the liberty of loading an instance of the SALV_WD_TABLE component behind the scenes when the application is first loaded—regardless of whether the ROLES tab were selected on screen at startup. However, if we rework the view assembly such that we nominate an EmptyView view as the default view, the TABLE interface view would be loaded only when the corresponding navigation plug is fired at runtime.

Since embedded interface views carry along with them the added baggage of their overarching component, we need to be even more careful about making sure the views are loaded only when they're truly needed. As we've seen in this section, we can achieve this fairly easily with a navigation plug and a little bit of planning. Alternatively, in rare cases, we can turn to dynamic programming techniques to gain even more control over the initialization process.

17.2.4 Frontend Delegation

Whenever you have an N-tier architecture like the one employed by SAP, there's a certain amount of trade-off among the different tiers in terms of performance. For example, to reduce the stress on the database tier in an SAP system, it's a common practice to scale out the application tier by adding additional application servers. That way, some of the burden of data crunching can be farmed out to dedicated application servers.

Similarly, in some cases, it can be beneficial to delegate certain tasks to the presentation tier. Here, for example, we might want to defer simple screen processing tasks to the client's user agent. That way, the application avoids a server roundtrip, and everybody wins. In this section, we'll look at some ways of achieving this sort of frontend delegation with WDA.

> **Note**
>
> Of course, the basic assumption here is that the client is up to the job, and that may not always be the case in the world of mobile clients we live in today.

Uniform Rendering Light Speed (URLS)

One of the quickest and easiest ways to delegate screen processing tasks to the frontend is to enable SAP's new *Uniform Rendering Light Speed* (URLS) rendering technology. URLS, which is integrated into the Web Dynpro runtime environment, utilizes JavaScript, AJAX, and inline CSS behind the scenes to radically change the way WDA applications are rendered by web browsers.

> **Note**
>
> See SAP Note 1107662 for information about which versions of the AS ABAP support URLS, specific features, and so on.

In particular, URLS offers up significant performance boosts by:

- Loading JavaScript and CSS resources on demand. Thus, less time is wasted downloading files that aren't being used.

- Enhancing certain UI elements with client-side scripting technology so that certain operations (e.g., sorting) can be performed on the frontend without a server roundtrip.

- Using AJAX technology to implement so-called "flicker-free" screens (more in this in the next section).

These days, most AS ABAP systems have URLS turned on by default, so there's usually nothing we have to do in order to reap the benefits of this new rendering technology. However, if you're on an older system, you may have to explicitly turn on URLS by:

- Applying the `sap-wd-lightspeed` URL query string parameter (e.g., `http://.../sap/wdaapp?sap-wd-lightspeed=X`)

- Configuring the standard `WDLIGHTSPEED` application parameter, as shown in Figure 17.6

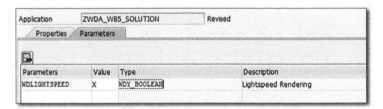

Figure 17.6 Enabling Lightspeed Rendering in a WDA Application (Part 1)

▶ Utilizing the SAP standard application WD_GLOBAL_SETTING to turn on URLS by default for all WDA applications in the system (see Figure 17.7)

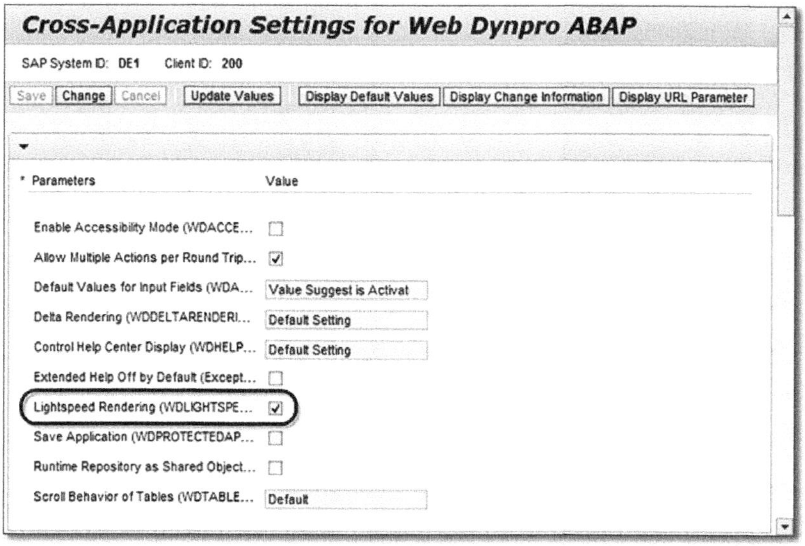

Figure 17.7 Enabling Lightspeed Rendering in a WDA Application (Part 2)

Delta Rendering

One of the most powerful features of the new URLS rendering framework is *delta rendering*. Delta rendering combines AJAX technology with some enhanced features of the Web Dynpro runtime environment to enable "flicker-free" screens, in which only the portions of the screen that change are updated during the rendering process.

To understand how delta rendering works, let's consider the rendering lifecycle of a simple reporting application. As you can see in Figure 17.8, the view assembly for our sample applications consists of three views:

▶ A selection-screen view, which contains all the UI elements needed to input search criteria

▶ A results view, which displays the search results in a Table UI element

▶ A top-level view, which organizes the view assembly according to the layout shown in Figure 17.8

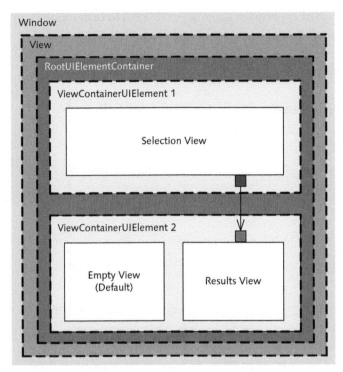

Figure 17.8 Understanding Delta Rendering Technology

Now, under normal circumstances, the entire view assembly shown in Figure 17.8 would be reloaded each time a change happens on screen that triggers a server roundtrip. So, for example, if we were to trigger the onSelect event of a DropDownByKey element in the selection screen view, the entire screen would be updated. As you'd expect, this can prove expensive if the Table element contains a large amount of data.

With delta rendering, it's a different story. In this case, each of the constituent views can be updated separately. For instance, if a change is made to the selection-screen view, only that view is updated; the results view is left untouched. Similarly, if we were to sort the contents of the Table element in the results view, only this view would be refreshed.

Behind the scenes, delta rendering works by keeping tabs on which views have become *dirty*. Therefore, in order to take advantage of this functionality, we must be careful not to introduce changes that toggle this flag unnecessarily. Examples of such changes include:

- Avoidable changes to context nodes or attributes (e.g., because of lazy programming techniques)
- Changes to UI elements made within the WDDOMODIFYVIEW() hook method
- Superfluous navigation requests or messages

Besides the programming practices outlined above, we can often avoid excessive screen refreshes by reorganizing our view assemblies. For example, if we have a page that contains several heavyweight UI elements, such as the Table UI element, it probably makes sense to move each of those Table elements into its own view. That way, each Table view can be updated independently.

As is the case for the URLS technology upon which it's based, delta rendering is enabled by default in most modern AS ABAP systems. However, we can control its usage on an application-by-application basis using the standard WDDELTAREN-DERING application parameter or the sap-wd-DeltaRendering URL query string parameter. More information about these features and delta rendering in general can be found in the SAP Help Portal (*http://help.sap.com*) by performing a search on the phrase "delta rendering."

Working with Islands Technology

In rare cases, we may encounter application requirements that call for a user interface that requires little to no interaction with the backend. In these situations, we can potentially improve the performance of the application quite a bit by utilizing the Adobe Flash Islands or Microsoft Silverlight Islands integration technologies. In this case, the bulk of the UI is developed using Adobe Flash or Microsoft Silverlight and the WDA application plays the role of carrier. On the frontend, users can interact directly with the embedded RIA application without having to incur the overhead of constant server roundtrips.

17.2.5 Compressing HTTP Transmissions

At the end of the day, WDA applications end up transmitting a lot of data over HTTP. Since much of the data in question is text (i.e., HTML markup), we can reduce the size of the transmission feeds quite a bit by compressing the contents of the HTTP response messages. We can do this by configuring the COMPRESSION property of the Web Dynpro runtime service in Transaction SICF, as shown in Figure 17.9. Whenever this property is set to the value Yes, the Web Dynpro runtime environment will apply a GZIP compression on the content before it's sent back to the user agent—that is, provided that the user agent will accept such compression. Otherwise, it simply passes back the data in its uncompressed form as usual.

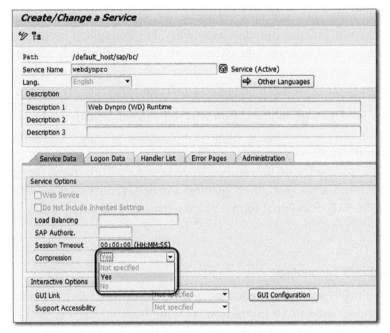

Figure 17.9 Turning on GZIP Compression in the WDA Runtime

How Do I know if a Client's Web Browser Supports GZIP Compression?

Most contemporary web browsers support GZIP compression out of the box. However, one way to verify this is to check the HTTP request message issued from your browser to see if the `accept-encoding: gzip` header is provided. We'll look at ways of achieving this in Section 17.3.3.

17.3 Performance Analysis Tools

When troubleshooting performance issues, it really helps to have the right set of tools to diagnose the problem at hand. In this section, we'll look at some of the tools available to assist us with performance tuning exercises.

17.3.1 Web Dynpro–Specific Monitoring Tools

The first set of tools we'll consider is the Web Dynpro–specific tools that can be used to trace the performance of various parts of the WDA application. As we'll observe, one of the nice things about these tools is that, because they're mostly browser-based, they can be used side by side with a running WDA application to gather performance metrics in real time.

> **Note**
>
> All the tools described in this section are based on the URLS rendering technology described in Section 17.2.4. Therefore, if you're running an older version of the AS ABAP, you may not have access to these tools.

Web Dynpro Trace Tool

The Web Dynpro trace tool is perhaps the most comprehensive of all the Web Dynpro–specific monitoring tools and can be activated in one of two ways:

- Within a running WDA application, you can activate the trace tool by simultaneously pressing the `Ctrl` + `Shift` + `Alt` + `C` key sequence.
- Alternatively, you can activate the tool within the SAP GUI by executing Transaction WD_TRACE_TOOL. As you can see in Figure 17.10, this option provides more configuration options for us to determine what gets traced and for which user.

When the Web Dynpro trace tool is activated, a little floating window like the one shown in Figure 17.11 launches. As you can see, the window contains a toolbar with functions that can be used to display various elements of the running trace, export the trace as a ZIP file, and so on.

After the trace is completed, you can download the trace as a ZIP file to your local machine and unpack the files. Here, the trace content is organized into folders: a couple of high-level folders, as well as individual folders, for each server roundtrip. The folders themselves contain a combination of HTML and XML files you can view by double-clicking on the Index.html file created in the root folder of the ZIP archive. This will open a frameset window like the one shown in Figure 17.12. From here, you can look at various trace artifacts, including the ones described in Table 17.1.

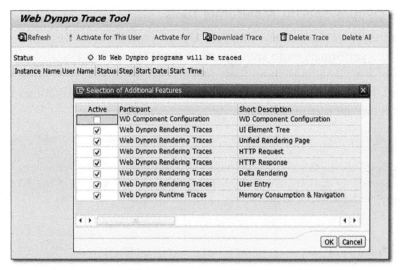

Figure 17.10 Activating the Web Dynpro Trace Tool

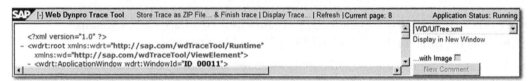

Figure 17.11 Working with the Web Dynpro Trace Tool

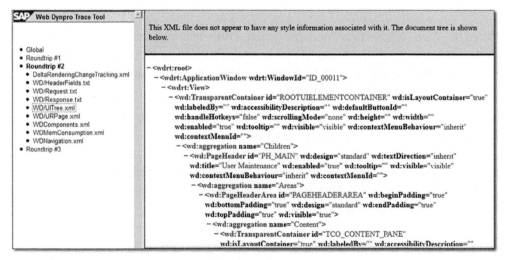

Figure 17.12 Viewing a Trace Created by the Web Dynpro Trace Tool

Trace File Name	Description
DeltaRenderingChangeTracking.xml	This file contains trace information collected by the delta rendering framework. Here, you can see why certain views were refreshed and the line(s) of code that caused the view to be flagged as "dirty."
WD/HeaderFields.txt	This file contains a list of all the HTTP header fields passed during a particular HTTP roundtrip.
WD/Request.txt	This file contains the complete HTTP request message submitted to the server during an HTTP roundtrip.
WD/Response.txt	This file contains the complete HTTP response message returned to the client during an HTTP roundtrip.
WD/UITree.xml	This file contains an XML-based representation of the UI element hierarchy at a particular point in time.
WD/Components.xml	For multi-component WDA applications, this file contains a complete listing of the constituent WDA components.
WD/MemConsumption.xml	As the name suggests, this file contains details about the memory consumed within the application at a particular point in time.

Table 17.1 Selected Artifacts within a Web Dynpro Trace Archive

Note
If you're troubleshooting performance issues related to an SAP standard-delivered WDA application, it's very likely that SAP will ask you to attach the ZIP file produced by the trace tool to any customer messages you have open with them. This information provides their support staff with the information needed to troubleshoot the problem internally.

Performance Monitor

If all you need to do is take a quick peek at some basic performance statistics, the performance monitor tool is the tool of choice. This tool can be activated in one of two ways:

- Within a running WDA application, the performance monitor can be activated by simultaneously pressing the ⌈Ctrl⌉ + ⌈Shift⌉ + ⌈Alt⌉ + ⌈R⌉ key sequence.

- Alternatively, we can enable the tool when an application is started, using the `sap-wd-perfMonitor` URL query string parameter (e.g., `http://.../sap/wdaapp?sap-wd-perfMonitor=X`).

In either case, the performance monitor loads into a tiny frame in the top right-hand corner of the browser window, as shown in Figure 17.13. From here, we can expand the window to display additional information by clicking on the >> link highlighted in Figure 17.13. Figure 17.14 demonstrates what the full view of the performance monitor looks like on screen.

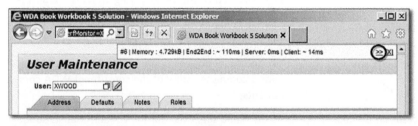

Figure 17.13 Accessing the Performance Monitor Tool (Part 1)

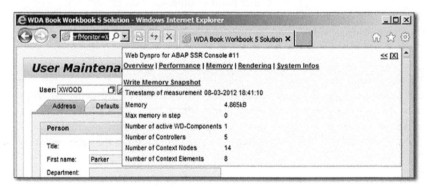

Figure 17.14 Accessing the Performance Monitor Tool (Part 2)

As you can see in Figure 17.14, the performance monitor provides basic statistical information in the areas of overall performance, memory consumption, rendering, and so on. Of particular interest is the WRITE MEMORY SNAPSHOT function shown in Figure 17.14. This function outputs a memory snapshot to the backend so it can be reviewed within the Memory Inspector tool. We'll take a brief look at the Memory Inspector tool in Section 17.3.2.

Nesting Analysis

If you think your performance problems are due to excessive nesting in the UI element hierarchy, the nesting analysis tool may be of use. You can activate this tool by simultaneously pressing the [Ctrl] + [Shift] + [Alt] + [O] key sequence.

Figure 17.15 shows what the tool looks like when it's activated. The tool provides a color-based overlay, which highlights various HTML containers. The color scheme can be interpreted as follows:

▶ HTML <table> elements are represented using red boxes.

▶ HTML <div> elements are represented using blue boxes.

▶ HTML <span> elements are represented using green boxes.

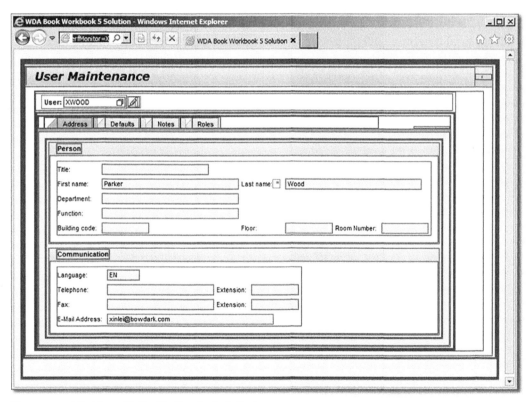

Figure 17.15 Working with the Nesting Analysis Tool

From a performance perspective, HTML <table> elements usually take longer to render than <div> or <span> elements. Therefore, if you see an unusual number of red boxes in the nesting analysis display, it might be an indication that you need to revisit the setup of your UI element hierarchy. Here, it could be that you have too many nested container elements, or maybe that a more efficient layout (e.g., FlowLayout instead of MatrixLayout) should be used.

DOM Analysis

Internally, web browsers store HTML markup within a tree-like data object whose structure is described by the W3C's *Document Object Model* (DOM). Besides enabling the direct access of HTML elements via JavaScript, DOM also provides us with some unique insight into the complexity and organization of an HTML document. Here, we can look at how the HTML document is constructed and determine whether we have too many instances of a particular element, and so on.

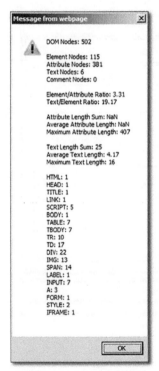

Figure 17.16 Working with the DOM Analysis Tool

We can view the DOM tree generated by the Web Dynpro runtime environment by turning on the DOM analysis tool, which we can activate by simultaneously pressing the $\boxed{\text{Ctrl}}$ + $\boxed{\text{Shift}}$ + $\boxed{\text{Alt}}$ + $\boxed{\text{D}}$ key sequence. When the tool is activated, a popup like the one shown in Figure 17.16 appears. Here, we can see the breakdown of HTML element usages, the total number of nodes within the tree, and more.

17.3.2 ABAP Monitoring Tools

Frequently, the source of a poorly performing WDA application can be traced down to the ABAP layer. Here, we could be talking about something as small as a slow-running ABAP Objects class method or as large as a system-wide resource shortage. Whatever the case might be, you'll find that there are a number of tools we can utilize to diagnose the problem.

In this section, we'll highlight some of the more commonly used tools in this space. Since this book is focused primarily on WDA programming, though, our coverage will be brief. If you're interested in learning more about these tools and basic ABAP performance tuning in general, we highly recommend *ABAP Performance Tuning* (Gahm, SAP PRESS, 2009).

Runtime Analysis

If you've been coding in ABAP for a while, you're probably familiar with the runtime analysis tool (Transaction SE30). This tool can be used to closely analyze various types of ABAP development objects. So, if you suspect that a model class or function module is the source of a performance bottleneck, the runtime analysis tool can probably help you isolate the problem in a hurry.

These days, the runtime analysis tool can be used for more than just plain ABAP code; it can also be used to measure the performance of WDA applications. We can do this by performing the following steps:

1. Open the WDA application you want to trace in the ABAP Workbench (Transaction SE80) and select the GOTO • HTTP SERVICE MAINTENANCE menu option, as shown in Figure 17.17.
2. This will take you to Transaction SICF and the filtered view shown in Figure 17.18. From here, you'll select the service node for your WDA application and then choose the EDIT • RUNTIME ANALYSIS • ACTIVATE menu option.

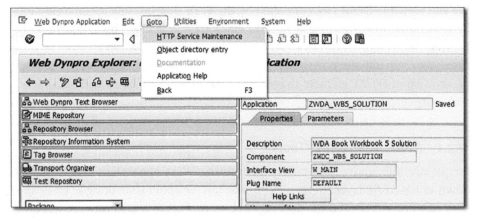

Figure 17.17 Activating the Runtime Analysis for a WDA Application (Part 1)

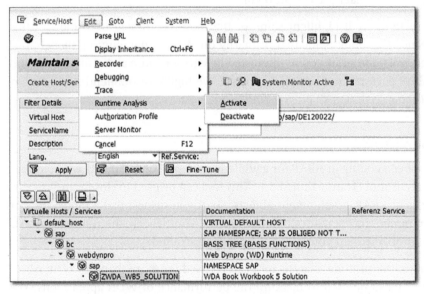

Figure 17.18 Activating the Runtime Analysis for a WDA Application (Part 2)

3. Next, you're prompted with the ACTIVATE RUNTIME ANALYSIS FOR URL dialog box shown in Figure 17.19. Here, you can configure the parameters as necessary to ensure that the runtime analysis is only turned on for a particular user (for example). Once you confirm the settings, you can click the ACTIVATE button to enable the analysis session.

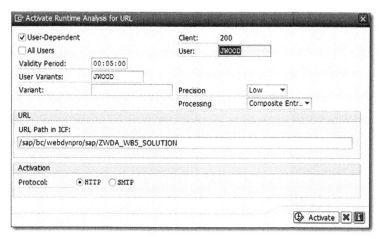

Figure 17.19 Activating the Runtime Analysis for a WDA Application (Part 3)

4. After the analysis session is activated, you can launch the WDA application and step through the various functions you want to profile. Then, once you're finished with the test, you can return to Transaction SICF and select the EDIT • RUNTIME ANALYSIS • DEACTIVATE menu option (see Figure 17.18).

5. Finally, once the analysis session is complete, we can review the results in Transaction SE30 as usual. Here, we simply select the target measurement within the EVALUATE tab, as shown in Figure 17.20, and use the familiar toolbar functions to view the trace, export it, and so on.

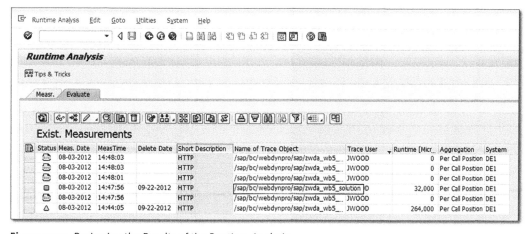

Figure 17.20 Reviewing the Results of the Runtime Analysis

Memory Inspector

The Memory Inspector tool comes in handy when we need to analyze the amount of memory utilized by a WDA application. Though such memory snapshots can be created in several different ways, we've already demonstrated a fairly straight-forward mechanism for creating these snapshots in Section 17.3.1. Here, we simply utilize the performance monitor tool to produce a snapshot of a running WDA application. Then, we can review the snapshot in detail by executing Transaction S_MEMORY_INSPECTOR. Figure 17.21 illustrates what these snapshots look like within the Memory Inspector tool.

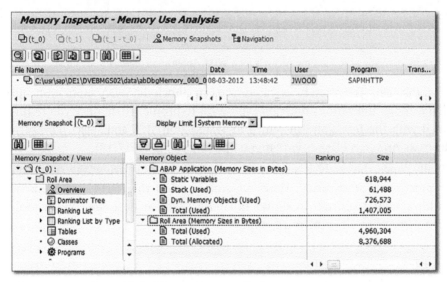

Figure 17.21 Working with the Memory Inspector Tool

Workload Monitor

The workload monitor tool (Transaction STAD) is useful in situations when we need to collect precise measurements of how long individual steps are taking within a server roundtrip. Here, we can see a breakdown of CPU time, processing time, and so on.

Performance Analysis

The performance analysis tool (Transaction ST05) allows us to apply more general traces, such as SQL traces, HTTP traces, and so on.

17.3.3 HTTP Monitoring Tools

As we mentioned earlier, sometimes slow performance with WDA applications has nothing to do with the application itself. Instead, the slow response times may be due to a sluggish network connection. To figure this out, we need to monitor low-level HTTP communications in both directions. That way, we can gain some insight into where the communication is breaking down.

In this section, we'll look at two classes of HTTP monitoring tools: client-side tools and server-side tools. Collectively, these tools should help us (or the project Basis staff) to pinpoint the source of the problem.

Server-Side Monitoring Tools

Though there are several monitoring tools on the market that allow us to monitor the HTTP traffic on a given application server host, we can likely accomplish everything we need to right inside the AS ABAP using Transaction SICF. For example, if we suspect that the problem might be located somewhere deep within the ICM, we can turn on an ICM trace by performing the following steps:

1. Open up Transaction SICF, navigate to the target service node (i.e., the Web Dynpro runtime node), and select the EDIT • TRACE • ACTIVATE TRACE menu option, as shown in Figure 17.22.

2. Then, in the ACTIVATE TRACE FOR URL dialog box shown in Figure 17.23, we're presented with options for configuring the scope of the trace. Once you're satisfied with the selections, click the ACTIVATE button.

3. Once the trace is turned on, we can open the WDA application as usual and test several server roundtrips.

4. After the test is complete, we can deactivate the trace by returning to Transaction SICF and selecting the EDIT • TRACE • DEACTIVATE TRACE menu option.

5. Finally, we can review the results by selecting the EDIT • TRACE • DISPLAY TRACE menu option. As you can see in Figure 17.24, this kind of trace includes a lot of low-level details that probably don't mean very much to the average ABAP developer. However, the information collected here can be quite useful for system administrators and/or SAP support.

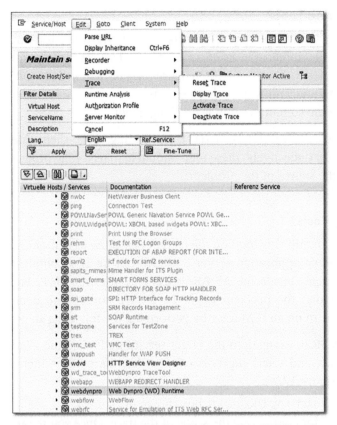

Figure 17.22 Turning on an ICM Trace in Transaction SICF (Part 1)

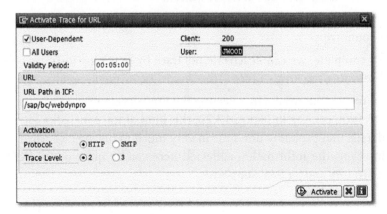

Figure 17.23 Turning on an ICM Trace in Transaction SICF (Part 2)

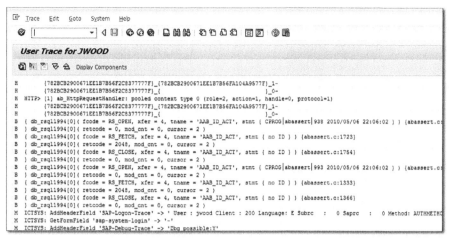

Figure 17.24 Displaying an ICM Trace

In addition to the low-level ICM trace, we also have the option of creating HTTP recordings. In this case, we can monitor HTTP traffic for particular users and see the actual HTTP request and response messages exchanged across the network. To turn on HTTP recordings, perform the following steps:

1. Open Transaction SICF, navigate to the target service node (i.e., the Web Dynpro runtime node), and select the EDIT • RECORDER • ACTIVATE RECORDING menu option.

2. This brings up the ACTIVATE RECORDING dialog box shown in Figure 17.25. Here, we're presented with parameters to adjust the scope of the recording. Once you're satisfied with your selection, click the ACTIVATE button.

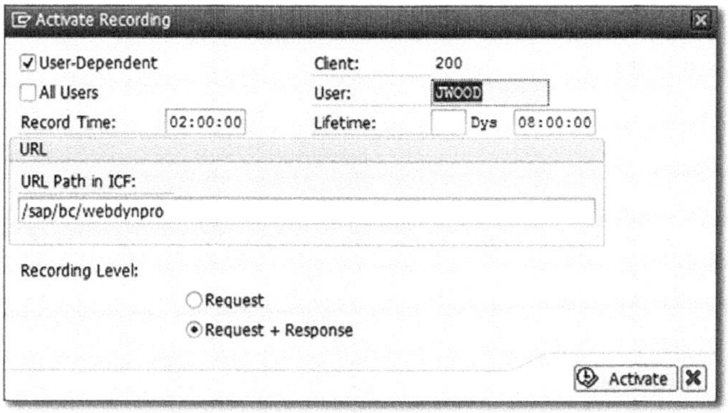

Figure 17.25 Activating an HTTP Recording within the ICF (Part 1)

697

3. After the recording is activated, you can open the WDA application and generate some HTTP traffic. Or, if the problems are user specific, you can have the user access the application and record their session instead.

4. Then, once the test is complete, return to Transaction SICF and deactivate the recording by navigating to the target service node and selecting the EDIT • RECORDER • DEACTIVATE RECORDING menu option.

5. Finally, to review the recording, select the EDIT • RECORDER • DISPLAY RECORDING menu option in Transaction SICF. This brings you to the screen shown in Figure 17.26. Within this screen, you can select a server roundtrip instance and use the provided toolbar functions to display the HTTP request/response messages, and so on.

Figure 17.26 Displaying the Results of an ICF Recording

Client-Side Monitoring Tools

The server-side monitoring tools provided in Transaction SICF can go a long way toward identifying the source of network latency issues. However, if we're to obtain a complete picture, we must also look at the issue from the perspective of the client. For this task, we can enlist the aid of client-side HTTP monitoring tools.

If you perform a Google search on the phrase "HTTP monitoring tools," you'll find a number of tools available online for this purpose; some freeware, others commercial. These tools basically allow you to monitor HTTP transmissions from the perspective of the client. Here, you can see the HTTP messages as they're transmitted over the wire, as well as basic statistical information, which can be helpful for determining which leg of the communication chain is running slower than usual.

Figure 17.27 shows an example of one of the most popular HTTP monitoring tools at work: the HTTPWatch tool provided by Simtec, Ltd. You can download a freeware version of this tool online at *http://www.httpwatch.com*. Another popular freeware tool in this space is WireShark, which can be downloaded at *http://www.wireshark.org*.

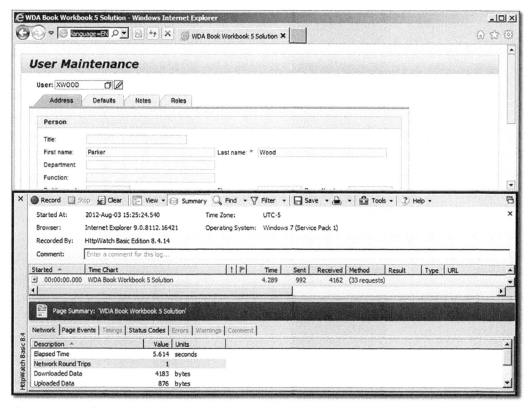

Figure 17.27 Working with the HTTPWatch Tool

17.4   Performance Tuning Checklist

In time, most of the performance tuning measures described in this chapter will become second nature to you. Nevertheless, whenever you face a particularly troublesome performance problem, it's helpful to have a checklist you can consult to make sure no stone has been left unturned. Fortunately, SAP provides just such a checklist in the SAP Help Portal (*http://help.sap.com*). To find this checklist, perform a search on the phrase "checklist for high-performance WDA programming."

17.5   Summary

In this chapter, we learned some valuable tools and techniques we can use to performance-tune WDA applications. Though we sincerely hope you never have to face the kinds of performance problems that require you to use these tools, it's nice to know that they're around if you need them.

Development Workbooks

W1 Displaying Basic Contact Information for a User

In Chapter 3, we provided a step-by-step demonstration of the creation of a basic WDA application that could be used to display user contact information. At that stage of the book, we glossed over many of the nitty-gritty details as we attempted to provide a big-picture view of the WDA application development process. Fourteen chapters later, you'll no doubt find yourself much better equipped to take another pass at this on your own.

W1.1 Requirements Overview

For our first exercise, we'll be creating a WDA application that can be used to display basic contact information for a user maintained in the AS ABAP system database. As you can see in Figure W1.1, this simple application provides an input field that can be used to select a user ID and a form containing the user address and contact information. To view the contact information for a particular user record, users simply plug in the target user's ID value into the USER input field and then hit the [Enter] key.

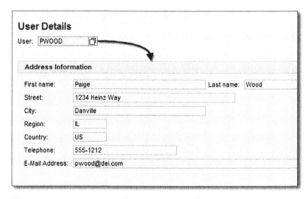

Figure W1.1 Displaying User Contact Information on Screen

In addition to the basic requirements outlined above, the application should also provide the following functionality:

- An input help for the USER field so that users can conveniently locate the user ID of the user they want to display.

- In order to maximize reuse, it's desirable to design the ADDRESS INFORMATION form in such a way that it could be leveraged elsewhere within the system. For example, we might want to display user contact information in a popup window in another application.

- The user value should be parameterized such that the selected user ID can be proposed as a URL query string parameter. Also, if no such parameter is provided, the application should default to the current user.

W1.2 Design Approach

Even for a simple application like this one, it pays to have a design approach in hand before proceeding. Therefore, the upcoming sections highlight important topics of the application design.

W1.2.1 Modeling the Application Data

Though there are several ways to retrieve the user contact information that will be displayed on screen, perhaps the easiest way to get at the data is to leverage the BAPI_USER_GET_DETAIL function provided by SAP. This BAPI function only requires a single piece of input: the user name of the target user. Since this will be provided via the USER input field at the top of the screen (see Figure W1.1), it should be a fairly trivial matter to implement the service call within a controller method.

Naturally, the resultant data will need to be stored within a controller context. Figure W1.2 demonstrates how the context might be organized. For simplicity's sake, it makes sense to define the context nodes and attributes in terms of the BAPI module parameter types. That way, it's easier to transfer the data back and forth.

In order to satisfy the input help requirement for the USER input field, be sure to configure the Input Help Mode property of the corresponding context attribute. For example, notice that we've plugged in the USER_COMP search help from the ABAP Dictionary for the USER.USERNAME context attribute in Figure W1.3. Of course, any of the input help techniques described in Chapter 10 can be used here.

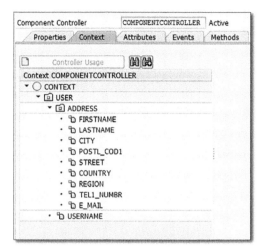

Figure W1.2 Modeling the Application Data in the Context

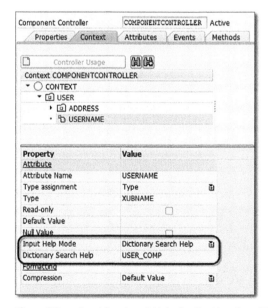

Figure W1.3 Providing Input Help for the User InputField

W1.2.2 Defining the User Interface

As you can see in Figure W1.1, the view layout for the user contact application is fairly straightforward, consisting of an InputField for the user name and a Group element that contains the user address form fields. Given the relative simplicity of this view layout, it's tempting to organize these UI elements into a single view. However, if we split these two element groups into two views, we can leverage the address form to satisfy the reuse requirement described in Section W1.1.

Figure W1.4 demonstrates how this separation can be achieved using a `ViewContainerUIElement` element. Here, we're using the `ViewContainerUIElement` to embed a separate address view into the view layout. Ultimately, this will yield the view layout depicted in Figure W1.1. However, splitting the address form out into a separate view also allows us to define a separate standalone window that only contains the address view. This separate window can be leveraged by external applications, as demonstrated in Chapter 9.

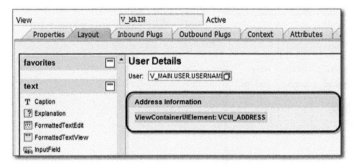

Figure W1.4 Using a ViewContainerUIElement to Organize the View Layout

W1.2.3 Event Handling

As we learned in Section W1.1, the user name of the user being displayed within the application can be provided in several different ways:

▶ By default, the current user will be preselected when the application is first loaded.

▶ A user name can be provided as a URL query string parameter to the WDA application.

▶ Users can explicitly select a user by filling in the USER input field shown in Figure W1.1.

In the upcoming sections, we'll consider how these different selections can be achieved.

Preselecting a User Name in an Inbound Plug Method

As you may recall from Chapter 6, WDA applications associate a URL with an interface view of a particular WDA component. Here, the link is established by selecting an inbound plug of the target interface view. At runtime, the event handler method of this inbound plug will be fired during the application startup process. Thus, it provides us with an excellent opportunity to preselect the target user name. Of course, in order to do this, we need to know which user to load.

According to the application requirements, we should select the current user by default. However, if a user name is provided with the application parameters, this user should be loaded instead. Easy enough, right? If you are stuck, refer back to Section 6.1.2.

Responding to User Selections on Screen

Frequently, search forms like the one being created in this workbook exercise provide some sort of button that allows users to execute a search. However, as you can see in Figure W1.1, there is no button defined within the view layout. Instead, the expectation is that the data will be loaded automatically when users enter a user name in the USER field. So, we must focus our attention on events defined by the InputField element.

W1.3 Solution

The solution for this workbook exercise can be found in the ZWDC_WB1_SOLUTION component provided with the book's code bundle. Here, pay attention to the definition of the W_USER_ADDRESS interface view because it will be leveraged in Workbook 4.

W2 Creating a Fully Functional User Maintenance Application

In Chapters 7 and 8, we introduced a user maintenance application that was used as a medium for demonstrating the functionality of various UI element types. At that stage of the book, the details of the application itself took a backseat to learning the ins and outs of various UI element types. However, now that we've had an opportunity to work through these issues, we're ready to take a closer look at how such WDA applications are implemented at the macro level. Therefore, in this workbook exercise, we'll explore the creation of a fully functional user maintenance application.

W2.1 Requirements Overview

From a requirements perspective, our user maintenance application bears many similarities to Transaction SU01, an SAP standard. So, rather than reinventing the wheel, we'll simply create a lightweight version of this application for the purposes of this exercise. Figure W2.1 shows the initial screen of Transaction SU01. As you can see, the initial screen consists of a USER input field and a toolbar containing functions related to user maintenance (e.g., CREATE, CHANGE, and DISPLAY, among others).

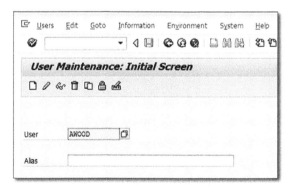

Figure W2.1 Maintaining Users in Transaction SU01 (Part 1)

Figure W2.2 shows what the user maintenance screen looks like. Here, various elements of the user data are logically grouped together on separate tabs (e.g., ADDRESS, LOGON DATA, SNC, and so on).

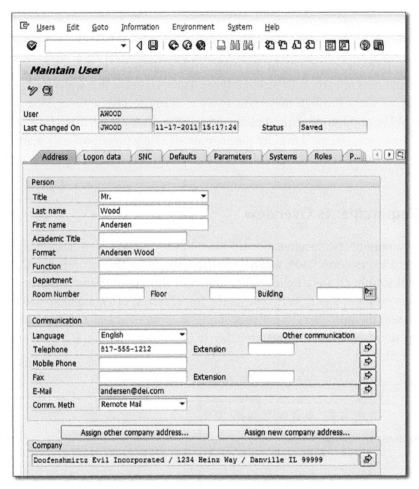

Figure W2.2 Maintaining Users in Transaction SU01 (Part 2)

Figure W2.3 shows what the initial screen of the WDA counterpart application looks like. As you can see, we've pared the set of supported functions down to just the essentials: CREATE, CHANGE, and DISPLAY.

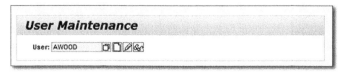

Figure W2.3 Initial Screen for WDA User Maintenance Application

Once a user record is selected on the initial screen, users can open the record in the editor screen shown in Figure W2.4. Here, user details are provided on three separate tab pages: ADDRESS, DEFAULTS, and NOTES. The ADDRESS tab, which is the initial tab depicted in Figure W2.4, consists of a series of input fields containing user contact information (much like the application created in the previous exercise).

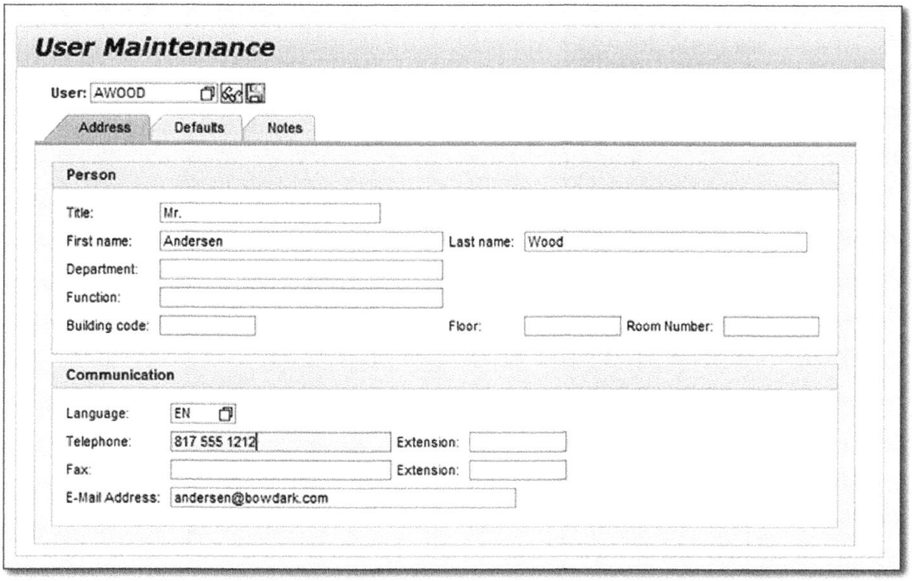

Figure W2.4 Editor Screen for WDA User Maintenance Application (Part 1)

Figure W2.5 shows what the DEFAULTS tab looks like. As you can see, this tab utilizes several different UI element types, including dropdown lists, a radio button group, and a checkbox.

Figure W2.5 Editor Screen for WDA User Maintenance Application (Part 2)

Besides the basic information captured on the ADDRESS and DEFAULTS tabs, the custom user maintenance application also contains a NOTES tab, in which users can enter notes about a particular user account. As you can see in Figure W2.6, the note text is captured in a `FormattedTextEdit` element, which supports rich text editing.

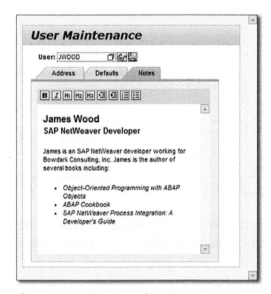

Figure W2.6 Editor Screen for WDA User Maintenance Application (Part 3)

W2.2 Design Approach

When you break down the requirements outlined in Section W2.1, you can see that none of the individual requirements are particularly complex in and of themselves. Instead, the devil is in the details of putting all the different pieces together. In this section, we'll consider some of the design challenges that the user maintenance application presents.

W2.2.1 Building an Application Model

If we start at the model layer and work our way outward, the first step in the design process is to come up with a workable application model. Here, we must seamlessly integrate data from two distinct sources:

▶ The basic user information comes from the AS ABAP user master database via a series of BAPI functions. In particular, we're using three different BAPI modules:

   ▹ To create new user accounts, we're using BAPI_USER_CREATE1.

   ▹ Changes to user accounts are posted using BAPI_USER_CHANGE.

   ▹ To read the details of a particular user account, we're using BAPI_USER_GET_DETAIL.

▶ The user notes information is stored in a custom Z-table outside the user master database. In the code bundle, we've provided a table called ZWDA_USER_NOTES for this purpose.

Though it would be possible to weave this information together within the methods of a global controller, there are several advantages to building a standalone model class outside Web Dynpro:

▶ The standalone model can be used elsewhere in the system (e.g., for interface development, other GUI applications, and so on).

▶ It simplifies the WDA application by separating UI concerns from lower-level model details. Not only does this allow the two development streams to occur in parallel, but it also makes it possible to test the model logic by itself before the WDA application is complete (e.g., using ABAP Unit).

▶ As stated in the online help documentation, the methods of regular ABAP Objects classes process much more efficiently than their WDA controller counterparts. So, there are performance advantages to be gained by factoring out the application model like this.

In the solution for this exercise, you can see that we've built a class called ZCL_ WDA_USER_MODEL for this purpose. This class provides a number of convenience methods which greatly simplify the interaction points between the WDA application and the underlying data sources.

W2.2.2 Defining the Context

Once the application model is defined, the next step is to model the user data in the context. Figure W2.7 shows how we set up a USER node in the exercise solution for this purpose. Here, notice that we've aligned the type of the nodes with the corresponding BAPI parameter types (e.g., BAPIADDR3). While this isn't a strict requirement, it certainly simplifies the transfer of data between the context and the application model.

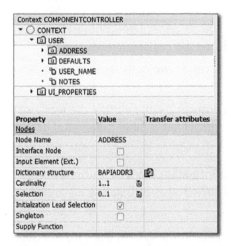

Figure W2.7 Modeling the User Data in the Context

In addition to the user data, another thing we need to keep track of in the context is the application mode. Here, for example, we need to know if fields are editable on screen and if certain toolbar buttons are visible and/or enabled. Figure W2.8 shows how the exercise solution has created a node called UI_PROPERTIES within the component controller for this purpose. As users execute specific actions on the frontend, this node will need to be updated accordingly. We'll look at the implications of this more closely in Section W2.2.4.

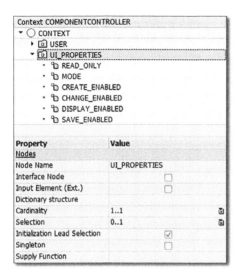

Figure W2.8 Defining a Context Node to Track Application Mode Details

W2.2.3 Designing the User Interface

Technically speaking, there are many different ways to design the user interface for the user maintenance application. One option would be to create one big, monolithic view to define the entire view layout. Another option would be to create separate views for each tab. As you can see in Figure W2.9, we chose the latter approach for the exercise solution because this option provides the most flexibility. Here, notice that we're using a default empty view to reveal the V_EDITOR editor view whenever users select from one of the actions defined in the top-level toolbar. This indirection allows for the transition you see depicted between Figure W2.3 and Figure W2.4.

Window Structure	Description
▾ ☐ W_MAIN	
▾ ☐ V_MAIN	Main View
▾ ☐ VCUI_MAIN	
▸ ☐ EMPTYVIEW	
▾ ☐ V_EDITOR	Editor View
▸ ☐ VCUI_ADDRESS	
▸ ☐ VCUI_DEFAULTS	
▸ ☐ VCUI_NOTES	
· IP_DEFAULT	Default Inbound Plug
▸ OP_TO_EDITOR	Outbound Plug to the Editor View
· DEFAULT	

Figure W2.9 Defining the Window Structure for the Application

W2.2.4 Application Mode Handling

In Section W2.2.2, we touched on the need to be able to track the application mode as users trigger actions on the frontend. Here, there are several basic requirements we must take into account:

▶ The SAVE button in the application toolbar should only be visible in situations when there's something to save. For instance, it should not be visible when a user record is being viewed in display mode.

▶ In display mode, all the input fields should be grayed out.

▶ It should be possible to toggle back and forth between change mode and display mode. Further, whenever such a switch occurs, the UI should be updated accordingly (e.g., fields are enabled/disabled as necessary).

As demonstrated in Figure W2.8, the exercise solution uses a context node called UI_PROPERTIES to track these details. Of course, in order for these updates to be synchronized with the frontend, we must bind the relevant UI elements with the corresponding context attributes. For example, in Figure W2.10, you can see that we're using the UI_PROPERTIES.CREATE_ENABLED element to control the visibility of the CREATE button in the application toolbar. As you might expect, there are several other properties that need to be configured in order to achieve the desired functionality.

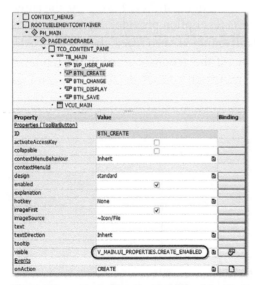

Figure W2.10 Controlling the Visibility of Application Toolbar Buttons

W2.3 Solution

The solution for this workbook exercise can be found in the `ZWDC_WB2_SOLUTION` component provided with this book's code bundle.

W2-3 Solution:

W3 Showing User Role Assignments

In this workbook exercise, we'll pick up where Workbook 2 left off by enhancing the user maintenance application to show user role assignments. Such an exercise will provide us with an opportunity to work with the complex Table element described in Chapter 8.

W3.1 Requirements Overview

Overall, the requirements for this workbook exercise are fairly straightforward. As you can see in Figure W3.1, we want to expand the user maintenance application developed in the previous exercise by adding a new tab called ROLES, which will display all the selected user's role assignments in a Table element. This table should provide the following features:

▶ Users should be able to click on a particular table column to sort the role assignments in ascending or descending order.

▶ Users should be able to filter the contents of the role assignment table using a filter row, as shown in Figure W3.1.

▶ Users should be able to display role details using a Popin, as demonstrated in Figure W3.1.

W3.2 Design Approach

Since this exercise builds upon the application created in the previous exercise, most of the basic infrastructure is in place already. Therefore, our primary focus for this exercise is defining the new ROLES tab and the Role Assignments table shown in Figure W3.1. In the upcoming sections, we'll look at how this new tab page can be defined.

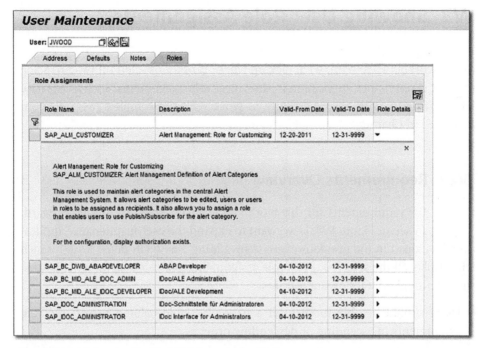

Figure W3.1 Enhancing the User Maintenance Application

W3.2.1 Defining the Context

In order to display a user's role assignments, we must extend the USER context node created in the previous exercise to include a child ROLES node. As you can see in Figure W3.2, the cardinality for the USER.ROLES node should be 0..n, so that zero or more role assignments can be displayed on the screen. Also, notice that we've defined a child node called ROLE_DETAILS in the exercise solution. This node contains the role long text description displayed in the aforementioned Popin element.

Besides the role data itself, we also need a couple of context nodes to keep track of various Table-related properties. Figure W3.3 shows that we've defined two nodes called TABLE_PROPERTIES and FILTER for this purpose. Refer back to Section 8.3.2 for details about what these nodes are used for.

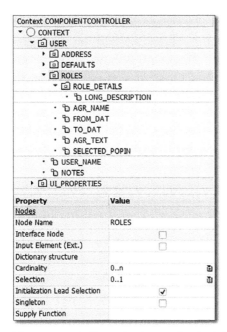

Figure W3.2 Defining the Context for the Roles Tab

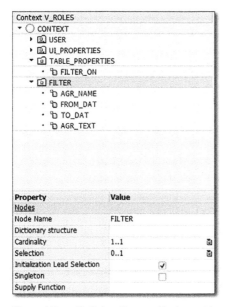

Figure W3.3 Defining Context Nodes to Keep Track of Table Properties

W3.2.2 Configuring the Table Element

Once the requisite context nodes are set up, the configuration of the `Table` element itself should be relatively straightforward. Figure W3.4 shows what the finished product looks like in the View Designer tool. Here, you can see that, in addition to the normal `TableColumn` elements, we've also defined:

► A `TablePopinToggleCell`, which provides the arrow icon used to expand and collapse the `TablePopin` (see Figure W3.1).

► A `TablePopin` and an underlying content area.

► A `ToolBar` element and a `ToolBarToggleButton` that can be used to turn the filter row on and off.

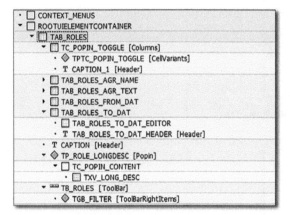

Figure W3.4 Configuring the Table Element in the View Designer Tool

W3.2.3 Turning on Sorting and Filtering

As we learned in Chapter 8, we have two options when it comes to sorting and filtering:

► We can use the events defined within the `Table` element as a point for integrating our own custom sorting and filtering logic.

► We can leverage the out-of-the-box sorting and filtering functionality provided by SAP in the `CL_WD_TABLE` runtime class of the `Table` element.

In the latter case, we can tap into the canned functionality by accessing the `_METHOD_HANDLER` instance attribute of the `CL_WD_TABLE` runtime class. This attribute points to an object of type `IF_WD_TABLE_METHOD_HNDL`. These references can be obtained via the WDDOMODIFYVIEW() hook method of the view where the Table element is displayed. From here, we can use methods from the IF_WD_TABLE_METHOD_HNDL interface to apply the sorting/filtering logic.

W3.2.4 Defining the TablePopin

For the most part, the process of defining the TablePopin is the same as the one described in Section 8.3.2. As you can see in Figure W3.5, the content area for the TablePopin consists of a TransparentContainer and a TextView element to display the role long text.

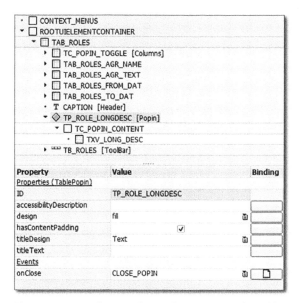

Figure W3.5 Configuring the onClose Event on the TablePopin Element

W3.3 Solution

The solution for this workbook exercise can be found in the ZWDC_WB3_SOLUTION component provided with this book's code bundle.

W4 Developing a Custom User Report

In Chapter 9, we considered some of the potential benefits of applying a component-based approach to WDA application design. In particular, we observed that the reuse of existing WDA components not only increases developer productivity, but also improves the overall quality of the finished product.

In order to reinforce these concepts, we'll be developing a custom user report in this workbook exercise that leverages the services of several different WDA components.

W4.1 Requirements Overview

From a functional perspective, the user report we'll be developing is positioned as a web-based substitute for the SAP standard transaction S_BCE_68001393 (USERS BY ADDRESS DATA). As you can see in Figure W4.1, the report layout is organized as follows:

▸ In the top half of the screen, a series of selection fields are provided to support user lookups using address-related selection criteria.

▸ In the bottom half of the screen, an ALV table is used to display the selection results.

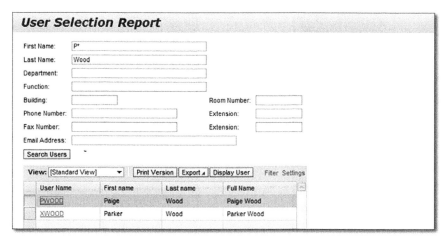

Figure W4.1 Basic Layout of the User Selection Report

In addition to the basic reporting requirements, the user selection report calls for a couple of additional bells and whistles:

▶ The report should support fuzzy logic searches using the familiar asterisk (*) wildcard character (see Figure W4.1).

▶ Users should be able to display the contact information for a particular user record in a popup window, as shown in Figure W4.2. It should be possible to access this popup window in two different ways:

  ▷ By selecting the user record in the list and clicking on a DISPLAY USER button

  ▷ By clicking on the hyperlink contained within the USER NAME column (see Figure W4.2)

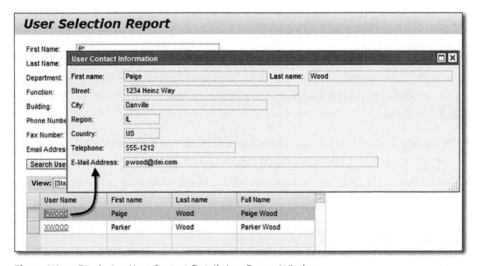

Figure W4.2 Displaying User Contact Details in a Popup Window

The final requirement for the user report is that its query model be *reusable*. Here, the goal is to define a general query model that can be used as a data supplier for many types of user-related reports. Examples of such reports might include:

▶ Users by account validity period

▶ Users having particular role assignments

▶ Users whose accounts are locked or unlocked

▶ Users having particular system assignments in SAP Central User Administration (CUA)

W4.2 Design Approach

The design of layered applications like the user report calls for a methodical approach in which we:

1. Lay out the component boundaries.

2. Locate and/or design the constituent WDA components.

3. Wire the components together and fill in any gaps that may remain.

In the upcoming sections, we'll consider each of these steps in turn.

W4.2.1 Defining the Component Architecture

As we set out to design our report application, the first order of business is to identify the roles and responsibilities assumed by the various collaborating WDA components. Once these boundaries are established, the rest of the application should fall in line pretty easily.

Though there are many ways to break up the application design, the component diagram depicted in Figure W4.3 demonstrates how we organized the participating WDA components in the exercise solution. Here, we have a main component called ZWDC_WB4_SOLUTION that leverages the services of three additional WDA components:

▶ ZWDC_WB4_MODEL
This faceless component provides a self-contained, reusable application query model. We'll explore how this model is designed in Section W4.2.2.

▶ SSALV_WD_TABLE
This SAP standard component is used to produce the ALV table shown at the bottom of the report screen depicted in Figure W4.1.

▶ ZWDC_WB1_SOLUTION
This is the WDA component we developed in the first workbook exercise. We'll reuse its user interface to produce the popup dialog window shown in Figure W4.2.

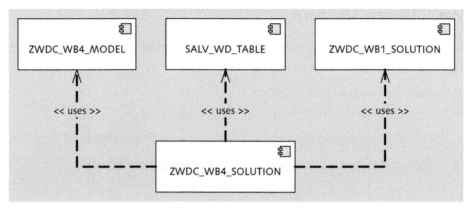

Figure W4.3 WDA Component Diagram for the User Report Application

W4.2.2 Constructing a Reusable Query Model

As described in Section W4.1, one of the requirements of the user report is that we construct a flexible and reusable query model. While such a model could certainly be built using standalone ABAP Objects classes, function modules, and so on, we can get even more reuse if we wrap this query model up as a faceless component like the ZWDC_WB4_MODEL component depicted in Figure W4.3. Here, the faceless component assumes the responsibility of transferring data between the Web Dynpro context and the backend data model so that leveraging components can quickly tap into the query model using context node mappings.

Behind the scenes, the faceless component can utilize the SAP standard function BAPI_USER_GETLIST to generate the various queries. Here, selection parameters are captured within the SELECTION_RANGE table parameter, which is defined like a range table. Reading through the code comments in the BAPI_USER_GETLIST module, we can see that the search fields it supports are defined in terms of field provided with the BAPI_USER_GET_DETAIL function module. Given these similarities, it makes sense to define the context hierarchy for the faceless component in terms of the relevant parameter types from BAPI_USER_GET_DETAIL. Figure W4.4 illustrates how we did this in the ZWDC_WB4_MODEL component provided with the exercise solution.

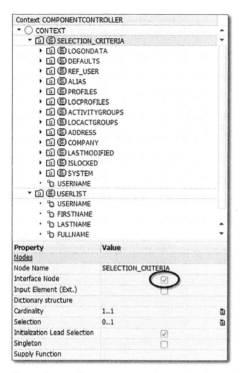

Figure W4.4 Defining the Context Node Hierarchy for the User Query Model

Looking at the context node hierarchy depicted in Figure W4.4, you can see that the exercise solution defines two context nodes:

▶ `SELECTION_CRITERIA`
This node contains all the various query parameters supported by the query model.

▶ `USERLIST`
This node is designed to store the query results from `BAPI_USER_GETLIST`.

At runtime, these context nodes will be used to transfer data back and forth between the faceless component and the report components that use it as a data supplier. Of course, in order for this to work, we must configure the `Interface Node` property on the context nodes, as illustrated in Figure W4.4.

Once the context nodes are in place, the only thing left to define in the faceless model component is an interface method leveraging components can use to perform the user lookup operation. As you can see in Figure W4.5, this step basically amounts to defining an instance method in the component controller and selecting the `Interface` property.

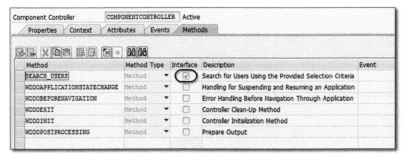

Figure W4.5 Defining an Interface Method to Conduct the Search

Figure W4.6 illustrates the basic data flow between the faceless model component and leveraging components at runtime. As you can see, data is transferred implicitly between the components using context node mappings, as described in Chapter 9. Therefore, once the context node mappings are established, the only thing a using component needs to do in order to execute a query is call the `SEARCH_USERS()` method from the faceless component's component interface.

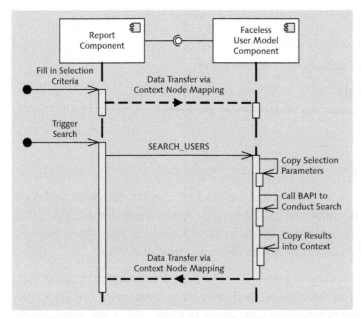

Figure W4.6 Data Exchange with the Faceless Model Component

W4.2.3 Designing the User Interface

As we observed in Section W4.1, the view layout for the user report is split up into two distinct areas:

▶ The top half of the screen contains a form that allows users to enter various selection parameters. This form is defined in terms of the SELECTION_CRITE-RIA.ADDRESS node illustrated in Figure W4.4.

▶ The bottom half of the screen embeds an ALV table used to display the user query results.

Figure W4.7 illustrates how this layout can be defined within a window element. Here, a main view called V_MAIN is using the ViewContainerUIElement element to embed two subviews:

▶ The VCUI_SELECTION element embeds a custom view called V_SELECT, which contains the selection parameter form.

▶ The VCUI_REPORT element embeds two views:

  ▷ An empty view displayed by default when the application is first loaded. The use of a default empty view here is optional but allows us to apply a common UI design pattern in which screen elements are only revealed when needed.

  ▷ The TABLE interface view from the SAP standard SALV_WD_TABLE component. This interface view displays the ALV table on the screen.

Window Structure	Description
▾ 🗖 W_MAIN	
▾ 🗖 V_MAIN	Main View
▾ 🗖 VCUI_REPORT	
▸ 🗖 EMPTYVIEW	
▸ 🗖 TABLE	ALV Table Interface View
▾ 🗖 VCUI_SELECTION	
▸ 🗖 V_SELECT	View Containing User Selection Screen
• 🖮 DEFAULT	

Figure W4.7 Defining the View Layout for the User Selection Report

W4.2.4 Coordinating the Event Flow

Once all the requisite WDA components are in place, the final piece to the puzzle is to wire up all the events that will be triggered at runtime. With our user report, there are three such events we must account for:

- ▶ The first event is the `Button.onAction` event, which is triggered whenever users click on the SEARCH USERS button in the selection form (see Figure W4.8). Whenever this event is triggered, two things need to happen:
  - ▶ First, the `SEARCH_USERS()` method of the faceless model component must be invoked to execute the user query.
  - ▶ Then, once the query is complete, an outbound plug must be triggered to load the `TABLE` interface view from the `SALV_WD_TABLE` component.
- ▶ Within the ALV table containing the query results, an event is triggered whenever users display a user record by clicking on the `Display User` button. Since this button is dynamically defined within the ALV component's toolbar, the report component must intercept this event by registering an event handler method for the `ON_FUNCTION` event of the `SALV_WD_TABLE` component's interface controller.
- ▶ Since users also have the option of displaying the details of a user record by clicking on the link attached to the user name, the report component must also listen for the `ON_CLICK` event of the `SALV_WD_TABLE` component's interface controller.

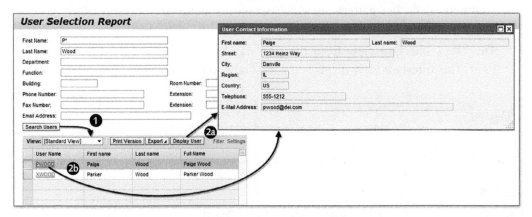

Figure W4.8 Defining the Event Flow for the User Report

The event handler methods for the `ON_FUNCTION` and `ON_CLICK` events of the ALV component are tasked with displaying the user contact information form created in the first workbook exercise. Refer back to Section 9.2.5 for a refresher on how this is accomplished.

W4.3 Solution

The solution for this workbook exercise can be found in the `ZWDC_WB4_SOLUTION` component provided with this book's code bundle.

W5 Implementing Special Features

Oftentimes, the difference between having a really good WDA application and a really bad WDA application comes down to how well we take care of the little things that guide users toward meeting their objectives. For example, if we think users may have a difficult time filling in the contents of a particular form field, we should provide them with an input help to guide them toward selecting the proper value. Or, if a user makes a mistake, we should provide an error message that helps them correct the problem and proceed.

In this workbook exercise, we'll see how to achieve such qualities in our WDA applications by expanding upon the user maintenance application developed in Workbooks 2 and 3. These subtle changes will help transform the application from a basic prototype into a full-fledged, production-quality application.

W5.1 Requirements Overview

As we mentioned earlier, this workbook exercise expands upon the user maintenance application developed in Workbooks 2 and 3. From a requirements perspective, we'll take the existing application as a baseline and add/implement the following features:

▶ An input help in the USER field on the main screen to assist users in finding the user master record for a particular user

▶ Checks to ensure that users don't try to create pre-existing user records or modify/display records that don't already exist

▶ Checks to make sure that users enter data in all the required fields of the user master record

▶ Checks to make sure that users enter valid values in free-form text fields such as the TELEPHONE, FAX, and E-MAIL ADDRESS fields

In addition to the changes outlined above, we also want to provide users with a confirmation dialog box to advise them of data loss in case they make changes to a user record and then click on the DISPLAY button (see Figure W5.1). This implies that we must keep track of any changes made to a user record within the application session.

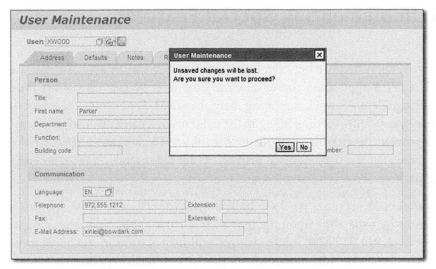

Figure W5.1 Prompting Users to Save Their Changes in a Popup Window

W5.2 Design Approach

From a design perspective, we'll be using the solution from Workbook 3 as a baseline for adding the features outlined in Section W5.1. Therefore, in the up-coming sections, our focus will be on locating the places within the application where the new requirements need to be implemented and looking at the steps required to do so.

W5.2.1 Providing Input Help Support

As we learned in Chapter 10, input helps can be attached to InputField elements in a variety of ways. Most of the time, they're automatically derived from the data element in the ABAP Dictionary used to define the type of the context attribute bound to the InputField element's value property. However, if the data element in question doesn't have a search help attached to it, we must manually assign an input help mode in order to provide input help support on screen. One way to achieve this would be to search for a compatible search help for a data element by opening the ABAP Dictionary and selecting the familiar WHERE-USED LIST feature, as shown in Figure W5.2 and Figure W5.3.

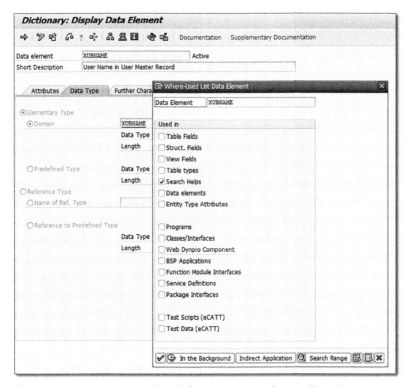

Figure W5.2 Locating a Search Help for a Given Data Element (Part 1)

Where-used Data Element XUBNAME in Search helps (61 Hits)

Complete List

Search help	Short description
☐ S_MODIFIER	Search Help for scpractp-modifier
☐ USALIAS	User alias
☐ USER_ADDR	Users by address data
☐ USER_ADDR_WD	User According to Address Data
☐ USER_AGRP	Users by Roles
☑ USER_COMP	Users by Logon Data
☐ USER_CUA_PROFILE	Users by System-Specific Profiles
☐ USER_CUA_ROLE	Users by System-Specific Roles
☐ USER_CUA_SYSTEMS	Users by Systems
☐ USER_GROUP	Users by User Groups (General)
☐ USER_HELP	Help to get valid R/3 users
☐ USER_LOGON	Users by Logon Data
☐ USER_PROF	Users by Profiles
☐ USREFUSER	Reference User
☐ WTY_F4_AUTNA	F4 Help for Name of Authorizer
☐ WTY_F4_CLERK	Search Help Person Responsible
☐ WTY_F4_CREABY	F4 Help for Person who Created Warranty Claim

Figure W5.3 Locating a Search Help for a Given Data Element (Part 2)

Once we locate a search help in the ABAP Dictionary, we can assign it to the target context attribute by configuring the `Input Help Mode` property, as shown in Figure W5.4.

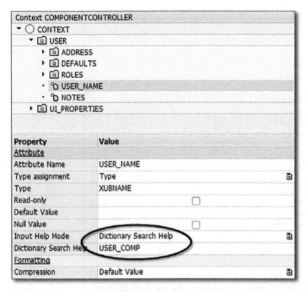

Figure W5.4 Manually Assigning a Search Help from the ABAP Dictionary

W5.2.2 Defining Field-Level Validations

In general, the process of applying field-level validations consists of two steps:

1. In the view that contains the fields in question, we must implement the validation logic within the `WDDOBEFOREACTION()` method.

2. Then, for any fields containing errors, we need to issue an error message on screen. Here, we want to prevent the user from proceeding until the error situation is corrected.

In the case of required field checks, we can save ourselves a few steps using the static `CHECK_MANDATORY_ATTR_ON_VIEW()` method of class `CL_WD_DYNAMIC_TOOL`, as described in Chapter 10. For other validations, we can use regular ABAP Objects code to verify user input. For example, in Listing W5.1, you can see how we're using regular expressions to validate that e-mail addresses are entered in the form *user@somedomain.ext.*

> **Note**
>
> For more information about regular expressions and their support in ABAP, check out *ABAP Cookbook* (Wood, SAP PRESS, 2010).

```
method WDDOBEFOREACTION.
  DATA lo_nd_address TYPE REF TO if_wd_context_node.
  DATA lo_el_address TYPE REF TO if_wd_context_element.
  DATA ls_address TYPE wd_this->Element_address.
  DATA lt_attributes TYPE string_table.

  "Validate fields for proper input:
  lo_nd_address =
    wd_context->path_get_node( path = `USER.ADDRESS` ).
  lo_el_address = lo_nd_address->get_element( ).
  lo_el_address->get_static_attributes(
    IMPORTING static_attributes = ls_address ).

  ...

  IF NOT ls_address-e_mail IS INITIAL.
    IF cl_abap_matcher=>matches(
        pattern = `^[A-Z0-9._%+-]+@[A-Z0-9.-]+\.[A-Z]{2,4}$`
        text = ls_address-e_mail
        ignore_case = abap_true ) EQ abap_false.

      REFRESH lt_attributes.
      APPEND 'E_MAIL' TO lt_attributes.
      CALL METHOD wd_assist->report_element_error_message
        EXPORTING
          message_text      = `Invalid email address.`
          element           = lo_el_address
          attributes        = lt_attributes
          cancel_navigation = abap_true.
    ENDIF.
  ENDIF.
endmethod.
```

Listing W5.1 Using Regular Expressions to Validate an E-Mail Address Field

In the example code shown in Listing W5.1, you can see how we're alerting users to an error in an e-mail address entry using the REPORT_ELEMENT_ERROR_MESSAGE()

method. Here, the population of the CANCEL_NAVIGATION parameter ensures that the user can't proceed until the error is corrected.

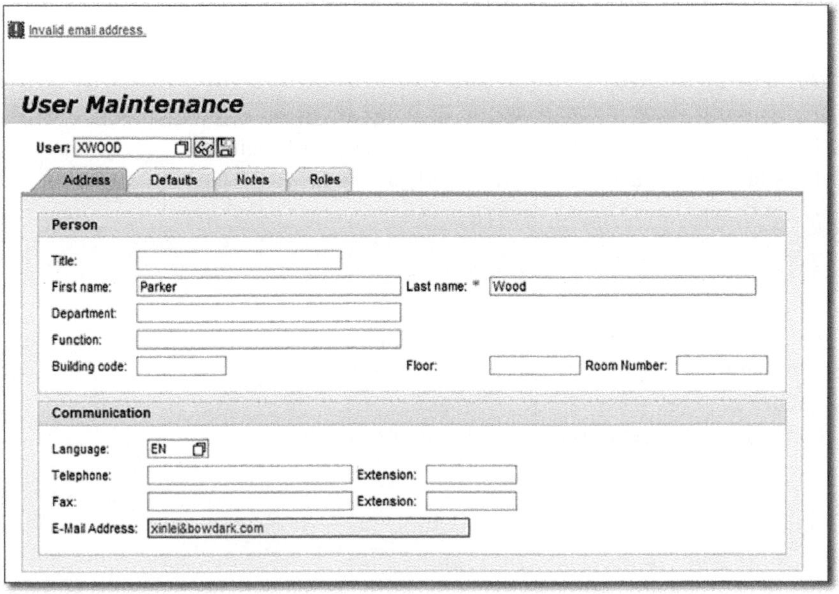

Figure W5.5 Attaching an Error Message to an InputField Element

W5.2.3 Tracking Changes to User Records

At first glance, the prospect of having to track changes made to user records may seem a bit tedious. However, if you recall that SAP provides us with a context change log to track changes such as this, the process is not really all that daunting. If you refer back to Section 5.4.6, you should find everything you're looking for to meet the first half of this requirement.

Once we establish that changes have occurred, the next step is to stop what we're doing and display a popup dialog box like the one demonstrated in Figure W5.1. For this, we can use the CREATE_POPUP_TO_CONFIRM() method of the IF_WD_WINDOW_MANAGER interface to create the popup window (refer back to Section 10.3 for details). Then, depending on the selection made by the user, we can determine whether or not to proceed by implementing logic in the corresponding action handler methods.

W5.3 Solution

The solution for this workbook exercise can be found in the `ZWDC_WB5_SOLUTION` component provided with this book's code bundle.

W6 Using Component-Based Development Techniques

As we've seen, the declarative programming model employed by Web Dynpro allows us to develop fully functional web applications in a short amount of time. However, if we depend on the toolset alone, we'll eventually reach the limits of what we can achieve, productivity-wise. Therefore, in order to speed things along, we need to come up with ways to reuse what we already have. Within the WDA programming environment, we do this using component-based development techniques.

In this exercise, we'll consider how component-based development techniques can be used to develop a simple reporting application. As you'll see, once we line up all the requisite components, the application itself falls into place quite quickly.

W6.1 Requirements Overview

For this exercise, we'll be developing a basic flight search application based on the familiar SAP flight model used in many SAP demonstrations. Here, we'll be using the standard BAPI module `BAPI_FLIGHT_GETLIST` to do the heavy lifting behind the scenes. With this in place, our focus will be more on developing the various screens for the tool.

Figure W6.1 shows what the flight search tool looks like on the screen. As you can see, the screen layout consists of a flight selection form and a results table. Beyond these basic requirements, we must also account for the following:

► Input helps must be provided for each of the three selection fields. In the case of the AIRLINE field, we can use an existing search help from the ABAP Dictionary. However, the requirements on the other two fields are a little more involved:

  ▸ The FROM and TO fields are used to represent the departure airport and arrival airport values, respectively. Since users may not know the airport codes off the top of their heads, we need to provide a flexible input help which will allow them to search for airport codes using several different attribute types (e.g., city, region, country, and so on).

▷ The flight model allows us to search for flights using a complex date range. Therefore, the FLIGHT DATE selection field must be defined as a select option.

▸ Users want to be able to export the flight search results, apply filters, etc. Therefore, the search results should be rendered in an ALV table.

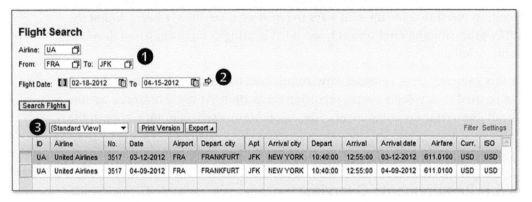

Figure W6.1 Flight Report Overview

W6.2 Design Approach

With component-based designs, we must first line up the WDA components we plan to use and then figure out how to integrate them inside a main component. From here, it's usually a matter of wiring an event here or there to finish out the final product.

W6.2.1 Designing an Airport Lookup Input Help

As we learned in Section W6.1, one of the requirements for our flight search application is to provide users with a flexible input help solution that will allow them to search for airport codes using various selection criteria. Since SAP does provide a table called SCITAIRP that contains this data, we could conceivably build such an input help using a search help from the ABAP Dictionary. However, this still doesn't quite get us where we want to go, flexibility-wise.

Instead, our design approach will be to create a freely programmed input help solution, as described in Section 10.1.3. Not only does this give us ultimate flexibility in the design process, but it also makes it easier for us to reuse the solution in other application scenarios.

Once we define the shell of the input help component and the IWD_VALUE_HELP component interface, the next step is to build out the query model. Here, we could build our own query engine on top of the SCITAIRP table. However, if you perform a quick search online, you'll find that there are several web-service–based query engines we can also leverage for this purpose. One such API is AirportCode, which is available online at *http://airportcode.riobard.com/about#api*. This REST-based API makes it very easy to perform complex airport code lookups using keyword-like semantics.

> **Note**
>
> Since this is a book on WDA programming, we won't get into the specifics of consuming REST-based services, etc. We have, however, provided a fully functional model class that simplifies the way that you interact with this service in this book's code bundle: ZCL_WDA_AIRPORT_QUERY. If you're interested in learning more about how these calls are implemented, you can also check out *ABAP Cookbook* (Wood, SAP PRESS, 2010).

Figure W6.2 demonstrates what the finished product for our airport lookup component looks like. Here, we've provided a single InputField element, which contains the keyword used to perform the search. Users can enter data in this field and then trigger the search by hitting the Enter key. Then, they can choose the proper airport code from the results and hit the SELECT button to confirm their selections.

Figure W6.2 Designing the Screen Layout for the Input Help Component

W6.2.2 Integrating the Used Components

Once we've defined our custom airport code lookup component, we have all the requisite used components in place:

▸ The newly-created custom airport lookup component will be used to build the input help from the FROM and TO fields in the selection form shown in Figure W6.1.

▸ The WDR_SELECT_OPTIONS component will be used to build the FLIGHT DATE selection field shown in Figure W6.1.

▸ The SALV_WD_TABLE component will be used to build the ALV table containing the flight search results.

So, in order to pull everything together, we simply need to define our main component and perform the following steps:

1. First, we need to define component usages for each of the used components, as shown in Figure W6.3.

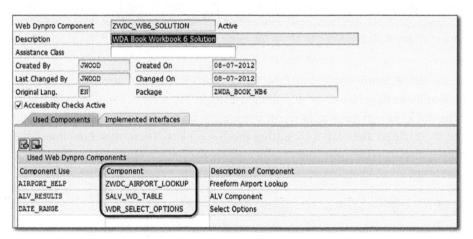

Figure W6.3 Defining Component Usages in the Main Component

2. Next, we need to assign the custom airport code lookup component as the input help of choice for the context attributes sitting behind the FROM and TO fields (see Figure W6.4).

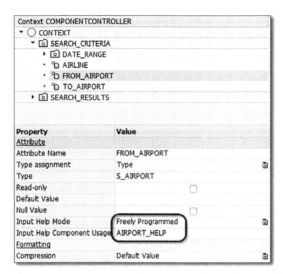

Figure W6.4 Integrating the Airport Code Lookup into the Context

3. To integrate the select option and ALV table into the view layout, we need to define a couple of `ViewContainerUIElement` placeholder elements. These elements will allow us to embed the target interface views of the `WDR_SELECT_OPTIONS` and `SALV_WD_TABLE` components.

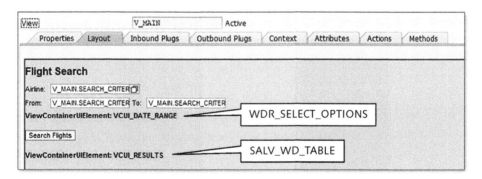

Figure W6.5 Embedding Interface Views from the Used SAP Components

4. We also have some initialization work to do within the view, which embeds the `WDR_SELECT_OPTIONS` component (e.g., the `V_MAIN` view shown in Figure W6.5). Here, we need to define the range table that will be used to capture the FLIGHT DATE selection criteria on screen. This task can be performed in the `WDDOINIT()` method and is described at length in Section 10.1.4.

5. Lastly, we need to define an external context mapping to map the flight search results to the ALV table output. This step is described in detail in Section 9.2.4.

Once these basic steps are completed, all that's left to do is define an event handler method that will trigger the flight search (e.g., function BAPI_FLIGHT_GETLIST). Then, at runtime, the main component will launch the application, and the used components will play their respective roles when called upon.

W6.3 Solution

The solution for this exercise can be found in the ZWDC_WB6_SOLUTION component provided with this book's code bundle.

W7 Configuring an FPM Application

In Chapter 14, we examined the Floorplan Manager as both an alternate and complementary methodology for creating WDA applications. In this workbook exercise, we'll put that concept to the test by creating a WDA application without developing our own component. Instead, we'll configure a FPM application that utilizes one of the Generic User Interface Building Blocks (GUIBBs) provided by the FPM framework.

W7.1 Requirements Overview

In this exercise, we'll be creating a simple address book application that allows a user to look up user contact information in the system by supplying search criteria for a first and last name. Structurally, this application will have a layout that displays selection screens and search functionality in the top half of the application, and a search results table in the bottom half of the application, as shown in Figure W7.1.

Figure W7.1 Layout of the FPM Application

If we were creating a component from scratch, we'd have to create and configure a view that supports this layout. In FPM, this layout is already supported by the search GUIBB component, which we plan to utilize in our design. Therefore, our requirements boil down to an issue of data in this instance. We want our application (the search component) to provide the following:

▶ Search attributes/selection fields for searching by the first and last name of a user.

▶ Search results for displaying the last name, first name, telephone number, and email address of the users found, shown in that order in the results table.

W7.2 Design Approach

We'll be basing our application design on the Object Instance Floorplan (OIF), which will contain the aforementioned search component. In order to implement this design, we'll need to perform each of the following activities:

1. Implement a feeder class for the search component.

2. Configure our floorplan application.

3. Configure the search GUIBB within our floorplan.

4. Configure the IDR component within our floorplan.

W7.2.1 Implementing a Feeder Class for the Search GUIBB

Configuration of a search GUIBB component mandates that a feeder class be provided for the component that implements IF_FPM_GUIBB_SEARCH. This class, in turn, describes the search and results data to be used in the search component and performs the actual search, supplying data back to the component. In this exercise, we'll be implementing our search feeder class as ZWDA_SEARCH_FEEDER.

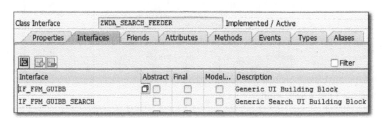

Figure W7.2 Interfaces Defined in the Search Feeder Class

> **Note**
>
> As you may have noticed in Figure W7.2, our search feeder class ZWDA_SEARCH_FEEDER also implements interface IF_FPM_GUIBB. This is brought in as a dependency of IF_FPM_GUIBB_SEARCH.

In order to implement the search feeder class, we'll need to supply code for the following methods:

▶ GET_DEFINITION

This method describes configuration options for the search, including which attributes may be searched and which data may be displayed as a search result.

▶ PROCESS_EVENT

This method conducts the actual search itself.

▶ GET_DATA

This method returns the search results data to the search GUIBB component when called.

Describing Search Attributes and Results

The easiest way to define/describe your search attributes and results data is to define each data set as a data type and return their descriptions by means of the DESCRIBE_BY_NAME or DESCRIBE_BY_DATA methods of class CL_ABAP_STRUCTDESCR.

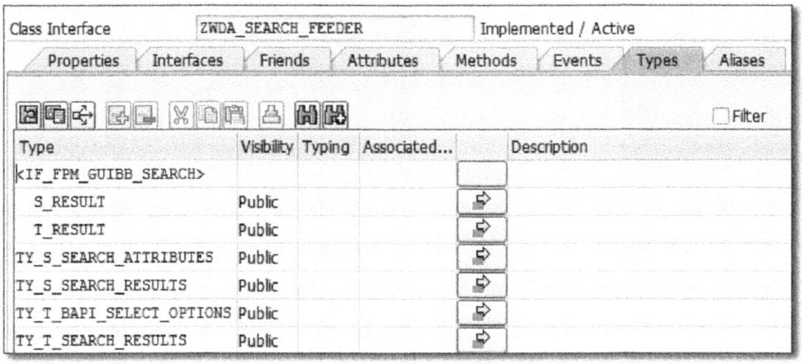

Figure W7.3 Types Defined in the Search Feeder Class

As you can see in Figure W7.3, we've defined types TY_S_SEARCH_ATTRIBUTES and TY_S_SEARCH_RESULTS to serve this purpose. Their descriptions are returned as the appropriate exporting parameters of the GET_DEFINITION method.

Searching For and Returning Data

As mentioned above, the PROCESS_EVENT method is where your search is conducted. In this method, you search for user data by means of the BAPI call BAPI_USER_GETLIST and the support classes we created for our earlier workbooks. The search result data is, in turn, stored as a class attribute in our feeder class so that it may be accessed later by use of the GET_DATA method.

W7.2.2 Configuring the FPM Application

Now that the hard work is done and we have our search feeder class, we may configure our FPM application. We'll create our application and its configuration objects by means of the FPM Application Creation Tool. This is called by running WDA application FPM_CFG_APPL_CREATION_TOOL.

In this tool, we'll need to supply an application name and specify that we wish to use the Object Instance Floorplan (OIF). Clicking the PROPOSE button will propose configuration IDs for each of the component configurations we'll be undertaking in the creation of this application. Figure W7.4 shows the configuration objects that we'll create for this application.

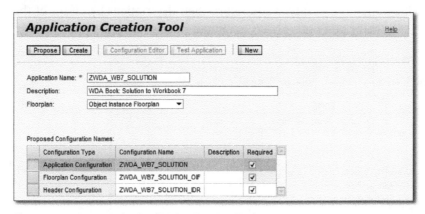

Figure W7.4 Running the Application Creation Tool

Once all the configuration objects have been specified and created, we'll proceed to configure our floorplan. We do this by executing the Configuration Editor for the floorplan configuration object we created.

There are two primary activities we'll need to conduct in this configuration:

1. Remove the predefined START button from our application.

2. Add a search GUIBB component to the floorplan.

Removing the Default Start Button

Object Instance Floorplans come with a preconfigured START button available on their toolbars. Since we have no use for this button (to navigate or process events) in our application, we can safely remove it by viewing its attributes and clicking the DELETE button.

Adding the Search GUIBB

You can add the search GUIBB component to the FPM application by adding a UIBB to the screen that utilizes the `FPM_SEARCH_UIBB` component. You'll also need to define a component configuration for this component, as shown in Figure W7.5.

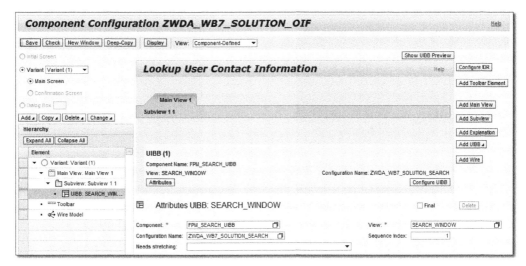

Figure W7.5 Search GUIBB Component Attributes within the FPM Application

W7.2.3 Configuring the Search GUIBB Component

You may configure the search GUIBB component by clicking the CONFIGURE UIBB button in the FPM Component Editor. In our search component, we have a small number of configuration tasks to undertake:

1. Configure the feeder class.

2. Configure the search attributes.

3. Configure the search results.

Once these tasks are complete, the search GUIBB's configuration should resemble Figure W7.6.

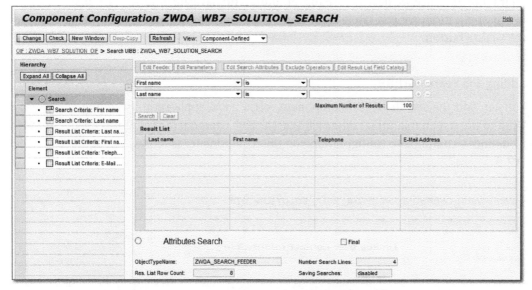

Figure W7.6 The Search Component Configuration Editor

Configuring the Feeder Class

You'll be prompted when first entering the search component's Configuration Editor to specify the feeder class for the component, as shown in Figure W7.7. You may alternatively click the EDIT FEEDER button to launch the same dialog.

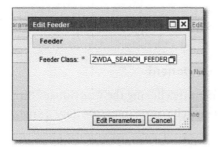

Figure W7.7 Configuring a Feeder Class

The search component's entire configuration is based on the implementation of your feeder class. As with the search component itself, the Component Editor also uses the feeder class to determine which search attributes and results data are available for use.

Configuring Search Attributes

You can configure search attributes in the editor by selecting the EDIT SEARCH ATTRIBUTES button. A dialog appears in which you may add, remove, and order the available search attributes for your component. Here, we want to select only the FIRSTNAME and LASTNAME attributes for display, as in Figure W7.8.

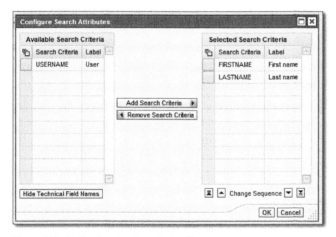

Figure W7.8 Configuring Search Attributes

Configuring Search Results

You can configure search results in the Component Editor by selecting the EDIT RESULT LIST FIELD CATALOG button. As with the edit search attributes functionality, a dialog appears in which you may add, remove, and order the available search result fields for your component. For our application, we'll want to view the LASTNAME, FIRSTNAME, PHONE_NUM, and EMAIL_ADDR fields, as shown in Figure W7.9.

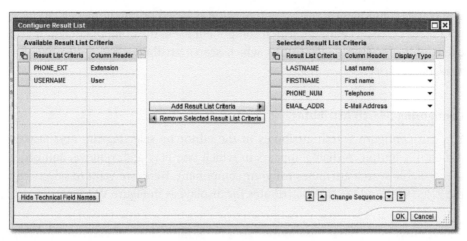

Figure W7.9 Configuring Search Results

W7.2.4 Configuring the IDR Component

OIF components are by default supplied with a header (IDR) component that describes the activity that the user is performing and a screen title for the application. For our application, we'd like to supply a custom title for the screen, which can be supplied by editing the APPLICATION TITLE field of the IDR BASIC UI element in the IDR component's Configuration Editor, as shown in Figure W7.10.

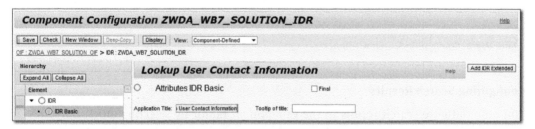

Figure W7.10 Configuring the Header Component

W7.3 Solution

The solution for this workbook exercise can be found in the ZWDC_WB7_SOLUTION component provided with this book's code bundle.

W8 Integrating WDA with Flash

As we discussed in Chapter 15, Web Dynpro has become quite flexible in its ability to integrate with other technologies and platforms. And in each subsequent release of WDA, more integration features are being added one at a time. One of the most popular and steadfast of these features, though, remains WDA's ability to integrate with Adobe Flash, which allows Adobe Flex–based Rich Internet Application content to integrate into your Web Dynpro applications.

In this workbook exercise, we'll take a closer look at an integration scenario involving these technologies and specifically look at how to fire an event in a Flash application so that it triggers an action on the Web Dynpro end. Orchestrating such integrations takes just a little bit of coordination.

W8.1 Requirements Overview

In this exercise, we'll be integrating a Flash-based CAPTCHA component into a fictitious user registration form much like you might see on any number of websites across the Internet. The form will supply inputs for registration information (in this case, a first and last name) and challenge you to verify that you're a human by identifying the characters displayed on a system-generated image, complete with noise.

The code for generating the CAPTCHA image will be supplied by an independent ActionScript class, so we won't delve into that particular piece of the puzzle. Instead, we'll focus on the mechanics of how to prepare a WDA application to receive an event from a Flash application, and vice versa.

If you examine Figure W8.1, you'll notice that there really isn't that much to laying out this application in a Web Dynpro component view. At a glance, you'll at least require the following:

- A first-name input field and matching context value
- A last-name input field and matching context value

- A `ViewContainerUIElement` to encapsulate the CAPTCHA component's `Flash-Island` container
- A view containing the `FlashIsland element`

Figure W8.1 The Registration Form and CAPTCHA

We intend to generate the CAPTCHA security code in the Flash application but check it on the WDA side using an event, so we'll also require the following:

- A supporting `GACEvent` and `GACEventParameters` as elements of our `FlashIsland`. The parameters will contain copies of the challenge code generated by our Flash application and the user-supplied security code.
- An action in our `FlashIsland view` to which to bind our `GACEvent`.

W8.2 Design Approach

The design of this application breaks into four major pieces: the registration fields of the WDA form, the Flash application content, the `FlashIsland` element's structure and content, and the backing action handler for the event fired. We'll forgo discussing how to structure the WDA form and on-screen content of the Flash application and instead concentrate on how the integration pieces work. This leaves calling the event from the Flash application, configuring the FlashIsland to respond to the event, and handling the event in our action handler.

W8.2.1 Calling the WDA Event from the Flash Application

Calling our event from the Flash application takes just a single method call in the right place. The FlashIsland.fireEvent method takes parameters for a reference to the FlashIsland application firing the event, an event name bound in our GACEvent control, and any event parameters (which are similarly bound to GACEventParameter controls). Figure W8.2 shows the code snippet from our Adobe Flex application that fires the submit event.

```
FlashIsland.fireEvent(
    this, "submit", {securityCode: captcha.securityCode, challengeCode: this.inpChallengeCode.text});
```

Figure W8.2 Firing the Event from the CAPTCHA Application

W8.2.2 Creating the FlashIsland View

FlashIsland views are created by supplanting the TransparentContainer element that usually forms the ROOTUIELEMENTCONTAINER of a view with a FlashIsland element. As we learned in Chapter 15, this is done by means of the SWAP ROOT ELEMENT functionality found in the context menu of the element. A compiled version of the CAPTCHA application is supplied to us as *captcha.swf* and should be specified in the FlashIsland element's swfFile property in order to link the two entities.

Additionally, as we discussed in Chapter 15, in order to enable eventing from a FlashIsland into WDA application, we need to structure GAC controls in the layout of the FlashIsland element that bind to the data we're sending from the Flash application. Figure W8.3 illustrates how we do this for this application.

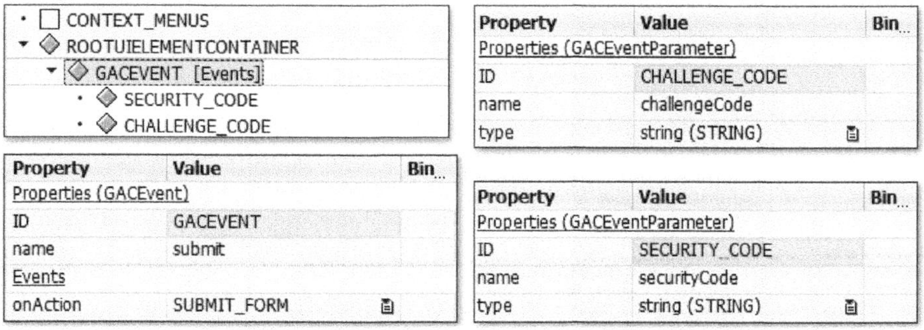

- ☐ CONTEXT_MENUS
- ▼ ◇ ROOTUIELEMENTCONTAINER
  - ▼ ◇ GACEVENT [Events]
    - · ◇ SECURITY_CODE
    - · ◇ CHALLENGE_CODE

Property	Value	Bin
Properties (GACEvent)		
ID	GACEVENT	
name	submit	
Events		
onAction	SUBMIT_FORM	🗐

Property	Value	Bin
Properties (GACEventParameter)		
ID	CHALLENGE_CODE	
name	challengeCode	
type	string (STRING)	🗐

Property	Value	Bin
Properties (GACEventParameter)		
ID	SECURITY_CODE	
name	securityCode	
type	string (STRING)	🗐

Figure W8.3 GAC Controls in the FlashIsland View

Note that for the GACEvent control, we bind submit as its name, and for each of the GACEventParameter controls, we bind challengeCode and securityCode as their names. These correspond to the event and parameter names we supplied in our call to the FlashIsland.fireEvent method in our Flash application. Additionally, we define the action SUBMIT_FORM in the GACEvent as the action called when this event is fired.

W8.2.3 Handling the SUBMIT_FORM Event

The key design element we have to be aware of in the action handler for SUBMIT_FORM is how to reference the parameter data. Parameter data is stored in the WDEVENT parameter supplied to the handler. We extract this data by making calls to one of the GET_DATA methods in the object. In this case, we call the GET_STRING method in order to return the event parameters as string data:

```
lv_security_code = wdevent->get_string( 'securityCode' ).
lv_challenge_code = wdevent->get_string( 'challengeCode' ).
```

From there, it's a matter of acting on the data we've received. Figure W8.4 and Figure W8.5 show status messages being returned in the MessageArea element we defined in the application for successful and unsuccessful attempts at submitting the security code.

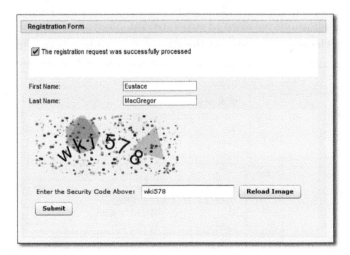

Figure W8.4 Successful Processing of the Security Code

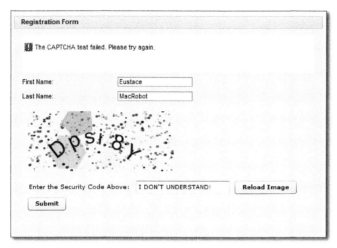

Figure W8.5 Unsuccessful Processing of the Security Code

W8.3 Solution

You can find the solution for this workbook exercise in the ZWDC_WB8_SOLUTION component provided with this book's code bundle. The Adobe Flex application used to create the CAPTCHA application is also supplied in the code bundle.

Appendices

Appendices

A   Debugging WDA Applications

When you get right down to it, WDA applications have a lot of moving parts. Therefore, as we attempt to debug applications, it can be difficult to get to the root of the problem without the help of a good debugger tool. Luckily, SAP provides us with an excellent debugger tool that can be used to diagnose not only regular ABAP code, but also various aspects of WDA applications.

A.1   Activating the ABAP Debugger Tool

Before we can take advantage of all the features of the ABAP Debugger tool, we must first figure out how to activate it within our WDA applications. In this section, we'll consider several different methods of achieving this.

A.1.1   Configuring the New ABAP Debugger

In release 6.40 of AS ABAP, SAP overhauled its classic ABAP Debugger tool, replacing it with a new tool called the *new ABAP Debugger*. Among other things, the technology innovations in this new debugger make it easier for SAP to incorporate new features into the tool. Therefore, when working with newer ABAP-based technologies like WDA, it makes sense to utilize the new ABAP Debugger tool wherever possible.

> **Note**
>
> We'll see evidence of the ease of incorporating new features shortly, when we look at the new Web Dynpro Debugger tool in Section A.2.

As of release 7.0 of AS ABAP, the new ABAP Debugger is turned on by default. You can confirm this setting by opening the ABAP Workbench tool in Transaction SE80 and selecting the UTILITIES • SETTINGS... menu path. This opens the USER-SPECIFIC SETTINGS dialog box shown in Figure A.1. From here, you can confirm the active debugger tool for your user profile in the radio button group within the ABAP DEBUGGER field group.

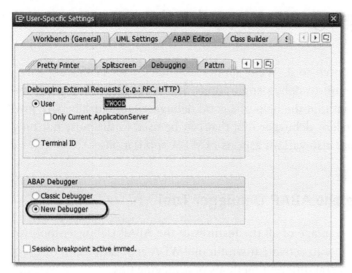

Figure A.1 Turning on the New Debugger in the ABAP Workbench

A.1.2 Setting External Breakpoints

One of the fundamental differences between web-based WDA applications and dialog applications based on classic Dynpro technology is that WDA application sessions are initiated via *external* HTTP requests. For the most part, the intricacies of these not-so-subtle differences in access points are managed internally by SAP. However, one thing we have to keep in mind as developers is that there are now two different types of breakpoints we can set when debugging ABAP code:

- **Session breakpoints**
  Session breakpoints are used to debug requests triggered within the same user session the breakpoints are set in. For example, if we want to debug an ABAP report program in Transaction SE38, we might set a session breakpoint at the beginning of a particular subroutine and then launch the program by clicking the EXECUTE button. In this regard, session breakpoints are functionally equivalent to the kinds of breakpoints that were set within the classic ABAP Debugger tool.

- **External breakpoints**
  External breakpoints, on the other hand, are used to set breakpoints in ABAP code that's not launched within the current user session, but rather via a user session created for an HTTP request, RFC request, and so on.

As you've probably guessed by now, external breakpoints are the breakpoint type of choice for debugging WDA applications. So, if we want to debug a particular controller method, we can do so by performing the following steps:

1. First, we need to log on to the AS ABAP system where the WDA application resides and open the Web Dynpro Explorer tool (Transaction SE80).

2. Next, since all the WDA application logic resides within controller methods, we must identify the target controller method and then open it in the Controller Editor tool.

3. Within the method itself, we can set an external breakpoint by placing the cursor on an executable line within the code and clicking the SET/DELETE EXTERNAL BREAKPOINT button (see Figure A.2). Alternatively, we can save ourselves a mouse click by simultaneously hitting the Ctrl + Shift + F12 key sequence.

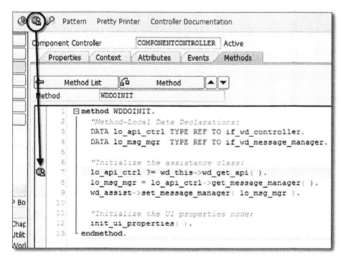

Figure A.2 Setting an External Breakpoint

4. Finally, once we're done with the external breakpoint, we can remove it by returning to the Controller Editor and clicking on the SET/DELETE EXTERNAL BREAKPOINT button once more (or by simultaneously hitting the Ctrl + Shift + F12 key sequence).

Once an external breakpoint is set, we can launch the WDA application as usual (e.g., via a direct URL, a Portal iView, or by running a test inside the ABAP Workbench). Then, when the program logic reaches the defined external breakpoint(s), a new session window pops up to display the ABAP Debugger tool. From here, we can begin stepping through the code as usual, as shown in Figure A.3.

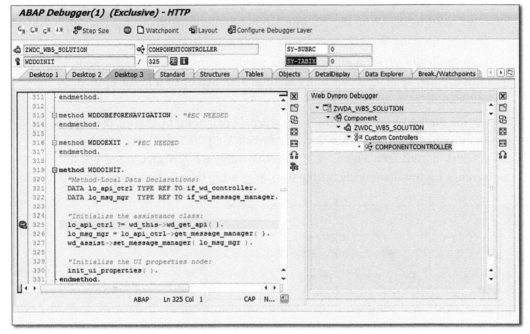

Figure A.3 Debugging a WDA Application

A.1.3 Debugging from the Context Menu

The ability to set external breakpoints is great if we know enough about the WDA application we're debugging to figure out the approximate location within the code where we need to begin debugging. However, if we're debugging a WDA application delivered by SAP or another developer, we might not know enough about the application to know where to begin.

In these circumstances, it's nice to be able to start debugging directly within the application at the point where we think the problem starts (e.g., at the point a particular button is clicked or an event occurs). For example, if we want to start debugging from within a classic Dynpro application, all we have to do is enter the ⍈/⍈+⍈h⍈ key sequence in the command field and hit the ⍈Enter⍈ key (see Figure A.4).

Then, when the next function code is triggered, the ABAP Debugger tool opens automatically and allows us to begin debugging from that point in the code forward.

Figure A.4 Setting an Ad Hoc Breakpoint within the SAP GUI

Within the WDA environment, we can achieve a similar ad hoc debugging functionality by tacking on the URL query string parameter /H=X to the end of the application URL when a WDA application is loaded. At first glance, this innocuous parameter doesn't appear to do anything. However, with this parameter in place, we now have the option of activating the ABAP Debugger in ad hoc fashion by simply right-clicking on the screen and choosing the ACTIVATE DEBUGGER menu option from the standard context menu, as shown in Figure A.5.

Figure A.5 Debugging from the Context Menu in a WDA Application

To demonstrate how this works, let's imagine we've chosen the ACTIVATE DEBUGGER • WDDOBEFOREACTION menu option on the screen shown in Figure A.5. Once this function is turned on, the ABAP Debugger tool launches automatically whenever an event is triggered on the frontend (e.g., a button is clicked, etc.). In this scenario, the Debugger will pick up with the first line of the WDDOBEFOREACTION() method of the view that triggered the event. We can then begin debugging within this method and trace through the application logic from that point forward.

> **Executing Debugging Scripts**
>
> If you've worked with the ABAP Debugger tool before, you may be familiar with the BREAKPOINT AT... functions provided within the application toolbar. Here, we can set breakpoints to see when particular statement types (e.g., the SELECT statement) are executed or messages are raised. To some extent, we can achieve this kind of functionality with WDA application debugging by executing *debugging scripts*. You can find more information about available debugging scripts and how to use them within the SAP Help Library (*http://help.sap.com*). Here, simply perform a search using the term "Web Dynpro ABAP debugging with debugging scripts."

A.2 Working with the Web Dynpro Debugger Tool

For the most part, the process of debugging a controller method is the same as the one we'd use to debug a regular ABAP Objects class method. Here, we can sequentially step through the code, look at the contents of controller attributes, view the current program call stack, and so on. This standard functionality serves us well when debugging regular ABAP code.

> **Note**
>
> Since this is standard behavior of the ABAP Debugger tool, we won't get into the details of this here. However, you can find plenty of detailed information about these functions in the SAP Help Library online at *http://help.sap.com*. From there, perform a search on the phrase "new ABAP debugger."

However, when it comes to WDA applications, there are other aspects of the application we need to account for. Recognizing this, SAP has embedded a specialized tool called the *Web Dynpro Debugger* within the new ABAP Debugger.

To enable the Web Dynpro Debugger tool within a debugging session, perform the following steps:

1. Within a Debugger session, click the NEW TOOL button contained within the toolbar on the right-hand side of the screen (see Figure A.6).

2. This opens the NEW TOOL dialog window shown in Figure A.7. From here, expand the SPECIAL TOOLS folder and double-click on the WEB DYNPRO node to load the new tool into the selected desktop tab.

Figure A.6 Enabling the Web Dynpro Debugger Tool (Part 1)

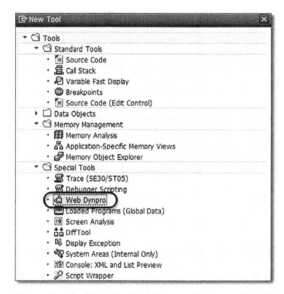

Figure A.7 Enabling the Web Dynpro Debugger Tool (Part 2)

Figure A.8 shows what the Web Dynpro Debugger tool looks like on the screen. As you can see, the main WDA component for the application is loaded into a tree-like view, which allows us to debug various Web Dynpro–specific artifacts, such as views, windows, controller contexts, used components, and so on.

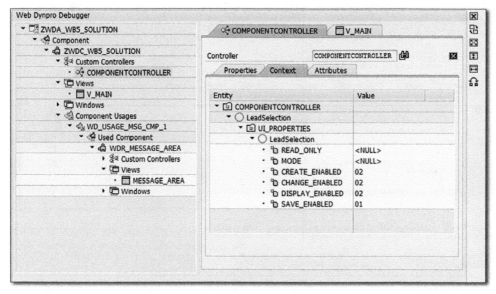

Figure A.8 Working with the Web Dynpro Debugger Tool

B   The Authors

James Wood the founder and principal consultant of Bowdark Consulting, Inc., an SAP consulting firm specializing in custom development and training. James is also an SAP Mentor and the author of several best-selling SAP-related titles.

Before starting Bowdark in 2006, James was a consultant at SAP America, Inc. and IBM Corporation where was involved in many large-scale SAP implementations. To learn more about James and the book, please check out *http:// www.bowdark.com*.

Shaan Parvaze is an IT software developer who has been working with SAP technologies for the past five years, principally in the areas of SAP NetWeaver Portal and SAP NetWeaver Process Integration. He is a graduate of the University of Texas at Arlington and work and lives in Fort Worth, Texas. This is his first book.

Index

Interested in reading more?

Please visit our website for all new
book and e-book releases from SAP PRESS.

www.sap-press.com